Introduction to
Public Administration

INTRODUCTION TO PUBLIC ADMINISTRATION

A BOOK OF READINGS

J. Steven Ott
University of Utah

E. W. Russell
Victoria University of Technology

Editors

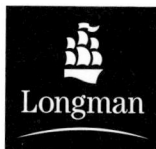

Longman

New York San Francisco Boston
London Toronto Sydney Tokyo Singapore Madrid
Mexico City Munich Paris Cape Town Hong Kong Montreal

Publisher: Priscilla McGeehon
Senior Acquisitions Editor: Eric Stano
Marketing Manager: Megan Galvin-Fak
Production Manager: Mark Naccarelli
Project Coordination, Text Design, and Electronic Page Makeup: WestWords, Inc.
Cover Designer/Manager: John Callahan
Senior Manufacturing Buyer: Dennis J. Para
Printer and Binder: R. R. Donnelley & Sons, Co.
Cover Printer: Coral Graphics, Inc.

For permission to use copyrighted material, grateful acknowledgment is made to the copyright holders on pages 584–588, which are hereby made part of this copyright page.

Library of Congress Cataloging-in-Publication Data

Introduction to public administration : a book of readings / J. Steven Ott and E. W. Russell, editors.
    p. cm.
    Includes bibliographical references.
    ISBN 0-321-07055-0
    1. Public administration. I. Ott, J. Steven. II. Russell, E. W. (Edward W.)

    JF1351 156 2000
    351—dc21

                                              00-044976

Please visit our website at http://www.awl.com

ISBN 0-321-07055-0

1 2 3 4 5 6 7 8 9 10 — DOH — 03 02 01 00

CONTENTS

13   PUBLIC BUDGETING   479

14   EVALUATION AND MEASURING PRODUCTIVITY 523

15   HONOR AND ETHICS   555

PREFACE

Introduction to Public Administration: A Book of Readings introduces students to the complexities of administering government organizations that engage in a surprisingly wide array of activities and provide an enormous range of services mostly for the purpose of improving the quality of life in the United States—or preventing its deterioration. Instead of writing a textbook about public administration, however, we decided to have the "masters" tell the public administration story in their own words. There are already enough very good introductory public administration textbooks available on the market today. (See References at the end of this Preface for a partial listing.)

The primary purpose for *Introduction to Public Administration* is to constitute a complete course package when used as a supplement to any solid public administration textbook. Because of the approach we used in designing the book and selecting readings, however, it also could stand on its own in public administration courses at the upper-division undergraduate or graduate level.

Our tasks as book editors were:

1. create a clear vision of what this collection of readings would accomplish;
2. select previously published articles and chapters that "tell the story" well;
3. edit-down reprinted readings to make them more readable and to help students focus in on the central ideas that make the reading worth including; and
4. write introductory essays that provide "frameworks" for the topic that is the focus of each chapter.

We believe that we have selected some of the most insightful, interesting, and useful articles and book chapters that can be found about the nature, scope, structures, functions, problems, and challenges facing public administration at the turn of the twenty-first century. We hope that you agree.

Each chapter addresses an important set of long-standing, historic, functions, structures, or issues from a variety of contemporary perspectives. "This is . . . a time when public administrators must face the future. Change is coming too rapidly to stand in the present and face toward the past."[1] Thus, we address "standard" public administration topics but in the context of the turn of the millenium. The essays that open each of the 15 chapters introduce the important issues, put major controversies in context, highlight unresolved debates, and explain what students should be looking for as they read the reprinted articles.

The summary of chapter titles and the authors and dates of reprinted readings below reveals the scope, depth, and currency of the book's coverage—and its compatibility with many of the textbooks that are widely used in introductory public administration courses today. (A complete listing of authors and titles is in the Table of Contents.)

Chapter

1 **Defining Public Administration**
    Woodrow Wilson (1887), Frank Marini (1998), Camilla Stivers (1998)

2 **The Practice of Public Administration**
    David H. Rosenbloom (1986), Andrew Gray and Bill Jenkins (1995), Fred W. Riggs (1998)

3 **The Cultural and Political Environment**
    of Public Administration and Policy-Making
    Charles E. Lindblom (1959), P. M. Jackson (1990), Kenneth J. Meier (1997)

4 **Reinventing the Machinery of Government**
    John J. DiIulio, Jr. (1995), B. Guy Peters (1996), Graeme Hodge (2000)

5 **Intergovernmental Relations**
    Dale Krane (1993), David B. Walker (1995), Janet E. Kodras (1997)

6 **Management and Organization Theory**
    Michael Barzelay (1992); Henry Mintzberg (1996); Harold F. Gortner, Julianne Mahler, and Jeanne Bell Nicholson (1997)

7 **Organizational Behavior**
    John Paterson (1983), Marvin R. Weisbord (1987)

8 **Managerialism and Performance Management**
    Arie Halachmi and Marc Holzer (1993), Marc Holzer and Kathe Callahan (1998), Steven Cohen and William Eimicke (1998)

9 **Strategic Planning and Management in Public Administration**
    Henry Mintzberg (1994), John M. Bryson (1995), Mark H. Moore (1995)

10 **Leadership and Accountability**
    Barbara S. Romzek and Melvin J. Dubnick (1987), Larry D. Terry (1995), Norma M. Riccucci (1995)

11 **Personnel Management**
    Mark W. Huddleston and William W. Boyer (1996), Rex L. Facer II (1998), Richard C. Kearney and Steven W. Hays (1998)

12 **Social Equity**
    H. George Frederickson (1990), Gregory B. Lewis (1997), James D. Slack (1997)

13 **Public Budgeting**
    Aaron Wildavsky (1978), Philip G. Joyce (1996), James J. Gosling (1997)

14 **Evaluation and Measuring Productivity**
    Susan C. Paddock (1998), Evan M. Berman (1998), City of Charlotte, NC. (1999)

15 **Honor and Ethics**
    James B. Bowman and Russell L. Williams (1997), Guy B. Adams and Danny L. Balfour (1998)

Five themes that are of paramount importance to public administration in the twenty-first century are addressed directly in the reprinted readings and also are woven into chapter introductions wherever they are appropriate:

- globalization,
- impacts of information technology,
- the movement of decisions to lower levels of government ("devolution") and down through government hierarchies ("empowerment"),
- delivery of government services by private sector organizations ("diffusion" to non-profit and for-profit organizations), and
- the opportunities and challenges of diversity.

In order to impress upon students that "globalization" of public administration is more than a vague notion, for example, five of the reprinted readings address issues that are equally salient in Australia, New Zealand, Canada and Great Britain as well as the U.S. The message of globalization, however, is reinforced by the fact that the authors of these articles are citizens of these countries.[2]

The chapter titles and the cross-cutting themes should make two of our strongest assumptions about public administration quite evident:

- Public administration is much more than the application of business administration tools to the management of government agencies. "No, an introduction to public administration must in at least two ways go beyond an inventory of management techniques. It must, first, place these techniques in the context of the public sector . . . . Second, an introduction must make crystal clear the highly political environment of American public administration."[3]
- In public administration, values and ethics are central to everything. "There is something very special about public administration: your work in public organizations is distinguished by its pursuit of democratic values, and this concern affects nearly everything you do as a public manager."[4] Ethical issues are an aspect of daily life in public administration. "Indeed every act of every public servant, at whatever level of government or in any related organization, has an important ethical dimension."[5]

Criteria for Selection

Finding enough "good" readings to include in *Introduction to Public Administration* was not a difficult task. Our problem was deciding which of many excellent readings would best help students understand and appreciate contemporary public administration. Several criteria were used to make decisions about which readings to include in this book.

The first "test" that any reading had to pass was "yes" answers to two questions:

- Does the reading provide a reason or reasons why public administration exists in its current form, and/or why public organizations engage in (or refrain from engaging in) particular types of activities?

- Should the serious student of public administration be expected to be able to identify and understand the authors' central themes—the crux of their arguments?

Second, each reading had to make a statement that has had a noticeable impact on the field of public administration. This criterion does not eliminate controversial readings—quite the contrary. This criterion simply requires that a reading must make a statement that cannot be ignored.

Third, the reading had to fit the vision and scope of this book. It had to address issues or ideas that are of long-standing importance to the field of public administration but from a contemporary perspective.

Finally, the article or chapter had to be readable. Students who have already had reason to peruse the literature of public administration will appreciate the importance of this criterion.

Acknowledgments

We wish that we could acknowledge everyone who contributed ideas, insights, support, challenges, and constructive criticisms during the creation and development of this volume. Space and propriety, however, require that we limit our statements of appreciation to individuals who played central roles in shaping our vision and preliminary ideas into a cohesive anthology. Professors Colin Clark, Deputy Dean, Faculty of Business and Law, Victoria University of Technology; Albert Hyde, the Brookings Institution; Frederick Lane, City University of New York; Jay Shafritz, University of Pittsburgh; Richard Green, University of Wyoming; and F. Ted Hebert and James H. Gosling, University of Utah. We also are deeply appreciative of the numerous and varied contributions made by Jared C. Bennett, University of Utah and Lisa A. Dicke, Texas Tech University. Jared helped in our searches for suitable articles to reprint, wrote drafts of two chapter essays, helped review proofs, and aided in the production of the manuscript in countless ways. We also enthusiastically thank John Tripotseris, Andrea Hill, and others on the reference staff at the Victoria University of Technology library and the State Library of Victoria for their cheerful and skillful help. And, finally, we thank the reviewers of this collection while it was in manuscript form: John C. Bretting at University of Texas-San Antonio; Patricia Fredrickson at Boise State University; William Gangi at St. John's University; Michael Hail at University of North Carolina-Greensboro; Peggy Jackson at Goleden Gate University; M.A. Peterson at Washburn University; Douglas Shumaron at Miami University of Ohio; and Zachary Smith at Northern Arizona University.

E. W. Russell   J. Steven Ott
Victoria University of Technology   University of Utah

Notes

1. Cooper, Phillip, J., Linda P. Brady, Olivia Hidalgo-Hardeman, Albert Hyde, Katherine C. Naff, J. Steven Ott, and Harvey White. (1998). *Public Administration for the Twenty-First Century*. Fort Worth, TX: Harcourt Brace, p. x.
2. See these readings that are reprinted in this book: Andrew Gray and Bill Jenkins, "From Public Administration to Public Management: Reassessing a Revolution?"; P.M. Jackson, "Public Choice and Public Sector Management"; and, John Paterson, "Bureaucratic Reform by Cultural Revolution."
3. Starling, Grover. (1998). *Managing the Public Sector* (5th ed.). Fort Worth, TX: Harcourt Brace, p. ix.
4. Denhardt, Robert B., and Joseph W. Grubbs. (1999). *Public Administration: An Action Orientation* (3rd ed.). Fort Worth, TX: Harcourt Brace, p. 1
5. Denhardt, Robert B. (1999). *Public Administration: An Action Orientation* (3rd ed.). Fort Worth, TX: Harcourt Brace, p. x.

A PARTIAL LISTING OF VERY GOOD TEXTBOOKS IN PUBLIC ADMINISTRATION

Balanoff, Howard. (1996). *Public Administration* (4th ed.). Guilford, Conn.: Dushkin.

Cooper, Phillip J., Linda P. Brady, Olivia Hidaldgo-Hardeman, Albert C. Hyde, Katherine C. Naff, J. Steven Ott, and Harvey White. (1998). *Public Administration For the Twenty-First Century.* Ft. Worth, TX: Harcourt Brace.

Denhardt, Robert B., & Joseph W. Grubbs. (1999). *Public Administration: An Action Orientation* (3rd ed.). Ft. Worth, TX: Harcourt Brace.

Fesler, James W., and Donald F. Kettl. (1996). *The Politics of the Administrative Process* (2nd ed.). New York: Chatham House.

Gordon, George J., and Michael E. Milakovich. (1998). *Public Administration in America* (6th ed.). New York: St. Martin's.

Henry, Nicholas. (1998). *Public Administration and Public Affairs* (7th ed.). Upper Saddle River, NJ: Prentice-Hall.

Rosenbloom, David H. (1998). *Public Administration: Understanding Management, Politics, and Law in the Public Sector* (4th ed.). New York: McGraw Hill.

Shafritz, Jay M., and E. William Russell. (2000). *Introducing Public Administration* (2nd ed.). New York: Addison Wesley Longman.

Starling, Grover. (1998). *Managing the Public Sector* (5th ed.). Ft. Worth, TX: Harcourt Brace.

Stillman, Richard J. (2000). *Public Administration: Concepts and Cases* (7th ed.). Boston, Mass.: Houghton Mifflin.

INTRODUCTION TO
PUBLIC ADMINISTRATION

1

DEFINING PUBLIC ADMINISTRATION

There is no single, generally-accepted, definition of *public administration,* and perhaps there never will be.[1] In this chapter, we explain why this is so, and while the absence of a single definition may be frustrating, it at least partially reflects healthy "growing pains" of a young, complex, and thus highly interesting field of academic study and practice.

> *Public administration* may be defined as *all processes, organizations, and individuals . . . associated with carrying out laws and other rules adopted or issued by legislatures, executives, and courts.*[2] (Emphasis in original.)
>
> Public administration is so vast that there is no way to encompass it all with only one definition.[3]
>
> Public administration, like many human endeavors, is difficult to define. . . . In part, this is because public administration covers such a vast amount of activity. . . . It was pointed out some time ago that any one-paragraph or even one-sentence definition of public administration is bound to prove temporarily mind-paralyzing.[4]
>
> To define a subject is to fix its boundaries or, if those turn out to be fuzzy, to identify its essence, its core character. But for public administration this has proved so intractable a problem that its scholarly study is said to be suffering a "crisis of identity."[5]

All of us who teach public administration have our own sense of what *it* is, and most of us would agree about many aspects of a definition. "Public administration does involve *activity,* it is concerned with *politics* and *policy-making,* it tends to be concentrated in the *executive* branch of government, it does differ from private [business] administration, and it is concerned with *implementing the law.*"[6] On the other hand, we also disagree spiritedly about where the "boundaries" of public administration lie and about the relative importance of various dimensions of public administration.

To an extent the absence of agreement about what public administration is (and is not) represents a mild case of "identity crisis" that all relatively young professions must pass through[7]—just as teenagers who are learning to be adults must struggle through difficult times. A second reason for the lack of agreement is that public administration is so all-encompassing that it is extraordinarily difficult to draw boundaries around it. A short listing of some "things" that public administration *is* only provides a glimpse of how much territory it covers and how difficult it is to establish its outer limits:

- a *field of academic study* (for example, a Masters of Public Administration degree program) *and* a *broad area of professional practice* (for example, city managers, state budget directors, and human resource managers in school districts);
- a *sub-field of political science* that emphasizes public sector values and the inherently political aspects of administering government agencies, *and* the *application of business management tools and techniques to government operations;*
- a "fourth branch" of government that is (or should be) *subordinate to elected officials, and* the *core of permanent, professional, substantive, policy expertise in government;*
- the "action" part of government—the *arm of government that implements* legislated public policy, *and* the *arm of government that uses (or should use) professional, substantive, policy expertise to influence public policy;*
- government agencies that intrude in business practices (for example, require businesses to protect employees from health hazards) (*regulate*), *and* agencies that help victims of hurricanes, floods, and earthquakes (*provide public services*).
- government employees who inspect restaurants for health hazards and repair city streets (*direct provision of public services*), *and* nonprofit organizations that contract with government agencies to provide services to vulnerable populations such as the aging, individuals with mental retardation and chronic mental illness, and youth who are at high risk of gang involvement (*outsourced public services*);

Rosenbloom groups the numerous existing definitions of public administration into three types: *political, managerial* and *legal.*[8] Shafritz and Russell[9] are more expansive. They have created eighteen definitions clustered in four categories (a few with tongue-in-cheek titles), *political, legal, occupational and managerial definitions:*

Political Definitions of Public Administration
- Public administration is what government does.
- Public administration is both direct and indirect.
- Public administration is a phase in the public policymaking cycle.
- Public administration is implementing the public interest.
- Public administration is doing collectively that which cannot be so well done individually.

Legal Definitions of Public Administration
- Public administration is law in action.
- Public administration is regulation.
- Public administration is the king's largesse.
- Public administration is theft.

Managerial Definitions of Public Administration
- Public administration is the executive function in government.
- Public administration is a management specialty.
- Public administration is Mickey Mouse.
- Public administration is art, not science—or vice versa.

Occupational Definitions of Public Administration
- Public administration is an occupational category.
- Public administration is an essay contest.
- Public administration is idealism in action.
- Public administration is an academic field.
- Public administration is a profession.

The readings that are reprinted in this chapter offer an excellent introduction to the numerous and varied dimensions of the field of public administration, so we will not dwell on the topic. But, we do not want to leave readers feeling frustrated or negative about public administration simply because there is not a consensus about a definition of the field. Complexity and ambiguity are pervasive realities in the twenty-first century. Public administration is—and always has been—an inherently complex and ambiguous field. Thus, an ambiguous and complex field currently faces an environment full of ambiguities and complexities. Complexity and ambiguity, however, create opportunities as well as frustrations for public administration. "It may seem surprising, but there has never been a better time to be a public administration professional. Of course, it is also probably the most difficult time to be a member of our profession as well."[10]

Public administration *is* personal idealism in action. It *is* where party platforms, campaign rhetoric, and press releases about "what government should do" end and actions to effect change are implemented. Public administration *is* the concrete steps that governments take, often in partnership with nonprofit and for-profit organizations, to improve the quality of life in communities and to prevent its deterioration. Thus, public administration *is* helping persons with disabilities to live as independently as possible, fighting fires, creating multimodal urban transportation systems, and protecting "green space" as expanding communities encroach upon what were farms, forests, wetlands, and ranches.

Why would anyone choose public administration for a career? Most individuals enter public administration occupations because they are personally committed to some aspect of the public interest. There are many career opportunities that offer higher incomes in industry and retail businesses. Careers in public administration are for people who care and want to make a difference.

READINGS REPRINTED IN THIS CHAPTER

"Public Administration" by Frank Marini[11] is a comprehensive introductory overview that summarizes public administration's definitional problems, its historical development, how it is configured in the U.S., its struggle for identity and to achieve legitimacy, and its future. Marini proposes a definition: "(1) The occupational sector, enterprises, and activities having to do with the formulation and implementation of policy of governmental and other public programs and the management of organizations and activities involved. (2) The academic field concerned with the study of, improvement of, and training for the activities mentioned in (1)." Marini does not stop with his first definition and attempts to draw boundaries. "It refers on the one hand to the administration or management of matters which have principally to do with the society, polity, and its subparts which are not essentially private, familial, commercial, or individualistic, and on the other hand to the disciplined study of such matters."

Public administration includes "the planning, formulating, modifying, and urging of goals and purposes" for the substance of public policy as well as the management functions of public agencies, such as personnel management, bookkeeping, and collecting taxes. Marini cautions against thinking narrowly about public administration—as something that occurs only in governmental organizations. "There have been developments such as governmental or quasi-governmental activities which compete with private sector activities or provide benefits through use of a price mechanism. . . . There are also devices such as public corporations [for example, AMTRAK], quasi-public corporations [such as the U.S. Postal Service], public-private cooperative enterprises, and government contractual arrangements with nongovernmental organizations. . . ." These types of developments and arrangements are integral parts of public administration in the twenty-first century—but also are a primary reason why the boundaries around public administration are blurred.

Marini identifies six reasons for the existing concerns about the field's identity and legitimacy: (1) questioning and doubts that are typical in the formative stages of academic disciplines and fields; (2) concern about whether public administration indeed is a profession; (3) inability to identify theories and concepts that unify the field; (4) feelings of "disconectedness" between academic public administration and public administration as practitioner-oriented concerns, occupations and activities; (5) "ambivalence about bureaucracy, hierarchy, and instrumental relationships"; and (6) unease about the legitimate political role of public administration.

Woodrow Wilson's 1887 article, **"The Study of Administration,"**[12] is widely regarded as the essay that signaled the beginning of the field of public administration. Wilson was a political science professor and president of Princeton

University who subsequently was elected governor of New Jersey and president of the United States.[13] "The Study of Administration" originated from his often-quoted concern that "it is getting harder to *run* a constitution than to write one." Wilson argued that the administration of government would be more manageable and efficient if it were removed and shielded from political influences, a notion that became known in later years as the *politics/administration dichotomy.* "Most important . . . is the truth . . . that administration lies outside the proper sphere of *politics.* Administrative questions are not political questions."

"The field of administration is a field of business," Wilson wrote, urging the creation of "a science of [public] administration which shall seek to straighten the paths of government, to make its business less unbusinesslike, to strengthen and purify its organization, and to crown its duties with dutifulness."

As a political scientist, Wilson knew that the United States was lagging behind several European nations in creating efficient government administrative structures, systems, and practices. "It is harder for democracy to organize administration than for monarchy" because democracies must be responsive to public opinion. "Lessons on how to administer government better could be learned from a wide variety of sources, including governments with whom we did not share values, like the Prussian bureaucracy."[14] Because Wilson believed strongly that administration could and should be separated from politics, he also believed that the United States could safely "learn administration from the Prussian and French (Napoleonic) autocracies without being infected by their political principles."[15] All that was needed was to "filter [the science of administration we borrowed from other nations] through our constitutions, only to put it over a slow fire of criticism and distill away its foreign gases."

What public administration is, depends on the perspective of the observer. **Camilla Stivers'** essay, **"Feminist Theory of Public Administration,"**[16] presents an important perspective that had not been articulated prior to the mid-1980s and that can still prompt vigorous debate. Stivers explains how feminist theories "use gender as a lens through which to analyze critically women's current status and role in public agencies, bring to light ways in which gender bias inhabits ideas and practices in the field, and formulate new theoretical approaches." Stivers identifies two types of feminist theories: *descriptive theories,* "based on empirical study, [that] report on how gender influences current practice in public agencies, especially its effect on women's access to and status in public agency employment"; and, *conceptual theories* that "call into question the frameworks within which public administration is typically understood." Whereas descriptive theories "take for granted existing modes of thought in public administration and examine the extent to which women have gained access to the world of practice," conceptual theories are based on the premise "that existing [male] perspectives, for all their apparent objectivity, contain hidden gender biases. Taking gender into account, therefore, involves more than simply adding women to public agencies; instead it entails rethinking fundamental theoretical assumptions, approaches and concepts. . . . New modes of thought are required, ones that call into question the neutrality of such central ideas as professionalism, leadership, and the public interest." Public administration is very different "things" when observed through the lenses of Woodrow Wilson, Frank Marini, and Camilla Stivers.

NOTES

1. For a comprehensive review of public administration definitions, see Richard Stillman II, *Public Administration: Concepts and Cases* (7th ed.). Boston: Houghton Mifflin, pp. 1–4.
2. Gordon, George J., and Michael E. Milakovich. (1995). *Public Administration in America* (5th ed.). New York: St. Martin's, p. 6.
3. Shafritz, Jay M., and E. William Russell. (2000). *Introducing Public Administration* (2nd ed.). New York: Addison Wesley Longman, p. 5.
4. Rosenbloom, David H. (1998). *Public Administration: Understanding Management, Politics, and Law in the Public Sector* (4th ed.). New York: McGraw-Hill, p. 4. (In this excerpt, Rosenbloom cites Dwight Waldo, "What is Public Administration?")
5. Fesler, James W., and Donald F. Kettl. (1996). *The Politics of the Administrative Process* (2nd ed.). New York: Chatham House, p. 7.
6. Rosenbloom, David H. (1998). *Public Administration: Understanding Management, Politics, and Law in the Public Sector* (4th ed.). New York: McGraw-Hill, pp. 5,6.
7. Fesler, James W., and Donald F. Kettl. (1996). *The Politics of the Administrative Process* (2nd ed.). New York: Chatham House, p. 7.
8. Rosenbloom, David H. (1998). *Public Administration: Understanding Management, Politics, and Law in the Public Sector* (4th ed.). New York: McGraw-Hill, p. 6.
9. Shafritz, Jay M., and E. William Russell. (2000). *Introducing Public Administration* (2nd ed.). New York: Addison Wesley Longman, pp. 6–31.
10. Cooper, Phillip, J., Linda P. Brady, Olivia Hidalgo-Hardeman, Albert Hyde, Katherine C. Naff, J. Steven Ott, and Harvey White. (1998). *Public Administration for the Twenty-First Century*. Fort Worth, TX: Harcourt Brace, p. viii.
11. Marini, Frank. (1998). "Public Administration," in Jay M. Shafritz (Ed.), *International Encyclopedia of Public Policy and Administration* (pp. 1782–1788). Boulder, Colo.: Westview.
12. Wilson, Woodrow. (June 1887). "The Study of Administration." *Political Science Quarterly, 2*(2), 197–222.
13. Miewald, Robert D. (1998). "Woodrow Wilson," in Jay M. Shafritz (Ed.), *International Encyclopedia of Public Policy and Administration*. Boulder, Colo.: Westview, p. 2410.
14. Cooper, Phillip, J., Linda P. Brady, Olivia Hidalgo-Hardeman, Albert Hyde, Katherine C. Naff, J. Steven Ott, and Harvey White. (1998). *Public Administration for the Twenty-First Century*. Fort Worth, TX: Harcourt Brace, p. 7.
15. Fesler, James W., and Donald F. Kettl. (1996). *The Politics of the Administrative Process* (2nd ed.). New York: Chatham House, p. 20.
16. Stivers, Camilla. (1998). "Feminist Theory of Public Administration," in Jay M. Shafritz (Ed.), *International Encyclopedia of Public Policy and Administration* (pp. 881–884). Boulder, Colo.: Westview.

1

Frank Marini

PUBLIC ADMINISTRATION

1. The occupational sector, enterprises, and activities having to do with the formulation and implementation of policy of governmental and other public programs and the management of organizations and activities involved. 2. The academic field concerned with the study of, improvement of, and training for the activities mentioned in 1.

Public administration refers to two distinguishable but closely related activities: (1) a professional practice (vocation, occupation, field of activity), and (2) an academic field which seeks to understand, develop, criticize, and improve that professional practice as well as to train individuals for that practice. The simple meaning of the term is quite direct: it refers on the one hand to the administration or management of matters which have principally to do with the society, polity, and its subparts which are not essentially private, familial, commercial, or individualistic, and on the other hand to the disciplined study of such matters. In this simplest meaning, public administration has to do with managing the realm of governmental and other public activities. This simple definition conveys the essence of public administration and probably covers the vast majority of activities and concerns of contemporary public administration.

Such a simple view, though, needs modification to account for at least two important considerations: First, it must be recognized that professional management of the public's affairs involves not only management in the narrowest sense (keeping the books, handling personnel decisions, implementing decisions which have been made elsewhere in the politico-socio-economic systems, etc.), but also significantly involves the planning, formulating, modifying, and urging of goals and purposes of much of public affairs. Second, it must be recognized that some matters of public administration are handled in ways which are not purely private but are also not precisely governmental.

The first consideration—that public administration is involved in the substance of policy as well as in the implementation of policy decisions—is frequently alluded to with terms such as the demise of the politics-administration dichotomy, the impossibility of value-free public administration, and the need for proactivity by public administrators. These terms reflect the widespread, though not universal, belief or allegation that it is no longer, if ever it was, defensible to interpret public administration as solely involved in technically objective solutions or in the neutral implementation of decisions made by nonadministrative parts of the political system (e.g., partisan leadership; electoral processes; party processes; partisan bargaining; and parliamentary, legislative, and judicial institutions). This belief and related understandings have led to significant public administration attention to policy and policy process. Some have felt a need for a rubric which emphasizes such a policy focus and which might also encompass or indicate receptivity to areas of studies which are closely related (e.g., planning, urban affairs, economic analysis, public policy analysis), and terms such as public affairs are sometimes used for this purpose. In general, though, public administration still functions as the umbrella term throughout the world, though it must be realized that the term implies a broader range of concerns and activities than the narrow meaning of management or administration may convey.

The second consideration—that not all public administration occurs in and through governmental organizations—also has led to a broadening of the meaning of public administration. At various times in the past of public administration it has seemed that its essence and activities could be identified by referring to nonmarket approaches to social purposes, but this perspective has been mitigated by the recognition that public programs and benefits could be developed through and provided with some market characteristics. Thus there have been developments such as governmental or quasi-governmental activities which compete with private sector activities or provide benefits through use of a price mechanism; sometimes water, utilities, sewers, health care, education, and other benefits are provided in this way. There are also devices such as public corporations, quasi-public corporations, public-private cooperative enterprises, and government contractual arrangements with nongovernmental organizations to provide certain benefits or perform certain functions. Indeed, even for large parts of the world where the private-public distinction has not been as prevalent or obvious as other places (for example, where the economy is essentially directed or nonmarket), the movement toward market or marketlike mechanisms for the provision of public goods is increasingly a matter of rhetoric, planning, or action.

When these considerations are taken into account, public administration is probably best defined as the practice and study of the professional formulation and influence of public policy and the implementation of such policy on a regular and organized basis on behalf of the public interest of a society, its civic subparts, and its citizenry.

DEVELOPMENT OF THE FIELD

It is usual to date the contemporary social scientific awareness of bureaucracy (a term which can include both private, or "business," administration and public administration) with the work of the German social scientist Max Weber (1864–1920). Such dating, though, is more a matter of convenience or recognition of important scholarly influence than of historical accuracy.

In the United States, it is usual to credit the reformism of the Populist and Progressive era of politics (about 1880–1920) and especially Woodrow Wilson's academic article "The Study of Administration" (in the *Political Science Quarterly* in 1887) for the systematic and self-conscious development of the field of public administration. It is usual also to identify the early years of U.S. public administration with scientific management, a school of thought largely attributed to Frederick Winslow Taylor (1856–1915) which emphasized a task analysis and efficiency approach to management; and with the subsequent human relations movement, which emphasized the human and social aspects of work environments and motivations somewhat in contradistinction to the scientific management movement. Both of these latter movements had their origins in industrial and business management, but were very influential on public administration in the United States and around the world. The period of U.S. history between the Great Depression and the World War II (about 1929–1945) is commonly held to represent U.S. public administration in a self-confident–though some also say naive–phase; this period is frequently referred to in the United States and elsewhere as the period of classical public administration or orthodox public administration. The dynamics of the Cold War competition between the United States and Western allies and the USSR and its allies, and the manifestation of this competition in various forms of technical assistance, aid in economic development, and administrative assistance had an impact upon public administration. In the 1960s and 1970s, much of the world of science and technology came under attack. In the United States, these decades and their challenges have come to be interpreted against the backdrop of the civil rights movement (and related movements such as feminism), Vietnam War activism, the "new left," anti-institutionalism, and particular manifestations of youth rebellion. Other parts of the world also experienced similar movements, frequently exacerbated by issues of neocolonialism, nationalism, anti-institutionalism, environmentalism, anti-technologism, and general critiques of scientific and technological perspectives and, indeed, the entirety of "modernity." All of these matters had effects upon politics, the social sciences, and public administration. In the United States and elsewhere, many of these developments were accompanied by significant critiques of public administration. One manifestation of this was a dialogue about the need for fundamental rethinking in public administration (and, for some, the need for a "new public administration"). In the last couple of decades, this had been augmented by tremendous technological developments (e.g., in computer applications and in communications developments) on the one hand, and ever more sophisticated philosophical and methodological interpretations asserting that we are transcending "modernity" in ways which call much of our contemporary understanding and technological approaches into question on the other hand. At the present time, public administration worldwide is in creative tension and undergoing rapid change and attempts at reconceptualization. What the effects of all this will be over time, or what the next developmental stage will be, is unclear but generally appears to have an energizing effect upon the field.

CONFIGURATION OF THE FIELD

Public administration is sometimes treated as though it is one of the social sciences, a discipline in some sense. As the number of programs offering doctoral degrees in the field has increased, this interpretation has gained strength.

In the United States, it is relatively unusual for public administration to be a free-standing degree program at the baccalaureate level (though there are some well-established and prestigious programs of this sort–especially in schools of public affairs, schools of management, or schools of public administration–and this approach may be on the increase). The more traditional and still usual pattern is for baccalaureate education in public administration to be a major or minor specialization within a political science degree program. Master-level degrees are increasingly emphasized as desirable or expected credentials for full commitment to professional careers in many fields (e.g., not only in business administration and public administration, but also in fields such as education, social work, nursing, and education where the appropriate degree for professional entry was once the baccalaureate), and the master's degree—usually, but not always, the master of public administration (MPA)—is becoming the recognized degree for those who aspire to careers in public administration. It should be remembered, though, that public organizations and activities cover virtually the whole spectrum of contemporary specialities and that the educational background and specialties of public administrators therefore reflect this diversity.

As modern and contemporary public administration evolved, it tended to develop a more or less regular set of subfields, approaches, and topical interests. These generally have to do either with the functional and technical specializations of public administration, with specific methods and approaches, or with the phenomena of specific locales and issue areas of public administration.

Thus, public administration has some subfields which deal with concerns which, in one form or another, have been part of the field since its earliest days. Budget and finance (how to provide, handle, and account for material resources), personnel (the policies and management of human resources), planning, operations management, organizational design and management, communications and communications systems, record-keeping, accounting of various kinds, reporting of various kinds and for a variety of purposes land clientele, internal and external public relations, and a host of similar concerns constitute some of the technical and functional foci of the field. In addition to these, there are various concerns dealing with the environment and context of administration: the constitutional and legal context; the context of the political, economic, and societal structure, requirements, and processes; the values, history, traditions, and habits of the society and its components; the values, history, requirements, and processes of the organizations, programs, and components of specific relevance at any given time; and many other such factors (as well as their interrelationships).

There are also specializations and foci having to do with the specific form and level at which administration occurs: international administration; national administration; federal/confederal administration, state/province administration, district/department/sector administration; city, county, and local administration; intergovernmental and interorganizational administration; "not for profit" administration; and so forth. Issue areas present other topics and specializations: police, fire, schools, military, medical, environmental, technology and technology transfer, science and scientific applications, government-business-industry cooperation, and a host of other specific issue concerns spawn specializations of knowledge, application, training, and experience.

When one realizes that all these (and many more) can be viewed as components of a huge matrix where any one (or more) can be related to any other one (or more), the complexity and variety of the field of public administration is suggested.

Public Administration as a Cultural and Social Phenomenon

The phenomena of public administration are also objects of study for purposes other than the development of public administration. That is, public administration can be the focus of study of other disciplines or concerns, much as religion can be a topic of investigation for a sociologist who is not religious and has no interest in improving religious experience for the godly. Thus, complex organizations, bureaucracy, and a variety of organizational, administrative, and policy phenomena constitute topics of interest to scholars from a variety of disciplines, fields, and perspectives. Economists, sociologists, political scientists, philosophers, historians, students of literature and of communications and rhetoric, and a host of other academic specialists find public administration and its phenomena worthwhile objects of investigation. The field of public administration, for its part, contributed to, profits from, and incorporates such studies.

Concern for Identity and Legitimacy

A characteristic of public administration in recent decades has been a concern for the identity or legitimacy of the field. This may, in fact, be several separable concerns, which are frequently subsumed under the idea of "identity crisis." There are at least six aspects of this concern: (1) questioning and clarification which is typical of the formation of disciplines and fields; (2) concern over whether public administration is, properly speaking, a profession; (3) unease about theoretical unification, (4) puzzling effects of the applied nature of the field or the fact that the field has a professional or occupational concern as well as a scholarly or academic concern; (5) ambivalence about bureaucracy, hierarchy, and instrumental relationships; and (6) concern about the political legitimacy of public administration.

The Wilson essay frequently cited as an example of the birth of a self-aware field of public administration in the United States was concerned precisely and explicitly with the question of the identity of a field of study and practice. The development of the field as a focus for study and training, concerning as it did an emphasis upon a new field or an interdisciplinary field, obviously had to focus on the continual definition of itself and on the distinguishing of itself from other foci and fields; this would seem true of all such developments, though it is sometimes not remembered in discussions of the development of fields which have been long established.

Though questions about the autonomy of the field may be less seriously raised than they have been in the past, they are still encountered from time to time and from several directions. For example, while a generic approach (i.e., the idea that administration or management is essentially the same field regardless of whether it is applied to business, education, health institutions, social work or social services, and so on) may not be as strongly asserted as it once was, the basic idea is still encountered in various forms.

Countervailing interpretations are indicated by professional and organizational conferences, associations, and journals which project public administration as a subfield in the discipline of political science. As indicated earlier, such dynamics seem to be a normal part of configuration and reconfiguration of intellectual enterprises generally. It is likely that public administration has as much integrity and clarity about its enterprise as most other fields have at a comparable stage of development; it seems unlikely that worry over precise disciplinary status should be more of a hindrance to public administration than it has been or is to other fields.

Sometimes worry over the issue of professional status is part of the perceived identity crisis. Thus, it is sometimes asked whether public administration is or can aspire to be a profession, and frequently this is framed with specific reference to traditional professions. Though such a question may have interesting implications, there seems to be a developing consensus that it is important to articulate appropriate professional standards, expectations, and ethics without worrying unduly about whether the field is a profession in all the senses of the traditional professions (e.g., law, medicine, and religious ministry). Still, questions about professional status have contributed to the sense some have of identity crisis.

A related aspect of this identity insecurity is concern over unifying theory: it is frequently said that public administration lacks a unifying theory such as some other fields or disciplines are alleged to have. It is true that public administration may tend to draw from a more multidisciplinary pool of knowledge than some fields, though even this is more often than not exaggerated (as reflection upon the developing edges of even hard sciences would suggest). It may be true that the practitioner connection gives public administration a somewhat more eclectic appearance than some fields; but, again, this eclecticism and its related complexities and nuances may be more usual in the development of fields than is sometimes recognized (as reflection upon the diversity of investigations and applications in most of the social or human sciences may suggest). As to theoretical unity or clear dominant paradigms, it is likely that the presence of such in many fields, as well as its absence in public administration, may be regularly overstated.

The fact that the field of public administration is both an academic endeavor and a professional field is sometimes thought to limit the field's disciplinary possibilities. Thus some suggest that public administration should be thought of as an applied field of practice and training, while basic research and education should be recognized as taking place in other fields which are thought to be more clearly disciplines or sciences. Sometimes the suggestion is made—most notably identified with Dwight Waldo—that public administration may be a field, discipline, or science in the way that medicine is; and that like medicine, it may be both a scientific and practitioner concern which draws on such other fields of learning as it finds fruitful to its own purposes and activities.

Perhaps the most important aspect of the concern about legitimacy and identity of the field has to do explicitly with the question of political legitimacy. Long ago, most debate about whether a specific government was legitimate or not would have rested upon questions of the line of succession or mystical or religious indication of the identity of the legitimate ruler. For much of the present-day world—and certainly most of the world in which public administration would have conscious identity—the question of governmental legitimacy turns on the public good (in many cases expressed in terms of the interest of the citizenry or even the will of the people). Under this understanding of legitimacy, questions of the legitimacy of public administration (essentially nonelected skill-based participants in rule) are difficult. A traditional answer to the problem posed has been that the public administrators bring their skills, training, and job experience to serve the purposes and directions indicated by the peoples' representatives (who frequently, and especially within representative governments, have been selected through some devices, such as elections, in which the citizens have had a voice). This is sometimes referred to as administrative neutrality: the idea that civil servants will bring their knowledge and skills to the service of whichever party or set of individuals is chosen to govern from time to time. This answer is still the largely unquestioned theory of public administration legitimacy in many parts of the world. Where public administration has been interpreted more frequently as having large aspects of discretion, policy formulation responsibilities, and relatively autonomous leadership roles, though, the possibility or appropriateness of neutrality has been increasingly called into question. This has left the field of public administration with the need to understand and explicate precisely how public administrators are or can be legitimate with reference to the citizenry and duly established political orders. Working out the important ramifications of such questions leads to dialogue and debate about the foundations of public administration legitimacy, and this leads some to articulate a sense that the field is in search of its role, identity, and purpose.

When these and other aspects—the mix, priority, and relative weight of specific aspects varies from context to context and polity to polity—of public administration identity are given serious and continuous deliberation and debate, it is understandable that fundamental questions about the status of public administration take on critical importance. The issues and the dialogue are not presently at rest, and they are not likely to be in the foreseeable future.

FUTURE OF THE FIELD

Though the field of public administration is perennially concerned about the identity and security of the field, the future and identity seem secure even if the exact intellectual configuration cannot be precisely predicted.

The "practice" of public administration is affected everywhere by political and resource changes. Visible aspects of such changes at the present time are concerns over the resources devoted to governmental and public activities (taxes, the portion of the economy devoted to governmental or public sector activities, etc.); increased interest in many places in introducing greater aspects of market factors into heretofore non-market public sector activities; continued interest in countering hierarchical and impersonal ("red tape," etc.) aspects; and continued concern about responsibility and accountability to the citizenry and its interests. The practice of public administration also experiences today, as it always has, the challenges of technological developments. Such concerns and interests bespeak possible changes in public administration, but they probably do not threaten the existence or identity of the practice, occupations, or vocations of public administration.

The "academic" part of public administration has continually undergone change, and in recent history it has continually interpreted such change as fundamental or as a matter of identity and essence. Intellectual history and the sociology of knowledge would suggest that we should expect the study of public administration to be buffeted by the winds of intellectual change, growth, and challenge (as all active fields of thought will be). Thus, public administration will participate in, and be influenced by, developments in virtually all areas of human thought. Presently, the field is visibly influenced not only by incremental developments of preexisting themes and directions, but also by the host of intellectual, philosophical, methodological, epistemological, and esthetic developments which are loosely grouped under labels such as postmodernism. The field has always been influenced by, and participated in, the intellectual climate and dialogue of its times. It will continue to do so. And this will be a sign, not particularly of crises of identity or future, but rather of vitality and engagement.

BIBLIOGRAPHY

Gladden, E. N., 1972. A History of Public Administration. 2 vols. London and Portland, OR: Frank Cass and Co., Ltd.

Lynn, Naomi B. and Aaron Wildavksy, eds., 1990. Public Administration: The State of the Discipline. Chatham, NJ: Chatham House.

Mill, John Stuart, ([1861] 1991). Considerations on Representative Government. Buffalo, NY: Prometheus Books.

Mosher, Frederick C., ed., 1975. American Public Administration: Past, Present, Future. University: University of Alabama Press.

Perry, James L., ed., 1989. Handbook of Public Administration, 2nd ed. 1996 San Francisco: Jossey-Bass Inc.

Shafritz, Jay M. and Albert C. Hyde, eds., 1992. Classics of Public Administration. 3d ed. Pacific Grove, CA: Brooks/Cole.

Wilson, Woodrow, 1887. "The Study of Administration." Political Science Quarterly, vol. 2 (June).

2

Woodrow Wilson

THE STUDY OF ADMINISTRATION

I SUPPOSE that that no practical science is ever studied where there is no need to know it. The very fact, therefore, that the eminently practical science of administration is finding its way into college courses in this country would prove that this country needs to know more about administration, were such proof of the fact required to make out a case. It need not be said, however, that we do not look into college programmes for proof of this fact. It is a thing almost taken for granted among us, that the present movement called civil service reform must, after the accomplishment of its first purpose, expand into efforts to improve, not the *personnel* only, but also the organization and methods of our government offices: because it is plain that their organization and methods need improvement only less than their *personnel*. It is the object of administrative study to discover, first, what government can properly and successfully do, and, secondly, how it can do these proper things with the utmost possible efficiency and at the least possible cost either of money or of energy. On both these points there is obviously much need of light among us; and only careful study can supply that light.

Before entering on that study, however, it is needful:

I. To take some account of what others have done in the same line; that is to say, of the history of the study.

II. To ascertain just what is its subject-matter.

III. To determine just what are the best methods by which to develop it, and the most clarifying political conceptions to carry with us into it.

Unless we know and settle these things, we shall set out without chart or compass.

I.

The science of administration is the latest fruit of that study of the science of politics which was begun some twenty-two hundred years ago. It is a birth of our century, almost of our own generation.

Why was it so late in coming? Why did it wait till this too busy century of ours to demand attention for itself? Administration is the most obvious part of government; it is government in action; it is the executive, the operative, the most visible side of government, and is of course as old as government itself. It is government in action, and one might very naturally expect to find that government in action had arrested the attention and provoked the scrutiny of writers of politics very early in the history of systematic thought.

But such was not the case. No one wrote systematically of administration as a branch of the science of government until the present century had passed its first youth and had begun to put forth its characteristic flower of systematic knowledge. Up to our own day all the political writers whom we now read had thought, argued, dogmatized only about the *constitution* of government; about the nature of the state, the essence and seat of sovereignty, popular power and kingly prerogative; about the greatest meanings lying at the heart of government, and the high ends set before the purpose of government by man's nature and man's aims. The central field of controversy was that great field of theory in which monarchy rode tilt against democracy, in which oligarchy would have built for itself strongholds of privilege, and in which tyranny sought opportunity to make good its claim to receive submission from all competitors. Amidst this high warfare of principles, administration could command no pause for its own consideration. The question was always: Who shall make law, and what shall that law be? The other question, how law should be administered with enlightenment, with equity, with speed, and without friction, was put aside as "practical detail" which clerks could arrange after doctors had agreed upon principles.

This is the reason why administrative tasks have nowadays to be so studiously and systematically adjusted to carefully tested standards of policy, the reason why we are having now what we never had before, a science of administration. The weightier debates of constitutional principle are even yet by no means concluded; but they are no longer of more immediate practical moment than questions of administration. It is getting to be harder to *run* a constitution than to frame one.

There is scarcely a single duty of government which was once simple which is not now complex; government once had but a few masters; it now has scores of masters. Majorities formerly only underwent government; they now conduct government. Where government once might follow the whims of a court, it must now follow the views of a nation.

And those views are steadily widening to new conceptions of state duty; so that, at the same time that the functions of government are every day becoming more complex and difficult. The idea of the state and the consequent ideal of its duty are undergoing noteworthy change; and "the idea of the state is the conscience of administration." Seeing every day new things which the state ought to do, the next thing is to see clearly how it ought to do them.

This is why there should be a science of administration which shall seek to straighten the paths of government, to make its business less unbusinesslike, to strengthen and purify its organization, and to crown its duties with dutifulness. This is one reason why there is such a science.

But where has this science grown up? Surely not on this side the sea. Not much impartial scientific method is to be discerned in our administrative practices. The poisonous atmosphere of city government, the crooked secrets of state administration, the confusion, sinecurism, and corruption ever and again discovered in the bureaux at Washington forbid us to believe that any clear conceptions of what constitutes good administration are as yet very widely current in the United States. No; American writers have hitherto taken no very important part in the advancement of this science. It has found its doctors in Europe. It is not of our making; it is a foreign science, speaking very little of the language of English or American principle. It employs only foreign tongues; it utters none but what are to our minds alien ideas. Its aims, its examples, its conditions, are almost exclusively grounded in the histories of foreign races, in the precedents of foreign systems, in the lessons of foreign revolutions. It has been developed by French and German professors, and is consequently in all parts adapted to the needs of a compact state, and made to fit highly centralized forms of government; whereas, to answer our purposes, it must be adapted, not to a simple and compact, but to a complex and multiform state, and made to fit highly decentralized forms of government. If we would employ it, we must Americanize it, and that not formally, in language merely, but radically, in thought, principle, and aim as well. It must learn our constitutions by heart; must get the bureaucratic fever out of its veins; must inhale much free American air.

On this side the sea we, the while, had known no great difficulties of government. With a new country, in which there was room and remunerative employment for everybody, with liberal principles of government and unlimited skill in practical politics, we were long exempted from the need of being anxiously careful about plans and methods of administration. We have naturally been slow to see the use or significance of those many volumes of learned research and painstaking examination into the ways and means of conducting government which the presses of Europe have been sending to our libraries. Like a lusty child, government with us has expanded in nature and grown great in stature, but has also become awkward in movement. The vigor and increase of its life has been altogether out of proportion to its skill in living. It has gained strength, but it has not acquired deportment. Great, therefore, as has been our advantage over the countries of Europe in point of ease and health of constitutional development, now that the time for more careful administrative adjustments and larger administrative knowledge has come to us, we are at a signal disadvantage as compared with the transatlantic nations; and this for reasons which I shall try to make clear.

Judging by the constitutional histories of the chief nations of the modern world, there may be said to be three periods of growth through which government has passed in all the most highly developed of existing systems, and through which it promises to pass in all the rest. The first of these periods is that of absolute rulers, and of an administrative system adapted to absolute rule; the second is that in which constitutions are framed to do away with absolute rulers and substitute popular control, and in which administration is neglected for these higher concerns; and the third is that in which the sovereign people undertake to develop administration under this new constitution which has brought them into power.

Those governments are now in the lead in administrative practice which had rulers still absolute but also enlightened when those modern days of political illumination came in which it was made evident to all but the blind that governors are properly only the servants of the governed. In such governments administration has been organized to subserve the general weal with the simplicity and effectiveness vouchsafed only to the undertakings of a single will.

The English race, consequently, has long and successfully studied the art of curbing executive power to the constant neglect of the art of perfecting executive methods. It has exercised itself much more in controlling than in energizing government. It has been more concerned to render government just and moderate than to make it facile, well-ordered, and effective. English and American political history has been a history, not of administrative development, but of legislative oversight,—not of progress in governmental organization, but of advance in law-making and political criticism. Consequently, we have reached a time when administrative study and creation are imperatively necessary to the well-being of our governments saddled with the habits of a long period of constitution-making. That period has practically closed, so far as the establishment of essential principles is concerned, but we cannot shake off its atmosphere. We go on criticizing when we ought to be creating. We have reached the third of the periods I have mentioned,—the period, namely, when the people have to develop administration in accordance with the constitutions they won for themselves in a previous period of struggle with absolute power; but we are not prepared for the tasks of the new period.

Such an explanation seems to afford the only escape from blank astonishment at the fact that, in spite of our vast advantages in point of political liberty, and above all in point of practical political skill and sagacity, so many nations are ahead of us in administrative organization and administrative skill. Why, for instance, have we but just begun purifying a civil service which was rotten full fifty years ago? To say that slavery diverted us is but to repeat what I have said—that flaws in our constitution delayed us.

Of course all reasonable preference would declare for this English and American course of politics rather than for that of any European country. We should not like to have had Prussia's history for the sake of having Prussia's administrative skill; and Prussia's particular system of administration would quite suffocate us. It is better to be untrained and free than to be servile and systematic. Still there is no denying that it would be better yet to be both free in spirit and proficient in practice. It is this even more reasonable preference which impels us to discover what there may be to hinder or delay us in naturalizing this much-to-be-desired science of administration.

What, then, is there to prevent?

Well, principally, popular sovereignty. It is harder for democracy to organize administration than for monarchy. The very completeness of our most cherished political successes in the past embarrasses us. We have enthroned public opinion; and it is forbidden us to hope during its reign for any quick schooling of the sovereign in executive expertness or in the conditions of perfect functional balance in government. The very fact that we have realized popular rule in its fullness has made the task of *organizing* that rule just so much the more difficult. In order to make any advance at all we must instruct and persuade a multitudinous monarch called public opinion,—a much less feasible undertaking than to influence a single monarch called a king. An individual sovereign will adopt a simple plan and carry it out directly: he will have but one opinion, and he will embody that one opinion in one command. But this other sovereign, the people, will have a score of differing opinions. They can agree upon nothing simple: advance must be made through compromise, by a compounding of differences, by a trimming of plans and a suppression of too straightforward principles. There will be a succession of resolves running through a course of years, a dropping fire of commands running through a whole gamut of modifications.

Wherever regard for public opinion is a first principle of government, practical reform must be slow and all reform must be full of compromises. For wherever public opinion exist it must rule. This is now an axiom half the world over, and will presently come to be believed even in Russia. Whoever would effect a change in a modern constitutional government must first educate his fellow-citizens to want *some* change. That done, he must persuade them to want the particular change he wants. He must first make public opinion willing to listen and then see to it that it listen to the right things. He must stir it up to search for an opinion, and then manage to put the right opinion in its way.

The first step is not less difficult than the second. With opinions, possession is more than nine points of the law. It is next to impossible to dislodge them. Institutions which one generation regards as only a makeshift approximation to the realization of a principle, the next generation honors as the nearest possible approximation to that principle, and the next worships as the principle itself. It takes scarcely three generations for the apotheosis. The grandson accepts his grandfather's hesitating experiment as an integral part of the fixed constitution of nature.

So much, then, for the history of the study of administration, and the peculiarly difficult conditions under which, entering upon it when we do, we must undertake it. What, now, is the subject-matter of this study, and what are its characteristic objects?

II.

The field of administration is a field of business. It is removed from the hurry and strife of politics; it at most points stands apart even from the debatable ground of constitutional study. It is a part of political life only as the methods of the counting-house are a part of the life of society; only as machinery is part of the manufactured product. But it is, at the same time, raised very far above the dull level of mere technical detail by the fact that through its greater principles it is directly connected with the lasting maxims of political wisdom, the permanent truths of political progress.

The object or administrative study is to rescue executive methods from the confusion and costliness of empirical experiment and set them upon foundations laid deep in stable principle.

It is for this reason that we must regard civil-service reform in its present stages as but a prelude to a fuller administrative reform. We are now rectifying methods of appointment; we must go on to adjust executive functions more fitly and to prescribe better methods of executive organization and action. Civil-service reform is thus but a moral preparation for what is to follow. It is clearing the moral atmosphere of official life by establishing the sanctity of public office as a public trust, and, by making the service unpartisan, it is opening the way for making it businesslike. By sweetening its motives it is rendering it capable of improving its methods of work.

Let me expand a little what I have said of the province of administration. Most important to be observed is the truth already so much and so fortunately insisted upon by our civil-service reformers; namely, that administration lies outside the proper sphere of *politics*. Administrative questions are not political questions. Although politics sets the tasks for administration, it should not be suffered to manipulate its offices.

This is distinction of high authority; eminent German writers insist upon it as of course. Bluntschli,[1] for instance, bids us separate administration alike from politics and from law. Politics, he says, is state activity "in things great and universal," while "administration, on the other hand," is "the activity of the state in individual and small things. Politics is thus the special province of the statesman, administration of the technical official." "Policy does nothing without the aid of administration;" but administration is not therefore politics. But we do not require German authority for this position; this discrimination between administration and politics is now, happily, too obvious to need further discussion.

There is another distinction which must be worked into all our conclusions, which, though but another side of that between administration and politics, is not quite so easy to keep sight of: I mean the distinction between *constitutional* and administrative questions, between those governmental adjustments which are essential to

---

[1]Politik, S. 467.

constitutional principle and those which are merely instrumental to the possibly changing purposes of a wisely adapting convenience.

One cannot easily make clear to every one just where administration resides in the various departments of any practicable government without entering upon particulars so numerous as to confuse and distinctions so minute as to distract. No lines of demarcation, setting apart administrative from non-administrative functions, can be run between this and that department of government without being run up hill and down dale, over dizzy heights of distinction and through dense jungles of statutory enactment, hither and thither around "ifs" and "buts," "whens" and "howevers," until they become altogether lost to the common eye not accustomed to this sort of surveying, and consequently not acquainted with the use of the theodolite of logical discernment. A great deal of administration goes about *incognito* to most of the world, being confounded now with political "management," and again with constitutional principle.

Perhaps this ease of confusion may explain such utterances as that of Niebuhr's: "Liberty," he says, "depends incomparably more upon administration than upon constitution." At first sight this appears to be largely true. Apparently facility in the actual exercise of liberty does depend more upon administrative arrangements than upon constitutional guarantees; although constitutional guarantees alone secure the existence of liberty. But—upon second thought—is even so much as this true? Liberty no more consists in easy functional movement than intelligence consists in the ease and vigor with which the limbs of a strong man move. The principles that rule within the man, or the constitution, are the vital springs of liberty of servitude. Because dependence and subjection are without chains, are lightened by every easy-working device of considerate, paternal government, they are not thereby transformed into liberty. Liberty cannot live apart from constitutional principle; and no administration, however perfect and liberal its methods, can give men more than a poor counterfeit of liberty if it rest upon illiberal principles of government.

A clear view of the difference between the province of constitutional law and the province of administrative function ought to leave no room for misconception; and it is possible to name some roughly definite criteria upon which such a view can be built. Public administration is detailed and systematic execution of public law. Every particular application of general law is an act of administration. The assessment and raising of taxes, for instance, the hanging of a criminal, the transportation and delivery of the mails, the equipment and recruiting of the army and navy, *etc.*, are all obviously acts of administration; but the general laws which direct these things to be done are as obviously outside of and above administration. The broad plans of governmental action are not administrative; the detailed execution of such plans is administrative. Constitutions, therefore, properly concern themselves only with those instrumentalities of government which are to control general law. Our federal constitution observes this principle in saying nothing of even the greatest of the purely executive offices, and speaking only of that President of the Union who was to share the legislative and policy-making functions of government, only of those judges of highest jurisdiction who were to interpret and guard its principles, and not of those who were merely to give utterance to them.

This is not quite the distinction between Will and answering Deed, because the administrator should have and does have a will of his own in the choice of means for accomplishing his work. He is not and ought not to be a mere passive instrument. The distinction is between general plans and special means.

There is, indeed, one point at which administrative studies trench on constitutional ground—or at least upon what seems constitutional ground. The study of administration, philosophically viewed, is closely connected with the study of the proper distribution of constitutional authority. To be efficient it must discover the simplest arrangements by which responsibility can be unmistakably fixed upon officials; the best way of dividing authority without hampering it, and responsibility without obscuring it. And this question of the distribution of authority, when taken into the sphere of the higher, the originating functions of government, is obviously a central constitutional question. If administrative study can discover the best principles upon which to base such distribution, it will have done constitutional study an invaluable service. Montesquieu did not, I am convinced, say the last word on this head.

To discover the best principle for the distribution of authority is of greater importance, possibly, under a democratic system, where officials serve many masters, than under others where they serve but a few. All sovereigns are suspicious of their servants, and the sovereign people is no exception to the rule; but how is its suspicion to be allayed by *knowledge*? If that suspicion could be but be clarified into wise vigilance, it would be altogether salutary; if that vigilance could be aided by the unmistakable placing of responsibility, it would be altogether beneficent. Suspicion in itself is never healthful either in the private or in the public mind. *Trust is strength* in all relations of life; and, as it is the office of the constitutional reformer to create conditions of trustfulness, so it is the office of the administrative organizer to fit administration with conditions of clear-cut responsibility which shall insure trustworthiness.

And let me say that large powers and unhampered discretion seem to me the indispensable conditions of responsibility. Public attention must be easily directed, in each case of good or bad administration, to just the man deserving of praise or blame. There is no danger in power, if only it be not irresponsible. If it be divided, dealt out in shares to many, it is obscured; and if it be obscured, it is made irresponsible. But if it be centred in heads of the service and in heads of branches of the service, it is easily watched and brought to book. If to keep his office a man must achieve open and honest success, and if at the same time he feels himself intrusted with large freedom of discretion, the greater his power the less likely is he to abuse it, the more is he nerved and sobered and elevated by it. The less his power, the more safely obscure and unnoticed does he feel his position to be, and the more readily does he relapse into remissness.

Just here we manifestly emerge upon the field of that still larger question,—the proper relations between public opinion and administration.

To whom is official trustworthiness to be disclosed, and by whom is it to be rewarded? Is the official to look to the public for his meed of praise and his push of promotion, or only to his superior in office? Are the people to be called in to settle administrative discipline as they are called in to settle constitutional principles? These questions evidently find their root in what is undoubtedly the fundamental problem of this whole study. That problem is: What part shall public opinion take in the conduct of administration?

The right answer seems to be, that public opinion shall play the part of authoritative critic.

But the *method* by which its authority shall be made to tell? Our peculiar American difficulty in organizing administration is not the danger of losing liberty, but the danger of not being able or willing to separate its essentials from its accidents. Our success is made doubtful by that besetting error of ours, the error of trying to do too much by vote. Self-government does not consist in having a hand in everything, any more than housekeeping consists necessarily in cooking dinner with one's own hands. The cook must be trusted with a large discretion as to the management of the fires and the ovens.

The problem is to make public opinion efficient without suffering it to be meddlesome. Directly exercised, in the oversight of the daily details and in the choice of the daily means of government, public criticism is of course a clumsy nuisance, a rustic handling delicate machinery. But as superintending the greater forces of formative policy alike in politics and administration, public criticism is altogether safe and beneficent, altogether indispensable. Let administrative study find the best means for giving public criticism this control and for shutting it out from all other interference.

There is an admirable movement towards universal political education now afoot in this country. The time will soon come when no college of respectability can afford to do without a well-filled chair of political science. But the education thus imparted will go but a certain length. It will multiply the number of intelligent critics of government, but it will create no competent body of administrators. It will prepare the way for the development of a sure-footed understanding of the general principles of government, but it will not necessarily foster skill in conducting government. It is an education which will equip legislators, perhaps, but not executive officials. If we are to improve public opinion, which is the motive power of government, we must prepare better officials as the *apparatus* of government. If we are to put in new boilers and to mend the fires which drive our governmental machinery, we must not leave the old wheels and joints and valves and bands to creak and buzz and clatter on as best they may at bidding of the new force. We must put in new running parts wherever there is the least lack of strength or adjustment. It will be necessary to organize democracy by sending up to the competitive examinations for the civil service men definitely prepared for standing liberal tests as to technical knowledge. A technically schooled civil service will presently have become indispensable.

I know that a corps of civil servants prepared by a special schooling and drilled, after appointment, into a perfected organization, with appropriate hierarchy and characteristic discipline, seems to a great many very thoughtful persons to contain elements which might combine to make an offensive official class,—a distinct semi-corporate body with sympathies divorced from those of a progressive, free-spirited people, and with hearts narrowed to the meanness of a bigoted officialism. Certainly such a class would be altogether hateful and harmful in the

United States. Any measures calculated to produce it would for us be measures of reaction and of folly.

But to fear the creation of a domineering, illiberal officialism as a result of the studies I am here proposing is to miss altogether the principle upon which I wish most to insist. That principle is, that administration in the United States must be at all points sensitive to public opinion. A body of thoroughly trained officials serving during good behavior we must have in any case: that is a plain business necessity. But the apprehension that such a body will be anything un-American clears away the moment it is asked, What is to constitute good behavior? For that question obviously carries its own answer on its face. Steady, hearty allegiance to the policy of the government they serve will constitute good behavior. That *policy* will have no taint of officialism about it. It will not be the creation of permanent officials, but of statesmen whose responsibility to public opinion will be direct and inevitable. Bureaucracy can exist only where the whole service of the state is removed from the common political life of the people, its chiefs as well as its rank and file. Its motives, its objects, its policy, its standards, must be bureaucratic. It would be difficult to point out any examples of impudent exclusiveness and arbitrariness on the part of officials doing service under a chief of department who really served the people, as all our chiefs of departments must be made to do.

The ideal for us is a civil service cultured and self-sufficient enough to act with sense and vigor, and yet so intimately connected with the popular thought, but means of elections and constant public counsel, as to find arbitrariness or class spirit quite out of the question.

III.

Having thus viewed in some sort the subject-matter and the objects of this study of administration, what are we to conclude as to the methods best suited to it—the points of view most advantageous for it?

We are a practical people, made so apt, so adept in self-government by centuries of experimental drill that we are scarcely any longer capable of perceiving the awkwardness of the particular system we may be using, just because it is so easy for us to use any system. We do not study the art of governing: we govern. But mere unschooled genius for affairs will not save us from sad blunders in administration. Though democrats by long inheritance and repeated choice, we are still rather crude democrats. Old as democracy is, its organization on a basis of modern ideas and conditions is still an unaccomplished work. The democratic state has yet to be equipped for carrying those enormous burdens of administration which the needs of this industrial and trading age are so fast accumulating. Without comparative studies in government we cannot rid ourselves of the misconception that administration stands upon an essentially different basis in a democratic state from that on which it stands in a non-democratic state.

So far as administrative functions are concerned, all governments have a strong structural likeness; more than that, if they are to be uniformly useful and efficient, they *must* have a strong structural likeness. A free man has the same bodily organs, the same executive parts, as the slave, however different may be his motives, his services, his energies. Monarchies and democracies, radically different as they are in other respects, have in reality much the same business to look to.

But, besides being safe, it is necessary to see that for all governments alike the legitimate ends of administration are the same, in order not to be frightened at the idea of looking into foreign systems of administration for instruction and suggestion; in order to get rid of the apprehension that we might perchance blindly borrow something incompatible with our principles.

We can borrow the science of administration with safety and profit if only we read all fundamental differences of condition into its essential tenets. We have only to filter it through out constitutions, only to put it over a slow fire of criticism and distil away its foreign gases.

I know that there is a sneaking fear in some conscientiously patriotic minds that studies of European systems might signalize some foreign methods as better than some American methods; and the fear is easily to be understood. But it would scarcely be avowed in just any company.

It is the more necessary to insist upon thus putting away all prejudices against looking anywhere in the world but at home for suggestions in this study, because nowhere else in the whole field of politics, it would seem, can we make use of the historical, comparative method more safely than in this province of administration. Perhaps the more novel the forms we study the better. We shall the sooner learn the peculiarities of our own methods. We can never learn either our own weaknesses or our own virtues by comparing ourselves with ourselves. We are too used to the appearance and procedure of our own system to see its true significance. Perhaps even the English system is too much like our own to be used to the most profit in illustration. It is best on the whole to get entirely away from our own atmosphere and to be most careful in examining such systems as those of France and Germany. Seeing our own institutions through such *media*, we see ourselves as foreigners might see us were they to look at us without preconceptions. Of ourselves, so long as we know only ourselves, we know nothing.

Let it be noted that it is the distinction, already drawn, between administration and politics which makes the comparative method so safe in the field of administration. When we study the administrative systems of France and Germany, knowing that we are not in search of *political* principles, we need not care a peppercorn for the constitutional or political reasons which Frenchmen or Germans give for their practices when explaining them to us. By keeping this distinction in view—that is, by studying administration as a means of putting our own politics into convenient practice, as a means of making what is democratically politic towards all administratively possible towards each,—we are on perfectly safe ground, and can learn without error what foreign systems have to teach us. We thus devise an adjusting weight for our comparative method of study. We can thus scrutinize the anatomy of foreign governments without fear of getting any of their diseases into our veins; dissect alien systems without apprehension of blood-poisoning.

Our own politics must be the touchstone for all theories. The principles on which to base a science of administration for America must be principles which have democratic policy very much at heart. And, to suit American habit, all general theories must, as theories, keep modestly in the background, not in open argument only, but even in our own minds,—lest opinions satisfactory only to the standards of the library should be dogmatically used, as if they must be quite as satisfactory to the standards of practical politics as well. Doctrinaire devices must be postponed to tested practices. Arrangements not only sanctioned by conclusive experience elsewhere but also congenial to American habit must be preferred without hesitation to theoretical perfection. In a word, steady, practical statesmanship must come first, closet doctrine second. The cosmopolitan what-to-do must always be commanded by the American how-to-do-it.

Our duty is, to supply the best possible life to a *federal* organization, to systems within systems; to make town, city, county, state, and federal governments live with a like strength and an equally assured healthfulness, keeping each unquestionably its own master and yet making all interdependent and co-operative, combining independence with mutual helpfulness. The task is great and important enough to attract the best minds.

This interlacing of local self-government with federal self-government is quite a modern conception. It is not like the arrangements or imperial federation in Germany. There local government is not yet, fully, local *self*-government. The bureaucrat is everywhere busy. His efficiency springs out of *espirit de corps*, out of care to make ingratiating obeisance to the authority of a superior, or, at best, out of the soil of a sensitive conscience. He serves, not the public, but an irresponsible minister. The question for us is, how shall our series of governments within governments be so administered that it shall always be to the interest of the public officer to serve, not his superior alone but the community also, with the best efforts of his talents and the soberest service of his conscience? How shall such service be made to his commonest interest by contributing abundantly to his sustenance, to his dearest interest by furthering his ambition, and to his highest interest by advancing his honor and establishing his character? And how shall this be done alike for the local part and for the national whole?

If we solve this problem we shall again pilot the world. There is a tendency—is there not?—a tendency as yet dim, but already steadily impulsive and clearly destined to prevail, towards, first the confederation of parts of empires like the British, and finally of great states themselves. Instead of centralization of power, there is to be wide union with tolerated divisions of prerogative. This is a tendency towards the American type—of governments joined with governments for the pursuit of common purposes, in honorary equality and honorable subordination. Like principles of civil liberty are everywhere fostering like methods of government; and if comparative studies of the ways and means of government should enable us to offer suggestions which will practicably combine openness and vigor in the administration of such governments with ready docility to all serious, well-sustained public criticism, they will have approved themselves worthy to be ranked among the highest and most fruitful of the great departments of political study. That they will issue in such suggestions I confidently hope.

3

Camilla Stivers

FEMINIST THEORY OF PUBLIC ADMINISTRATION

The theory that interprets or explains public administration or its various aspects from a feminist perspective. Although feminism includes a wide range of viewpoints, most, if not all, feminists maintain a critical perspective on women's current economic and social status and prospects, employ gender as a central element in social analysis, and are committed to the idea that men and women should share equally "in the work, in the privileges, in the defining and the dreaming of the world" (Lerner 1984, p. 33). Feminist theories of public administration, then, use gender as a lens through which to analyze critically women's current status and role in public agencies, bring to light ways in which gender bias inhabits ideas and practices in the field, and formulate new theoretical approaches.

Two types of feminist theory can be observed in the literature of public administration. Descriptive theory, based on empirical study, reports on how gender influences current practice in public agencies, especially its effect on women's access to and status in public agency employment, and sometimes attempts to account for observed differences between men's and women's employment experiences. Conceptual theory aims to use gender to rethink the existing philosophy of public administration, focusing on such issues as the politics-administration dichotomy, public bureaucratic structure and practice, the bases for defending the legitimacy of the administrative state, professionalism, leadership, and citizenship in public administration. Initial feminist theorizing in public administration was largely descriptive; more recent literature includes both descriptive and conceptual theories.

DESCRIPTIVE THEORIES

In comparison to closely related fields such as political science and business management, public administration was relatively slow to develop feminist perspectives, but beginning in the mid-1970s work began to appear that documented federal, state, and local government discrimination against women in public employment. This early work notably included a 1976 symposium in *Public Administration Review* edited by Nesta M. Gallas on "Women in Public Administration." Gallas was serving at the time as the first female president of the American Society for Public Administration (ASPA). In addition to two articles assessing the status of women in ASPA itself, the symposium included analyses of why so few women had by that time managed to land top jobs in federal agencies; the role of affirmative action in overcoming employment discrimination against women; strategies to help women administrators perform effectively; and the idea of women's rights as a basis for public policy.

An example of the type of comparative analysis referred to by Stewart is Mary E. Guy's edited collection (1992), which presents results of several studies finding consistent differences between the status of men and women managers in the governments of six states with widely varying political cultures, thus suggesting the persistence of factors that work against the equality of women in public employment. The articles in the collection, reflecting the focus on differences between men's and women's status characteristic of descriptive feminist theory, cover career patterns, personal characteristics, the impact of domestic responsibilities on individuals' ability to cope with work demands, mentoring, sexual harassment, and management style preferences and behaviors. Guy has concluded: "Only through a process of significant change and reform can we expect to see a more equitable balance between the numbers of female and male managers in state agencies" (p. 211). Her recommended strategies include job enrichment for women managers, mentoring, eliminating sexaul harassment, job restructuring to facilitate family obligations, and promoting child care and family leave policies.

CONCEPTUAL THEORIES

Descriptive theories take for granted existing modes of thought in public administration and examine the extent to which women have gained access to the world of practice, but conceptual theories call into question the frameworks within which public administration is typically understood. The basic premise of conceptual feminist theories is that existing perspectives, for all their apparent objectivity, contain hidden gender biases. Taking gender into account, therefore, involves more than simply adding women to public agencies; instead it entails rethinking fundamental theoretical assumptions, approaches, and concepts.

An early example of this approach to the theory of public administration is that of Robert B. Denhardt and Jan Perkins (1976), who argued that mainstream organizational analysis works from within a paradigm in which the reigning means-ends model of rationality, though purportedly universal-neutral, is in actuality culturally masculine. Denhardt and Perkins suggested that feminist theory provides an alternative paradigm in which process replaces task as the primary orientation, and hierarchy is challenged by an egalitarian framework. They noted that simply adding women to public organizations will not be enough to dislodge the "administrative man" paradigm; instead, a change of consciousness is necessary, one that replaces traditional ideas of professional expertise with the feminist notion of the authority of personal experience as the ethical basis of administrative practice.

Kathy Ferguson (1984) expanded the idea that liberal reforms, such as increasing the number of women in management positions, is not enough to end gender bias in public administration; real change entails a new approach grounded in the historical-cultural experiences of women. Ferguson argued that to encounter bureaucracy on its own terms, such as by integrating women into public organizations, precludes a decisive attack on typical bureaucratic patterns of hierarchy. Only women's "marginal" perspective, which has emerged as a result of their historical exclusion from the public realm, offers the hope of real transformation, redefining notions of power, rationality, and leadership. As Ferguson has noted, "To challenge bureaucracy in the name of the values and goals of feminist discourse is to undermine the chain of command, equalize the participants, subvert the monopoly of information and secrecy of decision-making, and essentially seek to democratize the organization" (pp. 208–209).

Suzanne Franzway, Dianne Court, and R. W. Connell (1989) brought feminist theory to bear on the idea of the bureaucratic state, viewing it as an agent in sexual politics, maintaining and perpetuating through its policies gender bias in society at large and, in turn, being shaped by this bias. The bureaucratic state, in other words, is not "outside" society but enmeshed in it, including its patterns of gender relations. The authors maintained that no theory of the state can avoid issues of sex and gender; they are present, if not always visible, as grounding assumptions or limitations to argument. The bureaucratic state supports the interest of men over those of women not only directly through policies but also ideologically, through characterizing what are actually gender-biased state processes as being simply impersonal and neutral.

Camilla Stivers (1993) presented a feminist reading of the literature on the legitimacy of the administrative state, a central theme of current public administration scholarship. She argued that ideas of expertise, leadership, and virtue that mark defenses of administrative power have culturally masculine features that privilege masculinity over femininity. This characteristic masculinity of public administration, though ignored by most theorists, contributes to and is sustained by gender bias in society at large. In Stivers' (1993) view, "As long as we go on viewing the enterprise of administration as genderless, women will continue to face their present Hobson's choice, which is either to adopt a masculine administrative identity or accept marginalization in the bureaucratic hierarchy" (p. 10).

Even though scholars of public administration tend to praise its differences from private business, Stivers argued, the publicness of public administration is problematic because of the historical and theoretical exclusion of women from the public sphere, which has barred issues such as the division of household labor from policy debate. The administrative state can only function as it does because women bear a lopsided share of the burden of domestic work, without which society would grind to a halt; thus public administrative structures and practices depend for their coherence and their effectiveness on the oppression of women.

Conceptual theorists agree that simply adding women to the bureaucracy will not be enough to end enduring patterns of gender bias; instead, new modes of thought are required, ones that call into question the neutrality of such central ideas as professionalism, leadership, and the public interest. The extent to which administrative agency policies and practices can change will also depend partly on such larger social transformations as the sexual division of labor in the household, a sphere that shapes and is shaped by the administrative state.

BIBLIOGRAPHY

Denhardt, Robert B., and Jan Perkins, 1976. "The Coming Death of Administrative Man." *Public Administrative Review*, vol. 36, no. 4 (July-August): 379–384.

Eyde, Lorraine, D., 1973. "The Status of Women in State and Local Government." *Public Personnel Management* (May-June): 205–211.

Ferguson, Kathy E., 1984. *The Feminist Case Against Bureaucracy*. Philadelphia: Temple University Press.

Franzway, Suzanne, Dianne Court and R. W. Connell, eds., 1989. *Staking a Claim: Feminism, Bureaucracy and the State*. Sydney, Australia: Allen and Unwin.

Gallas, Nesta M., ed., 1976. "A Symposium: Women in Public Administration." *Public Administration Review*. vol. 36. no. 4 (July-August): 347–389.

Guy, Mary E., ed., 1992. *Women and Men of the States: Public Administrators at the State Level*. Armonk, NY: M. E. Sharpe.

Hall, Mary M., and Rita Mae Kelly, eds., 1989. *Gender, Bureaucracy, and Democracy: Careers and Equal Opportunity in the Public Sector*. Westport, CT: Greenwood Press.

Lerner, Gerda, 1984. "The Rise of Feminist Consciousness." In E. M. Bender, B. Burk, and N. Walker, eds., *All of Us Are Present*. Columbia, MO: James Madison Wood Research Institute, Stephens College.

Mohr, Judith, 1973. "Why Not More Women City Managers?" *Public Management* (February-March): 2–5.

Stewart, Debra, 1990. "Women in Public Administration." In Naomi B. Lynn, and Aaron B. Wildavsky, eds., *Public Administration: The State of the Discipline*. Chatham, NJ: Chatham House.

Stivers, Camilla, 1993. *Gender Images in Public Administration: Legitimacy and the Administrative State*. Newbury Park, CA: Sage.

2

THE PRACTICE OF PUBLIC ADMINISTRATION

Public administration is one of the most diverse, significant and personally satisfying fields in which to work. While executives in private corporations, or professionals such as dentists or brain surgeons, may bring home more income and become wealthier, public administrators have the satisfaction of working for wider goals. Their work extends beyond self-enrichment, and in doing so they often face truly demanding issues and complexities. They must learn to work within the democratic political process by which competing interests have to be balanced for the common good.

WORKING FOR THE COMMON GOOD

This key idea can be traced right back to 1789 when, in the Preamble to the Constitution, the founding fathers spoke of "forming a more perfect Union" that would establish justice, ensure domestic tranquillity, provide for the common defense, secure the blessings of liberty and "promote the general welfare." David H. Rosenbloom says that this commitment to the general welfare "may seem too vague to convey anything of a specific nature, but generally it includes a commitment to economic development and to the provision of services by the government for the purpose of advancing the common good."[1] When the Preamble refers to "domestic tranquillity," this includes law and order as well as the justice and defense functions.

Over the decades, many additional functions have been added to the scope of public administration. Early additions included financial and economic management activities; later additions included activities to do with public education, health and welfare, environmental protection, and safe air and space travel. All of these activities are managed by public administrators who, more often than not, are individuals whose primary motivation is serving the common good.

PUBLIC CHOICE THEORY

The public choice view of the work of public administrators is controversial. An influential group of "new right" theorists proposes that public administrators seek primarily to satisfy their own desires for income, power and status. They use their positions in public agencies for their own selfish ends. These theorists conclude that we should structure and arrange our public services to minimize opportunities for this to happen. We should transfer as many decisions and services as possible out of government to individuals in the community. As few government services should be provided as possible, leaving people to spend their own money rather than finance public purposes through taxes. If a public service must be provided, these theorists argue for the "user pays" principle, or for "vouchers" as the basis to allocate services. By so doing, maximum choice would be left to individuals, and the minimum discretion and power would be left to "self-serving bureaucrats."

As a practicing public administrator, you will find among your colleagues and among the public with whom you deal some people who are motivated by the more optimistic of these views—people who see their work as truly serving the public. You may also encounter individuals who are out to serve only themselves, as well as legislators and members of the public who cannot understand how any broader motivation could exist.

THE ADMINISTRATIVE STATE

Regardless of the range of purposes individual public administrators may be pursuing, political decisions over the years have cumulated to build what F. Morstein Marx has termed "the administrative state."[2] According to Rosenbloom, "the essence of the administrative state and the need for large scale administrative action lie in the policy choice of governments to undertake action themselves to achieve their ultimate political goals."[3] Apart from the progressive addition of governmental functions over the years, governments also decided to "place heavy reliance upon direct provision of services and functions by government as opposed to reliance solely upon the manipulation of subsidies for private action."[4]

This direct service approach underlies some of the long-term growth in the U.S. public sector to the level where public employees now number in the millions. And, it was against this assumption—that services should be provided directly by government—that Osborne and Gaebler directed their famous *reinventing government* line that government should "steer, not row."[5]

The *reinventing government reform movement* of the late 1980s and 1990s literally has changed the way the practice of public administration occurs in many American jurisdictions, often by questioning the means rather than the ends. Direct delivery of services by government has thus given way to privatization. (See also Chapter 4.) A surprising variety of public services are contracted out into the business and nonprofit sectors—transforming many public administrators from persons who delivered services into persons who plan, arrange, and monitor contracts for services that are delivered by employees of private organizations on behalf of government. (See also Chapter 14.) The American administrative state is still with us, but its role has taken an increasingly managerial turn over the past two decades.

THE GLOBAL MOVE TOWARD PUBLIC MANAGEMENT

There have been tidal changes washing over America's public administration as "reinventing government" has become a dominant "movement" in cities, counties, states, and Washington, D.C. The same "movement" is equally pervasive in many other countries around the world, usually under the label of *new public management* or *administrative reform*.[6] In all of these reforms, a move away from direct delivery of services by government toward increased use of privatization or contracting-out has been a central theme. There are other important themes as well, however. These include: the replacement of essentially tenured, lifetime, government employment with shorter term contracts; and, a shift away from a wide view of public administration as a field set in its own ethical framework and political context toward a narrower, financially-dominated paradigm in which the focus is on the achievement of specific results. As a result, the practice of public administration as a lifetime career with a distinctive culture has receded markedly in many countries in the last two decades.

DISTINCTIVE FEATURES OF THE AMERICAN PRACTICE
OF PUBLIC ADMINISTRATION

Looking at global trends makes it easier to see what is "local" and what is "distinctive." The United States has always been known for its commitment to free enterprise and individual initiative. Paradoxically, it has also always been a nation committed to collective purposes, with a remarkably strong and enduring tradition of energetic public policy-making and resourceful implementation of public policy by professional public administrators. Other countries have often sought to copy America's model of government, but in many respects they cannot. The U.S. model of public administration is a product of our unique environment, history, traditions, values, laws and Constitution.

Fred W. Riggs, a long-time student of comparative public administration, argues that U.S. public administration occurs within a fairly unique instance of the presidentialist or "separation of powers" system. Riggs argues that the Pendleton Act of 1883 introduced "a new and uniquely American kind of bureaucrat, someone who was neither a mandarin nor a retainer, but rather someone evaluated on training and experience to occupy a particular position rather than a youth recruited for a lifetime career service with upward mobility assured."[7] Globalization promotes introspection of this kind. As ideas about public service reform spread from country to country, academicians and practitioners wonder why practices that are successful here do not work there. Consultants travel internationally to provide advice on public administration, but from where should they draw their models? The readings reprinted in this chapter by Gray and Jenkins, and Riggs bring these issues sharply into focus.

READINGS REPRINTED IN THIS CHAPTER

The **"Rise of the American Administrative State"** is the provocative title of the excerpt we have chosen from **David H. Rosenbloom's** writings. Rosenbloom traces the purposes of American government back to the 1789 Preamble to the Constitution and lays out the political roots and the legal and managerial origins of the American administrative state. The public administrator practices in a field where political, legal and managerial influences are pervasive, and Rosenbloom describes the interplay among these forces.

Andrew Gray and Bill Jenkins' article, **"From Public Administration to Public Management: Reassessing a Revolution"** (published in the British journal, *Public Administration*),[8] places the immense changes of the American "reinvention movement"—reinvention, privatization, and downsizing—in the context of global changes in the theory and practice of public administration. Gray and Jenkins' searching analysis leads them to conclude that the new public management "has developed an analytical agenda based heavily on the concepts and theories of public choice economics (and associated fellow travelers such as Osborne and Gaebler)."[9] They warn of the risks of accepting new public management in isolation. "We can employ the tenets of traditional public administration to add a necessary constitutional dimension to the theories and prescriptions of public management."[10]

Fred W. Riggs seeks to identify what is unique in American public administration by looking at two variables: bureaucratic power and performance in a presidentialist (separation of powers) system in, **"Public Administration in America: Why Our Uniqueness is Exceptional and Important."**[11] Riggs explains that the American system of public administration differs markedly from all other presidentialist regimes as well as from all parliamentary systems. He concludes that only with a deeper understanding of what is unique in the U.S. system will it be possible to "work more effectively for better public administration at home and also understand what we can and cannot usefully do overseas."

The practice of public administration can be one of the most satisfying of all career choices. Today, however, the practice of public administration exists in a global setting amid a welter of change with over-riding concerns about resource constraints and ever-present scrutiny by legislators, media and the public. If you can handle this kind of complexity and change in an environment of globalism, the practice of public administration may be the career for you.

NOTES

1. Rosenbloom, David H. (1998). *Public Administration: Understanding Management, Politics and Law in the Public Sector. 4th ed.,* New York: McGraw-Hill, p. 48.
2. Morstein Marx, Fritz. (1957). *The Administrative State.* Chicago: University of Chicago Press.
3. Rosenbloom, David H. (1998). *Public Administration: Understanding Management, Politics and Law in the Public Sector. 4th ed.* New York: McGraw-Hill, p. 49.
4. Rosenbloom, David H. (1998). *Public Administration: Understanding Management, Politics and Law in the Public Sector. 4th ed.,* New York: McGraw-Hill, p. 50.
5. Osborne , David, and Ted Gaebler. (1992). *Reinventing Government.* New York: Addison-Wesley, p. 25.
6. See, for example, Richard C. Kearney and Steven W. Hays. (Fall 1998). "Reinventing Government, The New Public Management and Civil Service Systems in International Perspective." *Review of Public Personnel Administration, 18*(4), 38–54 (reprinted in Chapter 11).
7. Riggs, Fred W. (1998). "Public Administration in America: Why Our Uniqueness is Exceptional and Important." *Public Administration Review, 58* (1), 28.
8. Gray, Andrew, and Bill Jenkins. (1995). "From Public Administration to Public Management: Reassessing a Revolution." *Public Administration, 73,* 75–99.
9. Gray, Andrew, and Bill Jenkins. (1995). "From Public Administration to Public Management: Reassessing a Revolution." *Public Administration, 73,* 93.
10. Gray, Andrew, and Bill Jenkins. (1995). "From Public Administration to Public Management: Reassessing a Revolution." *Public Administration, 73,* 95.
11. Riggs, Fred W. (1998). "Public Administration in America: Why our Uniqueness is Exceptional and Important." *Public Administration Review, 58*(1), 22–31.

4

David H. Rosenbloom

THE RISE OF THE AMERICAN ADMINISTRATIVE STATE

Today, there are perhaps 15 million civilian public employees in the United States. The growth of this number in the twentieth century and the development of large administrative components in governments at all levels are generally referred to as the "rise of the administrative state". The term "administrative state" is intended to convey several realities of contemporary government: that a great deal of the society's resources are spent on the salaries and functions of public administrators; that public administrators are crucial to the operation of contemporary government; that, as a whole, they are politically powerful; and that the nation has decided upon a course of attempting to solve its problems and achieve its aims through the use of administrative action. The growth of administrative power is a worldwide phenomenon that affects the nature of governments in virtually all nations.

THE POLITICAL ROOTS OF THE AMERICAN ADMINISTRATIVE STATE

The constitutional government of the United States came into existence in 1789 with some clearly stated formal goals. These are found in the Preamble to the Constitution, which reads:

> WE THE PEOPLE of the United States, in Order to form a more perfect Union, establish Justice, insure domestic Tranquillity, provide for the common defence, promote the general Welfare, and secure the Blessings of Liberty to ourselves and our Posterity, do ordain and establish this CONSTITUTION for the United States of America.

In this passage can be found some of the classic purposes of almost all contemporary nations: the desire to provide for the defense of the political community, for law and order, and for the general welfare. The latter may seem too vague to convey anything of a specific nature, but generally it includes a commitment to economic development and to the provision of services by the government for the purpose of advancing the common good. The idea that the state should provide such services did not develop in Western Europe until the 1660s, but now it is perhaps the most prominent feature of the administrative state. Thus, governments in the United States provide educational services, transportation services, communications services, and services intended to promote health and social and economic well-being in general.

The decisions to pursue these purposes in the first place is political. So is the choice of a means for achieving them. Several alternatives to government sponsor-

Growth of Federal Employment

Year:	Number of Employees	Year:	Number of Employees
1821	6,914	1911	395,905
1831	11,491	1921	561,143
1841	18,038	1931	609,746
1851	26,274	1941	1,437,682
1861	36,672	1951	2,482,666
1871	51,020	1961	2,435,808
1881	100,020	1971	2,862,926
1891	157,442	1981	2,865,000
1901	239,476		

Sources: Through 1951, U.S. Bureau of the Census and Social Science Research Council, *Statistical History of the United States from Colonial Times to the Present* (Stamford, Conn.: Fairfield Publishers, 1965), p. 710. Figures for 1961 and 1971 are from U.S. Civil Service Commission, *Annual Report*, pp. 78, 88, appendix A. The U.S. Bureau of the Census is the source for 1981.

ship of such services do exist. Governments could rely heavily upon private resources and incentives to serve their purposes. For example, private armies of mercenaries were once a common means of waging war or promoting national defense. Education was once a private or church-related endeavor. Taking care of individuals' health and welfare needs was once left up to families and churches. Private action has frequently been augmented by the provision of governmental financial assistance to those individuals whose actions promote general national goals. For instance, at one time mentally retarded person were "sold" to private individuals who would care for them at the least cost to the government, which was willing to pay for this service as part of its commitment to the common interest. Farm subsidies pay private farmers to use the nation's agricultural resources in the national interest. Today, some economists, such as Milton Friedman, argue that education should be supplied by private organizations through a scheme in which the parents of school children would receive tuition vouchers from the government. These could be used at any school the parents felt best suited their children's educational needs. Such an approach, it is argued, would create a greater incentive for schools to operate efficiently and effectively and would also maximize the freedom of parents to choose among competing educational services. Similarly, various incentives can be built into the government's system of taxation to promote individual behavior deemed in the common interest.

It is often feasible for the government to promote its objectives through reliance on private action and the manipulation of subsidies and incentives. But this is not always government's preferred choice of means. Sometimes—indeed, with increasing frequency in the twentieth century—governments seek to achieve their goals through direct public action. For instance, in the housing example, governments seek to assure that everyone is adequately housed by building and running public housing projects. Instead of paying private individuals to take care of the mentally retarded, governments build and operate mental health facilities for this purpose. Similarly, education, defense, and a host of other operations are undertaken by governments.

The essence of the administrative state and the need for large-scale public administration lie in the policy of governments to undertake organizational action themselves to achieve their ultimate political goals. It is commonly believed that the American founding fathers never anticipated that governments in the United States would become engaged in a great of administrative action. However, it is also clear that the Constitution itself indicates the preference for public action in some areas. For instance, it authorizes the federal government to establish post offices and post roads and to raise and direct an army and a navy. Even a brief review of the development of large-scale public administration in the United States during the past two centuries indicates the extent to which such direct administrative action has become increasingly commonplace.

In a thoughtful and succinct analysis, James Q. Wilson has identified several primary roots of the development of the contemporary American administrative state.[1] One was to provide a reliable postal service. The U.S. Post Office was not viewed as an end itself, but rather as a means of promoting economic development and national cohesion.

A second source of administrative growth has been the desire to promote economic development and social well-being through governmental action recognizing the needs of various sectors of the economy. For example, the Department of Agriculture was created in 1862 and the Departments of Commerce and Labor came into existence in 1913. More recently, the Department of Health, Education, and Welfare (now Health and Human Services) and the Departments of Housing and Urban Development, Transportation, Energy, and Education have been created to provide governmental goals in these economic and social areas of American life. Departments such as Agriculture, Labor, and Commerce are often called *clientele departments* because they deal largely with a relatively well-defined category of people who are generally assumed to have common economic interests.

Another source of administrative growth has been defense. The Departments of War and Navy were created in the eighteenth century, but the military establishment did not emerge as the federal government's largest administrative operation until after World War II. Since that time, the Department of Defense has employed as many as a third of all civilian federal workers. Interestingly, this means that about half of all federal employees are employed in two agencies—Defense and the Post Office.[2]

In sum, the political roots of development of contemporary public administration in the United States lie primarily in two political choices made by the government and society. One was that government would exist to promote such objectives as the common defense, economic development, and the general welfare. This was a choice first made back in the late 1780s and reinforced subsequently on many occasions. Second has been the more recent choice of placing heavy reliance upon direct provision of services and functions by the government as opposed to reliance solely upon the manipulation of subsidies for private action. In addition to these factors, the Constitution expresses a desire to promote domestic tranquility, which brings us to what can be considered the legal roots of the contemporary administrative state.

NOTES

1. James Q. Wilson, "The Rise of the Administrative State," *The Public Interest*, 41 (Fall 1975): 77–103.
2. In the late 1970s there were about 980,000 employed in the Department of Defense and some 600,000 in the Postal Service. If the independent Veterans Administration were included in the defense establishment, approximately 200,000 would have to be added.

5

Andrew Gray and Bill Jenkins

FROM PUBLIC ADMINISTRATION TO PUBLIC MANAGEMENT: REASSESSING A REVOLUTION?

In March 1994, Vice President Gore of the United States presented a report to President Clinton entitled *From Red Tape to Results: Creating a Government that Works Better and Costs Less*. On reading its eight hundred recommendations to improve the US

Federal Government, President Clinton is reported to have observed 'government is broken' (Moe 1994, p. 111). A few months later, the UK Government published a White Paper on the Civil Service (Cm 2627, 1994). Stressing continuity and change, the document set out the key principles on which the Civil Service was seen to be based and to which the government claimed to be committed: integrity, political impartiality, objectivity, selection and promotion on merit and accountability through ministers to Parliament (Cm 2627, p. 1). However, against this framework of continuity it also stressed the need for the service to adapt to a changing world characterized by a sharper focus on management and performance, new staffing procedures and an overall cut in total civil service size.

These two initiatives were separate and distinct. Yet, drawing on common ideologies, they represent the practical face of the new public management and a critique of traditional public administration. Further, as a commentator on the Gore report noted, they also reflect the shifting theoretical focus in the study of public administration as 'all reports on government organization and management have as their basis some theory about the nature of government and about the management of that government' (Moe 1994, p. 111).

This last point is significant both for its explicit emphasis on theories of government and governance and for its implicit underlining of the *values* that underpin the study and practice of both public administration and the public management. Thus it is important to recognize that neither the study nor practice of public administration or public management can be divorced from politics. As Caiden has argued, 'all public administration is political; it is an instrument of politics and political values dominate' (1994, p. 126). Such an argument also highlights the question of values and the importance of identifying them in any study of what 'public management' or indeed 'traditional public administration' might be. Although, the focus of this article is on developments in the United Kingdom, it would be wrong to neglect the worldwide debate embracing the theory and practice of public administration in contexts that include at least Australia, Canada, New Zealand and the United States. In each of these countries the traditional theories and practices of public administration are under attack from reform agendas and appear driven by what, on the surface at least, seem to be common ideologies and strategies. Further, in each there has been much talk of administrative revolutions and paradigm shifts.

It is against this background that this article seeks to explore the evolution of public management and public administration in the UK in terms of *both* theory *and* practice. Such breadth of coverage cannot be comprehensive but is necessary since it is the relationship (and often separation) between ideas and practice that is important. To establish whether a revolution in a Kuhnian sense has taken place may not be all that fruitful but it may help to discern what value shifts have taken place and their consequences.

The article will therefore consider the development of traditional public administration and the subsequent emergence of public management as a field by charting its links to and possible divorce from public administration. We then discuss in greater detail the way public management offers structural solutions to administrative problems, the rise of financial management as a major influence on public management theory and practice and the emphasis on quality and entrepreneurship. Finally, the conclusion attempts to portray the strengths and weaknesses of public management as an approach to the study and practice of public administration and government. This will hopefully facilitate the identification of core problems and assist in establishing an agenda for what is to be done.

THE EMERGENCE OF PUBLIC MANAGEMENT: REDEFINING A FIELD?

It is a point of continuing debate whether the study of public administration can in any circumstance be graced by a disciplinary label. Rhodes (1995), for example, has argued that the study of British public administration was traditionally insular, dominated for a long period by an institutionalist tradition characterized by an interest in administrative engineering but a distaste for theory. As Rhodes also observes, this position emphasized, albeit in a traditional sense, the political and ethical context of administration: public administration existed within a wider framework of accountability relationships and political and moral responsibilities. We might add to this the way government and public administration was seen as linked within a framework of administrative law which, while not formalized in the sense of continental Europe, was important.

It is within such a framework that the values attributed to the UK civil service and so recently re-articulated by the government (Cm 2627, 1994) can be analysed in that they represent an ideal and perhaps an idealized world where the administrative practice is set in a traditional structure of parliamentary accountability. This almost Weberian model of administrative structures—hierarchical, neutral, technocratic, salaried, pensioned, and rule bound—was perhaps not often analysed as such but was seen as an adequate and necessary model for the UK political system. Hence, while there might be calls for structural and procedural reforms there was generally consensus both on the relationship between the polity and the administrative world and the values that public administration should promulgate and represent. Traditionally, then, British public administration as an academic subject was seen as an adjunct of the study of politics and its practice was dominated by generations of politicians and administrators who operated within a consensus on the political context of administration and the structures required to service such a combination of political and administrative values.

It may be argued that such a portrayal is too broad-brush, neglecting the historical sweep of political and administrative developments including the wartime experience, the post-Second World War welfare expansion and the administrative reforms that sought to reshape traditional assumptions and analysis (Hennessy 1989, 1993; Rhodes 1995). However, for a substantial period, reform of both the study and practice of public administration took place within a consensus regarding both the context of the political-administrative relationship and the basic values underlying administrative behaviour. In the last decade or so, with the rise of what is now termed the new public management, this is no longer the case.

This shift in focus in the study of public administration may be illustrated from its literature. One of the standard texts for students of public administration in the 1970s, for example, was *The Administrative Process in Britain* by Brown (1970, with a second edition co-authored by Steel 1979). This text focused on central government, especially the history of civil service reform, theories of decision making and organizational behaviour, and a set of problem areas, including planning, the machinery of government and 'management'. This discussion of management in the second edition is brief (25 pages) but includes sections on accountable management and hiving off central government activities. As such this text represents the study of public administration in transition with the traditional under pressure from a desire to inject a theoretical dimension and a shift in focus. By and large, however, the text reflects the consensus outlined above.

Less than two decades later we find *Public Sector Management* by Flynn (1993) as a standard text. The contrast with Brown and Steel could not be more striking. The first three chapters address the perceived crisis in the British public sector and the remainder deal with aspects of public management in practice including markets and prices, performance measurement, and 'a user-oriented service'. The first reference in Flynn's bibliography is to the Adam Smith Institute, the second the Audit Commission and the last to Williamson's *Markets and Hierarchies* (1975).

One should hesitate from drawing easy conclusions from such a comparison. However, this simple exercise indicates how public management has, to a considerable extent, redefined the focus, language and theoretical basis of study of the public sector, drawing on literatures and ideas often external to traditional public administration. As noted above, the reasons for this include the insularity and fragmented focus, organization and theoretical underpinning of the subject. As a consequence it has been reactive rather than proactive, open to colonization by marauding theoretical hordes and changing agendas, often driven by outside forces. This situation has also been compounded by the fact that the links between theory and practice have also been weak.

It can be argued that the rise of public management as a threat to the study of public administration can be traced to the late 1960s and early 1970s, a period charted by Rhodes as an age of 'eclecticism' (1995). This period undoubtedly was characterized by the efforts of many academics to strengthen the analysis of UK central and local administration through the application of decision making and organization theory and the development of policy analysis and policy studies (Hogwood 1995). Yet these reform efforts rarely questioned the fundamental links between political and administrative structures, the roles of government and the value basis of the public service. Structural reform efforts remained within the accepted consensus while debates in the academic community as to the place of organization theory in public administration and the relationship between public administration and management studies, while at times acrimonious, were generally accommodated within current structures and values (Rhodes 1995).

Generally, then, this period was characterized by a confidence shared by practitioners and academics that the practice of public administration could be reformed effectively by a combination of strategic management, structural reorganization to create more responsive and accountable units, and the development of better personnel management systems. In embracing these beliefs, the study of public administration widened to accommodate not only political scientists but also organization theorists and other management specialists, all seeking to contribute to the field. In the early

1970s at least, there were also attempts to place the study of administration on a firmer theoretical footing (Dunsire 1973; Keeling 1972; Self 1972). These were followed by efforts to develop policy analysis (Jenkins 1978; Hogwood and Gunn 1984) and provide a clearer understanding of the internal politics of administrative organizations, an interest stimulated by the pathbreaking study of Heclo and Wildavsky on the operations of the UK Treasury (1974).

However, the political agenda was even at this time changing and with it the framework both of politics and public administration. In particular, the failure to control the economy led to the rejection of old solutions for the management of the state and a search for new methods of control (Smith 1994). This in turn was accompanied by a changing political ideology, particularly on the right, that broke with the old consensus (Kavanagh 1987). Thus, even in the mid–1970s (and before the dawn of the Thatcher era) policy analysis and its related prescriptions had been rejected in the political world in favour of a focus on management and control, particularly of resources.

From these small beginnings, the erosion of traditional administration and the development of public management have developed at a remarkable pace and by the 1990s have emerged as a world-wide movement (Hood 1990, 1991; *Governance* 1990; Pollitt 1990; Schick 1990). Its foundations lie in redefining the role of government for example as a 'steerer' rather than a 'rower' (Osborne and Gaebler 1993) and approaching macro-economic policy via control of public spending.

The emergence of public management as a supplement to or even replacement of traditional public administration therefore begins with a political theory of the role of the state in modern life (Dunleavy and O'Leary 1987). The debate engendered is complex and detailed but for the sake of simplicity can be seen to range from the conservative call for a smaller state through the socialist demand for a more responsive state to more radical demands for a more empowering state where real power is devolved to lower level organizations and citizens (Hambleton 1992). The importance of distinguishing between such visions (and they appear in other shades and combinations) is that they represent different ideological positions and sets of values (Hood 1991). Thus while reform strategies appear similar they may represent different *political* stances; i.e. such strategies are *not* neutral (further see below).

Linked with this ideological analysis is a theoretical onslaught on traditional public administration, led principally by economists and management scientists, aided and abetted by practitioners of personnel management (now termed human resource management) and by those who argue more generally that the arts of private sector management should be transposed to the public sector in the name of improving efficiency. If none of this is new (Rhodes 1995), it is now an integrated and sustained attack on what is perceived as the 'failure' of traditional government and public administration. Moreover, this intellectual baggage (or selected elements of it) has been harnessed by many political actors as a means to promulgate and fashion their ideological vision of the state (Pollitt 1990).

As a consequence of the latter, the new public management is often used to redefine politics rather than simply improve state management within current structures. This approach is illustrated by the work of think tanks such as the Institute of Economic Affairs (IEA) and the Adam Smith Institute. In contrast, economic analysis that has focused on the nature of the state as a mechanism for service provision and delivery may simply and less radically seek to improve the relative efficiency of its operations. Hence, as various writers have pointed out (Taylor Gooby and Lawson 1993a; Le Grand 1990, 1993; Levacic 1993), questions can be raised on failings arising from the monopolistic nature of state provision and co-ordination of activities. Solutions to such problems include creating markets, charging for services, liberalizing administrative regimes and even privatizing (Heald 1983; Vickers and Yarrow 1988). In separate but related critiques, management accountants have characterized traditional systems as lacking accountability for resource use and contributing to inefficiency. They have proposed delegated financial management to remedy this and reorganize institutional budgeting (Hopwood and Tompkins (eds.) 1984). Meanwhile, the motivation and incentive systems of traditional public organizations (incremental pay scales, career systems, job security) have also been attacked and reforms advocated which focus on performance-related reward systems and management against targets.

Hence, for its advocates, public management represents less an addition to the traditional practice of public administration in the UK than intellectual and practical means to achieve true 'cultural change' by which the old internal order is swept away (Dunsire 1995). This coming together of political ideology, economic theory and perspectives from private sector management lie behind the last decade of change in the UK public sector and include the mission to eliminate waste (Hennessy 1989; Metcalfe and Richards 1990), introduce delegated financial management (Gray and Jenkins 1991, 1993a), develop performance measurement (Carter 1991) and create executive agencies (Davies and Willman 1991), citizens' charters and regimes of market testing (Connolly et al. 1994; Doern 1993). Thus the Head of the UK Civil Service, Sir Robin Butler (1992, 1993) and the former Civil Service Minister (Waldegrave 1993) can talk of an administrative revolution involving the federalization of central government administrative structures.

Yet does this emergence of public management represent the development of a new paradigm in either theory or practice? Undoubtedly its rhetoric suggests so and its advocates champion change over stability. However, as a commentator on recent US reforms points out:

> To say that we are living in a rapidly changing world . . . is simply to recite a truism under the guise of intellectual insight. Change is an instrumental value and like efficiency, another instrumental value, has no normative content until linked with another concept or objective. What we need today therefore is to think what we really expect from our government (Moe 1994, p. 119).

This political dimension of the new public management, however, is often swept away in the UK by the language of its reforms and those who claim to contribute to its theories. In particular the reform agenda is often predicated on the basis of a distinction between politics and administration that resuscitates in a novel way that some earlier reformers thought to be misplaced and outdated dichotomy (Dunsire 1973; Self 1972; Ham and Hill 1993). From this perspective, public management is offered as neutral or transferable technology to improve the public sector without offending traditional values. Hence it offers a return to the classical view of public administration in which administrative structures are simply 'providers' of services and activities determined in the political sphere (Efficiency Unit 1988). The validity of this position can and should be questioned (see below).

The new public management has brought with it a new epistemology, a redefinition of accountability and a fresh batch of seers. The issue of epistemology is dealt with by Dunsire (1995). It is worth emphasizing, however, that a focus on cost, price, market, customer and similar terms constitutes not simply a re-labelling as an introduction of different (and often dominant) values into the dialogue of public administration. This is often at the expense of professional groups (and their own languages) who in the past controlled particular areas of administrative life (for example, education, health, housing) (Richards 1992). Indeed the thrust of the reform agenda is almost unhesitatingly hostile to the values of traditional public sector professionals. Yet the outcome of such changes has often not been so much the deprofessionalization of administrative life as the superimposition of a new 'management' cadre over established professional groups thus redefining the internal and external politics of administrative organizations.

The reconceptualization of accountability is based on this epistemology as well as on the dictates of what has been termed the new managerialism (Pollitt 1990). Thus in a decentralized, target-driven world of public management, responsibility and performance are often redefined in individualistic ways driven by particular conceptions in terms such as efficiency, effectiveness and quality which reflect the beliefs and values of the new faith (Jackson 1993; Likierman 1993). Moreover, faith is not too strong a word to describe public management and its growth. Many of its advocates are clearly true believers in the power and sanctity of markets or the ability of other nostrums to rescue what they perceive as the theoretically weak and misconceived field of public administration. They would replace the traditional emphasis on *public* administration by commitments to excellence, quality, flexibility, responsiveness, and mission.

The consequences of these developments of the study of British public administration have included the redefining, isolating or relocating the study of public administration as public management, the drawing of a number of new actors into the area and the restructuring of the relevant literature. The location of public management studies is increasingly, therefore, not traditional university departments of political science but business schools (e.g., London, Aston, Warwick), dedicated research institutes (e.g., Institute of Local Government Studies, School of Advanced Urban Studies), various professional bodies that attempt to link the world of theory, practice and consultancy (The Public Management Foundation and Public Finance Foundation) and even various polemical 'think tanks' (Adam Smith Institute, European Policy Forum, Institute for Economic Affairs, Institute for Public Policy Studies). These organizations vary widely but they often share an approach and perspective that differ radically from organizations that supported public administration in a more traditional sense (e.g., the former Royal Institute of Public Administration). Many also promote a literature that has its own distinctive signature and focus while traditional journals have grafted on public management sections to stimulate practitioner interest (e.g. *Public Administration*), or adjusted their content to reflect changing concerns in specific professional areas (*Local Government Studies, Policy and Politics*). Practitioner journals have, of necessity, followed management trends if selectively (*The Health Services Journal, Local Government Chronicle* and *Public Finance* (formerly *Public Finance and Accountancy*).

But how far do all these developments represent the development of a unique area different from traditional public administration? Has the context and content of the field of study simply changed or is public management an area with distinct characteristics from public administration? Such questions are less academic quibbles as prerequisite enquiries in understanding the logic of recent developments and assessing the current study and practice of public management. Public administration is based on an acceptance of a political model of parliamentary government and a professional and essentially bureaucratic model of state structures and operations. Neither its alleged failures nor the superiority of alternative administrative arrangements should be taken for granted, especially when arguments are expressed in apolitical terms. What is important about the theory and practice of traditional public administration is the value system embraced and served. What we need to know of public management and its new agenda are its values and basic assumptions. With this in mind we proceed to an examination of some of the developments in both the theory and practice of public management.

STRUCTURES FOR PUBLIC MANAGEMENT

There is a growing literature on public management in the UK. The more generalist has a distinct flavour from what has gone before in public administration (e.g., Flynn 1993; Pollitt and Harrison (eds.) 1992) even if other texts takes a more traditional approach discussing developments in specific areas (e.g., civil service, local government, education) under a public management guise (e.g., Taylor and Popham (eds.) 1989). Moreover, much of the literature is more specialist, dealing with recent reforms in areas such as health care (Harrison *et al.* 1990), the welfare services (Taylor-Gooby and Lawson (eds.), 1993b) or local government (Walsh 1989). Much of this offers incisive analysis of recent public sector reforms and changes many of which, if not all, have been driven by a mission to change the structures of public sector organizations and reshape relationships with the political world on the one hand and the public on the other.

Within all the above has been a common concern with organizational structures. This has been a traditional issue for the study of public administration for decades (Self 1972; Dunsire 1973, 1995) although, as Rhodes (1995) illustrates, theoretical concerns with structural reform (e.g., as in the classical management theory) initially had limited impact. However, in the 1960s and 1970s an interest in organization theory, policy analysis and management attempted to refocus the study of public administration on such issues as structures for strategic planning, policy implementation and policy co-ordination. In addition, the concern with strategic financial management (as reflected in such innovations as planning programming budgeting (PPB)) also had a structural emphasis in its attempts to refocus and integrate hierarchical organizational structures (e.g., via corporate planning). The practical expression of these concerns in this period were giant merged Whitehall departments, mechanisms of corporate review (e.g., the Central Policy Review Staff), local government reorganization, social service departments and the restructuring of the National Health Service.

Undoubtedly many of these reforms were driven by a technocratic agenda, based on ideas of rational decision making and the perceived inefficiencies of political structures (e.g., failures to define goals, or to evaluate options, etc). Nevertheless, within the conventional study and practice of public administration the role of the state was rarely questioned, a minority task undertaken only by those of more radical (usually left wing) persuasion (Ham and Hill 1993).

In the late 1970s and throughout the 1980s, however, these consensus approaches were ferociously attacked for their theoretical weakness and practical failures. In their place came an emphasis on markets, flexible and responsive organizations and decentralization. In the lexicon of public sector studies the word 'management' began to usurp 'administration'.

Even if the evidence for discrediting the ideas of traditional administration and the values underpinning the so called 'bureaucratic' paradigm (Kernaghan 1993; Osborne and Gaebler 1993) seems often more assumed than demonstrated (Jordan 1994), the attack which emerged from the Chicago School of Political economy (e.g., Friedman), the Austrian School of Political Economy (e.g., Von Hayek), public choice (Buchanan, Tullock, Niskanen) and neo-classical economic was fierce (Dunleavy 1991; Flynn 1993; Le Grand 1990, 1993; Levacic 1993; Taylor Gooby and Lawson 1993a). This set of ideas (or perhaps selective interpretations of them) became powerful influences on British politicians and public sector reformers while also shaping the new agenda of public management studies. Hence, while public management theory is not the exclusive preserve of public choice or economic theory, it frequently draws on these disciplines for its structural diagnosis and prescription. In essence, this analysis identifies state involvement as encouraging monopolies, suppressing entrepreneurial behaviour, limiting choice, overproducing unwanted services and encouraging waste and inefficiency. In contrast, markets encourage competition, maximize choice and freedom, increase efficiency (in its various forms), coordinate fragmented activities via the price mechanism and create conditions for entrepreneurial behaviour to flourish. Such solutions are not necessarily seen as unproblematic and some role for state and administration is acknowledged, but only as a 'facilitator' and minimalist regulator for market systems.

The practice of public management is seen, therefore, to need structures which encourage the creation of external and internal markets whenever possible. This means investigating a range of options ranging from privatization and market testing to the purchaser-provider split, the concept of the 'enabling' authority and the contracting state (further see Hardin 1992; Stewart 1993). That such strategies have captured the political agenda is immediately clear. Whether there exists empirical evidence to support the claims made on their behalf is another matter. Perhaps, as Goodsell notes (1993, p. 86), 'A good sales pitch does not go into the messy details or carefully weighed pros and cons.' Nevertheless, there has been no formal effort, for example, to evaluate the introduction of the internal market in health care in the UK nor any assessment of the adequacy of its theoretical assumptions (J. Butler 1992; Hunter 1994). Further, in areas of public life such as contracting-out or market testing, the supporting evidence for the universal success of such innovations is far from overwhelming (Audit Commission 1993b).

In these and other areas there is considerable controversy over the conceptual basis on which any assessment can be made, a fact that illustrates the conflicting value positions underlining the public management debate. This is compounded by a tendency to blur or eliminate the distinctions between the public and private sectors (government as a business) and perhaps, as importantly, often to treat the public sector as homogenous in organizational terms rather than a differentiated system of organizations with different tasks, values and relationships often linked into complex policy networks (Prior 1993). Thus, the mission to impose a new 'culture' on public sector organizations via structural solutions based on market theory often fails to analyse the old culture or the underlying value structures and administrative politics or, if it does recognize it, seeks to depoliticize it by fragmenting the organizational world into quasimarkets and a contract culture (Dunleavy and Hood 1994).

Market-based theory often pays little attention to the internal structures of organizations or simplifies these away in the rhetoric of public choice. As an antidote, or perhaps in sheer need for a defence against the more extreme ideas thrust upon them, practitioners in the UK public sector have turned for salvation to contemporary literatures emerging from organizational management consultants especially in the United States. Based mainly but not exclusively on the experience of private companies, this literature has also shaped the structural doctrines of public management through the works of Peters and Waterman (1982), Peters (1988, 1992), Waterman (1994), Kanter (1983, 1989) and, most significantly in the public sector itself, Osborne and Gaebler (1993). An almost exclusively North American product (though see Kay 1993), this literature focuses on how organizations can survive in an increasingly hostile environment (political, economic and social), adjust to change or, in the title of one of Peters' later works, 'thrive on chaos'. The authors' answer is that the old command and control structures (reminiscent of Weberian organizations) have become redundant with the need for organizations that are more flexible and adaptable. This in turn is achieved by the flatter and more focused structures which encourage entrepreneurial rather than bureaucratic management and more flexible personnel regimes.

Although criticized for exaggeration, simplification and selective use of anecdotal evidence, Peters and Waterman (1982) were hugely influential. In the early 1980s, for example, it was easy to gain the impression that this was the only management text that UK senior civil servants had read, so common was their reference to it. Similarly, the Audit Commission used the 7S framework (which identifies organizational success with the seven elements of strategy, structure, staff, management style, systems and procedures, shared values, and skills) to promote 'excellence' in local government.

In the 1990s, however, the cult of Peters and Waterman appears to have been replaced by that of Osborne and Gaebler, the major literary influence behind Vice President Gore's report discussed at the start of this article. For Osborne and Gaebler, the reinvention of government requires structures which are 'mission rather than rule-driven', 'decentralized' and 'entrepreneurial'. This analysis has much in common with that of Peters' later work (1988) and also that of another US management guru Rosabeth Moss Kanter. Indeed the Kanter model (1989) of successful organizations designed around a small core overseeing a flatter fragmented structure has recently become fashionable in British central government and local authorities. Kanter claims that these structures are more responsive to external forces and changes, facilitate closer personnel identification (the creation of an organizational culture), and encourage entrepreneurship (albeit in a limited sense). The fact that they are often seen to be cheaper ('restructuring' as a euphemism for cutting staff) is also probably significant, especially at a time when shedding numbers from the public sector has become a matter of high political priority.

The new theories of public management therefore appear to unite in attacking the traditional bureaucratic model of administrative structure and advocating efficiency and responsiveness through some form of decentralization. Such ideas, in theoretical terms at least, often prescribe greater 'freedom' for administrative organizations and their members. They attack the restrictive nature of central controls and rule-bound systems that are considered to restrict prized values such as entrepreneurship, staff empowerment and client sensitivity. However, as Hambleton (1992) notes, while different analysts may agree on this diagnosis and advocate decentralization as a solution to such problems, the form and nature of 'decentralization' favoured may vary. Decentralization via markets liberates both organizations and customers, the latter expressing their freedom through choice in the market place (e.g., parents and schools). In contrast, administrative decentralization does not reject state delivery of services but seeks to create organizations more consumer (or citizen) responsive while retaining control over political strategy and service distribution. Thus its structures follow the Kanter model with a small core that has strategic responsibilities and co-ordinates the highly differentiated and sharply focused organizational unit of service delivery. Political decentralization goes further in promoting 'empowerment' by providing structures where financial and decision-making control is pushed down the organization and sometimes outwards to clients involving them in the operation of services. Hambleton notes, not surprisingly, that while administrative decentralization is often a fashionable strategy (e.g., amongst UK local authorities) political decentralization may often be discussed but is rarely practised.

This analysis is clearly not definitive but demonstrates the differing ideologies that can underlie public management theory and from here filter into practice. Thus a seemingly common reform strategy, decentralization, may emerge from different ideological positions and value sets, each leading to different frameworks of analysis and offering differing structural solutions. Public management theory is therefore neither coherent nor neutral; rather, it represents a different political perspective not only on the structure and functioning of public organizations but also on the political basis of the public sector itself.

In its most radical form the difference between the public management agenda for the structuring of public sector organizations and that of traditional public administration begins with the assumption that the current political system is inefficient. Further, what has previously been positively valued (e.g., bureaucratic routines and professional codes of conduct) are assessed as costs rather than as benefits. This analysis is also transposed to networks of organizations (better fragmented) as well as to internal structures (better individualized and destabilized). Thus, efficiency is valued over accountability and responsiveness over due process.

This perspective undoubtedly has its strengths but is also based on a universal and neo-managerial view of government and its processes. We now turn to discuss some of these, notably the recent emphasis of finance and performance management as well as the focus on quality and entrepreneurship.

FINANCIAL AND PERFORMANCE MANAGEMENT

A survey of the traditional literature on public administration in the UK (e.g., Brown and Steel 1979; Greenwood and Wilson 1989) reveals little on the *internal* financial and informational workings of public sector organizations and even less on systems of personnel management. Even a concern with the public as consumers and customers was rare indeed. Such matters were seen either as dull and distant from policy concerns or as the bailiwick of specialist literatures. This is even true of the more theoretical public administration literature of the 1970s (Dunsire 1973; Keeling 1972; Self 1972) and, notwithstanding the work of Heclo and Wildavsky (1974), it was not until the 1980s that finance and expenditure (mainly in terms of public expenditure management) became a subject deemed worthy of detailed consideration and even then only by a select group of specialist economists and political scientists (Heald 1983; Hood and Wright (eds.) 1981).

Meanwhile at the more micro-level there was intensive but perhaps transient interest in organizational budgetary reform (e.g. planning programming and budgeting (PPB)) and, in the wake of the Fulton Committee's Report into the Civil Service, some support for improved accounting and management techniques promulgated by enthusiasts such as Garrett (1972). Some, but not all of this, appeared on the political agenda as experiments in programme budgeting and evaluation but few of these reforms were long lived. Instead, as 'big governments faced hard times' (Hood and Wright 1981) from the early 1970s, the prevailing economic voices that gained political attention in the UK were writers such as Bacon and Eltis (1976), US public choice economists such as Buchanan, Downs and Niskanan, and emerging think tanks such as the Adam Smith Institute and the Centre for Policy Studies. These were to change the political agenda and focus, aided by populist voices which claimed that financial management in the public sector was characterized by waste and inefficiency (Chapman 1978).

Faced with deepening crises of public expenditure the prime policy goal of government in the UK and elsewhere became the control of public finances. The importance of this cannot be over-estimated both in terms of the internal management techniques called upon to serve this objective and of the regimes of personnel management that accompanied it. In brief, between the late 1970s and early 1980s there was a conscious shift of political emphasis from the management of policy to financial control and a search for mechanisms to serve this end. Practical developments such as delegated financial management and individualized personnel management systems therefore represent strategies developed to support a particular set of political values and agenda. Further, the theories deemed necessary to service this agenda were those of management accounting and finance rather than any identifiable sub-discipline of traditional public administration.

In the practice of public management, the 1980s and 1990s have become the age of the financial manager. Accounting, budgeting and auditing have dominated the discourse about the delivery of public services and changed the language and rules of resource allocation in areas as diverse as education, health, and policing both in the UK and overseas (Cothran 1993; Gray et al. (eds.) 1993b; Schick 1990). The theoretical literature used to legitimize this transformation has been drawn frequently from the fields of academic accounting and, to a lesser extent, the work of economists interested in the public sector and public management processes (Jackson 1982, Hopwood and Tomkins (eds.) 1984).

The most significant practical impact of these changes has been the emergence of accountable management and regimes of performance measurement. Even if defining accountable management precisely has its difficulties, it is clearly based on a management accounting theory that commends the decentralizing of responsibility for resource use within organizations by identifying individuals and holding them responsible for budgets and performance (Gray et al. 1991). Backed up by the development of information systems to enhance top management control, accountable management is therefore concerned with 'the economics of public sector delivery' (Humphrey et al. 1993, pp. 14-15) and aims to change the nature of public sector management processes. It is also, in the view of some of its academic advocates, a way of liberating managers from over rigorous central controls. Hence 'entrepreneurial' budgeting (Cothran 1993) is seen as a device where budget holders can use resources in a creative and innovative way to serve their needs within accepted limits of accountability.

In a similar way, the growing literature on performance measurement appears to play out old debates in a new arena. How can effectiveness be measured and performance assessed in a world of ambiguous or conflicting objectives? Does the easy to measure drive out the more difficult? Indeed, the emphasis on measurement, performance and cost has been one of the prime causes of the labelling of this financial focus of public management theory and practice as 'managerialism' and 'neo-Taylorism' and criticized accordingly (Pollitt 1990). However, as Flynn (1993, ch. 8) also points out, performance cannot be ignored and, if any organization is to learn and progress, mechanisms for assessing performance at different levels and different ways are necessary. This is clearly the position of writers such as Jackson (1993) and Carter (1989, 1991, 1992) who make a strong case for the development of performance measures and indicators while noting the difficulties in developing such systems in the public sector (recognized also by Pollitt 1986, 1988 and Likierman 1993).

This picture, however, has now dramatically changed not least since the achievement of a political vision of a public sector based on fragmented financial structures and a contract culture is deemed to require the dismantling and federalizing of professional and occupational groups. Hence the practical agenda of public management includes a vision of personnel management dominated by contracts and performance-related reward schemes and the 'opening-up' of appointment systems to both public and private sector candidates.

Given its current fashionable status, one might have expected a substantial empirically based literature on the merits or otherwise of performance-related reward systems. Such evidence, however, appears at best limited both at home and abroad. In a recent review, for example, Ingraham notes that 'the diffusion of pay-for-performance has been based less on careful analysis and evaluation than on a perception of success in other settings, informal communication among bureaucratic and elected decision makers and perhaps wishful thinking' (1993, p. 348). Ingraham goes on to note the fact that reviews of the effects of performance-related pay in the US (commissioned by the Office of Personnel Management) and by bodies such as the Organization for Economic Co-operation and Development (OECD) demonstrate that many of the assumptions held about the effectiveness of performance-related reward systems appear to have little empirical foundation. The author then concludes that what is required is an assessment of what systems *public* organizations need rather than what *private* organizations do. This should involve integrating such innovations closely into other reforms and into the reality of public sector work (1993, pp. 354–55).

QUALITY, EMPOWERMENT AND ENTREPRENEURSHIP

Over and above financial and performance management, both the theory and (sometimes) practice of public management identifies a commitment to quality and clients within organizational systems that empower managers and offer scope for entrepreneurial activity. The advocacy of such characteristics emerges seamlessly from the models of 'excellent' organizations discussed above and to a lesser extent on from the management accounting literature of delegated budgeting.

The discovery of quality is a by-product of a developing strand of general management thinking that links organizational *success* with a concern for quality. Beginning with questions on the reasons for the dominance of Japanese industry, this has moved from a focus on product quality through a flirtation with techniques such as quality circles to the rediscovery of the works of Edwards Deming (1986) and his concept of Total Quality Management (TQM). This approach, first offered as a way forward for private industry in the USA, has been transferred to government (Carr and Littman 1990). It is now the subject of a fast growing literature on public management (Morgan and Murgatyrod 1994). Yet, as in performance-related pay, questions have been raised concerning its appropriateness to public sector organizations unless redesigned to take account of government's unique circumstances (Swiss 1992).

The underlying problem with an emphasis on quality is that no-one is against it but definitions depend on values and circumstances (e.g., what is a quality health service?) (Walsh 1991a). Similar problems characterize other aspects of the new public management lexicon such as 'empowerment' and 'entrepreneurship'. The literature of the new management, both public and private, extols the virtue of systems where rules are relaxed and opportunities given for organizational members to take the initiative in the interests of providing a quality service. But who is to determine what quality means? It is clear from any study of the established literature on organizational behaviour and psychology, especially in the areas of motivation and organizational design, that there exists a firm theoretical basis for some aspects of these prescriptions. What is less clear, however, is how far the general and often anecdotal arguments of writers such as Osborne and Gaebler can be applied *generally* to public sector organizations and more particularly to their *political* context. Thus, for example, the complaint of advocates of the agency initiative in UK central government is that 'freedoms' granted are in fact severely constrained to the extent that such new systems may be characterized less by the 'empowerment' of public managers as by the centralizing of control and the displacing of blame (Dopson 1993; Mellon 1993).

This last point is of importance not least since it indicates the potential of public management or at least the *use* of some of its ideas to depolitize the operations of the governmental process and to redefine accountability relationships. In this there is a sharp difference between the ideas that sustain theory and practice in traditional public administration and those of public management. As was outlined earlier, traditional visions of public service place this within a system of accountability relationships that while sometimes ill defined (e.g., the firm line between politics and administration) do place administrators as accountable to the public through the political system. In the new world, however, it appears possible not only for politics and administration to be 'separate' but 'separated' with the former actors entering a 'blame free' zone, leaving administrative actors in the front line. It would be unwarranted and unwise to blame public management for this situation but it is as unwise to see traditional public administration structurally and theoretically to have failed or to regard the development of public management simply as a linear progression from an old to a new world. The central point of interest of the Kuhnian vision of a paradigm shift is that it represents a discontinuity rather than a continuity in value systems. Our contention is less that a paradigm shift has taken place but rather that competing visions exist that in many ways remain separate and distinct. Whether they can be drawn together is an issue we now address in the conclusion.

CONCLUSION

Over two decades ago, Ridley wrote that there was cause for discontent in the subject public administration. 'It is reasonable to ask', he observed.

> 'whether progress in the field of public administration is more likely to come in response to a demand from administrators or whether demand itself depends on the existence of a recognized *subject*. . . . If administrators are to ask for more than instruction in a miscellaneous bag of techniques, if they are to ask for something actually called public administration, they must surely first see the existence of an integrated discipline clearly different from other disciplines which between them offer the miscellaneous techniques they currently study' (1972, p. 68, emphasis in original).

At the time of Ridley's comments, public administration was still the preserve largely of political science and constitutional law. It had enjoyed an opportunity to use these disciplines to forge a clearly defined and at least interdisciplinary subject with its own territories and conceptual and methodological framework. Yet neither before nor since have those in the positions of academic leadership sought to seize this opportunity. It will not return. Yet in some ways this may not matter as both traditional public administration and public management may never be more than foci for study in which a variety of disciplines make a contribution. It may thus be more important to seek ways in which these fields can be integrated rather than remain as mutually exclusive areas occupied by different academic communities with differing theoretical values and prescriptions.

The need for such a move may be urgent since in terms of practice, the advance of public management may be unstoppable. As Prior has observed:

> It is arguable that the fundamental change that has occurred in the public sector is not the replacement of one broadly uniform set of arrangements with another uniform set, but the fracturing of the public sector into a plethora of different sets of arrangements with few common features. It is then questionable whether the term 'public sector' is any longer useful as a generic analytical concept (1993, p. 459).

Given this reality, there is little to be gained by harking back for a return to some lost world of public administration or of simply offering a blanket critique of the new public management which would in no way be deserved. Rather, it is necessary to examine the strengths and weakness of the public management approach and to assess whether there are aspects of traditional public administration that need to be 'rediscovered' and incorporated into its framework (Goodsell 1993).

As outlined above and clearly articulated by other commentators, public management differs from traditional public administration. It has developed an analytical agenda based heavily on the concepts and theories of public choice economics (and associated fellow travellers such as Osborne and Gaebler) and strands of corporate management thinking that attempt to define the structures and processes of 'excellent' or 'well-performing' organizations in rapidly changing and complex economic and social environments. Although, as Aucoin (1990) points out, such perspectives are not necessarily complimentary, such a theoretical approach has identifiable strengths. It meets the need for a variety of alternative organizational structures and delivery systems to be recognized (contingency theory is alive and well—even Burns and Stalker (1961) are to be reprinted!) and for the motivation of staff and relations between organizations and the clients they serve to be given high priority. Further, the exploration of alternative financial/budgetary arrangements may clarify and redefine the politics of the budgetary process, while a focus on goals and results, together with an interest in institutionalized systems of evaluation, have the potential at least of creating the 'learning' organizations sought for so long by advocates of strategic management. The progressive and attractive aspects of public management theory therefore stress decentralization, deregulation and delegation within a framework of executive models of centralization, co-ordination and control (Aucoin 1990, pp. 119–25).

Theories of public management also have identifiable weaknesses both individually and in terms of their ability to be drawn together into some conceptual 'gestalt' that might qualify for the term paradigm. In particular their often apolitical perspective may lead to a downgrading of values considered important in both theorizing about and reforming systems of public administration. Examples of such difficulties include the championing of results over administrative processes, the imposition or substitution of economic values for legal values and a conception of accountability that replaces or redefines traditional mechanisms by quasi-markets and producer / consumer relationships (Caiden 1994; Kernaghan 1993; Moe 1994). A fundamental basis of government and traditional public administration in most states is the role of law and its attendant regulations. However, commenting on US experience, Moe argues that in the entrepreneurial paradigm results come first, processes second or never. He adds that this represents a fundamental misunderstanding of government where 'if certain laws, and implementing regulations, hinder effective and responsible management, we should amend those laws and regulations' (1994, p. 115).

When discussing management changes in British government in the early 1980s, Metcalfe and Richards (1990) argued that the application of reform techniques represented 'an impoverished conception of management'. This may still be true for public management theory since its approaches often avoid any discussion of mechanisms of governance. On this point Hood (1991) has called for an assessment of public management in terms of what he terms administrative values since this one will allow judgment on 'good administration' separate from political values that deal with the role of state in society. That such a distinction must remain artificial has been stressed in different contexts by Ranson and Stewart (1988, 1989), Walsh (1991b) and Moe (1994). The agendas of these writers differ but their case for the distinctiveness of the public sector and the values it represents rests on such features as collective choice in the polity, equity, citizenship and collective action as a policy instrument. In different ways these are features of the agenda of traditional public administration. Their presence in the lexicon of public management is somewhat less predictable.

As Aucoin has pointed out, the changing political agenda of the last decade and the emergence of public management has led to tensions and even contradictions in models of governance and administration. Thus theoretical divergence within public management itself (i.e., between public choice and the managerialist perspective) may result in principles of organizational design and management that push in opposite directions (centralization and decentralization, co-ordination and deregulation, control and delegation). He also notes that these perspectives may have 'radically different understandings of the "politics" which underlie the exercise of management functions' (1990, p. 127).

This issue of resolving the political dimension of public management is one of the core problems in both the theory and practice of public management. So too is the development of a capacity to deal with the values particular to the public sector outlined above. In this, public management may need the stimulus of traditional public administration just as much as the latter doubtless required that of many of the concepts and theories of public management.

So what of a future agenda? First, the theoretical approaches of public management have to be recognized and studied for what some (although not all) of them are—distinctive contributions to economic and political thought. Dunleavy (1991) was exemplary in recognizing this about public choice theory and provides a model for others to follow. Second, and as outlined above, we can employ the tenets of traditional public administration to add a necessary constitutional dimension to the theories and prescriptions of public management. Third, there must be a willingness to examine, test and, if appropriate, adopt the conceptual and methodological frameworks which the new approaches to the field are bringing with them and to employ them more rigorously to help forge an empirically based range of theories that bring together both public administration and public management. This seems to apply especially to the practical and political implications of basing the management of public service on some form of separation of policy and execution and the resulting organizational fragmentation. Unless both public management and public administration seek to do this a consequence will be government and, more widely, a public sector which continues to be ill-informed, where the implementation of reform changes may lead to perverse results and where public disillusionment with government and administration will continue to increase.

REFERENCES

Accounting, Auditing and Accountability. 1993. Special Edition on 'Accounting, accountability and the "New" UK public sector', 6, 3.

Aucoin, P. 1990. Administrative reform in public management: paradigms, principles, paradoxes and pendulums', *Governance* 3, 2, 116-37.

Audit Commission. 1988. *Performance review in local government: a handbook for auditors and local authorities.* HMSO: London.

————. 1989. *Loosing an empire, finding a role.* London: HMSO.

————. 1993a. *Putting quality on the map: measuring and appraising quality in the public sector.* Occasional Paper No. 18, March.

————. 1993b. *Realising the benefits of competition.* London: HMSO.

Bacon, R. W. and W. A. Eltis. 1976. *Britain's economic problem: too few producers,* 2nd edn. London: Macmillan.

Bogdanor, V. 1993. 'The democratic deficit', *The Guardian* 14 June.

Brown, R. G. S. and D. Steel. 1979. *The administrative process in Britain* (2nd edn.). London: Methuen.

Burns, T. and G. M. Stalker, 1961. *The management of innovation.* London: Tavistock.

Butler, J. 1992. *Patients, policies and politics.* Buckingham: Open University Press.

Butler, Sir Robin. 1992. 'The new public management: the contribution of Whitehall and academia', *Public Policy and Administration* 7, 3, 1-14.

————. 1993. 'The evolution of the civil service: a progress report', *Public Administration* 71, 3, 395-406.

Caiden, G. S. 1994. 'Administrative reform: American style', *Public Administration Review* 54, 2, 123-8.

Carr, D. K. and I. D. Littman. 1990. *Excellence in government: total quality management into the 1990s.* Arlington, VA: Coopers and Lybrand.

Carter, N. 1989. 'Performance indicators: "backseat driving" or "hands-off" control', *Policy and Politics* 17, 131-8.

————. 1992. 'Learning to measure performance: the use of indicators in organizations', *Public Administration* 69, 1, 85-101.

Carter, N., R. Klein and P. Day. 1992. *How organisations measure success: the use of performance indicators in government.* London: Routledge.

Chapman, L. 1978. *Your disobedient servant.* Harmondsworth: Penguin.

Cmnd 3638. 1968. *The civil service* (The Fulton Report). London: HMSO.

Cm 1599. 1991. *Raising the standard: the Citizen's Charter.* London: HMSO.

Cm 1730. 1991. *Competing for quality.* London: HMSO.

Cm 2280. 1993. *Inquiry into police responsibilities and rewards* (The Sheehy Report), London: HMSO.

Cm 2627. 1994. *The civil service: continuity and change.* London: HMSO.

Connolly, M., Penny McKeown and G. Milligan-Byrne. 1994. 'Making the public sector user friendly?: a critical examination of the Citizen's Charter', *Parliamentary Affairs* 47, 1, 23–37.

Cothran, D. A. 1993. 'Entrepreneurial budgeting: an emerging reform', *Public Administration Review* 53, 5, 445–54.

Davies, A. and J. Willman. 1991. *What next?: agencies, departments and the civil service.* London: Institute of Public Policy Research.

Deming, W. Edwards. 1986. *Out of the crisis.* Cambridge. MIT Press.

Doern, G. Bruce. 1993. 'The UK Citizen's Charter: origins and implementation in three agencies', *Policy and Politics* 21, 1, 17–30.

Dopson, S. 1993. 'Are agencies an act of faith? The experience of HMSO', *Public Money and Management* 13, 2, 17–23.

Dunleavy, P. and C. Hood 1994. 'From old public administration to new public management', *Public Money and Management* 14, 3, 9–16.

Dunleavy, P. and B. O'Leary. 1987. *Theories of the state: the problems of liberal democracy.* London: Macmillan.

Dunleavy, P. 1991. *Democracy, bureaucracy and public choice.* London: Harvester Wheatsheaf.

Dunsire, A. 1973. *Administration: the word and the science.* Oxford: Martin Robertson.

————. 1995. 'The state of the discipline: administrative theory', in R. A. W. Rhodes (ed.) 'British Public Administration: the state of the discipline', *Public Administration* 73, 1, 1–15.

Efficiency Unit. 1988. *Improving management in government: the Next Steps.* (The Ibbs Report). London: HMSO.

Flynn, N., 1993. (2nd edn.) *Public sector management.* London: Harvester Wheatsheaf.

Garrett, J. 1972. *The management of government.* Harmondsworth: Penguin.

Goodsell, C. T. 1993. 'Reinvent government or rediscover it?' *Public Administration Review* 53, 1, 85–7.

Governance. 1990. Special edition on 'Managerial reform' 3, 2, 115–218.

Gray, A. G. and W. I. Jenkins with A. C. Flynn and B. A. Rutherford. 1991. 'The management of change in Whitehall: the experience of the FMI', *Public Administration* 69, 1, 41–59.

Gray, A. G. and W. I. Jenkins, 1993a. 'Markets, managers and the public service', ch. 1 in P. Taylor-Gooby and R. Lawson (eds.), *Markets and managers.* Buckingham: Open University Press.

Gray, A. G., W. I. Jenkins and R. V. Segsworth (eds.). 1993b. *Budgeting, auditing and evaluation.* New Brunswick: Transaction Publishers.

Greenwood, J. and D. J. Wilson. 1989. *Public administration in Britain today* (2nd edn.). London: Unwin Hyman.

Ham, C. and M. J. Hill. 1993. *The policy process in the modern capitalist state* (2nd edn.). London: Harvester Wheatsheaf.

Hambleton, R. 1992. 'Decentralisation and democracy in UK local government', *Public Money and Management,* July/September, 9–20.

Hardin, I. 1992. *The contracting state.* Buckingham: Open University Press.

Harrison, S., D. Hunter and C. Pollitt. 1990. *The dynamics of British health policy.* London: Unwin Hyman.

Heald, D. 1983. *Public expenditure.* Oxford: Martin Roberson.

Heclo, H. and A. Wildavsky. 1974. *The private government of public money.* London: Macmillan.

Hennessy, P. 1989. *Whitehall.* London: Secker and Warburg.

―――. 1993. *Never again.* London: Vintage Books.

Hogwood, B. and L. Gunn. 1984. *Policy analysis in the real world.* Oxford: Oxford University Press.

Hogwood, B. 1995, 'Public policy', in R. A. W. Rhodes (ed.). 'British Public Administration: the state of the discipline'. *Public Administration* 73, 1, 59–73.

Hood, C. and M. Wright (eds.). 1981. *Big government in hard times.* Oxford: Martin Robertson.

Hood, C. 1990. 'De Sir Humphrying the Westminster model of bureaucracy: a new style of governance', *Governance* 3, 2, 204–14.

―――. 1991. 'A public management for all seasons?', *Public Administration* 69, 1, 3–19.

Hopwood, A. and C. Tompkins (eds.). 1984. *Issues in public sector accounting.* London: Philip Allan.

Humphrey, C., P. Miller and R. W. Scapens. 1993. 'Accountability and accountable management in the UK public sector', *Accounting, Auditing and Accountability* 6, 3, 7–29.

Hunter, D. 1994. 'Why the world should be wary', *The Guardian*, 9 March.

Ingraham, P. W. 1993. 'Of pigs in pokes and policy diffusion: another look at pay-for-performance', *Public Administration Review* 53, 4, 348–56.

Jackson, P. M. 1982. *The political economy of bureaucracy.* Oxford Philip Allen.

―――. 1993. 'Public service performance evaluation: a strategic perspective', *Public Money and Management* 13, 4, 9–14.

Jenkins, W. I. 1978. *Policy Analysis.* Oxford: Martin Robertson.

Jordan, G. 1994. 'Reinventing government but how will it work?', *Public Administration* 72, 2, 271–9.

Kanter, R. M. 1983. *The change masters.* New York: Simon and Schuster.

―――. 1989. *When giants learn to dance.* London: Unwin Hyman.

Kavanagh, D. 1987. *Thatcherism and British politics: the end of consensus?* Oxford: Oxford University Press.

Kay, J. 1993. *The foundations of corporate success.* Oxford: Oxford University press.

Keeling, D. 1972. *Management in government.* London: George Allen and Unwin.

Kernaghan, K. 1993. 'Reshaping government: the post-bureaucratic paradigm', *Canadian Public Administration* 36, 4, 636–44.

Kuhn, T. 1970. *The structure of scientific revolutions.* Chicago: University of Chicago Press.

Le Grand, J. 1990. *Quasi-markets and social policy.* Bristol: School of Advanced Urban Studies.

―――. 1993. *Quasi-market and community care.* Bristol: School of Advanced Urban Studies.

Levacic, R. 1993. 'Markets as co-ordinate devices', ch. 2 in R. Maidment and G. Thompson (eds.), *Managing the United Kingdom.* London: Sage.

Likierman, A. 1993. 'Performance indicators: twenty early lessons from managerial use', *Public money and management* 13, 4, 15–22.

Local Government Chronicle. 1993. 'Gore's own guru', 4 July.

Mellon, E. 1993. 'Executive agencies: leading change from the outside in', *Public Money and Management* 13, 2, 25–31.

Metcalfe, L. and S. Richards. 1990. *Improving public management.* 2nd edn. London: Sage.

Moe, R. C. 1994. 'The reinventing government exercise: misinterpreting the problem, misjudging the consequences', *Public Administration Review* 54, 2, 111–22.

Morgan, C. and S. Murgatroyd. 1994. *Total quality management in the public sector.* Buckingham: Open University Press.

Morgan, G. 1986. *Images of organizations*. Newbury Park, California: Sage.

————. 1993. *Imaginization*. Newbury Park, California: Sage.

Osborne, D. and T. Gaebler. 1993. *Reinventing government*. New York: Plume Books.

Peters, T. J. and R. H. Waterman. 1982. *In search of excellence*. New York: Harper and Row.

————. 1988. *Thriving on chaos*. London: Pan Books.

————. 1992. *Liberation management*. London: Macmillan.

Pollitt, C. 1986. 'Beyond the managerial model: the case for broadening performance assessment in government and the public services', *Financial Accountablility and Management* 2, 3, 155-70.

————. 1988. 'Bringing consumers into performance measurement', *Policy and politics* 16, 2, 77-87.

————. 1990. *Managerialism and the public services*. Oxford: Blackwell

Pollitt, C. and S. Harrison (eds.). 1992. *Handbook of public services management*. Oxford: Blackwell.

Poole, K. P. 1978. *The local government service*. London: George Allen and Unwin.

Prior, D. 1993. 'In search of the new public management', *Local Government Studies* 19, 3, 447-60.

Ranson, S. and J. D. Stewart. 1989. 'Citizenship and government: the challenge for management in the public domain', *Political Studies* 37, 5-24.

Rhodes, R. A. W. 1994. 'The hollowing out of the state: the changing nature of public service in Britain', *Political Quarterly* 65, 2, 138-51.

————. 1995. 'From institutions to dogma: tradition, eclecticism and ideology in the study of British public administration', *Public Administration Review* forthcoming.

Richards, S. 1992. 'Changing patterns of legitimation in public management', *Public Policy and Administration* 7, 3, 15-28.

Ridley, F. F. 1972, 'Public administration: cause for discontent', *Public Administration* 50, 1, 65-77.

Schick, A. 1990. 'Budgeting for results: recent developments in five industrialized countries', *Public Administration Review* 50, 26-34.

Self, P. 1972. *Administrative theories and politics*. London: Unwin Hyman.

Smith, T. 1994. 'Post-modern politics and the case for constitutional renewal', *Political Quarterly* 65, 2, 128-37.

Stewart, J. D. 1986. *The new management of local government*. London: George Allen and Unwin.

————. 1992. *Accountability to the public*. European Policy Forum.

————. 1993. 'The limitations of government by contract', *Public Money and Management* 13, 3, 7-12.

Stewart, J. D. and S. Ranson. 1988. 'Management in the public domain', *Public Money and Management* 2, 13-19.

Stewart, J. D. and K. Walsh. 1992. 'Change in the management of public services', *Public Administration* 70, 4, 499-518.

Swiss, J. E. 1992, 'Adapting total quality management (TQM) to government', *Public Administration Review* 52, 4, 356-62.

Taylor, I. ad G. Popham (eds.). 1989. *An introduction to public sector management*. London: Unwin Hyman.

Taylor-Gooby, P. and R. Lawson. 1993a 'Where we go from here: the new order in welfare', ch. 9 in *Markets and managers*. Buckingham: Open University Press.

Treasury, HM 1992. *Executive agencies: a guide to setting targets and measuring performance*. HM Treasury.

Vickers, J. and G. Yarrow. 1988. *Privatization: an economic analysis.* London: MIT Press.

Waldegrave, W. 1993. 'The myth of the democratic deficit', *Public Finance and Accountancy* 16 July , 6–7

Walsh, K. 1989. *Marketing in local government.* Harlow: Longman.

————. 1991a. 'Quality and public services', *Public Administration* 69, 4, 503–14.

————. 1991b. 'Citizens and consumers: marketing and public sector management', *Public Money and Management* 11, 2, 9–16.

Waterman, R. H. 1994. *The frontiers of excellence.* London: Nicholas Brealey.

Williamson, O. 1975. *Markets and hierarchies.* New York: Free Press.

6

Fred W. Riggs

PUBLIC ADMINISTRATION IN AMERICA: WHY OUR UNIQUENESS IS EXCEPTIONAL AND IMPORTANT

The *comparative* study of public administration ought to include the United States as well as other countries. We often hear that because our system of governance is unique it cannot be compared with any other. Is that not paradoxical? How can we know it is unique except by comparisons? If we only knew about our own system, we might think it was not exceptional and that all systems of governance work like ours— or ought to. Indeed, that is the implied premise of works by our colleagues that describe public administration in America as though is reflects universal principles, applicable anywhere. And was that not the premise of Americans who went abroad to teach and advise other governments, especially in the new states that emerged when the industrial empires collapsed?

THE COMPARATIVE STUDY OF AMERICAN PUBLIC ADMINISTRATION

After the Second World War, when former colonies formed new states, Americans began to go abroad to help Third World countries improve their administrative performance as a means to help them accomplish their development goals. Many of us naively assumed that our knowledge of public administration, based on our experiences in America, would equip us to help others in less developed countries improve their administrative performance.

In fact, we generalized pretentiously by writing about Public Administration on the basis of what we knew about public administration in America. Most scholars naturally focus on administration in their own countries. But none of us should claim that what we see at home can, by itself, justify a universally relevant theory of Public Administration. Not to be comparative is to be naively parochial.

Only the comparative study of American administration can liberate us from that kind of parochialism. Moreover, such comparisons need to focus on the relevant experience of countries that have adopted our own constitution principles rooted in the separation of powers. Comparisons with parliamentary regimes are interesting, but they cannot help us gain a deeper understanding of ourselves. Only after we make appropriate comparisons, can we justifiably talk about *public administration* in general.

THE AMERICAN EXCEPTION

The exceptionalist argument claims that America is so different from other countries—geographically, culturally, economically, socially, religiously, historically—that it cannot be compared (Lipset, 1996). That logic would make it impossible to compare any countries, all of which are unique in key ways. The trick it to compare countries that are different and analyze those differences in meaningful ways.

For example, why have American appointed officials, headed by military officers, never seized power in the United States? Is this not the most striking difference between the American experience and that of other presidentialist (separation of powers) constitutional systems?

POWER AND PERFORMANCE

To explain the American exception we need to consider two variables: bureaucratic power and performance. In general, these variables are positively correlated: the more powerful a bureaucracy, the greater its capacity to administer. By contrast, a powerless bureaucracy, under single-party domination, is administratively incompetent (Riggs, 1997b). However, there is a ceiling on this relationship. Beyond a certain level, when bureaucratic power becomes politically dominant—as it does, by definition, in a bureaucratic policy—the lack of effective controls by nonbureaucratic institutions destroys its administrative capacity. Corruption, laziness, and ignorance ultimately destroy any dominant bureaucracy that cannot be effectively controlled by other institutions (Riggs, 1973).

In all democracies, these controlling institutions are representative, centering on an elected assembly and a responsible head of government. However, I believe the fusion of powers in a parliamentarist regime enables it to manage a more powerful bureaucracy than any presidentialist (separation of powers) system. This is because the unity of authority principle inherent in any cabinet (parliamentarist) system of government permits more effective control over a bureaucracy than does the separation-of-powers (presidentialist) principle. From the bureaucratic perspective, disunity at the top often confuses and frustrates officials, undermining their morale and ability to coordinate their work. This is scarcely a new idea; others have written about it (for example, Kaufman, 1981; Rosenbloom, 1983; and Newland, 1987). Nevertheless, the deeper implications of this structure were not appreciated, even by John Rohr whose superb analysis of the implications of a separation-of-powers constitutional framework for American public administration suffers form its lack of comparisons, especially with other presidentialist regimes (Rohr, 1986).

Disunity at the top has major administrative costs. Conflict between branches (magnified by clashes between the components of each branch) hampers effective administration. It also blocks policy making, as we know from the frequent gridlocks which occur even in the United States where, I believe, our oligarchic practices make political decision making easier than in other presidentialist regimes. Study of the experience of these regimes reveals that their inability to shape policies and control their bureaucracies lies at the root of the problem of maintaining their democratic institutions. They cannot empower their bureaucracies enough to ensure competent public administration without, at the same time, making them so powerful that they can overthrow the regime when serious crises arise. The separation of powers principle also hampers their ability to make good public policy decisions and to make optimal use of the bureaucratic resources they have available to them.

To explain the American exception, therefore, we need to understand how its bureaucracy has been kept weak enough not to be able to seize power, but strong enough to administer reasonably well. Part of the answer lies in two basic variables that affect bureaucratic power and performance: experience and coordination. Long-term experience in public service gives appointed officials specialized knowledge about how to solve difficult problems and it also enhances their power potential. Rotation of assignments among different agencies and levels of governance from the center to the periphery enables officials to increase their capacity to exercise power and also to coordinate their work more effectively than when they have worked only in one specialized field. A more detailed discussion of bureaucratic power can be found elsewhere (Riggs, 1991b).

MANDARINATES

The administrative class in Great Britain is a familiar example of a bureaucratic system that combines long-term experience and position rotation. Its members are recruited by tough entrance examinations. Their subsequent careers enable them to advance, step by step, from junior to senior posts rotating between the center and localities and different ministries. Finally, as senior undersectretaries, they become distinguished generalists and advisers to the cabinet as coordinators and policy experts. These permanent undersecretaries can facilitate policy formation by a government much better than any collection of short-term patronage appointees or specialists familiar with only one type of government service. A similar system obtains in Canada (Campbell and Szablowski, 1979).

The basic principles involved in this type of bureaucracy are not new. They were invented about two thousand years ago in China and evolved into that country's famous mandarinate. It helped maintain the stability and integrity of long-term Chinese dynasties. When the British learned that is was difficult to maintain effective control over their distant empire in India, they borrowed the Chinese design. Only later, after they became increasingly impatient with the problems generated by the patronage system they had used to govern England did they decide to import the mandarin system from India where it had been elaborated in their Indian Civil Service. Similar reforms were carried out in virtually all other parliamentary governments, but they could not be implemented in the United States. Instead, we have developed a distinctive type of public bureaucracy that combines short-term patronage appointees with long-term officials who specialize in particular subject fields and staff services.

Had we adopted the mandarin principle in our bureaucracy, I believe it would have led to the collapse of presidentialist democracy in this country. Career mandarins would probably have gained power gradually, by nonviolent means, because no government based on the separation of powers can effectively manage a mandarin bureaucracy. Mandarinates are intrinsically powerful because of their long-term experience in diverse fields of administration. A White House office fully staffed by mandarins could easily dominate a president—heavy reliance on transients selected by and loyal to the chief executive are needed to avoid that outcome. Mandarins assigned to congressional committees also could probably control their policies.

A mandarinate is too powerful to be controlled by any constitutional regime based on separation of powers. The two 20th century examples—South Korea and South Vietnam—fell victims to bureaucratic domination soon after they were created. By contrast, the countries under American military administration after World War II that were permitted to restore parliamentary governance—Japan and Germany—already had mandarinates. But the new regimes were able to control them. This helps explain why, in both countries—despite the near total destruction caused by World War II—governmentally supported economic growth has proceeded so rapidly that they have become industrial superpowers.

PATRONAGE

In order to understand the unique form of bureaucracy found in America today we need to learn more about how patronage systems work. They prevail to the present day in almost all other presidentialist regimes, and survived in the United States in a modest way even after the passage of the Pendleton Act in 1883. Actually, all modern states were born with patronage bureaucracies. During the 19th century, most parliamentary regimes were able to replace them with mandarin-type systems. However, no presidentialist regime could make (or could afford to make) this transformation.

To understand how the U.S. experience differed form that of other presidentialist regimes, were need to consider two different forms of patronage. The original and still the most widespread form of patronage involves long-lasting appointments filled without assurances of tenure. This is what we had during the first 30 years or so of our existence until rotation in office was institutionalized by Andrew Jackson, as Leonard White has explained (1954, 5, 12–13). The word, retainer, identifies such people quite well. During most of the 19th century, a different type of patronage system based on short-term patronage appointments became the norm in America. This kind of rotation system, which relies on transients (in-and-outers), continues to prevail in the United States at top levels of the bureaucracy. Both are patronage appointees and most presidentialist regimes still rely mainly on retainers rather than transients to staff their bureaucracies.

Initially, retainers were nonthreatening to presidentialist regimes. So long as the functions of government were relatively simple, they could easily be learned or improved "on-the-job" and experience paid off so it was clearly expedient to retain "work horses" who could pull the barges of state. Having experienced officials became increasingly important as the problems generated by industrialization became more complicated.

This means that as entrenched retainers became more indispensable to presidentialist regimes, their propensity to organize informally to protect their jobs made them more and more powerful. They never established trade unions since without job security, anyone seeking to organize a union could readily be discharged. However, they could easily resist changes that threatened their perquisites, such as international projects to install a civil service system (Ruffing-Hilliard, 1991). More dramatically, secret cabals and cliques, especially among military officers, could become the incubators of successful coups. By contrast, in America, the replacement of retainers by transients undermined the capacity of patronage appointees to seize power. A classic description of transients in the American bureaucracy can be found in Heclo (1978), but without a comparative framework, the political significance of this kind of patronage system is not discussed.

GROWING COMPLEXITY

In the United States the patronage system became more and more corrupt and incompetent while the new problems generated by industrialization compelled the government to adopt increasingly complicated policies. It became apparent to members of Congress that a fundamental reform in the civil service was needed. The result, after a long struggle, was the enactment of the Pendleton Act in 1883 (Van Riper, 1958). Although only an ordinary act of Congress, this law has had fundamental consequences (Riggs, 1986).

The act introduced a new and uniquely American kind of bureaucrat, someone who was neither a mandarin nor a retainer, but rather, someone evaluated on training and experience to occupy a particular position rather than a youth recruited for a life-long career service with upward mobility assured. Congressional responsiveness to local constituencies was reflected in a provision of the act that required the nationwide distribution of appointments; this shrewd move was based on the West Point precedent that ensured patronage for all members of Congress while blocking the appointment of Ivy League graduates, the sons of affluent easterners who could, indeed, have established a mandarinate had the British model been followed, as originally proposed. Although opposition to elitism was often mentioned as a reason for the American rejection of the mandarin model, its political consequences for the survival of democracy in America were profound.

Our lack of a comparative framework is reflected in the fact that we have no specific term for this unique invention. Civil servant is a generic term that includes mandarins so it is not specific enough to characterize the distinctively American type of civil servant. The word "functionary" is often used in a pejorative sense to refer to a kind of bureaucrat trapped by repetitive office routines so we cannot borrow it. However, we might avoid the pejorative connotation of this word by using "functionist" instead to refer to the distinctively American type of career official who is recruited and promoted to work in a specific functional domain. Gradually, after 1883, more posts in the American public services were staffed by functionists. For the most part, American Public Administration schools and theories are dedicated to the training of future functionists—they focus their attention on the problems fucntionists will face as government officials. This focus excludes military officers who already had well-established training programs prior to the Pendleton Act. It also excludes the transients whose continuing appointment for high-level posts in the American bureaucracy largely explains the inherent political weakness of our bureaucracy. Reliance on functionists also means that basic policy areas—agriculture, engineering, transportation, communications, health, education, etc.—cannot be a focus of Public Administration training because, simultaneously, professional schools in these functional areas have emerged in all the state universities where the opportunity to prepare for public service became increasingly important.

In time, many functionists became professionals in the sense of this word intended by Wilson (1989). Their bureaucentric orientations combined with loyalty to the externally generated norms of their professional associations and schools meant that they would not be interested in the formation of bureaucracy-wide informal organizations. Assurances of tenure meant they lacked the motivation of retainers to organize informally to defend their long-term interests. It also meant that most functionists in government service do not identify themselves as bureaucrats or public administrators—they prefer to think of themselves as engineers, agriculturists, public health doctors, ect., choosing professions that link them with their private-sector counterparts and associations.

After subtracting the mainstream professions, what was left over for Public Administration was mainly staff services—personnel, finance, public relations, organization and methods—the bread and butter of our field. As ASPA has discovered, it is quite difficult in this environment to find many people who identify themselves with the "profession" of Public Administration. More attractive identities are available to them in the main-line professions, or in the subfields identified as staff services, each of which, I think, has associations with more members that ASPA can attract under the broad rubric of public administration professionals.

The external links of American functionists with a private sector profession also permit many of them to become nonpartisan transients, entering and leaving government service in professional roles, including those of university professors. In sum, the development of a functionist bureaucracy enabled the American government to enjoy the services of increasingly specialized long-termers without taking the risk that they might form cabals to control or oust the government. We feel so secure about the permanence of our presidentialist (separation of powers) constitutional system that we never think about the possibility of a coup d'etat. The spread of functionalism in America also meant that the quality of public administration in specific niches could improve radically, giving us an impression of administration prowess. The fact that the system makes interprogram coordination or metapolicy development so difficult came to be viewed as a challenge that we ought to be able to solve rather than as an inescapable liability inherent in the formula that permits our fragile constitutional system to survive. We also learned to see subgovernments as regrettable accidents but not as deep-rooted manifestations of this basic system nor as an inherent feature of all presidentialist regimes that are able to survive. We therefore view bureaucratic politics as a type of game or challenge that is peculiar to the American regime rather than as a necessary feature of any constitutional regime based on the separation of powers (Rourke, 1991; Seidman, 1980).

CONCLUSION

Because the risk of bureaucratic revolts was eliminated in America, it is not even discussed in our textbooks on Public Administration. We assumed that all bureaucracies could be essentially "nonpolitical" instruments of public policy, subservient to the basic political choices made by some kind of representative government. Our myth of a dichotomy between politics and administration permitted us to distance ourselves from political questions and also from political science as a discipline. It also allowed us to ignore the growing prevalence in the Third World of bureaucratic politics, regimes in which appointed officials, led by military officers, were politically dominant. We tended to overlook the political role of all public bureaucracies (Riggs, 1963).

Our current emphasis on "development management" points to parallels in business administration where politics is viewed as irrelevant. This focus enables us, in our schools and departments of Public Administration, to assume that we have some kind of universally relevant and valuable expertise that can be applied everywhere, in any system of governance. By ignoring problems of military administration and our own continuing reliance on patronage in public office for top-level appointees, we can focus on the management and role of functionists, especially in the staff services, as equivalent to the while field of Public Administration. There are exceptions to this generalization, but it remains essentially true.

Ultimately we can overcome ethnocentrism only by learning to view our own American system of public administration in a comparative context. That will enable us to understand the uniqueness of such historical experiences as the Jacksonian revolution and the Pendleton Act. When we become more aware of the basic ways in which our system of governance differs from that of other presidentialist regimes—and from all parliamentary systems—we will also learn what is unique about it and which of our practices can be usefully exported and which are relevant only at home. We will also discover, I think, that some of the reforms we would most like to carry out at home will undermine the viability of our system of government. International comparison will help us understand the constitutional risks inherent in many such reforms.

REFERENCES

Arora, Ramesh K. (1992). *Politics and Administration in Changing Societies: Essays in Honour of Professor Fred W. Riggs.* New Delhi: Associated Publishing House.

Braibanti, Ralph, ed. (1969). *Political and Administrative Development.* Durham, NC: Duke University Press.

Campbell, Colin and George J. Szablowski (1979). *The Superbureaucrats: Structure and Behavior in Central Agencies.* Toronto: Macmillan.

Gable, Richard W. and J. Fred Springer (1976). *Administering Agricultural Development in Asia: A Comparative Analysis of Four National Programs*. Boulder, CO: Westview Press.

Heady, Ferrel (1996). *Public Administration: A Comparative Perspective*. 5th ed. New York: Marcel Dekker.

Heady, Ferrel and Sybil L. Stokes, eds. (1962). *Papers in Comparative Public Administration*. Ann Arbor, MI: Institute of Public Administration, University of Michigan.

Heaphey, James J., ed. (1971). *Spatial Dimensions of Development Administration*. Durham, NC: Duke University Press.

Heclo, Hugh (1978). *A Government of Strangers: Executive Politics in Washington*. Washington, DC: Brookings Institutions.

Kaufman, Herbert (1981). *The Administrative Behavior of Federal Bureau Chiefs*. Washington, DC: Brookings Institution.

Kornberg, Allan and Lloyd D. Musolf, eds. (1970). *Legislatures in Developmental Perspective*. Durham, NC: Duke University Press.

Linz, Juan (1990a). "The Perils of Presidentialism." *The Journal of Democracy* 1(1): 51–69.

————. (1990b). "The Virtues of Parliamentarism." *The Journal of Democracy* 1(4):84–91.

Lipset, Seymour Martin (1997). *American Exceptionalism: A Double-Edged Sword*. NY: W. W. Norton.

Montgomery, John D. and William J. Siffin, eds. (1966). *Approaches to Development: Politics, Administration and Change*. New York: McGraw-Hill.

Newland, Chester (1987). "Public Executives: Imperium, Sacerdotum, Collegium?" *Public Administration Review* 47(1): 45–56.

Przeworski, Adam, Michael Alvarez, Jose Antonia Cheibub, and Fernando Limongi (1996). "What Makes Democracies Endure?" *Journal of Democracy* 7 (1): 39–55.

Report of a Conference on Comparative Administration (1952). Princeton, NJ, Sept. 12–14. Convened by the Public Administration Clearing House.

Riggs, Fred W. (1957). "Agraria and Industria: Toward a Typology of Comparative Administration." In William J. Siffin, ed., *Toward the Comparative Study of Public Administration*. Bloomington, IN: Indiana University Press, 23–116.

————. (1961). *The Ecology of Public Administration*. Bombay: Asia Publishing House. Published under the auspices of the Indian Institute of Public Administration, New Delhi.

————. (1963). "Bureaucrats and Political Development." In Joseph LaPalombara, ed. *Bureaucracy and Political Development*. Princeton, NJ: Princeton University Press, 120–167.

————. (1964). *Administration in Developing Countries: The Theory of Prismatic Society*. Boston: Houghton Mifflin.

————. (1966). *Thailand: The Modernization of a Bureaucratic Polity*. Honolulu: East-West Center Press.

————. (1968). "Administration and a Changing World Environment." *Public Administration Review* 28(4): 348–361.

————. ed. (1970). *Frontiers of Development Administration*. Durham, NC: Duke University Press.

————. (1971). *Final Report: Comparative Administration Group, American Society for Public Administration*. Honolulu: Social Science Research Institute.

————. (1973). "Legislative Structures: Some Thoughts on Elected National Assemblies." In Allan Kornberg, ed., *Legislatures in Comparative Perspective*. New York: McKay, 39–93.

————. (1974). *Prismatic Society Revisited*. Morristown, NJ: General Learning Press.

————. (1976a). "Comparative Administration: The U.S. Tradition." Unpublished paper presented at the ASPA conference, Washington, D.C., April 1976.

————. (1976b). "The Group and the Movement: Notes on Comparative and Development Administration." *Public Administration Review* 36(6): 648–654.

————. (1980). "The Ecology and Context of Public Administration: A Comparative Perspective." *Public Administration Review* 40(1): 107-115.

————. (1981). "Cabinet Ministers and Coup Groups: The Case of Thailand." *International Political Science Review* 2(2): 159-188.

————. (1982). "Politics of Bureaucratic Administration." In Krishna K. Tummala, ed., *Administrative Systems Abroad*. Washington, DC: University Press of America, 392-410.

————. (1986). "The Survival of Presidentialism in America: Para-Constitutional Practices." *International Political Science Review* 9(4): 247-278.

————. (1988). "Bureaucratic Politics in the U.S." *Governance*. 1(4): 343-379.

————. (1991a). "Public Administration: A Comparativist Framework." *Public Administration Review* 51(6): 473-477.

————. (1991b). "Bureaucratic Links between Administration and Politics." In Ali Farazmand, ed., *Handbook of Comparative and Development Public Administration*. New York: Marcel Dekker, 587-509.

————. (1993). "Fragility of the Third World's Regimes." *International Social Science Journal* 45(2): 199-243.

————. (1994a). "Bureaucracy and the Constitution." *Public Administration Review* 54(1): 65-72.

————. (1994b). "Bureaucracy: A Profound Perplexity for Presidentialism." In Ali Ferazmand, ed., *Handbook on Bureaucracy*. New York: Marcel Drekker, 97-148.

————. (1994c). "Presidentialism in Comparative Perspective." In Mattei Dogan and Ali Kazancigil, eds. *Comparing Nations: Concepts, Strategies, Substance*. Oxford, UK: Oxford University Press, 72-152.

————. (1995a). "Ethnonational Rebellions and Viable Constitutionalism." *International Political Science Review* 16(4): 375-404.

————. (1995b). "Presidentialism: A Problematic Constitutional System." In L. V. Carino, ed., *Conquering Politico-Administrative Frontiers: A Festschrift Honoring Raul de Guzman*. Quezon City, Philippines: University of the Philippines Press, 541-562.

————. (1996). "Viable Constitutionalism and Bureaucracy: Theoretical Premises." *Journal of Behavioral and Social Sciences*. 1995(2): 1-35. Tokyo: Tokai University.

————. (1997a). "Bureaucracy and Viable Constitutionalism." In Abdo Baaklini and Helen Desfosses, eds., *Designs for Democratic Stability: Studies in Viable Constitutionalism*. Armonk, NY and London: M. E. Sharpe, 95-125.

————. (1997b). "Coups and Crashes: Lessons for Public Administration." In Ali Farazmand, ed. *Modern Systems of Governance: Exploring the Role of Bureaucrats and Politicians*. Thousand Oaks, CA: Sage, 8-47.

————. (1997c). "Modernity and Bureaucracy." *Public Administration Review* 57(4): 347-353. (Abridged version of paper presented at the Dwight Waldo symposium, Maxwell School, Syracuse University, July 1996).

————. (1997d). "Presidentialism vs. Parliamentarism: Implications for Representativeness and Legitimacy." *International Political Science Review* 18(3): 253-278.

————. (1997e). "Coping with Modernity: Constitutional Implications." UNESCO/MOST Discussion paper. www2.hawaii.edu/~fredr/6-mstza.htm.

————. (1997f). "The Modernity of Ethnic Identity and Conflict." *International Political Science Review*. In press. www2.hawaii.edu/~fredr/7-isala.htm.

Rohr, John A. (1986). *To Run a Constitution: The Legitimacy of the Administrative State*. Lawrence, KS: University Press of Kansas.

Rosenbloom, David H. (1983). "Public Administration Theory and the Separation of Powers." *Public Administration Review* 43(3): 219-227.

Rourke, Francis E. (1991). "American Bureaucracy in a Changing Political Setting." *Journal of Public Administration: Research and Theory* 1(2): 111-129.

Ruffing-Hilliard, Karen (1991). "Merit Reform in Latin America," In Ali Farazmand, ed., *Handbook of Comparative and Development Public Administration*. New York: Marcel Dekker, 301–312.

Seidman, Harold (1980). *Politics, Position and Power: The Dynamics of Federal Organization*. New York: Oxford University Press.

Thurber, Clarence E. and Lawrence S. Graham, eds. (1973). *Development Administration in Latin America*. Durham, NC: Duke University Press.

Tummala, Krishna K. (1995). "Fred W. Riggs and Comparative Administration." *Public Administration Review* 55(6): 581–582.

United Nations, Technical Assistance Program (1961). *A Handbook of Public Administration: Current Concepts and Practice with Special Reference to Developing Countries*. NY: UN Department of Economic and Social Affairs.

Van Riper, Paul (1958). *History of the United States Civil Service*. Evanston, IL: Row, Peterson.

Waldo, Dwight, ed. (1970). *Temporal Dimensions of Development Administration*. Durham, NC: Duke University Press.

Weidner, Edward W., ed. (1970). *Development Administration in Asia*. Durham, NC: Duke University.

White, Leonard D. (1951). *The Jeffersonians*. New York: Macmillan.

———. (1954). *The Jacksonians*. New York: Macmillan.

Wilson, James Q. (1989). *Bureaucracy: What Government Agencies Do and Why They Do It*. New York: Basic Books.

3

DECISION MAKING IN PUBLIC ADMINISTRATION

In Chapter 2, we discussed some of the ways in which public administration is conducted within a framework of political purpose. Hopefully, that purpose is the common good. We also noted Gray and Jenkins' warning that public administration consists of far more than simply public choice economics and "new public management." Public administration is a profession that has constitutional, political and ethical dimensions that extend it well beyond the more limited concerns of business management for cutting costs and maximizing shareholders returns.

IS PUBLIC ADMINISTRATION THE CLASSIC CASE OF "BOUNDED RATIONALITY"?

The broader dimensions of public decision making become obvious by looking at some of the debates that have been studied by wave after wave of students of public administration. Consider first the debate about *rational decision making* that was advanced by Herbert A Simon in his classic book, *Administrative Behavior,* first published in 1945. Although Simon claimed he wrote *Administrative Behavior* for "administrators and executives in business and government,"[1] is clear that he wrote it primarily for public administrators. The first two chapters of the book were published originally in *Public Administration Review,* the journal of the American Society for Public Administration, and in it Simon depicts and analyses rationality and its limits in a way that speak directly to public administrators. Simon argues that administrative decisions are made within a framework of bounded rationality. He also makes the important distinction between *economic man* and *administrative man.* Economic man is a person as imagined by economists. Economic man selects the best alternative from among all available options. By contrast, *administrative man* recognizes that the world he perceives is a "drastically simplified model of the buzzing, booming confusion that constitutes the real world."[2]

Administrative decisions are about rational choice from among alternatives; "good" administrative decisions are adapted realistically to public benefit ends—just as "good" business decisions are calculated to realize financial gain.[3] In Simon's view, the public administrator makes decisions in pursuit of public benefit ends, choosing between alternatives in a complex world using a process that is rational but limited. It is an approach to decision making that most public administrators readily recognize. Despite Simon's persuasive argument, however, making "the most rational choice possible" continues as a *leitmotif* or dominant theme in the literature and practice of public administration. Decades after Simon wrote *Administrative Behavior*, the designers of PPBS placed "the analytical comparison of alternatives" at the center of the budgeting process. In so doing, they continued this often-rancorous debate. Practicing public administrators also continue it when they place cost-benefit studies for alternative freeway routes before a government or a municipality.

OR GOOD OL' DEMOCRATIC "MUDDLING THROUGH"?

In America, public administration is conducted in a setting of democratic politics, of lobbying and dealing. In a pluralist society such as ours, there is not a single interest to be pursued but many to be balanced. Charles Lindblom's writings about decision making highlight the need to depict public decision making as an unplanned, step-by-step process—"incremental" as he terms it. (We have reprinted Lindblom's early classic article, "The Science of Muddling Through,"[4] in this chapter.) *Incrementalism* reflects the small and gradual changes that are more characteristic of government decision making in democratic pluralism than in a centrally planned economy. Just as many public administrators readily identify with Simon's world of bounded rationality, they also identify time and again with the "muddling through" world of public administration as depicted by Lindblom and his followers.[5]

PUBLIC ADMINISTRATION UNDER CHALLENGE

During the last fifteen years of the twentieth century, the public choice school of economists opened a pervasive questioning of traditional assumptions about public administration and the very purposes of government. (We introduced public choice economic theory in Chapter 2, and it arises again in Chapter 4.) Public choice and its "offspring movement," "new public management" have arguably posed the greatest challenge to public administration this century and also have resulted in its greatest recent transformation. Today students must compare and contrast the depictions of public administrators in a democracy as described by traditional public administration with depictions of public administrators as put forward by the public choice economists and their followers. The reading by P. M. Jackson[6] that is reprinted in this chapter, tackles this problem.

OR DOES THE FAULT LIE WITH THE CRITICS?

Two decades of public choice-inspired denigration of public administration and successive cutbacks in government have caused an endless repetition of ex-President Ronald Reagan's aphorism: "Government is not part of the problem, it is the problem." However memorable and appealing this "sound bite" may have been to Reagan's followers, this largely unwarranted slur has hardly inspired public administrators to work long hours and do their best for their country. Kenneth Meier takes up from that position. "There are no more . . . silver bullets that will slay the bureaucracy dragon and magically improve governance. Most of the dragons have starved to death; few of the bullets hit anything."[7] Meier's conclusion: It is more likely that governance is the problem, not bureaucracy. Welcome to yet another heated debate about the public administrator's role!

READINGS REPRINTED IN THIS CHAPTER

This chapter contains three outstanding articles that introduce two key debates about the nature of public decision making.

Charles E. Lindblom's 1959 article, **"The Science of Muddling Through,"**[8] is a "classic" article that is a pleasure to pass on to a new generation of students. In many respects "The Science of Muddling Through" is a direct rejoinder to Herbert Simon's[9] "rational-comprehensive decision making" argument and an argument for "the method of successive limited comparison"[10] *incrementalism*—for short. *Rational-comprehensive decision making* ("root") relies on theory, undertakes comprehensive analysis, and separates means and ends. *Successive limited comparisons decision making* ("branch") reduces or eliminates theory, drastically limits analysis, and sees means and ends as intertwined.

In the second reading, **"Public Choice and Public Sector Management"**, **P. M. Jackson** argues that public sector economics and public sector management should complement one another more than they do. Writing in 1990—at the peak of the international popularity of public choice economics and "new public management"—Jackson argues that the public choice perspective provides important insights for understanding public policy and public decision making. In Chapter 2, Gray and Jenkins wrote about the inadequacy of the "new public management" approach that, they argued, lacked the breadth of public administration. In this chapter, Jackson counter-argues that public sector management needs to be informed by the teachings of public choice economists. Jackson shares with Lindblom a belief that "good management practice needs to be predicated upon sound theory."[11]

Kenneth Meier's 1997 article, **"Bureaucracy and Democracy: the Case for More Bureaucracy and Less Democracy,"** is a rejoinder to the many "bureaucrat bashers" who are the political counterparts of the academic public choice economists. To the extent that the so-called "bureaucracy problem" in the U.S. is instead a governance problem, government reformers should focus on the reform of governance and elected bodies, not only on the bureaucracy. If there is a problem with decision making, it is appropriate to look at the legislatures and council chambers as well, and not assume that all problems lie with public administrators. These articles by Jackson and Meier provide very different ways of thinking about public administration and perspectives on government reform.

The readings in this chapter thus demonstrate unequivocally how public administration in a democracy sits in the middle of heated debates about how a democratic society governs itself—or how it should govern itself.

NOTES

1. Simon, Herbert A. (1945/97). *Administrative Behavior.* New York: Macmillan, p. x.
2. Simon, Herbert A. (1945/97). *Administrative Behavior.* New York: Macmillan, p. xxv.
3. Simon, Herbert A. (1945/97). *Administrative Behavior.* New York: Macmillan, p. 62.
4. Lindblom, Charles E. (Spring 1959). "The Science of Muddling Through." *Public Administration Review, 19,* 79–88.
5. In the readings in this chapter, we have included two gems from a rich mine of thinking and writing. In later chapters there are several more excellent contributions on this subject by Henry Mintzberg (in Chapters 6 and 9) and Aaron Wildavsky (in Chapter 13). Mintzberg and Wildavsky are equally skeptical about rational administration carried to inflexible extremes.
6. Jackson, P. M. (1990). "Public Choice and Public Sector Management." *Public Money and Management, 10,* 13–20.
7. Meier, Kenneth J. (1997). "Bureaucracy and Democracy: The Case for More Bureaucracy and Less Democracy." *Public Administration Review, 57*(3), 194.
8. Lindblom, Charles E. (Spring 1959). "The Science of Muddling Through." *Public Administration Review, 19,* 79–88.
9. Simon, Herbert A. (1945/97). *Administrative Behavior.* New York: Macmillan, p. 62.
10. Lindblom, Charles E. (Spring 1959). "The Science of Muddling Through." *Public Administration Review, 19,* 81.
11. Jackson, P. M. (1990). "Public Choice and Public Sector Management." *Public Money and Management, 10,* 20.

7

Charles E. Lindblom

THE SCIENCE OF "MUDDLING THROUGH"

Suppose an administrator is given responsibility for formulating policy with respect to inflation. He might start by trying to list all related values in order of importance, e.g., full employment, reasonable business profit, protection of small savings, prevention of stock market crash. Then all possible policy outcomes could be rated as more or less efficient in attaining a maximum of these values. This would of course require a prodigious inquiry into values held by members of society and an equally prodigious set of calculations on how much of each value is equal to how much of each other value. He could then proceed to outline all possible policy alternatives. In a third step, he would undertake systematic comparison of his multitude of alternatives to determine which attains the greatest amount of values.

In comparing policies, he would take advantage of any theory available that generalized about classes of policies. In considering inflation, for example, he would compare all policies in the light of the theory of prices. Since no alternatives are beyond his investigation, he would consider strict central control and the abolition of all prices and markets on the one hand and elimination of all public controls with reliance completely on the free market on the other, both in the light of whatever theoretical generalizations he could find on such hypothetical economies.

Finally, he would try to make the choice that would in fact maximize his values.

An alternative line of attack would be to set as his principal objective, either explicitly or without conscious thought, the relatively simple goal of keeping prices level. This objective might be compromised or complicated by only a few other goals, such as full employment. He would in fact disregard most other social values as beyond his present interest, and he would for the moment not even attempt to rank the few values that he regarded as immediately relevant. Were he pressed, he would quickly admit that he was ignoring many related values and many possible important consequences of his policies.

As a second step, he would outline those relatively few policy alternatives that occurred to him. He would then compare them. In comparing his limited number of alternatives, most of them familiar from past controversies, he would not ordinarily find a body of theory precise enough to carry him through a comparison of their respective consequences. Instead he would rely heavily on the record of past experience with small policy steps to predict the consequences of similar steps extended into the future.

Moreover, he would find that the policy alternatives combined objectives or values in different ways. For example, one policy might offer price level stability at the cost of some risk of unemployment; another might offer less price stability but also less risk of unemployment. Hence, the next step in his approach—the final selection—would combine into one the choice among values and the choice among instruments for reaching values. It would not, as in the first method of policy-making, approximate a more mechanical process of choosing the means that best satisfied goals that were previously clarified and ranked. Because practitioners of the second approach expect to achieve their goals only partially, they would expect to repeat endlessly the sequence just described, as conditions and aspirations changed and as accuracy of prediction improved.

By Root or by Branch

For complex problems, the first of these two approaches is of course impossible. Although such an approach can be described, it cannot be practiced except for relatively simple problems and even then only in a somewhat modified form. It assumes intellectual capacities and sources of information that men simply do not possess, and it is even more absurd as an approach to policy when the time and money that can be allocated to a policy problem is limited, as is always the case. Of particular importance to public administrators is the fact that public agencies are in effect usually instructed not to practice the first method. That is to say, their prescribed functions and constraints—the politically or legally possible—restrict their attention to relatively few values and relatively few alternative policies among the countless alternatives that might be imagined. It is the second method that is practiced.

Curiously, however, the literatures of decision-making, policy formulation, planning, and public administration formalize the first approach rather than the second, leaving public administrators who handle complex decisions in the position of practicing what few preach. For emphasis I run some risk of overstatement. True enough, the literature is well aware of limits on man's capacities and of the inevitability that policies will be approached in some such style as the second. But attempts to formalize rational policy formulation—to lay out explicitly the necessary steps in the process—usually describe the first approach and not the second.

The common tendency to describe policy formulation even for complex problems as though it followed the first approach has been strengthened by the attention given to, and successes enjoyed by, operations research, statistical decision theory, and systems analysis. The hallmarks of these procedures, typical of the first approach, are clarity of objective, explicitness of evaluation, a high degree of comprehensiveness of overview, and, wherever possible, quantification of values for mathematical analysis. But these advanced procedures remain largely the appropriate techniques of relatively small-scale problem-solving where the total number of variables to be considered is small and value problems restricted.

Accordingly, I propose in this paper to clarify and formalize the second method, much neglected in the literature. This might be described as the method of *successive limited comparisons*. I will contrast it with the first approach, which might be called the rational-comprehensive method.[1] More impressionistically and briefly they could be characterized as the branch method and root method, the former continually building out from the current situation, step-by-step and by small degrees; the latter starting from fundamentals anew each time, building on the past only as experience is embodied in a theory, and always prepared to start completely from the ground up.

Let us put the characteristics of the two methods side by side in simplest terms.

Assuming that the root method is familiar and understandable, we proceed directly to clarification of its alternative by contrast. In explaining the second, we shall be describing how most administrators do in fact approach complex questions, for the root method, the "best" way as a blueprint or model, is in fact not workable for complex policy questions, and administrators are forced to use the method of successive limited comparisons.

---

[1] I am assuming that administrators often make policy and advise in the making policy and am treating decision-making and policy-making as synonymous for purposes of this paper.

Rational-Comprehensive (Root)	Successive Limited Comparisons (Branch)
1a. Clarification of values or objectives distinct from and usually prerequisite to empirical analysis of alternative policies.	1b. Selection of value goals and empirical analysis of the needed action are not distinct from one another but are closely intertwined.
2a. Policy-formulation is therefore approached through means-end analysis: First the ends are isolated, then the means to achieve them are sought.	2b. Since means and ends are not distinct, means-end analysis is often inappropriate or limited.
3a. The test of a "good" policy is that it can be shown to be the most appropriate means to desired ends.	3b. The test of a "good" policy is typically that various analysts find themselves directly agreeing on a policy (without their agreeing that it is the most appropriate means to an agreed objective).
4a. Analysis is comprehensive; every important relevant factor is taken into account.	4b. Analysis is drastically limited: i) Important possible outcomes are neglected. ii) Important alternative potential policies are neglected. iii) Important affected values are neglected.
5a. Theory is often heavily relied upon.	5b. A succession of comparisons greatly reduces or eliminates reliance on theory.

INTERTWINING EVALUATION AND EMPIRICAL ANALYSIS (1B)

The quickest way to understand how values are handled in the method of successive limited comparisons is to see how the root method often breaks down in *its* handling of values or objectives. The idea that values should be clarified, and in advance of the examination of alternative policies, is appealing. But what happens when we attempt it for complex social problems? The first difficulty is that on many critical values or objectives, citizens disagree, congressmen disagree, and public administrators disagree. Even where a fairly specific objective is prescribed for the administrator, there remains considerable room for disagreement on sub-objectives.

Administrators cannot escape these conflicts by ascertaining the majority's preference, for preferences have not been registered on most issues; indeed, there often *are* no preferences in the absence of public discussion sufficient to bring an issue to the attention of the electorate. Furthermore, there is a question of whether intensity of feeling should be considered as well as the number of persons preferring each alterna-tive. By the impossibility of doing otherwise, administrators often are reduced to de-ciding policy without clarifying objectives first.

Even when an administrator resolves to follow his own values as a criterion for decisions, he often will not know how to rank them when they conflict with one an-other, as they usually do.

How does one state even to himself the relative importance of these partially con-flicting values? A simple ranking of them is not enough; one needs ideally to know how much of one value is worth sacrificing for some of another value. The answer is that typically the administrator chooses—and must choose—directly among policies in which these values are combined in different ways. He cannot first clarify his values and then choose among policies.

A more subtle third point underlies both the first two. Social objectives do not always have the same relative values. One objective may be highly prized in one cir-cumstance, another in another circumstance. If, for example, an administrator val-ues highly both the dispatch with which his agency can carry through its projects *and* good public relations, it matters little which of the two possibly conflicting values he favors in some abstract or general sense. Policy questions arise in forms which put to administrators such a question as: Given the degree to which we are or are not al-ready achieving the values of dispatch and the values of good public relations, is it worth sacrificing a little speed for a happier clientele, or is it better to risk offending the clientele so that we can get on with our work? The answer to such a question varies with circumstances.

The value problem is, as the example shows, always a problem of adjustments at a margin. But there is no practicable way to state marginal objectives or values except in terms of particular policies. That one value is preferred to another in one decision situ-ation does not mean that it will be preferred in another decision situation in which it can be had only at great sacrifice of another value. Attempts to rank or order values in general and abstract terms so that they do not shift from decision to decision end up by ignoring the relevant marginal preferences. The significance of this third point thus goes very far. Even if all administrators had at hand an agreed set of values, objectives, and constraints, and an agreed ranking of these values, objectives, and constraints, their marginal values in actual choice situations would be impossible to formulate.

Unable consequently to formulate the relevant values first and then choose among policies to achieve them, administrators must choose directly among alter-native policies that offer different marginal combinations of values. Somewhat paradoxically, the only practicable way to disclose one's relevant marginal values even to oneself is to describe the policy one chooses to achieve them. Except roughly and vaguely, I know of no way to describe—or even to understand—what my relative evaluations are for, say, freedom and security, speed and accuracy in governmental decisions, or low taxes and better schools than to describe my prefer-ences among specific policy choices that might be made between the alternatives in each of the pairs.

In summary, two aspects of the process by which values are actually handled can be distinguished. The first is clear: evaluation and empirical analysis are intertwined;

that is, one chooses among values and among policies at one and the same time. Put a little more elaborately, one simultaneously chooses a policy to attain certain objectives and chooses the objectives themselves. The second aspect is related but distinct: the administrator focuses his attention on marginal or incremental values. Whether he is aware of it or not, he does not find general formulations of objectives very helpful and in fact makes specific marginal or incremental comparisons.

As to whether the attempt to clarify objectives in advance of policy selection is more or less rational than the close intertwining of marginal evaluation and empirical analysis, the principal difference established is that for complex problems the first is impossible and irrelevant, and the second is both possible and relevant. The second is possible because the administrator need not try to analyze any values except the values by which alternative polices differ and need not be concerned with them except as they differ marginally. His need for information on values or objectives is drastically reduced as compared with the root method; and his capacity for grasping, comprehending, and relating values to one another is not strained beyond the breaking point.

Relations Between Means and Ends (2b)

Decision-making is ordinarily formalized as a means-ends relationship: means are conceived to be evaluated and chosen in the light of ends finally selected independently of and prior to the choice of means. This is the means-ends relationship of the root method. But it follows from all that has just been said that such a means-ends relationship is possible only to the extent that values are agreed upon, are reconcilable, and are stable at the margin. Typically, therefore, such a means-ends relationship is absent from the branch method, where means and ends are simultaneously chosen.

Yet any departure from the means-ends relationship of the root method will strike some readers as inconceivable. For it will appear to them that only in such a relationship is it possible to determine whether one policy choice is better or worse than another. How can an administrator know whether he has made a wise or foolish decision if he is without prior values or objectives by which to judge his decisions? The answer to this question calls up the third distinctive difference between root and branch methods: how to decide the best policy.

The Test of "Good" Policy (3b)

In the root method, a decision is "correct," "good," or "rational" if it can be shown to attain some specified objective, where the objective can be specified without simply describing the decision itself. Where objectives are defined only through the marginal or incremental approach to values described above, it is still sometimes possible to test whether a policy does in fact attain the desired objectives; but a precise statement of the objectives takes the form of a description of the policy chosen or some alternative to it. To show that a policy is mistaken one cannot offer an abstract argument that important objectives are not achieved; one must instead argue that another policy is more to be preferred.

So far, the departure from customary ways of looking at problem-solving is not troublesome, for many administrators will be quick to agree that the most effective discussion of the correctness of policy does take the form of comparison with other polices that might have been chosen. But what of the situation in which administrators cannot agree on values or objectives, either abstractly or in marginal terms? What then is the test of "good" policy? For the root method, there is no test. Agreement on objectives failing, there is no standard of "correctness." For the method of successive limited comparisons, the test is agreement on policy itself, which remains possible even when agreement on values is not.

Agreement on policy thus becomes the only practicable test of the policy's correctness. And for one administrator to seek to win the other over to agreement on ends as well would accomplish nothing and create quite unnecessary controversy.

If agreement directly on policy as a test for "best" policy seems a poor substitute for testing the policy against its objectives, it ought to be remembered that objectives themselves have no ultimate validity other than they are agreed upon. Hence agreement is the test of "best" policy in both methods. But where the root method requires agreement on what elements in the decision constitute objectives and on which of these objectives should be sought, the branch method falls back on agreement wherever it can be found.

In an important sense, therefore, it is not irrational for an administrator to defend a policy as good without being able to specify what it is good for.

NON-COMPREHENSIVE ANALYSIS (4B)

Ideally, rational-comprehensive analysis leaves out nothing important. But it is impossible to take everything important into consideration unless "important" is so narrowly defined that analysis is in fact quite limited. Limits on human intellectual capacities and on available information set definite limits to man's capacity to be comprehensive. In actual fact, therefore, no one can practice the rational-comprehensive method for really complex problems, and every administrator faced with a sufficiently complex problem must find ways drastically to simplify.

In the method of successive limited comparisons, simplification is systematically achieved in two principal ways. First, it is achieved through limitation of policy comparisons to those policies that differ in relatively small degree from policies presently in effect. Such a limitation immediately reduces the number of alternatives to be investigated and also drastically simplifies the character of the investigation of each. For it is not necessary to undertake fundamental inquiry into an alternative and its consequences; it is necessary only to study those respects in which the proposed alternative and its consequences differ from the status quo. The empirical comparison of marginal differences among alternative policies that differ only marginally is, of course, a counterpart to the incremental or marginal comparison of values discussed above.[2]

---

[2]A more precise definition of incremental policies and a discussion of whether a change that appears "small" to one observer might be seen differently by another is to be found in my "Policy Analysis," 48 *American Economic Review* 298 (June, 1958).

RELEVANCE AS WELL AS REALISM

It is a matter of common observation that in Western democracies public administrators and policy analysts in general do largely limit their analyses to incremental or marginal differences in policies that are chosen to differ only incrementally. They do not do so, however, solely because they desperately need some way to simplify their problems; they also do so in order to be relevant. Democracies change their policies almost entirely through incremental adjustments. Policy does not move in leaps and bounds.

The incremental character of political change in the United States has often been remarked. The two major political parties agree on fundamentals; they offer alternative policies to the voters only on relatively small points of difference. Both parties favor full employment, but they define it somewhat differently; both favor the development of water power resources, but in slightly different ways; and both favor unemployment compensation, but not the same level of benefits. Similarly, shifts of policy within a party take place largely through a series of relatively small changes, as can be seen in their only gradual acceptance of the idea of governmental responsibility for support of the unemployed, a change in party positions beginning in the early 30's and culminating in a sense in the Employment Act of 1946.

Party behavior is in turn rooted in public attitudes, and political theorists cannot conceive of democracy's surviving in the United States in the absence of fundamental agreement on potentially disruptive issues, with consequent limitation of policy debates to relatively small differences in policy.

Since the policies ignored by the administrator are politically impossible and so irrelevant, the simplification of analysis achieved by concentrating on policies that differ only incrementally is not a capricious kind of simplification. In addition, it can be argued that, given the limits on knowledge within which policy-makers are confined, simplifying by limiting the focus to small variations from present policy makes the most of available knowledge. Because policies being considered are like present and past policies, the administrator can obtain information and claim some insight. Nonincremental policy proposals are therefore typically not only politically irrelevant but also unpredictable in their consequences.

The second method of simplification of analysis in the practice of ignoring important possible consequences of possible policies, as well as the values attached to the neglected consequences. If this appears to disclose a shocking shortcoming of successive limited comparisons, it can be replied that, even it the exclusions are random, policies may nevertheless be more intelligently formulated than through futile attempts to achieve a comprehensiveness beyond human capacity. Actually, however, the exclusions, seeming arbitrary or random from one point of view, need be neither.

ACHIEVING A DEGREE OF COMPREHENSIVENESS

Suppose that each value neglected by one policy-making agency were a major concern of at least one other agency. In that case, a helpful division of labor would be achieved, and no agency need find its task beyond its capacities. The shortcomings of such a system would be that once agency might destroy a value either before another agency could be activated to safeguard it or in spite of another agency's efforts. But the possibility that important values may be lost is present in any form of organization, even where agencies attempt to comprehend in planning more than is humanly possible.

The virtue of such a hypothetical division of labor is that every important interest or value has its watchdog. And these watchdogs can protect the interests in their jurisdiction in two quite different ways: first, by redressing damages done by other agencies; and, second, by anticipating and heading off injury before it occurs.

In a society like that of the United States in which individuals are free to combine to pursue almost any possible common interest they might have and in which government agencies are sensitive to the pressures of these groups, the system described is approximated. Almost every interest has its watchdog. Without claiming that every interest has a sufficiently powerful watchdog, it can be argued that our system often can assure a more comprehensive regard for the values of the whole society than any attempt at intellectual comprehensiveness.

Mutual adjustment is more pervasive than the explicit forms it takes in negotiation between groups; it persists through the mutual impacts of groups upon each other even where they are not in communication. For all the imperfections and latent dangers in this ubiquitous process of mutual adjustment, it will often accomplish an adaptation of policies to a wider range of interests than could be done by one group centrally.

Note, too, how the incremental pattern of policy-making fits with the multiple pressure pattern. For when decisions are only incremental—closely related to known policies, it is easier for one group to anticipate the kind of moves another might make and easier too for it to make correction for injury already accomplished.[3]

Even partisanship and narrowness, to use pejorative terms, will sometimes be assets to rational decision-making, for they can doubly insure that what one agency neglects, another will not; they specialize personnel to distinct points of view. The claim is valid that effective rational coordination of the federal administration, if possible to achieve at all, would require an agreed set of values[4]—if "rational" is defined as the practice of the root method of decision-making. But a high degree of administrative coordination occurs as each agency adjusts its policies to the concerns of the other agencies in the process of fragmented decision-making I have just described.

For all the apparent shortcomings of the incremental approach to policy alternatives with its arbitrary exclusion coupled with fragmentation, when compared to the root method, the branch method often looks far superior. In the root method, the inevitable exclusion of factors is accidental, unsystematic, and not defensible by any argument so far developed, while in the branch method the exclusions are deliberate, systematic, and defensible. Ideally, of course, the root method does not exclude; in practice it must.

---

[3]The link between the practice of the method of successive limited comparisons and mutual adjustment of interests in a highly fragmented decision-making process adds a new facet to pluralist theories of government and administration.

[4]Herbert Simon, Donald W. Smithburg, and Victor A. Thompson, *Public Administration* (Alfred A. Knopf, 1950), p. 434.

Nor does the branch method necessarily neglect long-run considerations and objectives. It is clear that important values must be omitted in considering policy, and sometimes the only way long-run objectives can be given adequate attention is through the neglect of short-run considerations. But the values omitted can be either long-run or short-run.

SUCCESSION OF COMPARISONS (5B)

The final distinctive element in the branch method is that the comparisons, together with the policy choice, proceed in a chronological series. Policy is not made once and for all; it is made and re-made endlessly. Policy-making is a process of successive approximation to some desired objectives in which what is desired itself continues to change under reconsideration.

Making policy is at best a very rough process. Neither social scientists, nor politicians, nor public administrators yet know enough about the social world to avoid repeated error in predicting the consequences of policy moves. A wise policy-maker consequently expects that his policies will achieve only part of what he hopes and at the same time will produce unanticipated consequences he would have preferred to avoid. If he proceeds through a *succession* of incremental changes, he avoids serious lasting mistakes in several ways.

In the first place, past sequences of policy steps have given him knowledge about the probable consequences of further similar steps. Second, he need not attempt big jumps toward his goals that would require predictions beyond his or anyone else's knowledge, because he never expects his policy to be a final resolution of a problem. His decision is only one step, one that if successful can quickly be followed by another. Third, he is in effect able to test his previous predictions as he moves on to each further step. Lastly, he often can remedy a past error fairly quickly—more quickly than if policy proceeded through more distinct steps widely spaced in time.

Compare this comparative analysis of incremental changes with the aspiration to employ theory in the root method. Man cannot think without classifying, without subsuming one experience under a more general category of experiences. The attempt to push categorization as far as possible and to find general propositions which can be applied to specific situations is what I refer to with the word "theory." Where root analysis often leans heavily on theory in this sense, the branch method does not.

The assumption of root analysis is that theory is the most systematic and economical way to bring relevant knowledge to bear on specific problem. Granting the assumption, an unhappy fact is that we do not have adequate theory to apply to problems in any policy area, although theory is more adequate in some areas—monetary policy, for example—than in others. Comparative analysis, as in the branch method, is sometimes a systematic alternative to theory.

Suppose an administrator must choose among a small group of policies that differ only incrementally from each other and from present policy. He might aspire to "understand" each of the alternatives—for example, to know all the consequences of each aspect of each policy. If so, he would indeed require theory. In fact, however, he would usually decide that, *for policy-making purposes*, he need know, as explained above, only the consequences of each of those aspects of the policies in which they differed from one another. For this much more modest aspiration, he requires no theory (although it might be helpful, if available), for he can proceed to isolate probable differences by examing the differences in consequences associated with past differences in policies, a feasible program because he can take his observations from a long sequence of incremental changes.

THEORISTS AND PRACTITIONERS

This difference explains—in some cases at least—why the administrator often feels that the outside expert or academic problem-solver is sometimes not helpful and why they in turn often urge more theory on him. And it explains why an administrator often feels more confident when "flying by the seat of his pants" than when following the advice of theorists. Theorists often ask the administrator to go the long way round to the solution of his problems, in effect ask him to follow the best canons of the scientific method, when the administrator knows that the best available theory will work less well than more modest incremental comparisons. Theorists do not realize that the administrator is often in fact practicing a systematic method. It would be foolish to push this explanation too far, for sometimes practical decision-makers are pursuing neither a theoretical approach nor successive comparisons, nor any other systematic method.

It may be worth emphasizing that theory is sometimes of extremely limited helpfulness in policy-making for at least two rather different reasons. It is greedy for facts; it can be constructed only through a great collection of observations. And it is typically insufficiently precise for application to a policy process that moves through small changes. In contrast, the comparative method both economizes on the need for facts and directs the analyst's attention to just those facts that are relevant to the fine choices faced by the decision-maker.

With respect to precision of theory, economic theory serves as an example. It predicts that an economy without money or prices would in certain specified ways misallocate resources, but this finding pertains to an alternative far removed from the kind of policies on which administrators need help. On the other hand, it is not precise enough to predict the consequences of policies restricting business mergers, and this is the kind of issue on which the administrators need help. Only in relatively restricted areas does economic theory achieve sufficient precision to go far in resolving policy questions; its helpfulness in policy-making is always so limited that it requires supplementation through comparative analysis.

SUCCESSIVE COMPARISON AS A SYSTEM

Successive limited comparisons is, then, indeed a method or system; it is not a failure of method for which administrators ought to apologize. None the less, its imperfections, which have not been explored in this paper, are many. For example, the method is without a built-in safeguard for all relevant values, and it also may lead the decision-maker to overlook excellent policies for no other reason than that they are not suggested by the chain of successive policy steps leading up to the present. Hence, it ought to be said that under this method, as well as under some of the most sophisticated variants of the root method—operations research, for example—policies will continue to be as foolish as they are wise.

Why then bother to describe the method in all the above detail? Because it is in fact a common method of policy formulation, and is, for complex problems, the principal reliance of administrators as well as of other policy analysts. And because it will be superior to any other decision-making method available for complex problems in many circumstances, certainly superior to a futile attempt at superhuman comprehensiveness. The reaction of the public administrator to the exposition of method doubtless will be less a discovery of a new method than a better acquaintance with an old. But by becoming more conscious of their practice of this method, administrators might practice it with more skill and know when to extend or constrict its use. (That they sometimes practice it effectively and sometimes not may explain the extremes of opinion on "muddling through," which is both praised as a highly sophisticated form of problem-solving and denounced as no method at all. For I suspect that in so far as there is a system in what is known as "muddling through," this method is it.)

One of the noteworthy incidental consequences of clarification of the method is the light it throws on the suspicion an administrator sometimes entertains that a consultant or adviser is not speaking relevently and responsibly when in fact by all ordinary objective evidence he is. The trouble lies in the fact that most of us approach policy problems within a framework given by our view of a chain of successive policy choices made up to the present. One's thinking about appropriate policies with respect, say, to urban traffic control is greatly influenced by one's knowledge of the incremental steps taken up to the present. An administrator enjoys an intimate knowledge of his past sequences that "outsiders" do not share, and his thinking and that of the "outsider" will consequently be different in ways that may puzzle both. Both may appear to be talking intelligently, yet each may find the other unsatisfactory. The relevance of the policy chain of succession is even more clear when an American tries to discuss, say, antitrust policy with a Swiss, for the chains of policy in the two countries are strikingly different and the two individuals consequently have organized their knowledge in quite different ways.

If this phenomenon is a barrier to communication, an understanding of it promises an enrichment of intellectual interaction in policy formulation. Once the source of difference is understood, it will sometimes be stimulating for an administrator to seek out a policy analyst whose recent experience is with a policy chain different from his own.

This raises again a question only briefly discussed above on the merits of like-mindedness among government administrators. While much of organization theory argues the virtues of common values and agreed organizational objectives, for complex problems in which the root method is inapplicable, agencies will want among their own personnel two types of diversification: administrators whose thinking is organized by reference to policy chains other than those familiar to most members of the organization and, even more commonly, administrators whose professional or personal values or interests create diversity of view (perhaps coming from different specialties, social classes, geographical areas) so that, even within a single agency, decision-making can be fragmented and parts of the agency can serve as watchdogs for other parts.

8

P.M. Jackson

PUBLIC CHOICE AND PUBLIC SECTOR MANAGEMENT

THE ROLE OF PUBLIC SECTOR ECONOMICS

Public sector economics plays an important role in providing a firm foundation for the general principles of public sector management. Indeed, at a more general level it is economics which establishes most of the principles of general management. Public sector economics contributes to the design of fiscal institutions and the formulation of public policies. It lies at the centroid of the Trinity: theory, institutions and policy. This is insufficiently appreciated, especially by those who practise management. Lest this be regarded as an act of academic imperialism by economists, the balance should be immediately redressed by pointing out that economists have paid insufficient attention to the problems and issues of management. The theme of this essay is that a stronger symbiotic relationship between those involved in public sector economics and those concerned with the issues of public sector management would produce the synergy necessary to advance the quest for improved efficiency and effectiveness in the public sector.

Academic research is by definition devoted to replacing legends with truth, and replacing myth with reality. However, there are some areas where myths are particularly tenacious and no more so than when it comes to "management". The combination of theory with facts ensures that management by slogan is minimized. Whilst theory without facts might be regarded as sterile, practice without theory is usually blind. In this age of "guruspeak," and the encapsulation of complex ideas into memorable and elegant epigrams, theory reminds us that quotable aphorisms do not have the general applicability often supposed and that such statements are, therefore, of little value to managers who face real problems. What public sector economics attempts to do is to get behind the slogans and aphorisms and to set out the essential elements which are necessary to design public sector organizations, establish management techniques, and formulate policy.

If management is about achieving an organization's objectives through efficient, effective, and morally acceptable processes, then economics has much to contribute to the formulation of management principles. Economists, however, have not been effective publicists of their trade. Moreover, some economists have failed to appreciate the limitations of their approach, especially when it comes to the implementation of their policy plans.

Too often, economists erect unnecessary barriers by publishing their research in an arcane and impenetrable language. They often write for other economists, forgetting that there are important issues, including public sector management, which might benefit from their approach to problem identification and problem-solving. Thus the social value of economics is reduced.

The methodology of economics is powerful in showing those areas where markets are a superior form of social organization and where there is, therefore, no role for government. Where, however, there is a role for government, public sector economics is useful in helping to identity that role and in defining the more important policy instruments which are both necessary and sufficient in achieving specific policy objectives. Public sector economics, however, is at its weakest when it is asked how public policies might be performed effectively. "How" questions involve issues of implementation and the organizing principles of management, and, with few exceptions (for example Simon, Lindblom, Leibenstein and Williamson), economists have remained silent on these issues.

If the economist is to present useful prescriptions for social policy, and for public sector management, then more attention must be given to evolving methods that can be used not only to guide what the government's role might be, but also how that role might be played. More attention needs to be given to figuring out what rules might meet the ends of "rough justice" and also "rough efficiency", rather than complaining that the world is not organized in a way that will enable the implementation of the rigorous first-best rules of evaluation. If the economist is not sufficiently careful in matching up theory with context then the result can be a bias towards getting the right answer to the wrong question.

THE ROLE OF THE ECONOMIST

What is the role of the public sector economist when it comes to discussing matters of public sector management? What are the areas of competence over which the economist might have some command, and, therefore, something useful to say? To answer these questions it is useful to have some idea of the subject matter of public sector economics.

Public sector economics bring together two branches of economics. These are *welfare economics*, with its emphasis upon efficiency theorems and issues of distributive justice, and *public finance* which is concerned with matters of tax incidence and the effects of taxation upon private sector behaviour. Welfare economics and public finance in combination provide powerful analytical tools when it comes to designing fiscal institutions and public policies.

Starting from the welfare economics proposition that market failure brings about a departure from the Pareto efficient resource allocations (i.e. essentially prices equal to marginal costs) of the first-best world of perfect competition, economists have designed policies to bring about improvements in efficiency. Thus, the catalogue of policies would include pollution taxes to correct the market failures of externalities; subsidies to ensure that certain public goods are adequately consumed; optimal taxes that minimize the deadweight losses or distortions caused by tax systems; and regulations which bring individual self-interest serving behaviour closer to collective objectives of the common good.

More recently, public sector economics has employed the analysis of welfare economics to understand public sector behaviour, rather than focusing solely upon private sector market failure. Critics of an active role for government, such as libertarians, have long pointed out that public sector failure is just as important as market failure. The public sector is essentially a monopolist which is divorced from the discipline of competitive market forces. This state of affairs can be a source of inefficiency within the public sector, unless fiscal institutions are designed in such a way that adequate systems of accountability and control ensure that the organizations of the public sector are managed efficiently.

Designing appropriate incentive and information structures for the management of public sector institutions is a new and challenging role for the economist. This is where the public sector economist and those involved in public sector management should work closely together. The application of the intellectual infrastructure of welfare economics to the problems of internal organization has in recent years brought forth a number of significant innovations which have changed the structure and the character of the public sector (see, for example, Leibenstein, 1987).

Efficient allocation of resources requires decisions to be well informed. The information revolution that has taken place in the public sector can be found in Whitehall, in local governments and the NHS. Whilst the revolution is in no sense complete, public sector decision-makers are now better informed than ever before.

PURSUING SOCIAL JUSTICE

Minimization of allocative and X-inefficiencies is only one string to the bow of the public sector economist. Economic analysis shows that it is possible to produce efficient market or pseudomarket allocations which are ethically unacceptable. Competitive markets are quite capable of producing efficient outcomes in which some individuals have insufficient resources to survive! The policy objectives of allocative and X-inefficiencies, therefore, need to be traded off against the objective of distributive justice. That trade-off needs to be identified and defined. How much efficiency is given up by pursuing an improvement in the distribution of welfare? The public sector economist is in a strong position to help articulate the dimensions of this policy problem. This is not to say that hard and fast guidelines, or measures of welfare gains compared to efficiency losses, are available. To suppose otherwise would be misleading. The economist is, however, in a strong position to force a number of issues into the decision frame such as, for example, to raise the question "what are the distributive objectives of the policy?" Is the objective to pursue a utilitarian policy of the greatest good for the greatest number, or to maximize a weighted sum of each individual's welfare (if so which weights are to be used?) or is the objective to pursue a strategy of maximizing the welfare of the least well-off in society?

It should be immediately clear that simply by asking this series of questions the policy decision becomes both more complex and richer. Introduction of issues of distributive justice goes some way to counter the criticisms made by political scientists of the economist's rational model of decision-making. Of course economists have always recognized the importance of distributive justice and the efficiency/equity trade-off (Okun, 1975), and it was unfortunate that some political scientists, such as Self (1975), took the debate down a blind alley by failing to recognize that.

POLITICAL ECONOMY

The role of the public sector economist in decision-making was usefully set out many years ago by Eckstein (1961, p. 445). "The economist must interpret the desires of the policy people whom he is serving and express them in analytical form as an objective function. He then seeks to maximize this function given the empirical relations in the economy and the institutional constraints that may be appropriate to the analysis. In this manner the economist can play the role of technician, of bringing technical equipment to bear upon policy problems with maximum effectiveness". This state-ment is, however, subject to misinterpretation. It does not imply that the economist has a ready-made set of techniques which will automatically make decisions, thereby rendering decision-makers obsolete. The economist *qua* economist does not judge whether the objectives of the decision-maker are ethically acceptable. Rather, eco-nomic analysis helps the decision-maker to explore fully the implications of pursuing one set of policy objectives.

Some economists, such as Tinbergen (1956), minimize the role of the economist simply to that of providing data to the policy-maker. For example, the economist in his framework would determine the values of the instrumental variables required to hit a clearly specified set of policy targets. Experience has, however, shown that this approach is somewhat idealized. Policy targets are not sufficiently well defined and the economist has an important role to play in making them clearer. This can be done in the case of cost benefit analysis, for example, by varying the distributional weights in the objective function and thereby providing the decision-maker with information of the form, "here is a menu of potential policy outcomes, choose from it".

Serving up alternative menus or policy opinions is necessary, but not sufficient, for informed decision-making. There remains the issue of determining the criteria against which the policy options are to be ranked. Many economists have in the past shied away from that problem claiming that it is for others to come up with such cri-teria. As Shultze (1968) has pointed out such economists: "serve only to rationalise what is being done and lose their potential as educators . . . [and] become "yes men" in the halls of political economy" (p. 9).

If economists are to design efficient and effective policies, and if they are, as policy analysts, to assist in the evaluation of policies, then they require criteria founded in a logical framework. A minimum requirement is to be able to say whether or not a policy is acceptable on economic criteria. The changes that have taken place as part of the managerial revolution which has swept through the public sector over the past 10 years are superficially plausible as means of improving efficiency and enhancing perfor-mance. But have these changes been adequately designed? How should contracts be formulated; what principles should guide the choice of discount rate for cost benefit calculations; what choice of discount rate for cost benefit calculations; what rules determine the costing of hospital specialties; how should the prices of public services be set; under what conditions will devolved budgeting improve efficiency? These and many more questions remain. The introduction of so many of the new methods of public sector management and decision-making are based on faith. Policy managers need policy analysts to provide them with the firm foundations of why they should do X rather than Y. For the public sector economist as policy analyst these firm foundations are to be found in economic theory.

The role of public sector economic is, therefore, to inform the debate about public policy and the design of fiscal institutions. This does not, however, just mean informing politicians, civil servants and public sector managers. It also includes the wider policy community, for example pressure groups. Public sector economics should help to raise the level of public debate which is essential for the operation of an effective democracy. James Madison in *The Federalist Papers* (1790) recognized this when he argued that social statistics were vital to inform social legislation, a point which is confirmed by modern advocates of social policy indicators (see MacRae 1976; and MacRae and Wilde, 1979).

IN PRAISE OF THEORY

Nothing is quite so practical as a good theory (Lewin, 1945). Theory in the social sciences, especially economic theory, is frequently attacked by practitioners because its function is so often misunderstood. Others, especially those outside of the discipline of economics, wrongly believe that there is an oversupply of competing theories and paradigms in economics. Economists suffer the butt of jokes such as, "if you lay all of the economists in the world end to end you will never reach a conclusion". The amount of disagreement amongst research economists, as compared to political economy commentators and scribblers, is much less than is often supposed. Indeed, that economists do not agree on policy prescriptions is a reflection of the complexity and uncertainty of the world in which we live and for which policy has to be designed. Policy rules are contingent upon a reality which unfolds with uncertainty. Other disciplines, even the hard sciences, have their controversies: what is the origin of the universe; what is the cause of cancer? Recently, forensic evidence provided to a court of law has been found wanting.

Do public policies promote the general welfare of citizens? Will policy X have an impact upon the welfare of a specific group of citizens? To answer these questions, and more, practitioners frequently adopt a set of policy indicators (for example educational attainment; mortality; economic indicators). But how robust are these indicators; what are the causal relations between these statistics and individual well-being (welfare)? What implicit social values do these indicators reflect? What is the set of causal links between public policies and individuals' welfare? These questions are often regarded as troublesome by politicians and some career policy advisers whose interests lie in providing a quick fix to social problems. It is the role of theory to challenge and to question the adequacy of existing practice and to improve the quality of the arguments in the policy debate. Far from being impractical, theory is extremely practical and an appreciation of how to use theory in formulating policy arguments will lead to improved practice.

Economic theory's contribution to policy analysis and design is to provide an understanding of events and phenomena within the domain of public policy. Understanding and explanation of events is not, however, synonymous with prediction. Even when phenomena (consider, for example, earthquakes) are understood it is not always possible to predict when the phenomenon will next occur. Recently, chaos theory has taught that in complex systems small perturbations can build up to large events. Whilst an understanding of the processes and dynamics of a system is of importance for purposes of control and manipulation, it does not follow that the precise timing of events can be predicted. Instead, statements of future events must be made in probabilistic terms, i.e. if conditions X and Y prevail then there is a probability that Z will occur. An assessment of the probabilities informs managers and decision-makers. Thus, forecasts of economic and social events must not be regarded as having probabilities of unity assigned to them (i.e. complete certainty) instead the forecaster needs to inform the decision-maker of the probability (confidence) of the forecast being correct. The further a socioeconomic event lies into the future, the lower is the probability that its forecast will be accurate.

A useful theory must encompass the event which is to be explained: the event(s) should not contradict the theory. Furthermore, useful theories are those which are communicable to others. If an event can be incorporated into a theory then it means that the event (phenomenon) is understood. If it cannot be so incorporated then the event is not understood and the theory is not as general as might have been supposed. Policy interventions require an understanding of the events which lie in the policy domain: they require an understanding of the causal processes which gave rise to the event. Such understanding can only be the result of systematic research within a wider conceptual framework. This reduces the chances of futile and misdirected interventions which often result in catastrophic outcomes. There is nothing quite so practical as a good theory. Sound theory is a line of first defence against madmen and cranks. Policy managers need policy analysts and policy analysts need sound theory.

Theorists start from axioms, i.e. generally agreed upon basic statements of the real world. A theorist seeks to find out of those propositions which are presented as policy statements are deducible from a set of these elementary axioms. Put another way—what does the world actually have to look like for the proposition to be true? It is at this point that the assumptions upon which a theory is predicated come in. Different assumptions in conjunction with the basic axioms produce different propositions.

The basic axioms used by the economist are that decision-makers are rational and that individuals are the best judge of their own welfare. This means nothing other than that either preference orderings are well defined, or that individuals have reasons for the choices that they make. Rationality also means that the choices which are made by individuals are logically consistent. Typical assumptions relate to whether or not the decision-maker is fully informed when making choices; whether decisions are made in a total system or a partial system at a single moment in time or inter-temporally; whether or not the future is known with certainty; and the extent to which market structures are perfectly competitive or monopolistic. To assume, as the public choice theorists do, that politicians and bureaucrats have preferences is an axiom. Making statements about the objective function of politicians and bureaucrats, i.e. that they are vote maximizers or budget maximizers, is to make assumptions. Different assumptions will generate different propositions (hypotheses) which might, if they are in a suitable form and if data are available, be tested (with a view to refutation) empirically. A theory provides a coherent framework within which the implications of different assumptions can be analysed.

The aim of theory is not to describe reality. It is to understand that reality. By necessity, abstraction from reality is required for understanding. Thus, the charge, often made by practitioners, that a theory is unreal is a weak criticism. Simon, Lindblom and Wildavsky have frequently taken economists to task for the strong form of rationality that they suppose economists to subscribe to. However, their alternative representation of rationality is a "red herring". Modern economic theory recognizes explicitly that rationality is bounded because the world is too complex and because the information requirements for decision-making over the complete choice set would make the whole exercise prohibitively costly. Of course, individuals statisifice because they do not have the wit to maximize. Such statements can be reformulated as an act of local maximization subject to the constraints of limited and costly means of computation. Individuals adopt routinized personal and organizational decision-making as long as these decisions produce acceptable (satisfactory) outcomes. However, individuals also engage in search behaviour: they look for new processes, systems and outcomes. There is organizational learning and adaptation. The introduction of the FMI and systems of devolved resource allocation are attempts to generate more reliable information to expand the boundary of choice in the public sector. Search will continue as long as it is worthwhile to do so—provided the expected pay off exceeds search costs.

The axiom of methodological individualism frees the economist from making bizarre statements about collective decision-making. It asserts that individuals make decisions, not a mystical entity or a ghostly spirit of the collectivity. To assume otherwise takes the practitioner into the Hegelian mists where travellers end up lost forever to reason or science. The axiom of individual rationality does not imply a collective rationality. Indeed, one of the most powerful propositions which economists have to offer management theory is that of Arrow's impossibility theorem. Arrow demonstrated that starting from a reasonable set of statements about individual behaviour it is impossible to find a rule which will enable the aggregation of individual preferences into a collective preference that results in consistent collective choices. Arrow's analysis, along with that of Duncan Black's study of committee decision-making and Sen's general analysis of collective choice, forces managers, especially those in the public sector, to consider quite carefully how collective (committee) decisions should be made. What voting rules will produce allocative and ethically acceptable outcomes? (See Arrow, 1963; Black, 1958; and Sen, 1970.) These are issues which cannot be ignored, and theory, especially at a high level of abstraction, helps to clarify them.

The analysis of collective action using modern game theory, in addition to recognizing the aggregation problem outlined by Arrow, reveals that decisions which are rational from an individual's perspective often cease to be rational when considered in the context of collective interaction. There is a tyranny of small decisions which, when they are combined, produce adverse outcomes. This applies to market situations, as well as to bureaucratic decisions. The profit-maximizing behaviour of one factory owner which generates environmental pollution may be tolerable, but the collective outcome of many producers behaving in a similar way is not if it means destruction of the ozone layer. What is being described here is the familiar prisoner's dilemma problem (see Brown and Jackson, 1990, pp. 5–8). Again, theory at this level of abstraction is of practical importance. It throws into relief the need to consider carefully the circumstances under which individual behaviour should be regulated. This in turn forces questions about what form that regulation should take. The theory also challenges the libertarians who argue that institutions both in the public and the private sectors should be designed in such a way as to leave individuals free to make their own decisions.

RIGHTS, FREEDOMS AND INCENTIVES

Public sector theorists cannot avoid abstract debates about individual's rights. Libertarians, such as Hayek, Friedman, or Nozick, constantly challenge the existence of the public sector on the grounds that public sector institutions and policy interventions infringe individual freedoms and liberties. Public sector managers should be familiar with the basis of such arguments.

Hayek and the radical subjectivists argue that it is insufficient to judge or evaluate policy, or indeed any event, solely in terms of outcomes or consequences. The means through which choices are made must be also evaluated—choice of an end is not the complete revelation of preference. When individuals choose a means they are expressing a preference. No-one would disagree that the evaluation of means is as important as the evaluation of outcomes. However, often Hayek *et al.* seem to argue that the means through which choices are made are more important. They evaluate social choice mechanisms with reference to the extent to which they are based on individual choices. If individual preferences are constrained or over-ridden, as in the case of regulated behaviour or bureaucratic decision-making, then the loss of individual freedom and liberty, which such means of decision-making entail, is regarded as being too great and alternative forms of social organization (especially *laissez-faire* markets) are sought.

Are the libertarians right to suggest that individual rights to freedom and liberty are of paramount importance? Most would agree that, wherever possible, it is best if individuals are given the freedom to determine their own destiny. That, however, is a right to a particular type of freedom or liberty, what Berlin (1958) called "negative freedom", i.e. freedom from interference by others. However, there is another dimension to freedom which libertarians ignore and that is the right to "positive freedom"—freedom to be able to do certain things: a right to have basic needs satisfied. A legitimate role for government, therefore, is to provide for positive freedom goods such as basic education and basic health. The decisions which remain are to determine the form in which that provision should be made, either by direct public provision or via the payment of income support and the level of provision.

Another dimension to positive freedom is that which is associated with citizenship rights. Such rights give individuals, as citizens, access to participate in the determination of the formation of laws. Some writers, such as de Tocqueville (1835), have argued that this is an essential part of human dignity (i.e. citizens direct themselves), and that such rights extend positive freedom. This love for the laws (what Montesquieu called *vertu*) is a public good—it is the basis of the civic humanist tradition of thought about republican rule.

Marshall (1964) set out to define citizenship rights in a comprehensive manner. Citizenship rights encompass civil rights (freedom of speech and equality before the law), political rights (universal suffrage) and social rights (guaranteed levels of health, education etc.). These rights move members of society towards an egalitarian social order. It is, however, an objective of libertarians to reduce these rights. Following Hayek, they argue that inequality is a requisite for economic development. Inequality is inevitable and acceptable. It generates the incentives required for progress through entrepreneurial actions.

Public policies have the potential to create incentive and disincentive effects. Theory, however, demonstrates that matters are seldom as clear cut as Hayekians would have us believe. It is insufficient to assert, as they do, that the extension of citizenship rights and positive freedoms reduce the potential for growth and development. These claims must be grounded in theory and that theory must be tested empirically.

Over the past 20 years public sector economists have done much to refine the analysis of the incentive effects of public policies. In particular, they have examined the impact of various forms of taxation upon the supply of hours of work, savings, investment and risk-taking. These magnitudes are important inputs to the process of economic growth and development. What this research agenda tends to conclude is that whilst taxes do distort private decision-making the disincentive effects are not as large as is often assumed. This means that improvements in welfare (income) distribution can be achieved without giving up too much economic efficiency or economic growth (see Atkinson and Stiglitz, 1980; and Brown and Jackson, 1990).

Are individuals always the best judge of their own welfare as methodological individualism asserts? Generally speaking, the answer is, yes they are. But individuals are not always adequately informed, nor do they have the technical skills to make decisions that will serve their best interests. Others have the competence and information to make decisions on their behalf. This is the "principal-agent" relationship, in which the agent makes decisions on behalf of the principal in the principal's interest. The doctor/patient and lawyer/client relationships are examples of principal and agent. For this relationship to be effective, the principal must "trust" the agent. Trust is, however, a commodity which can be short in supply, so that once again there is a potential regulatory role for government to monitor and control some of the more significant principal-agent relationships.

PRACTICAL THEORY

What insights do these examples of theoretical considerations provide for the practically minded public sector manager? Theory liberates us from slack and lazy thinking; from rhetoric and from aphorisms. It liberates us from those practitioners who, for their authority and legitimacy, appeal to judgement gained from years of practical experience.

Theory makes possible an orderly and coherent deepening of understanding. Without understanding, it is difficult to persuade others in the long term. The value of rhetoric only lasts as long as people can be fooled.

Theory imposes structure and pattern; it creates metaphors and *gestalts*. It helps us to order the facts of a complex reality: "science is facts, just as houses are made of stone . . . but a pile of stones is not a house and a collection of facts is not necessarily science" (Poincare, 1903).

Theories, however, cannot account for or explain all phenomena. That which remains hidden from understanding constitutes the research agenda. Such understanding is not only hidden from the theorist, it is also hidden from those of practical affairs. Acknowledgment of our ignorance and acceptance of the complexity of the world would make for more humble and less extravagant policy. It would reduce the probability of creating in the future the great planning disasters of the past. This involves recognizing the boundary constraints of our theories, i.e. is the set of propositions true in all contexts and for all moments in time? Contingency theory forces us to recognise the probabilistic nature of the world in which policies are designed and implemented.

PUBLIC CHOICE AND BUREAUCRATIC FAILURE

The public choice perspective is now recognized as a distinct approach to the study of economic policy and public sector decision-making. Pioneered by the Nobel Prizewinning economist, James Buchanan, and his principal collaborator Gordon Tullock, public choice theory extends the standard welfare economics model of public sector economics and provides an economic analysis of politics, democracy and bureaucracy (see Mueller, 1989).

What is public choice theory? Buchanan's critique of the standard welfare economics approach to economic policy and discussions of the economic role of the state is that it uses theoretical constructs, such as a "social welfare function", in an uncritical way. To say that policy-makers, when they are designing policies, aim to maximize a social welfare function is too abstract if the intention is to understand the policy-making process. Equally, arguments such as policy-makers are motivated to serve the "public interest" are too vague. Public choice theorists seek to focus attention more narrowly on such questions as: whose interests are served by the policy, which interests dominate and why?

Rather than concentrating upon "optimal policies", which by definition are those which maximize a social welfare function, subject to a number of restrictive contextual assumptions regarding the perfection of markets etc., Buchanan and his followers search for "good decision rules". This search for decision rules brings public sector economics closer to the interests of public sector management.

Buchanan argues that the welfare economics approach takes a naive view of the political process. It is straightforward to demonstrate why markets fail (see Brown and Jackson, 1990). This has been used to justify and legitimize government intervention, for example to correct externalities such as pollution, or to regulate monopolies. Such prescriptions are, however, made in the absence of any assumptions about the behaviour of politicians or bureaucrats. What Buchanan has done though the public choice framework is to demonstrate that there is not an *a priori* reason to suppose that governments will improve the allocative efficiency of markets through policy interventions. This is a powerful result which challenges much of the standard thinking about the desirability of public policy. If the efficiency losses of public sector interventions exceed the efficiency losses of market failure then why bother intervening?

Central to the public choice argument is the requirement that "man" does not become a different species in the voting booth, or in a bureaucracy, or in a central bank compared to his behaviour in the market place. Individuals acting as politicians are assumed to behave in a way which will maximize their chances of election—this will influence the way in which they design policies. Bureaucrats are not administrative eunuches, they have their own objective function which they seek to maximize (Niskanen, 1971; and Jackson, 1982), and central bankers do not blindly serve the objectives of monetary policy but instead have managerial interest (see Mayer, 1987).

Many political scientists object to the public choice approach to theorizing about political behaviour. Several reasons are given for this objection, especially that the assumptions are unrealistic. This does not, however, cut much ice. There are many different public choices each depending upon the initial assumptions used. The basic issue, however, is would, for example, a Marxist public choice theory come up with significantly different conclusions? What Buchanan *et al.* have done is to push open a door leaving a basic question to be answered: "under what conditions will government policy interventions improve upon the allocative efficiency of the market?" It is this question which lies at the heart of the design of public sector institutions, and much of public sector management. Those who are not in sympathy with the public choice approach need to articulate their own framework, which will not only encompass that fundamental question, but which will also provide an answer to it.

If politics is the study of the resolution of the conflicts of interests of different pressure groups then a constitution must be found within which such resolutions can be achieved efficiently and effectively, such that each interest group will find it to their own long run advantage to accept the constitution's constraints. The search for a constitution, a set of decision rules and political constraints, is to be found in Buchanan's more recent work (Brennan and Buchanan, 1980).

When discussing the tax constitution for Leviathan, Brennan and Buchanan distinguish between the design of the fiscal constitution and the setting of tax rates within that constitution. The fiscal constitution is based upon the basic principles of taxation that a typical taxpayer would prefer, given the assumption that after the constitution has been set any government will seek to maximize tax revenues within the bounds set by the constitution. For Brennan and Buchanan, taxpayers will prefer narrow tax bases, rather than comprehensive bases, and progressive, rather than proportional, tax structures.

The public choice perspective and the attention given to the formulation of fiscal constitutions and decision rules has much to offer public sector management. A fiscal constitution could be extended to include the rules governing budget decision-making: the voting rules for choosing public policies that involve the preferences of future generations; and the organizational structure of central-local government relations. The economic analysis of bureaucracy, and its focus of attention upon non-market decision-making within hierarchies, is ripe for extension to incorporate the problems of designing internal markets and systems of performance measurement. "Bureaucratic failure" is an expression of the fact that the internal organizational structure of public sector agencies, their incentive structures and their information systems, are inadequate to deliver public services efficiently and effectively. Poor performance and low value for money come about because of bureaucratic failures.

It would, however, be a false claim to suppose that public sector economics has an instant answer to these problems of bureaucratic failure. The current research agenda does, however, offer some hope that fresh insights will be provided for these problems. Attention is currently being given to the design of contracts; the design of internal incentive structures and the design of demand revelation systems (Laffont, 1988).

CONCLUSIONS

Public sector economics and public sector management share a common set of interests: the promotion of an efficient allocation of resources within the public sector, the minimization of bureaucratic failure, and the design of efficient and ethically acceptable fiscal institutions and policies.

Good management practice needs to be predicated upon sound theory, and public sector economics and public choice theory can provide public sector managers with the insights that will enable them to define their management problems more clearly.

To achieve the goal of improved public sector performance, the channels of communication between those who practice public sector management and those who study public sector economics need to be widened. A closer relationship between these two groups offers improvements in public sector efficiency and value for money.

REFERENCES

Arrow, K.J. (1963). *Social Choice and Individual Values*. Yale University Press, New Haven.
Atkinson, A.B. and Stiglitz, J.E. (1980). *Lectures on Public Sector Economics*, McGraw Hill, London.
Berlin, I. (1958). *Two Concepts of Liberty*. Clarendon Press.
Black, D. (1958). *Theory of Committees and Elections*. Cambridge University Press, Cambridge.
Brennan, G. and Buchanan, J.M. (1980). *The Power to Tax: Analytical Foundations of a Fiscal Constitution*. Cambridge University Press, Cambridge.
Brown, C.V. and Jackson, P.M. (1990). *Public Sector Economics*. 4th Edition. Basil Blackwell, Oxford.
Eckstein, O. (1961). *Water Resource Development: The Economics of Project Evaluation*. Harvard University Press, Cambridge.
Jackson, P.M. (1982). *The Political Economy of Bureaucracy*. Philip Allen, Oxford.
Jackson, P.M. (1990). A survey of modern welfare economics. In J. Moroney: *Modern Economic Analysis*. Manchester University Press.
Laffont, J.J. (1988). *Fundamentals of Public Economics*. The MIT Press, London.
Leibenstein, H. (1987). *Inside the Firm: The Inefficiencies of Hierarchy*. Harvard University Press, Cambridge.
Lewin, K. (1945). The Research Centre for Group Dynamics at MIT. *Sociometry*, Vol. 8.
MacRae, D. (1976). *The Social Function of Social Science*. Yale University Press, New Haven.

MacRae, D. and J. Wilde (1979). *Policy Analysis for Policy Decisions*. Duxbury, North Scituate.

Marshall, T.H. (1964). *Class, Citizenship, and Social Development*. Doubleday, New York.

Mayer, T. (1987). The debate about monetarist policy. *Kredit and Kapital*. Vol. 20, pp. 281–302.

Mueller, D.C. (1989). *Public Choice*. Cambridge University Press, Cambridge.

Niskanen, W. (1971). *Bureaucracy and Representative Government*. Aldine-Atherton, Chicago.

Okun, A. (1975). *Equality and Efficiency*. Brookings Institution, Washington, D.C.

Poincare, J.H. (1903). *La Science et l'hypothese*. E. Flammarion. Paris.

Rawls, J. (1971). *A Theory of Justice*. Harvard University Press.

Schultze, C. (1968). *The Politics and Economics of Public Spending*. Brookings Institution, Washington D.C.

Self, P. (1975). *Econocrats and the Policy Process*. Macmillan, London.

Sen, A.K. (1970). *Collective Choice and Social Welfare*. Oliver and Boyd. Edinburgh.

Tinbergen (1956). *Economic Policy: Principles and Design*. North Holland, Amsterdam.

de Tocqueville, A. (1835). *Democracy in America*. World Classics Edition, Oxford, 1965.

9

Kenneth J. Meier

BUREAUCRACY AND DEMOCRACY: THE CASE FOR MORE BUREAUCRACY AND LESS DEMOCRACY

The United States is facing a serious problem with the interface between its bureaucracy and its electoral institutions.[1] Politicians often run for office by campaigning against the bureaucracy.

Missing in the political debates is any serious assessment of bureaucracy, its performance, its pathologies, or its promise.[2] In comparison to other industrialized democracies, however, the United States bureaucracy appears to be much smaller and leaner (Rose, 1985). It relies more on the private sector to deliver goods and services.

It is composed of technocrats rather than administrative elites. And, I will argue that it is both reasonably effective and at the same time highly responsive to legitimate political demands.

The problems in American government, in my view, are not problems of bureaucracy but problems of governance.[3] In contrast to what is adequate (some might even argue excellent) performance by the bureaucracy (Goodsell, 1983), the performance by our electoral institutions has been dismal. As an illustration, Congress and the president have been engaged in a futile 25-year battle to balance the budget.

Tilting at economically forecasted windmills, different Congresses and different presidents have agreed to balance the budget (Gramm-Rudman); have acquiesced in deficits nearing three hundred billion dollars; have perpetrated the myth that one can balance the budget without either raising taxes or cutting spending; have on numerous occasions shut down the federal government; but have accomplished little more than to make Alan Greenspan's job more difficult. As the electoral institutions have eliminated the feasibility of sensible fiscal policy, a bureaucracy (the Federal Reserve) has compensated. In the policy fields of health care, affirmative action, budget deficits, crime, drugs, and so on, electoral institutions have been unable either to provide a deliberative forum for resolving political conflicts, or to adopt good public policy.[4] The only political consensus appears to be that bureaucracy is bad and needs to be restricted. The irony of the situation is that as the electoral branches stalemate, they act against the bureaucracy—the one part of government that has a capacity to govern.

PUBLIC ADMINISTRATION'S SINS ARE SINS OF OMISSION

The governance problem can be blamed in part on the field of public administration. We readily and enthusiastically helped to reorganize, reform, and reinvent bureaucracy. We have worked suboptimizing wonders on the bureaucracy but have long since passed the point of diminishing marginal returns. There are no more, if there were any, silver bullets that will slay the bureaucracy dragon and magically improve governance in the United States. Most of the dragons have starved to death; few of the bullets hit anything.

Intellectually the field of public administration made two mistakes that contributed to our current governance problem. First, in rejecting the politics/administration dichotomy, public administration was unambitious in its territorial claims. As scholars, we were happy to argue that the administrative process was inherently political and, therefore, we confined our study to bureaucratic politics. With few exceptions (e.g., Mazmanian and Sabatier, 1989; Linder and Peters, 1987), we have never recognized that the political branches of government had administrative components and that the real problem with the politics/administration dichotomy is that we only study part of the policy process. That we study both the political and the administrative within the bureaucracy is good, but it still yields an incomplete view of governance.

Public administration needs to overcome its bad choice on the politics/administration dichotomy and return to its pre–1950 reformist roots. The field of public administration, epitomized by the New York Bureau of Municipal Research, was at one time part of a larger reform tradition. That tradition of pragmatic liberalism with progressive ideas (Anderson, 1990) produced the merit system, the secret ballot, direct election of senators, and city manager government. It was concerned with governance, not with a narrow view of public administration.

To correct our first error, I suggest we redefine the field of public administration to encompass the design, evaluation, and implementation of institutions and public policy. These topics should be added to our long-term interests in policy evaluation and implementation.

The second error of ambition made by academic public administration occurred contemporaneously with its declaration of independence from political science.[5] At the height of the behavioral revolution in political science, public administration rightly perceived that it was unwanted in political science (Waldo, 1987, 94; also Brown and Stillman, 1986). Many public administration scholars shifted their loyalties, others stayed within political science with the goal of recreating an empirical public administration within political science.[6] Those who separated from political science left the broader reform tradition to political scientists, implicitly assuming that as they shifted their focus to bureaucratic institutions of governance political scientists would continue to deal with the problems of democracy at the interface between bureaucracy and electoral institutions. Political scientists instead focused on individual behavior in the quest for the definitive study of presidential elections.[7] Public administrators who remained in political science busily built a solid empirical study of bureaucracy, but they also neglected the political institutions side of governance. There are no great normative theories of bureaucracy in political science, by which I mean theories about what the role of bureaucracy *should* be in governance.[8]

OK, THAT'S A NICE IDEA, BUT WHAT DOES IT MEAN?

Within this view of public administration, I revisit the question of the relationship between bureaucracy and democracy in the contemporary United States.[9] I will look at this problem from the perspective of institutions and institutional design. The look is quite frankly normative as well as empirical; it seeks to define what we should study and what we should proselytize.

Bureaucracy

Bureaucracies are permanent, goal-oriented open systems, and all these characteristics are important for understanding the relationship between bureaucracy and electoral institutions. Bureaucracies are structured around policy-oriented goals (see Simon, 1947; Barnard, 1938; Wilson, 1989).[10] Because bureaucracies are built around goals, what others call a mission, they quite naturally resist tasks that do not fit within these goals.

Bureaucratic permanence (or more aptly its stability since bureaucracies can be, and at times are, eliminated—e.g. the Civil Aeronautics Board, the Interstate Commerce Commission, the Resolution Trust Corporation), the use of merit-oriented procedures, and the ability to exploit economics of scale mean that bureaucracies become storehouses of expertise. They can learn over time (Lebovic, 1995; Sabatier and Jenkins-Smith, 1993), specialize beyond the capabilities of the electoral branches of government, and hire or contract for needed expertise.

The open-systems element of bureaucracy has consequences for a bureaucracy existing in a democracy. The norms of democracy grant policy-making legitimacy to electoral institutions, not to bureaucracy.[11] While bureaucracy can at times claim to represent the interests of individuals, bureaucracies are not inherently representative institutions and lack the imprimatur of elections.[12]

As open systems, however, bureaucracies both shape their environment and respond to it. In general, bureaucracies are fairly responsive institutions as long as what the environment demands of them is consistent with their mission, their capabilities, and the norms of democratic policy making.[13] The democratic norms of the policy process also define methods for influencing bureaucracy. The more the attempts to influence the bureaucracy are consistent with the norms of democracy, the less likely they are to generate resistance. That is, clear legislation passed by Congress and signed by the president is difficult to resist since both institutions are performing their defined constitutional role. Attempts to change policy by changing department heads have less legitimacy but are still acceptable if such changes are within the scope of the agency's mission.

Given the development of bureaucracies as goal-oriented open systems within a democracy, I would posit a normative institutional rule for bureaucracy. Bureaucracies perform best and can contribute the most to the policy-making process when 1) they are given clear goals by electoral institutions, 2) they are allocated adequate resources, and 3) they are given the autonomy[14] to apply their expertise to the problem.[15] This normative rule applies to all stages of the policy process. In the agenda setting or policy adoption phase of policy making, this demands a policy advocacy role. Bureaucracy contributes to the political debate to the extent it can provide informed commentary on policy problems and how they might be solved.

Electoral Institutions

Congress and the presidency are also open systems although it is unclear if they are goal-oriented or merely composed of goal-oriented individuals. Because they rely on elections, these institutions have less control over their institutional boundaries. Electoral institutions, as a result, are less likely to be as homogeneous as bureaucracies since they are less able to use the normal means that organizations use to recruit, socialize, and train their members.[16] Whether members of electoral institutions have goals of re-election or of policy, there will be greater tension between the institution and its members than in a bureaucracy.

The key skill of the electoral institutions is serving as forums for deliberation. They aggregate the political interests in the nation and provide a forum for the conflict between these interests in which they can be focused and perhaps resolved, either through compromise or through majoritarian fiat. In the process of representing interests, electoral institutions set public policy goals or, put in more organizational terms, resolve goal conflict among the demands from the organization's environment (that they do not always do so has long been known; see Seidman, 1970).[17]

While bureaucratic institutions can be designed to resolve political conflict—the National Labor Relations Board is a good example—bureaucracy has no inherent advantages in this role. If anything, the bureaucracy is far less suited to this role than are electoral institutions. This position reflects the consensus of both scholars who think that neutral competence is the end of bureaucracy (Goodnow, 1900) and those who advocate responsive competence (Wood and Waterman, 1994).

SO WHAT IS THE PROBLEM?

The fundamental problem of governance that has generated the continual state of crisis in political/bureaucratic relationships is that the electoral branches of government have failed as deliberative institutions; they have not resolved conflict in a reasoned manner. At times they do not resolve conflict and at other times they have done so in a manner that undercuts effective public policy.[18] The policy failures of Congress and the president are legion.

Failure to establish new policy is not the only area where political institutions have failed. At times policies have contradictory goals, and these are left to the bureaucracy to grapple with as best it can. Affirmative action is one such policy, and many others could be found in agricultural policy and social welfare policy.

The failure to resolve goal conflict with informed public policy is exacerbated by the development of the continual campaign for office. Presidential candidates now start their campaigns a minimum of two years before the election. Members of Congress campaign, raise money, and run for office on a continual basis. The greater emphasis on campaigns has attracted individuals with high levels of campaigning skills, not necessarily the skills that are valuable in governance.

Political problems are enhanced by what is a decline in commitment to the institutions of governance. Uslaner (1993) finds that current member of Congress are less likely to identify with Congress as an institution than past members were. This decline in identification results in less deference to institutional rules, more personal attacks on other members and the institution, more confrontation and less cooperation, and more concern with district and thus electoral benefits than institutional and policy benefits.

The method of staffing the institutionalized presidency has similar consequences. As part of the administrative presidency, recent recruits to the executive office have had to meet the test of personal loyalty to the president. As a result, staff members are loyal not to the institution of presidency but to the person who is president (Hart, 1995, 145; Hinckley, 1985, 131–136). While such personal loyalty is not necessarily bad, it can lead individuals to overlook the role the institution plays in governance and the limits on that institution. On frequent occasions such forms of personal loyalty produce an Oliver North.

Unwilling or unable to resolve political conflict, when political institutions opt for policy action it is in areas where goals are generally not in conflict. In such areas as drug abuse and drunk driving, for example, there is only one politically acceptable side to the debate. Such policies are popular because they are easy to understand and appear to be electorally rewarding. Since there is no goal conflict, facts are irrelevant to the debate and we have a type of process that I call "the politics of sin" (Meier, 1994).[19] Politicians compete with each other to adopt more extreme policies; the normal tempering role of bureaucracy, the application of expertise to policy and policy proposals, is lacking. Little rational deliberation is done, and the policies that are normally adopted are destined to fail because either the policy problem is not understood or the policy itself is poorly designed.

Policy failure then leads to greater cynicism among the public. Cynicism in turn leads to a renewed quest for magic bullets—those policies that will somehow quickly and cheaply solve the problem. Solving crime by building more jails; improving education by relying on vouchers; balancing the budget by eliminating waste, fraud, and corruption; and reinventing government by contracting out services are current magic bullets.

LESS DEMOCRACY AND MORE BUREAUCRACY

Our basic problem of governance is that the long running interplay between bureaucracy and expertise on one hand, and responsiveness and democracy (read electoral institutions) on the other hand, has swung too far in the direction of democracy. We now demand not just that bureaucracy be responsive to electoral institutions, but that it be hyperresponsive; that it respond to political demands whether or not those demands are consistent and whether or not they are expressed through politically legitimate channels. Bureaucracy is being asked to resolve political conflict, a function it performs poorly at best. The scapegoating and resource reductions have surely dissipated some of the bureaucratic capacity essential for effective governance. If we are also going to ask bureaucracy to solve political problems, then even greater capacity is necessary. The solution to the governance problem in the United States is to have more bureaucracy and less democracy.

The argument for less democracy is so un-American that nothing less than fundamental political change is required.[20] I do not have the solution, but let me suggest some items as a first step in the debates.

1. Redesign our political system to resolve rather than exacerbate conflict. The establishment of an elaborate set of checks and balances was a triumph of libertarian political thought perfectly appropriate in the eighteenth century. While these procedural checks should make majority tyranny less likely,[21] they also prevent the resolution of political conflicts and the adoption of good public policy. I suggest we examine the more unified political structures and corporatist processes of many European countries. In such systems politicians, bureaucrats, and interested citizens all actively participate in the discussion, design, and implementation of public policy.

2. Lengthen the time frame for public policy making. Frequent elections—a reform of Jacksonian democracy—do create an incentive for elected officials to be responsive. They also create, however, a short-term focus and are not conducive to a good policy process.

3. Restrict and perhaps even eliminate political appointees. Quite clearly, the responsiveness of bureaucracies to electoral institutions is not a function of the number of political appointees (e.g., England, Australia). A large number of political appointees sets a layer of incompetence between elected officials and the career bureaucracy. The Senior Executive Service should be restricted to career personnel, and political appointees should be limited to agency heads only.

4. Assess rationally the trend in contracting out governmental functions. Both markets and bureaucracies do some things well and some things poorly. Neither is a universal solution. Uninformed reliance on the private sector will consistently let government capacity waste away (O'Toole, 1989) and frequently spawn an epidemic of corruption (Perry and Wise, 1990).

5. Evaluate critically the agency's policies so as to contribute effectively to the policy debate. Bureaucracy's normative role in public policy suggests that bureaucracy serves best when it exploits its information and expertise advantages. If agencies fail to exploit these advantages, they may pander to politicians by offering them solutions that will not work.

6. Bring the institutionalized presidency under the merit system. If organizations such as the Office of Management and Budget can faithfully serve presidents of different ideologies, then similar organizations can run the White House and other parts of the institutionalized presidency.

7. Replace the current public philosophy of neoclassical economics and its sole value of efficiency. We need a public philosophy that unites rather than divides, that enhances rather than destroys public institutions, that values rather than denigrates public service.

8. Reorient our education programs from training entry-level civil servants to training policymakers.

CONCLUSION

The bureaucracy problem confronting the United States is in reality a governance problem (Frederickson, 1997, especially ch. 3). The bureaucracy, by most objective standards, is performing fairly well while the electoral institutions seem to be deteriorating. To solve this problem, public administration needs to revisit its past and reincorporate the study of electoral institutions into the field. This suggests a normative orientation, with public administration concerned with how governance should be structured and operated rather than just how the bureaucracy should implement public policy.[22] If the argument is correct, that the primary problem facing the United States is governance, then public administration must redefine its focus because no other discipline, field, or profession is concerned with these problems.

NOTES

1. In this essay I will use the term electoral institutions rather than political institutions to refer to Congress and the presidency because I believe that bureaucracy is also a political institution. "Electoral institutions" is used merely as a convenient collective description of these institutions. Little will be said about the courts, since I do not feel they are a democratic institution (Meier, 1993a, 162–167; see also Brown and Stillman, 1986, 177).

2. There have been academic debates on this topic, most recently the Blacksburg Manifesto (see Wamsley et al., 1990; and the response by Kaufman, 313–315) and before that the New Public Administration (Frederickson, 1990). My argument is distinct from previous ones because I seek to reform both politics and administration.

3. I am using the term governance in the same sense that Aristotle used politics; it is the process of governing society in a generic sense. I do not use it to describe the process whereby bureaucracy is minimized and policy is privatized either through exchanges or contracts. The many nuances of the contemporary use of "governance" are cogently discussed in Frederickson (1997). My prescriptions are 180 degrees away from those of most scholars using the term. Like Frederickson I seek to conserve institutions of governance not destroy them (see also Terry, 1990).

4. These conflicts are exacerbated by the system of checks and balances at the federal level; however, the problem appears at the state and local levels also.

5. Or was kicked out depending on one's point of view.

6. That movement has been a success. Within political science, public administration is now viewed as a field that is quantitatively sophisticated and on a par with other subfields of political science (see the work of Wood, 1988; Wood and Waterman, 1994; Scholz and Wei, 1986; Krause, 1994; Moe, 1985). A subgroup within political science has also taken mathematical and formal approaches to the same end (see Bendor and Moe, 1985; Bendor, 1994; Epstein and O'Halloran, 1994). This success, however, has had at best modest impact on dissertations in the field.

7. In the second edition of The Administrative State, Waldo (1984, xlii) notes that no new studies of the separation of powers seem to have been written since the first edition. The early works on the separation of powers discussed in The Administrative State come closest

to being normative theories of institutions and looking at the administrative side of political institutions.

8. A third error was made when public administration rightly rejected logical positivism. In the process it confused a tool of positivism, quantitative methods, with the philosophy itself. The philosphy was sterile, but the tool can be used to merge values with facts rather than separate them (see Meier and Keiser, 1996).

9. By democracy I am referring to overhead democracy and control of the bureaucracy by electoral institutions. There are other forms of democracy, such as direct political participation in bureaucratic governance or having bureaucracy play an active role in the representation process (see Wamsley et al., 1990; Meier, 1993a, ch. 7).

10. I consider the notion that an organization's primary goal is to survive is trivially true. Organizations cannot attain their goals if they do not survive, but survival alone is fairly meaningless since it will deprive the organization of any methods of motivation other than monetary ones.

11. By making this statement, it should be clear that I am not advocating administrative supremacy as many accuse the Blacksburg Manifesto of doing. Electoral institutions in a democracy are the legitimate institution for setting policy goals and resolving political disputes. These roles, however, are restrained by the Constitution. As a result I characterize electoral institutions' interventions in the administrative process as ranging from highly legitimate (legislation) to of questionable legitimacy (*ex parte* contacts).

12. Whether bureaucracy should represent individuals is an interesting normative question that needs to be addressed in public administration.

13. At times electoral institutions ask bureaucracy to do a job but fail to provide it with the resources to do so. Immigration control is an obvious example, as is regulating consumer products. When and why this is done are interesting questions, but they need far more space than this essay permits.

14. Autonomy for an open system means that electoral institutions do not micromanage the bureaucracy. It does not mean that bureaucracy should be left unchecked.

15. I recognize that this rarely happens in practice.

16. The work on the institutionalization of Congress suggests that the institutional coherence of Congress has varied over time. At times, the institution *per se* appears to be able to get individual members to submerge some of their goals for the greater institutional good. At other times, Congress appears to be little more than a collection of individuals (Uslaner, 1993).

17. Criticizing democratic institutions for not making good public policy is somewhat unfair since they are designed to be democratic rather than to produce good public policy. At the same time, the survivability of democracy rests, at least in part, on its ability to produce good public policies.

18. My feeling is that it is better to not resolve the conflict than to resolve it in an uninformed way. The latter results in the "politics of sin," while the former suggests that a resolution in the future is possible. This assumes, of course, that policy is not delegated to the bureaucracy without an effort to set goals and resolve conflict.

19. An alternative but similar view of such policies can be seen in the work of Schneider and Ingram (1993). They argue that social constructions create incentives for politicians to pursue policies focused on those designated as deviants.

20. In another context Rosenbloom (1983, 224) noted that we cannot synthesize the different values of public administration (which he defined as management, politics, and law) because they reflect integral parts of our political culture. His warning is relevant here.

21. I am skeptical, given my work on "sin politics," that majority tyranny is not highly likely in a fragmented political system. While fragmentation is thought to constrain such policies, in

actuality it may limit fast action only to those areas where knowledge exists by revelation—not by empirical analysis.

22. One potentially promising area is institutional rational choice, which attempts to determine what the impact of various political and bureaucratic structures might be (Knott and Miller, 1987; Moe, 1989). While I do not always agree with the findings of this literature, it is asking the right questions.

REFERENCES

Anderson, Charles W. (1990). *Pragmatic Liberalism.* Chicago: University of Chicago Press.

Barnard, Chester (1938). *The Functions of the Executive.* Cambridge, MA: Harvard University Press.

Bendor, Jonathan, and Terry M. Moe (1985). "An Adaptive Model of Bureaucratic Politics." *American Political Science Review* 79: 755-774.

Brown, Brack, and Richard J. Stillman II (1986). *A Search for Public Administration: The Ideas and Career of Dwight Waldo.* College Station, TX: Texas A&M University Press.

Epstein, David, and Sharyn O'Halloran (1994). "Administrative Procedures, Information, and Agency Discretion." *American Journal of Political Science* 38: 697-722.

Frederickson, H. George (1990). "Public Administration and Social Equity." *Public Administration Review* 50: 228-237.

_____. (1997). *The Spirit of Public Administration.* San Francisco, CA: Jossey-Bass.

Goodnow, Frank J. (1900). *Politics and Administration.* New York: Macmillan.

Goodsell, Charles T. (1983). *The Case for Bureaucracy.* Chatham, NJ: Chatham House.

Hart, John (1995). *The Presidential Branch from Washington to Clinton.* Chatham, NJ: Chatham House.

Hinckley, Barbara (1985). *Problems of the Presidency.* Glenview, IL: Scott, Foresman.

Knott, Jack, and Gary Miller (1987). *Reforming Bureaucracy: The Politics of Institutional Choice.* Englewood Cliffs, NJ: Prentice-Hall.

Krause, George A. (1994). "Federal Reserve Policy Decision Making: Political and Bureaucratic Influences." *American Journal of Political Science* 38: 124-144.

Lebovic, James H. (1995). "How Organizations Learn." *American Journal of Political Science* 39: 835-863.

Linder, Stephen H., and B. Guy Peters (1987). "A Design Perspective On Policy Implementation: The Fallacies of Misplaced Prescription." *Policy Studies Review* 6: 459-475.

Mazmanian, Daniel A., and Paul A. Sabatier (1989). *Implementation and Public Policy.* Lantham, MD: University Press of America.

Meier, Kenneth J. (1993a). *Politics and the Bureaucracy: Policymaking in the Fourth Branch of Government.* 3d ed. Pacific Grove, CA: Brooks/Cole.

_____. (1994). *The Politics of Sin: Drugs, Alcohol, and Public Policy.* Armonk, NY: M.E. Sharpe.

Meier, Kenneth J., and Lael R. Keiser (1996). "Public Administration as a Science of the Artificial:" A Methodology for Prescription." *Public Administration Review* 56 (5): 459-467.

Moe, Terry M. (1985). "Control and Feedback in Economic Regulation: The Case of the NLRB." *American Political Science Review* 79: 1094-1117.

_____. (1989). "The Politics of Bureaucratic Structure." In John E. Chubb and Paul E. Peterson, eds., *Can Government Govern?* Washington, DC: The Brookings Institution, 267-324.

O'Toole, Laurence J., Jr. (1989). "Goal Multiplicity in the Implementation Setting: Subtle Impacts and the Case of Wastewater Treatment Privatization." *Policy Studies Journal* 18:1-21.

Perry, James L., and Lois Recascino Wise (1990). "The Motivation Bases of Public Service." *Public Administration Review* 50: 367-373.

Rose, Richard (1985). *Public Employment in Western Nations*. Cambridge, MA: Cambridge University Press.

Rosenbloom, David H. (1983). "Public Administration Theory and the Separation of Powers." *Public Administration Review* 43: 219–227.

Sabatier, Paul A., and Hank C. Jenkins-Smith (1993). *Policy Change and Learning: An Advocacy Coalition Approach*. Boulder, CO: Westview Press.

Schneider, Anne, and Helen Ingram (1993). "Social Construction of Target Populations: Implications for Politics and Policy." *American Political Science Review* 87: 334–347.

Scholz, John T., and Feng Heng Wei (1986). "Regulatory Enforcement in a Federalist System." *American Political Science Review* 80(4): 1249–1270.

Seidman, Harold (1970). *Politics, Position and Power*. New York: Oxford University Press.

Simon, Herbert A. (1947). *Administrative Behavior*. New York: Free Press.

_____. (1952). "'Development of Theory of Democratic Administration': Replies and Comments." *American Political Science Review* 46: 494–503.

Terry, Larry D. (1990). "Leadership in the Administrative State." *Administration and Society* 21: 395–413.

Uslaner, Eric M. (1993). *The Decline of Comity of Congress*. Ann Arbor, MI: University of Michigan Press.

Waldo, Dwight (1984). *The Administrative State*. 2d ed. New York: Holmes and Meier.

_____. (1987). "Politics and Administration: On Thinking About a Complex Relationship." In Ralph Clark Chandler, ed., *A Centennial History of the American Administrative State*. New York: Free Press.

Wamsley, Gary, Robert N. Bacher, Charles T. Goodsell, Philip S. Kronenberg, John A. Rohr, Camilla M. Stivers, Orion F. White, and James Wolf (1990). *Refounding Public Administration*. Newbury Park, CA: Sage.

Wilson, James Q. (1989). *Bureaucracy: What Government Agencies Do and Why They Do It*. New York: Basic Books.

Wood, B. Dan (1988). "Principals, Bureaucrats, and Responsiveness in Clean Air Enforcements." *American Political Science Review* 82: 213–234.

Wood, B. Dan, and Richard W. Waterman (1994). *Bureaucratic Dynamics: the Role of Bureaucracy in a Democracy*. Boulder, CO: Westview.

4

REINVENTING THE MACHINERY OF GOVERNMENT

Anyone who visits Washington, D.C. or a state capital will be struck by the scale and monumental stature of the major public buildings—the Capitol, the Treasury, the Pentagon, the State Department. These buildings house and symbolize part of the "machinery of government"—the set of structural and procedural arrangements used by the national, state and local governments to advise on policy, deliver services, and safeguard the personal and property rights of citizens. Some of the older and larger national agencies have 200-year histories. Many agencies though have been created more recently as government has faced new issues such as civil rights in the 1950s and environmental protection in the 1970s. Since 1980, legislators, public executives, business leaders, scholars and reformers all have focused on streamlining and reinventing these "machines of government" with the aim of leaner, more efficient and more focused services.

THE ARCHITECTURE OF ADMINISTRATION

The U.S. Constitution provided the basic design for the machinery of government in America by dividing government into the executive, legislative and judicial branches. This separation of powers was designed to protect individual liberty against the perceived danger of a government machine that was too efficient or too ruthless. The framers of the Constitution were worried about the protection of citizens' rights—not about the efficiency of government. Now 230 years later, we feel great frustration when the checks and balances designed by the framers produce gridlock and frustration rather than efficient decision-making and service delivery.

Each of the three branches of American national government has its own machinery, and similar structures and procedures are found in all state and local governments as well. The *Executive Branch* is the most complex part of the national machinery of government. It includes the Executive Office of the President, 14 major national departments, and many independent and partially independent commissions, boards, and corporations.

There are 10 major offices within the Executive Office of the President, many of which were placed there after one of the hundreds of investigations over history recommended strengthening the in-house advisory resources available to the president and his administration. Examples include the Office of Management and Budget and the National Security Council. The 14 Executive Departments that form the core of the Executive Branch machinery of government rarely change, such as the Departments of Defense, Health and Human Services, and Commerce. Their heads, "Secretaries," form the president's cabinet. Finally, there are the numerous independent and partially-independent commissions, boards and corporations, that conduct public business, regulate parts of the economy, and protecting citizens' rights, including for example the Interstate Commerce Commission, the U.S. Commission on Civil Rights, and the Federal Reserve Board. Change is much more frequent in this third part of the machinery of the Executive Branch of government, where agencies that have outlived their usefulness may be abolished periodically.

The machineries that serve the *Legislative Branch* (Congress) and the *Judicial Branch* (the federal courts) are less extensive and complicated than in the Executive Branch. They too, though, have their intricacies. Some important agencies such as the General Accounting Office (GAO), the Administrative Office of the U.S. Courts, the Congressional Budget Office (CBO) and the Government Printing Office (GPO) are located there because of the special responsibilities they have to the Congress and the courts.

WAVES OF REFORM AND REINVENTION

Over the last 70 years the national government has experienced a never-ending succession of commissions, committees, inquiries and consultants who have diligently suggested ways to make the machinery of government more efficient or effective. Back in the 1930s, the Brownlow Committee emphasized changes that would strengthen the President's hand. The Reorganization Act of 1939, which flowed from the Brownlow Committee's work, created the Executive Office of the President and the Bureau of the Budget (later expanded by President Nixon into the Office of Management and Budget). A decade later, the two Hoover Commissions, chaired by former President Herbert Hoover, continued the efforts to streamline the Executive Branch. The first Hoover Commission (1947 to 1949) resulted in further strengthening of the powers of the presidency and the Executive Branch; the second (1953 to 1955) called for massive privatization of government activities, but it was too far ahead of its time and brought little change.

The theme of privatization resurfaced with President Ronald Reagan's 1982 "Private Sector Survey on Cost Control," chaired by businessman J. Peter Grace and thus popularly known as "the Grace Commission." Despite highly visible support from President Reagan and its $75 million cost, the Grace Commission misfired badly and very little positive resulted from it.

The decade of the 1990s witnessed several new sustained reform efforts for the machinery of government. W. Edwards Deming's "Total Quality Management" (TQM), which had been widely adopted in industry during the 1980s, and the highly popular and influential 1992 book, *Reinventing Government,* by David Osborne and Ted Gaebler kick-started the process. The "National Performance Review" (NPR) led by Vice President Al Gore continued through the second Clinton-Gore administration, giving rise to many new innovative reform structures and processes, such as the National Partnership for Reinventing Government. Although NPR has numerous critics, it led to significant cost savings, cultural changes, and ways of doing government's business.

CURRENT REINVENTION THEMES

Several themes have dominated the government reinvention movement of the 1990s and early 2000s in the US's version of a wave of reform thinking loosely termed "the new public management." Despite considerable "hype," the U.S. has lagged behind several other countries on this cutting-edge reform front. New Zealand, Australia, and Great Britain were the early leaders in "the new public management" movement, introducing many innovations during the 1970s and 1980s. Key ideas associated with "the new public management" have included:

- privatization of many government activities;
- downsizing of public bureaucracies;
- an emphasis on government making policy ("steering") rather than delivering services ("rowing");
- greater use of nonprofits in service delivery;
- deregulation;
- reduced bureaucratic complexity;
- the decline of the politically neutral career public service; and
- an emphasis on measuring, reporting and rewarding performance.

The sources of these changes have included political-economic theories such as "public choice," "organizational economics," and "agency theory"; political initiatives such as those undertaken by President Reagan with the Grace Commission and the Clinton-Gore administration with the National Performance Review; and management concepts largely imported from industry, such as outsourcing and pay-for-performance.

READINGS REPRINTED IN THIS CHAPTER

The first reading reprinted here is **Guy Peters'** global overview of proposals for new forms of governance, **"Changing States, Governance, and the Public Service,"** from his 1997 book, *The Future of Governing: Four Emerging*

Models. Peters cautions that not all reforms are necessarily for the better. If, for example, efficiency is the sole focus of reforms, other cherished values may be sacrificed in the process. These "costs of change" should be recognized and included in the analysis when considering whether to implement reforms.[1] He identifies six enduring principles or "old chestnuts" that have guided thinking about the public service in the U.S. and its governance:

- a civil service based on the concept of politically neutral competence;
- the appropriateness of hierarchical and rule bound bureaucracy that provides predictability, universality, and probity;
- permanence and stability of service, within a lifetime commitment;
- an institutionalized civil service governed as a corporate body;
- high levels of internal regulation; and
- equality of outcomes.

Peters argues that in the application of reforms, governments have often adopted practices that may have worked in industry or taken reforms "off the shelf" without sufficient regard for the vision of governance. Peters presents four models of governance that underlie most current public sector reform proposals:

- Market Government
- Participative Government
- Flexible Government, and
- Deregulated Government[2]

Peters' insightful categorization reminds us of the dangers of piecemeal, contradictory, and incomplete reform agendas. Are Peters' concerns warranted? Are we risking losing our nation's long-standing concern for equity, justice, and individual rights in our determination to increase government's efficiency? Are the priorities of the Constitution's framers nothing more than historic relics? Can we find reforms that increase efficiency without endangering our democratic form of government? These issues are open to debate. Peters' chapter raises important questions about the future of governing.

In the second reading, **"Learning to Get the Balance in Privatization,"**[3] **Graeme Hodge** assesses the conclusions of a comprehensive international study assessing the results of privatization and contracting out in a number of countries, not just America. Hodge argues that in considering a major reform such as privatization, we must pay attention not only to theory, and to the aims of a reform process, but to the results experienced as implementation progressively takes place. Using this philosophy, Hodge undertook perhaps the most comprehensive and rigorous study of contracting out yet—relying "not on newspaper reports, anecdotes or government ideology,"[4] but on the available international empirical evidence. The results of this study, later corroborated elsewhere, was that early predictions of savings from contracting out as high as 20-30% were much higher than the average measured saving, of more like 6%. Hodge's study is full of interesting conclusions—but the most interesting aspect of all is that they result from looking at the evidence carefully and widely—not just adding another opinion to the pile.

John Dilulio's chapter **"Works Better and Costs Less? Sweet and Sour Perspectives on the National Performance Review,"**[5] provides a glimpse behind the hype as he describes how the National Performance Review process was initiated and operated in its first two years. How much was NPR "hype," and how much real achievement? Separating hype from results in practice is a classic problem when assessing the outcomes of any governmental reform program.

This chapter focuses on the cutting edge of public sector change. It introduces ideas and beliefs about a variety of reform models and theories, but it is also about the implementation of change and accountability in government. It asks when and how to change—and to change carefully. It cautions that efficiency should not be the only goal of public sector reform. If we are not careful with reform, we risk destroying values of lasting importance and, perhaps, our distinctive form of democratic governance.

NOTES

1. Peters, B. Guy. (1997). *The Future of Governing: Four Emerging Models.* Lawrence Kans.: University Press of Kansas, p. 4.
2. Peters, B. Guy. (1997). *The Future of Governing: Four Emerging Models.* Lawrence Kans.: University Press of Kansas, p.19.
3. Hodge, Graeme A. (2000), "Learning to Get the Best from Privatization," in G. A. Hodge, *Privatization: An International Review of Performance* (pp. 229–247). Boulder, Colo.: Westview.
4. Hodge, Graeme A. (2000), "Learning to Get the Best from Privatization," in G. A. Hodge, *Privatization: An International Review of Performance.* Boulder, Colo.: Westview, pp. 232–233.
5. Dilulio Jr., John J. (1995). "Works Better and Costs Less? Sweet and Sour Perspectives on the National Performance Review, "in D. F. Kettl and J. J. Dilulio (Eds.), *Inside the Reinvention Machine: Appraising Governmental Reform* (pp. 1–6). Washington DC: The Brookings Institution.

10

B. Guy Peters

CHANGING STATES, GOVERNANCE, AND THE PUBLIC SERVICE

Governance is a scarce commodity. Governments have created a vast array of institutions designed to exercise collective control and influence over the societies and economies for which they have been given responsibility. Those efforts at institution-building have certainly provided comparative politics with an interesting array of data, but it is much less clear that they have moved any closer to solving the problems of regulating the behavior of people and organizations. If anything, these efforts at governance may be less successful now than were similar efforts in the past. There has been some loss of government's policy autonomy to external actors, such as international organizations and amorphous international markets, at the same time that an apparent popular resistance to being governed has sharply increased. Political leaders in the world today must ask whether what they do in their national capitals has much effect in shaping the lives of their citizens.

Fortunately, governments, government leaders, and their civil servants continue attempting to find better ways of governing. I say fortunately not just because these efforts keep students of the public sector occupied but also because there is a great capacity to do good for citizens, individually and collectively, through effective public action. It is now fashionable to malign government and the people working in it and to point out gleefully all their failures. Such skepticism and cynicism are cheap; great commitment and courage are required to continue attempting to solve problems that almost by definition exceed the capacity of any individual or private actor to solve. If the problems had been easy or profitable, they probably would have remained in the private sector, and government would never have been made to cope with them. Despite the popular mythology, government is rarely imperialistic, nor does it look for new problems to solve; governments are more likely to be handed the poisoned chalice of an insuperable problem.[1]

It remains crucial for governments, and the individuals who constitute them, to continue their search for innovative mechanisms for making government work better and to serve society better. This effort must be carried on even in the face of "ill structured" (H. A. Simon 1973) or "intractable" (Schon and Rein 1994) or "wicked" (Dunn 1988) problems and often in the service of a mass public that neither recognizes nor appreciates the effort involved. Contemporary public servants are neither martyrs nor saints, but they are individuals charged with continuing to make collective decisions and to enforce previous decisions on behalf of the public interest.

The leaders of government are also charged with reforming and improving the internal performance of their organizations. Many of the efforts at reform that I will discuss have been internally generated, an indication that the public sector is not resisting change, as many of its critics assume, but in some cases is actually leading the way for change (Tellier 1990; B. Peters and Savoie 1994; Derlien 1995). Of course, there are at least as many reforms that have been imposed from the outside, some of which have indeed been resisted vigorously by the entrenched civil service. There is no monopoly on virtue or vice in the world of administrative reform.

Understanding administrative reform in turn requires understanding the traditional model of governance that is the backdrop against which attempts at reform must be viewed. Rather than evolving from a set of intellectual principles, this model tended to evolve from practice and rarely has been articulated as a distinct model. Despite its lack of an intellectual foundation, the traditional model was once thought to be the way in which the public sector should be organized, and indeed it worked rather well for decades. During the height of optimism about government's capacity to solve social problems, for example, the 1950s through the early 1970s, the basic model for governance appeared to require little fundamental debate. The task then was to refine the model, make it more "rational" with techniques such as program budgeting (Novick 1965) and cost-benefit analysis (Mishan 1988), and then merely to let the governing system continue to produce effective policies and continued socio-economic improvements.

Certainly some conservative politicians and thinkers did raise questions about the virtues of those (by then) traditional ideas about government and especially about the increased role of the public sector (Friedman 1962; Hayek 1968; Sawer 1982). For most people in and out of government, however, the parameters of acceptable public action then were broad and well established. There was a pervasive belief the government could regulate the economy through taxing and spending and that it had sufficient economic resources to ameliorate social problems such as poverty, sickness, and poor education. The fifties and sixties were the period of the "mixed-economy welfare-state," of "treble affluence" (Rose and Peters 1978), and of the promise of an ever-brighter future through public action.

The fifties and sixties were also the period of consensus politics (Kavanagh and Morris 1994) in most countries of Western Europe and North America, and both scholars and practical politicians proclaimed the "end of ideology" and the creation of a "post-industrial society" (Gustafsson 1979).[2] Even a conservative such as Richard Nixon would say, "We are all Keynesians now," and would attempt to create new social programs (Spulbar 1989) rather than roll such programs back as subsequent Republican presidents and congresses attempted to do.[3] Similarly, Christian Democrats in Germany could preach the virtues of the "social market economy" as a desirable alternative to unbridled capitalism (Peacock and Willgerodt 1989). Clearly something has changed in the economy and in the popular mind since that time, and with that change has come a change in the definition of what constitutes good government and acceptable public administration.

TRADITIONAL PUBLIC ADMINISTRATION: THE OLD-TIME RELIGION

Dwight Waldo (1968) once wrote that public administration has had so many identity crises that in comparison the life of the average adolescent appeared idyllic. Waldo was discussing public administration as an academic discipline, but its contemporary practice displays much of the same uncertainty. Questions about its practice include such basic issues as the structure of government, management of those structures, and the proper role of public administration in governance (Harmon 1995). Many traditional certainties about government and the public service are now either totally altered or are subject to severe scrutiny.

Rather than being singular, the old model of public administration is actually a number of different concepts (Richards 1992), and at least six old chestnuts have guided our thinking about the public service and its role in governance (B. Peters and Wright 1996). These six ideas clearly are no longer as canonical as they once were.[4]

The sometimes forgotten aspect in the discussion of alternative approaches to public management is that these principles evolved over a long period and generally represent responses to a number of problems that existed in public administration in earlier times. Indeed, there is a real chance that some of the problems for which the old chestnuts were designed may reappear once they are replaced with more modern conceptions about how to run government.

Reforms solve problems existing at one time, often in the process creating a new set of problems that may generate subsequent reforms (Kaufman 1978; Aucoin 1990; B. Peters 1995a). Moreover, a word of caution about administrative reform does not mean that the old ways of running government were necessarily better. The appeal to prudence simply points out that these approaches to public management did solve certain problems, albeit creating some additional ones. Overturning the older modes of administering, though solving some problems, may in the process revive older difficulties and perhaps even create new ones. If the potential costs of discarding the existing system of public administration are not recognized, then change may appear entirely too attractive.

An Apolitical Civil Service

The first of the six principles is the assumption of an apolitical civil service, and associated with that the politics-administration dichotomy and the concept of "neutral competence" (Kaufman 1956) within the civil service. The basic idea is that civil servants should not have discernible political allegiances and that they should be able to serve any master, i.e., any government of the day. The civil servant may have views about particular policies and is almost expected to, as a member of an organization responsible for making and implementing policies (Aberbach, Putnam, and Rockman 1981). But they are not expected to have partisan views that might lead them to be disloyal to a government of one complexion or another.

The principle of an apolitical civil service has been largely an Anglo-Saxon preoccupation, compared to administration in other industrialized democracies (Silberman 1993). However, even in countries with a more overtly politicized civil service, such as Germany and France (Derlien 1991; Bodiguel and Rouban 1991), the concept of competence ranks at least as high as political allegiance in the selection of civil servants. Similarly, the civil services of the Scandinavian countries tend to be less overtly politicized than that of Germany, but even there political allegiances are often known or assumed (Ståhlberg 1987). The characteristic common to these civil service systems is that objective qualifications are the first hurdle for recruitment, and political considerations follow those.

Although depoliticization of the civil service has been very much an Anglo-American concern, it is also a rather recent administrative value. In the United States, for example, the spoils system dominated recruitment until the mid-1880s, and even then the number of merit appointments under the Pendleton Act (1883) was rather small (Skowronek 1982; Ingraham 1995a). By 1904 only half of the total federal employment was under the merit system, and most of that was in lower-level clerical positions (Johnson and Liebcap 1994, 30–33). In the United Kingdom the merit system was initiated only slightly earlier than in the United States, although it spread throughout the administrative system more quickly (Parris 1969). The historical record in other Anglo-American democracies is not significantly different, as patronage appointments were either replaced by merit gradually under British rule from the end of the nineteenth century or as former colonies institutionalized merit systems quickly after gaining independent status (Braibanti 1966; Koehn 1990).[5]

Associated with the concern for maintaining an apolitical personnel system was the argument that politics and administration were, and more importantly, should be separate enterprises. In the United States this principle was stated first by Woodrow Wilson (1887) and restated more forcefully by Goodnow (1900). In the United Kingdom the argument was also advanced, first implicitly in the Northcote-Trevelyan Report (1853) on the civil service and then later in the Haldane Report (Machinery of Government Committee 1918) on the structure of government. In both countries the argument was that the job of the civil service was to implement the decisions made by the political masters and to do so without questioning the sagacity of the decisions.[6] Other Anglo-American political systems have had similar apolitical civil services and have encountered the same problems of increased politicization.

Despite the ideological advocacy of an apolitical civil service, it is increasingly clear that civil servants do have significant, if not necessarily dominant, policy roles in most contemporary governments (B. Peters 1992; Kato 1994; Plowden 1994). It is also clear to most analysts that governance is better, on average, because they do (Terry 1995). The policy role of civil servants is most obvious at the implementation stage, where the role of implementors in determining real policies occurred as early as the 1930s (Gulick 1933; Almond and Lasswell 1934). In addition to the policy that emerges from "street-level bureaucrats" (Lipsky 1980; Adler and Asquith 1981) dealing with individual cases, the public bureaucracy has a more systematic role in making public policy through implementation. The recognition of the empirical reality of the role of the bureaucracy in governance and of the benefits that arise from that involvement has not prevented the continuing ideological advocacy of separating politics and administration, however.

The manifest policymaking role of the public bureaucracy arises most clearly in the promulgation of "secondary legislation," "regulations" in the language of American government. Very few legislatures in the world are capable of writing laws that specify the necessary details for complex policy areas and thus depend upon their bureaucracies to fill in that legal and technical content. In the United States, for example, although Congress passes only a few hundred bills each year, something approaching 5,000 final rules are passed annually.[7] The accumulation of rules over the years has produced over 10,000 pages of them in the *Code of Federal Regulations* for agriculture policy alone (Kerwin 1994, 18–19). In other industrialized democracies the volume of secondary legislation appears no less; even in the European Union there are approximately ten times as many rules written as pieces of primary legislation adopted (Blumann and Soligne 1989).

The civil service also has a significant, if now threatened, role as policy advisers at the formulation stage. Although ministers may be elected to make policy decisions, they may lack the capacity to do so effectively (Blondel 1988). Even in countries where civil servants are generalists by education and career patterns, through experience they can gain greater command of the details of policy than can ministers who are in office for only a short time (B. Peters 1992). And the role of the civil service in policy formulation and advice is perhaps even more crucial within developing and transitional governments, in which the need for expertise and the demands for a "committed bureaucracy" are that much greater (B. Peters 1995a; Hesse 1993).

The problem then becomes how to structure government in ways that recognize the reality, and even the desirability, of the significant policy role for civil servants while simultaneously preserving the requirements of democratic accountability. This is a difficult balance for designers of government institutions to achieve, especially given the historical legacy of thought concerning the neutrality of the civil service and the current reality of public demands for enhanced accountability (Day and Klein 1987; Cooper 1995). Furthermore, political leaders have become ever more aware of the policy role of civil servants and in response often have attempted to minimize that role (Aberbach and Rockman 1988; C. Campbell 1993). Reducing the role of the civil service has been done partly for ideological reasons (they were perceived either as too far right or left) or simply for reasons of preserving institutional differences.

The struggle over competence and authority in making public policy is now more obvious to individuals working within government, as well as to citizens, than in the past. The politicization of the functions of the civil service, if not the members of the civil service themselves, may make the delicate balance of competent policymaking even more difficult to maintain. Years of one-party domination mean that current civil servants are often identified with the policies of that particular party. Further, the prevailing assumption, if not always the reality, is that civil servants must accept the party line of the incumbent government or face termination.

Hierarchy and Rules

The second significant change in attitudes toward the traditional model of government is the decline of assumptions about hierarchical and rule-bound management within the public service and about the authority of civil servants to implement and enforce regulations outside it. The neat Weberian model of management (Wright and Peters 1996) does not apply within public organizations as it once did, and in its place a variety of alternative sources of organizational power and authority are to be found. The market, as one example, is an increasingly significant standard against which to compare the structure and performance of government organizations (Lan and Rosenbloom 1992; Hood 1990; Boston 1991). Though it can be argued that the inherent differences between the public and private sectors are crucial to understanding governance (Savoie 1995b; Self 1993; Perry and Rainey 1988), even governments on the political left have implemented market-based reforms.[8]

For transitional and developing regimes the demands for greater economic efficiency in the public sector must be balanced against the needs to create some of the predictability, universality, and probity associated with Weberian bureaucracy. The changes being introduced in industrialized countries are based on the assumption that the employees implementing market-based reforms will have at least some of the public-service values that have informed the civil service. Without those values, market-oriented reforms run the risk of justifying corruption and becoming a publicly sponsored version of the excesses of capitalism. Those excesses to some extent have occurred already in the former Soviet Union and may well emerge in other transitional regimes. These aberrations, unfortunately, have not been entirely absent from the industrialized democracies in which market-oriented reforms have been implemented.[9]

There are other challenges to hierarchy. Alternative to the market model, as well as to traditional models of bureaucracy, is the "dialectical" or participatory organization. Scholars and reformers have discussed this model for a number of years, but government organizations are now being placed under increasing real pressure to accommodate the interests of lower-level employees, as well as those of their clients, into their decisionmaking processes (Barzelay 1992). This change in management is at once a manipulative mechanism for increasing efficiency and a genuine moral commitment to participation (Thomas 1993). Whether the participation is authentic or not, it is difficult for an organization to deny involvement and access to its employees and even to its clients.

Contemporary public organizations also must negotiate social compliance with their decisions and compliance with contracts for service delivery instead of implementing public programs directly through law and other authoritative means. The spread of network conceptualizations in the social sciences has been paralleled by a proliferation of network practices in governance (Scharpf 1991; Kenis and Schneider 1991). No longer can governments impose their wills through legal instruments and, if necessary, coercion; they must now work to achieve an outcome approaching consensus among a large group of self-interested parties who have some influence over the policy. Governing in most industrialized democracies has become a process of bargaining and mediating rather than applying rules (Kooiman 1993).

Civil servants increasingly are expected to make their own decisions about what constitutes the public interest, and they at times are compelled to make determinations diametrically opposed to the stated policies and desires of their nominal political masters.[10] If civil servants and other appointed officials are indeed to become entrepreneurial then they must become less dominated by the dictates of these masters. If this approach were practiced, it would alter fundamentally ideas of accountability as well as ideas of management in the public sector, especially in the Westminster democracies (G. Wilson 1994).

Changes such as these make the role of civil service managers even more difficult that it has been and leave the role of civil servants within governments more ambiguous. Further, the general absence of a formalized normative structure in government may make preserving accountability increasingly difficult (*Public Money and Management* 1995).

For developing and transitional regimes these changes are even more problematic than for the industrialized countries. Bureaucracies in European and North American countries are searching for ways to become more entrepreneurial and less constrained by red tape, but governments in many developing and transitional regimes have different challenges. The problem for many governments in such regimes is in creating the Weberian and rule-directed bureaucracies that are now being supplanted in the industrialized regimes. Applying the earlier characterization of bureaucracies in transitional regimes by Fred Riggs (1964) as "prismatic," one of the challenges of public management in contexts of low universality of rules is to ensure equality and uniformity of those rules.

Permanence and Stability

The third change in the assumptions about governance and the public bureaucracy concerns the permanence and stability of the organizations within government (Kaufman 1976). Employment as a public servant is usually conceptualized as being a lifetime commitment, a "social contract," with civil servants trading a certain amount of income for secure employment (Hood and Peters 1994). Joining a public organization is sometimes seen as joining a Japanese corporation once was—as lifetime employment. The permanence of public organizations is frequently overestimated (B. Peters and Hogwood 1988), but it has been an important partial truth about government. Increasingly, this pattern of permanent organization is being attacked. The growing recognition of the dysfunctions of permanence and the realization that many significant social and economic problems currently exist within the interstices of public organizations have led to some discussion of alternative forms of government organization.

The character of the alternative organizational structures remains somewhat inchoate at present. In particular, ideas about task forces, "czars," interdepartmental committees, and similar structures have generated options for achieving more flexible governance.[11] Another possibility is the "virtual organization" as a means of linking a range of individuals, and with them institutional interests, to be employed across a range of government organizations. Given the spread of information technology, the necessity for people to be in a common setting in order to share the characteristics of an organization has diminished. Therefore, forming alternatives to traditional organizations has become practical.

For individual public employees, organizational methods would also be diverse, with contracting and consultancy arrangements, temporary employment at peak times (for tax and recreational employees, for example), and an increasing number of positions clearly not intended to be tenurable. In the senior civil service the idea of a distinctive career structure is now being questioned and abandoned, even in countries such as the United Kingdom, in which the civil service has been very much a group apart from other employment streams. The Treasury—long the homeland of the mandarin—has embarked on a process of reducing its own staff and thinking about how best to involve outside talent in its own work (HMSO 1993; HMSO 1994a).

The traditional sense of permanence in public organizations is being questioned from several perspectives. In one view, a change is simply a means of deprivileging the civil service during a time in which almost all organizations and employees are being confronted with downsizing and other threats to their existence. Another view holds that permanence and stability tend to ossify policy lines and to make coordination of policies more difficult. If temporary organizational structures were more common, the change could have two benefits. First, it would enable more organizational experimentation in solving problems (D. Campbell 1982) without the fear that a future dinosaur was being created (Kaufman 1976). Second, it could permit the creation of organizations with primarily coordinative tasks that could address a particular problem of interaction among programs and organizations and then disappear. The conventional wisdom would argue that government organizations would not disappear, but neither has there been much real attempt to create such organizations explicitly.[12]

Governments of developing countries appear even more affected by the permanence of public organizations and employment. Government is a major employer in these countries, especially for the relatively small professional and educated segments of the society. It is difficult for any government to dismiss existing workers, but it also may perceive the need to hire additional, politically loyal personnel. It may make sense to dismiss existing employees, however, if they have been compromised by their participation in a regime with serious human rights abuses (B. Peters 1995a). In any case, the tendency for public employment to be conceptualized as permanent presents real problems for these governments.

An Institutionalized Civil Service

The fourth fundamental assumption undergirding traditional public administration is that there should be an institutionalized civil service that is governed as a corporate body. This concept is a somewhat recent development in some industrialized democracies, with patronage or personal service to the crown or both being the older model for managing the state. For the intellectual father of contemporary bureaucracies, Max Weber (1958; see also Mommsen 1989), the development of authority and bureaucracy—beginning with charismatic and traditional authority using patrimonial organizations and ending with rational-legal authority employing bureaucratic organizations—represented the development of the modern state (especially in Germany). Although some analysts consider it central to political modernity, the concept of a distinctive and professional civil service has been brought into question in a number of countries seeking to establish a more committed and activist civil service.

In addition to the impermanent government organizations being created, the personnel commitments of government also have become less permanent. Government organizations increasingly expand and contract to meet variable demands for work, for example, in tax offices or recreation programs. Although this style of personnel management may save money, it produces several empirical and normative questions for public managers and policymakers. Temporary employment for a significant portion of the public labor force may produce even more difficulties for citizens than the presumed indifference of permanent employees. Citizens will have to cope with public employees who may lack the commitment to service and other public values that in most instances have characterized the career civil service. At a more practical level, temporary employees may lack the training and information necessary to do their jobs properly.

Even if the civil service system itself has not been challenged, the manner in which it traditionally has been managed is being questioned. For example, one of the common principles of personnel management in the public sector has been a uniform set of grades for personnel throughout the civil service, based upon their qualifications, the difficulty of their assigned tasks, or both, with relatively equal pay within each grade. Advancement was to be based upon merit, demonstrated either by performance on the job or by a series of examinations. It is now less clear that merit is to be measured within the context of the public service and the public sector, as forces and priorities of the market are being used to test the worth of individuals and of policies.

Internal Regulation

The fifth chestnut is that the civil service should be acquiescent and respond almost without question to policy directives issued by its nominal political masters. This demand goes beyond mere political neutrality. Many of the problems associated with government, and especially with public bureaucracy, are a function of controls imposed by political leaders seeking greater control and accountability (Kaufman 1977; Walters 1992a). Government organizations are generally among the most stringently regulated in any society (J. Wilson 1989), especially in Anglo-American democracies. Therefore, if the skills and entrepreneurship of public employees could be engaged more freely, then government is likely to be able to perform more efficiently and effectively (Osborne and Gaebler 1992).

It is less clear that deregulation is the most appropriate response to the needs of developing and transitional regimes. Certainly many of these governments have been characterized by extremely high levels of internal regulation (Beyme 1993) that have stifled creativity and produced problems in dealing with citizens. Further, in many instances international organizations and private-sector lenders are pressing for loosening restraints on government action. Still, deregulation may not be the most appropriate response for the governments of transitional countries. The need in these regimes generally is for greater predictability and accountability rather than for the increased entrepreneurship demanded in more developed regimes.

Equality

The sixth characteristic of the traditional model of governance and public administration holds that there should be as much equality of outcomes as possible. Personnel management stresses equal pay and conditions of employment for similarly qualified employees across the civil service. And there are strong norms that the decisions made by the public service with respect to its clients should be as similar as possible: clients with the same objective characteristics should receive the same benefits. In this Weberian conception of bureaucracy the civil servant applies the rules *sine irae ac studio* to produce equitable outcomes for all clients (Thompson 1975).

This conception of equality of services and outcomes is also being questioned, through several related types of reform. First, market-oriented reforms have tended to decentralize and disaggregate government departments and to provide an enhanced amount of autonomy to managers. The assumption is that these managers will still be obliged to follow the laws of the programs they administer. There does appear, however, to be much greater room for discretion, which is especially important if it is seen as possibly saving money for government. In this view the creation of differential levels and patterns of service creates a quasi market of sorts, so that citizens can exercise some choice over what they will receive (and perhaps what they will pay for) from government.[13]

The attacks on equality of services also arise from another quarter and are based on the participatory ethic in relationship to public services and public employment. The concept here is to empower lower-echelon workers in organizations and enable them to make more autonomous decision about services. The argument is that the rigidity of bureaucratic structures designed to ensure greater equality of services for clients restricts the freedom of employees to "self-actualize" on the job and to make more creative and humane decisions about their clients. If the shackles of rigidity are removed, then public employees will be happier and will also deliver better services to their clients. Particularly for social services, programs that were intended to be humane and helpful have become bureaucratized (in the pejorative sense of that term) and frequently harm (if only in subtle ways) in addition to helping their clients (Smart 1991). Further, some proponents of the models of administrative reform argue for the empowerment of clients so that they can make more of their own decisions, a reform that may be diametrically opposed to the empowerment of the workers administering their benefits (see pp. 52–54).

The issue of equality also raises important questions about accountability and the law. Do clients want the outcomes of their demands for service to be contingent upon getting the "right" worker? Do other taxpayers want public employees to have so much latitude in delivering the services that are paid for with tax money? Is it legal (or ethical) for people with the same characteristics and the same rights to be treated differently by government, or are these other public values equally or more important than the values of empowerment? Unfortunately, these issues too often are not addressed in the contemporary debates about change in the public sector.

Rather than looking back to vestiges of past thinking about governance, I shall explore several alternative paths for the development of the public service. By examining the development of alternative models of the state that are emerging in practice, readers can look at the implications of these models of governance for the civil service. Except for the market model, they have not been articulated in a comprehensive form; they have appeared more clearly in government documents than in the academic literature. Thus they will have to be extracted almost as ideal types from academic and practical discussions of governing.

There is some similarity of analyses and prescriptions across the alternatives, although the meanings attached to the prescriptions may be quite different in each model. Most reforms have the effect, however, of "hollowing out" the state and making it, and particularly the career public service, a less significant actor in society (R. Rhodes 1994; Milward, forthcoming). Yet interestingly, one of the approaches to changing the government may have the (probably unintended) consequence of enhancing both the powers of government and of the civil service. Although the focus is on alternatives, one possible model is a vigorous restatement of the status quo ante. For many civil servants, and for some politicians, the "old-time religion" may still be the best way to run a government, even if they must face massive skepticism from the public.

VISIONS OF THE STATE AND GOVERNANCE

Few governments have remained untouched by the wave of reform that has swept through the public sector over the past several decades. The magnitude of reform undertaken in most political systems may have been unprecedented, at least during peacetime, but the reforms themselves also have tended to be extremely piecemeal and unsystematic (B. Peters and Savoie 1994a). The absence of clear visions and integrated strategies may partly explain why the results of the reforms have tended to disappoint so many of their advocates (Caiden 1990; Ingraham 1995b). Apparently, governments often have selected "off the shelf" reforms derived from one set of assumptions (implicit or explicit) at the same time they selected other reforms based upon quite different, or even directly contradictory, premises. The political and administrative leaders made these selections expecting all the changes to work well together. Yet it is little wonder that in practice the sets of reforms not only have not worked together in a large number of instances but that at times the interactions also have proven to be negative.

My task is to explicate several more integrated visions of possible futures for the state and its bureaucracy. The nature of each vision will, in turn, influence the manner in which governance, considered more broadly, would be practiced if such an administrative regime were to be implemented in toto. These reform agendas must not be considered in isolation from other political and cultural movements in society. For example, the emphasis on market models for reforming government represents but one strand of thinking about the need to inculcate the market approach into a whole range of social institutions, such as universities (Tully 1995). Likewise, the drive for making administration more participatory is but a part of a general ethos (largely contradictory to the market model) stressing greater opportunities for participation in the very same institutions.

If the implications of these alternative visions are more fully explored, understood, and contrasted with the traditional conceptualizations of governance, then there is some possibility of producing more effective planned change in government. There is certainly no guarantee of success even with more coherent programs, and the possibility that even the best-planned administrative changes will be diverted and subverted is inevitably present (March and Olsen 1983).

The practical significance of this exercise, however, will be secondary since my primary purpose is to enhance an understanding of what has been happening with governance as well as an understanding of the future implications of the alternative conceptions. Gaining a clear understanding of contemporary reforms is not easy. Speaking of the changes occurring in British government, Sue Richards argues:

> It is a confusing picture of changing patterns of behaviour, of informal and emergent rules, and of shifting power plays. We need greater clarity so public managers and other practitioners of public service may be assisted in their understanding, and so that a wider public may have better access to these changes (1992, 15).

It appears almost certain that the status quo ante is no longer a preferred option in the public sector, in Britain or anywhere, so it is essential to understand the patterns that are emerging. Academic and practitioner-analysts must explore the assumptions of those models, along with the particular proposals derived from those assumptions. Without that analysis and interpretation, it will be difficult to comprehend the emerging form of the state in society—both industrialized and transitional—and to think about the fundamental problems of governing in the twenty-first century.

A concern with alternative visions should not be read to mean that any of these schemes is superior to the traditional model of the civil service in governance. I tend to think that that is not the case, although certainly the traditional model is far from perfect and could be made to function better. I also assume that continuing reform in government is likely, or even inevitable in the current political climate, and if that reform is to occur it is more likely to be effective if the reforms are systematic and integrated. One should also remain cognizant of the internal contradictions inherent within some of these approaches to governance. It may be that, as in H. Simon's now classic discussion (1947) of the "proverbs of administration," there are also "proverbs of reform" that are equally contradictory (Kaufman 1978; B. Peters 1996). Current thinking about the complexities of the public service, even when guided by a relatively strong set of theoretical assumptions, tends toward constructing situational rather than systematic remedies. This emphasis can be seen most clearly in cycles of reform: centralization efforts follow decentralization followed by yet another round of decentralization.

Nevertheless, the context within which any particular vision of governance is to be implemented must be considered. For transitional regimes in Central and Eastern Europe perhaps a Weberian system of highly constrained administration may be the most suitable tool for restoring some legitimacy to government (Hesse 1993: Derlien and Szablowski 1993). The values inherent in that system may need to be institutionalized first, to be followed by the more marketized systems of administration. The politicization and extreme arbitrariness of the old system may have to be purged from people's minds before a more decentralized administrative system can be legitimate.

Yet some Third World regimes that have been dominated by a bureaucracy (perhaps in the pejorative sense of the word) may find the alternative models just as applicable and desirable as do the industrialized countries (Grindle and Thomas 1991). One difficulty in the reform process has been that the advocates of reforms have assumed that "one size fits all" and that any government could be improved by the institutionalization of their preferred new pattern. Indeed, some of the problems with reforms, such as "reinvention" (Osborne and Gaebler 1992) in the United States, arise from the reforms being based on assumptions about government derived from the experiences of small local governments that may be inappropriate from central governments.

Through the development of these four alternatives to the traditional system of governance, the implications and prescriptions of each vision for several aspects of governing can be examined. Most basic is the diagnosis of the problem. Reform efforts imply a desire for change, and each of the four alternatives contains a clear idea about the source that is producing problems in the public sector. Thus, the models attempt to take the (often) vague sense of uneasiness and malaise that citizens feel about their governments and translate it into a specific cause-and-effect relationship. As with any attempt to impose such a construction on complex social and political institutions, this exercise often produces some oversimplification. The identification of a cause, however, also produces the clarity that may be needed to engage in the complex and difficult battles to reform government.

The other four dimensions of analysis are more specific conceptualizations of problems and particularly of alternatives to the status quo. The second dimension is structure: How should the public sector be organized? Governments have tended to be organized in a hierarchical manner, the principal format being large departments headed by a cabinet minister. This pattern remains the default option in most governments, but there is also a variety of alternative structures being introduced, more or less successfully, in almost all political systems. Thus, the structure of government is no longer the given that it once was, and scholars and practitioners should think about the options available and the relationships of structural decisions to the several emerging models of governance. Although some students of organizations tend to see structure as a relatively insignificant aspect of making an organization effective, I will argue that structure needs to be coordinated with other aspects of governance if the public sector is to be effective.

The third dimension of the models is management: How should the members of the public sector be recruited, motivated, and managed, and how should its financial resources be controlled? A clearly articulated model for personnel management has dominated thinking in the public sector. The thinking about structure has tended to question the conventional wisdom while largely retaining it, but in personnel management the dominant pattern has been to eliminate the old ways. These changes tend to replicate personnel management in the private sector and also tend to weaken the long-term commitment of government to its employees. Working for the public sector is now less different from working for the private sector, and one should think about the implications of those changes.

Similarly, there has been a dominant managerial ethos about the control of resources through budgeting and purchasing rules, which have tended toward the ex ante control of decisions by powerful central agencies. In this view management was largely a central function, with other actors following the direction of the central masters. There might have been some latitude for personal decisions by organizational heads, but the principal managerial tasks were carried out by conforming to rules rather than by exercising discretion. The emerging models of governing tend to shift the thinking about management toward greater autonomy and discretion for lower-echelon officials.

The fourth dimension focuses on the conception of the policy and the policy process: What should the role of the career public service be in the policy process, and more generally how should government seek to influence the private sector? These questions involve a variety of difficult issues about the procedures through which government should make its decisions as well as the content of those decisions. Too often, those two issues are conflated, with the assumption that certain actors (civil servants) will produce certain types of policies (interventionist). Therefore, more market-based instruments (vouchers, for example) that keep the bureaucrats out are preferable. Further, it is necessary to examine the impact of internal rules and regulations, such as civil service laws, in the policy process as the means that legislatures and judiciaries use to ensure that policies are made appropriately, if not always quickly.

These four emerging visions of governance each contain some conception of the public interest and an overall idea of what constitutes good government. The conceptions are often implicit in the models, but they are certainly apparent after a little reflection. Each has an answer to the question, "How should government govern, and what should it do?" This concern for the public interest is perhaps the most important component of the entire exercise, given that the fundamental question that anyone in government should be asking is whether the programs of reform adopted and the outcomes of the policy process are likely to benefit the public more than the system that is being abolished. All the reformers do believe that their changes will be for the best, although they often operate with very different conceptions of the public interest.

NOTES

1. We should separate imperialism *within* government—organizations fighting for control of problems and budgets—from more overt imperialism—government searching for problems to solve. The former is much more common that the latter.
2. There may now be a substitute consensus developing around the market (Grice 1995).
3. Nixon did, of course, attempt to curb some of the power of the existing bureaucracy and can hardly be considered a benign figure in America politics, but it is also too easy to ignore some of his domestic policy achievements.
4. For an excellent discussion of the (no longer?) conventional wisdom, see K. Walsh and Stewart (1992) for the United Kingdom and Stillman (1991) for the United States.
5. The implementation of merit ideals has been far from perfect in many of these settings, but the principles do tend to be enshrined in law.
6. It should be remembered, however, that at least for Wilson and the other Progressives, public administration was superior to politics: administration could be studied and reformed scientifically; politics was more an art (see Doig 1983).
7. The Republican Contract with America is pledged to reduce the volume and intrusiveness of rulemaking activity, but that may be difficult to do in any modern government.
8. Indeed, the most radical use of the variety of market-based reforms available to government was implemented by the Labour government of New Zealand (Scott, Bushnell, and Sallee 1990). More recently, the Social Democratic government in Sweden has undertaken a number of market-oriented changes in governance, and Tony Blair, leader of the Labour party in Britain, now accepts many of the administrative changes imposed during the Thatcher years.
9. Even some Conservatives now argue that the same excesses have occurred during the privatization of public utilities in the United Kingdom, as directors have awarded themselves massive salary increments with little or no control (Riddell 1995). The tales of scandals in privatized firms in Italy are also legion.
10. This autonomous role is not unfamiliar in the United States but is extremely unusual and threatening in Westminster systems. The Ponting affair in Britain and the Al-Mashat case in Canada are important examples of the significance of this change in the Westminster norms of governing (Chapman 1993; Sutherland 1991).
11. This pattern is already used rather widely in several European systems (see, for example, Fournier [1987] and his discussion of coordination within French government). In other settings—task forces, projets de mission, Projektgruppen, and a variety of other organizations—devices are used to coordinate and manage cross-cutting issues (Timsit 1988).

12. When there have been such attempts, the record appears to indicate that they have closed down generally as intended. Even if they did not, the real culprit would appear to be the legislatures that continued to fund them.
13. This is similar to the Tiebout model of local taxation and expenditure in public finance (see Tiebout 1956).

BIBLIOGRAPHY

Aberbach, J. D., R. D. Putnam, and B. A. Rockman (1981). *Politicians and Bureaucrats in Western Democracies.* Cambridge: Harvard University Press.
_____. (1988). Mandates or Mandarins? Control and Discretion in the Modern Administrative State. *Public Administration Review* 48: 607–12.
_____. (1989). On the Rise, Transformation, and Decline of Analysis in U.S. Government. *Governance* 2: 293–314.
Adler, M., and S. Asquith (1981). *Discretion and Power.* London: Heinemann.
Almond, G. A., and H. D. Lasswell (1934). Aggressive Behavior by Clients Toward Public Relief Administrators. *American Political Science Review* 28: 643–55.
Aucoin, P. (1990). Administrative Reform in Public Management: Paradigms, Principles, Paradoxes and Pendulums. *Governance* 3: 115–37.
Barzelay, M. (1992). *Breaking Through Bureaucracy.* Berkeley: University of California Press.
Beyme, K. von (1993). Regime Transition and Recruitment of Elites in Eastern Europe. *Governance* 6: 409 -25.
Blondel, J. (1988). Ministerial Careers and the Nature of Parliamentary Government: The Cases of Austria and Belgium. *European Journal of Political Research* 16: 51–71.
Blumann, C., and A. van Soligne (1989). La commission, agent d'exécution du droit communitaire: La Comitologie. In *La commission au couer du système institutionel des Communautés Européenes*, ed. J-V. Louis and D. Waelbroeck. Brussels: Universite de Bruxelles, Institut d'etudes Europeenes.
Bodiguel, J.-L., and L. Rouban (1991). *Le fonctionnarie detrône?* Paris: Presses de la Fondation Nationale des Science Politiques.
Boston, J. (1991). The Theoretical Underpinnings of State Restructuring in New Zealand. In *Reshaping the State*, ed. J. Boston et al. Auckland, New Zealand: Oxford University Press.
Braibanti, R. J. D. (1966). *Asian Bureaucratic Systems Emergent from the British Imperial Tradition.* Durham, NC: Duke University Press.
Caiden G. (1990). *Administrative Reform Comes of Age.* Berlin: Aldine de Gruyter.
Campbell, C. (1983). The Search for Coordination and Control: When and How Are Central Agencies the Answer? In *Organizing Government, Government Organizations*, C. Campbell and B. G. Peters. Pittsburgh: University of Pittsburgh Press.
_____. (1993). Public Service and Democratic Accountability. In *Ethics in Public Service*, ed. R. A. Chapman. Edinburgh. University of Edinburgh Press.
Campbell D. T. (1982). Experiments as Arguments. *Knowledge: Creation, Diffusion, Utilization* 3: 327–37.
Derlien, H.-U. (1991). Horizontal and Vertical Coordination of German EC-Policy. *Hallinnon Tutkimus* 27: 3–10.
_____. (1995). Germany. In *Learning from Experience: Lessons of Administrative Reform*, ed. J. Olsen and B. G. Peters. Pittsburgh: University of Pittsburgh Press.
Derlien, H.-U., and G. Szablowski (1993). *Regime Transitions, Elites and Bureaucrats in Eastern Europe.* Oxford: Blackwell.

Dunn. W. N. (1988). Methods of the Second Type: Coping with the Wilderness of Conventional Policy Analysis. *Policy Studies Review* 7: 720–37.

Friedman, M. (1962). *Capitalism and Freedom*. Chicago: University of Chicago Press.

Goodnow, F. J. (1900). *Politics and Administration: A Study in Government*. New York: Macmillan.

Grindle, M. S., and J. W. Thomas (1991). *Public Choices and Policy Change: The Political Economy of Reform in Developing Countries*. Baltimore: Johns Hopkins University Press.

Gulick, L. (1933). Politics, Administration and the "New Deal." *Annals of the American Academy of Political and Social Science* 169 (September): 45–78.

Gurwitt, R. (1992). A Government That Runs on Citizen Power. *Governing* 6 (3): 48–54.

Gustafsson, B. (1979). *Post-Industrial Society*. London: Croom Helm.

HMSO (1988). *Improving Management in Government: The Next Steps*. London: HMSO.

_____. (1993). *Career Planning and Succession Planning*. London: HMSO.

_____. (1994a). *The Civil Service: Continuity and Change*. London: HMSO, CM. 2627.

Harmon, M. M. (1995). *Responsibility as Paradox: A Critique of Rational Discourse on Government*, Thousand Oaks, CA: Sage.

Hayek, F. A. von (1968). *The Constitution of Liberty*. London: Macmillan.

Hesse, J. J. (1993). From Transformation to Modernization: Administrative Change in Central and Eastern Europe. *Public Administration* 71: 219–57.

Hood, C. (1989). The Tools of Government. Chatham, NJ: Chatham House.

_____. (1990). De-Sir Humphereying the Westminster Model of Bureaucracy. *Governance* 3: 205–14.

Hood, C., B. G. Peters, and H. Wollmann (1995). Public Management Reform: Putting the Consumer in the Driver's Seat. Unpublished paper, London School of Economics.

Ingraham, P. W. (1987). Building Bridges or Burning Them? The President, the Appointees and the Bureaucracy. *Public Administration Review* 47: 425–35.

_____. (1995a). *The Foundation of Merit: Public Service in American Democracy*. Baltimore: Johns Hopkins University Press.

_____. (1995b). Quality Management in Public Organizations: Prospects and Dilemmas. In *Governance in a Changing Environment*, ed. B. G. Peters and D. J. Savoie. Montreal: McGill/Queens University Press.

Johnson, R. N., and G. D. Liebcap (1994). *The Federal Civil Service System and the Problem of Bureaucracy*. Chicago: University of Chicago Press.

Kato, J. (1994). *The Problem of Bureaucratic Rationality: Tax Politics in Japan*. Princeton: Princeton University Press.

Kaufman, H. (1956). Emerging Doctrines of Public Administration. *American Political Science Review* 50: 1059–73.

_____. (1976). *Are Government Organizations Immortal?* Washington, D. C.: Brookings Institution.

_____. (1977). *Red Tape: Its Origins, Uses and Abuses*. Washington, D.C.: Brookings Institution.

_____. (1978). Reflections on Administrative Reorganization. In *Setting National Priorities: The 1978 Budget*, ed. J. A. Pechman. Washington, D.C.: Brookings Institution.

_____. (1991). *Time, Chance, and Organizations*. 2d ed. Chatham, NJ: Chatham House.

Kavanagh, D., and P. Morris (1994). *Consensus Politics: From Atlee to Major*. Oxford: Blackwell.

Kenis, P., and V., Schneider (1991). Policy Networks and Policy Analysis: Scrutinizing a New Analytical Toolbox. In *Policy Networks: Empirical Evidence and Theoretical Considerations*, ed. B. Marin and R. Mayntz. Boulder, CO: Westview.

Kerwin, C. M. (1994). *Rulemaking: How Government Agencies Write Law and Make Policy*. Washington, DC: CQ Press.

Koehn, P. H. (1990). *Public Policy and Administration in Africa: Lessons from Nigeria*. Boulder, CO: Westview Press.

Kooliman, J. (1993). Governance and Governability: Using Complexity, Dynamics and Diversity. In *Modern Governance*, ed. J. Kooliman. London: Sage.

Lan, Z., and D. H. Rosenbloom (1992). Public Administration in Transition? *Public Administration Review* 52: 535-37.

Lipsky, M. (1980). *Street-level Bureaucracy.* New York: Russell Sage Foundation.

Machinery of Government Committee (1918). *Report.* Cmnd. 9320. London: HMSO. Haldane Report.

March, J. G., and J. P. Olsen (1983). Organizing Political Life: What Administrative Reform Tells Us About Governing. *American Political Science Review* 77: 281-97.

Milward, H. B. (forthcoming). Symposium on the Hollow State: Capacity, Control and Performance in Interorganizational Settings. *Journal of Public Administration Research and Theory.*

Mishan, E. J. (1988). *Cost-benefit Analysis: An Informal Introduction.* 4th ed. London: Unwin-Hyman.

Mommsen, W. J. (1989). *The Political and Social Theory of Max Weber: Collected Essays.* Oxford: Polity Press.

Northcote, S., and Trevelyan, C. (1853). *Report on the Organization of the Permanent Civil Service.* Reprinted as Appendix B. Vol. 1, Committee on the Civil Service *Report* (The Fulton Report). London: HMSO, 1968.

Novick, D. (1965). *Program Budgeting, Program Analysis and the Federal Budget.* Cambridge: Harvard University Press.

Osborne, D., and T. Gaebler (1992). *Reinventing Government.* Reading. MA Addison-Wesley.

Parris, H. (1969). *Constitutional Bureaucracy.* London: George Allen and Unwin.

Peacock, A. T., and H. Willgerodt (1989). *Germany's Social Market Economy: Origins and Evolution.* Basingstoke, UK: Macmillan.

Perry, J., and H. G. Rainey (1988). The Public-Private Distinction in Organization Theory: A Critique and a Research Strategy. *Academy of Management Review* 13.

Peters, B. G. (1985). Administrative Change and the Grace Commission. In *The Unfinished Agenda for Civil Service Reform*, ed. C. H. Levine. Washington, DC: Brookings Institution.

———. (1992). Public Policy and Public Bureaucracy. In *History and Context in Comparative Public Policy*, ed. D. Ashford. Pittsburgh: University of Pittsburgh Press.

———. (1995a). The Politics of Bureaucratic Change in Transitional Governments. *International Social Science Journal*, 147: 122-36.

———. (1996). The Antiphons of Administrative Reform. Unpublished paper, Department of Political Science, University of Pittsburgh.

Peters, B. G., and B. W. Hogwood (1985). In Search of the Issue-Attention Cycle. *Journal of Politics* 47: 238-53.

———. (1988). Births, Deaths and Marriages: Organizational Change in the U.S. Federal Bureaucracy. *American Journal of Public Administration* 18: 119-33.

Peters, B. G., and J. Loughlin (1995). State Traditions and Administrative Reform. Paper, Department of Political Science, University of Pittsburgh.

Peters, B. G., and D. J. Savoie (1994a). Civil Service Reform: Misdiagnosing the Patient. *Public Administration Review* 54: 418-25.

———. (1994b). Reinventing Osborne and Gaebler: Lessons from the Gore Commission. *Canadian Public Administration* 37: 302-22.

Peters, B. G., and Wright, V. (1996). The Public Bureaucracy. In *The New Handbook of Political Science*, ed. R. E. Goodin and H. D. Klingemann. Oxford: Oxford University Press.

Plowden, W. (1994). *Ministers and Mandarins.* London: Institute for Public Policy Research.

Public Money and Management (1994). Reorganizing Local Government, 14, 1 (theme issue).

———. (1995). Fraud and Corruption in the Public Sector, 15, 1 (theme issue).

Rhodes, R. A. W. (1992). Local Government Finance. In *Implementing Thatcherite Policies: Audit of an Era*, ed. D. Marsh and R. A. W. Rhodes. Buckingham, UK: Open University Press.

_____. (1994). The Hollowing Out of the State. *Political Quarterly* 65: 138-51.

Richards, S. (1992). Changing Patterns of Legitimation in Public Management. *Public Policy and Administration* 7: 15-28.

Riggs, Fred W. (1964). *Administration in Developing Countries*. Boston: Houghton-Mifflin.

Rose, R., and B. G. Peters (1978). *Can Government Go Bankrupt?* New York: Basic Books.

Savoie, D. J. (1990). *The Politics of Public Spending in Canada*. Toronto: University of Toronto Press.

_____. (1995b). *Central Agencies: Looking Backward*. Ottawa: Canadian Centre for Management Development.

Sawer, M. (1982). Political Manifestation of Australian Libertarianism. In *Australia and the New Right*, ed. M. Sawer. Sydney: George Allen and Unwin.

Scharpf, F. W. (1989). Decision Rules, Decision Styles and Policy Choices. *Journal of Theoretical Politics* 1: 149-76.

_____. (1991). Die Handlungsfähigkeit des Staates am Ende des zwanzigsten Jahrhunderts. *Politische Vierteiljahrschrift* 4: 621-34.

Schon, D., and M. Rein (1994). *Frame Reflection: Resolving Intractable Policy Issues*. New York: Basic Books.

Self, P. (1993). *Government by the Market?* Boulder, CO: Westview.

Silberman, B. S. (1993). *Cages of Reason: The Rise of the Rational State in France, Japan, the United States and Great Britain*. Chicago: University of Chicago Press.

Simon, H. (1947). *Administrative Behavior*. New York: Free Press.

Skowronek, S. (1982). *Building a New American State: The Expansion of National Administrative Capacity, 1877-1920*. Cambridge: Cambridge University Press.

Smart, H. (1991). *Criticism and Public Rationality: Professional Rigidity and the Search for Caring Government*. London: Routledge.

Spulbar, N. (1989). *Managing the American Economy: From Roosevelt to Reagan*. Bloomington: Indiana University Press.

Ståhlberg, K. (1987). The Politicization of Public Administration: Notes on the Concepts, Causes and Consequences of Politicization. *International Review of Administrative Science* 53: 363-82.

Tellier, P. M. (1900). Public Service 2000: The Renewal of the Public Service. *Canadian Public Administration* 33: 123-32.

Terry, L. D. (1995). *Leadership of Public Bureaucracies: The Administrator as Conservator*. Thousand Oaks, CA: Sage.

Thomas, J. C. (1993). Public Involvement and Government Effectiveness. *Administration and Society* 24: 444-69.

Thompson, V. A. (1975). *Without Sympathy or Enthusiasm: The Problem of Administrative Compassion*. University: University of Alabama Press.

Tully, S. (1995). Finally, Colleges Start to Cut Their Crazy Costs. *Fortune* 131 (8): 110-14.

Waldo, D. (1968). Scope of the Theory of Public Administration. *Annals of the American Academy of Political and Social Sciences* 8:1-26.

Walters, J. (1992a). How Not to Reform Civil Service. *Governing* 6 (2): 30-34.

Weber, M. (1958). Bureaucracy. In *From Max Weber: Essays in Sociology*, ed. H. H. Gerth and C. W. Mills. New York: Oxford University Press.

Wilson, G. (1994). The Westminster Model in Comparative Perspective. In *Developing Democracy*, ed. I. Budge and D. McKay. London: Sage.

Wilson, J. Q. (1989). *Bureaucracy*. New York: Free Press.

Wilson, W. (1887). The Study of Administration. *Political Science Quarterly* 2: 197–222.
Wright, V., and B. G. Peters (1996). Public Administration: Change and Redefinition. In *New Handbook of Political Science*, ed. R. E. Goodin. Oxford: Oxford University Press.

11

Graeme A. Hodge

LEARNING TO GET THE BALANCE IN PRIVATIZATION

Pressures for greater privatization within public sector activities have occurred as part of a much broader context. This context has been international in scope, and has been part of a wider move of government organizations away from the traditional practices of administration, towards a style of managing for results. Processes of contracting and competitive testing are now becoming well developed in many areas—at least by the look of the guidelines appearing.[1] Likewise, the processes of selling enterprises have also been further developed.

My focus in this chapter is on the leanings from the international evidence on privatization and on the policy implications of these. Human services, information technology outsourcing, refuse collection, history, and politics each have something to teach us if we seek to get the best value balance from privatizing public sector services. In striving to deliver better services, whether through the sale of enterprises or through contracting out, a learning approach is desirable. The task is to observe, to analyze, and to question as we move forward.

I will firstly look at the question of a learning philosophy, and contrast this against other philosophies operating inside reforming public agencies. Some comments on theories will then be made. These theories underpin the thrust towards privatization, and it would be a sensible part of our learning to discuss the extent to which the predictions of these theories appear to have been met, in retrospect. Next, I will look at the broad meta-analytic findings from my work on contracting out services and the policy implications of these to public sector services as a whole. As a part of this, I will explore the practices of private companies as well. Finally, I will look at the meta-analytic findings of enterprise sales. Based on these, I will investigate some of the policy implications and suggest tentative directions for future privatization reforms.

THE LEARNING PHILOSOPHY

The first thing that might be said about many government reforms—whether they be privatization or the strengthening of competition—is that within the dimension of economics, the aims of reforms are nearly always laudable. In theory, for instance, privatization should encourage more efficient market behavior, and competition should drive down prices through greater innovation and intelligent production. It is not so much the aims of reforms on which we ought to base our discussions, however, but the reality of achievements in reform as well as the reality of the extent to which existing circumstances are changed for the better or worse. In a sense, privatization, competition or other public sector reforms can become like motherhood. No one would argue against them in principle. Nonetheless, political leaders continue to argue that such reforms are urgently needed, and that they must proceed without being slowed by messy debate. The more ardently the suggestion is made that we "take this reform pill because it's good for you," the more we might want to look at the extent to which the community as the patient benefits from the medicine.

Of course, in asking questions in today's managerial climate, individuals run the risk of being labeled as someone who is "against us": There appears to have been an increasing tendency to be either with privatization reformers or against them these days—a kind of "us and them" syndrome. It is as if government reform was just a military operation requiring complete compliance from all cogs within the machine rather than reform implementation being the output of an evolutionary and adaptive process as suggested two decades ago (Majone and Wildavsky 1978, Browne and Wildavsky 1984), or a learning process as authors such as Senge (1992) suggest more recently.

But learning requires a commitment to open evaluation and careful assessment. Which evaluations of, say, competition policy ought we believe? Do we take the political evaluation in which selective results are advertised and through which we are told yet again that contracting and competition reforms are good for us—just trust me . . . benefits will trickle through! On the other hand, should we believe the concerns from rural citizens who saw a wave of increased bank fees and reduced postal services?

There is no doubt that all nations need to be more cognizant of finite resources and competitiveness in the face of globalization. The question, however, is not whether this need exists, but the real extent of the problem, its priority against other competing public policy issues, and how best we might simultaneously improve our use of resources and our competitiveness whilst being equitable. It is an inherently political question and is thus one of balance. Focusing simply on getting the best value for our limited resources, it would seem to make healthy sense if we were to base our proposed strategies on our learnings to date from empirical implementation. So, in the area of competitive tendering and contracting, what does the theory say? What does the evidence say? Likewise, for the sale of enterprises, what are the lessons?

THEORY

There [is] a large amount of theoretical and conceptual information providing a framework for the privatization of government services. These conceptual bases have included theories of public choice, transaction cost economics, and managerialism, to name three. These three areas have in common a philosophy that people are inherently selfish, and that economic interests provide the primary motivation and lubricant of human behavior. For contracting out government services, they also suggest that firms ought to minimize the costs of transacting their business by being careful about whether services are provided using in-house staff or through external parties.

These academic theories have been exceedingly influential in providing supporting frameworks to underpin political reforms, but understandably, have also been the subject of much ideological and academic debate.

Those supporting moves towards a greater use of the private sector argue that, in line with the predictions of public choice theoretical ideas, government organizations are often captured by those who traditionally supply the services of the organization, and that in the absence of the profit motive, bureaucrats in government maximize the size of their own bureau rather than maximizing benefits to customers or citizens. In other words, bureaucrats look after their own interest, not the public interest. Proponents point out that organizations need to more carefully analyze decisions on whether to provide services using in-house resources or else buy services from external sources through a contract. In an age where corporate planning objectives, targets, and activity-based costing are becoming the norm, they argue that the role of government nowadays should be viewed as establishing high-level objectives and developing policies, rather than actually delivering the services per se. As Osborne and Gaebler (1993) put it, government ought to "steer not row."

Those not supporting greater use of the private sector in the provision of public services point out that public choice ideas are used selectively. Thus, for example, the potential for self-interest to lead to service cost reductions is emphasized, rather than the potential of self-interest to lead to higher management salaries, or to underpin a greater willingness by managers to be more obedient to a specific political direction for the sake of bonus payments. Again, the pressure of self-interest leading to greater innovation and entrepreneurship is emphasized rather than self-interest leading to increased fraud and corruption, the reality that cozy relationships between businesses and ministers from political parties do occur, and the propensity for more information to be deemed commercial-in-confidence to ensure secrecy. Furthermore, they also argue that this theory is interesting, but it is just that: only a theory. Policy choices for public organizations ought to be based not on a set of theories, but on the basis of our past experience of what has worked well and what has not. Ideologically charged perfect theory always wins in a comparison with an imperfect current reality.

Notions of managerialism also underpin current reforms. The phrase "managing for results" encapsulates this philosophy in which objectives are established, strategies developed, programs are organized and resourced, and then performance is measured in terms of the efficiency and effectiveness of achieving objectives. Its central tenets extend these principles, emphasizing management skills, quantified performance targets, and devolution. Further, it encompasses the separation of policy from implementation, commercial from noncommercial functions, and the use of private sector practices such as corporate plans, short term contracts, monetary incentives, and cost-cutting. Benefits of this approach have included stronger partnerships with the private sector, greater cost consciousness in the knowledge of actual costs of delivering activities and products, and economic savings. This set of ideas has also, however, been criticized as an ideology that assumes that better management will prove an effective solvent for a wide range of economic and social ills (Pollitt 1993). Improvements to the productivity of public services have encouraged the view that management improvements can solve problems and make decisions previously conceived of as political in nature. The unquestioning application of techniques may well amount to simplistic ideology, but whether we agree with this or not, a narrowed emphasis on quantified targets and measures has often occurred at the expense of more fundamental areas such as relationships and community.

THE EFFECTIVENESS OF CONTRACTING OUT SERVICES

How should we interpret the research conclusions on the effectiveness of contracting out government services? How did the benefits compare to the theoretical predictions? What are the policy implications here?

Focusing not on newspaper reports, anecdotes, or government ideology, my study looked at the available international empirical measurements that have been made of service quality and costs under contracting. In essence, my research revealed several learnings. These were generally far more measured than much of the current policy discourse on the subject of contracting and outsourcing. I observed firstly that a significant average saving of around 6 percent (12 percent)[2] is probably experienced in contracting public sector services overall. This modest average cost saving was in contrast to the 20 to 30 percent often quoted by proponents of contracting, by some management consultants, or as seen in press and advertising statements. That said, the bulk of the documented evidence on contracting related to strong savings in the areas of garbage collection, cleaning, and maintenance services (i.e., between 19 and 30 percent). These findings supported the idea that large cost savings can be made for these specific areas.

For many other services however, particularly those more difficult to define and measure, little or no savings were found from the empirical evidence (which varied between an 8 percent saving and a 24 percent increase). Although this finding could have been influenced by the availability of only a few research measurements, even when combined as a group, little significant cost savings were evident. Statistically, cost savings available from different services were found to be quite different (i.e., heterogeneous). These findings were enlightening, and contrasted the claims of privatization proponents who espouse contracting out all government services as a cure-all solution to public sector ills.

In terms of service quality, the little empirical evidence available indicated that, on average, service quality was unaffected by contracting. Sometimes it was better, sometimes not. This implied that the claims of both sides were extreme. Service quality was not as a rule generally improved, as claimed by one side, or reduced, as claimed by the other.

Of more importance was the finding that contracting either in-house or outside the organization both led to cost savings. Thus, service specification and competition appeared to be the drivers of efficiency, not the sector doing the work. This finding is an important one. The question of gains achievable by enabling private provision in preference to public provision seemed to be resolved through the learning that gains were possible by contracting with either sector. Such an assessment of private sector versus public sector efficiency has major implications for policy reforms to the extent that competition and contracting policy is seen as an agenda to transfer service provision to the private or market sector rather than simply to improve value for money.

A significant flow-on also seemed to operate in that agencies not contracting services, but in areas adjacent to those doing so, showed cost reductions of around four-fifths that for areas contracting out. The presence of beneficial flow-on effects from areas subject to contracting to those adjacent to these reforms was interesting. Evidently, although these areas were not themselves actually contracting out services, the threat of competition and the acquisition of new financial performance knowledge itself also led to real performance improvements. Again, such a finding has implications for the use of contracting as a public sector reform. It is not necessary to contract all services comprehensively in order to achieve extensive cost savings. A little bit of contracting reform appears to go a long way.

The review of contracting research findings also indicated that some unfortunate social impacts occurred with contracting reforms. Women and minority groups appeared to bear the brunt of contracting efficiencies consistently from the international studies. To the extent that governments continue to see themselves as having a role in matters of equity as well as economic reform, this trade-off will need to be recognized explicitly in policymaking. Likewise, the potential for businesses to exert undue influence over political decisions, as well as the lack of transparency due to arrangements now being deemed "commercial-in-confidence," were also both seen to be real risks in the review.[3] Again, reform policies espousing cost savings through contracting need to be aligned with actions to protect and strengthen checks and balances on government. The review concluded that contracting-out decisions for governments were clearly more than simply commercial in nature. The inclusion of social impacts, the recognition of business influence in political decisionmaking, and issues such as conflicts of interest and commercial-in-confidence need to be given more attention than has been evident to date.

Several of these areas deserve some further exploration under our learning philosophy, particularly where there may be implications for future contracting reforms.

Cost Savings

The first point is that large differences still appear to arise as new evidence on contracting cost savings comes to light. We might recall that the early economic studies of Domberger, Meadowcroft, and Thompson (1986, 1987) were instrumental in the field and suggested that contracting either in-house or externally was likely to result in cost savings of around 20 percent for garbage collection and cleaning services. This work was the source of the now popular "20 percent rule." Interestingly, more recent surveys of public sector managers have also consistently reported sizeable savings of around 20 percent or more from the use of competitive contracting over a range of service types. Examples here include:

- average reported cost savings from Domberger's CTC Consulting Group of 20 percent, 20 percent, and 26 percent for surveys of managers in the Australian states of New South Wales, Western Australia, and Victoria,[4] and

- reported average savings of between 26 percent and "one-third" for defense-related services in Canada, United Kingdom, and Australia (Howard 1998, Badelow 1988).[5]

Against these reports are the more modest average cost savings of around 6 percent found in the research in this book, as well as in other recent international surveys. These have included two further major survey reports from high-profile management consulting companies—the PA Consulting Group (1997) and Deloitte and Touche Consulting Group (1997)—both of which have similarly reported more modest cost-savings estimates for outsourcing. These international surveys suggest that average cost savings were likely to be very modest, at around 2 to 10 percent, to the extent that they exist at all. PA Consulting, for instance, reported an average cost reduction for outsourcing contracts outside the area of information technology (IT) at 10 percent for private firms. For IT, the PA Consulting report put the average cost reduction reported in Australia at just 2 percent, whilst Deloitte and Touche, looking at both private and public organizations, were even more circumspect. They noted that for their recent survey as well as earlier surveys, "then, as now, significant savings are rarely realized" for IT outsourcing. Recent support for more modest cost-savings estimates has also come from further international research into information technology outsourcing. Willcocks (1998) looked at 116 companies in the U.S. and Britain that pursued large-scale, single-vendor outsourcing contracts. His study reported that some 53 percent of these companies were not making savings from outsourcing, and that a total of some 64 percent of companies either regarded outsourcing as a failure (37 percent) or had mixed results (27 percent). Most organizations were reported to have underestimated the cost of outsourcing and the number of people and capabilities needed to oversee the project.

The contrast between these two sets of findings is striking. Reasons for this difference are largely unknown, though we might surmise several. The veracity of cost-savings reports from managers may well be questionable on the grounds that those answering the questionnaires have a dubious personal incentive for accuracy in reporting. Are managers always more optimistic than accurate when a manager's salary depends on implementing reforms to the system? To what extent might it have been possible for managers to simply report the more successful contracts rather than all contracts undertaken? This would presumably apply to both public sector and private sector surveys, although the gap between optimism and accuracy may be greater in the public sector, where reform may be seen as a political rather than a solely commercial issue. The other reason for doubting the veracity of cost-savings reports from public sector managers is that more formal evidence of savings such as reduced departmental budget levels has not been consistently observed. The cost-savings claims seem to have little or no correlation with real budget reductions. It may be that such differences are due to the use of different survey or research methods or else the study of quite different services. It may also be a reflection of the degree to which such estimates continue to vary wildly or continue to be based on differing assumptions.[6] Differences may also have arisen due to the differing savings that might be expected from outsourcing activities from the public and private sectors, particularly if one assumes, for instance, that private sector activities are always inherently more efficient, and hence smaller cost savings could be expected when private firms outsource.

An alternative interpretation of this discrepancy between more modest cost-savings results and others is that higher levels of savings are indeed accurate, and show that contracting is simply a strong lever for changed workloads, service levels, and production arrangements. It is useful to recall that the strongest correlation in the research was the simple relationship always found in studies between the amount of work done and the cost of that work. In other words, all other things being equal, a company will, on average, get what it pays for. Thus, when we hear of, say, a 40 percent cost saving through contracting out services, the strongest probability in my mind is that we are not doing in future what we did in the past. In all likelihood, we have carefully reviewed what work is really required, along with the levels of service, and it has been restructured. Desirable reform to our services and practices is at issue here, not necessarily the use of contracting out the service per se. Having said this, of course, it must also be added that contracting is indeed a powerful lever for such change to service levels, quality levels, and staffing levels and structures. There is no doubt that most workplaces have the potential for reviewing work outputs, as well as improving practices and procedures. This may be particularly so in cases such as defense services, which may have tended to be more insulated from budget-cutting pressures that have driven efficiencies in other areas of the public sector over the past decade or so.

There is a further alternative interpretation. Perhaps the two statements "contracting is accompanied by large cost savings" and "contracting alone results only in modest cost savings" are both partly true. In other words, contracting many services may well result in cost-savings gains on average, partly through the contracting process and partly through the thorough review of outputs and levels of service, as well as the restructuring activities that almost inevitably accompany contracts. The truth of contracting may well be in the middle, rather than at either extreme.

DO CONTRACTING BENEFITS OUTWEIGH COSTS IN PUBLIC SECTOR SERVICES?

A central observation made in this research based on the international empirical evidence suggested that cost savings for contracting out different public sector services were likely to be varied rather than simply being identical. Our findings were that nontraditional services experienced lower real cost savings on outsourcing. Cautionary advice relating to problems with applying competitive contracting in areas such as human services has also arisen in Victoria through the social sector (People Together Project 1998, Rance 1999). With this knowledge, we might proceed with the guiding philosophy of caution. But why, on a theoretical basis, might we expect differing effectiveness for contracting reforms for different services?

Importantly, what is left undiscussed by many outsourcing proponents is the difficult to measure cost of transactions, the ongoing costs associated with managing contracts (or governance costs), and the overall costs to the organization of organizing market competition and undertaking the transition to the new arrangements. This is an increasingly important area of the debate—particularly for complex services that can be difficult to define and tricky to measure. In general, none of these costs are well researched, let alone openly debated.[7]

Some of the theoretical ideas of Williamson (1975) as well as others are useful here, however. His transaction cost analysis theory adopted five main building blocks as a basis for explaining the development of large vertically integrated firms in capitalist economies. Paradoxically, this theory, which explains why private companies produce the majority of their services in-house, is one of the most useful foundations for exploring the effectiveness of outsourcing public sector services. Williamson's argument is that firms aim to minimize the costs of transacting their business. He suggests that this aim can often be achieved by vertical integration, that is, by taking over either the firms to whom they sell or else their suppliers. He sees large hierarchical firms in capitalist economies as being the result of these firms aiming to minimize transaction costs. Governance structures is a branch of transaction cost theory, and this theoretical area deals with alternative forms of organization structure, the contracting processes employed to undertake services, and the resulting transaction costs (Spicer et al. 1991). This area of theory dates back to the work of Ronald Coase over half a century ago (Coase 1937). The conceptual building blocks to the theory of transaction cost economics include uncertainty, frequency, asset specificity, measurability of attributes, bounded rationality, and opportunism (Ashton 1998). These may have potential relevance in the application of outsourcing to many public sector services. Uncertainty refers to the inability to foresee or control changes in the contractual environment. Contracts are unavoidably incomplete in the face of uncertainty and the limits to human rationality. The concept of frequency simply says that when few transactions occur between two parties, more general (and cheaper) governance structures will be adopted even though this will be less than ideal. The notion of asset specificity refers to the extent to which resources required to complete the transaction can be productively used elsewhere. Measurability is necessary to reduce the scope for opportunism. The greater the complexity of measurement, the greater the cost of writing, negotiating, and monitoring contracts.

What are the implications of this theory for contracting public sector services? Ashton (1998), for instance, notes that if transactions are infrequent, asset-specific, difficult to measure, or involve uncertainty, then the splitting of purchasers and providers inside an organization is likely to involve larger transaction costs. Ashton's work looked particularly at the area of health services, but parallels are still likely to exist with many other public sector services. After all, characteristics such as uncertainty, asset specificity, measurability of attributes, bounded rationality, and opportunism have been central to some public sector services for centuries. The suggestion is therefore that contracting for some services may not enhance, and may even reduce, the efficiency of public sector services because the additional transaction costs are likely to outweigh any gains in technical efficiency.

Aspects of this theory have of course been contested,[8] whilst acknowledging the contribution to our understanding of alternative governance structures.

De Hoog (1990) looks at the notion of the competitive market as the basis for producing business outputs, and assesses the belief that the competition paradigm is the optimum when employing contracts. She argues that the competition model for contracting is but one of three, as show in Figure 11.1.

FIGURE 11.1   *Models for Contracting Services*

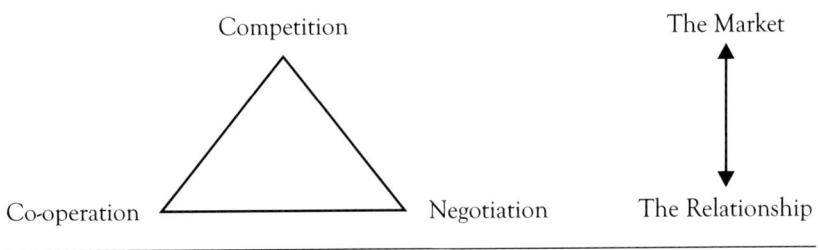

She stresses that "there is no one best way to contract for services." Each model for contracting has its advantages and its weaknesses. Competition, for instance, stresses the complete specification of services, wide solicitation, and objective award decision and monitoring procedures. It can give financial benefits under certain assumptions, and certainly requires the use of powerful service-definition tools. However, its disadvantages in some public sector service areas include the fact that multiple suppliers may not exist, transaction costs can be high, and a complete specification of services may simply not be practical or even possible. Relational contracting through either the negotiation or cooperation models, on the other hand, involves contracting with one or a few suppliers of your choice, partly specifying services, and then negotiating on the services to be delivered. The contractor chosen may well have had a long-term relationship with the client. The advantages of these types of contracts are that a limited number of suppliers are usually involved, transaction costs are low, and that uncertainty and complexity can be well accommodated. The disadvantages of such contracts are that the contracting process is more susceptible to decisions being made through "cozy" relationships or political allies, processes are typically closed with fewer systemic control mechanisms, and that, overall, familiarity risks breeding complacency. Thus, it is not surprising that the use of partnering or cooperative models may be seen by proponents of outsourcing as desirable, whilst to others such arrangements are criticized as being too cozy. Drawing on De Hoog's work, some truth exists in both claims.

Looking to the future, it could be questioned whether we now have some re-learning to do. To the extent that we continue applying contracting to everything that moves, we are bound to rediscover what the private sector found out decades ago. For the majority of business production transactions, relationship contracts (using cooperation with a limited number of external parties, or else using negotiation with in-house staff) are likely to be far more cost effective than full market testing.

PRIVATE SECTOR FIRMS AND MARKETS

Another learning from this research was that savings and reform gains were possible through contracting with either the public or the private sectors, rather than solely through one or the other. What do the ideas of transaction cost economics and, for that matter, notions of the market and the popular purchaser/provider split model contribute to our understanding of how contracting may help to provide better public sector services? There notions do have direct application in contemplating the range of future delivery mechanisms. For instance, the use of both the negotiation and cooperation models in preference to the competition model may offer an alternative framework enabling the use of in-house teams, or the coproduction of services with another public or not-for-profit agency, under appropriately specified service contracts. Indeed, it may well be that the future direction taken in contracting out government services—as we rediscover the real cost of transactions—is to repackage contracting in terms of public-private partnerships or strategic alliances in the fashionable consulting jargon. To the extent that this becomes the case, we will of course run the risk of cozy relationships and undue influence from organization or corporate interests.

On the issue of relying more on private sector energies and market forces, it is often difficult to separate out the rhetoric from the reality—the politics from the practice. We all recognize that a large part of the political process is concerned with the rhetorical and the symbolic. But at least some attempt to try to separate the two is desirable if we are to determine the cost advantages possible through reengineering, restructuring, or reduction of services, as well as through the policy of outsourcing. Indeed, it is a prerequisite if we are to learn how to get the best value for our resources through the notion of the competitive market or, alternatively, the use of cooperation or negotiation. We might reflect on the practices of private sector companies and ask why, in the information technology area, for example, do Australian private companies currently outsource only 29 percent of their activities?[9] Again, why are only 15 percent of business support functions outsourced internationally?[10] Looking at all company expenditures, why would almost four out of five dollars spent stay in-house?[11] Transaction costs most likely have a lot to do with it. Relying on previously formed personal relationships that have worked out in the past is much more efficient than repeatedly going through a process of competitive tenders for the sake of fairness. It may well be that government agencies ought to go through competitive tendering processes to get business out to the private sector market, but to the extent that such processes are likely to increase transaction costs, and reduce resources available for other activities, this needs to be recognized explicitly. If business functions such as information technology, which are now seen as not belonging in government, result in negligible cost gains or cost increases when outsourced, the role of government has simply been remixed rather than reformed or reinvented. Rather than using contracting as a sensible business tool, and recognizing the beneficial flow-ons likely from judicious use of such reforms, it has been used as an element of a command structure driving by an ideology.

PROBITY, ACCOUNTABILITY, AND GOVERNANCE

Another learning from this research recognized the existence of social impacts and the possibility of undue business influence in political decisionmaking. Focusing on the latter of these two issues, it was suggested that a more contractual state led to issues such as conflict of interest and commercial-in-confidence rising in prominence. At the present time, when we are applying the contracting philosophy in a wholesale manner across all public sector service, I have no doubt we will be rediscovering some of the lessons of the past. Many of these lessons are likely to relate to issues of commercial-in-confidence, probity, conflicts of interest, tender processes, and the range of other different expectations that the community holds for the public sector compared to private companies. Let us be clear: It is not one political leaning or other that is at issue here. It is the need to be continually vigilant to balance our personal and political behavior with our desire for better organizational productivity and growth. It is the need to understand why the rigidity of public sector tender and procurement processes may well prevent the public sector from always achieving the benefits that the private sector can gain from outsourcing.[12]

The issue of accountability also seems to be a significant sleeper. It is typically over-simplified into terms of basic financial or customer interests alone, rather than the interests of citizens, of democratic process, or of advocacy roles for industry or local communities. Are some public sector services complex and not necessarily amenable to the simple-linear-sequential business model? I suspect so. Establishing the community's expectations on the potential roles of nongovernment or private companies across a breadth of services from justice through to human services or defense may be sensible here. Applying a cautious "learn as we progress" approach may therefore be the most sensible option in redefining our organizational arrangements, although I suspect we will continue to learn about the real impacts of changes from telephone calls to ministers, from adverse newspaper reports, and through political dynamics.

We certainly now know that it is physically possible to outsource just about anything. Although possible, whether it is sensible or desirable for good governance is another question.

The future for governance and accountability is likely to be somewhat predictable in some senses. Simply watch the incentives. If we learn anything from public choice ideas, it is that incentives to individuals are a strong determinant. So, what are the incentives relating to outsourcing? Wilson (1989) suggests, in his book *Bureaucracy: What Government Agencies Do and Why They Do It*, that when the military purchases new systems of any sort it puts in train a procurement bureaucracy designed not for efficiency but to avoid making a bad or unfair decision. This reputedly amounts to more than 1,200 pages of Federal Acquisition Regulation and Defense Regulation Acquisition as well as other DOD directives, Congressional authorization, and unwritten guidance! Incentives are designed to avoid waste, fraud, and abuse. As a consequence, almost everyone in the U.S. Defense "system" has an incentive, according to Wilson, "to overstate the benefits and understate the costs of new systems." We are not purchasing new defense systems here, but the point is still worthy of consideration. New service delivery systems are indeed being purchased by managers whose personal incentives are intimately bound up within the need for the reform itself to be seen as successful. What *are* the behavioral incentives at work here, and for whom are they working?

Looking forward again, the future environment is also likely to continue to involve a balance of both sectors—rather than one dominating the other. The history of many nations reminds us that contracting out services is not new at all for the public sector. One hundred years ago, Australia witnessed the well-developed practice of competitive contracting and tendering, honed over several decades, being interrupted by a

Royal Commission which, in 1896, found widespread malpractice in the contracting-out system, including schedule rigging and inferior work. This led to the use of direct (in-house) labor forces. Subsequent decades saw periodic swings towards and away from the average in-house and external labor mix. In terms of history, therefore, perhaps we ought to regard ourselves as simply being further along a path of "well-rehearsed argument" on the effectiveness, efficiency, and probity of these two types of service production systems (McIntosh, Shauness, and Wettenhall 1997).

THE EFFECTIVENESS OF SELLING ENTERPRISES

Looking now at the sale of enterprises, how should we interpret the research conclusions here? Were the benefits promised in theory realized, and what are consequential policy implications?

Again, this research essentially revealed several learnings. These generally followed the flavor of previous narrative reviews, but with some additional nuances as well. We found firstly that reported labor productivity improvements had been significant following privatizations—consistent with reductions in overmanning. Importantly, though, these productivity gains were interpreted as having been due mainly to the changing external environment, with only a small part of this gain being associated with the enterprise sale itself. Having said this, we observed that the labor-productivity gains reported for privatizations were significantly greater than those meager gains measured from nationalizations in the United Kingdom. Thus, although we might conclude that productivity gains from enterprise sales have not been as large as we had hoped, reported gains have certainly outstripped those for nationalizations. These changes are broadly in line with our expectations that privately owned firms should generally have higher labor productivity.

We also observed that significant improvements in enterprise financial performance were reported with privatizations. In particular, we saw better returns on sales and returns on equity being reported. Improvements in financial performance reported for different countries varied markedly, with effect sized for Chile over three times those produced for the United Kingdom. Looking also at some limited effect-size data for privatization as a reform compared to nationalization as a reform, we found that financial performance improvements were not different from a statistical perspective. This was a surprise. Likewise, the reported financial improvements that accompanied privatization tested as not significantly different from those measured in control groups that were not privatized. I concluded here that, although reported firm financial performance did improve significantly, there is real doubt as to whether privatization per se caused them. These findings were unexpected, and did not conform to my prior expectations.

Next, the firm's investment behavior was analyzed. We concluded here that, on average, a positive association was present after privatizations. In other words, reported capital investment increased following privatization. Returns to shareholders were also on average significantly positive, with returns to the United Kingdom shareholders being much greater than those in Chile. Evidently, firms invested more after privatization, and people who invest in the initial float did well.

The last of our economic interests concerned the broader question of national economic performance. Here, the data did not support a simple direct link between the size of the private sector and economic growth. In all likelihood, the connection, assuming there is one, is probably more sophisticated and subtle.

On the social-performance dimension, most narrative assessments of service prices concluded that promises of price reductions and greater competition had not generally been delivered. This was due to a preoccupation with ensuring a rapid and politically successful transfer of ownership. The high profile of benefits promised to citizens in this area contrasted the low profile and few measurements made to date. The narrative review revealed service-quality findings on both sides, with some services better and some worse. For the one available study, British Telecom, a positive service-quality improvement was found on average. Of great interest was the analysis of the impacts of regulatory intensity and public accountability requirements for this case. Here, the meta-analysis suggested that the performance-improvement effects from enhanced regulatory and public accountability requirements were several times that associated with the change in ownership. In other words, these measurements suggested that the best payoffs for improved performance from the customer's perspective were most likely to come from strengthening regulatory conditions and enhancing accountability requirements for firms rather than from the transfer of ownership. Although these findings must be regarded as preliminary, they are also fundamentally important, and deserve more research attention in the future.

Returning to observations of social aspects of privatization, I concluded that the social contours of inequality appear unfortunately to have deepened. Low-income consumers have generally been affected more than others. Emphasizing growing disparities, employment reductions were witnessed along with simultaneous growth in executive remuneration levels. Indeed, there has been a noticeable theme of winners and losers with privatization. Sure, the spread of individual incomes appears to have widened. But on a national scale, my review also noted cases where a whole country was expected to lose, in contrast to the handsome gains made by international investors. The theme of winners and losers is undeniable.

What are the implications here? In a sense, it is simply a relearning of an old maxim. Identifying the winners and losers of policy decisions as separate groups is part of good policy analysis. Its absence is part of power and political opportunism. Openness to such information is part of achieving a better balance in future privatizations compared to those of the past.

Privatization is obviously a strategy that is inherently political. It brings into relief clashing values. As such, the future of the public-private mix is one in which the community itself will continue to make choices, as well as political leaders. One of the first lessons for any privatization researcher is that there are no accurate economic theories, no equations, and little quantitative guidance as to what belongs inside government and what does not. The role of government is contestable, and as such it boils down largely to a community choice. Thus, we might initially find it surprising that whilst the French buy their water from private companies, Sydney citizens are not likely to consider doing so following a series of water-quality scares in the late 1990s in which water from a recently privatized treatment plant had to be boiled before drinking.[13] Whilst Australian citizens have bought alcohol from private companies, Canadians have traditionally insisted that the government own such outlets. Whilst Australia has been busily privatizing its major airports, the New Zealand government has been paralyzed over the refusal by the New Zealand community to allow such remaining privatizations. Whilst many governments talk of post office privatization, almost none have done so. And so on. The "right balance" of private and public sector activities appears to be as much a community, and hence a political, choice as it is an economic or financial one.

Even if the presumed economic and social benefits of privatization evaporate, or are only marginal, the sale of public enterprises is still likely to be far easier for governments than cutting public expenditure, or announcing tax increases in the short term. Irrespective of the degree of which privatization proceeds are used by governments to meet policy objectives such as public debt reduction or else are used in the pursuit of other recurrent policy directions, it is politically attractive. From the perspective of broad community interests, too, there is also no doubt that unless catastrophic service difficulties or outrageous price increases occur, a change in ownership will continue to be seen by end-user consumers as an issue of little concern. The more that postprivatization service or quality levels are debated with no clear or obvious consensus, the more privatization will continue to be smart politics.

Returning again to the review conclusions, we noted that a common risk with all privatization programs was the allegation of corruption. Further, we concluded that whether such allegations are proven, doubts over corruption and cronyism are likely to linger when reformist governments create an atmosphere of less openness in the availability of information.

Conclusions

So, where does all this leave us? What are the implications of these empirical findings, theoretical ideas, and discussion points? Clearly, there are real cost savings to be gained on average through establishing competitive contracting arrangements, albeit that savings are likely to be quite different for different services. Contracting either in-house or externally can both be effective. Moreover, in traditional service areas such as cleaning, refuse collection, and maintenance, contracting should already be in place. Expecting contracting to be a panacea for all public sector services, though, would be foolish. Some are difficult to accurately specify and measure, or are infrequent and uncertain. These may attract greater governance costs. In considering current trends in outsourcing and contracting, a bigger question also needs to be addressed. When contracting reforms are applied to governments in a wholesale manner, there is a real danger that the market/contracting model will be emphasized at the expense of sensible alternatives such as "cooperation" or "negotiation" with in-house or external teams. A series of alternative options for establishing the cost effectiveness and relative competitiveness of services exist. These range from the simple establishment of business units (with their own service contracts at specific unit costs, business plans, and competitive comparisons), benchmarking comparisons, the periodic adoption of business-process reengineering for restructuring operations, as well as the more well known competitive tendering and outsourcing options. Formally contracting through the market is only one of the modes of establishing the competitiveness of operations. There is certainly a current trend amongst managers to adopt without question quantitative techniques promising management improvements and believing that these can somehow solve problems and make decisions previously conceived of as political in nature. I should emphasize again that the international literature and empirical findings on privatization as contracting out services do not suggest that competitive contracting is always inappropriate. Neither do they say that competitive contracting always is. Careful application of this strategy with targets based on our learnings to date is likely to yield greater benefits than a blanket application based on ideology.

On the question of enterprise sales, the promised benefits of private ownership appear to have exceeded the measured gains to date. Nonetheless, there has been much to learn from privatizations that have occurred worldwide to date. Perhaps the overwhelming message from measurements taken of past privatizations was the need for a healthy degree of skepticism. Whilst it is now possible to privatize just about anything, it is not necessarily sensible. The recurring theme of "winners and losers" that seems to inevitably follow privatization reforms is worrying, as is the speed and inevitability with which such reforms are sold to the populace. Much of the journey on which we are embarking as we reshape government is being undertaken on faith. We need to recognize that the results are not all one way. In researching the two most common forms of privatization, I have adopted a multidimensional approach to performance, and have attempted to arrive at conclusions in an open and transparent manner. Having used an innovative statistical analysis technique as well as previous findings in the field, our experience teaches us that the impacts of privatization are manifold. There is, no doubt, much to be gained for communities and citizens through the judicious use of privatization as well as other reforms, and through careful structuring of market and regulatory arrangements. But differences between the theory of privatization on the one hand and the reality on the other remain. One size will not usually fit all. A learning approach is needed as we go, in order to get the right balance. We now know that the common question, Does privatization work? requires a supplementary request for clarification before any reliable assessment can be made. "Work? . . . Work for whom?"

NOTES

1. The Australian Department of Defence is, for instance, up to the fifth edition of its market-testing Commercial Support Program (CSP) guidelines, these having been shaped by eight years of learning and development, decades of experience overseas and following reviews such as that of the National Audit Office. Likewise, there are several comprehensive sets of guidelines around, such as those for outsourcing issued by the Victorian government.

2. Recall that, averaged over all available international measurements (most of which related to local government garbage collection, cleaning, and maintenance services), a mean cost saving of around 12 percent was found, but averaged over services (equally weighted) a mean of around 6 percent was found.

3. Not listed in the findings above was the strongest (and obvious) statistical observation continually found in studies between the amount of work done and the cost of that work.

4. Sources for cost savings were as follows: NSW Treasury (1993) reported a cost saving of 20 percent, CTC Consulting (1994) likewise found a cost saving of 20 percent, and Williamson (1998) reported a cost savings of 26 percent.

5. The standing of these cost-savings estimates is likely to have been increased by the Australian Industry Commission's comprehensive report on this subject as well (Industry Commission 1996).

6. In the case of the Defence Department's Commercial Support Program, it reported cost savings of "one-third," for instance. The Australian National Audit Office (1998, pp. 32–33), however, came to the conclusion that "the level of reported savings . . . has limited value as an indicator of performance" and although this CSP estimate may be a rough guide to overall costs, it "does not have sufficient verifiable support to be used as a benchmark."

7. One exception to this has been the Department of Treasury and Finance (1997) survey, which reported the costs of managing outsourced contracts at between 1.6 and 11.3 percent, with an average of 1.9 percent.

8. Such criticisms include limited predictive and explanatory power, the looseness of the definition of "transaction cost," and the fact that the actual growth of large firms over the past century can be attributed mainly to the pursuit of market power and to the various mechanisms of government support. It suffers from the criticisms leveled at the key assumption of the self-interested individual, as well.

9. Interestingly, this figure of 29 percent from PA Consulting (1997) is identical to the proportion of IT activities presently outsourced in Australian public sector organizations.

10. See PA Consulting (1997, p. 9).

11. See ibid., p. 4.

12. It is also the need to somehow wrestle with the tension between rigid public sector tendering processes, in which a rock solid specification is developed, for instance, with the reality that the majority of complex outsourcing contracts may well need to be renegotiated partway through the contract period. Some 80 percent of companies that had outsourced IT activities for contract periods of five years apparently renegotiated their contracts after only one year, according to one recent report (Robertson 1998, p. 5).

13. The speed at which both the media and the public can jump to conclusions (whether fair or not) as to the cause of such water-quality reductions is indicative of the sensitivity of the privatization issue and the sensitivity to the removal of such basic services.

REFERENCES

ANAO. 1998. *Commercial Support Program: Department of Defense, Audit Report Number 2.* Australian National Audit Office: Canberra, pp. 32–33.

CTC Consulting 1994. *Competitive Tendering and Contracting in the West Australian Public Sector.* Sydney: University of Sydney.

Department of Treasury and Finance. 1995. *Government Business Enterprises Reform in Victoria: A Guide to the First Three Years October 1992–September 1995.* Privatizations and Industry Reform Division, Department of Treasury and Finance, State Government of Victoria, December.

————. 1997. *Victorian Outsourcing Activity Survey: 1995–96.* Outsourcing and Contract Management Unit, Melbourne, December.

Industry Commission. 1996. Competitive Tendering and Contracting by Public Sector Agencies. Australia. January.

Mottram, M. 1999. The Corporate Umpire. *The Age*, News Extra (July 17), p. 2.

NSW Treasury. 1993. Competitive Tendering and Contracting in the NSW Budget Sector: Survey Findings. NSW Treasury, December.

PA Consulting Group, 1997. *Strategic Sourcing Survey 1998: Australia in the International Context*, Melbourne.

Robertson, R. 1998. Contract Details are the Secret to Success. *Australian Financial Review*, Outsourcing Special Report, p. 5.

12

John J. DiIulio, Jr.

WORKS BETTER AND COSTS LESS? SWEET AND SOUR PERSPECTIVES ON THE NPR

ON DECEMBER 19, 1994, a front-page story in the *New York Times* declared "Clinton Turns to Gore's Proposal for Faster, Cheaper Government."[1] As leaders of the Republican-controlled 104th Congress vowed to raze the federal government (for example, to abolish the Department of Housing and Urban Development), President Clinton redoubled his efforts to reinvent it (for example, to cut HUD's staff by thousands and consolidate its scores of programs into just four). The president sought "to prove that his Administration can shrink the bureaucracy and was doing so long before the Republican electoral triumph" of November 8, 1994.[2]

The smashing Republican victory in the midterm congressional elections of 1994 changed the politics of reforming the federal bureaucracy in ways that increased the chances of congressional support for some form of the administration's civil service personnel, procurement, downsizing, and reorganization efforts.

REINVENTING, RAZING, OR REFORMING GOVERNMENT?

The question, however, is whether a legislative-executive bidding war to raze or reinvent government is necessarily conducive to meaningful efforts to reform the federal service in a manner that improves performance and spares the public purse. Based on a careful analysis of the first year of the administration's reform efforts, this [chapter] provides some preliminary answers.

On September 7, 1993, the Clinton administration released the first report of its National Performance Review (NPR), headed by Vice President Al Gore. Entitled *From Red Tape to Results: Creating a Government That Works Better and Costs Less*, the NPR report contained 384 major recommendations for improving performance in the federal bureaucracy. The recommendations covered twenty-seven federal agencies and fourteen "government systems," including budgeting practices, information technologies, personnel procedures, and procurement regulations."[3]

THE RUSH TO REINVENTION

The NPR got off to a fast start, attracted an enormous amount of favorable media attention, and won early praise and encouragement from academics, union leaders, and policymakers of both parties.

The report was issued on Labor Day, just six months after the NPR initiative was announced, and less than nine months into the new administration. Inside government, the vice president made impassioned "reinvention" speeches before workers in each agency. Outside it, he waged a public relations campaign for the NPR that included several high-profile television appearances. Most memorable was CBS's "Late Night with David Letterman," during which he dramatized wasteful tests of government-issue products by shattering an ostensibly overpriced ashtray.[4]

On the day the NPR report was released, the president joined the vice president on the White House lawn for a widely televised briefing and photo opportunity in which they were flanked by forklifts loaded with government personnel manuals and related "red tape" documents.[5] At least at the outset, the NPR was a pure public relations triumph, resulting in a quick twelve-percentage-point bounce in Clinton's approval ratings.[6]

Intellectually, the NPR was animated by journalist David Osborne and former city manager Ted Gaebler's *Reinventing Government*, a treatise that stood the field of public administration on its head by identifying ways that government could alter or eliminate civil service personnel and procurement systems and become less top-heavy, more decentralized, and more committed to serving "customer interests."[7] Every generation of public service reformers has included some who believe that government can and should be run like a business. But Osborne and Gaebler went farther, arguing not only that government should borrow successful business approaches such as total quality management but that government should "reinvent" itself so that the "entrepreneurial spirit" could grow from within and new, performance-oriented organizational cultures could take root.

Like *Reinventing Government*, and unlike any other government-sponsored public service reform document on record, the NPR report made its way on to the *New York Times* best sellers' list and was quickly reprinted by several for-profit publishers. Many previous efforts to reform the federal service did make headlines and also made a positive difference. For example, the President's Committee on Administrative Management (the Brownlow committee) of the 1930s and the two Commissions on Organization of the Executive Branch (the first and second Hoover commissions) of the 1940s and 1950s left indelible organizational marks on the federal government and were treasured moments in the golden age of American public administration. But no previous government or private commission on the federal service—including the NPR's two immediate predecessors from the 1980s, the Executive Committee of the Private Sector Survey on Cost Control in the Federal Government (the Grace commission) and the National Commission on the Public Service (the Volcker commission)—captured public attention in quite the way the NPR did.

Beyond the favorable public reception, many of the early political and academic responses to the NPR report were quite favorable. In Congress, the initial Republican response to this early effort by a Democratic administration showed a degree of bipartisan spirit that, with the exception of the final vote on the North American Free Trade Agreement, was nowhere else in evidence during the first year of the Clinton presidency.[8] Republican Senator William V. Roth, Jr., endorsed the thrust of the report, stating that it "offered some important recommendations" that "provided an excellent starting point for reorganizing, streamlining, and reforming federal program structure and operations."[9]

In December 1993 the General Accounting Office (GAO) issued an analysis of the NPR report's 384 major recommendations; it officially agreed with 262, offered no comment (for lack of sufficient information) on 121, and rejected only 1. (The GAO rejected the NPR's recommendation for a creation of a multiagency coordinating council within the Department of Labor.)[10] The Alliance for Redesigning Government of the National Academy of Public Administration (NAPA) bolstered efforts to get policymakers, the public, the academic community, and the press to "really take the NPR's message seriously."[11] A number of prominent journalists, including nationally syndicated columnist David Broder, wrote highly favorable articles about the NPR's promise and progress.[12] And the NPR was acknowledged as a model for reform efforts abroad.[13]

MUCH MOTION, LITTLE REINVENTION?

But it was not long before these largely favorable early returns on the NPR were swamped by political problems and negative reviews. As the first year of the NPR drew to a close, there were basically two schools of thought about it, one on balance positive, the other on balance negative. On the one side were those who, like public management expert Laurence E. Lynn, Jr., found problems with the NPR but concluded that

> the Gore report already has been catalytic, and public administration is enlivened by a palpable new energy. Properly mobilized on behalf of good policies, the movement to reinvent government will enter the history of administrative reform as a useful step forward.[14]

On the other side were those who, like former NAPA trustees Herbert N. Jasper and Anita F. Alpern, looked "favorably on the intent and general direction" of the NPR but concluded that

> the report is flawed by a number of omissions, inconsistencies, and questionable judgments. Further, the implementing actions to date . . . contain significant defects. . . . We think it contains both good and bad ideas, and a lot of overblown rhetoric which is mostly irrelevant to solving federal management problems.[15]

By the end of the NPR's first year, however, the negative perspective had found many more adherents than the positive one. Many came to the conclusion that the NPR report was, in the words of budget analysts Louis Fisher and Albert J. Kliman, "rife with contradictions, misstatements, and inaccuracies that call into question the overall quality of the report."[16]

Politically, the rush to reinvention began to stall just two months after the NPR report was released with such great political fanfare.[17] The haste with which the report was prepared became a source of criticism and embarrassment for the NPR. For example, most of the footnotes in the NPR report were to "accompanying reports" that were not released until months later and varied greatly in quality.[18] Another embarrassment came when, in early congressional hearings on the NPR, administration spokespersons were unable to explain precisely how the NPR had arrived at a work force reduction target of 252,000 (since revised upward to 272,900).[19]

Although trivial in their own right, such journalistic quibbles and political nitpicks were magnified beneath the thick lens of cautions, criticisms, and quasi-moral condemnations that eventually surrounded the NPR. Among other things, the NPR was criticized for overstating potential cost savings and for ignoring what many believed to be the twin sources of government's burdensome personnel and procurement regulations, namely, the proliferation of political appointees within the executive branch and the rise of legislative micromanagement within Congress. And the NPR was charged with everything from an abject failure to understand the Constitution to a complete misreading of the lessons of private-sector and state and local government reforms.[20]

ASSESSING GOVERNMENTAL REFORM

In August 1994 the Brookings Center for Public Management released a report on the NPR's first year. The report drew an enormous amount of media attention, which in turn quickly transformed the report into a "report card." When the NPR's own first-year report was released in September 1994, the press pushed the vice president to give the effort a single grade. He gave it a "B+."[21]

Whatever the administration and the 104th Congress make of the NPR, let no one suppose that meaningful reform can occur in defiance of certain basic facts. For example, at 2.1 million employees, the federal civilian work force is smaller today than it was in 1960.[22] Then as now, nine out of ten federal civilian workers lived outside the Washington, D.C., metropolitan area. The only part of the federal bureaucracy that has consistently grown over the last three decades is the ranks of political appointees. That has happened under presidents of both parties and shows no sign of abating. Every major domestic federal program enacted since the end of World War II has been administered directly not by federal workers but by state and local government employees and networks of private contractors. The Reagan administration made several serious efforts to "devolve" responsibility for social programs to the states. But those efforts did not, in the end, limit the scope of these programs, shrink their overall budgets, change the behavior of program staff or clients, or decrease the number of government employees who were responsible for administering them. Finally, while many, perhaps most, federal agencies could function well with less staff, some federal agencies and subunits within given agencies clearly need more staff to monitor pensions, manage prisoners, or perform other nontrivial functions.

No strategy for reforming federal bureaucracy can succeed unless it confronts these realities. As Donald F. Kettl argues[23] in its first year the NPR took some important first steps on the road to real reform. But the biggest political and administrative challenges are yet to come.

NOTES

1. Todd S. Purdham, "Clinton Turns to Gore's Proposal for Faster, Cheaper Government," *New York Times*, December 19, 1994, pp. A1, B10.
2. Ibid p. A1.
3. National Performance Review, *From Red Tape to Results: Creating a Government that Works Better and Costs Less* (Government Printing Office, 1993).
4. Stephen Barr, "Bureaucracy Review Opens with a Rally," *Washington Post*, April 16, 1993, p. A23; and Mike Mills, "Clinton and Gore Hit the Road to Build a Better Bureaucracy," *Congressional Quarterly Weekly Report*, September 11, 1993, pp. 2381–89.
5. Mills, "Clinton and Gore Hit the Road," p. 2385.
6. Richard Benedetto, "Key to Gaining Ground Is Sticking to Basics," *USA Today*, September 27, 1993, p. A1.
7. David Osborne and Ted Gaebler, *Reinventing Government: How the Entrepreneurial Spirit Is Transforming the Public Sector* (Reading, Mass.: Addison-Wesley, 1992); David Osborne, "Government That Means Business," *New York Times Sunday Magazine*, March 1, 1992, pp. 20-28: and David Osborne, "Reinventing Government: Creating an Entrepreneurial Federal Establishment," in Will Marshall and Martin Schram, *Mandate for Change* (New York: Berkley Books, 1993).
8. For example, see Republican Senator Charles E. Grassley, "Reinventing Government, The Final Verdict," *Vital Speeches of the Day*, vol. 60 (January 1, 1994), pp. 167-70.
9. William V. Roth, Jr., "Reinventing Government: Maintaining the Momentum," *Public Manager*, vol. 22 (Winter 1993-94), pp. 15-17. At that time, Roth was the ranking minority member of the Senate Committee on Governmental Affairs.
10. General Accounting Office, *Management Reform: GAO's Comments on the National Performance Review's Recommendations*, OCG-94-1 (December 1993).
11. Alliance for Redesigning Government, "Rego, for Real?" *Public Innovator*, no. 1 (December 1993), p. 4.
12. David S. Broder, "Reinvention Dissenters," *Washington Post*, March 16, 1994, p. A19.
13. B. Guy Peters and Donald J. Savoie, *Reinventing Osborne and Gaebler: Lessons from the Gore Commission* (Ottawa: Canadian Centre for Management Development, November 1993).
14. Laurence E. Lynn, Jr., "Government Lite," *American Prospect*, no. 16 (Winter 1994), p. 144.
15. Herbert N. Jasper and Anita F. Alpern, "National Performance Review: The Good, the Bad, the Indifferent," *Public Manager*, vol. 23 (Spring 1994), p. 27.
16. Louis Fisher and Albert J. Kliman, "The Gore Report on Budgeting," *Public Manager*, vol. 22 (Winter 1993-94), p. 19-22.
17. Stephen Barr, "On Capitol Hill, 'Reinventing Government' Is Off to a Crawling Start," *Washington Post*, November 24, 1993, p. A15.
18. Guy Gugliotta, "Look for the New Titles from Reinvention Press," *Washington Post*, February 1, 1994, p. A19.
19. See Tom Shoop, "Targeting Middle Management," *Government Executive*, vol. 26 (January 1994), p. 11; and Stephen Barr, "Senators Uneasy about 'Buyout' for Bureaucrats," *Washington Post*, October 20, 1993, p. A27.

20. For a small but representative sample of critical commentary on the "reinvention movement" and the NPR, see Ronald C. Moe, "Let's Rediscover Government, Not Reinvent It," *Government Executive*, vol. 25 (June 1993), pp. 46-48, 60; John J. DiIulio, Jr., "Mothers of Reinvention: Why Gore's Red-Tape Reformers Won't Save Money," *Washington Post*, August 22, 1993, p. C1; Charles T. Goodsell, "Did NPR Reinvent Government Reform?" *Public Manger*, vol. 22 (Fall 1993), pp. 7-10; Paul Glastris, "Whose Government is Gored?" *New Republic*, October 11, 1993, pp. 33-34; David Segal, "What's Wrong with the Gore Report," *Washington Monthly*, November 1993, pp. 18-23; David H. Rosenbloom, "Editorial: Have An Administrative Rx? Don't Forget the Politics!" *Public Administration Review*, vol. 53 (November-December 1993), pp. 503-07; Paul A. Volcker and others, "An Open Letter on the Report of the National Performance Review," National Commission on the Public Service, Washington, February 14, 1994; Ronald C. Moe, "The 'Reinventing Government' Exercise: Misinterpreting the Problem, Misjudging the Consequences," *Public Administration Review*, vol. 54 (March-April 1994), pp. 125-36; and Peri E. Arnold, "Reform's Changing Role: the National Performance Review in Historical Context," paper prepared for Woodrow Wilson International Center for Scholars, April 12, 1994.

21. Transcript 362 of *Prime Time Live*, ABC News, August 11, 1994, p. 9.

22. National Performance Review, *Human Resource Management: Accompanying Report* (GPO, 1993), p. 1; and James Q. Wilson and John J. DiIulio, Jr., *American Government: Institutions and Policies*, 6th ed. (Lexington, Mass.: D.C. Heath, 1994), p. 393.

23. Donald F. Kettl, *Reinventing Government? Appraising the National Performance Review*, A Report of the Brookings Institution's Center for Public Management, CPM 94-2 (Brookings, August 1994).

5

INTER-GOVERNMENTAL RELATIONS

No features of U.S. government better encapsulate American expectations and fears of government than our systems of federalism and inter-governmental relations (IGR). Just as the U.S. Constitution avoided threats to liberties by spreading powers across three separate branches of government (see Chapter 4), it also established a complex structure of rights and relationships among different levels of government to protect sub-national governments.

FEDERALISM

The system of federalism was established by the Constitution. James Bryce explains: "It has long been agreed that the only possible form of government for America is a federal one."[1] The chief alternative to a federal system of government is a unitary system, as in France or Japan, where there are no state governments and all significant power lies with the national government. Such systems may be good for getting things done and for focusing accountability. They avoid overlap and duplication between levels of government, and have no need for co-ordination between levels of government or complex systems of federal state financial relations. But non-unitary federal systems offer great strengths in terms of enhancing diversity—of recognizing the variances among aspirations, values and resources that people hold in different communities and corners across this nation. Our system of federalism places significant democratic governments in every city and crossroads and, by so doing, the potential risk of a remote and unresponsive tyrannical government is reduced.

INTER-GOVERNMENTAL RELATIONS (IGR)

Inter-governmental Relations (IGR) refers to the less formal, day-to-day interactions among employees at all levels of government, as they work to solve problems or capitalize on opportunities—within the framework of the system of federalism. Four over-arching principles define the IGR in the United States:

- *Constitutional government:* all of our governments operate under well defined written constitutions;
- *Formal federalism:* a well-crafted yet evolving set of principles for the policy and fiscal relationships between levels of government;
- *The diversity of governments:* thousands of governments form the total picture: one federal government, 50 state governments, and countless municipal, county, and regional multi-purpose and single purpose governments;[2] and
- *Pervasive democracy:* elections, policies and the principle of representation underlie governments at all levels and in all forms;

Because Americans do not like or trust centralized government power, we have instead a proliferation of governments serving many purposes that never wholly interlock with one another. Our formal and informal systems and structures for inter-governmental relations are designed to improve and streamline connections, but they carefully avoid centralizing power or detracting from the rights of participating governments and their constituents. Our chosen approach to federalism and IGR is pervasively democratic. Level upon level of governments have their own voters, candidates, charters or constitutions, policies and mandates. Inter-governmental relations thus consist of endless conversations among employees and representatives with differing constituencies and interests.

The approach to federalism in the U.S. embodies the hopes and aspirations of many generations and communities of Americans. It is the combination of structures and processes we have created to achieve common purposes that cross-jurisdictional boundaries. Every school board, for example, is a monument to a community's wish to afford its children access to a good education. Every water district, hospital district, and sewer district serves a purpose that could not be met effectively through established municipal or county governments. Every special purpose agency at the national, state, and local level represents a hope that common action across levels of government can achieve a broad aspiration, such as protecting the community from organized crime or environmental degradation. Federalism defines the structures and the "rules." Inter-governmental relations (IGR) is how the machinery of government actually works—how government employees work across boundaries so that many different existing representative governments can play their part in securing worthy ends for their citizens.

As we saw in Chapter 4, however, American individualism has always caused us to be skeptical about the capability of government to deliver on these hopes. The founders of the republic were mindful of the history of British tyranny when they drafted a Constitution that divided power between branches and levels of government. Poets and writers, from Thoreau to Ayn Rand, have expressed doubts about what government could deliver. According to Thoreau, "that government is best which governs least." More recently, President Ronald Reagan expressed the feelings of a generation and his particular political constituency when he declared that government is not part of the problem, it *is* the problem. IGR is an important part of the machinery that helps a non-unitary system of government to work smoothly—which wasn't entirely designed to do so in the first place.

THE CONSTITUTIONAL BASIS

The fundamental document of federalism and inter-governmental relations in America is the U.S. Constitution of 1789, the oldest written constitution continuously in force in the world. The Constitution assigns powers to the various branches and levels of government. It:

- creates a federal system in which there is a national government and states;
- allocates some powers to the national government, while reserving other powers for the states; and;
- provides guidance and limits when the Supreme Court is considering altering the respective powers of the national or state governments.[3]

Thus, the Constitution is the starting point for understanding any aspect of federalism and inter-governmental relations.

DIVERSITY

One of the most important reasons why our particular form of federalism and IGR continues to work well is that it encourages and allows for diverse aspirations and approaches. Just as our market economy produces a kaleidoscope of innovation (the decentralized dynamism of the Internet is one key expression), the U.S. system of decentralized government stimulates these same values. Diversity in innovation allows people to pursue what is important to them. Thus, the State of Oregon has a "Livability Initiative," and the City of Charlotte, North Carolina uses the "Balanced Scorecard" to keep track of its city government. (See the reading about Charlotte's "Balanced Scorecard" that is reprinted in Chapter 14.) No one tells the State of Oregon or the City of Charlotte that it must do these things. In most activities that affect the quality of lives, no two localities are required to do the same things or in the same ways. Federalism and IGR encourage and support diversity. There are gated communities that are almost outside the reach of local government in one area, and there are cities in which urban policies are the central concerns of citizens in another. This diversity of governments reflects—and advances—diversity among communities. Communities, counties, states, and regions are largely free to solve problems in their own way. They are not forced into a single national model of public provision.

PERVASIVE DEMOCRACY

The conversations that make up inter-governmental relations in America are conversations among democratically constituted bodies. Thus the particular versions of federalism that have evolved in the U.S., from "marble-cake" to "picket fence" and from "permissive" to "protected," are circumscribed by the respect that is given to representatives chosen by the people. Our approach to inter-governmental coordination and cooperation, financial assistance and mandates are, ultimately, adjustments among bodies that have in common an allegiance and accountability to electors.

READINGS REPRINTED IN THIS CHAPTER

In **"American Federalism, State Governments and Public Policy,"** Dale Krane examines public policy-making within the framework of what he calls "America's most distinctive political invention—federalism."[4] Often analyses of public policy formation and analyses of American federalism occur in two separate watertight compartments. "While not 'forgetting' federalism completely," says Krane, "policy textbooks pay brief homage to America's federal government."[5] Only since the revitalization of state governments after the 1960s and concurrent growing demands to devolve public policy, has federalism truly reemerged on the public policy agenda. According to Krane, "American federalism is more than a maze of institutions: it is a matrix of reciprocal power relations." Thus, the separate strands of federal studies and policy analysis must be better woven together. "American Federalism, State Governments and Public Policy," suggests how this process might proceed.

The reading from **David Walker's** book, ***The Rebirth of Federalism: Slouching toward Washington,***[6] provides a uniquely well-informed and detailed analysis of the current state of U.S. federalism and inter-governmental relations. Walker characterizes "Permissive Federalism"—which he sees as "an accurate but also unpleasant description for any faithful federalist."[7]

The U.S. system remains one-nation centered, but states have developed their roles in ways that have led toward an effectively cooperative form of federalism. States, however, still must cope with many unfunded mandates and program conditions that sometimes place significant burdens on them. Reduced federal funding to states has not produced a corresponding reduction in federal oversight and regulation. Walker sees the seeds of a "fearful new federalism" in the structure of many grant programs, with conflicting roles and tensions between managers at both levels of government. In relation to "hollowed out government"—the attempt in the 1980s to scale back national government and to rely on external providers—Walker perceives areas where only a "thin red line" of administrative competence remains to oversee programs at the national level.

These factors add up to a "Permissive Federalism" in which federal and state governments share power, but the states' share rests on the "permission and permissiveness of the federal government." This outcome is repugnant to Walker. Neither the federal policy process, federal finances, nor the clusters of functional interests in Washington, can cope with the challenges of national policy making. Sub-national governments must have a "due measure" of policy discretion to face contemporary policy challenges. Walker therefore argues for a "Protected Federalism," and his article sets out a range of reforms and measures that could bring this about. Walker's reform proposals are presented in detail because they provide a concrete basis for discussion.

In **"Restructuring the State: Devolution, Privatization, and the Geographic Redistribution of Power and Capacity in Governance,"**[8] Janet Kodras explains how restructuring the scale or scope of government through devolution or privatization will redraw the map of governance. As the national government passes responsibilities to the states or to the private sector, many repercussions will follow. There will be "geographic disparities in the role and effect of government in accordance with the capacity of institutions and groups in particular places" to take on functions that previously had been administered in Washington.

Kodras predicts that restructuring will alter federalism and will have differential impacts depending on local government capacity. "The current restructuring of the US government [is] a process whereby the state renegotiates its dual role with capital and with civil society . . . .[with] important implications for locally based states, private nonprofit organizations and social movements."[9] She concludes: "Most Americans would agree in principle that one's health, affluence, and well-being should not depend on one's zip-code, [yet] there exists little overall consensus as to how the responsibilities of the state should be divided."[10] "Restructuring the State" reminds us that the shifting nature of federalism needs to be aligned with the shifting balance of responsibility among the public, private and nonprofit sectors. As these balances change, there will be geographic, social, and political winners—and losers.

The readings that are reprinted in this chapter demonstrate the richness and, above all, the centrality of inter-governmental relations for American government and public administration. Some IGR issues are as old as the nation. Others are contemporary products of globalization, privatization, downsizing, devolution, and numerous other sweeping trends of change that are pervading the practice of public administration at the turn of the millennium.

NOTES

1. Bryce, James (Viscount). (1933). *The American Commonwealth*. New York: Macmillan, p. 243.
2. Not to mention tribal governments and territorial governments.
3. Particularly in the Bill of Rights and, subsequently over the decades, through court opinions.

4. Krane, Dale. (June 1993). "American Federalism, State Governments and Public Policy: Weaving Together Loose Theoretical Threads." *PS: Political Science and Politics,* 186.

5. Krane, Dale. (June 1993). "American Federalism, State Governments and Public Policy: Weaving Together Loose Theoretical Threads." *PS: Political Science and Politics,* 187.

6. Walker, David B. (1996). *The Rebirth of Federalism: Slouching toward Washington.* New York: Chatham House.

7. Walker, David B. (1996). *The Rebirth of Federalism: Slouching toward Washington.* New York: Chatham House, p. 328

8. Kodras, Janet E. (1997). "Restructuring the State: Devolution, Privatization, and the Geographic Redistribution of Power and Capacity in Governance," in L. A. Staeheli, J. E. Kodras, and C. Flint (Eds.), *State Devolution in America: Implications for a Diverse Society* (pp. 79–96). Thousand Oaks, CA: Sage.

9. Kodras, Janet E. (1997). "Restructuring the State: Devolution, Privatization, and the Geographic Redistribution of Power and Capacity in Governance," in L. A. Staeheli, J. E. Kodras, and C. Flint (Eds.), *State Devolution in America: Implications for a Diverse Society.* Thousand Oaks, CA: Sage, p. 90.

10. Kodras, Janet E. (1997). "Restructuring the State: Devolution, Privatization, and the Geographic Redistribution of Power and Capacity in Governance," in L. A. Staeheli, J. E. Kodras, and C. Flint (Eds.), *State Devolution in America: Implications for a Diverse Society.* Thousand Oaks, CA: Sage, p. 93.

13

Dale Krane

AMERICAN FEDERALISM, STATE GOVERNMENTS, AND PUBLIC POLICY: WEAVING TOGETHER LOOSE THEORETICAL THREADS

Decisions about the provision and delivery of public goods and services take place within the framework established by America's most distinctive political invention—federalism. Author after author reminds students and scholars alike that policy making can be understood only from an intergovernmental perspective. But to use a term such as "intergovernmental policy making" thrusts one into two distinctive analytic worlds which, at best, are loosely woven together.

Many conventional models of policy making give little place to federal arrangements or to the factors that sustain American federalism. Equally problematic, efforts to model federalism often do not take advantage of the conceptually more developed policy making literature. An unfortunate consequence of this "separateness" is the regular appearance of policy studies with hypotheses or conclusions that could have been easily explained or predicted had the author been more familiar with the corpus of work available on American federalism.

Compounding this lack of conceptual integration between federalism and policy-making studies is the continuing tendency to downplay or even ignore the activities and influence of state governments. To use states as an observational unit of analysis is not the same as granting state governments the explanatory status of a "structural variable" (Scheuch 1969; Ragin 1987).

Although information about states comprises the data bases for numerous inter-governmental and policy analyses, nevertheless, states are not accorded an explanatory role commensurate with their impact on public policy.

"FORGOTTEN FEDERALISM"

Hamilton and Wells (1990, 1) unabashedly declare that "federalism is simply too often forgotten." A quick perusal of common public policy textbooks confirms their assessment. While not "forgetting" federalism completely, policy textbooks pay brief homage to America's federal government. Federalism is depicted as a con-textual feature which conditions the behavior of individuals and groups, typically expressed as "federalism disperses power" or " . . . permits policy diversity." This ritualistic recognition of federalism includes some combination of the following topics: reasons for federalism, historical eras, the grant system, and the complica-tions for policy makers. Seldom are students presented with a conceptual frame-work or a model that links the components of federal organization to the formulation, adoption, or implementation of policy. By forgetting the considerable body of writing on American federalism, policy analysts continue to produce re-search findings that could have been easily explained or derived from the intergov-ernmental literature.

MODELS OF POLICY FORMULATION

Of course, the manner and the degree to which federalism/intergovernmental rela-tions intertwine with policy making depends on the phase of the policy process one has under consideration. Widely accepted models of policy formulation such as iron triangles, issue networks, and agenda-building offer scant reference to federal arrange-ments or to the diversity or subnational cultures and place-based interests that dynam-ically support and are sustained by American federalism. PIGs, or intergovernmental lobbies, are categorized as just one more interest group in the "policy soup." Cer-tainly, states and localities behave as pressure groups; but their constitutional status empowers them with legitimate authority not exercised by other types of groups as well as institutional access not available to other interests.

With so many competing policy models, it is only natural that some conceptual devices do a better explanatory job than others. Iron triangles, for example, offer little heuristic value in explaining specific instances of state officials derailing presidential initiatives, such as the National Governors Association's bipartisan resistance that doomed Reagan's "turnback and swap" proposal to devolve programs *to* the states. On the other hand, diffusion of innovation models offers clear insights into the growing influence of state policy initiatives that arrive on the national agenda and are ultimately adopted (e.g., education reform, environmental protection, health care, and "workfare").

Even agenda-setting models, probably the most sophisticated framework for exploring policy formulation, downplay the impact of the federal matrix. State government officials, because of their place in American federalism, have a number of doors, not just windows, into the larger national policy process. Wright (1988, 275) identified nine issue areas in which governors can work to shape national policy. Governors also possess a freedom of action that encompasses personal contact with presidents, strategy sessions with their state congressional delegation, negotiations with federal administrators, and mobilization of public opinion in their home state and throughout the nation.

Other state government officials also possess the capacity and resources by which to influence national policy (see Krane 1993). A covert example of state power over national policy can be found in the 1991 reports from state capitals that state legislators were using the decennial process of redrawing congressional districts as a bargaining chip to extract policy promises form congressional incumbents. The point here is simple: policy models that assign federalism to a contextual role which only creates complications or obstacles to action miss the fundamental fact that subnational officials are actors whose preferences embody the interests of a particular jurisdiction. Put more simply, American federalism is more than a maze of institutions; it is a matrix of reciprocal power relations.

MODELS OF POLICY IMPLEMENTATION

Although implementation research from its earliest beginnings acknowledged the intergovernmental dimensions of the policy process, the role of state governments in policy implementation models has been cast in a curiously emasculated fashion. For example, top-down models view implementation as a rational-technical process of assembling the necessary elements needed to penetrate through "bureaucratic-political" layers to the policy's target beneficiaries. Successful top-down implementation depends on marshalling enough resources (money, trained personnel, facilities) to overcome the complexity of joint action, provided the national policy goals are sufficiently clear.

Bottom-up models stress the potential for deflection or distortion of national policy by local authorities. The encounter of street-level bureaucrats with program clients is reputed to be the defining moment that actualizes the policy mandate. Local action that is faithful to national objectives serves as the benchmark for successful bottom-up implementation. While bottom-up models recognize the autonomy granted to subnational authorities by federalism, these behavioral-realist models sometimes so narrow their conceptual focus as to obscure the impact of state government on local actions. For example, the administration of welfare programs over the past twenty years has changed in important ways as a result of state government takeover of the old county welfare office. This change in turn affects the ability to integrate welfare reform with education, training, and employment programs, many of which remain locally based.

What is conceptually striking about many implementation models (of either direction) is the lack of attention to two of the earliest and best articulated frameworks, both of which begin with the attributes of the federal system. Pressman (1975) developed a "donor-recipient" model of the grant-in-aid process that explicitly incorporated the interjurisdictional conflict, mutual dependence, and power asymmetry of American federalism. Williams (1980) set forth a "shared governance" model of the "uneasy partnership" within federal programs. Only with the "third generation" of implementation studies has the capacity of states and localities to act as "power wielders" (Pressman's term) been restored to the status of an explanatory variable.

A RESURGENCE OF STATE GOVERNMENTS AS AN EXPLANATORY VARIABLE

Lack of attention to American federalism in explanations of public policy may be coming to an end. The post–1960 revitalization of state governments, the growing demands to devolve public policy, and the national government's own fiscal distress have thrust state governments and American federalism back onto the agenda of both policy makers and model makers.

However, for the renaissance in federalism studies to continue, the loose weaving of federalism with policy models must be tightened. One can see the need for transcending the treatment of intergovernmental relations as a contextual variable in policy studies by reviewing the changing fortunes of American federalism in the premier policy textbook.

If one revisits the first edition (1972) of Thomas Dye's *Understanding Public Policy*, the widely used and influential undergraduate textbook, one finds no mention of federalism or intergovernmental relations. There is, however, a chapter devoted to "a systems analysis of state policies." A separate chapter on American federalism did not appear until the fifth edition (1984) and its historical (e.g., change in federalism from dual to cooperative) and descriptive (e.g., block versus categorical grants) treatment of federalism carried over to the sixth edition (1987). In the current seventh edition (1992, 307–10) Dye has added, for the first time, a section which analyzes through the lens of public choice theory the impact of intergovernmental competition on various types of policy (also see Dye 1990). No doubt this theoretical breakthrough is a harbinger of models to come, but improved theorizing about federalism also needs to be infused into models of the policy process.

Other signs that the paths of federalism and policy studies may be converging can be found in recent scholarship. Jack Treadway (1985) summarizes twenty years of politics versus environment debate over policy outputs and uses his critical review to produce a model of the state policy-making process that combines national and state level features (including state political culture). Thomas Anton (1989, v) proposes a "benefits coalition" framework to explain how ". . . the interrelationships among levels [of government] that are the defining characteristics of American public policies." Robertson and Judd's (1989) policy text adopts a "new institutionalism" approach which emphasizes the independent role of government in the policy making process. Paul Sabatier (1991), in laying out some directions for "better theories of the policy process," describes three models, each of which holds that government institutions are a critical explanatory variable for understanding public policy.

WEAVING TOGETHER LOOSE THEORETICAL THREADS

Research on American federalism, state governments, and public policy has produced two extensive fabrics of information that demonstrate it is possible to accumulate knowledge without substantial synthesis. In order to move toward more conherence and integration of federal studies with policy analysis, a number of epistemological problems will have to be addressed. The list offered here is not a complete itemization of the many sharp philosophical points that can snag the warp and woof of theory; instead the points raised here are illustrative of the challenges of weaving together the threads of different subfields.

One snag is the combined-effects" problem that is also encountered in the study of international relations. interaction between two (or more) governments or organizations requires (1) identification of the internal and external factors that account for phenomenon under study and (2) determination of the relative causal strength of each factor. These "combined-effects" produce another tangle: that of multiple units of analysis. Both policy and federal studies struggle with the linkage of individuals and institutions, especially when the boundaries of organizational or jurisdictional units are "blurred." Third, the dynamics of the policy process coupled with the flux in federal institutions tear at any static theory. To cope with change, an integrative model would have to focus on activities which shape institutions and policies over time, such as decision making. A fourth epistemological point that can rip the fabric of theory is overreliance on a single type of information (e.g., fiscal data). Working with a small number of data threads not only diminishes the richness of the theoretical pattern, but also reduces its generalizability; that is to say, the theoretical cloth produced will have too many holes.[1]

What kind of loom will weave together the threads of federalism and public policy? Over the last ten years there has been a lessening of the optimism that a theory of politics can be constructed by ignoring political institutions (March and Olsen 1984). The "new institutionalism" and the nascent theory of "policy design" share a theoretical concern with understanding the effects of different institutional structures on the behavior of individuals. The search for a "structural logic of policy" which ". . . will contribute to a more refined understanding of the role of institutional factors in policy design" (Linder and Peters 1990, 103) closely matches the message of the "new institutionalism"—"the organization of political life makes a difference." Efforts to increase the complementarity of rational choice models with institutional analysis appear to hold great potential for avoiding many of the snags to an integrative theory (Ostrom 1991).

Only by weaving together the separate strands of federal studies with policy analysis can instructors help their students understand why Martha Derthick (1992, 675), in delivering the 1992 Gaus Lecture, revealed that she was seriously thinking of petitioning a federal judge for the right to vote in California. The reason she offered for this secret desire was her realization that in many policy areas she was governed by the state of California, even though she lived in Virginia!

NOTE

1. The points raised in this paragraph derive from the discussions of shortcomings in political inquiry found in Gillespie and Zinnes (1982), especially the essays by Judith Gillespie, Brian Job, and J. Donald Moon.

REFERENCES

Anton, Thomas J. 1989, *American Federalism and Public Policy: How the System Works.* New York: Random House.

Beam, David R., Timothy J. Conlan, and David B. Walker. 1983. "Federalism: The Challenge of Conflicting Theories and Contemporary Practice." In *Political Science: The State of the Discipline,* ed. Ada W. Finifter, Washington, D.C.: The American Political Science Association.

Derthick, Martha. 1992. "Up-to-Date in Kansas City: Reflections on American Federalism." *PS: Political Science & Politics* 25: 671–75.

Dye, Thomas R. 1972. *Understanding Public Policy.* Englewood Cliffs, NJ: Prentice-Hall

Dye, Thomas R. 1990. *American Federalism: Competition among Governments.* Lexington, MA: D.C. Heath.

Finifter, Ada W., ed. 1983. *Political Science: The State of the Discipline.* Washington, DC: The American Political Science Association.

Gillespie, Judith A. and Dina A. Zinnes, eds. 1982. *Missing Elements in Political Inquiry: Logic and Levels of Analysis.* Beverly Hills, CA: Sage.

Hamilton, Christopher and Donald T. Wells. 1990. *Federalism, Power, and Political Economy: A New Theory of Federalism's Impact on American Life.* Englewood Cliffs, NJ: Prentice-Hall.

Hansen, Susan B. 1983. "Public Policy Analysis: Some Recent Developments and Current Problems." In *Political Science: The State of the Discipline,* ed. Ada W. Finifter. Washington, DC: The American Political Science Association.

Gillespie, Judith A. 1982. "Introduction: Some Basic Puzzles in Political Inquiry." In *Missing Elements in Political Inquiry: Logic and Levels of Analysis,* ed. Judith A. Gillespie and Dina A. Zinnes. Beverly Hills, CA: Sage.

Job, Brian L. 1982. "Synthesis: Problems and Prospect in Dynamic Modeling." In *Missing Elements in Political Inquiry: Logic and Levels of Analysis,* ed. Judith A. Gillespie and Dina A. Zinnes. Beverly Hills, CA: Sage

Krane, Dale. 1993. "State Efforts to Influence Federal Policy." In *Welfare System Reform: Coordinating Federal, State, and Local Programs,* ed. Edward T. Jennings, Jr. and Neal Zank. Westport, CT: Greenwood Press.

Linder, Stephen H. and B. Guy Peters. 1990. "The Design of Instruments for Public Policy." In *Policy Theory and Policy Evaluation: Concepts, Knowledge, Causes, and Norms.* chap. 7, ed. Stuart S. Nagel. Westport, CT: Greenwood Press.

MacManus, Susan A. 1991. "Federalism and Intergovernmental Relations: The Centralization versus Decentralization Debate Continues." In *Political Science: Looking to the Future,* Vol. 4: American Institutions, ed. William Crotty. Evanston, IL: Northwestern University Press.

March, James G. and John P. Olsen. 1984. "The New Institutionalism: Organizational Factors in Political Life." *American Political Science Review* 78: 734–49.

Moon, J. Donald. 1982. "Introduction: Two Views of Integrative Models." In *Missing Elements in Political Inquiry: Logic and Levels of Analysis*, ed. Judith A. Gillespie and Dina A. Zinnes. Beverly Hills, CA: Sage.

Ostrom, Elinor. 1991. "Rational Choice Theory and Institutional Analysis: Toward Complementarity." *American Political Science Review* 85: 237–43.

Pressman, Jeffrey L. 1975. *Federal Programs and City Politics: The Dynamics of the Aid Process in Oakland*. Berkely: University of California Press.

Ragin, Charles C. 1987. *The Comparative Method: Moving Beyond Qualitative and Quantitative Strategies*. Berkeley: University of California Press.

Robertson, David B. and Dennis R. Judd. 1989. *The Development of American Public Policy: The Structure of Policy Restraint*. Glenview, IL: Scott, Foresman.

Sabatier, Paul A. 1991. "Toward Better Theories of the Policy Process." *PS: Political Science & Politics* 2A: 147–56.

Scheuch, Erwin K. 1969. "Social Context and Individual Behavior." In *Quantitative Ecological Analysis in the Social Science*, ed. Mattei Dogan and Stein Rokkan. Cambridge, MA: The M.I.T. Press.

Treadway, Jack M. 1985. *Public Policy-making in the American States*. New York: Praeger.

Williams, Walter. 1980. *The Implementation Perspective: A Guide for Managing Social Service Delivery Programs*. Berkeley: University of California Press.

Wright, Deil S. 1988. *Understanding Intergovernmental Relations*, 3rd ed. Pacific Grove, CA: Brooks/Cole.

14

David B. Walker

THE REBIRTH OF FEDERALISM: SLOUCHING TOWARD WASHINGTON

To gauge the condition of our federalism at any particular time is rarely a simple task. And currently, it is devilishly difficult. Why? Because power and influences in the system are manifesting themselves in more areas of intergovernmental activity and in more consistent ways than ever before. Hence, the totally different contemporary interpretations of the character of today's federalism and the intergovernmental relations that flow from it. Single-factor explanations of the evolution of U.S. federalism usually have been found to be faulty, and in federalism's present highly conflicted condition, such an approach is at best a way to gain only a partial understanding of what makes the system tick.

To describe the system as still fully centralized, or newly decentralized; as cooperative, or resurgently competitive; as less regulated or more so; as activistic or retrenching; as overloaded or unburdened highlights the wide range of dynamic and antagonistic impulses that shape it.

What basic conclusions can be drawn concerning the many dimensions of intergovernmental interaction that compose today's immensely complex and conflicted system?

1. In terms of power relationships, our system remains basically a nation-centered one, certainly when compared to that of 1960 or even 1968; yet it is somewhat less centripetal than the system of 1980, thanks to the current constrained Federal fiscal and programmatic roles (but not the regulatory or preemptive ones); to certain prostate Supreme Court decisions; and to the growing state assertiveness, operational responsibilities, and leadership in curbing some of the more arbitrary Federal IGR actions.

2. Regarding intergovernmental operations, the states are far more the middle-level planners, administrators, and partial funders of national domestic programs than they were in 1960, 1970, or even 1980 because the scope of Federal grant programs was smaller in the first two years, and the local role was much larger in the last. This suggests no return to dual federalism but, superficially, a continuance of the pre–1961 cooperative federalism.

3. When some of the core processes that make up the vast operational IGR terrain are explored, the cooperative label is appropriate generally only for the older functions, where program goals have become consensual ones. In the financial relationships between and among the levels, the reduced level of Federal funding in nonentitlement, urban, and non-safety-net social programs has left the states and notably the localities in more strained financial shape. But, overall, the direct expenditures of the subnational governments are on par with Federal domestic expenditures, and despite the pain, this parity is a most welcome omen for those who seek signs of greater balance in any of the areas where federalism functions.

4. In operational federalism's regulatory realm, the weight of unilaterally added mandates by the national government on states and localities has not been lifted. Neither the deficit dilemma nor the State or Local Government Cost Estimates Act (1982) has nurtured a more responsible congressional behavior in this area. If anything, the deficit vise has resulted in more regs and costly specific program conditions (the expansion of Medicaid coverage, the Safe Drinking Water Act, the Immigration Reform and Control Act of 1986, to note a few of the more blatant examples); all contained provisions that heaped up sizable, unreimbursed fiscal burdens on state and some local governments;[1] this, in turn, has produced instances of states' probing for accounting loopholes in programs like Medicaid. In tandem with the revolution in intergovernmental regulation was the parallel push to preempt, with 280 such actions occurring between 1960 and 1991.[2] In constitutional terms, these actions amount to a steady erosion of the states' police powers and a further enhancement of the reach of Congress's regulatory arm.

5. The proposition that some analysts put forth that with reduced Federal grant funding in most program areas a comparable reduction would occur in the regulatory area has proved to be a myth. The Federal propensity in the eighties and nineties to fall back on mandates actually continued at the same high rate as it had in the roaring seventies. To some extent, the same scenario has been played out at the state level, with locals suffering most from the punitive, pass-the-buck policy, a policy that would have been unthinkable in the years of the "old party system."[3]

6. With grants management, the assignments since 1981 have been both easier and tougher. The return to a roughly one-to-fifty grant administrative relationship has

strengthened the supervisory role of Federal grants managers and the administrative tasks of their state counterparts as well. But the merger of the traditional grant distributive and program oversight roles with the more recent role of administering the new social regulations attached to these programs (with different but equally conflicting roles assigned to the state and local counterparts) violates all rules of proper management. This burden has become the fate of far too many Federal managers, generating tension, if not confrontation, between the administering groups at both levels. Where once the cooperative federalist ethic prevailed in the old grant programs, the seeds of suspicion and of a "fearful new federalism" have been sown.

7. Regarding the Federal agencies themselves, the full impact of "Hollow Government" and "government-by-proxy" at the national level has yet to be fully fathomed by most observers. Any objective assessment of the domestic agencies—whether direct providers of services or providers of grants and loans to other governments and agencies—would show clearly that the shortcomings of many of these units are largely a result of severe earlier personnel cuts and the extraordinary expansion in Federal reliance on third-party providers to implement policies, prompted largely by ideological initiatives in the eighties. The agency assignment has not been reduced, but staff has; in intergovernmental terms, this condition frequently has produced a situation where state agency people appear more professional, knowledgeable, and numerous than their Federal counterparts. It also has produced fundamental oversight problems regarding the operations of third-party organizations, especially with the proliferating Government Sponsored Enterprises (GSEs) with their billions of outstanding lending authority. A "thin red line" of administrative competence is not the best way to uphold the Federal position in current grant and loan management operations, especially in light of the new regulatory complexities Congress has thrust into the operations.

8. The "new politics" buried two very different theories of Federal bureaucratic behavior. Its centralizing propensities demolished the Grodzins-Elazar thesis that no president, Congress, or administrator would enact grants or conditions that were fundamentally subversive of state and local jurisdictional integrity because the noncentralized political system of the fifties and early sixties placed national policymakers in jeopardy if they took such actions.[4] In addition, Leonard D. White's extension of classical public administration precepts to cover grant administration also bit the dust somewhere in the middle of Johnson's Great Society years. The White theory held that Federal grant administrators possessed adequate controls to run the programs and to maintain accountability.[5] Given the number, variety, and controversial goals of many of the pressure group-conditioned grants enacted in the late sixties and especially the seventies, the White precept proved unworkable.

9. Even more to the point perhaps, the new political system with its coterie of special actors surrounding the individual candidate, the ever-present media, and plethora of pressure groups and PACs—while reflecting the nation's incredibly rich, multicultural but deeply divided pluralism—pretty nearly took over in the seventies, as Peterson and others have noted. Fiscal constraints placed curbs on some of the smaller groups in the eighties, but the gridlock of the eighties and

early nineties was as much a pressure-group-produced phenomenon as it was a mere matter of divided political control of the executive and legislative branches.[6] The phenomenon also was shaped by ideologies at both ends of Pennsylvania Avenue, with each sustained by its own cohorts of rabid factional partisans and of assorted pressure groups.

10. Among the pressure groups, the functional and centripetally oriented have tended to dominate, although the professional-technological, regulating, social-moralistic, and citizens' groups in most cases are not genuinely functional in character but just as centralizing as the other groups. Where does this leave the intergovernmental lobby? It leaves the lobby in a very precarious position: few allies, many actual and potential opponents, and techniques that do not differ materially from those of other lobbying groups. On rare occasions, as has been pointed out, it can score with Congress and the administration. And this effort is demeaning for a group that provides the major means for the national government to carry out most of its domestic policies. The IGR lobby is about all that is left of representational federalism, which once was the bulwark of state-local strength within the very confines of the central government.

11. With judicial federalism, an institutional force is encountered that plays a grander and greater adjudicatory function that any high court in any other system, whether federal or unitary. The assessment herein of the Supreme Court's recent record indicates another kind of deep division, but in this case between institutional and ideological judicial conservatives with a couple of neoliberals as spectators. There were a few liberal ideologues on the Court earlier and there are some conservative ideologues now, and neither group laced the Court's role, institutional integrity, and popular acceptance of its decisions at the core of their very different philosophies. Yet, the Court is one of the few institutions in our system that can be above politics, politicians, and specific interests—even though its members frequently were nurtured in such an atmosphere. The Court could play a salutary role in relieving the nation of some of its worst excesses, including the continuous centralization.

12. Finally, if a label is to be put on the current system of federalism, it is Michael Reagan's "Permissive Federalism." Though coined more than a dozen years ago, his description (and John Sanzone's) still captures most of the realities of current intergovernmental relations. There still is a sharing of power and authority between the two constitutionally recognized levels of government and the states' share rests largely "upon the permission and permissiveness of the national government."[7] For Reagan and others, this version of federalism was both accurately descriptive and normatively prescriptive. The basis for the interpretation was the belief that the national government should be dominant, that the interdependence involved give rise to mutual leveraging activities, that the states and localities "retain sufficient political strength to ensure that their views will be listened to by the national government," and that considerable discretion be permitted in the implementation of grant programs.[8] One may quibble with these points, especially those dealing with political strength and program discretion, but the description is all the more accurate because the states and localities do not possess

much political clout under the "new political system," and significant program discretion depends on the type of grant—certainly practically all of the big-ticket grants are heavily conditional and all grants are still enmeshed in crosscutting and other forms of regulation.

Missing in the Reagan and Sanzone analysis is an assessment of the Court's centralizing role, the powerful role of the key nonparty actors in the new political system, and the new regulatory and preemptive roles of the political branches of the national government. Yet, all of these trends only render "Permissive Federalism" all the more accurate as a description. The only modifiers that need to be noted are the few instances the intergovernmental lobby overturned or blunted national mandates, the recent but secondary Supreme Court decisions that favored the states and localities, and the informal administrative clout subnational governments possess as basic implementors of Federal domestic programs, along with the national government's inability to sack anybody working for these governments.

"Permissive Federalism," then, is an accurate portrayal of current intergovernmental power, political, judicial, and administrative trends, though it misses the "slouching towards Washington" that arrival of the "new political system" symbolizes. But as a normative interpretation, the Reagan view is repugnant to those who are concerned with the long-term vitality of our governance system and who find in the present arrangements inadequate constitutional, political, and representational protections for state and local governments. National policy-making and implementation must leave subnational governments with a due measure of policy discretion so they may help cope with the manifold challenges now confronting the country. Neither the Federal policy process, not Federal finances, nor the centralizing cluster of functional interests in Washington—singly or in combination—can cope with these challenges. Permissiveness is not enough. A freed-up and protected federalism is what is needed now, not the conflicts, ambivalences, and overloads that "Permissive Federalism" has nurtured.

FIVE PARADOXES

The above twelve summary findings and observations underscore the conflicted condition of federalism today, and they clearly reveal antagonisms within and among the four areas of analysis employed here: the operational, political, representational, and judicial. Others, relying on a one-or two-factor approach to assessment, do not find this multidimensional ambivalence in their analyses of the system. To highlight the variety of other contemporary interpretations, five paradoxes found in the recent record of Federal-state-local relations will be briefly probed.[9]

One debate that has emerged from very different readings of the record is *whether a state-centered system has been restored (or has always existed) or whether a nation-centered system has been strengthened (or has never really been dismantled).* In the final months of the Reagan presidency, a *Washington Post* headline read "States Assuming New Powers as Federal Policy Role Ebbs," and a lead article at about the same time in a state and local affairs journal carried the title "State Power Needn't Be Resurrected Because It Never Died."[10]

A second federalist debate has erupted over whether ours is *a competitive or cooperative federal system*. One argument for the competitive case holds that the 1981 Federal tax cuts, the repeal of General Revenue Sharing, and the rising deficit, along with other shackling development, have produced a situation where the national government no longer "can move into virtually any domestic area," no longer "possesses a towering fiscal advantage over the state and local governments," and must "now compete head on for the political and fiscal support of federalism's ultimate arbiters—the voters/taxpayers."[11]

A different version of the competitive thesis comes from Thomas Dye, who has enunciated a contemporary theory of competitive federalism that links public choice and the more traditional state-centered federalism theories. Dye finds several signs of the vigor of the competitive ethic in the provision and financing of domestic public services. Yet, he also cites the hurdles that hinder achievement of a more ideal free-market model, hurdles that need to be torn down.[12]

Yet another perspective on competitiveness has been advanced by Alice Rivlin. In *Reviving the American Dream*, she calls for a wholesale sorting out of governmental functions, and assigns to the states a long list of services—education, crime protection, physical infrastructure, job training, and so forth—that would constitute a "Productivity Agenda" in which differing competitive state approaches to providing these function would enhance the likelihood of their success.[13]

Contrasting collaborative views of the system come from other thinkers and from experience. Paul Peterson and his associates in an in-depth study of certain Federal grant programs over time concluded that the vigorous give-and-take between Federal and state and local administrators regarding grant conditions and objectives ultimately produces a rough kind of agreement, even in the case of redistributive aid programs. For Peterson and others, this in practice amounts to a contemporary version of cooperative federalism.[14]

A third controversy generating opposite IGR views is *whether the system has become a co-optive rather than a collaborative, decentralized one*. Proponents of the co-optive interpretation point to the national propensity for a quarter of a century to preempt and to regulate—and not merely the private sector in the latter regard but subnational governments as well. More preemptions since 1960 than the total from 1789 to 1960 and more than a quadrupling of the number of new social regs enacted in the sixties in both the seventies and the eighties are usually cited by those asserting the emergence of a co-optive Federal role in the system.

Contrary opinion holds most of the above arguments are exaggerations and do not reflect operational reality. This school of thought points to the expanded number of block grants, the Federal exit from certain program areas (notably the multistate and substate regional ones), the passive behavior of many Federal regulators, their small number in various of the key agencies, and the practical problem of their insisting on mandate compliance when money is lacking.

The question of *governmental activism or governmental constraint* has also been a source of dispute. Activism advocates point to the continuous growth in total governmental outlays as a percentage of GNP from 1960 through 1986 and a 4 percent decline from 1987 to 1990, but a rise to 41.8 percent by FY 1991, the highest in this period. They note that no proposed presidential budget since FY 1983 has ever been less than its immediate predecessor, and that the same is true of congressional budgetary actions. They emphasize the 42 percent hike in grant-in-aid outlays during the Bush years, surpassing the $193 billion mark in FY 1993 and signaling the end of the Reagan era's slowdown in grant growth. The activism group stresses the steady rise in the proportion of total aid for grants involving payments to individuals—rising from 35.7 percent of the 1960 total to 62 percent by FY 1993.

Those adhering to the governmental-constraint interpretation include supporters and opponents of downsizing public expenditures. Both usually agree that the rate of Federal program domestic growth from 1978 to the present was far below what it would have been if the annual growth rate of the midseventies had continued. Rather, they stress that there was a $19.2 billion aid reduction in constant dollars between 1978 and 1988 and a decline in aid as a proportion of state and local revenue to 17 percent. Even with the aid hikes under President Bush, the Federal share of subnational governmental revenues crept up to only 27 percent by FY 1993. Gramm-Rudman and especially the November 1990 agreement, most agree, did curb Federal budgetary outlays, though nowhere near what the constraints should have been.

A final point of major debate is *whether the federal system is overloaded or not.* By the end of the seventies, systemic overload was diagnosed as the chief malady afflicting the federal system.[15] The evidence cited then was the extraordinary expansion in national programs (that is, grants, loans, subsidies, regulations)—both major and many very minor—in the wide range of recipients, in grant conditions and regulations, in convoluted intergovernmental programmatic linkages, and in grant outlays. At the same time, there were too few Federal supervisory personnel, too few adequate controls, too few dollars, and too little accountability, given the advent of fungibility (that is, the inability to track the final program effects of Federal grant dollars). These fiscal administrative signs of overload gave rise to the impression that major policy-making had been centralized, even as implementation had been devolved for the most part.

From the perspective of the nineties many would contend that the system is still overloaded, not quite as much as it had been in 1980 but still overloaded. The gap between service demands and revenue receipts at the national level; the continuing influence of a centripetal interest group-dominated political system in Washington; the concomitant continuance of "slouching toward Washington"; the absence of effective party intermediaries and procedures to force a responsible reply to the systemic fiscal crisis; and the still largely centralizing and conservative court—all are current signs of an overloaded federal system.

The Federal propensity to slough off responsibilities to states and localities, to mandate without money, and to continue to rely on these governments to implement most of its domestic programs remains: No change here! And these continuities are part of the overload problem as well. Perhaps the major cause of this ongoing challenge is the popular habit, acquired largely in the seventies and eighties, of desiring a panoply of public programs but also of adhering to the now-venerable quotation of former senator Russell Long (D-La.): "Don't tax you, don't tax me, tax the man behind the tree."

The opposite view stresses the changes that have occurred since 1981. Reagan, after all, may not have succeeded in his New Federalism, but he barred a return to the seventies. The soaring deficits injected a kind of discipline into the system—not through a strengthening of parties but of congressional procedures that were intended to discipline. Gramm-Rudman and the November 1990 budget procedures, although far from perfect, did allow economy-minded legislators to exercise their franchise, and the Peterson probe showed that marginal (or true) pressure groups did suffer as a result.

WHY THESE CONFLICTING VIEWS?

A conflicting condition is one wherein, according to Webster, an emotional state exists characterized by indecision, restlessness, uncertainty, and tension. Well might one so describe the range of antagonistic assessments of U.S. intergovernmental relations today. Why this confusion? One answer is that there has been little agreement over the proper role and requisite needs of subnational governments, especially the states, in our federal system for over half a century, and there has been only glancing recognition that the states have been transformed over the past twenty-five years or so. The memories of rurally dominant, in some cases racist, and generally nonprogressive state governments die slowly. Related to this is the fact that no consensus has arisen since the New Deal over the proper Federal role in the federal system, other than economic action in hard times. The Reagan years, which some thought would settle the matter, left us in an even greater quandary about this issue than in 1980.

This not to say that the ambivalence in U.S. federalism today are a product only of conflicting intellectual interpretations and their impact. Far from it. The system to date, in fact, does reflect a simultaneous series of centralizing and devolutionary tendencies, of a co-optive national government and of less-shackled states, of competitive and collaborative administrative and political intergovernmental behaviors, of significant activism and of restraint, and of systemic overload and greater balance.

But how can this be? Part of the American political tradition has been the propensity to honor values that are basically incompatible, such as liberty and equality, individualism and group cooperation, and more recently, programmatic liberalism (support for individual governmental programs) and philosophic conservatism (hostility to big government). Present-day intellectual, institutional, and operational arenas of our system mirror a rich cluster of contradictions, and this really is nothing new. Yet, their number and destructive results are novel and merit attention.

What immediate causes contributed to this agenda of ambivalence? *The parlous condition of our economy and our public finances*, of late, is one major explanatory factor. On the one hand, the severe fiscal straits of the national government from 1982 until now have generated program cuts, eliminations, and a slow grant growth rate and an undergirding of a whole movement toward devolution. On the other hand, this same fiscal factor enhanced the earlier centripetal tilt in the system by promoting more regulations, more preemptions, more unfunded grant mandates, and more direct orders (that is, co-optive federalism's prime devices).

The economy, as such, produced a comparable result. State efforts during the recessions of 1981–1982 and 1990–1992 to institute self-help programs, attract foreign investment, curb and streamline government programs, and experiment with cost controls in health and hospital programs reflected noncentralizing undertakings and provided further evidence of state revitalization. When it came to matters of further Federal program cuts, prospective new mandates, the need to curb the dumping by foreign firms and other unfair trade practices harmful to industries in particular states, an inevitable reliance on heavy-duty representational efforts in Washington by members of the intergovernmental lobby occurred and occurs, and these were and are centralizing actions.

Another conditioner of our systemic inconsistencies is our *recently acquired new political system.* To generalize about the collective tendencies of the many, many actors in this system—the parties, especially the revamped national parties; the ever-expanding nationally based pressure-group complexes; the PACs; the media; the narrowly focused "iron triangles" of specific program concern; the unfocused, broadly constituted "issues networks" of wide policy involvement; and all of the hired hands that constitute a candidate's personal campaign organization—is a risky business. But, the focus of the overwhelming majority of these active political participants is national, and only incidentally state and local.

The reformed states are another new force, and one that provides one of the few firm foundations for noncentralization and devolution. With the financial, institutional, and representational reforms prompted both by forces from within and without, the states have become operationally indispensable to the overall workings of the system. In the seventies, they became again "the laboratories of democracy" after a forty-year hiatus; heavy revenue raisers despite earlier assertions that this could not or would not happen without a Federal tax credit; prime implementors of most Federal programs; increasingly more solicitous parents of their local governmental offspring; and policy innovators in such diverse areas as educational reform and finance, foreign trade and investment, hospital and health care reform, and consumer protection.

All this aside, the states by the very nature of our system have had to resort regularly to utilizing all the weaponry they can muster in Washington to ward off new conditions, resist more encroachments into their revenue reserves, avoid costly and undermining Court decisions, and fight off ruthlessly drafted new regulations. And these required actions of preservation contribute in their own way to centralization. Yet overall, the states' recent roles have served to enhance decentralization, cooperation, constraint, and a more balanced loading of the system.

The Supreme Court has served as a force that until recently, and like the new political actors, was centralizing. Since the early sixties its prime approach to interpreting the commerce and conditional spending powers and its assertive stance regarding the scope of the Fourteenth Amendment protections have produced a cumulative effect that was highly centripetal. Some reining in of the scope of the Fourteenth Amendment did occur during the Burger era, and Federal habeas corpus and Section 1983 appeals were curbed as the Court became more conservative in the eighties. These and other Court actions discussed earlier have balanced somewhat the status of the states' police powers, criminal justice processes, taxing authority and standing before the Court. All this weighs in moderately on the side of decentralization, interlevel comity, and judicial balance. But the Court's failure to date to provide any meaningful limits to the program and regulatory purposes to which the conditional spending power may be put, its equally permissive position on the commerce power, and its essentially modest procedural curb on Federal preemptions place its actions relating to elemental constitutional provisions affecting federalism on the centralizing, co-optive, confrontational, and overloaded side of the ambivalence agenda.

Finally at *the most elemental level of our social and political values,* yet another source of divergence arises. Libertarian concerns can generate a push to Washington when a First Amendment issue crops up, but the localities and states loom large when diversity and differences are the libertarian goals. Equity and egalitarian norms, which frequently conflict with libertarian norms, usually produce a thrust toward the center, but not when it is dominated by conservatives as it was in the eighties. Promising economic growth can lead to an international focus along with a state and regional one. Fearful economic protectionism, however, can lead only to Washington, and the help it can provide. Social issues of a moral, behavioral, or even religious nature may initially be fought out in state legislatures and courts, but if the issue is deeply controversial with vehement protagonists and rabid opponents, Congress and the Supreme Court ultimately will become involved. These battles over different values in our multicultural, superpluralistic society, along with public-finance, programmatic, administrative, and broadly systemic disputes, help explain some of the basic reasons for this mix of divergent tendencies within contemporary federalism. And in terms of the conflicting values issue, the emphasis sometimes is on the centralizing, co-optive, activist, overloaded side of the agenda and sometimes on the other, with decentralization, competition, and systemic balance being strengthened. In the main, the latter have not scored all that well in this current intergovernmental period.

IS FEDERALISM STILL A CORE VALUE?

The general findings and observations, along with the intellectual and operational ambivalence in the system, suggest both health and neglect regarding federalism. Tensions can be creative and conflict may be constructive, but hot ideological debates; unilateral power grabs, and resulting efforts to manipulate accounts and to discover loopholes in the rules are destructive. Moreover, they underscore the ways in which thoughtless neglect of the prerequisites of a resourceful federalism are expressed. A more balanced and better buttressed federalism can be a basis for resolving many of our most serious public issues; a conflicted one is not.

This brings up the question of whether federalism is still a core value in the American creed. It certainly was for all but the past thirty years of this republic's history, but what of it now? Intellectually, most of us do not see recent centripetal developments as part of an inevitable evolution to a unitary system. At the same time, compared with all the older authentic federal systems, ours alone provides continuing examples of a central government moving unilaterally against its own constituent governments. Is this premeditated centralization or a mindless neglect of the fundamental ground rules of a healthy federalism?

In what ways, then, is ours still a federal system? And why are they crucial to comprehend?

1. Societally, the American electorate, although increasingly subject to the pressures of homogenization, is still differentiated territorially. Popular attitudes on a range of topics—taxes, social issues, levels of regulation, public-services support—still vary on a regional and state-by-state basic, but not as much as a generation ago.

2. Attitudinally, the public's belief system even now embodies a hostility to big government, to enhancing governmental power, and to more governmental intrusion, despite its adherence to views that in practice add up to the opposite of all these attitudes.

3. In terms of economic modernization, the extraordinary expansion of small, frequently technically based entrepreneurial firms; of territorially targeted communication systems; and of differentiated state and local responses to educational, economic, public-finance, environmental, and consumer concerns suggests that a monolithic centralizing trend is not the inevitable result of increasing specialization, growing interdependence, and greater technological/informational advances. Moreover, states have proven to be more resourceful in economic development ventures than in central government.

4. Among the many interest groups now influencing policy in Washington, there are some that do understand the role of our territorial governments, their indispensability, and their renaissance, and there are some that reflect a deep anxiety about the national financial plight and the need for more retrenchment.

5. Fiscally, the revenue systems of the three levels are still, to a large degree, separated, and in good times the state-local sector constitutes a major force for fiscal resiliency.

6. Administratively, the national government since the 1960s and to greater degree than during the New Deal, has relied on states and, to a lesser degree, the localities to implement most of its domestic service and regulatory programs. If evolution toward a unitary system were really sought and deemed politically feasible, this heavily devolved pattern of implementation would not occupy the paramount position in today's system that it does, and most of state government would be mere adjuncts of well-staffed, fully supervising Federal agencies, which is not the case.

7. Judicially, the Supreme Court has begun to enumerate a clearer conception of the need for states that are not totally shackled, although this, as yet, is not its dominant stand.

8. Local governments, to a greater degree than has been the case since the early sixties, are more cognizant of their organic interdependence with and dependence on their states.

These eight noncentralizing features of contemporary American federalism—although significant—still leave the constituent governments and their localities at the mercy of unilateral interventions actions of national government officials and to the hostile pressure tactics of interest groups in Washington that do not defer to the federalist principle. After more than twenty-one decades of development, federalism ought to mean more than a cultural attachment and sentiment. Its operational, fiscal, educational, testing, and social diversity advantages also should be appreciated.

AN AGENDA FOR REFORM

A revitalized federalism, then, is needed to free up the Federal government from its fixation with minutiae, with concerns and political complexes that are not national, and with all the other distractions that enfeeble it. Can federalism facilitate a strengthening of the federal system and of the national government? Of course, it can. But first the new political system needs to be scrapped; it should be clear by now what ought to be done. The states, as has been demonstrated throughout this analysis, have done well in the realm of operational federalism, and their record in this practical world of programs, personnel, and funding would be even better if they were less constrained by the cumulative effects of Federal regulations, preemptions, grant mandates, and judicial dictates. To strengthen the states where they are weak, to reduce Federal authority where it is overreaching, but to enhance it where it is enfeebled—these are the three basic goals of any genuine program for federalism reform. Remember, for the states, all that is sought is to put them on a par with their counterparts in Australia, Germany, and Switzerland (Canada's provinces have been given too much power over the past three decades). A freeing up of the states and of the national government is the thrust of what is needed now, along with the accompanying hope that the localities would also benefit from these systemic liberations.

To circumvent some of the current ambivalences in the system and to end some of the distrustful, destructive, and self-defeating intergovernmental behavioral patterns that are found in so many areas of interlevel activities, a new unshackling strategy is required. Changes then are needed on four fronts.

First, *focus on the weaknesses of constitutional federalism*; it is time for the Supreme Court to take seriously its mandate from Hamilton in Federalist 78, from Madison and Oliver Ellsworth in the First Congress, and from Marshall as chief justice that the umpiring responsibility in a federal system is one of its most fundamental assignments. It should learn from its sister high courts in Karlsruhe, Ottawa, and Canberra that centralization may be countenanced in certain areas, and constituent government rights must be protected in others. It should come to grips with the fact that judicial passivity in the conditional spending, commerce, and supremacy clause areas leaves it to the political branches of the national government to determine the reach of their own powers therein.

The country needs Court decisions of a landmark character in these areas to reflect a long overdue balancing of national and federalist values. In addition, Article V's state-initiated amendatory option needs to be sanitized so that it actually may be used. Madison did not deem it appropriate to leave the first phase of amending our basic charter solely to the Congress of the United States. It is time to make alive what is dead constitutional law. Such a safeguard is a minimum and traditional one. It is urgently needed now to begin to curb the cavalier and careless approach to asserting national power that has prevailed over the past three decades. It should begin by two-thirds of the states legislatures adopting common and carefully phrased resolutions petitioning Congress to issue a call for a constitutional convention to consider this one fundamental issue.

Second, *mount a variety of efforts to overcome the feeble condition of most state and local parties.* Compared to the sixties, state parties today are far more likely to provide services to their candidates, to perform electoral mobilization undertakings , to conduct public opinion polls, to publish newspapers or bulletins, and to raise money. But vital as these functions are, they are not enough to counteract the arrival of a large number of new interest groups in state capitals that began during the Reagan years nor to help recapture control over formerly party functions. This should mean drives to curb or even eliminate the detailed state codes of regulation that govern practically every aspect of party activity at both the state and local levels.

Third, *states and localities need to reassert themselves in the representational sphere.* State and local organizations should attempt to

- ensure that the Federal regulation of lobbying act (1993) with its exemption of public-interest groups and tightened rules for private-sector lobbyists is effectively implemented.
- amend the Federal Advisory Committee legislation of 1974 to place public-interest groups in an exempt status. Such groups should be given preferred status in grant rule making, modifications, and policy-development decisions. This legislation places the very implementators of most Federal domestic programs on par with all the self-centered interest groups in the Republic.
- beef up the Federal Fiscal Note legislation of 1982 so that the "guesstimates" may be called for during or after subcommittee deliberations and that a point of order may be made on the floor if this requirement is not met.
- develop specific judicial arguments for State-Local Legal Center briefs that would fix parameters around the conditional spending and preempting powers.
- demonstrate clearly, when severely provoked, the state's overwhelmingly paramount operational role and the impotence of the Federal agencies to carry out the will of Congress by having the remaining states that participate in voluntary partial preemption programs, like OSHA, withdraw in a dramatic fashion from the program. After a decent interval all states would, when cause was shown, file suites in Federal district courts throughout the land citing the Federal agency's failure to implement the legislation. A way is needed to assert the states' operational power in the political and judicial spheres, and this might be one.

The last suggestion may sound fairly drastic, but the national government and the politics in which it is enmeshed must be freed form the folly of petty power plays; of dozens of puny project grants that functionally add up to nothing but pork and politics; of unreimbursed regulations on states and localities; of Federal regulating agencies that lack the personnel and sometimes the professionalism to carry out a direct regulatory role; of a Supreme Court that hands down a decision on patronage that is almost totally ignored, save for the local jurisdiction that figured in the case. A strange mix exists here of real and empty threats, of pretentious and pharisaic behavior. Yet, all are completely possible, even in an era of fiscal stringencies, because the Federal role in the federal system still seems endless though its resources are finite. Hence, the gap between promise and the performance in Washington and the basic source of many of the ambivalence analyzed earlier.

A stronger intergovernmental representation, then, is needed at the national level to inject some programmatic reality into the frequently fuzzy understanding there of governmental operations, to voice the territorial perspective amidst the cacophony of the functional clusterings, and in this process, to help unburden both the Federal and subnational governments from the special pleaders. Perhaps the greatest obstacles to achieving this kind of systemic representational undertaking are the deep division between and among members of the state and local groupings, who tend to forget that unity—rare though it is—has produced positive results. The natural propensity on the part of state and local leaders is to focus on the immediate and to put off pondering the long-term effects of current conflicting developments.

Were these strengthening representational reforms to come about, the national government could be unburdened of the need to resort to brazenness, bluff, and bluster to convey the image of being the senior partner in the federalism drama, in that the intergovernmental groups would not have to tolerate such unbecoming behavior. The states and localities also would be better protected against unreimbursed mandates, arbitrary regulations, and court cases that denigrate the special jurisdictional and operational status that is theirs. Ideally, a relationship rooted in the rough parity that nearly prevails now in the domestic expenditures areas should emerge.

Of prime concern is the operational sphere of intergovernmental relations, and it is in this fiscal, functional, and administrative realm of shared governmental operations that many of the ultimate results of the dynamics in the judicial, political, and representational spheres are seen. It is also in this sphere that many ambivalent tendencies manifest themselves: centralization and devolution, cooperation and competition, co-option and collaboration, activism and inaction. Yet, it also is here that a better balance between the center and the periphery can be clearly discerned.

The healthy signs include the enhanced fiscal, policy, and implementation roles of the states; the Federal-state collaboration in such recent legislative enactments as ISTEA and the Clean Air Act Amendments; the devolution to the states of greater administrative authority under certain environmental programs; and the improved intergovernmental administration caused by the reduction in bypassing and the disappearance of the "funny-money" syndrome. Above all, the reduced Federal domestic expenditure role coupled with the increasing state-local share of domestic outlays from their own revenues underlies a new and more balanced trend in intergovernmental operations.

The negative aspects of this recent record include a rush to regulate and mandate at both the national state levels, which has engendered anger and distrust at all the subnational levels; a reemergence of deep interlevel entanglements because of this development; a rapid pickup in preemptions; a hollowing out of Federal domestic agencies by personnel cuts, regulations, and politicization; the understandable tendency on the part of many states to probe for loopholes in order to avoid compliance or to save money; and the increasing fragmentation of local government, which provides a continuing source of functional weakness at this level.

The Federal aid package has acquired some features that are new and menacing and others that are old and disreputable. Among the former is the ever-growing proportion of payments to individuals soaring from 36 percent in FY 1960 to 62 percent in FY 1993, and a corresponding decline in the share of grant monies going for physical capital projects, which experienced a sharp drop form 47 percent to 17 percent during the same period. This course dramatizes the extraordinary drop-off in grants to governments for governmental functions and a nearly uncontrollable rise in the states' role as administrators and partial funders of transfer payments to people. Another vital aspect of the Federal grant package is that although the number of programs continues to grow chiefly for congressional and interest-groups' entrepreneurial reasons, in 1993 thirty-seven programs out of 593 accounted fro over 90 percent of the FY 1993 dollar total, and just four—Medicaid, food stamps, family support welfare, and the highway obligation ceiling—represented over two-thirds of the total. Put differently, there is an extraordinary number of small formula and especially paltry project grants that explains the explosion in the number of grants. Yet, their impact, save for those involving highly specialized and objectively targeted research and demonstration projects, is mostly political in the narrowest sense of the word. Moreover, the degree to which many grants (such as higher education project grants and certain highway programs) now are subject to congressional earmarking further undercuts a claim to legitimate national concern with these aspects of the grant enactment process.

Reforms of one sort or another are clearly suggested by the above and other IGR operational findings presented elsewhere. At the very minimum, state and local officials should be granted more discretion in implementing Federal grant programs, and the earlier recommendations dealing with better consultation, mandate review, and preemption should be instituted.[16] Additionally, the earlier IGR machinery within the executive branch should be reestablished, and President Clinton has begun doing this.

At a higher level of political risk are recommendations that call for the elimination of all categorical grants that provide less than 5 percent of total state-local program outlays, the merger of dozens of small grants so they at least reach this threshold level, and the creation of block grants in various areas now dominated by categoricals (for example, education of the handicapped, special education, vocational education, higher education scholarships, library programs). Moreover, and assuming a continuation of Medicaid as a separate shared program, Congress and the administration should encourage state demonstration projects that broaden health coverage by liberalizing and streamlining the waiver process.[17] The Employment Retirement Income Security Act of 1974 (ERISA) should be amended so as to encourage, not hinder, state efforts to require employers to provide a specific health plan or to pay state-imposed premium taxes.[18]

Shifting to the equally significant state-local relations arena, all states should enact legislation to establish state-level advisory commissions on intergovernmental relations (ACIRs) to provide—as more than half the states have—neutral turf on which state and local officials may meet, identify, and debate outstanding interlevel sources of tension, and it is hoped, come up with proposals for resolving such issues. Finally, states and their respective city and county associations should join with their ACIRs to probe the fundamental jurisdictional dilemma that excessive numbers of small nonviable local units create, and come up with ways and means of overcoming their dysfunctionality.

Turning now to the most ambitious of the reform propositions, many believe the time has come to apply some basic surgery to the intergovernmental system, so that federalism becomes part of the solution to, not a cause of, the nation's basic economic, fiscal, administrative, and program problems. In light of the Federal deficit; the still-unsure economy; the health care industry's sopping up annually of 14 percent of GNP and accounting for half of every triple-digit Federal deficit; and the staggering challenge of reconciling the goals of various of our social policies with contrary goals implicit in some of the above, it is time to revisit the "sorting-out" proposals.

Unlike its predecessors, the argument here is not made solely on the basis of improved program administration through devolution, as it was in Eisenhower's time; nor solely on the basis of decongesting a heavily overloaded system for the sake of greater functional effectiveness and greater equity, as the Advisory Commission on Intergovernmental Relations proposed in 1981;[19] not solely on the basis of Reagan's "Big Swap" 1982 State of the Union proposal, which was largely rooted in an ideological thrust to get several grant programs, including most of welfare, back to the states (but Medicaid would have been nationalized);[20] nor solely on the basis of resolving the nation's current economic and fiscal nightmares, as Alice Rivlin has recently and persuasively advocated,[21] though this clearly enters into any current argument for "dividing the job." Among the other reasons for advocating a sensible "Big Swap" now are these:

- The national government's role in national affairs is infinitely more unpredictable, less understandable, and obviously a consumer of unusual amounts of presidential and congressional time, given the wide-ranging uncertainty of a post-cold war world; hence, the need to unburden it of what now seems to be extraneous or secondary domestic issues that the states and localities are perfectly capable of handling.

- The states need to be unburded too—of arbitrary deficit-driven mandates, of unnecessary preemptions, and of being treated as pressure groups rather than full partners. A realigning of present entangled servicing roles would further underscore the need for this unshackling.

- The functioning local governments—not the feeble, the tiny, or the very limited though ostensibly general-purpose units—need some unburdening too. A sensible realigning of servicing and regulatory responsibilities to the states could reduce Federal intrusions into local America and reestablish a rare singular and constitutionally proper local reliance on the states for various needed aids, freedoms, and proper regulations.

- Above all perhaps, the entire system needs a severe slashing of the extent of interest-group focusing on and lobbying in the nation's capital. The much publicized national gridlock, in truth, was just as much a matter of irreconcilable interests and of rigid ideologies as it was of political differences or systemic weaknesses. With the elimination and devolution of a host of programs that do not belong on the nation's agenda but do belong on that of subnational governments—all of which must live with balanced budgets—the impression of total national ascendancy in most policy areas will be readjusted to the realities of a system that has acquired a new equilibrium.

- Finally, with health and welfare reform as major components of the Clinton administration agenda, not to mention grappling with the deficit and the need for a more dynamic economy, major contemporary reasons present themselves for considering the very real possibility of harnessing a revamped federal system to aid, if not solve, these great public policy challenges.

What in broad-brush terms should be considered in a "Big Swap" for the nineties? The first thing to ponder is that over the past thirty years, as underscored above, *we have already experienced a major sorting out of basic fiscal and servicing assignments.* Despite the jumble of programs and shifts in their objectives, the Federal government's overall domestic focus has been on people, not on place or territorial governments, nor on the program needs of such governments. And this sorting out at the Federal level by the allocation of relatively small amounts of aid funds for nontransfer-payment programs, and the compensating actions at the state and local levels underscore the capacity of the latter governments to cope quite well with a variety of functions that fall under what Alice Rivlin calls "The Productivity Agenda": public infrastructure, job training, education reform, housing, rural services, and economic development.[22] For profound altruistic, experiential, and self-interested reasons, state and local officials as they confront the rigors of economic restructuring have no difficulty in melding these servicing areas into a scheme that along with those of sister states produces a competitive and productive response to what otherwise would be potentially crippling challenges. These, after all, are program areas where the national government has not been especially successful.

For the Federal government, research and development, central information gathering, some transportation functions (that is, air traffic control, some highways), some income-maintenance programs, and above all the jobs of reforming the most expensive and least effective health system in the world and of dealing with the deficit would be exclusively left to it. Shared Federal-state programs would continue in the areas of the environment, natural resources, probably AFDC (depending on the outcome of the welfare-reform proposals), higher education, and student grants and loans.

With this swap, the states would lost the bulging burden of the Medicaid matches but acquire full responsibility (in partnership with their localities in some functional areas) for the devolved Federal programs for primary and secondary education, job training, community and economic development, housing, social services, most highways and other transportation, juvenile justice, and drug control.[23] The Federal government would be left with the challenging assignments of reacquiring the capacity to implement its own traditional exclusive program responsibilities in an effective fashion, and of dealing with health reform, the economy, and the deficit.

At some point, once the dust has settled a bit from the flurry of program reassignments, it should develop a Federal-state equalization fund to even out the fiscal discrepancies among the states that emerge after the devolutions and nationalizations. The relief from Medicaid, for example, would help the affluent states far more than it would the middling ones, given the differences in their respective participation rates. All this still adds up to a heavy Hamiltonian agenda for the country's central government, but one that with the new freedom that this sorting out provides has a good chance of being addressed.

A LAST WORD

The "Permissive Federalism" designation was used to describe the actual power relations between the central and the state and local governments. It was deemed an accurate but also an unpleasant description for any faithful federalist. Should the proposals advanced here receive recognition and be acted on in the near future, the designation "Protected Federalism" will be appropriate, and a rebirth of American federalism will have been achieved. Moreover, the incidence of "slouching toward Washington" would be slashed significantly. And this would be in keeping with the intent of the Founders, the thrust of our political tradition, the lessons that foreign federal systems teach us, and the basic policy problems confronting the nation.

NOTES

1. Jack P. Greene, "The Background of the Articles of Confederation," *Publius* 12 (Fall 1982): 18–19.
2. Ibid., 20–25.
3. See ibid., 24.
4. Richard H. Leach, *American Federalism* (New York: Norton, 1970), 30.
5. These included contact with the committee on appeals of the Privy Council in cases of judicial appeal; with the Board of Trade on legislative review and disallowance matters; with the treasury and customs commissioners regarding the colonial customs service; with the High Court of Admiralty on marine and violations-of-trade-act cases; and with the secretary of state for the Southern Department on military, foreign policy, and royal gubernatorial matters.
6. Quoted in Alpheus T. Mason, *Free Government in the Making: Readings in American Political Thought* (New York: Oxford University Press, 1949), 130–31.
7. Alfred H. Kelly, Winfred A. Harbison, and Herman Belz, *The American Constitution: Its Origins and Development*, 6th ed. (New York: Norton, 1983), 56.
8. Greene, "The Background of the Articles of Confederation," 29–32.
9. Ibid., 30.
10. Ibid., 33.
11. Jack Rakove, "The Legacy of the Articles of Confederation," *Publius* 12 (Fall 1982): 48.
12. Ibid., 50.
13. See Andrew C. McLaughlin, *A Constitutional History of the United States* (New York: Appleton, 1935), 125.
14. Rakove, "The Legacy of the Articles of Confederation," 52.
15. Greene, "The Background of the Articles of Confederation." 43.
16. McLaughlin, *A Constitutional History*, 185.
17. See Clinton Rossiter, *The American Presidency* (New York: Harcourt, Brace & World, 1959), 76ff.
18. Ibid., 77.
19. Benjamin F. Wright, *Consensus and Continuity* (Boston: Boston University Press, 1958), 34–35.
20. See McLaughlin, *A Constitutional History*, 180–81.
21. See Wright, *Consensus and Continuity*, 32.
22. See McLaughlin, *A Constitutional History*, 185–86.
23. Ibid., 190.

15

Janet E. Kodras

RESTRUCTURING THE STATE: DEVOLUTION, PRIVATIZATION, AND THE GEOGRAPHIC REDISTRIBUTION OF POWER AND CAPACITY IN GOVERNANCE

The search for appropriate division of responsibility within and between the public and private sectors is an ongoing process in the American federal system, a political struggle rooted in the U.S. Constitution. Recent trends have favored reducing the role played by the national government as it sheds selective responsibilities to state and local administrations, private firms, nonprofit organizations, civic groups, and households. Determining who benefits and who loses from the current wave of devolution and privatization is speculative until after the fact, but one repercussion is already apparent: The current reductions in the scale and scope of the American state will increase geographic disparities in the role and effect of government in accordance with the capacity of institutions and groups in particular places to take on functions previously coordinated by the national government. The capacity to assume these responsibilities is defined by the extent to which fiscal resources, expertise, infrastructure, and political will exist, or can be developed, within specific locales. In this sense, capacity for governance is geographically and historically produced, reflecting the place-specific and time-accumulated material resources and discursive practices that sustain and justify actions of the state and civil society.

STRATEGIES OF STATE CHANGE

Governmental restructuring is manifested in complex and highly differentiated ways, focusing on different facets of economic and social life. Across all such realms, state change is currently promulgated through three primary strategies: devolution, privatization, and dismantling. Each of these is defined below as a foundation for discussion to follow.

Devolution refers to the transfer, or decentralization, of government functions from higher to lower levels of the federal hierarchy. As a transformation internal to the state that alters the scale of activities, devolution redefines government responsibilities for regulating civil society, transfers authority across levels and administrative units of government, redraws the map of government costs and benefits, and changes accessibility and entitlement to government services. In shifting responsibilities and resources to lower tiers in the federal hierarchy, the national government still retains authority to set the direction for change, as "this complex subnational reconstitution of state power and regulatory structures is occurring within a set of political, discursive, an institutional parameters established by (or mediated by) the nation-state" (Peck, 1996, p. 3). Devolution is an inherently spatial process of state change—first, because the American federal structure is a hierarchical organization of territorially demarcated governments, and second, because the uneven development of different local states generates dissimilar initiatives in response to devolution according to local needs, perceptions, and abilities.

Privatization refers to the transfer of government functions to commercial firms and nonprofit organizations, thus substituting the private sector for components of the public sector. Examples of the government's encouragement of, and entanglements with, the private sector include the establishment of quasi-governmental corporations (e.g., the U.S. Postal Service, Amtrak); the employment of private contractors (e.g., for construction of the interstate highway system and other forms of infrastructure, contracts to assess and clean environmentally damaged properties); and the use of vouchers and subsidies to be spent in the commercial sector (e.g., food stamps, agricultural export incentives, Section 8 rent subsidies).

As these examples suggest, privatization incorporates a vast assortment of institutions into the business of government. The *for-profit sector* participates through direct corporate service providers (e.g., Hospital Corporation of America, Marriott Lifecare Retirement Communities, Corrections Corporation of America); corporate-established foundations (e.g., the Ford Foundation, J. Paul Getty Trust, Lilly Endowment, Inc.); and other corporate-supported organizations (e.g., Urban League, American Enterprise Institute, La Raza, Brookings Institution). The *nonprofit sector* includes nationally known entities (e.g., the Red Cross, United Way), as well as local voluntary organizations numbering in the tens of thousands. The importance of the nonprofit sector has reached the point that it is referred to as the *shadow state,* "a para-state apparatus comprised of multiple voluntary sector organizations, administered outside of traditional democratic politics and charged with major collective service responsibilities previously shouldered by the public sector, yet remaining within the purview of state control" (Wolch, 1990, p. xvi).

Privatization redefines the scope of government but does not eliminate its role altogether, because the state externalizes only selected functions to nongovernmental entities. At issue here is the proper relationship between the public and private spheres of American life—the extent to which the state should cast off service provision while retaining sovereign authority for policy making and oversight.

Finally, *dismantling* refers to the withdrawal of a government function no longer deemed appropriate for the state to provide. Dismantling is accomplished through the outright elimination of programs or by the more covert mechanisms of cutting financial support, allowing funding to fall behind the cost-of-living, or complicating regulatory procedures to the point that administration and oversight are rendered impossible. In the case of complete dismantling, the state reduces the scope of its activities; and these either cease to exist or fall to whomever will take responsibility. Private firms may see financial incentives to acquire government assets, such as mineral extraction firms purchasing Western public lands. Alternatively, responsibilities may fall to the domestic sphere. For example, the retraction of government responsibility for long-term health care, via Medicaid, would require many households to assume responsibility of family members who are elderly or severely disabled, regardless of their financial ability or competence to do so. Because the functions discarded by the government often fall to individuals, dismantling represents the most extreme form of spatial fragmentation under conditions of state change.

These three strategies of state change reflect important differences in the understood role and acceptability of government involvement in a given function. Devolution implies that a particular policy remains an accepted function of government, but that a different tier should hold responsibility for its provision; whereas privatization indicates that a given function should be performed within society but not by government. Dismantling occurs when the function is no longer deemed appropriate, whether for program-specific or broadly ideological reasons. Such "understanding" of the legitimate role of government is time- and place-specific; competing political groups seek to impose their particular vision of the acceptable functions of government in pursuit of larger agendas to decenter or recenter or recenter the national state.

Among those who seek to check the power of the national state, *devolutionists* argue that government should be "close to the people," because the local state has greater flexibility to efficiently address local needs and effectively satisfy local preferences (Bennett, 1990; Schwab, 1988). Others seek to diminish the role of the national state through privatization: *corporatists* contend that substituting the monopoly power held by the state with market competition introduced by private firms is more cost effective and responsive to consumer demand (Le Grand & Robinson, 1984); whereas *voluntarists* assert that nonprofit organizations are most deeply rooted in communities, fostering individuals' altruistic participation in civic life (Pines, 1982; Salamon, Musselwhite, & de Vita, 1986).

Proponents of a strong national state challenge each of these arguments. The leading response to the devolutionist perspective charges that local state control creates sharp inequities in government provision because those areas with the greatest need for services have the least resources, and often the least political will, to address those needs (Smith, 1986). Even when local governments do responds to local preferences, policies enacted to serve the interests in the local majority may fail to protect the economically and politically disenfranchised. Furthermore, while devolution of authority to state and local governments may appear to support local autonomy, in practice such responsibilities can create severe problems in policy making and financing at the local level. Delegating "knotty problems" to lower tiers displaces conflict away form the national government, which may engender local political battles and fiscal crises (Cockburn, 1977).

Among those opposing privatization of state functions, critics of the corporatist perspective hold that the competition assumed to make private firms more efficient than the government is often absent, so that the state has traditionally had to take on those very societal responsibilities that private suppliers shun (U.S. House of Representatives, 1991). These critics also hold that the government must retain control over policy making and oversight of private service providers to prevent fraud and abuse by those not directly accountable to the public (GAO, 1991).

The major argument against the voluntarism position is that nonprofit organizations, highly fragmented and oriented toward amenities for elites more than services for the needy, cannot be expected to substitute for the state's entitlement provision, have no prescribed obligation to national priorities, and cannot be held culpable for their actions (Wolpert, 1993).

Finally, several participants in the debate present a more refined perspective, arguing that the determination of how best to sort responsibilities between the public and private spheres, and within the federal hierarchy, cannot be resolved in the abstract, and that the choice must necessarily depend on the particular type of policy involved. DiIulio and Kettl (1995, citing Osborne, 1993) identify four policy domains where the national state should retain control, resisting devolution to states and localities:

> *Interstate Issues:* Problems cannot be solved without federal action because state and local governments lack leverage or incentives.
>
> *Uniform Standards:* Solutions require uniform standards (e.g., social security).
>
> *Destructive Competition:* Policies are so sensitive to competition between states or localities that such competition creates negative consequences that exceed the benefits of decentralization.
>
> *Fiscal Redistribution:* Solutions require redistribution of national resources to poor regions that lack them.

Peterson (1995) elaborates on these points, contending that policies encouraging economic development are best handled at state and local levels, while redistributive policies championing the social welfare are best controlled at the national level. He finds that interjurisdictional rivalry lies at the core of this division of responsibilities: Competition between state and local governments drives them to efficiently and effectively provide basic government services and promote their economic development, but this same competition engenders a "race to the boom" among state and local governments when held responsible for social welfare and other redistributive policies. Finally, Wolpert (1993) contributes to the debate over sorting responsibilities between the public and private sectors, finding that nonprofit organizations are well suited to contribute to amenities, such as the arts, in accordance with local preferences; but that they lack the resources and infrastructure to address critical local needs, such as social welfare, where the redistributive and risk-pooling capacity of the national government is needed.

These three primary strategies for restructuring the state, and the principles sustaining them, have been employed throughout American federal history, with each holding sway at particular points throughout this distinctive and dynamic experiment in the territorial dispensation of power and responsibility. I discuss these strategies of state restructuring in the following section that briefly traces development of the American federal system to the present moment of controversy.

DEFINING THE SCALE AND SCOPE OF THE FEDERAL STATE

As "the most geographically expressive form of all political systems," federalism is a distinctive spatial structure of governance that confers ultimate authority to no single level or branch of government as it seeks to balance power among the various components (Robinson, 1961). The American federal system is internationally distinguished for the explicit and distinct role played by governments in its subnational tiers; the total $3 trillion government budget in the United States consists of about half state and local expenditures and half federal spending (DiIulio & Kettl, 1995). In addition, almost 50% of all federal discretionary spending takes the form of grants to state and local governments (11%) or contacts to private sector organizations (37%) (DiIulio & Kettl, 1995).

Although the national government is currently the stronger partner in the American federal system, the 50 states and more than 80,000 local governments retain substantial control; and the distribution of benefits and burdens conferred by government is still largely a function of the jurisdiction in which one lives. The amount of taxes one pays, the penalty for committing a crime, the control over land use, the level of public school expenditures, the availability of public assistance, the extent of public subsidies for economic development and job growth, and myriad other regulations and rules shaping the lives of Americans vary substantially from place to place across the United States.

Alteration of the federal system, as currently under discussion, involves a geographic rearrangement of these benefits and burdens and thus a redistribution of power and resources among places. Even avowedly aspatial policies directed by the national government vary in their impact and effectiveness when implemented in different local jurisdictions (Kodras, 1990). Devolving federal responsibilities to state and local governments or shifting functions to a highly fragmented private sector greatly accentuates geographic variations in government provision.

The question of how best to divide responsibilities within the American federal system, first raised in the country's founding documents, has no final answer: "It cannot be settled by one generation, because it is a question of growth, and every new successive stage of our political and economic development gives it a new aspect, makes it a new question" (President Woodrow Wilson, cited in Malbin, 1996, p. 5). Accordingly, the power of the federal government has waxed and waned over the course of the 20th century. Its role expanded in the wake of the Great Depression in the 1930s, escalated during World War II, and increased further during the period of postwar economic growth in the 1960s. Efforts to reduce the power of the national government relative to the states grew during the Nixon administration it the 1970s, accelerated during the Reagan administration of the 1980s, and has taken on new force since the 1994 congressional election.

Over time, the national government has alternated the expansion and the retraction of its role by redefining its administrative partnerships with state and local governments (via changes in the types of magnitude of grants) and the private and nonprofit sectors (via alterations in contract activity). For example, the procurement of war supplies from private vendors and the promotion of technological innovation during World War II set the pattern of government contractual involvement with the private sector ever since. Its initial partnerships with defense and aerospace industries have expanded in the postwar era to include virtually every sector of government activity.

An important means by which the national government alters its relationship to state and local governments is changing the flow of funding, shifting between categorical grants, block grants, and general revenue sharing. *Categorical grants* (consisting of operating, capital, and entitlement programs) provide funds to state and local governments for a particular purpose designated by federal law. Specific program regulations constrain, but do no eliminate, state and local flexibility as categorical grants are implemented and administered in diverse place contexts (Pressman & Wildavsky, 1973). *Block grants* (federal stipends intended to address a general area of government activity) give subnational governments greater spending flexibility, and general revenue sharing (a lump sum payment with virtually no strings attached) concedes almost total discretion to governments at the subnational level.

Recent effort to strengthen the power of states and localities relative to the national government have focused on shifting from categorical to block grants, although the approaches have differed in important ways (Nathan, 1996). Whereas Nixon advocated converting operating and capital grants into block grants, he retained entitlement programs, arguing nationwide responsibility to preserve a basic safety net for the American population. Reagan's position was more complicated, but ultimately followed the pattern set by Nixon. In contrast, current efforts target the conversion of entitlement grants, which provide assistance wherever and whenever need is demonstrated, into general block grants with strict limits on funding and participation. This latest proposal represents a fundamental shift in the customary role of the federal government dating back to the New Deal of the 1930s.

In this and other ways, the year 1994 signaled an important moment in the history of American federalism as the election of a Republican majority in both houses, including a large number of activist conservatives, took the lead in challenging the power of the national state. The defining document of the 1990s effort to restructure government was House Republicans' *Contract with America.* This and related efforts advocate swift reduction in the size and scope of the national government, devolving federal responsibilities to state and localities, shifting functions to the private and nonprofit sectors, dismantling regulations, and, in some cases, eliminating programs and funding altogether.

The current effort to reduce the national state is not limited to congressional initiative, however (Malbin, 1996; Pagano & Bowman, 1995). In contrast to his party's traditional defense of the national government, President Clinton seeks a "middle path" that allows decentralization and state flexibility, yet retains safeguards guided at the national level. In addition, the U.S. Supreme Court has reasserted the principle of dual sovereignty, specified in the Bill of Rights, as a foundation for several recent rulings. The 50 states have taken contradictory positions, some celebrating the prospect of increased flexibility and others fearing the loss of revenues to undertake initiatives newly expected of them.

The current trend in restructuring federalism through devolution and privatization of functions previously held by the national state—a trend identifiable in various guises for more than 20 years—has distinctive implications for governance in different places across the country. I discuss the geographic consequences of current efforts at state restructuring in the following section.

LOCAL CAPACITY AND THE GEOGRAPHIC REDISTRIBUTION OF POWER

Evidence from previous efforts to reduce the scale and scope of the American state suggest that the current phase will increase geographic inequities in the role and effect of government, and that the resultant patterns will correspond with the capacity of institutions and groups in particular places to take on functions formerly coordinated by the national government.

> A decade of devolution and decentralization of federal programs has already yielded considerable disparity between places because states and municipalities vary in their

fiscal resources and willingness to compensate for federal cutbacks. Much of this effect could have been readily anticipated from public finance studies of fiscal federalism and the organization of the nonprofit sector. The decentralization strategy may potentially help to restrict central government growth, but it also reduces the prospects for consistently equitable remedies across America's communities by either public or nonprofit sectors. (Wolpert, 1993, pp. 37–38)

The capacity to take on responsibilities is defined by the extent to which fiscal resources, expertise, infrastructure, and political will exist, or can be cultivated, within particular localities. Over time, places take on distinctive economic characteristics (based on local resource endowments, production systems, class relations, etc.); political practices (grounded in factional ideologies, traditions of party dominance, local civic and philanthropic traditions, etc.); and social relations (defined by race, ethnicity, gender, generation, etc.). Taken together, these conditions create specific institutional contexts—accretions of organizational experience and political seasoning, capital and infrastructure—that shape the capacity of governmental and nongovernmental organizations and groups in each jurisdiction, and indeed, the local sense of what is possible and appropriate for these entities to undertake. As a result, state and local governments, private corporations, nonprofit organizations, community groups, and individual households situated in different places vary considerably in their ability to respond to state restructuring at the national level. As these differences are thrown into sharp relief by devolution and privatization, the more affluent, experienced, and innovative hold a distinct advantage (Greenberg, Popper, & West, 1991).

Although the conditions defining institutional capacity are specific to place, they are by no means generated solely *within* a given place, but are instead developed through the evolving relationship of the place to the wider world. As opposed to the traditional definition of *place* as "a bounded and static portion of space," recent conceptualizations treat place as open and mutable, shaped by forces telescoping inward as global processes are transcribed and translated into local contexts. Defining place in terms of its relations to other places, the outside as constitutive of the inside (Massey, 1994; Mouffe, 1995), suggests that institutional capacities *in* place are created as global capitalist production, national government practices, and societal conventions are differentially refracted into specific local contexts. Furthermore, institutional capacities evolve over time, "by layer upon layer of interconnections with the world beyond" (Massey, 1994, p. 8). As a result, places differ in their ability to address local needs because they are dependent on their particular position within the world economy; and although this position can change, it is heavily constrained by previous layers of investment and political experience that define the capacity to address those needs.

Seen in this light, places are highly vulnerable to alterations in the larger political economy. The current drive toward global economic integration in the midst of a two-decade slowdown in productive expansion compels change in the operation of firms and governments placed around the world as each seeks to reposition itself within the intensifying competition. The result is a fundamental transformation in the global political economy, a rearrangement of the *geographic* relations between capital, the state, and civil society.

Of the three, *capital* has become the most mobile. Although some segments of capital, such as local real estate envelopment (see Cox & Mair, 1988), remain more place-bound and locally dependent than others, such as international finance (see Warf, 1996), capital has increased its ability to play across the global stage, situating its practices in particular places as it finds profitable sites for production (Harvey, 1982; Peck, 1995). In contrast to the growing international operation of important segments of capital, states remain largely confined to jurisdictional boundaries. *National states* increasingly operate within a global economy that they are unable to control (Clark & Dear, 1984) as nation-based fordist production, regulated by the Keynesian welfare state, yields to globally extensive postfordist production, emancipated through deregulation by the neoliberal state (Jessop, 1993; Peck & Tickell, 1994). The neoliberal restructuring of the national state, taking the particular forms of devolution and privatization in the United States, passes greater responsibility onto *local states*, which are even less capable of exerting power within a globalized economy. Finally, despite the prospect of migration or some individuals, *civil society* remains the most place-bound and locally dependent, due to material, familiar, and emotional ties to community (Beynon & Hudson, 1993; Cox & Mair, 1998). David Harvey (1989) nails the point: "Labor power has to go home every night" (p. 19). These interconnected trends—globalizaiton of capital, devolution and privatization of the state, and localization of civil society—shift power increasingly toward capital (Offe, 1985; Peck, 1995; Storper & Walker, 1989), an asymmetrical power relation termed "glocalization" by Swyngedouw (1992).

Even this cursory review of the shifting geographic relations between capital, the state, and civil society helps us to understand the current restructuring of the U.S. government as a process whereby the state renegotiates its dual role with national governments in an era of economic globalization has important implications for locally based states, private nonprofit organizations, and social movements.

First, local states are left with less control to position themselves within a volatile global economy, even as the national state passes off additional responsibility for them to attempt this (Peck & Tickell, 1994). Devolution of the national state does open new "regulatory spaces" for local initiative, and the geographic consequences of this particular mode of restructuring will reflect the reflective capacities of local states to respond, as discussed above. But these regulatory spaces will be constrained in all placed by competitive pressures imposed by global capital and reinforced by neoliberalism in the national state (Peck, 1955). The accelerating global mobility of capital accentuates fine distinctions between places (Harvey, 1989) and exerts "economic discipline" on locales to conform to its demands (Harvey, 1985). The ensuing rivalry for investment among local states will require reducing the regulatory role previously played by government, while the taxes that underwrite governmental assistance will be kept to a minimum to ensure the area's ability to attract and retain firms. John Agnew (1987) asks the telling question: "Who dares to provide public services when the tax base may move?" (p. 188). The likely scenario, then, is a "geographically uneven drift" toward lower state involvement in the well-being of local populations (Peck, 1995, p. 224). Thus, local states subject to the demands of global capital increasingly restructure their own role to ensure that pliant labor forces and adequate infrastructural bases are available to capture and retain mobile capital. Only in those rare place-contexts where capital is overwhelmingly place-bound and locally dependent does the local state have relative autonomy within the larger economic transformations (Cox, 1991; Miller, 1994).

Second, the nonprofit sector is an insufficient substitute for the local state in this situation, given the localism and limited capacity of most voluntary organizations (Wolch, 1990; see also Wolpert, this volume). Just as the national state shifts responsibility without power to local states, it calls on the nonprofit sector to assume a greater role in social provision as it reduces financial support to those organizations (Karger & Stoesz, 1994). As the national government privatizes many previous responsibilities and withdraws funding, local voluntary organizations become increasingly dependent on the community in which they are located, and consequently, the less affluent, experienced, and innovative communities, where needs for assistance are greater, are least able to address those needs.

Finally, local social movements have relatively little maneuverability in the current era of economic globalization and state restructuring. The extent to which they can exert any power whatsoever is a function of their own capacity set within the particular geographic and historical context in which they operate, especially the political opportunity structures that have evolved in place over time to empower non-governing groups (Miller, 1994). The unique and changing relationship of the social movement to the local state is especially important, part of the larger process whereby civil society seeks to capture the state in serving its interests (see Mitchell, this volume and Wright, this volume). Furthermore, the history of conflictual politics between groups in a particular locale will play an important role in defining the specific response of each locality to economic globalization and state restructuring, and new conflicts—and coalitions—may arise in response to particular initiatives because power relations are most open to reconfiguration during periods of rapid political change. There are, nevertheless, limits to the power of local social movements in the present era. As devolution and privatization of the national state "subjects labor to global discipline, locally applied" (Peck, 1995, p. 256), rising job insecurity, declining wages and benefit packages, and the need to work longer hours limit the financial resources and time available to individuals who might contribute to such coalitions. Once again, the less affluent and politically experienced individuals will suffer the greatest risk.

Recent research has begun to document the processes whereby local social movements creatively use scale to build power, flexibly defining the arena for political action and directing their efforts to that level most open to change. For example, Herod (in press) examines the postwar history of the International Longshoremen's Association, representing East Coast waterfront workers. In response to political and economic changes in the shipping industry, the ILA devised an explicitly geographic strategy, forcing a change in bargaining practices from portspecific agreements to a master contract that held for a time at the national level. Herod argues that struggles over the scale at which groups negotiate have very real consequences, in this case rewriting the economic landscape of the industry, "workers' applied geography." Cross-scale and trans-local alliances have begun to appear in local states, nonprofit organizations, and social movements spanning the political spectrum as each seeks to augment its power. The combined processes of economic globalization and state restructuring stack the odds against these local entities, but their ability to prevail is place-and time-specific (Miller, 1994).

CONCLUSION

I have reviewed the primary strategies for state restructuring in American federal history and have considered the consequences of the current round of devolution and privatization for localities seeking to compete in an intensifying international arena. At the core of this ongoing search for the appropriate balance of power is the issue of geographically distributing authority and resources within the federal hierarchy, which responds to the diverse map of regional conditions and political cultures, yet protects national norms valued in a common American political culture.

Although most Americans would agree in principle that one's health, affluence, and well-being should not depend on one's zip code (Green, 1989, p. 460), there exists little overall consensus as to how the responsibilities of the state should be divided. Indeed, few Americans seem to appreciate how current changes in the scale and scope of the American state will affect their lives, much less how this effect will depend on the place where they live. Above all, the American people need to "rediscover government" (DiIulio and Kettl, 1995, p. 65), separating the actual successes and failures of the state from the barrage of rhetoric that obscures its role. Beyond that, political elites and citizens need to recognize that the implications of state restructuring will differ considerably from place to place across the country, reflecting spatial variations in the resources and capacities of public and private institutions to manage these changes, and given the great geographic complexity of the American people whose lives will be altered by the outcome. These patterns and trends deserve careful study; and their analysis and documentation should guide the difficult decisions that are being made not only in Washington, DC, but also in city halls and town meetings across the country.

REFERENCES

Agnew, J. (1987). *The United States in the world-economy: A regional geography.* Cambridge, UK: Cambridge University Press.

Bennett, R. (Ed.). (1990). *Decentralization, local governments, and markets.* Oxford, UK: Oxford University Press.

Beynon, H., & Hudson, R. (1993). Place and space in contemporary Europe: Some lessons and reflections. *Antipode, 25,* 177–190.

Clark, G., & Dear, M. (1984). *State apparatus: Structures and language of legitimacy.* Boston: Allen and Unwin.

Cockburn, C. (1977). *The local state.* London: Pluto Press.

Cox, K. (1991). Questions of abstraction in studies in the new urban politics. *Journal of Urban Affairs, 13,* 267–280.

Cox, K. & Mair, A. (1988).Locality and community in the politics of local economic develop-ment. *Annals, Association of American Geographers*, 78, 307–325.

Cox, K. & Mair, A. (1991). From localised social structures to localities as agents. *Environment and Planning, A*, 23, 197–213.

DiIulio, J.,& Kettl, D. (1995). *Fine print: The Contract with America, devolution, and the administrative realities of American federalism.* CMP Report 95-1. Washington, DC: Brookings Institution.

General Accounting Office (GAO). (1991). *Government contractors: Are service contractors performing in-herently governmental functions?* GGD-92-11. Washington, DC: Government Printing Office.

Green, M. (1989). State attorneys general move in: Filling the deregulatory vacuum. *Nation*, 249, 441, 458–460.

Greenberg, M., Popper, F., & West, B. (1991). The fiscal pit and the federalist pendulum: Ex-plaining differences between states in protecting health and the environment. *Environmen-talist*, 11, 95–104.

Harvey, D. (1982). *The limits to capital.* Oxford, UK: Basil Blackwell.

Harvey, D. (1985). *The urbanization of capital.* Baltimore, MD: Johns Hopkins University Press.

Harvey, D. (1989). *The urban experience.* Oxford, UK: Basil Blackwell.

Herod, A. (in press). Labor's spatial praxis and the geography of contract bargaining in the U.S. East Coast longshore industry, 1953–1989. In H. Leitner & S. Silvern (Special Issue Eds.), *Political Geography, 15.*

Jessop, B. (1993). Towards a Schumpeterian workfare state? Preliminary remarks on post-Fordist political economy. *Studies in Political Economy, 40,* 7–39.

Karger, H., & Stoesz, D. (1994). *American social welfare policy: A pluralist approach.* White Plains, NY: Longman.

Kodras, J. (1990). Economic restructuring, shifting public attitudes, and program revision: The pol-itics underlying geographic disparities in the Food Stamp Program. In J. Kodras & J. P. Jones III (Eds.), *Geographic dimensions of U.S. social policy* (pp. 218–236). London: Edward Arnold.

Le Grand, J., & Robinson, R. (Eds.). (1984). *Privatization and the welfare state.* London: Allen and Unwin.

Leitner, H., & Silvern, S. (Special Issue Eds.). (in press). *Political Geography, 15.*

Malbin, M. (Ed.). (1996). Symposium: American federalism today. *Rockefeller Institute Bulletin.* New York: Nelson A. Rockefeller Institute of Government.

Massey, D. (1994). *Space, place, and gender.* Minneapolis: University of Minnesota Press.

Miller, B. (1994). Political empowerment, local-central state relations, and geographically shift-ing political opportunity structures. *Political Geography*, 13, 393–406.

Mouffe, C. (1995). Post-Marxism: Democracy and identity. *Environment and Planning, D: Society and Space*, 13, 259–265.

Nathan, R. (1996). The devolution revolution. *Rockefeller Institute Bulletin.* New York: Nelson A. Rockefeller Institute of Government.

Offe, C. (1985). *Disorganized capitalism: Contemporary transformations of work and politics.* Cam-bridge, MA: Polity.

Osborne, D. (1993). A new federal contract: Sorting out Washington's proper role. In W. Mar-shall & M. Schram (Eds.), *Mandate for change* (205–261). New York: Berkley.

Pagano, M., & Bowman, A. O'M. (1995). The state of American federalism, 1994–1995. *Pub-lius: The Journal of Federalism*, 24, 1–21.

Peck, J. (1995). *Work-place: The social regulation of labor markets.* New York: Guilford.

Peck, J. (1996, April). *Permeable welfare? Workfare politics and the deconstruction of Canada's work-welfare regime.* Paper presented at the Crises of Global Regulation and Governance Conference, Athens, GA.

Peck, J., & Tickell, A. (1994). Searching for a new institutional fix: The *after*-Fordist crisis and the global-local disorder. In A. Amin (Ed.), *Post-Fordism: A reader* (280-315). Oxford, UK: Basil Blackwell.

Peterson, P.E. (1995). *The price of federalism.* Washington, DC: Brookings Institution.

Pines, B. (1982). *Back to basics: The traditionalist movement that is sweeping grassroots America.* New York: William Morrow.

Pressman, J., & Wildavsky, A. (1973), *Implementation: How great expectations in Washington are dashed in Oakland; Or, Why it's amazing that federal programs work at all, This being a saga of the Economic Development Administration as told by two sympathetic observers who seek to build morals on a foundation of ruined hopes.* Berkeley: University of California Press.

Robinson. K. (1961). Sixty years of federation in Australia. *Geographical Review, 51,* 1-20.

Salamon, L., Musselwhite, J., & de Vita, C. (1986). Partners in public service: Government and the nonprofit sector in the welfare state. In *Philanthropy, voluntary action, and the public good* (42-58). Washington, DC: Independent Sector Inc.

Schwab, R. (1988). Environmental federalism. *Resources, 88,* 6-9.

Smith, C. (1986). Equity in the distribution of health and welfare services; Can we rely on the state to reverse the "inverse care law"? *Social Science and Medicine, 23,* 1067-1078

Smith, N. (1993). Homeless/Global. Scaling places. In J. Bird, B. Curtis, T. Putnam, G. Robertson, & L. Tucker (Eds.), *Mapping the futures: Local culture, global change* (pp. 87-119). London: Routledge & Kegan Paul.

Storper, M., & Walker, R. (1989). *The capitalist imperative: Territory, technology and industrial growth.* Oxford, UK: Basil Blackwell.

Swyngedouw, E. (1992). The Mammon quest: "Globalization," interspatial competition, and the monetary order: The construction of new spatial scales. In M. Dunford & G. Kafkalas (Eds.), *Cities and regions in the New Europe: The global-local interplay and spatial development strategies* (39-67). London: Belhaven.

U.S. House of Representatives, Committee on the Budget. (1991). *Management reform: A top priority for the federal executive branch.* Serial #CP-4. Washington, DC: Government Printing Office.

Warf, B. (1996, April). *The hypermobility of capital and the collapse of the Keynesian state.* Paper presented at the Crises of Global Regulation and Governance Conference, Athens, GA.

Wolch, J. (1990). *The shadow state: Government and voluntary sector in transition.* New York: Foundation Center.

Wolpert, J. (1993). *Patterns of generosity in America: Who's holding the safety net?* New York: Twentieth Century Fund Press.

6

MANAGEMENT AND ORGANIZATION THEORY

How should government be organized and managed to deliver services? Everyone seems to enjoy "bashing" bureaucracies and bureaucrats, but bureaucracies (and bureaucrats) have stood the test of time. And although there are many things we don't know about government organizations and management, one thing we do know with certainty: nothing in, around, or about organizations survives for very long unless it serves useful purposes. If so, why does bureaucracy persist as the premier form of government organization (and also business organization) in the United States and around the world even though dissatisfaction with the performance of government bureaucrats is rampant. For many, frustration with government bureaucracies "has advanced into cynicism, anger, and perhaps even alienation from the organizations of our own governance."[1] This chapter deals with these types of questions. As you will discover quickly, however, government organizations are complex social/political/economic institutions, and the answers to questions about them are not always straight-forward.

WHAT IS AN ORGANIZATION?[2]

An *organization* is simply a social unit with some particular purposes. "The most common formal definition of an organization is a collection of people engaged in specialized and interdependent activity to accomplish a goal or mission."[3] These definitions, though, say only that an organization consists of more than one person who join together (temporarily or permanently) to get something accomplished. Thus, according to these definitions, a few neighbors who decide to hold a block dance and pot-luck supper will form a simple organization, probably without giving much thought to the fact that they did so. Fielding a little league baseball team or establishing a homeowners association requires a slightly more complex organization. The festival or association organizers probably will want to establish an organization structure, complete with officers, lines of authority, a means for orderly replacement of officers, fiscal responsibilities, and a means for resolving grievances. As the things people want to accomplish become larger, more complex, more costly, require more people with more skills, and last for longer periods of time, the organizations they create become commensurately more complex also.

The basic components of organizations have not changed very much over the centuries. All organizations have explicit or implicit purposes, attract participants, acquire and allocate resources to accomplish their purposes—often among competing interests and activities, establish some form of structure to assign and coordinate tasks, and permit some members to lead or manager others.

HOW AN ORGANIZATION IS MANAGED REFLECTS BOTH ITS ENVIRONMENT AND THE ORGANIZATION "MODEL"

Despite the constants of organizations over the centuries, their purposes, forms and shapes, rules, ways of doing things, and techniques for coordinating work, have varied widely and changed dramatically over the years. These constants and changes in structure and practices are inevitable, because organizations reflect the worlds they are in. Organizations are a part of their culture.[4] When, for example, white males control virtually all power in a society, its organization structures and practices will be designed to allow white males to have similar dominance within organizations.[5] Likewise, when a society becomes "fed up" with rigidity, impersonality, and non-responsiveness in its large government agencies, pressures will mount to shrink government and make its agencies more flexible and responsive to the people they serve. Thus, during the 1980s and 1990s, city, state, and national governments in the United States and elsewhere moved surprisingly swiftly to "re-engineer," "devolve," "re-invent," "contract-out," and to otherwise replace large government bureaucracies with less rigid forms of government organizations and with private contractors.[6]

The form or "model"[7] of organization also influences how the people in them are managed. As organizations become more formal, the ways people are managed tend to follow suit. Informal agreements give way to policies and procedures which ensure that employees are treated equitably and fairly, but that management retains certain rights to make and impose decisions for the good of the entire organization.

Although the management and leadership in government organizations share many characteristics and functions with management and leadership in private businesses, there are important differences in emphasis. The title of an article by Graham Allison says it well: "Public and Private Management: Are They Fundamentally Alike in All Unimportant Respects?"[8]

ORGANIZATIONS REQUIRE STRUCTURE AND RULES

No one sets out intentionally to create a complex, "formal" organization. How many times have you heard a group of people say as they start a little league baseball team, a neighborhood cleanup campaign, or a new business:

"Let's keep this simple and informal. We all know each other. We don't need a lot of rules and things." Sometimes things work out well. More often than not, though, the well-meaning participants discover (sooner or later) that they need to have some "rules" in order to get things done—and to protect their individual and collective rights. Rules are needed to make certain people know who is responsible for what, to coordinate activities, and to limit the scope of peoples' activities and decisions. Consider for example: Does any one participant—or small group of participants—have the right to make decisions and financial commitments that obligate the others? Are all participants "empowered" equally? Does everyone agree on this? Does everyone have the time (and the stomach) to make all decisions by consensus? If I withdraw my participation, do I have any rights? How can we remove someone from the organization who is doing things that the others (or a majority of the others) don't like? All too often, the need to have structures and procedural "rules" in place to cope amicably with these types of questions, isn't understood until after problems have arisen.

Obviously, government agencies are more formal than the types of organizations we have been discussing. When they are created, it is with the understanding that structures, rules and procedures will be needed. Citizens and employees want to know—need to know—what they can expect from government bureaus. Goodwill among the participants will not suffice.

ORGANIZATION THEORY IS . . . .

We have been discussing organizations and management, but we need to start with some basics. What is *organization theory?* First, a *theory* is simply a proposition or group of propositions that seeks to explain or predict something. *Organization theory,* then, is a set of propositions that seeks to explain or predict the relationships among "things" in and around organizations. "Organization theory focuses on the formal and informal structures, internal dynamics, and surrounding social environments of complex human organizations."[9]

If we wanted to know why the introduction of a new computer network has not increased productivity as had been expected, we would need to find organization theories that explain relationships among different types of networked electronic communications, the interaction between messages communicated electronically and human motivation, and productivity. Likewise, if we wanted to know why women do not advance into leadership positions in certain types of state government organizations, we would need to find and use organization theories that are able to deal with this type of issue, perhaps theories by Joan Acker,[10] Kathy Ferguson,[11] and Camilla Stivers.[12] Organization theories by Max Weber, Frederick Winslow Taylor, Luther Gulick, Douglas McGregor,[13] Henry Mintzberg[14] or Michael Barzelay[15] wouldn't be of any use in this quest. They don't look at the right relationships among variables in organizations—the variables and relationships that would help answer our question.

WHY CLASSICAL ORGANIZATION THEORY
HAS SURVIVED FOR CENTURIES

Hierarchy is a concept "based on the distinction between the roles of superior and subordinate. The superior is expected to exercise authority over the subordinate."[16] *Bureaucracy* is a special form of hierarchy that has survived over the centuries because it is "the single best form of organization yet devised for providing consistency, continuity, predictability, stability, deliberateness, efficient performance of repetitive tasks, equity in dealing with the public and employees, rationalism, and professionalism."[17] Bureaucracy is *the* ideal form of organization for protecting government employees and career managers from the pressures of partisan politics on administrative decision-making. Bureaucracies are built on the "foundations" of: *professionalism*—hiring and retaining qualified employees who have the needed job skills and knowledge—with the ability to make decisions and do government's work free from political influence; continuity; consistency; equity; and *accountability*—"answerability" to higher public officials and through them to the general public.[18]

Classical organization theory, of which *bureaucracy* is a key element, remained essentially *the only* theory of organization until World War II, and it remains the most prevalent form of organization for governments—as well as in businesses—around the world. Classical organization theory is the base from which virtually all other theories of organization have been built. Bureaucracy as described by Max Weber,[19] the German sociologist who is still considered the most authoritative writer on bureaucracy, was neither a description of reality nor a statement of his preference. It was instead an "ideal type" with carefully defined characteristics: "the specialization function; the requirement that the hiring and promotion of officials be based solely on expertise; that authority be exercised through a centralized hierarchical chain of command; and the development of an intricate system of rules to cover all possible actions and to minimize discretion."[20]

The original reasons for the emergence of classical organization theory and bureaucracy can be traced back long before Weber's writing, to the industrial revolution and Adam Smith's concepts of "specialization and division of labor."[21] Classical theory was refined and "bloomed" during the first-half of the twentieth century with major contributions by Weber, Frederick Winslow Taylor's "scientific management,"[22] and Henri Fayol[23] and Luther Gulick,[24] who separately developed "general principles of organization" in France and the United States.

THE TENETS OF CLASSICAL ORGANIZATION THEORY WERE
APPROPRIATE FOR THE TIMES

The fundamental tenets of classical organization theory, as developed by Weber, Taylor, Gulick, Fayol and others, and that persist today, are:

1. Organizations exist to accomplish production-related and economic goals.
2. There is one best way to organize for production, and that way can be found through systematic, scientific inquiry.
3. Production is maximized through specialization and division of labor.
4. People and organizations act in accordance with rational economic principles.[25]

These tenets were fitting for the harsh realities of the 1800s and early 1900s, because it was not until the mid-twentieth century that industrial workers in the United States and Europe began to enjoy basic rights as organization citizens. "Workers were viewed not as individuals, but as interchangeable parts in an industrial machine whose parts were made of flesh only when it was impractical to make them of steel."[26] As the world has changed, organizations and organization theory have adapted also—but never completely letting go of the tenets and features of the classical organization theory—of bureaucracy.

ORGANIZATION THEORY—OR ORGANIZATION THEORIES?

By now, it should be quite evident: "Organizations are different creatures to different people. . . . Organizations are 'defined' according to the contexts and perspectives peculiar to the person doing the defining."[27] Thus there is no single organization theory. There cannot—and should not be—for at least two fundamental reasons: First, organizations are such enormously complex social/economic/political systems, that multiple perspectives are needed to understand the numerous relationships and variables in and around them. Second, different types of theories are needed for different purposes.

Government organizations have changed dramatically since World War II, and organization theories have also. Myriad "schools" or "paradigms" of organization theory have emerged to help us understand government organizations and why they—and the people in and around them—act in the ways they do. For example, greatly increased knowledge about and appreciation for human behavior, including leadership, motivation, group behavior, inter-group conflict within and between organizations, the effects of organizations on people (in particular the effects of bureaucracy on people), uses of power in relations, and the effects of organizational culture on employees all contributed to ascendance of the "human relations school" of organization theory in the late 1950s and early 1960s—a school of organization theory that departed radically from the tenets of classical organization theory.[28] Since the decade of the 1960s, some of the new "paradigms" of organization theory have included systems theories, critical theories, "modern" structural theories, cultural theories, feminist theories, rational choice theories, post-modern theories, and . . . on . . . and . . . on.[29]

ORGANIZATION AND MANAGEMENT THEORY IN THE TWENTY-FIRST CENTURY

Classical organization theory was "right" for the environment of the industrial revolution, but it isn't adequate for government organizations of today. The events, happenings, and contexts of the 1960s, '70s, '80s, and '90s caused changes in peoples' expectations about government agencies. The "flower children era" of the 1960s, the introduction of personal computers in the 1970s and the explosion of their use in the 1980s and 1990s, the loss of national self-confidence in the U.S. in the 1980s, and the population waves of "baby boomers" and "gen x' ers" in the 1990s, all have created major challenges for government organizational forms as we have known them for centuries. Government organizations have been changing—and not just "on the margin." The "rules of the game" have changed for how they are structured, managed, and how they get tasks done. Public management and organization theories have followed suit.

> Three major [groups of] theories challenge the hierarchical authority model. One, rooted in the dynamics of human relations, condemns the impersonality of bureaucratic hierarchies and so pleads for the humanizing of organizations. The second, rooted in the realities of political life, yields a pluralistic model. The third, noting how extensively a government delegates authority to other governments, to private organizations, and to mixed public-private enterprises, calls for a third-party administration model.[30]

All five of the "themes" that we have identified throughout this book as having important impacts on public administration, are directly affecting management and organization theory at the turn of the twenty-first century. Four of the five are having particularly great and lasting effects on public management and organization theory and deserve mention:

- information technology,
- the movement of decisions to lower levels of government ("devolution") and down through government hierarchies ("empowerment"),
- delivery of government services by private sector organizations ("diffusion" to nonprofit and for-profit businesses), and
- population diversity.

Organizations and organization theories reflect their environments. This is especially true for public organizations that exist in the political-legal-economic-social-power environment of government.

READINGS REPRINTED IN THIS CHAPTER

Michael Barzelay's 1992 chapter, **"Beyond the Bureaucratic Paradigm,"** provides an excellent example of how these themes are influencing the structures and processes of public organizations and management. Barzelay uses several administrative service agencies in Minnesota State government to explain how and why bureaucracy has become an inadequate form of governmental organization in an era when people want and expect business-like responsiveness and a "customer satisfaction" orientation from government employees. According to Barzelay, authority to make decisions has been "pushed" down the Minnesota government hierarchies, lower-level employees have been "empowered" to make decisions "on the spot" in order to satisfy clients, and activities. Printing services and the motor pool—service activities that had been operated as monopolies by state employees for decades and that other agencies had been required to use—were contracted out to private businesses. Other state agencies were turned loose to buy administrative services from whatever source has the best price and the best service quality—public or private. Networked computers have proved able to coordinate activities that had always been coordinated before by supervisors, and supervisors of supervisors. Numerous supervisory positions thus were eliminated, and incumbents were reassigned.

"The Pivotal Controversies," by **Harold F. Gortner, Julianne Mahler, and Jeanne Bell Nicholson,** analyzes four of the important on-going controversies that have been swirling around public organization theory for years: (1) law and legal authority; (2) rationality and efficiency; (3) psychological and social relations; and (4) politics and power relations. They conclude: "It is not enough for public managers to know all about the psychological and sociological theories related to complex organizations. When any attempt is made at application of these theories . . . , it is essential to understand the legal and political environment in which that attempt is being made. . . . Public organization theory must address all four perspectives in the controversy to develop a comprehensive picture of the bureau and how it works." In other words, organization theory is "messy"—it is complex and disorderly. *Public* organization theory is even more so.

Henry Mintzberg, a highly influential writer on business organizations, offers interesting views on why it is important to organize and manage government and nonprofit organizations *not* like businesses, in **"Managing Government—Governing Management."** The widely-shared mis-belief that "capitalism has triumphed [in the world] is now throwing the societies of the West out of balance, especially the United Kingdom and the United States. That the imbalance will favor private rather than state ownership will not help society." Mintzberg identifies four roles all citizens fill at times as members of a society: customers, clients, citizens, and subjects. "Customers are appropriately served by privately owned organizations, ... [but] when it comes to citizen and subject activities, we should stray beyond the state-ownership model only with a great deal of prudence." Because of these basic differences among citizen roles, Mintzberg argues that government needs to be managed differently. Adoption of "business school models" of management is not simply inappropriate, it is dangerous.

NOTES

1. Cooper, Phillip J., Linda P. Brady, Olivia Hidalgo-Hardeman, Albert C. Hyde, Katherine C. Naff, J. Steven Ott, and Harvey White. (1998). *Public Administration for the Twenty-First Century.* Fort Worth, Texas: Harcourt Brace, p. 203.

2. A parallel discussion of organization theory in the nonprofit sector is in, J. Steven Ott (Ed.), *The Nature of the Nonprofit Sector.* Boulder, Colo.: Westview, 2000.
3. Gortner, Harold F., Julianne Mahler, and Jeanne Bell Nicholson. (1997). *Organization Theory: A Public Perspective* (2d. ed.). Fort Worth, Texas: Harcourt Brace, p. 2.
4. Shafritz, Jay M., and J. Steven Ott (2001). "Introduction." In J. M. Shafritz & J. S. Ott (Eds.) *Classics of Organization Theory* (5th ed.) Fort Worth, Texas: Harcourt Brace.
5. See Camilla Stivers' article that is reprinted in Chapter 1, "Feminist Theory of Public Administration," or her 1993 book, *Gender Images in Public Administration: Legitimacy and the Administrative State.* Newbury Park, Calif.: Sage.
6. See the readings reprinted in Chapter 4, in particular, "Changing States, Governance, and the Public Service," by Guy B. Peters (1996).
7. A "model" has "considerable utility in discussing what an organization is. . . . Unlike a definition, a model does not represent an attempt to express the basic, irreducible nature of the object, and is a freer approach that can be adapted to situations as needed. . . . Thus it is with organizations." Nicholas Henry (1995). *Public Administration and Public Affairs* (6th ed.) Englewood Cliffs, NJ: Prentice Hall, p. 52.
8. Allison, Graham T. (February 1980). "Public and Private Management: Are They Fundamentally Alike in All Unimportant Respects?" *Proceedings of the Public Management Research Conference, November 19–20, 1979.* Washington, DC: Office of Personnel Management, OPM Document 127–53-1, pp. 27–38.
9. Gordon, George J, and Michael E. Milakovich. (1995). *Public Administration in America* (5th ed.). New York: St. Martin's Press, p. 164.
10. Acker, Joan. (1992). "Gendering Organizational Theory," in A. J. Mills and P. Tancred (Eds.), *Gendering Organizational Analysis.* Newbury Park, Calif.: Sage.
11. Ferguson, Kathy E. (1984). *The Feminist Case Against Bureaucracy.* Philadelphia: Temple University Press.
12. An article by Camilla Stivers, "Feminist Theory of Public Administration," is reprinted in Chapter 1; or see her 1993 book, *Gender Images in Public Administration: Legitimacy and the Administrative State.* Newbury Park, Calif.: Sage.
13. McGregor, Douglas M. (1960). *The Human Side of Enterprise.* New York: McGraw-Hill.
14. Mintzberg, Henry. (May–June 1996). "Managing Government—Governing Management." *Harvard Business Review,* 75–83.
15. Barzelay, Michael. (1992). *Breaking Through Bureaucracy: A New Vision for Managing in Government.* Berkeley: University of California Press.
16. Starling, Grover. (1998). *Managing the Public Sector* (5th ed.). Fort Worth, Texas: Harcourt Brace, p. 64.
17. Cooper, Phillip J., Linda P. Brady, Olivia Hidalgo-Hardeman, Albert C. Hyde, Katherine C. Naff, J. Steven Ott, and Harvey White. (1998). *Public Administration for the Twenty-First Century,* (Ch. 8: "Managing Public Organizations"). Fort Worth, Texas: Harcourt Brace, p. 201.
18. See the readings reprinted in Chapter 10, and Kevin Kearns (1996), *Managing for Accountability: Preserving the Public Trust in Public and Nonprofit Organizations.* San Francisco: Jossey-Bass.
19. Weber, Max. (1922). "Bureaucracy," in H. Gerth and C. W. Mills (Eds.), *Max Weber: Essays in Sociology.* Oxford, UK: Oxford University Press.
20. Gortner, Harold F., Julianne Mahler, and Jeanne Bell Nicholson. (1997). *Organization Theory: A Public Perspective* (2d. ed.). Ft. Worth, Texas: Harcourt Brace, p. 4.

21. Smith, Adam. (1776). *The Wealth of Nations,* Chapter 1, "Of the Division of Labor."
22. Taylor, Frederick Winslow. (1911). *The Principles of Scientific Management.* New York: Norton.
23. Fayol, Henri. (1949). *General and Industrial Management* (C. Storrs, Trans.). London: Pitman. (Originally published in France in 1916 as *Administration Industrielle et Generale.*)
24. Gulick, Luther, and Lyndall Urwick. (1937). *Papers on the Science of Administration.* New York: Institute of Public Administration.
25. Bolman, Lee G., and Terrence E. Deal. (1997). *Reframing Organizations: Artistry, Choice, and Leadership* (2nd ed.). San Francisco: Jossey-Bass.
26. Shafritz, Jay M., and J. Steven Ott. (2001). "Classical Organization Theory," in J. M. Shafritz, and J. S. Ott (Eds.) *Classics of Organization Theory* (5th ed.) Fort Worth, Texas: Harcourt Brace, p. 31.
27. Henry, Nicholas. (1995). *Public Administration and Public Affairs* (6th ed.) Englewood Cliffs, NJ: Prentice Hall, p. 52.
28. Ott, J. Steven. (Ed.). (1996). *Classic Readings in Organizational Behavior* (2d. ed.). Fort Worth, Texas: Harcourt Brace.
29. For information about these "schools" or "paradigms," see Jay M. Shafritz, and J. Steven Ott. (Eds.). (2001). *Classics of Organization Theory* (5th ed.) Fort Worth, Texas: Harcourt Brace; or Harold F. Gortner, Julianne Mahler, and Jeanne Bell Nicholson. (1997). *Organization Theory: A Public Perspective* (2d. ed.). Fort Worth, Texas: Harcourt Brace.
30. Fesler, James W., and Donald F. Kettl. (1996). *The Politics of the Administrative Process* (2nd ed.). New York: Chatham House, p. 45.

16

Michael Barzelay

BEYOND THE BUREAUCRATIC PARADIGM

Imagine how government would work if almost every operating decision—including the hiring and firing of individuals—were made on partisan political grounds; if many agencies spent their entire annual appropriations in the first three months of the fiscal year; if appropriations were made to agencies without anyone having formulated a spending and revenue budget for the jurisdiction as a whole; and if no agency or person in the executive branch had authority to oversee the activities of government agencies.

This state of affairs was, in fact, the norm in the United States in the nineteenth century. That it sounds so chaotic and backward to us is due to the success of early twentieth-century reformers in influencing politics and administration at the city, state, and federal levels. As a result of their influence, most Americans take for granted that administrative decisions should be made in a businesslike manner, that the executive branch should be organized hierarchically, that most agency heads should be appointed by the chief executive, that the appropriations process should begin when the chief executive submits an overall budget to the legislature, that most positions should be staffed by qualified people, that materials should be purchased from responsible vendors based on objective criteria, and that systems of fiscal control and accountability should be reliable.[1]

The political movements favoring this form of bureaucratic government emerged partly in response to the social problems created by the transformation of the United States from an agrarian and highly decentralized society to an urban, industrial, and national society.[2] For government to address social problems in an efficient manner, reformers said repeatedly, government agencies needed to be administered much like the business organizations that, at the time, were bringing about the industrial transformation.[3] For Americans supporting the reform and reorganization movements, bureaucracy meant efficiency and efficiency meant good government.[4]

Bureaucratically minded reformers also placed a high value on the impersonal exercise of public authority. To this end, they argued that actions intended to control others should be based on the application of rules and that no action should be taken without authorization. When official's actions could not be fully determined by applying rules, professional or technical expertise was to be relied on to make official action impersonal.[5] This outlook extended to hiring and purchasing. The consistent application of universal rules embodying the merit principle was expected to assure that government officials would act competently on behalf of the public interest, while simultaneously undermining the power of the party machines that dominated politics *and* administration.[6] The consistent application of universal rules in purchasing was expected to reduce government's operating costs and to have similar political consequences.[7]

The values of efficiency and impersonal administration along with prescriptions for putting them into practice in government constituted a compelling system of beliefs in the early twentieth century. This system may be termed the *bureaucratic reform vision.*

PERSISTENCE OF THE BUREAUCRATIC PARADIGM

The bureaucratic reform vision lost its hold on the political imagination of the reform constituency once civil service and executive budgeting had been put into place and the Great Depression posed new and pressing collective problems. As a belief system about public administration, by contrast, the bureaucratic reform vision survived—although not wholly intact—such political changes as the Great Society and Reaganism and a series of efforts to improve management in government including systems analysis, management by objectives, and zero-based budgeting. Among the legacies of the bureaucratic reform movements are deeply ingrained habits of thought.[8] These habits of thought and the belief system that supports them are referred to in this book as the *bureaucratic paradigm.*[9] . . .

Unraveling the Bureaucratic Paradigm

The bureaucratic paradigm has been criticized by intellectuals since the 1930s. . . . Nonetheless, many of the beliefs of the bureaucratic paradigm have escaped serious challenge.[10]

The most important recent conceptual challenge to the bureaucratic paradigm arising in the world of practice is the notion that government organizations should be customer-driven and service-oriented. A recurring aspiration of public managers and overseers using these concepts is to solve operational problems by transforming their organizations into responsive, user-friendly, dynamic, and competitive providers of valuable services to customers. Thinking in terms of customers and service helps public managers and overseers articulate their concerns about the performance of the government operations for which they are accountable. When supplemented by analysis of how these concepts have been put into practice in other settings, reasoning about customers and service helps managers generate alternative solutions to the particular problems they have defined as meriting attention. In many instances, the range of alternatives generated in this fashion is substantially different from that yielded by reasoning within the bureaucratic paradigm.[11]

Many public officials, alert to the power of these conceptual resources in the contemporary United States, are identifying those whom they believe to be their customers and are using methods of strategic service management to improve their operation.[12] For example, the U.S. Army Recruiting Command has developed an extremely sophisticated strategy to attract its external customers—qualified young Americans—to join the military.[13] This strategy is designed to satisfy these customers' needs for guaranteed future employment, occupational training, immediate income, self-esteem, individuality, and fair treatment so as to meet the internal customers' needs for a high-quality workforce. The Army recruiting operation's key service concept—reinforced by television advertising—is to provide external customers a "guaranteed reservation" for "seats" in training programs for specific military occupations. To support this service concept, Army contractors engineered a sophisticated information system known as REQUEST. Operated by specialized recruiters referred to as guidance counselors, the REQUEST system customizes the Army's offer of multiyear membership, employment, training, immediate cash, and other benefits. The more attractive the recruit—as judged from a battery of standardized tests—the better the offer. This example plainly illustrates how one government organization, in attempting to implement public policies—in this case, maintaining a large standing army capable of fighting wars and staffing it with volunteers—puts the customer-service approach into practice. . . .[14]

Formulating an Alternative

The concept of customer-driving service organization is thus a tool used increasingly by public officials to define and solve problems.[15] At a higher level of generality, this concept also provides many of the resources needed to formulate a coherent alternative to the bureaucratic paradigm.[16] The outlines of this alternative and its mode of identifying and attacking the vulnerabilities of the bureaucratic paradigm are already coming into focus. The following paired statements highlight the main rhetorical battle lines:[17]

- A bureaucratic agency is focused on its own needs and perspectives. A customer-driven agency is focused on customer needs and perspectives.
- A bureaucratic agency is focused on the roles and responsibilities of its parts. A customer-driven agency is focused on enabling the whole organization to function as a team.
- A bureaucratic agency defines itself both by the amount of resources it controls and by the tasks it performs. A customer-driven agency defines itself by the results it achieves for its customers.
- A bureaucratic agency controls costs. A customer-driven agency creates value net of cost.
- A bureaucratic agency sticks to routine. A customer-driven agency modifies its operations in response to changing demands for its services.
- A bureaucratic agency fights for turf. A customer-driven agency competes for business.
- A bureaucratic agency insists on following standard procedures. A customer-driven agency builds choice into its operating systems when doing so serves a purpose.
- A bureaucratic agency announces policies and plans. A customer-driven agency engages in two-way communication with its customers in order to assess and revise its operating strategy.
- A bureaucratic agency separates the work of thinking from that of doing. A customer-driven agency empowers front-line employees to make judgments about how to improve customer service and value.[18]

The fact that this kind of rhetoric is coming into common use suggests that a new alternative to the bureaucratic paradigm—one that builds on much prior practical and intellectual work—is now available. As this alternative becomes well-formulated and well-accepted, it may become the frame of reference for most efforts to diagnose operational problems in the public sector and to find solutions to them. The time is ripe, therefore, to define as carefully as possible what this alternative is. *Breaking Through Bureaucracy* takes on this task.[19]

THE POST-BUREAUCRATIC PARADIGM IN HISTORICAL PERSPECTIVE

. . . To understand the structure and workings of the newer paradigm well enough to improve public management requires attention and thoughtfulness but not the honed skills of an analytic philosopher or social linguist. The new paradigm, we suggest, can readily be understood by working with the metaphor of an extended family of ideas. The image of an extended family is helpful because it indicates that each idea is somehow related to every other, and it implies that some concentration is required to identify just how. The same metaphor can be pushed much further.[20] Think of the new paradigm, as well as the bureaucratic one, as a generation within an extended family. Although the members of each generation may not enjoy equal standing, their relationships—like those between concepts in either paradigm—are not hierarchical. All the cousins may be compatible in many situations, but their personalities—much like the entailments of the concepts of incentives and empowerment—are likely to differ markedly. Furthermore, just as siblings and cousins seek to prove that they are individually and collectively different from their parents' generation, self-definitions of the new paradigm emphasize divergences from the bureaucratic paradigm. Generational differences in extended families and paradigms also reflect changes in the social, economic, and political environments in which they have lived. To pursue the metaphor one more step, just as the siblings and cousins are influenced more by the preceding generation than they care to see or admit, concepts in the new paradigm are deeply conditioned by their lineal relationships to concepts in the bureaucratic predecessor.

The most appropriate term for the new generation of the extended family of ideas about how to make government operations productive and accountable is the *post-bureaucratic paradigm*. This term implies that the post-bureaucratic paradigm is as multifaceted as its predecessor. An unrelated name would hide the fact that as a historical matter, the younger generation of ideas has evolved from the bureaucratic paradigm.

Table 16.1 depicts this evolution. This framework guides the effort to identify the post-bureaucratic paradigm and to place it in historical perspective.

TABLE 16.1
Comparing the Paradigms

Bureaucratic Paradigm	Post-Bureaucratic Paradigm
Public interest	Results citizens value
Efficiency	Quality and value
Administration	Production
Control	Winning adherence to norms
Specify functions authority, and structure	Identify mission, services customers, and outcomes
Justify costs	Deliver value
Enforce responsibility	Build accountability
	Strengthen working relationships
Follow rules and procedures	Understand and apply norms
	Identify and solve problems
	Continuously improve processes
Operate administrative systems	Separate service from control
	Build support for norms
	Expand customer choice
	Encourage collective action
	Provide incentives
	Measure and analyze results
	Enrich feedback

SHIFTING PARADIGMS

From the Public Interest to Results Citizens Value

. . . In the age of bureaucratic reform, when the effective demand for combating disease, building civil works, and accounting for public funds had just become significant, the presumption that decisions made in accord with professional standards were congruent with citizens' collective needs and requirements was reasonably defensible. This presumption is no longer reasonable to make. Government often fails to produce desired results from the standpoint of citizens when each professional community within government is certain that its standards define the public interest.

To stimulate more inquiry and better deliberation about how the work of government actually bears on citizens' volitions, the post-bureaucratic paradigm suggests that the specific rhetorical phrase "the public interest" should be confined to books on the history of American politics and administration. A desirable substitute expression is "results citizens value." Compared with its predecessor, the newer expression can be used to motivate more inquiry, clearer argumentation, and more productive deliberation about what results citizens collectively value. This rhetorical construction also conjures up the network of ideas about customer-focused organizations, emphasizes results over inputs and process, and implies that what citizens value cannot be presumed by professional communities in government.[21]

From Efficiency to Quality and Value

Leaders of the scientific management movement in the early twentieth century crafted and popularized a commonsense theory about the causes, nature, and significance of efficiency.[22] This commonsense theory rang true because it explained the industrial progress that characterized the age and because information about the workings of modern factories was widely known. It is a small step to infer that reformers used their knowledge of efficient industrial administration to inform their conception of efficient public administration. . . .[23]

Industry was not just a source of rhetoric about efficient government; reformers' understanding of the main ingredients of efficient government—reorganization, accounting systems, expertise, and cost control—was rooted in their knowledge about *industry.*[24] Reformers elaborated some ingredients into specific processes and techniques, such as careful delineation of roles and responsibilities, centralized scrutiny of budget estimates, centralized purchasing, work programming, reporting systems, and methods analysis. However, one key concept—the product—did not make the journey from industry to government.[25]

Since it excluded the concept of product, reformers' influential conception of efficient government was trouble waiting to happen. It encouraged the notorious bureaucratic focus on inputs to flourish and it permitted specialized functions to become worlds unto themselves. More specifically, an increase in efficiency could be claimed in government whenever spending on inputs was reduced, whereas it was much easier to argue in an industrial setting that cost reduction improved efficiency only when it led to a reduction in the cost per unit of output. Industrial managers may not have had an easy time keeping every specialized member of the organization focused on the product, but in this concept—embodied in the goods moving through the production stream and out the door—they at least had a way to think precisely and meaningfully about how integration of differentiated functions could achieve efficiency. . . .

Some minimal agreement on terms is necessary. First, the appropriate perspective from which these concepts should be defined is that of the customer. By this rule, the recurring definition of quality as conformance to customer requirements is acceptable. Second, net value should be distinguished from value by taking costs into account. By this rule, the claim that reducing expenditures is desirable needs to be scrutinized in terms of the effect on the cost *and* value of products and services. Third, the nonpecuniary costs borne by customers when coproducing services or complying with norms should be taken into account. By this rule, costs measured by conventional accounting systems should be adjusted in service or compliance contexts.

From Administration to Production

The bureaucratic reformers had a theory of how individual public servants contributed to efficient administration. The theory claimed that the purpose of administration was to solve public problems by implementing laws efficiently. Agencies performed their functions by subdividing responsibilities and assigning them to positions. Public servants, assigned to positions on the basis of merit, performed their responsibilities competently by applying their expertise.[26] This theory promised order and rationality in that new domain of public affairs denominated as administration[27] and nicely combined a political argument about administrative legitimacy with an organizational argument about efficiency. The theory also provided a reason to believe that the work of public servants served the public interest.

To some degree, this theory of work in the administrative branch of government lives on. Ask public servants to describe their work and many will reveal facts about their organization's functions and their own responsibilities. In order to communicate what the incumbent of a position does, some agencies compose titles mimicking the chain of command. For example, one senior manager in the Veterans Administration carried the title of Assistant Associate Deputy Chief Medical Director.

This strategy of defining work is failing to satisfy public servants. . . .[28]

The accumulating evidence that production is a powerful alternative to the idea of administration comes from the total quality management (TQM) movement. TQM provides employees with methods—such as process flow analysis—for identifying and improving production processes.[29] Most government employees whose experience with TQM concepts and methods has been positive are deeply committed to the idea of process analysis and control.[30]

By using methods of process analysis, employees can develop a shared visual representation of the organization without making any reference to its hierarchical structure or boundaries. What is more important is that through process analysis, individual employees can visualize and describe for others how their work leads to the delivery of a valuable service or product. And coworkers develop an understanding of—and appreciation for—the work each does.[31]

To guard against mistaken analogies between production in government and manufacturing, the post-bureaucratic paradigm suggests that the concept of production be rendered as service delivery.[32] This terminology reminds public servants of the complex and intimate relationship between process and product in service delivery: whereas the production of goods is a separate process from distribution and consumption, many services are produced, delivered, and consumed in the same process, often with customers participating as coproducers.[33]

From Control to Winning Adherence to Norms

Within the bureaucratic reformers' vision of government, control was the lifeblood of efficient administration. Control was considered to be so vital that the intention to strengthen it served as an effective major premise in arguments supporting a wide array of practices that deepened and extended the bureaucratic reforms. These practices included accounting systems, budgetary freezes, reorganizations, reporting requirements, and countless measures to reduce the exercise of discretion by most public servants. . . .

The formulators of the bureaucratic paradigm pursued the aims of order, rationality, impersonal administration, efficiency, and political accountability by instituting centrally controlled systems of rules. The focus on rules, commitment to centralization, and emphasis on enforcement spawned worrisome consequences, which have tended to make bureaucracy a pejorative rather than a descriptive term.

Rules.   The bureaucratic paradigm encouraged control activities to develop ever-denser networks of rules in response to changing circumstances or new problems.[34] When rule systems became extremely complex, staff operations of substantial size—located in both staff and line agencies—were needed to understand, administer, and update them.

Centralization.   The bureaucratic paradigm urged overseers to centralize responsibility and authority for making administrative decisions in the hands of staff agencies. Centralized staff operations generally lacked the capacity to process incoming requests quickly, either because their power in the budget process was slight or because they were committed to the idea of saving taxpayers money. As a further consequence, decisions made centrally did not take into account the complexity and variability of the situations confronted by line agencies.

Enforcement.   Staff agencies focused on enforcement were typically blind to opportunities to correct problems at their source.[35] For instance, agencies were often unable to comply with norms because their employees did not know how to apply them to specific situations. Many such compliance problems could have been solved by providing education and specific advice about how to improve administrative or production processes; however, compliance organizations stressing enforcement tended to underinvest in problem solving. Furthermore, an emphasis on enforcement unnecessarily set up adversarial relationships between control activities and compliers. This kind of relationship discouraged efforts to comply voluntarily with norms.[36]

In our view, after more than a half-century of use, the concept of control is so bound up with the obsolete focus on rules, centralization, and enforcement that continued use of the term is an obstacle to innovative thinking about how to achieve results citizens value.

Since achieving adherence to norms requires people to make choices among alternatives under conditions of complexity and ambiguity, compliance strategies should empower compliers to apply norms to their particular circumstance. Compliers become empowered, by definition, when they feel personally responsible for adhering to the norms and are psychologically invested in the task of finding the best way to comply. Taking personal responsibility for results is as crucial to making good compliance decisions as to delivering quality goods and services.

As analysts have discovered in studying the sources of productivity and quality in organizations, taking personal responsibility is substantially influenced by the work setting. In particular, researchers argue that employees are most likely to take personal responsibility at work when they receive clear direction about purposes and desired outcomes, education, coaching, material resources, feedback, and recognition.[37] These findings suggest that taking personal responsibility for adhering to norms is likely to be enhanced when compliers understand the purpose of the norms, obtain education and coaching about how to apply the norms to the situations they face, receive timely and useful information about the extent to which compliance is being achieved, and are recognized for their accomplishments.

Beyond Functions, Authority, and Structure

The bureaucratic paradigm defined organizations in terms of their assigned functions, delegated authority, and formal structure. Functions were abstract categories of work to be performed within the larger organizational machinery of government. Authority was the right to make decisions and demand obedience from subordinates on matters related to the grant of authority. Formal structure referred to the system of superior-subordinate relationships, which matched delegated authority with subdivided functions ultimately to the level of individual positions.

The critiques of this outlook are legendary. From a post-bureaucratic perspective, the central challenge of organizations is to channel human energies into thinking about and doing socially useful work. Public servants need better categories than functions, authority, and structure to meet this challenge. The concepts of mission, services, customers, and outcomes are valuable because they help public servants articulate their purposes and deliberate about how to adapt work to achieve them.[38] Missions are claims about the distinctive contribution an organization makes to the public good.[39] Services are the organization's products.[40] Customers are individuals or collective bodies—whether internal or external to the organization—to whom employees are accountable as parties to customer relationships.[41] Outcomes are precisely defined states of affairs that the organization intends to bring about through its activities.[42]

From Enforcing Responsibility to Building Accountability

. . . From a post-bureaucratic perspective, the most effective way to hold employees accountable is to make them feel accountable.[43] This route to accountability is attractive, in part, because employees want to be accountable. They want to be accountable because it is the only way for them, as for us all, to be important. . . .

Psychologists specializing in the study of work argue that employees feel accountable when they believe intended work outcomes are consequential for other people, receive information about outcomes, and can attribute outcomes to their own efforts, initiatives, and decisions.[44] Informed by this kind of argument, the post-bureaucratic paradigm values efforts by public managers and their overseers to bring about states of affairs in which public servants feel accountable for achieving desired results.

As a way to overcome the hierarchical and remedial thrust of accountability in the bureaucratic paradigm, attention should focus on the spectrum of working relationships, including the customer relationship, through which public servants create results citizens value. (Table 16.2 shows a classification scheme of working relationships.) From a post-bureaucratic perspective, accountability between the parties engaged in such working relationships should be a two-way street. For example, providers should be accountable to customers for meeting their needs for quality and value, while customers should be accountable to providers for clarifying their own needs and for giving feedback. . . .

TABLE 16.2
Working Relationships

Customer Relationships

Individual or organizational customers
- within the organization
- within government
- outside government

Collective customers
- within the organization
- within government
- outside government

Production Relationships

Coproduction relationships with customers

(continued)

TABLE 16.2
Working Relationships (continued)

Complier relationships
- within government
- between government and the public

Relationships with providers
- within government
- vendors

Team relationships
- between individuals
- between task groups
- between functions

Partner relationships
- within government
- between public and private sectors

Oversight Relationships

Relationships with executive branch leadership and their staffs
Relationships with legislative bodies, legislators, and staff
Relationships with courts

Membership Relationships

Employment relationships
- between employees and their organizational leaders
- between employees and their immediate superiors
- between employees and the employer

Communitywide relationships
- among agencies
- among public servants

Peer group relationships
- among executives
- among members of a professional specialty

From Justifying Costs to Delivering Value

Budgeting, according to the bureaucratic paradigm, was a process of arriving at annual spending plans. As part of the budgeting process, administrators were charged with the task of developing estimates of their organization's needs.[45] In practice, administrators assumed the task of developing convincing arguments that their needs in the upcoming budget year were greater than in the current one. The major categories of acceptable evidence for arguments about needs included current spending, expected increases in the cost of doing business, and the estimated cost of expanding the organization's level of activity. Upon receiving estimates of needs, central budget offices built arguments for the claim that the agency's costs were less than the estimated ones as part of an effort to judge whose claims for resources were most justified....[46]

Some advocates of the post-bureaucratic paradigm ... speculate that citizens are much more interested in the quality and value of public services than they are in costs; hence, it is mistaken for overseers to scrutinize costs during budget deliberations. They envision a world in which budget deliberations enable overseers to make informed purchases of services from agencies on behalf of the public. They further contend that improving the quality and value of public services can be achieved on a routine basis if agencies are expected to track changes in customer requirements and to improve productivity through better management of production processes; they point out that budget processes under the bureaucratic paradigm instead motivate public managers to spend their limited time justifying costs. From a post-bureaucratic perspective, it is urgent to work out the implications of these claims and speculations in theory and practice.

Beyond Operating Administrative Systems

Centralized staff agencies were institutional embodiments of the bureaucratic reform vision. By operating administrative systems, these organizations put into practice the concepts of efficiency, administration, and control. Their cultures and routines spawned many of the constraints and incentives facing line agencies, which from a post-bureaucratic vantage point now detract from government's ability to deliver results citizens value.

If the time has come to break through bureaucracy, centralized staff operations must be part of the process. In serving this purpose, centralized staff operations need to transform their organizational strategies. Just like line agencies, they can benefit from using the concepts of mission, services, customers, quality, value, production, winning adherence to norms, building accountability, and strengthening working relationships. More specifically, central staff operations should separate service from control, build support for norms, expand customer choice, encourage collective action, provide incentives, measure and analyze results, and enrich feedback in the context of all working relationships....

ROLE OF PUBLIC MANAGERS

The post-bureaucratic paradigm values argumentation and deliberation about how the roles of public managers should be framed. Informed public managers today understand and appreciate such varied role concepts as exercising leadership, creating an uplifting mission and organizational culture, strategic planning, managing without direct authority, pathfinding, problem setting, identifying customers, groping along, reflecting-in-action, coaching, structuring incentives, championing products, instilling a commitment to quality, creating a climate for innovation, building teams, redesigning work, investing in people, negotiating mandates, and managing by walking around.[47] As a contribution to current deliberation, we suggest that breaking through bureaucracy is a useful supplement to this stock of ideas. This concept alerts public managers to the need to take seriously the profound influence of the bureaucratic paradigm on standard practices, modes of argumentation, and the way public servants derive meaning from their work.

Historically aware public managers, committed to breaking through bureaucracy, will help coworkers understand that the bureaucratic paradigm mistakenly tended to define organizational purpose as doing assigned work. They will argue that a crucial challenge facing all organizations is to imbue work effort with purpose while thwarting the tendency to presume that current practices deliver as much value as possible. They will build capacity within and around organizations to deliberate about the relationship between results citizens value and the work done.

Public managers guided by the idea of breaking through bureaucracy should employ not only a combination of historical knowledge and post-bureaucratic ideas as tools to diagnose unsatisfactory situations and to spot inadequacies in arguments rooted in the bureaucratic paradigm, but should also deal creatively with the fact that many public servants are emotionally invested in the bureaucratic paradigm. Public servants, in our experience, are generally willing to move on to a newer way of thinking and practicing public management if they are convinced that the efforts they expended in past years will not become depreciated by the move. An effective way to overcome resistance to change stemming from this source is to make an informed argument that the presuppositions of the bureaucratic paradigm as played out in the organization's particular field of action were reasonable during most of the twentieth century, but that times have changed.[48]

NOTES

1. William F. Willoughby, *The Movement for Budgetary Reform in the States* (New York: D. Appleton, 1918); Leonard D. White, *Trends in Public Administration* (New York: Mc Graw-Hill, 1933); Lloyd M. Short and Carl W. Tiller, *The Minnesota Commission on Administration and Finance, 1925–39: An Administrative History* (Minneapolis: University of Minnesota Press, 1942); Fritz Morstein Marx, ed., *Elements of Public Administration*, 2d ed. (Englewood Cliffs, N.J.: Prentice-Hall, 1959); Barry Dean Karl, *Executive Reorganization and Reform in the New Deal* (Cambridge, Mass.: Harvard University Press, 1963); Aaron Wildavsky, *The New Politics of the Budgetary Process* (Glenview, Ill.: Scott, Foresman, 1988), 53-63.

2. Stephen Skowronek, *Building a New American State: The Expansion of National Administrative Capacities, 1877–1920* (Cambridge, England: Cambridge University Press, 1982).

3. See, generally, Jack H. Knott and Gary J. Miller, *Reforming Bureaucracy: The Politics of Institutional Choice* (Englewood Cliffs, N.J.: Prentice-Hall, 1987), and Robert B. Reich, *The Next American Frontier* (New York: Times Books, 1983). According to Yale sociologist Charles Perrow, "The founders of organizations of all types and reformers of those

that existed repeatedly held the industrial organization model—factories, by and large—
as the important social innovation of the time. And it truly was." "A Society of Organizations," *Estudios del Instituto Juan March de Estudios e Investigaciones* (Madrid) (October
1990): 33.

4. In the words of historian Barry Dean Karl, these movements' beliefs and actions (as well as
those of many New Dealers) were "in many respects a consequence of both industrialism
and nationalism. The chief value of centralization rested on the increase in efficiency
which it invariably seemed to bring to the growing urban and industrial chaos. But efficiency could also become identified with national purpose. The idea that human effort
could be wasted when undirected and uncontrolled . . . was central to the growing concern with efficiency, leadership, and planning." *Executive Reorganization and Reform*,
182–83.

5. An excellent contemporary restatement of this outlook is contained in Jerry L. Mashaw,
Bureaucratic Justice: Managing Social Security Disability Claims (New Haven, Conn.: Yale University Press, 1983). For a discussion of the concept of impersonal administration from a
sociological and historical perspective, see Charles Perrow, *Complex Organizations: A Critical Essay*, 3d ed. (New York: Random House, 1986), 1–29.

6. See Woodrow Wilson, "The Study of Public Administration," *Political Science Quarterly*
(June 1887): 197–202. See also Skowronek, *Building a New American State*, 47–84.

7. See Steven Kelman, *Procurement and Public Management: The Fear of Discretion and the Quality of Government Performance* (Washington, D.C.: American Enterprise Institute, 1990),
11–15.

8. Other key legacies are institutional arrangements, including hierarchical executive
branches and staff agencies, and organizational routines. These arrangements, agencies,
and routines embed certain habits of thought into people who work in government.

9. A definition of paradigm that fits this usage is "the basic way of perceiving, thinking, valuing, and doing associated with a particular vision of reality. A dominant paradigm is seldom if ever stated explicitly; it exists as unquestioned, tacit understanding that is
transmitted through culture and in succeeding generations through direct experience
rather than being taught." Willis Harmon, *An Incomplete Guide to the Future* (New York:
Norton, 1970), quoted in Joel Arthur Barker, *Discovering the Future: The Business of Paradigms* (St. Paul, Minn.: ILI Press, 1985), 13–14. A similar locution can be found in the literature on public administration: "Each of us lives with several paradigms at any given
time. . . . As it appears appropriate, each of us moves in and out of paradigms throughout
any work day, and with scarcely a thought about the belief and values systems that under-
gird them." Yvonna S. Lincoln, "Introduction," in *Organizational Theory and Inquiry: The
Paradigm Revolution*, ed. Yvonna S. Lincoln (Beverly Hills, Calif.: Sage, 1985), 30. The word
paradigm began to be used in natural scientific and social scientific communities after publication of Thomas S. Kuhn's *Structure of Scientific Revolutions* (Chicago: University of
Chicago Press, 1962).

10. The belief that politics and public administration are separate domains of social action
was central to the bureaucratic reform vision. This notion has been criticized for decades
by academics and educators. According to Wilson, "Political scientists never fail to remind
their students on the first day of class [that] in this country there is no clear distinction between policy and administration." *Bureaucracy*, 241. We suppose that these teachings have
had sufficient influence to merit focusing attention elsewhere. The bureaucratic paradigm's prescribed separation between substance and institutional administration *within*
the administration component of the politics/administration dichotomy has received inadequate notice and scrutiny.

11. Strictly speaking, in the public sector the concepts of *customer* and *service* are typically structural metaphors. Introducing new metaphorically structured concepts into an existing conceptual system makes a difference in how people reason. According to George Lakoff and Mark Johnson, "New metaphors have the power to create a new reality. This can begin to happen when we start to comprehend our experience in terms of a metaphor, and it becomes a deeper reality when we begin to act in terms of it. If a new metaphor enters the conceptual system that we base our actions on, it will alter that conceptual system and the perceptions and actions that the system gives rise to. Much of cultural change arises from the introduction of new metaphorical concepts and the loss of old ones. For example, the Westernization of cultures throughout the world is partly a matter of introducing the 'time is money' metaphor into those cultures." *Metaphors We Live By* (Chicago: University of Chicago Press, 1980), 145.

12. The forces making customer service attractive as a conceptual scheme include the emergence of services as the nation's leading sector, a climate that makes privatization in its various forms an ever-present possibility, public discontent with bureaucracy, renewed appreciation for market-oriented forms of social coordination, technological innovation (especially in information systems), directives from the Office of Management and Budget and the Office of the Secretary of Defense, and the availability of training monies. The list could be extended. The availability of training monies. The list could be extended. The social and intellectual history of the movement under way has yet to be written.

13. See the John F. Kennedy School of Government case study "The Army and REQUEST," by Steven Kelman.

14. The point of the example is not that the substitution of a customer orientation for the bureaucratic approach necessarily improves the operation of government; rather, it suggests that applying the customer approach is likely to alter what government agencies do, thereby changing the results of government operations. To evaluate whether the altered outcome constitutes an improvement requires an act of judgment and will. As an empirical matter, the judgment of the Army and its authorizers is that this application is desirable, on the whole.

15. See Ron Zemke, "Putting Service Back into Public Service," *Training* (November 1989): 42–49, on improvements in motor vehicle licensing and registration services. See Mary Faulk, "Customer Service and Other Unbureaucratic Notions" (Olympia: Department of Licensing, State of Washington, n.d., Mimeographed). The John F. Kennedy School of Government case study "Middlesex County Jury System," C16-86-656, is another illustration.

16. Excellent academic critiques of more general versions of the bureaucratic paradigm can be found in Perrow, *Complex Organizations,* Gareth Morgan, *Images of Organization* (Beverly Hills, Calif.: Sage, 1986), and Wilson, *Bureaucracy.* The service approach is not used by these prominent organizational theorists to critique the theory or practice of bureaucracy. Among the works we draw on in synthesizing the conceptual system of customer service are those written by business school academics and consultants: Theodore Levitt, "The Industrialization of Service," *Harvard Business Review* (September-October 1976): 63–74; Richard B. Chase, "Where Does the Customer Fit in a Service Operation?" *Harvard Business Review* (November-December 1978): 137–42; Thomas J. Peters and Robert H. Waterman, Jr., *In Search of Excellence: Lessons from America's Best-Run Companies* (New York: Warner, 1982); Geoffrey M. Bellman, *The Quest for Staff Leadership* (Glenview, Ill.: Scott, Foresman, 1986); James L. Heskett, *Managing in the Service Economy* (Boston: Harvard Business School Press, 1986); James L. Heskett, "Lessons in the Service Sector," *Harvard*

Business Review (March-April 1987): 118-26; Karl Albrecht, *At America's Service* (Homewood, Ill.: Dow Jones-Irwin, 1988); Christian Grönroos, "The Relationship Approach to Marketing in Service Contexts: The Marketing and Organizational Behavior Interface," *Journal of Business Research* 20 (1990): 3-11; William R. George, "Internal Marketing and Organizational Behavior: A Partnership in Developing Customer-Conscious Employees at Every Level," *Journal of Business Research* 20 (1990): 63-70; Christian Grönroos, *Service Management and Marketing: Managing the Moment of Truth in Service Competition* (Lexington, Mass.: Lexington Books, 1990); David E. Bowen, Richard B. Chase, Thomas G. Cummings, and Associates, *Service Management Effectiveness* (San Francisco: Jossey-Bass, 1990); and James L. Heskett, W. Earl Sasser, Jr., and Christopher W. L. Hart, *Service Breakthroughs* (New York: Free Press, 1990). The public sector literature on service management includes Charles C. Goodsell, ed., *The Public Encounter: Where State and Citizens Meet* (Bloomington: Indiana University Press, 1981).

17. The term *rhetorical* is not meant to be disparaging. On the contrary, rhetoric is a valuable way of mobilizing conceptual resources and evidence. See Giandomenico Majone, *Evidence, Argument, and Persuasion in the Policy Process* (New Haven, Conn.: Yale University Press, 1989). See also Alasdair Roberts, "The Rhetorical Problems of the Manager," paper presented at the Annual Research Conference of the Association for Public Policy Analysis and Management, San Francisco, October 1990.

18. The rhetoric of customer service is becoming ubiquitous in statements of mission and strategy by government organizations. See, for example, U.S. General Services Administration, "1991 Strategic Plan" (Washington, D.C., 1990). It is also becoming commonplace in articles written for public managers. See, for example, Organization for Economic Cooperation and Development, *Administration as Service: The Public as Client* (Paris, 1987); Zemke, "Putting Service Back into Public Service"; Steven Kelman, "The Renewal of the Public Sector," *American Prospect* (Summer 1990): 51-57; David Osborne, "Ten Ways to Turn D.C. Around," *Washington Post Magazine*, December 9, 1990, pp. 19-42; Barbara Bordelon and Elizabeth Clemmer, "Customer Service, Partnership, Leadership: Three Strategies That Work," *GAO Journal* (Winter 1990-91): 36-43; Monte Ollenburger and Jeff Thompson, "A Strategy for Service?" *Public Management* (April 1990): 21-23; George D. Wagenheim and John H. Reurink, "Customer Service in Public Administration," *Public Administration Review* (May-June 1991): 263-70; Tom Glenn, "The Formula for Success in TQM, " *Bureaucrat* (Spring 1991): 17-20; and Joseph Sensenbrenner, "Quality Comes to City Hall," *Harvard Business Review* (March-April 1991): 64-75. Professional associations of public administrators are bringing these ideas to the attention of their members. See, for example, the papers presented at the 1990 National Conference of the American Society for Public Administration, published in the Fall 1990 issue of *The Bureaucrat*. Executive education programs, furthermore, are increasingly using the concepts of customers and service. See Michael Barzelay and Linda Kaboolian, "Structural Metaphors and Public Management Education," *Journal of Policy Analysis and Management* (Fall 1990): 599-610.

19. In undertaking this task, it is well to bear in mind two observations made many years ago by legal theorist Karl N. Llewellyn. First, "it is hard to take things which are unconventional or otherwise unfamiliar to the addressee and to get them said so that they come through as intended. . . . I say we all know this, and we all try to canvass and prepare, to choose words well and to arrange them better, so that they may become true messengers." Second, "there are no panaceas." *The Common Law Tradition: Deciding Appeals* (Boston: Little, Brown, 1960), 401-3.

20. On mappings from source to target domains, see George Lakoff and Mark Turner, *More Than Cool Reason* (Chicago: University of Chicago Press, 1989), 57-65.

21. Some may criticize the use of any concept such as the public interest. Arguments can be found in the literature on public deliberation and public management to support our premise that if the public interest rhetorical category is suppressed, it should be replaced by a functionally similar idea. See Steven Kelman, *Making Public Policy: A Hopeful View of American Government* (New York: Basic Books 1987), 215. See also Robert B. Reich, ed., *The Power of Public Ideas* (Cambridge, Mass.: Harvard University Press, 1990); Dennis F. Thompson, "Representatives in the Welfare State," in *Democracy and the Welfare State*, ed. Amy Gutmann (Princeton, N.J.: Princeton University Press, 1988), 136–43; and Mark H. Moore, "Creating Value in the Public Sector," book manuscript in progress. Support for the premise that rhetoric contributes to deliberation can be found in such diverse works as Donald N. McCloskey, *The Rhetoric of Economics* (Madison: University of Wisconsin Press, 1985); Warren Bennis and Richard Nanus, *Leaders: Strategies for Taking Charge* (New York: Harper & Row, 1985); David Johnston, *The Rhetoric of Leviathan* (Princeton, N.J.: Princeton University Press, 1986); and Giandomenico Majone, *Evidence, Argument, and Persuasion in the Policy Process* (New Haven, Conn.: Yale University Press, 1989).

22. We simplify here by omitting discussion of the concept of economy. Economy was the watchword of those who wanted to reduce government expenditures and taxes; efficiency was highlighted by those who wanted to improve government performance. We also simplify the discussion of efficiency here by focusing on the scientific management movement and factory administration. For a more complete discussion of the concept of efficiency in early public administration, see Dwight Waldo, *The Administrative State*, 2d ed. (New York: Holmes and Meier, 1984).

23. By knowledge in this context we mean ordinary knowledge as discussed in Charles E. Lindblom and David K. Cohen, *Usable Knowledge: Social Science and Social Problem Solving* (New Haven, Conn.: Yale University Press, 1979), 12–14. On mappings from source to target domains, see Lakoff and Turner, *More Than Cool Reason*, 57–65.

24. "Systematic bookkeeping was revolutionizing control over industrial production, pointing out the direction not only of efficiency and greater profit but honesty as well." Barry Dean Karl, *Executive Reorganization and Reform in the New Deal* (Cambridge, Mass.: Harvard University Press, 1963), 35. In stressing the role of industry as a source domain of knowledge about efficient government, we do not claim that other sources of knowledge were irrelevant. Indeed, Karl points out that early reformers were influenced by city management in Germany and the British parliamentary system, although the influence of these models was mediated by knowledge of business and industry in the United States. See *Executive Reorganization and Reform*, 95–96. Karl also argues that the power of arguments about industrial practice was enhanced by moral outrage against corruption and waste. See *Executive Reorganization and Reform*, 141–43.

25. What explains this puzzle? One argument might be that the outputs of government are different from the outputs of factories. But that argument fails because the concept of product could have served as a structural metaphor—as it does today—in efforts to conceptualize the relation between organizational goals and organizational work. One might argue, against this view, that reformers did not know how to think metaphorically. But the concept of an efficient government entails the use of the structural metaphor "Government is industry." Whether reformers knew they were speaking metaphorically is largely irrelevant. We conjecture that the concept of product was left out because reformers were committed to rationalism and professionalism and shunned market processes and commercial values in the context of government. The influence of legal conceptions of organization was also felt.

26. On classical organization theory, see Gareth Morgan, *Images of Organization* (Newbury Park, Calif.: Sage, 1986), 19–38.

27. For a classic argument that administration is an identifiable domain of governmental activity, see Woodrow Wilson, "The Study of Administration," *Political Science Quarterly* (June 1887): 197–222.

28. National Commission on the Public Service, *Leadership for America: Rebuilding the Public Service* (Washington, D. C., 1989), 173–75.

29. For a discussion of process control, see Robert H. Hayes, Steven C. Wheelwright, and Kim B. Clark, *Dynamic Manufacturing: Creating the Learning Organization* (New York: Free Press, 1988), 185–341; and Heskett, Sasser, and Hart, *Service Breakthroughs*, 112–58.

30. This empirical claim cannot be substantiated on the basis of social scientific research. It rests on anecdotal evidence derived from extensive contact with public sector managers and from conducting field work for "Denise Fleury and the Minnesota Office of State Claims," John F. Kennedy School of Government case C15-87-744.0.

31. One interviewee for the Denise Fleury case reported that before engaging in process flow analysis, coworkers viewed one another as job categories; afterward, they viewed one another as people.

32. Some activities in government, such as minting currency and making weapons, are more like manufacturing than like service delivery. Most compliance activities are more similar to services than to manufacturing. *Winning compliance to norms* is an appropriate term for production in a compliance context.

33. The typical accounts of total quality management fail to make the vital distinction between industrial production and service delivery. For a discussion of this distinction, see James L. Heskett, *Managing in the Service Economy* (Boston: Harvard Business School Press, 1986). Indeed the source domains for total quality management practices are industries and utilities. Viewed at close range, the failure to make the service/industry distinction is a significant handicap of TQM.

34. For a discussion of frequent mismatches between rules and operational realities, see James Q. Wilson, *Bureaucracy*, 333–345; and Steven Kelman, *Procurement and Public Management: The Fear of Discretion and the Quality of Government Performance* (Washington, D.C.: American Enterprise Institute, 1990), 88–90.

35. As mentioned above, the total quality management movement has not focused on compliance processes. If such a focus were to be developed, it might begin by pointing out the similarities between enforcement approaches to compliance and inspection approaches to quality assurance. In diagnosing problems with the enforcement approach, experience with inspection could serve as a useful source domain. Similarly, as a heuristic device to structure a better approach to compliance, TQM's preferred alternatives to inspection should be used as a source domain. From a post-bureaucratic perspective, TQM should not be the only such source domain. Other source domains include the liberal and civic republican strands of American political theory and recent experience with service management.

36. For a discussion of this consequence of an enforcement orientation in the context of social regulation, see Eugene Bardach and Robert A. Kagan, *Going by the Book: The Problem of Regulatory Unreasonableness* (Philadelphia: Temple University Press, 1982), 93–119.

37. See J. Richard Hackman and Greg R. Oldham, *Work Redesign* (Reading, Mass.: Addison-Wesley, 1980).

38. Another valuable concept is strategy, especially as defined in Lax and Sebenius, *Manager as Negotiator*, 261–68.

39. This definition is influenced by Mark H. Moore, "What Sort of Ideas Become Public Ideas?" *The Power of Public Ideas*, ed. Robert B. Reich (Cambridge, Mass.: Harvard University Press, 1990), 55-83; and Ronald Jepperson and John W. Meyer, "The Public Order and the Construction of Formal Organizations," in *The New Institutionalism in Organizational Theory*, ed. Walter W. Powell and Paul J. DiMaggio (Chicago: University of Chicago Press, 1991), 183-203.

40. As mentioned above, services and products in the public sector are often defined metaphorically. The role of structural metaphors in public sector management thought and practice deserves substantial attention. For a beginning, see Michael Barzelay and Linda Kaboolian, "Structural Metaphors and Public Management Education," *Journal of Policy Analysis and Management* (Fall 1990): 599-610.

41. See the principles discussed in chapter 7.

42. The bureaucratic paradigm focused attention on functions and nonoperational goals rather than producing desired states of affairs. The term *outcome* has a different meaning in this context than in the academic public policy literature, where the concept of outcome generally refers to the ultimate intended consequences of a public policy intervention. As used here, an outcome can be proximate results of an organization's work. For example, desired outcomes of a plant management operation include clean buildings and satisfied customers.

43. The argument that accountability is a psychological state of affairs that can be influenced by the individual's environment is developed in Hackman and Oldham, *Work Redesign*, 71-98. In a similar vein, other social psychologists conclude on the basis of experiments that accountability raises "concerns about social evaluation, so that an individual's interest in appearing thoughtful, logical, and industrious overcomes motivation to loaf." See Elizabeth Weldon and Gina Gargano, "Cognitive Loafing: The Effects of Accountability and Shared Responsibility on Cognitive Effort," *Personality and Social Psychology Bulletin* (1988): 160, cited in Robert E. Lane, *The Market Experience* (Cambridge, England: Cambridge University Press, 1991), 49.

44. Hackman and Oldham, *Work Redesign*, 77-81. For a recent summary of the literature on intrinsic and extrinsic motivations at work, see Lane, *Market Experience*, 339-71.

45. Simon, Smithburg, and Thompson, *Public Administration*, 508-9.

46. Allen Schick presents a nuanced statement of this aspect of the bureaucratic paradigm: "Spending agencies usually behave as claimants, but most have procedures to conserve the resources available to them. . . . Similarly, the central budget office has a lead role in conserving resources, but it occasionally serves as a claimant for uses that it favors. It is not uncommon for the budget office to argue that some programs should be given more funds than have been requested." See "An Inquiry into the Possibility of a Budgetary Theory," *New Directions in Budget Theory*, ed. Irene S. Rubin (Albany: State University of New York Press, 1988) 65.

47. Among the many authors who have formulated, elaborated, restated, and/or popularized such concepts are Mary Parker Follett, Peter Drucker, Herbert Simon, Philip Selznick, Warren Bennis, Donald Schön, J. Richard Hackman, Harold Leavitt, James Q. Wilson, Rosabeth Moss Kanter, James Sebenius, James Heskett, Robert Behn, Philip Crosby, Thomas Peters, and Robert H. Waterman, Jr. These conceptual themes continue to be extended in the public management literature by such writers as Jameson Doig, Steven Kelman, Mark Moore, Ronald Heifetz, Philip Heymann, and Robert Reich.

48. The change process in Minnesota, described in chapters 3-5, accelerated after such arguments—informed by the results of the research leading to this book—were made.

17

Harold F. Gortner, Julianne Mahler, and Jeanne Bell Nicholson

THE PIVOTAL CONTROVERSIES

Organization theory is a disorderly and fascinating field (Waldo 1978). Each theory starts with a unique set of assumptions, asks a different set of basic questions, and, not surprisingly, arrives at different—sometimes diametrically opposed—answers. Nevertheless, certain themes are constantly addressed as the frantic debate among "public" organization theorists goes on. These controversies about, or perspectives on, organization in the public sector can be categorized under the following four general headings:

1. *Law and legal authority.* Public agencies are established by law to administer the law, and all of society is affected by the result. Therefore, questions pertaining to the interpretation and implementation of the law as it applies to public organizations and about how these organizations fulfill their mandated functions are of central importance and are subject to constant debate.
2. *Rationality and efficiency.* The public's material resources are used by public organizations. Therefore, how efficiently and rationally those resources are used is of utmost importance to everyone. Whether inside or outside those bureaus.
3. *Psychological and social relations.* Civil servants are human beings (even though some politicians might have us believe otherwise). Therefore, public managers must understand the psychological and sociological aspects of the organization if they are to accomplish good human resource management and achieve individual neutrality while maintaining high motivation and involvement among employees who cannot be rewarded in what are typical ways for the private sector. Psychological and social principles that apply to individuals and groups in organizations must be understood and then interpreted to fit the public milieu.
4. *Politics and power relations.* All public organization action takes place in a politically charged environment. Therefore, the decisions and actions of the principal actors in these organizations must be considered in a political context.

The second and third controversies noted are especially universal and must be considered in any discussion on organization theory although they must be interpreted in the context of the public sector. However, since public organizations exist for reasons (and have obligations) quite dissimilar to those in the private sector, the first and last of these pivotal perspectives assume a special significance that does not exist for organizations in the private sector. Although the reason for this emphasis on the law and the political environment should be relatively clear after reading the last chapter, it may be worthwhile to comment briefly on the importance of these two areas.

The law places serious limitations on the way public organization structures and functions can be instituted and carried out. While striving for optimal efficiency and the best possible social and psychological arrangements in the bureau, the public manager must always be cognizant of "what the law will let one do."

When dealing with the fourth controversy noted, students of public bureaucracy need to be aware of the assumptions and thinking behind the questions asked about organizations. These questions and their answers are political: they often express, implicitly or explicitly, criticism of the political system and the predominant culture, and agendas for change. Therefore, they rest on a particular set of assumptions about authority, conflict, power, and the proper criteria for choice within organizations. Any organizational theory, when applied to bureaus in the public sector, should be examined for such assumptions when it is studied and, especially, before attempting to apply it in the hope of improving management or changing the operations of any group or agency.

Similarly, the politically charged environment is a prominent factor that must be considered as public organization theory is examined. How does the theory take into account the existing political system, which, in turn, helps explain why bureaus currently function as they do? And is must be considered whenever an attempt is made to apply organization theory to a bureau. How will actors in the political environment interpret what is attempted, and how will they react to that effort given their political philosophy, position within the political system, and the perception that both factors give them of the world? How will the reactions of the political actors affect the implementation of any change? It must be recognized that different types of rationality (that is, several types of political and managerial rationality) exist based on different sets of basic values and on whether substantive or instrumental rationality is being considered. (Rationality will be discussed later in this chapter.) These different rationality systems are being used simultaneously in defining the goals of public bureaus and in assessing how "rational and efficient" they are.

Thus, it is the inclusion of the four controversies in this particular combination that makes public organization theory unique, especially the heavy emphasis that must be placed on the first and last principles. If, when studying organization theory, such an emphasis is not included, there is no way to recognize the special problems faced by public organizations or the special interpretations that must be understood when the traditional theories are applied to this unique sector of our society; it is the addition of these issues that creates additional problems for nonprofit and private organizations when they are carrying out public policy functions.

In the next section, after presenting two models of organization that will help us focus the discussion throughout this chapter, we will examine the four pivotal themes of public organization theory, and, finally, we will take a special look at the influence of political history on the bureau, on public organization theory, and on public management practice.

MODELS OF ORGANIZATION

Let us briefly present two models of complex organizations and how to manage them, the first the more traditional model of bureaucracy presented by Max Weber and widely accepted as the norm[1] for public organization, and the second a currently popular model of how to organize the successful private sector business organization.

Throughout the chapter, as we discuss the four controversies, we will refer to the two models. They will help us understand the larger field of organization theory and the application of its concepts to the workings of public organizations, and of equal importance, how the perspectives differ in importance within the private sector.

Probably the most influential model of organization ever presented is Max Weber's description of the internal characteristics of the "ideal type" bureaucracy. According to Weber, within the bureaucracy:

> The whole administrative staff under the supreme authority . . . consists, in the purest type of individual officials who are appointed and function according to the following criteria:
>
> 1. They are personally free and subject to authority only with respect to their impersonal official obligations.
> 2. They are organized in a clearly defined hierarchy of offices.
> 3. Each office has a clearly defined sphere of competence in the legal sense.
> 4. The office is filled by a free contractual relationship. Thus, in principle, there is free selection.
> 5. Candidates are selected on the basis of technical qualifications. In the most rational case, this is tested by examination of guaranteed by diplomas certifying technical training, or both. They are appointed, not elected.
> 6. They are remunerated by fixed salaries in money, for the most part with a right to pensions. Only under certain circumstances does the employing authority . . . have a right to terminate the appointment, but the official is always free to resign. The salary scale is primarily graded according to rank in the hierarchy; but in addition to this criterion, the responsibility of the position and the requirements of the incumbent's social status may be taken into account.
> 7. The office is treated as the sole, or at least the primary occupation of the incumbent.
> 8. It constitutes a career. There is a system of "promotion" according to seniority or to achievement, or both. Promotion is dependent on the judgment of superiors.
> 9. The official works entirely separated from ownership of the means of administration and without appropriation of his position.
> 10. He is subject to strict and systematic discipline and control in the conduct of the offices. (1947, 333–334)

This model describes major aspects of the structure of almost all organizations, and in those cases where it does not, the organizations are generally categorized or specifically recognized by the extent to which their structure varies from the bureaucratic standard. Built into this model is a series of assumptions about the functions of an organization within the larger society, the goals of the organization and where they

---

[1]The use of the term *norm* is solely descriptive. Weber's model describes the way public organizations look; it says nothing about how they should be structured or how they should operate. In fact, Weber decried such structure, but he described it in an objective and scholarly manner. Weber's use of the term *ideal type* means "the organization that most perfectly meets the criteria of bureaucracy," and not *the best* organization.

are established, and the individuals within the organization and how they think and act. For these reasons, the model may be described as "universal," or as an attempt to present facts and relationships that must be understood any time one talks about complex organizations, which has certainly been the case.

Over the last decade, total quality management (TQM) has swept through the business community. As American businesses felt the threat of foreign competition and the pressure for both efficiency and quality, the teachings of the "quality theorists," and especially W. Edwards Deming (1986), have been accepted by an increasing number of organizations and organization/management theorists. It is perhaps unnecessary to give much historical background to this movement; however, TQM is being "borrowed back" by Americans, after having been rejected earlier, and after it was developed and implemented during its first several decades by Japanese businesses.

There is a strong movement to bring TQM into government, with several state and local governments involved and the Federal Quality Institute working with agencies in the federal government. Elements of TQM appear in a variety of critiques of government organizations and operations, including but certainly not limited to Osborne and Gaebler's *Reinventing Government* (1992) and the report of the National Performance Review, *Creating a Government that Works Better & Costs Less* (1993).

Deming (1986) presents fourteen principles for successful total quality management (see Figure 17.1); however, the original principles were developed for manufacturing companies and need to be modified a bit to apply to governmental operations. According to James E. Swiss (1992), the TQM model for a "successful" government organization includes seven primary tenets.

1. The customer is the ultimate determiner of quality. If the product does not meet the desires of the customers, it is bad quality, no matter how "perfectly" made.
2. Quality should be built into the product early in the production process (upstream) rather than being added on at the and (downstream), Proper early, upstream design saves later redesigning or reworking and makes customers happier. TQM opposes mass inspections—quality is everyone's task, not someone's at the end of the process.
3. Preventing variability is the key to producing high quality. Quality slips when variation occurs. Therefore, process control charts that track deviation from the optimum are analyzed to prevent deviation in product or service.
4. Quality results from people working within systems, not individual efforts. The system usually creates quality slips, not individual. With committed people working together, it is a mistake to focus on individuals. The system should create intrinsic motivators that lead all workers to perform well.
5. Quality requires continuous improvement of inputs and processes. This continuous improvement should be in processes and inputs—not in outputs (defined as profits).
6. Quality improvement requires strong worker participation. The workers must do it right the first time, so managers and workers must work together "without fear."
7. Quality requires total organizational commitment. Managers must create an organizational culture where everyone focuses on consistently producing quality products and improving them constantly (Swiss, 1992, 357–358).

FIGURE 17.1   *Deming's Fourteen Points for Management*

1. Create constancy of purpose toward improvement of product and service, with the aim to become competitive and to stay in business, and to provide jobs.
2. Adopt the new philosophy. We are in a new economic age. Western management must awaken to the challenge, must learn their responsibilities, and take on leadership for change.
3. Cease dependence on inspection to achieve quality. Eliminate the need for inspection on a mass basis by building quality into the product in the first place.
4. End the practice of awarding business on the basis of price tag. Instead, minimize total cost. Move toward the single supplier for any one item, on a long-term relationship of loyalty and trust.
5. Improve constantly and forever the system of production and service, to improve quality and productivity, and thus constantly decrease costs.
6. Institute training on the job.
7. Institute leadership. The aim of supervision should be to help people and machines and gadgets to do a better job. Supervision of management is in need of overhaul, as well as supervision of production workers.
8. Drive out fear, so that everyone may work effectively for the company.
9. Break down barriers between departments. People in research, design, sales, and production must work as a team, to foresee problems of production and in use that may be encountered with the product or service.
10. Eliminate slogans, exhortations, and targets for the work force asking for zero defects and new levels of productivity. Such exhortations only create adversarial relationships, as the bulk of the causes of low quality and low productivity belong to the system and thus lie beyond the power of the work force.
11. a. Eliminate work standards (quotas) on the factory floor. Substitute leadership.
    b. Eliminate management by objective. Eliminate management by numbers, numerical goals. Substitute leadership.
12. a. Remove barriers that rob the hourly worker of his right of pride of workmanship. The responsibility of supervisors must be changed from sheer number to quality.
    b. Remove barriers that rob people in management and in engineering of their right to pride of workmanship. This means, *inter alia,* abolishment of the annual or merit rating and of management by objective.
13. Institute a vigorous program of education and self-improvement.
14. Put everybody in the company to work to accomplish the transformation. The transformation is everybody's job.

SOURCE: W. Edwards Deming. *Out of Crisis.* Cambridge, Mass.: Massachusetts Institute of Technology, Center for Advanced Engineering Study. 1986. pp. 23-28.

From these TQM principles comes a universal organizational and managerial model that the authors argue is the structure necessary for success in the competitive environment of capitalist free enterprise. This model, like Weber's, operates from a set of assumptions about the functions of organizations within the larger society, the goals of the organization and where they are established, and the individuals within the organization and how they think and act.

Both the Weberian and the TQM models more specifically address some, and de-emphasize others, of the four perspectives that we suggested are central to the study of public organizations. It is the thesis of this discussion that placing too much emphasis on any one of these perspectives is unproductive, whereas combining them creates a useful picture. After each perspective is examined separately, they must be brought to-gether in a meaningful synthesis.

THE CONTROVERSY AROUND FOUR PERSPECTIVES

Law and Legal Authority

We take it for granted that bureaus operate on a legal basis, or according to the law. We also recognize that the purpose of the bureau is to execute the law. However, we may fail on occasion to recognize that the effort to execute the law according to struc-tures and processes established by law may cause great difficulty for these agencies. The most obvious example of this difficulty is seen in law enforcement's attempt to control organized crime, where the strict limits placed on surveillance and collection of evidence and the broad interpretation of individual rights create problems for the police. Although *police departments* are derided for not doing a better job of control-ling organized crime, *police officers* also work under procedural proscriptions, strongly ascribed to by most citizens, that limit their ability to control that crime. Law enforce-ment must find a way to meet the goals established for it by society while staying within the procedural limits placed on it by that same society.

In a similar vein, it is not uncommon for legislative adversaries, once aware that they cannot block passage of a new program, to attempt to place it in an al-ready existing organization that is inimical or, at best, coldly neutral to that pro-gram. Another ploy regularly used by enemies of programs is to create, in the enabling act, procedures or structures that will hobble or make inefficient the de-livery of the service or good in the hope that they may reopen the debate about the issue at a later date with "proof" that the decision to create the program was a mis-take in the first place because of the problems that have been shown to exist in ad-ministering it.

That government and its bureaus should operate according to law is a widespread belief. Even in totalitarian states, the government and its agencies at least pay lip ser-vice to this idea and function under a constitution and laws that, though failing to guarantee some of the most important human rights, justify the legality of the im-posed order to the citizenry.

Today, however, we take for granted Abraham Lincoln's statement that we have a government of laws, not of men. The public bureaucracy is the administrative or imple-mentation and service arm of government, and it is based on laws. Laws establish the pol-icy direction, or the goals, of bureaus, thereby spelling out what output or results are expected. Likewise, laws define proper organizational structure, due process, reporting procedures, and conflict of interest. In other words, the law clarifies both structural and procedural questions. It even establishes the system by which personnel are selected, rewarded, or punished within the bureau.[2]

The centrality of law and the concomitant responsibility for the execution of the law required the development of the modern public bureau. This is especially true if it is assumed that bureaus should *react to and fulfill* citizen desires and demands rather than *create* social objectives because the bureaucracy is geared toward objectivity, independence from personal pressure, and control over discretionary actions by bureaucrats. Looking back at Max Weber's model of bureaucracy, or at his description of the internal characteristics of bureaucratic organizations, one can see how these characteristics help guarantee that public agencies will "automatically" obey the law.

A second aspect of the relationship between the law and bureaucracy becomes overwhelmingly apparent as we look at Weber's model and the ways in which it guarantees that the law will be the basis for bureau action. By examining Weber's criteria, we can clarify the way in which the bureaucratic system guarantees an inordinate focus by public employees on the law. Central to this point is the fact that each office has a clearly defined sphere of competence (criterion 3). And where is that sphere defined? In the law—if not in the enabling act, then in the rules, regulations, and other materials that are based on and interpret the inert law as it is put into action. Note also that bureaucratic officials are subject to authority only when it applies to their offices (criterion 1), these offices are at least their primary occupation (criterion 7), and the officials are entirely separated from ownership (criterion 9). These factors limit the possibility of conflict of interest; thus, employees of bureaus are under no other pressure except to know and obey the law. Furthermore, the fact that positions in the bureaucracy are filled by free contractual relationships (criterion 4) after being selected on the basis of technical qualifications (criterion 5) and are then paid fixed salaries in money (criterion 6) guarantees their loyalty. The officials are not forced to participate, and their rewards are fixed; therefore, no *person* has an undue claim on their services. They are not distracted by personal claims from the objective administration of the law. Finally, the hierarchical structure of offices (criterion 2) and the natural desire to advance in a career (criterion 8) mean that all officials are held accountable for their actions. Strict accountability breeds close adherence to the law, and deductive rules and rigorous control are the major objects of design and management.

Within the public sector, adherence to the law is central to all activities. Accountability and control, especially as spelled out in the law, are ensured by the structure of organizations. Structure, as portrayed in the organizational chart, is the formal aspect of organizational life, and if the chief executive or an external body such as the legislature wishes to have an impact on the operation of an agency, the primary line of attack is through changes in the law that force reorganization. Like-

---

[2]Although the laws specify all the elements of organization mentioned here, it must be understood that the elements may not, indeed cannot, be complete, concise, and clear in many if not most cases.

wise, the easiest and most direct way for top officials to make an imprint on their agencies is through reorganization. The result is instantaneous and visual, whereas attempts to influence the informal portion of a bureau take an indeterminate amount of time and often cannot be concretely measured. Nor are these officials often able to get the enabling law changed to accomplish the shift in agency direction that they would like. In addition, appointed officials, bringing with them a portfolio of experience from their prior positions (often from the private sector), are convinced that by restructuring the bureau they can increase the efficiency and effectiveness of the public agency. Such changes and "improvements" always appear, ultimately, in formal rules and regulations or some similar "lawlike" format.

Efficiency and Rationality

The principles of efficiency and rationality are grouped together here because many social theorists, especially during the first third of the twentieth century, used the terms almost interchangeably. Whether they realized the synonymity of the two concepts is unclear, but their recognition, or lack thereof, is not important to the major thrust of our argument. In the interest of clarity, we will first discuss the two principles separately. Then we will point out how they overlap.

Efficiency   In its simplest sense, efficiency equals maximization of productivity, or the greatest possible output for the least input. The founders of this school of administrative study came from both industry and public administration, with their ideas being adapted in both sectors. Let us look at the two approaches to this principle and then note the common assumptions from which the founders operated.

Frederick Taylor was interested in increasing productivity because everybody benefited from the result:

> It is perfectly clear that the greatest permanent prosperity for the workman, coupled with the greatest prosperity for the employer, can be brought about only when the work of the establishment is done with the smallest combined expenditure of human effort, plus nature's resources, plus the cost for the use of capital in the shape of machines, buildings, etc. (1947, 11)

Productivity was achieved by applying Taylor's interpretation of the scientific method to the man-machine system in industry. Since little had been done up to that time by way of systematically examining how men and machines interacted as a single task or process (series of tasks) was carried out, Taylor zeroed in on this most obvious factor.

Taylor's approach to the study of work soon became known as scientific management. He best defines the central concepts of this approach at the end of his treatise when he says that:

> It is no single element, but rather [a] combination, that constitutes scientific management, which may be summarized as:
>   Science, not rule of thumb.
>   Harmony, not discord.

Cooperation, not individualism.

Maximum output, in place of restricted output.

The development of each man to his greatest efficiency and prosperity. (1947, 141)

By using his version of the scientific method, Taylor was convinced that it was possible to discover the "one best way" to structure any job or process. With the discovery of the one best way, the principle of efficiency was realized.

Another group of individuals was attempting to apply scientific principles to administration, which Luther Gulick defines as "the phenomena of getting things done through cooperative human endeavor" (1937). Whereas politics is concerned with the process of getting elected to office and setting objectives for the country, Gulick argues that "administration has to do with getting things done; with the accomplishment of defined objectives" (1937, 191). If administration is removed from the value-laden field of politics, then a science of administration becomes possible.

The way to achieve that efficiency is by "scientifically" examining the structure of organizations, and this is what is done throughout Gulick and Urwick's *Papers*. Questions such as what is the proper span of control for a supervisor, what should be the basis for assigning supervisors over workers, and what principles should control the division, or structure, of large organizations are analyzed throughout the book in one of the first attempts to find the "one best way" to structure organizations to guarantee efficiency in both administration and production of goods or services.

Rationality   The principle of rationality was accepted as an undisputed law by all the writers mentioned. When Weber defines the phenomenon that he calls bureaucracy, he is simply describing the organizational construct that has been established to guarantee rationality. Taylor, Gulick, Urwick, and the other proponents of scientific management and scientific administration prescribe rational procedures and structures. Both groups, whether descriptive or prescriptive, accept the idea that what organizations seek and need is rationality. Rationality (the quality or state of having or being based on reason) is central to all organizations in our modern, technological, interdependent world. Nowhere is this idea more alluring than in the public sector because of the government's influence on all of society.

However, these theorists are over simplistic in their definition and perception of essential elements. This simplicity is best understood by examining the term *rationality* and by recognizing the narrowness of their definition as opposed to the complexity that exists when a full explication of the concept is given.

There are two levels of rationality: substantive and instrumental (Weber 1947). Substantive rationality is concerned with the ends that an organization attempts to achieve—what are the right, appropriate, or best goals to be sought? Instrumental rationality is concerned not with ends, but means, or *how* an organization attempts to achieve a given end or set of ends. The two levels are both essential, but the types of logic and analytic tools that are involved differ dramatically.

Weber recognizes the need for rationality as one of the central causes for the development of bureaucracy. Bureaucracy is a necessary result of the development of modern technology, with its incredible level of interdependence among all parts of society. Technological interdependence creates a requirement for stable, strict, intensive, and calculable interactions, and "it [bureaucracy] is superior to any other form [of organization] in precision, in stability, in the stringency of its discipline, and in its reliability" (Weber, 1947, 339). Like them or not, bureaucracies are rational, and since that principle is central to our lives, bureaucracies will continue to exist until a form of organization is discovered that improves on the delivery of this particular characteristic. All this discussion, however, focuses on instrumental rationality—getting things done efficiently—rather than on "what should be done," which is determined by the superior powers (the legislature, courts, and so on) outside the bureaucracy. This is especially true in the public sector.

The model presented by those advocating TQM also accepts much of the scientific management philosophy of Taylor: in their case, scientific methods are used to monitor performance and to identify points of high leverage for performance improvement. "TQM practitioners are expected to focus their attention on work processes rather than on outcome measures and to use scientific methods to improve those processes continuously" (Hackman and Wageman 1995, 325). Thus, although there is continuous improvement in performance, there is a "one best process" at any moment, arrived at rationally by teams of workers and managers through use of the scientific tools at their disposal, and it is to be followed by workers.

Substantive rationality plays a role in the internal decision-making process in the private sector—corporations do care about what they make and what affect their product has on society; however, the decisions about "what ought to be" are biased by the basic assumptions about the goals of businesses. If the product makes a profit and it is not illegal, then it is okay to carry on that activity, maximize productivity, and reap the available profit. Such ends are usually not appropriate for the public manager. There may be a vociferous debate about the impact of alcohol and tobacco products on the society at large, but perfectly legitimate businesses will continue to make those products until they are specifically banned from doing so. Public agencies generally cannot be involved in such debatable activities unless there is believed to be a need for the activity despite its questionableness, and then the goals of the operations are specifically stated, and procedures are stringently regulated.

In order to achieve the bottom-line success that is assumed to be the goal of all organizations. TQM advocates accept structures and procedures that would be highly questionable in the public sector. For example, they argue that it is rational to break the employees of the corporation into small, independent teams (under management direction) to examine the work being done and to make changes once agreement is achieved on optimum procedures. This step, of course, accepts the basic tenet that the organization should cater to its customers. Both of these eminently rational suggestions for corporations may raise howls of protest if implemented by many of their public counterparts (Swiss 1992). It can also be suggested to private managers that they remain in the business the company knows best and that the administrative structure be kept lean and simple (Peters and Waterman 1982). Such a focus on quality often leads to success and growth for a private company.

However, public managers often do not have the luxury of deciding such matters; therefore, such advice may very well be useless to them. The public served, and the services to be rendered, are often decided before the public manager begins to get involved in the decision-making process. Rago (1994) also points out that public agencies often pay a price for being successful.

Public administrators may focus on process and improve it dramatically,[3] but that does not guarantee more resources or more satisfaction from "customers." Still procedural efficiency and rationality are the goals of TQM, and these two terms continue to dominate public organization debate even when in new rhetorical clothing.

Rationality-efficiency   By closely examining the two approaches to organization theory, and by probing for the more basic assumptions on which the approaches are built, it becomes clear that though different terms are used, they are used in almost identical ways. TQM searches for efficiency in procedures and uses scientific methods to achieve the one current best way of production. Other theorists—Weber, Taylor, Gulick, and others—consider only the instrumental level of rationality, and they define rationality and efficiently identically. According to these theorists, "The efficient achievement of a single goal is technical rationality (Taylor), the maximum achievement of a plurality of goals is economic rationality (Gulick; Weber), and no other types of rationality are admitted" (Diesing 1962, 1). Substantive rationality is irrelevant; goals are established somewhere outside the organization or the part of the organization being considered. Technical rationality, as developed by Taylor, was specifically geared toward increased output for the same amount of input; that equals efficiency.

The issues of rationality, efficiency, or both, if they are in fact the same, are of great importance in the study of public organizations. Attempts to achieve rationality and efficiency must not be downplayed. However, focusing on such concepts inspires us to ask only some of the vital questions, and our horizons must expand, even when we are considering the place of reason or rationality in organizations. Both levels of rationality, and at least the five types of reason mentioned by Diesing, are required to understand or operate in a public organization.

Psychology and Social Relations

Interest in the social relations of organizations developed in part as a reaction to the formalistic approaches emphasized by the early students of management and organization and in part as the logical evolution of interest or curiosity by those who desired to examine all aspects of organizational life. The reaction to the formal emphasis and the ensuing recognition of the fact that informal relations within an organization are equal in importance to the structures and processes established by law or in writing occurred for at least

---

[3] TQM assumes top management support, but political officials operate under a different concept of rationality than do business officials (see the section in this chapter on "Politics and Power"). TQM focuses, ultimately, on economic factors—in the long term, businesses increase profits or gain a larger segment of the market. Public officials focus on the short term—the next election. They must get reelected, or the politician who appointed them must. There are few incentives for public officials to focus on management. For example, Joseph Sensenbrenner, the mayor of Madison, Wisconsin, and a public official who was committed to TQM in the 1980s enumerates the tremendous gains made in efficiency within the city. It gained him accolades from across the nation. "But this recognition was not enough to win me a fourth term. Other political factors were more compelling" (1991, 75).

three reasons. Some manager/scholars such as Chester Barnard (1938) began to point out that both a formal and an informal life existed side by side, if not intertwined, in the structure and functions of any organization, and that both aspects of organizational life had to be considered. At the same time, some of the programs attempting to reach the goals of increased productivity and rationality did not achieve the expected results (for example, the Hawthorne experiments, Roethlisberger and Dickson 1939). At least part of the reason for the failure of such efforts was the fact that after a certain point in the development of productivity programs and increasing rationality in structures, the individuals operating in the organizations began to resist further change. To comprehend the attitudes and reactions of employees, it became important to focus on both the individuals and groups in the organizations and how they interacted outside the formal structures and procedures. Finally, with the developing interest and skill in testing and evaluation of individuals, and to a certain extent groups, which was hastened and increased by the coming of World War II, it became obvious that the informal side of organization theory added a great deal to our knowledge about the total field.

Focus on Individual Behavior (the Psychological Approach)   The importance of examining the individual's skills and aptitudes (issues also important to Taylor) is recognized by everyone, but equally important is the study of individual traits and attitudes, with the second gaining major impetus from the "surprises" at Hawthorne. Central to the examination of individual skills and aptitudes is the area of testing and measurement. Personnel selection, for instance, has been one of the principle areas of interest to industrial and organizational psychologists since the field's earliest days. The goal of those involved in testing and measurement is to choose, from a larger group, the best individual or group of individuals to fill positions within an organization. These decisions are frequently based on tests that purport to measure one's ability to perform specified mental or physical tasks and to measure attitudes and personality traits or attributes that are believed to predict future success on the job.

Central to this issue is a series of questions, a sample of which are: What is the impact of the civil service system on recruiting top-notch individuals and then motivating them to do good work? How do bureau structures affect communication, decision making, and other functions? How do bureau structures affect communication, decision making, and other functions? How do people interact with the new technologies being introduced into bureaus? Organization structure, job design, and even the physical layout of offices have an impact on the way that individuals interact and carry out their tasks. All these factors then must be considered as organizational managers decide what is appropriate job preparation for applicants, and, for those already in the bureau, what kinds of preparation, training, and knowledge and skills are required for the new jobs being created by technological change or for promotion to higher positions.

Finally, the study of leadership focuses much attention on the individual: considerable effort has gone into the attempt to discover the personality characteristics or traits of leaders. Do individuals who become leaders have certain traits in common? Are certain traits always necessary in particular types of situations? These and similar questions are examined by students of leadership. When one examines history, it appears that some individuals were destined to become leaders, whereas others would never have risen to the top, no matter how hard they tried. This phenomenon has piqued the interest of all those who examine the leadership role.

Focus on Group Behavior (the Sociological Approach)   The common thread in every preceding case is the researchers' interest in the individual. A parallel interest exists in the role of the group and how it affects and is affected by the organization. The informal organization, which comprises groups that form outside or despite the formal structure, plays a significant part in determining the perceptions and attitudes of group members, as well as in establishing the values and norms of behavior. One of the early discussants of the importance of the informal aspects of organization was Chester Barnard (1938), who argued that informal organization preceded the formal in existence. Barnard also pointed out that each type of organization needed the other if both were to continue existing for a significant time because each fulfilled functions that could not be accomplished by the other.

Of course, the recognition of the importance of informal groups meant that a new fact of organization life had to be examined if we were to be fully cognizant of *all* the forces that influence organizations. The most inclusive term for this study is *group dynamics*, which is defined by Cartwright and Zander as "a field of inquiry dedicated to achieving knowledge about the nature of groups, the laws of their development, and their interrelations with individuals, other groups, and larger institutions" (1968, 4). From this research came numerous explanations of and theories about group behavior.

Closely related to the idea of organization culture and its impact is the understanding of leadership in the group context. Success in changing the attitudes and habits of individuals and groups usually depends on the commitment of the leaders: If they support change, it has a chance: if they do not support change, it probably will not occur. The relationship between groups and their leaders has become an increasingly important aspect to organization theory. Social exchange theory, for example, bases leadership effectiveness in a group not on formal position, but on the benefits the leader can generate for the group in return for his or her acceptance in the position (Jacobs 1971). In other words, leadership is a role or position granted by the group in exchange for services rendered. This and other similar theories point out the difference between management and leadership, the first being based on one's position in the bureaucratic hierarchy and the second on power relationships in a social situation (French and Raven 1958).

Only by understanding the group aspects of these processes can anyone claim to be knowledgeable about the theory of organizations or about how to apply that theory to group management.

Combining the Individual and the Group   Our understanding of organizations increases immensely by examining the individual or the group and how he or she or they interact with the organization. Perhaps even greater progress has been made by combining the various theories into a more comprehensive network. When one looks at theories about individuals in organizations, then adds the element of individuals in informal groupings that also are operating within the formal organization, and finally recognizes that the formal organizations themselves operate in larger environments where each organization may be thought of as an individual within the larger system, the complexity of organization theory is brought home rather forcefully.

On the other hand, advocates of TQM take a broader view of both individuals and organizations that recognized both formal and informal relationships. They encourage a formal structure that serves as the instigator and modulator of group process—both formal and informal—that flourishes as work teams focus on production processes. Management's job is to guarantee that the total organization, formal and informal, is focused on the major value of the firm (which is to guarantee satisfied customers). By recognizing that productivity occurs through people, this model emphasizes the importance of motivating employees. Demming, Juran, and the others recognize that a broad and multifaceted view of the psychological and social principles operating in any organization is necessary. The problem becomes one of figuring out what parts of their ideas can be applied in the public sector and how, and then using them.

Finally, the much-touted area of "organization development" is based on an attempt to apply all the theories in a way that will open communication channels, increase trust, and create a more democratic environment in organizations. Although there is a fierce debate about the feasibility and propriety of the objectives and about the methods used to achieve them, the debate is one that includes all the various aspects of organization theory. In a similar manner, TQM includes a broad interpretation of organization theory—that sometimes disagrees with commonly held ideas about motivation and reward, for example—and attempts to maximize quality in performance through the combination of human understanding and scientific methods. Therefore, these theories about organizational change and improvement encourage a scope of integration that is beneficial to those wishing to improve their understanding of how public bureaus work, regardless of what happens to the ideas generating the debate.

Politics and Power

Public organizations, which we refer to as bureaus, are unlike most others in one important way: The difference is the political setting in which public organizations function. In this area, most of the generic or universal models have failed; they simply do not deal with the issue of politics, and they interpret power as an internal phenomenon usually related to the area of leadership. Weber, when describing bureaucracy, spends little time in discussing power, and to the extent that he does discuss it, internal power relations are defined by the law and its formal interpretation in the hierarchy and in individual spheres of competence. Ultimate power and the relationship of each bureau with the others in society are determined either totally outside the organization or are considered by only those few in formal positions at the top of the hierarchy where such matters fall within their sphere of competence.

The adherents of TQM also ignore the subject of power and politics. Power relationships within the corporation remain basically the top-down system traditional to American industry. Since "quality" is ultimately a management responsibility . . . attempts to improve quality must begin at the top? (Hackman and Wageman 1995, 315). The success or failure of the TQM program depends on the wholistic implementation of the principles noted earlier, and this implementation is seen as an internal process. Nothing is said about the political environment within which the organization operates.[4]

Public employees operating at lower levels of bureaus, especially those in nonboundary-spanning positions, may nor recognize or care much about the political environment because the way they work may be somewhat similar to the way an employee in the private sector works. However, when one examines positions at higher levels of the bureau, or when the behavior of the public organization as an entity is the focus of attention, the political environment becomes an essential element in the equation. In this case, it is necessary to note the development of theories related to political values and power, which in turn have an impact on resource distribution, coalition building, and political goal setting and decision making. A grasp of these theories is essential to an understanding of the political factors that profoundly influence public organization.

The impact of political culture on perceptions and actions can be seen by comparing the views toward the civil service in Canada and the United States. Even though Canada and the United States both have a representative democratic form of government, a history that is predominantly related to Great Britain, and much in the way of a common cultural heritage, the structures and practices of the two governments vary substantially. It is doubtful that two geographically contiguous countries anywhere else in the world are so culturally alike, but there are still major misunderstandings (or a lack of understanding) between the two governments and the people who work in them. For example, when one of the authors spoke with Canadian civil servants who were attending an international conference on the future of public administration held in Quebec City during 1979, the Canadians were mystified by the strict enforcement of the Hatch Act, which limits political activities of federal employees in the United States. Canadian civil servants simply could not understand the necessity of such strict adherence to the act by their southern counterparts. In Canada, despite the clear prohibition of political activity in Section 32 of the Public Service Employment Act:

> Federal employees are in practice much more active than the Act allows. Yet, complaints about the political activity of public servants have been negligible. The political parties seem to have adopted an informal "live and let live" arrangement whereby no party complains about political activity by public servants. (Kernaghan 1975, 29)

---

[4]Private organizations also must pay attention to the political setting. An example that shows the difficulty that may be caused when two sociopolitical systems are involved is the case of international corporations giving bribes to government officials in foreign countries to gain contracts. Such behavior is a common practice in some countries, but the practice—even though taking place in another country and in an environment that accepts the behavior—causes an uproar in the United States and has been declared illegal by law. Businesspeople, therefore, must be politically sensitive and astute in their actions. Industries that are regulated by government or that depend on government for much of their business are naturally much more cognizant of the principles of politics and power; however, these are generally seen as external factors, only peripherally affecting internal operations.

If such differences exist in perceptions about what is necessary legal protection and proscription for public employees and the way those proscriptions are administered, it is obvious that the way public servants operate within the bureaucracy will also differ.

Likewise, political culture plays a major role in attempts to resolve the problem of acid rain in the northeastern United States and eastern Canada. While Canadian officials urge the United States to take firmer action against the industrial air pollution that is responsible for a major portion of the problem, members of the U.S. Congress bitterly complain that Canada should go home and strengthen its own laws. One of the major causes of this controversy is the different ways in which government agencies are expected to behave as they enforce laws. In the United States, government agencies are expected to enforce rules to the letter of the law, but no more.[5] And even then they are often opposed, often in the courts, by private corporations that, for whatever reason, wish to drag their feet concerning compliance. On the other hand, Canadian officials argue that their government agencies tend to operate in such cases through persuasion and gentlemen's agreements, and that, therefore, the overall level of compliance with air-pollution abatement goals is superior in Canada. Needless to say, the U.S. congressmen are hard to convince.

The culture of the political system is inextricably bound up with the existing governmental structure. A mayor-council or a council-manager form of government exists in a city not by chance, but because of the size of a community, the heterogeneity of its population, and the political values of the citizens in the community. (Smaller and middle-sized communities that are socioeconomically homogeneous tend to have manager-council governments, whereas larger and more socioeconomically heterogeneous communities tend to have mayor-council systems.) To a great extent, the structure of local government is a formalized statement of the citizens' values as they relate to such vital issues as political empowerment and decision making, communication, conflict resolution, and control. The structure, in turn, influences the procedures around and in the bureaus established to carry out city policy. Therefore, theories about how the political system works, who has access where, and what is considered "proper" within the political sphere are vital to understanding how public structure develops and is maintained.

PUBLIC ORGANIZATION THEORY TODAY

It is no wonder that a larger number of theories has appeared, given the multitude of perspectives from which to examine organizations. In most cases, we have a situation similar to that of the group of blind men who examined an elephant. Any one theory about public organizations may appear to be wrong, even ludicrously wrong, at least in

---

[5] There is much disagreement on what the letter of the law is. The constant debate over affirmative action and equal employment opportunity shows the drastic differences that can exist between politicians, civil servants, and the interested public in interpreting the law.

part because the theory focuses too closely on one particular aspect of the organization at the expense of the others.

By examining the full range of theories, we can move toward the creation of a set of perspectives useful to public administrators and students of public management.

In a similar vein, it is not enough for public managers to know all about the psychological and sociological theories related to complex organizations. When any attempt is made at application of these theories (and that is the prevalent goal), it is essential to understand the legal and political environment in which that attempt is being made. For example, public managers cannot use all the methods of motivation that are open to managers in the private sector. Likewise, many other theories about organization, when applied in the public sector, must be adjusted to meet the demands of the general political culture and the specific political actors that are relevant to the bureau in question. Public organization theory must address all four perspectives in the controversy to develop a comprehensive picture of the bureau and how it works.

REFERENCES

Barnard, Chester. *The Functions of the Executive.* Cambridge, Mass.: Harvard University Press, 1938.

Bentley, Arthur F. *The Process of Government: A Study of Social Pressures.* Chicago: University of Chicago Press, 1908.

Blau, Peter M. *The Dynamics of Bureaucracy.* Chicago: University of Chicago Press, 1955.

Boulding, Kenneth E. "General Systems Theory—The Skeleton of Science," *Management Science* 2, 1956: 197–208.

Buchanan, James M., and Gordon Tullock. *The Calculus of Consent.* Ann Arbor, Mich.: University of Michigan Press, 1962.

Carey, Alex. "The Hawthorne Studies: A Radical Criticism." *American Sociological Review* 32, 1967: 403–416.

Cartwright, Dorwin, and Alvin F. Zander. *Group Dynamics: Research and Theory.* New York: Harper & Row, 1968.

Creech, Bill. *The Five Pillars of TQM: How to Make Total Quality Management Work for You.* New York: Truman Talley Books/Dutton, 1994.

Dahl, Robert. *Who Governs? Democracy and Power in an American City.* New Haven: Yale University Press, 1961.

_____, and Charles E. Lindblom. *Politics, Economics and Welfare: Planning and Politico-Economic Systems Resolved into Basic Social Processes.* New York: Harper, 1953.

Demming, W. Edwards. *Out of the Crisis.* Cambridge, Mass.: MIT Center for Advanced Engineering Study, 1986.

_____. *The New Economics for Industry, Government, Education.* Cambridge. Mass.: MIT Center for Advanced Engineering Study, 1993.

Diesing, Paul. *Reason in Society: Five Types of Decisions and Their Social Conditions.* Urbana: University of Illinois Press, 1962.

Dye, Thomas R., and Harmon Ziegler. *The Irony of Democracy: An Uncommon Introduction to American Politics.* 9th ed. Belmont, Calif.: Wadsworth, 1993.

Fischer, Frank, ed. *Technocracy and the Politics of Expertise.* Newbury Park, Calif.: Sage Publications, 1990.

French, John R. P., and Bertram Raven. "The Bases of Social Power." In *Studies in Social Power.* ed. Dorwin Cartwright. Ann Arbor, Mich.: Institute for Social Research, 1958: 150-167.

Garvey, Gerald. *Facing the Bureaucracy: Living and Dying in a Public Agency.* San Francisco: Jossey-Bass Publishers, 1992.

Gortner, Harold F. "Values and Ethics." In *Handbook of Administrative Ethics,* ed. Terry L. Cooper. New York: Marcel Dekker, 1994: 373-390.

Gulick, Luther H., and Lyndall Urwick. eds. *Papers on the Science of Administration.* New York: Institute of Public Administration, 1937.

Hackman, J. Richard, and Ruth Wageman. "Total Quality Management: Empirical, Conceptual, and Practical Issues." *Administrative Science Quarterly* 40, 1995: 309-342.

Harmon, Michael M., and Richard T. Mayer. *Organization Theory for Public Administration.* Boston: Little, Brown, 1986.

Hummel, Ralph. *The Bureaucratic Experience.* 2nd ed. New York: St. Martin's Press, 1982.

Hunter, Floyd. *Community Power Structure: A Study of Decision Makers.* Chapel Hill: University of North Carolina Press, 1953.

Ishikawa, Kaoru. *What is Total Quality Control? The Japanese Way.* Englewood Cliffs, N.J.: Prentice Hall, 1985.

Jacobs, T. O. *Leadership and Exchange in Formal Organizations.* Alexandria, Va.: Human Resources Research Organization, 1971.

Janis, Irving L. *Victims of Groupthink.* Boston: Houghton Mifflin, 1972.

Juran, Joseph M. *Juran on Planning for Quality,* New York: Free Press, 1988.

Katz, Daniel, and Robert L. Kahn. *The Social Psychology of Organizations.* 2nd ed. New York: John Wiley & Sons, 1978.

Kaufman, Herbert. *The Forest Ranger.* Baltimore: The Johns Hopkins University Press, 1960.

Kernaghan, Kenneth. *Ethical Conduct: Guidelines for Government Employees.* Toronto: Institute of Public Administration, 1975.

Lens, Sidney. *The Military Industrial Complex.* Philadelphia: Pilgrim Press, 1970.

March, James, and Herbert A. Simon. *Organizations.* 2nd ed. Cambridge, Mass.: Blackwell, 1993.

Mosher, Frederick C., and Richard J. Stillman, eds. *The Professions in Government.* New Brunswick. N.J.: Transaction Books, 1982.

National Performance Review (U.S.). *Creating a Government that Works Better & Costs Less: Report of the National Performance Review.* Vice President Al Gore. New York: Time Books, 1993.

Osborne, David, and Ted Gaebler. *Reinventing Government: How the Entrepreneurial Spirit is Transforming the Public Sector.* Reading, Mass.: Addison-Wesley, 1992.

Ostrom, Vincent. *The Intellectual Crisis in American Public Administration.* Rev. ed. University. Ala.: University of Alabama Press, 1974.

Parsons, Talcott. "Suggestions for a Sociological Approach to the theory of Organizations." *Administrative Science Quarterly* 1, 1956: 63-85.

Peters, Thomas J., and Robert H. Waterman, Jr. *In Search of Excellence: Lessons from America's Best-Run Companies.* New York: Harper & Row, 1982.

Rago, William V. "Adapting Total Quality Management (TQM) to Government: Another Point of View." *Public Administration Review* 54, 1994: 61-64.

Roethlisberger, Fritz J. *Management and Morale.* Cambridge, Mass.: Harvard University Press, 1941.

————, and W. Dickson. *Management and the Worker.* Cambridge, Mass.: Harvard University Press, 1939.

Rossiter, Clinton, ed. *The Federalist Papers: Alexander Hamilton, James Madison, John Jay.* New York: New American Library, 1961.

Scott, Walter Dill. "How Suggestion Works on the Prospect's Brain." *Advertising & Selling* (May 1914): 11, 59.

Senge, Peter M. *The Fifth Discipline: The Art and Practice of The Learning Organization.* New York: Doubleday, 1990.

Sensenbrenner, Joseph. "Quality Comes to City Hall." *Harvard Business Review* 69, 1991: 64–75.

Simmons, Robert H. *Achieving Humane Organization.* Malibu, Calif.: Daniel Spencer Publishers, 1981.

Spiro, Herbert. *Responsibility in Government; Theory and Practice.* New York: Van Nostrand Reinhold, 1969.

Stokey, Edith, and Richard Zeckhauser. *A Primer for Policy Analysis.* New York: W. W. Norton, 1978.

Swiss, James E. "Adapting Total Quality Management (TQM) to Government." *Public Administration Review* 52, 1992: 356–362.

Taylor, Frederick W. *Principles of Management.* New York: Harper & Row, 1911.

———. *Principles of Scientific Management.* New York: W. W. Norton, 1947.

Thompson, James. *Organizations in Action.* New York: McGraw-Hill, 1967.

Truman, David. *The Governmental Process; Political Interests and Public Opinion.* New York: Alfred A. Knopf, 1951.

Waldo, Dwight. "Organization Theory: Revisiting the Elephant." *Public Administration Review* 38, 1978: 589–597.

Weber, Max. *The Theory of Social and Economic Organization.* Trans. and ed. A. M. Henderson and Talcott Parsons. New York: Oxford University Press, 1947.

Weisband, Edward, and Thomas M. Franck. *Resignation in Protest.* New York: Grossman Publishers/Viking Press, 1975.

Wilson, James Q. *Bureaucracy: What Government Agencies Do and Why They Do It.* New York: Basic Books, Inc., 1989.

Wilson, Woodrow. "The Study of Administration." *Political Science Quarterly* 2 (June 1887): 197–222. In *Classics of Public Administration,* ed. Jay M. Shafritz and Albert C. Hyde. Oak Park, Ill.: Moore Publishing, 1978.

18

Henry Mintzberg

MANAGING GOVERNMENT-GOVERNING MANAGEMENT

"Capitalism has triumphed." That was the pat conclusion reached in the West as, one by one, the communist regimes of Eastern Europe began to fall. It has become such an article of faith that we have become blind to its effects. Those effects are highly negative—indeed, dangerous—because the conclusion itself is wrong. In my view, we have confounded the whole relationship between business and government, and we had best clear it up before we end up no better off than the Eastern Europeans once were.

THE TRIUMPH OF BALANCE

Capitalism did not triumph at all; balance did. We in the West have been living in balanced societies with strong private sectors, strong public sectors, and great strength in the sectors in between. The countries under communism were totally out of balance. In those countries, the state controlled an enormous proportion of all organized activity. There was little or no countervailing force. Indeed, the first crack in the Eastern bloc appeared in the one place (Poland) where such a force had survived the Catholic Church.

The belief that capitalism has triumphed is now throwing the societies of the West out of balance, especially the United Kingdom and the United States. That the imbalance will favor private rather than state ownership will not help society. I take issue with Milton Friedman of the University of Chicago, who has been fond of comparing what he calls "free enterprise" with "subversive" socialism. The very notion that an institution, independent of the people who constitute it, can be free is itself a subversive notion in a democratic society. When the enterprises are really free, the people are not.

Indeed, there is a role in our society for different kinds of organizations and for the different contributions they make in such areas as research, education, and health care. The capitalism of privately owned corporations has certainly served us well for the distribution of goods and services that are appropriately controlled by open-market forces. The books published by Friedman and his colleagues are goods of that kind. But is their research? Or the health care received by poor people living near those professors' offices?

BEYOND PUBLIC AND PRIVATE

For as long as anyone cares to remember, we have been mired in a debate over the allocation of resources between the so-called private and public sectors. Whether it is capitalism versus communism, privatization versus nationalization, or the markets of business versus the controls of government, the arguments have always pitted private, independent forces against public, collective ones. It is time we recognized how limited that dichotomy really is.

There are *privately* owned organizations, to be sure, whether closely held by individuals or widely held in the form of market-traded shares. And there are *publicly* owned organizations, although they should really be called *state* owned, because the state acts on behalf of the public. We as citizens no more control our public organizations directly than we as customers (or as small shareholders) control the private ones. But there are two types of ownership that deserve equal attention.

First, there are *cooperatively* owned organizations, whether controlled formally by their suppliers (as in agricultural cooperatives), by their customers (as in mutual insurance companies or cooperative retail chains), or by their employees (as in some commercial enterprises, such as Avis). Indeed, all countries in the West, including the United States, are to a large extent societies of cooperatively owned organizations.

According to the National Cooperative Business Association, almost half of the U.S. population is directly served by some cooperative endeavor, and one in three people is a member of a cooperative. I did some work recently for a major U.S. mutual insurance company. The enterprise is vigorously competitive, yet it benefits from being cooperatively owned. Its executives are quick to point out just how important the absence of stock market pressures is for their ability to take a long-term perspective.

Secondly, we have what I call *nonowned* organizations, controlled by self-selecting and often very diverse boards of directors. These not-for-profit organizations are often referred to as nongovernment organizations (NGOs), but they are also nonbusiness and noncooperative organizations (NBOs and NCOs). Indeed, we are surrounded by nonowned organizations. Among them are many of our universities (including Friedman's University of Chicago), hospitals, charity organizations, and volunteer and activist organizations (the Red Cross and Greenpeace, for example).

From a conventional political perspective, the inclination might be to lay out these four forms of ownership along a straight line from left (state ownership) to right (private ownership), with cooperative ownership and nonownership in between. But I believe that would be a mistake because, here as elsewhere, extremes meet: It is the ends that are most alike. For example, from the point of view of structure, both private and state organizations are tightly and directly controlled through hierarchies—one emanating from the owners, the other from state authorities. In other words, we should fold that line over. What seems like a straight line is really more like a horseshoe.

As a horseshoe-shaped representation of the four forms of ownership would suggest, the leap between state and private ownership can be made more easily than a shift to nonownership or cooperative ownership. That may be why so much of our attention has focused on nationalization versus privatization. The leap is so simple: Just buy out the other side, change the directors, and keep going; the internal control systems remain intact. In Russia today, in many sectors, these leaps have been *too* simple: State control seems to have given way to equally devastating control by the private sector. A surer way of achieving balance—slower and more difficult but now being pursued successfully in some of the other Eastern European nations—is to make wider use of all four forms of ownership around the entire horseshoe.

Unfortunately, we in the West have not come to terms with the full range of possibilities. Because capitalism has supposedly triumphed, the private sector has become good, the public sector bad, and the cooperatively owned and nonowned sectors irrelevant. Above all, say many experts, government must become more like business. It is especially this proposition that I wish to contest. If we are to manage government properly, then we must learn to govern management.

CUSTOMERS, CLIENTS, CITIZENS, AND SUBJECTS

"We have customers," Vice President Al Gore announced early in his term in office. "The American people." But do you have to call people customers to treat them decently? We would do well to take a look at what *customers*, this now fashionable word, used to mean before the Japanese taught us a thing or two. The greatest of the U.S. corporations—those of the automobile industry—did not treat their customers very well. They long pursued deliberate strategies of planned obsolescence—a euphemism for building quality *out*. Moreover, at least one giant retail chain regularly used bait-and-switch tactics, luring in customers with low prices to sell them more expensive products. And in one well-known story, a famous consumer-products company, in order to sell more toothpaste, first made the opening in its tubes bigger and then marketed toothbrushes with longer heads!

Business is in the business of selling us as much as it possibly can, maintaining an arm's-length relationship controlled by the forces of supply and demand. I have no trouble with that notion—for cars, washing machines, or toothpaste. But I do for health care. For cars, washing machines, and toothpaste, most intelligent buyers can beware, as that expression goes; and we have protective mechanisms in place for buyers who cannot beware. But *caveat emptor* is a dangerous philosophy for health care and other complex professional services. Sellers inevitably know a great deal more than buyers, who can find out what they need to know only with great difficulty. In other words, the private ownership model, much as it provides "customers" with a wonderfully eclectic marketplace, does have its limits.

I am not a mere customer of my government, thank you. I expect something more than arm's-length trading and something less than the encouragement to consume. When I receive a professional service from government—education, for example—the label *client* seems more appropriate to my role. General Motors sells automobiles to its *customers*; Ernst and Young provides accounting services to its *clients*. In fact, a great many of the services I receive from government are professional in nature.

But, more important, I am a *citizen*, with rights that go far beyond those of customers or even clients. Most of the services provided by government, including highways, social security, and economic policy, involve complex trade-offs between competing interests. Tom Peters captures this idea perfectly with a story about getting a building permit to enlarge his house. I don't want some bureaucrat at City Hall giving me a hard time, he said in one of his newsletters. I want proper, quick, businesslike treatment. But what if my neighbor wants a permit to enlarge *his* house? Who's City Hall's customer then?

If I have rights as a citizen, then I also have obligations as a *subject*. The British, of course, retain official status as subjects of the crown—a throwback to the days when individuals forfeited much of their autonomy over their "nasty, brutish, and short" lives, as Thomas Hobbes put it, in return for the protection of the state. But, British or not, in one way or another we all remain subjects of our governments—when we pay taxes, allow ourselves to be drafted into armies, or respect government regulations for the sake of collective order.

Customer, client, citizen, and subject: These are the four hats we all wear in society. As customers and citizens, we enjoy a reciprocal, give-and-take relationship with government. Government's customers receive *direct services* at arm's length; its citizens benefit more indirectly from the *public infrastructure* it provides. But there is one major difference between government's customer-oriented activities and its citizen-oriented activities: frequency of occurrence. Review public sector activities carefully—for example, go over a government telephone directory—and you will find relatively little that fits the pure customer category. (And some of what does fit is rather unfortunate, such as lottery tickets. Do we really want our governments, like that toothpaste company, hawking products? Couldn't the current malaise about government really stem from its being *too much* like business rather than not enough?) In contrast, under the citizen category, you will find an enormous amount of activity in the form of public infrastructure: social infrastructure (such as museums), physical (such as roads and ports), economic (such as monetary policy), mediative (such as civil courts), offshore (such as embassies), and the government's own support infrastructure (such as election machinery).

As subjects and clients, we have relationships with government that are more one-sided. To paraphrase John F. Kennedy, the question for us as subjects is what we must do for our governments in the form of respecting state controls. In contrast, as clients who receive professional services, our question is about what the state provides to us. That government phone book reveals all kinds of activities under the subject category—policing, the military, regulatory agencies, and prisons. But more surprising is the prevalence of professional services that governments provide directly, or indirectly through public funding: all of the health care in some countries and much of it in others, much of education, plus other services such as meteorology.

Of course, not all government activities fit neatly into one of the four categories. Our national parks, for example, provide customer services (to tourists) and professional client services (to tourists stranded on mountain faces). Parks are also part of the public infrastructure we enjoy as citizens, and that fact requires us, as subjects, to respect the environment of the park. To take another example, the inmates of prisons are most evidently subjects. But they remain citizens with certain rights and, insofar as we believe in the role of rehabilitation, are clients as well. I introduce these four labels, therefore, not so much for classification as for clarification—to further our appreciation of the varied purposes of government.

Let me link the roles of customer, citizen, client, and subject to our earlier discussion. Customers are appropriately served by privately owned organizations, although cooperatively owned ones—such as mutual insurance companies—can often do the job effectively. Only in limited spheres is direct customer service a job for the state. When it comes to citizen and subject activities, we should stray beyond the state-ownership model only with a great deal of prudence. The trade-offs among conflicting interests in citizen activities and the necessary use of authority in subject activities mandate a clear role for the state.

The client relationship is perhaps more complicated. It is not clear that those professional services widely accepted as public—certain minimum levels of education and of health care, for example—are particularly effective when offered directly by government, let alone by private business. Neither one on its own can deliver all the nuanced requirements of professional services. Markets are crass; hierarchies are crude. Nonowned organizations or, in certain cases, cooperatively owned ones may serve us better here, albeit with public funding to ensure some equity in distribution. Incidentally, relying on cooperatively owned organizations for professional services is not unusual. Even such obviously commercial professions as accounting and consulting often deliver services through cooperatives—namely, professional partnerships.

THE MYTHS OF MANAGEMENT

We have seen that a balanced society requires various institutional forms of ownership and control and that within the public sector there is a wide range of roles for government. How, then, should government activities be managed? To answer the question, we first need to take a look at management itself—or at least at the popular myths about it.

Discussion of management is currently all the rage. I should really say Management, following the lead of Albert Shapero of Ohio State University, who years ago wrote an article titled "What MANAGEMENT Says and What Managers Do" (*Fortune*, May 1976).

Three assumptions underlie the Management view of management.

Particular activities can be isolated—both from one another and from direct authority. The principle derives from the private sector, where many corporations are divided into autonomous businesses, organized as divisions. Each unit has a clear mission: to deliver its own set of products or services. If it satisfies the goals set by the central headquarters, it is more or less left alone.

Performance can be fully and properly evaluated by objective measures. The goals that each activity must achieve can be expressed in quantitative terms: Both costs and benefits can be measured. (In business, of course, the criteria are financial, and costs and benefits are combined to set standards for profit and for return on investment.) That way, there can be "objective" assessment, which is apolitical in nature. The system cannot afford a great deal of distracting ambiguity or nuance.

Activities can be entrusted to autonomous professional managers held responsible for performance. "Let the managers manage," people say. Many have great faith in managers trained in the so-called profession of management. "Make them accountable. If they perform according to plan, as indicated by measurement, reward them. If they don't, replace them."

These assumptions, in my opinion, collapse in the face of what most government agencies do and how they have to work. To isolate government activities from direct hierarchical control in the manner that Management prescribes, there have to be clear, unambiguous policies formulated in the political sphere for implementation in the administrative sphere. In other words, policies have to be rather stable over time, and politicians (as well as managers of other agencies) have to stand clear of the execution of those policies. How common is that? How many government activities fit such a prescription?

Lotteries, to be sure, but what else? Less than you might think. Many government activities are interconnected and cannot be isolated. Foreign policy, for example, cannot be identified with any one department, let alone any one agency. There are, of course, public sector activities that can be isolated horizontally from one another more or less, as in the case of police or prison services. But can they be isolated vertically—from the political process? Certainly, there has been no shortage of effort to isolate them. A few years ago, the United Kingdom made its prison service an ostensibly autonomous executive agency and appointed a high-flying business manager to run it. Recently, in a major scandal, the manager was fired—apparently because he would not dismiss one of the wardens after a highly publicized escape of three inmates. On leaving, he complained to the press that there was more political control over the service after it became "autonomous" than before.

How many politicians are prepared to relinquish control of how many of their policies? And how many policies in government today can simply be formulated in one place to be implemented in another, instead of being crafted in an iterative process involving both politics and administration? *Learning* is another of the current buzzwords of Management. Well, this process of crafting policies *is* learning—mindlessly applying them is not. The belief that politics and administration in government—like formulation and implementation in corporate planning—can be separated is another old myth that should be allowed to die a quiet death.

Next consider the myth of measurement, an ideology embraced with almost religious fervor by the Management movement. What is its effect in government? Things have to be measured, to be sure, especially costs. But how many of the real benefits of government activities lend themselves to such measurement? Some rather simple and directly delivered ones do—especially at the municipal level—such as garbage collection. But what about the rest? Robert McNamara's famous planning, programming, and budgeting systems in the U.S. federal government failed for this reason: Measurement often missed the point, sometimes causing awful distortions. (Remember the body counts of Vietnam?) How many times do we have to come back to this one until we finally give up? Many activities are in the public sector precisely because of measurement problems: If everything was so crystal clear and every benefit so easily attributable, those activities would have been in the private sector long ago.

The fact is that assessment of many of the most common activities in government requires soft judgment—something that hard measurement cannot provide. So when Management is allowed to take over, it drives everyone crazy. And no one more so than the "customer," who ends up getting the worst of it.

Finally, there is the myth that the professional manager can solve everything: "Put someone properly trained in charge, and all will be well." We are so enamored of this cult of heroic leadership that we fail to see its obvious contradictions. For example, in the name of empowering the workers, we actually reinforce the hierarchy. So-called empowerment becomes the empty gift of the bosses, who remain firmly in charge. And those bosses, if knowledgeable about nothing but Management itself, sit in midair, all too often ignorant of the subject of their management. Such a situation just breeds cynicism. In mortal fear of not meeting the holy numbers, managers run around reorganizing constantly, engendering more confusion than clarification. In other words, our obsession with Management belies a good deal of the reality out there. Consequently, it distorts serious activities, as in the case of many public school systems that have been virtually destroyed by the power of the managerial hierarchy to direct classroom activities without ever having to teach anything.

MODELS FOR MANAGING GOVERNMENT

How then should government be managed? Let's consider five models. Each is marked by its own way of organizing government's controlling authority, or *superstructure*, and the activities of its agencies, or *microstructure*. (The budget authority would be part of the former, for example; an environmental protection agency, an example of the latter.) Some of the models are older, some newer. Some we could do with less of, despite their current popularity; others we could use more of, despite their unfamiliarity.

The Government-as-Machine Model. Government here is viewed as a machine dominated by rules, regulations, and standards of all kinds. This applies to the superstructure no less than to each of the microstructures. Each agency controls its people and its activities just as the agency itself is controlled by the central state apparatus. Government thus takes on the form of a hologram: Examine any one piece and it looks just like the rest.

This has been the dominant model in government, almost to the exclusion of everything else. As Frederick Taylor's "one best way," it was popularized in the 1930s in the public sector by Luther Gulick and Lyndall Urwick. Its motto might be Control, Control, Control. In fact, the term *bureaucrat*, for civil servant, comes from the influence of this model.

The machine model developed as the major countervailing force to corruption and to the arbitrary use of political influence. That is why it became so popular earlier in this century. It offered consistency in policy and reliability in execution. But it lacked flexibility and responsiveness to individual initiative, so now it has fallen out of favor. In one form or another, however, the machine model continues to dominate government.

The Government-as-Network Model. This is the opposite of the machine model: loose instead of tight, free-flowing instead of controlled, interactive instead of sharply segmented. Government is viewed as one intertwined system, a complex network of temporary relationships fashioned to work out problems as they arise and linked by informal channels of communication. At the micro level, work is organized around projects—for example, a project to develop a new policy on welfare or to plan for construction of a new building. Connect, Communicate, and Collaborate might be the motto of this model. Ironically, like the machine model, the network model is also holographic in that the parts function like the whole: Individual projects function within a web of interrelated projects.

The Performance-Control Model. Capital-letter Management finds its full realization in the performance-control model, the motto of which could be Isolate, Assign, and Measure. This model aims above all to make government more like business. But we need to be specific here because the ideal is not just any business. There is an assumption, not often made explicit, that the ideal is the divisional structure that conglomerates in particular have popularized. The overall organization is split into "businesses" that are assigned performance targets for which their managers are held accountable. So the superstructure plans and controls while the microstructures execute. All very tidy. But not necessarily very effective.

The ultimate effect is to reinforce the old machine model. In other words, the performance model decentralizes in order to centralize; it loosens up in order to tighten up. And tightening up comes at the expense of flexibility, creativity, and individual initiative. Thus the brave new world of public management all too often comes down to nothing more than the same old machine management—new labels on the old bottles. It works fine where machine management worked—sometimes even slightly better—but not anywhere else.

The Virtual-Government Model. Carry the performance model to its natural limit and you end up with a model that can be called virtual government. Popular in places like the United Kingdom, the United States, and New Zealand, virtual government contains an assumption that the best government contains an assumption that the best government is no government. Shed it all, we are told, or at least all that it is remotely possible to shed. In virtual government's perfect world, the microstructures (the activities of agencies) would no longer exist within government. All that kind of work would take place in the private sector. And the superstructure would exist only to the extent needed to arrange for private organizations to provide public services. Thus the motto of this model might be Privatize, Contract, and Negotiate. The model represents the great experiment of economists who have never had to manage anything.

The Normative-Control Model. None of the above models has succeeded in structuring social authority adequately. Perhaps that is because social authority is hardly about structures. "It's all so simple, Anjin-San," the confused British captain in *Shogun*, shipwrecked in a strange land, is told by his Japanese lover. "Just change your concept of the world." Exemplifying a different concept of the world, the normative-control model is not about systems but about soul. Here it is attitudes that count, not numbers. Control is normative—that is, rooted in values and beliefs.

The model is not well recognized in most Western governments these days, let alone in most Western businesses. It hasn't exactly worked badly for the Japanese, but the more they have demonstrated its superiority in direct competition with the West, the more the West has retreated into its old machine model—or newer versions of it—which works in precisely the opposite way. Once upon a time, however, when there was still the concept of public *service*, it was really the normative model that managed to keep the machine model functioning. In other words, service and dedication muted the negative effects of bureaucracy. But much of that attitude is now gone or going quickly.

There are five key elements that characterize the normative model:

- *Selection.* People are chosen by values and attitudes rather than just credentials.
- *Socialization.* This element ensured a membership dedicated to an integrated social system.
- *Guidance.* Guidance is by accepted principles rather than by imposed plans, by visions rather than by targets.
- *Responsibility.* All members share responsibility. They feel trusted and supported by leaders who practice a craft style of management that is rooted in experience. Inspiration thus replaces so-called empowerment.
- *Judgment.* Performance is judged by experienced people, including recipients of the service, some of whom sit on representative oversight boards.

The motto of the normative model might be Select, Socialize, and Judge. But the key to all is dedication, which occurs in two directions: by and for the providers of the service. Providers are treated decently and therefore respond in kind. The agencies can still be isolated horizontally, but vertical control by the superstructure is normative rather than technocratic. The model allows for radically different microstructures: more missionary, egalitarian, and energized; less machinelike and less hierarchical.

There is no one best model. We currently function with all of them. Tax collection would be inconceivable without a healthy dose of the machine model, as would foreign policy without the network model. And no government can function effectively without a significant overlay of normative controls, just as no government today can ignore the need to shed what no longer belongs in the public sector. Government, in other words, is an enormously eclectic system, as varied as life itself (because it deals with almost every conceivable facet of life).

But some models are for the better and some for the worse. We might wish to favor the better. We all recognize the excessive attention given to the machine model. But we should be aware of its resurgence in the performance model. This is not to dismiss the performance model. The quasi-autonomous executive agency is fine for many of the apolitical, straightforward services of government—such as the passport office. Let's just keep it there and not pretend it is some kind of new "best way."

We need to be more appreciative of the network model, which is necessary for so many of the complex, unpredictable activities of today's governments—much of policy making, high-technology services, and research, for example. But reliance on this model can also be overdone. In France, both public and private sectors have long been dominated by a powerful and interconnected élite who move around with a freedom and influence that is proving increasingly stifling to the nation. The network system in France could use a lot more agency autonomy to check the power of that élite.

It is my personal belief that we sorely need a major shift of emphasis to the normative model. As the Japanese have made clear, there is no substitute for human dedication. And although much of Western business needs to take this message to heart, it has become especially important in government—with its vagaries, nuances, and difficult trade-offs among conflicting interests. An organization without human commitment is like a person without a soul: Skeleton, flesh, and blood may able to consume and to excrete, but there is no life force. Government desperately needs life force.

I believe this conclusion applies especially to client-oriented professional services, such as health care and education, which can never be better than the people who deliver them. We need to free professionals from both the direct controls of government bureaucracy and the narrow pressures of market competition. That is why nonownership and some cooperative ownership seem to work so well in those areas.

GOVERNING MANAGEMENT

If any of these ideas make sense, then we must prove them feasible by beginning to temper the influence that business values and currently popular Management thinking have on other sectors of society. In other words, government may need managing, but management could use a little governing, too. Consider the following propositions:

- *Business is not all good: government is not all bad.* Each has its place in a balanced society alongside cooperative and nonowned organizations. I do not wish to buy my cars from government any more than I wish to receive my policing services from General Motors. And I would like to see both private and public sectors passed over, for the most part, in the *direct* delivery of health care in favor of nonowned and cooperatively owned organizations.

  Societies get the public services they expect. If people believe that government is bumbling and bureaucratic, then that is what it will be. If, in contrast, they recognize public service for the noble calling it is, then they will end up with strong government. And no nation today can afford anything but strong government. Isn't it time that all the knee-jerking condemnation of government in the United States stopped? As a Canadian who lives part of the year in France, I can testify that these negative attitudes are proving contagious, and they are doing none of us any good.

- *Business can learn from government no less than government can learn from business; and both have a great deal to learn from cooperative and nonowned organizations.* People in the public sector cope with their own kinds of problems: conflicting objectives, multiple stakeholders, and intense political pressure, for example. Yet their problems are becoming increasingly common in the private sector. Many of the most intelligent, articulate, and effective managers I have met work for government. Unfortunately, they are not very aggressive about letting their ideas be known. Businesspeople profit greatly when they listen to them.

- *We need proud, not emasculated, government.* Attacks on government are attacks on the fabric of society. We have individual needs, to be sure, but a society that allows them to undermine collective needs will soon destroy itself. We all value private goods, but they are worthless without public goods—such as policing and economic policies—to protect them.

  Making numerous political appointments is now considered a natural part of the U.S. political process. (This was not always the case: Such appointments are proportionately three times more common today than they were in the 1930s.[6] Each new administration simply replaces the top layers of the departmental hierarchies. I believe it is time that this was recognized for exactly what much of it is: political corruption; not technically illegal but nonetheless corrupting of a dedicated and experienced public service. It, too, stems from the mistaken belief that those who have managed something can manage anything (although many political appointees have managed only a few lawyers or research assistants).

- *Above all, we need balance among the different sectors of society.* This applies to attitudes no less than to institutions. Private sector values are now pervading all of society. But government and other sectors should be care-

---

[6]Donald J. Savoie, *Thatcher, Reagan, Mulroney: In Search of a New Bureaucracy* (Pittsburgh: The University of Pittsburgh Press, 1994).

ful about what they take from business. Business has probably never been more influential than it is now. In the United States, through political action committees and lobbying activities, institutional interests (not only business interests) put enormous pressure on the political system, reducing the influence of individuals. The system is out of control. My argument here is not against business as business; rather, it is for balance in society. We need balance among our four sectors, and we need to balance our public concerns as individuals with the private demands of institutions.

Today the prevailing mood supports the privatization of public services. Some of that thinking is probably useful. But a good deal of it is also just plain silly. And if we are so prone to scrutinizing what doesn't belong in government, shouldn't we be equally diligent in considering what doesn't belong in business? Take newspapers, for example. Can any democratic society afford to have all newspapers in the private sector, especially when they are concentrated in a few hands that can exercise great political influence should they choose? Other models of ownership can be found, indeed in some of the most prestigious newspapers in the world—for example, nonownership of *The Guardian* in England and multiple cooperative ownership (journalists and readers, alongside some institutions) of *Le Monde* in France. Let us not forget that the object of democracy is a free people, not free institutions. In short, we would do well to scrutinize carefullly the balance in our societies now, before capitalism really does triumph.

7

ORGANIZATIONAL BEHAVIOR

Organizational behavior is a field of applied research that seeks answers to practical questions about human behavior in organizational settings. It tries to determine how people adapt to life in organizations—what "makes people in organizations tick" while they are at work.

Whereas the field of *organization theory* (Chapter 6) focuses on the behavior of organizations as entities, *organizational behavior* looks instead at the attitudes, motivations, feelings, relationships, and behaviors of people and groups in organizations. Obviously, these two fields overlap, particularly in organization theory's "human resource theories"[1] and "power theories."[2] Organization theory, though, is mostly interested in the "big picture" of organizations—their structures and formal processes as institutions. Organizational behavior's central interests are the formal and informal behavior of individuals and groups at work.

Organizational behavior thus seeks answers to important practical questions about how to manage and supervise people effectively at work, such as:

- How can we increase the motivation and productivity of our employees? We have tried almost everything, but nothing works for very long.
- Why are some work units more productive, creative, or receptive to changes than others are? What can be done to help the less productive work groups be more receptive to making changes?
- If we could give pay incentives to our hourly employees, would it help decrease employee turnover and increase motivation and productivity?
- Should we be creating more "empowered" work teams,[3] or should we be giving our supervisors more authority to run their units "like a business"? Which would have better results?
- Are we doing long-term damage to our organization when we require work teams to compete with each other? Doesn't competition make everyone more efficient?
- What can we do to lower resistance to changes that we simply must make in our contracted nonprofit service providers?

- How can we do a better job of developing hourly employees into future supervisors?
- Electronic technology (e-mail and the web) allows many of our employees to telecommute (work at home), but it feels as though we are losing touch with them. Are our telecommuters being isolated and perhaps overlooked for challenging assignments and promotions? Are our supervisors prepared to supervise employees who telecommute and thus do not come into the office regularly?
- Would more diversity help employee morale and productivity, or would it just drive wedges between groups of employees?

The behavior and attitudes of people and groups in government and businesses are changing almost as rapidly as government organizations are changing. (See Chapters 4 and 6.) The effects of population diversity, information technology, globalism, devolution, contracting-out, and the constancy of change in government organizations are altering the dynamics of individual and group behavior in organizations (organizational behavior) and thus also are affecting the long-standing nature of relationships between people and the organizations for whom they work. For example, as governments increasingly contract-out public human services, many people who actually deliver public services to people with mental retardation and mental illness, victims of rape, and people with Alzheimer's disease and autism—our most vulnerable populations—often are not government employees. Many are employed by contracted nonprofit agencies and for-profit businesses. (See Chapters 4 and 8.) When government administrators do not directly supervise the service deliverers, how can they be certain that front-line caregivers are being properly selected, motivated, trained, communicated with, and monitored—for the protection of the clients they serve on behalf of the government agency?[4]

Whether people are employees or contracted agents, they are resources of their organizations. Some organizations manage people better than others. Others seem to go out of their way to alienate the people who work for them. But in the long term, does any of this truly matter, or is it simply a question of public relations or political correctness? Are "happy employees" better employees? Is pay the only thing that really matters to employees?

Is all of the rest of this "stuff" about leadership styles, incentives, group dynamics, and morale just "fluff"? No it isn't. How people are managed—treated—is key to the effectiveness of government agencies and nonprofit organizations. When people in organizations are understood and worked with as *whole people* rather than treated simply as *"tools" of production,* they produce greater returns to their organization and the people they serve. This is more difficult to achieve, however, than it may sound.

Humans are complicated beings. Humans at work in government agencies are even more complicated. "Happy" employees are not always productive employees. Poorly paid employees can be highly committed and loyal—under some circumstances. More communication can cause people to "close down" and "tune out." Some people work best in relatively autonomous, empowered, closely-knit work teams; others are most productive working at home and telecommuting; but some others do their best work when they are supervised directly and closely—once again, under certain circumstances. Differences in ethnic and cultural backgrounds create variations in needs and motivations at work. People do bring their emotions, fears, family problems, and concerns to the job, and emotions *do* affect what and how people do their job and how they relate to others around them—including the people who supervise them and the people they supervise. Employees do not leave their emotions, feelings and personal lives in the parking lot when they come to work—it doesn't matter what their supervisors (or you or we) believe they should do!

For all of these reasons and more, organizational behavior is more complicated than simply "understanding people" or "being nice" to people. Peoples' behavior at work is affected by powerful forces, such as their economic relationship with the organization; their jobs, careers, and identities are tightly inter-woven; and there are constraints on their behavior. Established structural roles, hierarchical relations, and on-going utilitarian functions, all influence leadership, motivation, relationships, communication—behavior in organizations.

Although researchers and managers have been interested in the behavior of people in organizations for a very long time, it has only been since the mid–1950s that our basic assumptions about the relationship between individuals and organizations have evolved into their current form.[5] Max Weber and Frederick Winslow Taylor, for example (see Chapter 6), were interested in people and how they could make organizations more effective. This does not mean that Weber and Taylor were organizational behaviorists. *Organizational behavior* is more than the study of people at work. It is also a perspective—a point of view—about what makes organizations work. It is built upon a set of "bedrock" values and deeply-held assumptions about the nature and worth of humans, "the basic purposes for organizations, their fundamental right to existence, the nature of their links to the surrounding environment, and—most important for organizational behavior—the whole of their relationships with the people who work in them."[6]

Two famous pioneers in the field, Fritz Rothlisberger and William Dickson, defined organizational behavior as:

> The study of human behavior, attitudes, and performance within an organizational setting; drawing on theory, methods, and principles from such disciplines as psychology, sociology, and cultural anthropology to learn about individual perceptions, values, learning capacities, and actions while working in groups and with the total organization; analyzing the external environment's effect on the organization and its human resources, missions, objectives, and strategies[7]

This remains an excellent definition for today—with the reminder to also add: "in government organizations that are struggling to cope with an environment of unparalleled change in globalism, diversity, information technology, devolution, empowerment, and diffusion."

READINGS REPRINTED IN THIS CHAPTER

The readings that are reprinted in this chapter emphasize four issues that are central in organizational behavior:

- Social pressures cause individual group members to conform;
- Effective work teams do not just happen, they must be built and nurtured;
- Making major changes in a government agency requires broad scope strategies that are more similar to military tactics and strategies than to organization theory; and
- If an organization is to become and remain effective, its members must engage in "generative learning," learning that enhances our capacity to create.

Most projects and tasks that are performed in government agencies have become too complex for individuals to work alone. Public administrators regularly "team up" with people who work in the same office, in other divisions or departments, from different levels of government, and the private sector. Work groups have become staple elements of modern public administration at the local, state, and national levels. A public administrator today must have well-honed technical or professional skills *and* highly developed group skills.

John Paterson's paper, **"Bureaucratic Reform by Cultural Revolution,"**[8] is a witty but deadly serious discussion about the extraordinarily difficult process of making "deep changes" in government agencies. Paterson identifies and discusses numerous structural and extra-structural barriers to change in government, including zealous protection of power, deeply entrenched stakeholders, territoriality, mistrust, "common interest in the maintenance of the [existing] system," deeply held values that are not connected with performance, promotion by seniority, and institutionalized systems of rewards. He argues, though, that these barriers do not make change impossible, they simply explain why there has been so little change in government agencies over the years. Paterson is optimistic, but realistic. Change in government agencies is possible, but a "cultural revolution approach" is necessary—an approach that allows changes to be made but without also hurting the agency's ability to provide services. "In effect it calls for a discontinuity in the political system, combined with continuity of the processes of production." The paper includes a "how-to manual" that draws on the military tactics and strategies of Sun Tzu, Miyamoto Musashi, Carl von Clausewitz, and Mao Tse-Tung. Paterson recommends specific steps, grouped into three levels of change activities: preparing the bases (for the change "wars"), strategy, and tactics. If all goes well, peace eventually may accompany change. "Peace becomes possible when you have captured all the territory, re-educated all the prisoners who are willing to become loyal citizens, and put to the sword those who remain unreconstructed. . . . Conflict is present in any social system, and will certainly exist, but it will be conflict about means rather than ends. . . . These are the preconditions for the next finite leap, from an organization which suffices, to one which is demonstrably excellent."

"Transforming Teamwork: Work Relationships in a Fast-Changing World," by **Marvin Weisbord,**[9] focuses on the need for organizations to build and support their working teams. "We call every work group a team even if they rarely see each other. 'Team' rivals 'quality' as a business cliché." But, effective teams do not just happen, they take work. Weisbord lists four conditions for successful team building:

1. Interdependence. The team is working on important problems in which each person has a stake. In other words, teamwork is central to future success, not an expression of ideology or some misplaced 'ought-to.'
2. Leadership. The boss wants so strongly to improve group performance the he or she will take risks.
3. Joint decision. All members agree to participate.
4. Equal influence. Each person has a chance to influence the agenda.

Weisbord identifies questions that "each person in a work group continually struggles with" that are never answered "and must be resolved over and over again," several approaches to team building, and the future of team building.

NOTES

1. See Chapter 3, "Human Resource Theory, or the Organizational Behavior Perspective," in Jay M. Shafritz, and J. Steven Ott. (Eds.). (2001). *Classics of Organization Theory* (5th ed.). Fort Worth, Texas: Harcourt Brace
2. See Chapter 6, "Power and Politics Organization Theory," in Jay M. Shafritz, and J. Steven Ott. (Eds.). (2001). *Classics of Organization Theory* (5th ed.). Fort Worth, Texas: Harcourt Brace
3. See for example, Jack D. Orsburn, Linda Moran, Ed Musselwhite, and John H. Zenger. (1990). *Self-Directed Work Teams: The New American Challenge.* Homewood, IL: Richard D. Irwin.
4. Ott, J. Steven, and Lisa A. Dicke. Summer 2000. "Important but Largely Unanswered Questions about Accountability in Contracted Public Human Services." *International Journal of Organization Theory & Behavior 3*(3 & 4), 283–317; also, Lisa A. Dicke, and J. Steven Ott. (June 1999). "Public Agency Accountability in Human Services Contracting." *Public Productivity & Management Review, 22*(4), 502–516.
5. Ott, J. Steven. (Ed.) (1996). "Introduction," in J. S. Ott (Ed.), *Classic Readings in Organizational Behavior* (2d ed.) (pp. 1–24). Fort Worth, Texas: Harcourt Brace.
6. Ott, J. Steven. (Ed.) (1996). *Classic Readings in Organizational Behavior* (2d ed.). Fort Worth, Texas: Harcourt Brace, p. 2.
7. Rothlisberger, Fritz J., and William J. Dickson. (1939). *Management and the Worker.* Cambridge: Mass.: Harvard University Press.
8. Paterson, John. (June 6, 1983). "Bureaucratic Reform by Cultural Revolution." Paper presented at a seminar of the Urban Research Unit, Research School of Social Sciences, The Australian National University. Note that Paterson wrote a "postscript" to the article for this book. It immediately follows the reprinted article.
9. Weisbord, Marvin R. (1991). "Transforming Teamwork: Work Relationships in a Fast-Changing World, Chapter 15 in M. R. Weisbord, *Productive Workplaces: Organizing and Managing for Dignity, Meaning, and Community* (pp.296–310). San Francisco: Jossey-Bass.

19

John Paterson

BUREAUCRATIC REFORM BY CULTURAL REVOLUTION[1]

INTRODUCTION

I have been engaged in an attempt to reshape a social system composed of about 1600 people, producing non-interruptible basic services to a clientele of about 400,000 people. The NSW Government is strongly committed to reform of bureaucracy, and general lines of government policy in this field have been derived.

Outside the bureaucratic arena, there is a large body of doctrine on organisation and management which should provide "the answer" on means of approach. Experience in action leads to the conclusion that there is a serious gap in the received doctrine. Indeed military doctrine and the theory of revolutionary war falls more naturally to hand than much of the teaching of the business schools. Reasons for this are explored, followed by an outline of an alternative and potentially more successful method.

DOCTRINE ON ORGANISATION AND ORGANISATIONAL CHANGE

There have always been a few individuals of genius with a clear, consistent, and operational understanding of organisation. These have included the really great statesmen, merchants, soldiers and clerics who have been documented, or less often, have documented themselves, from Alexander the Great onwards.

While the history of thought in this field often takes Taylorism (Taylor, 1911) as the point of departure, the Hawthorne Experiments (Mayo 1933, 1946) makes a more convincing operational claim on the "human" side.

In recent years the focus of attention has been on organisational culture, and a related fascination with the "Japanese" approach to organisation, where organisational norms and values play the vital role. Among a mass of recent discussion of varying quality, the take-home message seems to be that travel broadens the mind. Companies with "Japanese-like" attributes have been identified among some of the largest and most successful American corporations (Pascale and Athos 1981; Ouchi, 1981). Great tolerance of change coexists with, or rather, stems from, rock solid stability of the culture of the corporation.

The major deficiency of all these models is that they "work" best in already good organisations. When any improvement is made to an already good organisation (good being measured almost any way you like), the exponents of *almost* any school, and the

---

[1]Paper read at a seminar of the Urban Research Unit, Research School of Social Sciences, The Australian National University on 6 June 1983.

254   Organizational Behavior

consultants offering propriety packaged versions thereof, can legitimately claim the improvement as their own.

This loose proposition can be stated in a slightly more seemly manner by reference to the concept of organisational equilibrium (Simon, 1947). There may be a multitude of equilibrium points for any organisation, but only one or a few will be efficient. Non-efficient equilibria represent a form of organisational poverty trap. Piecemeal reform, under the rubric of any of the contending schools, and no matter how skillfully pursued, routinely fails. The pathological realities of organisational life subject the reform to reality testing as soon as the initiator leaves the scene.

It is easy to be more concrete. A reformed top management soon resorts to "management prerogatives" when faced with industrial opposition to dissemination of reform. A reformed work group soon becomes embittered and disillusioned when territoriality is enforced elsewhere, or when senior management resorts inappropriately to authority. Sensitivity-trained individuals soon stop "giving" when openness is abused, information withheld, or divisive tactics re-establish a climate of mistrust. Those whose performance has improved soon fall back on the darg when rewards go to non-contributors. And even when a fragile organisational fabric is woven around a superior equilibrium point, an economic downturn, loss of markets, or loss of the opportunities inherent in growth and profitability, test the robustness of the new structure, usually beyond its limit. "We've gone through all this together, and now I'm out of a job".

A common feature of received doctrine is the assumption that reform will be evolutionary in nature. "Someone" within the existing structure decides on change. Others are either encouraged or instructed to take part. All are supposed to gain, basically by improvements in returns and/or in the work environment, or both. Unfortunately there is a fatal flaw. From a structural angle some *must* lose unless the organisation is already in an efficient equilibrium, ie, is already an excellent organisation. The losses can take many forms. These include loss of authority by those who can only manage by fiat, disclosure of incompetence by those who know the system rather than knowing their jobs, devaluation of skills which were required in a sick organisation but are not required in a healthy one, loss of security of expectations, lost opportunities for petty graft, reduced opportunities for the quiet life, and lost empires. Sick organisations structure themselves to generate "positional goods" in the process of substituting means for ends. Restoration of health eliminates or redistributes positional goods into alignment with functional ends. So there are many stakeholders whose losses will exceed their gains, even if jobs, wages and salaries are guaranteed.

When organisational change represents only a small displacement from the prior equilibrium, all these stakeholders remain in place, with power largely unchecked. The forces for maintenance of the existing social system are strong. The time-honoured defensive tactic of passive resistance, delay, petty sabotage, and systematic disinformation, are costless and virtually riskless. Established networks remain fully efficient while new networks are ephemeral. The strategic advantage to the defence under all the common approaches to reformist attack is overwhelming. To create countervailing power which can even remotely match the power of "the system" is risky and difficult, whereas the defence is simple and riskless.

In spite of the strategic balance, many organisations do gradually improve. Consistent effort over a long period, forced rationalisation in times of adversity, gradual upgrading of personnel through effective recruitment and promotion, fortunate combinations of personalities, business growth which permits stakeholders to be bought off, and "environmental" influences, such as technological change, management education, professional values, all work toward slow improvement. People do die, retire, or leave, and roadblocks then disappear. It can be a long and costly process, but change by osmosis, by absorption of environmental influences, appears to be overwhelmingly the predominant source of organisational reform. Again all schools of thought can claim vindication in the post hoc examination of cases selected from the more successful organisations.

There is a gradual advance in "organisational technology" as new approaches diffuse, through professional bodies, the recent products of the education system, and the influence, direct and indirect, of developments abroad. In a competitive environment the rate of advance of individual organisations tends to cluster around the rate of technological progress. At the ends of the distribution a few do much better, and grow, and a few do worse, and die.

In a non-competitive environment there are few evident casualties, but a growing brigade of walking dead, a skewed distribution of advance, rather than a normal distribution around an environmentally determined mean. The advantage to the defence, powerful in any organisational setting, is further buttressed by statutory powers, and by the multi-objective function of government, which trades off competitive efficiency against a multitude of other considerations to which the private corporation needs pay no heed.

EXTRA-SKELETAL PROPS TO STABILITY

In any social structure, form is maintained by basic or "skeletal" elements; the equilibrium balance of contribution and reward gives each part a stake in the whole. Primary group loyalties and small group behaviours translate organisational behaviour into something different than the sum of the individual parts. Status and prestige derive from organisational roles per se. Power emerges as a survival requirement even if it is not externally mandated. Hierarchical power derives from ownership (directly or indirectly) in a private corporation, or from statute in a public one. Habit, as well as rules, establishes continuity of practice. Information is controlled to reinforce power as well as to meet survival needs. Initiation to sacred mysteries provides continuity of the organisational culture, and protects the organisationally sacred against the external profane.

These are common skeletal features of any social system. In a stable and unrationalised system they are buttressed by what might be called "extra-skeletal" or secondary sources of defence. Status is minutely differentiated, and detached from that which derives naturally from function. "The position", rather than "the job" is given exaggerated significance. Apart from minute differentiation in pay scales, and in the trappings of office, negative status symbols are imposed to bring trivial positive symbols into relief. Those at the bottom of the pecking order are made to feel it. Usually they are wages employees and women.

Empire building is a form of extra-skeletal protection; it gives the over-staffed manager and the redundant subordinates a common interest in maintenance of the system. With redundant numbers comes a scarcity of real work, boredom, displacement activities, individual performance anxiety and elaboration of rituals becomes a substitute for work as such. Skills prized by the organisation come to be those skills associated with ritual, rather than with direct production. Being unique to the particular organisation, performance anxiety is reinforced by a lock-in effect; key skills are non-transferable to other organisations.

In this setting, performance measurement of any kind becomes an anathema. The organisational culture is based on values largely unconnected with performance, and is threatened by anything which can permit performance measurement or comparison.

Similarly, it is threatened by task-oriented individuals; many of these leave. Those who for some reason stay are quarantined and tacitly certified insane. They commonly begin to exhibit signs of neurosis, which is comforting for members of the majority culture, or they become passive, absolutely or conditionally. This is not far fetched; many instances can be found. This legion of the damned does, however, represent a potential fifth column, and the walls of this asylum are zealously guarded.

Promotion by seniority ensures that responsible positions are filled by long service employees. The destabilising influence, and pre-emption of positional goods, caused by outside appointments is strenuously opposed by unions and management. Long service employees can be relied upon to have fully assimilated organisational values. Those reaching the highest positions by seniority know that they owe their good fortune to demographic factors rather than personal attributes or performance. They know that those who are stranded at lower levels suffered from the same causes. The prizes, in the form of position, are recognised and rigid hierarchical forms are observed, but since the incumbents succeeded by the luck of the draw, they rarely care to change the rules in any way, or to ask more from their subordinates than the system asked of them.

Positions are occupied passively; entitlements are grasped with both hands, but the prerogatives of management are tacitly accepted, by the managers and the managed, to be minimal. Management skills are minimal as they have never been favoured in training or promotion. Senior managers do what they did as junior officers. External stimuli for change typically draw the reaction "The union would not accept it", which really means "I don't like it". The union becomes a extra-skeletal prop to the system.

Key practices are given the force of law by incorporation in industrial awards and registered agreements. Industrial relations personnel are often drawn untrained from the ranks. They are often outclassed by union representatives, and if not, are limited by their brief. The unions win even when their grounds are weak. Industrial relations, while being superficially prone to conflict, is more often symbiotic in nature and the arbitration system becomes further extra-skeletal protection.

Finally, in the case of government bodies providing services to the public, the threshold of pain to the government is a strategic instrument for system maintenance. Most ministers are suspicious of the bureaucracies over which they exert a control but, in the majority of cases, that control is nominal. Unions count on government capitulation if vital services are interrupted.

Management knows that a minister can become vulnerable if unsatisfactory aspects of performance come to light. All but the most alert ministers are affectively co-opted into the "tell 'em nothing" strategy which comes easily to the official. Once a minister has agreed to the first cover-up, the minister becomes a hostage to the organisation, and a potentially destabilising influence is neutralised. The minister is dragged into service as a further prop.

CHANGE BY CULTURAL REVOLUTION

The analysis so far does not lead to the conclusion that nothing can be done. It does help explain why so little has happened over the years, even in the face of ministerial aspirations and public discontent. Public inquiries, changes of chief executive, "good government" movements and the rest not withstanding, the successes have been few, and the stability of most government bodies has been phenomenal.

If the defences available to a social system are sufficient to resist piecemeal reform, the obvious solution is to destabilise that system to the extent that those defences become ineffective. That part is easy. The trick is to do it without seriously affecting the continuing production of services. That requires a combination of art and science. Taking a political analogy, the task is no different from that of the revolutionary who seeks to transform the structure of power in the summer while ensuring that the population does not starve in the following winter. In effect it calls for a discontinuity in the political system, combined with continuity of the processes of production. A number of measures are obvious. The strategy outlines here is premised on having the authority of the chief executive available, though not necessarily on *being* the chief executive officer.

The measures required can be arbitrarily divided into resources requirements or "bases", strategy, and tactics. A system fully equipped with the normal "skeletal" requirements for stability, and with a comprehensive armoury of "extraskeletal" defences can only be radically reconstructed if these are all attacked. The system is a simultaneous one and must in principle be attacked by a comprehensive onslaught on all the major defences. In practice resources for the attack will be minimal at the outset, so that choice between measures will be required. The notes which follow are organised in hierarchical, and to some extent serial form. This is more reflective of the limitations of human cognition than of the nature of the task, or the experience of participating in it. No apologies are made for the imperative mood that follows. It is of course presented in a light-hearted vein, with apologies to Sun Tzu (490 BC), Musashi (1644), Clausewitz (1832) and Mao (1936).

(i) Preparing the Bases

- Win the support of you minister; it will need to be earned. No minister will tie his fortunes to a ratbag. Ministerial confidence depends on performance, some shared values, effective communications, the attitudes of other ministers and caucus, all of whom distrust bureaucracy. They see the world through different, and usually clearer eyes than most bureaucrats, at least in the broad perspective. It is vital to think like government, whilst possessing the full armoury of bureaucratic skills. Radical change without political support is impossible.

- Speak directly and often to employees as a whole. In an organisation of any size it is impossible to know everyone personally, but it is possible, in a sense, to be known. Walk about a lot, use large meetings, social occasions, and internal news channels. All of these bypass the established channels of "the system" which will distort your messages and misrepresent your intentions. Be open to anyone who wants to talk to you. Do no paper work during business hours—just talk, see and be seen. There is plenty of time before 8.00am and after 5.00pm to push paper. During business hours build your cadres and school them in revolution. By doing so you will learn of an organisational weakness every day. Find a new tactical opportunity and win a new recruit to the revolutionary cause every day.

- Allow the counter-revolutionaries no hostages. You must be personally untouchable. Be self-denying with perks of office, scrupulous with petty cash, and avoid any sexual contact which cannot stand the light of day. Admit all errors immediately; do not pretend to knowledge you do not have and never procrastinate. Document everything or you will offer phantom hostages which can materialise as if real.

- Build your prestige outside the organisation. Bureaucratic systems shun the light of day, fearing the hostile gaze of the public and the politician. Turn this to your advantage by exposing everything. Understand the media and use it to build external support. This places the most robust bureaucratic system on the defensive, delivers prizes to your political masters and confirms their support. It will bring you some allies in the wider bureaucracy, who will become your spies. It will weaken and deflect the blows of your enemies who come to fear the loss of their own anonymity if they move against you, as they will.

- Symbolic significance attaches to your every act, at every moment of each day. Every act will be minutely scrutinised by those around you, and every act must carry a symbolic message. You must be the symbolic model of all that you want the organisation to become. The symbolic message must be strong, clear and simple to minimise scope for distortion in interpretation and retelling. You are on a stage, and every gesture must be exaggerated so it can be clearly seen from the back stalls.

- It goes without saying that you must be well read and well practised in the basic organisational and interpersonal skills, that you must revel in danger, and perform best under stress. You must be physically robust. Without these attributes you will fail, and should not have been appointed in the first place.

(ii) STRATEGY

- Organisational performance must never get worse in the process of being made better. Find the elements of the existing system which can be attacked with little cost. Isolate them as far as possible by exploiting existing divisions, and be ruthless in your onslaught. As one prop falls another becomes the point of maximum stress. Attack that in turn. Do not be provoked into precipitate action, and never let a chance go by. There will be some lucky breaks; be opportunistic.

- At the outset the system of production will be obscure to you. Tread warily as you analyse it. At the start you will rely on observation, theory and experience. As time passes you will learn the technology, identify strategic problems and opportunities, find individual strengths and weaknesses, and discover the course for long-term productivity improvement. In a traditional organisation little will be measurable at the outset. Establish benchmarks and formal systems of performance measurement. Transform accounting into management information and transform engineering data into performance measurement. Make maximum possible use of internal expertise, but be quick to bring in external expertise when interval resources are lacking. When you are confident of your direction write a corporate plan and make it the organisational bible.

- Senior management must be reformed first. Many incumbents will be useless, but all should be tested. The testing process can speed the departure of those who must go, and can build the confidence of those who measure up. Deal harshly with passive resistance, and brutally with sabotage. You will encounter both; either if left unchecked will destroy you. Be tender with those who try, even if they are incompetent. Treasure each one who is competent and loyal. When your senior management has been purged and rebuilt, talk every day to every one, but give each one great autonomy of action and forgive every admitted mistake. Encourage cooperation between them and strongly discourage competition. Share information fully, and never apply "divide and conquer" tactics to your loyal cadres; reserve such tactics for the key points of resistance.

- If you have ten immediate subordinates who are capable and loyal, your effectiveness is immediately multiplied tenfold. If each develops ten such subordinates within his or division, your effectiveness is multiplied 100 fold. With one or two further replications of this exponential process, you will have completely transformed the largest organisation. Even one weak link in the top ten will leave part of the old system untouched. This can form a rallying point for the forces of reaction, permitting their symbolic presence to infect and disrupt the exponential process right across the organisation. Even the outpost of reaction can threaten the revolution.

These are the key elements of strategy; unremitting attack on weak points of the old system, development of the system of production, and exponential multiplication of your own visions through the growth of loyal cadres. The strategic base must be in your mind at all times, or inconsistent actions and ambiguous messages will abound. The revolutionary process will be retarded and may fail altogether. Your day to day ac-

tivities, however, will be dominated by tactical considerations, which make an instinc-
tive and comprehensive grasp of strategy the more vital.

(iii) TACTICS

- *Duration:* The time required to complete the transformation depends primarily
  on the size of the organisation. Allow one year for each round in the exponential
  process. Thus 10–50 people one year, 50 to 500 two years, 500–5000 three years,
  and 5,000 to 50,000 four years. Each recruit should also average one conversion
  per month or about ten per year. Less than this will give respite to the old system,
  while more will be difficult to achieve thoroughly, until disorder breaks out in
  the ranks of the old system.
- *Timing:* While duration is determined by large numbers and probabilities, timing
  depends on discrete events and is intrinsically unpredictable. For example, if one
  senior manager is recruited on the first day, that manager may complete the second round of exponentiation in the first year, while another may not be replaced
  for a month, or a year so the second round starts much later. It is dangerous to allow any element to lag too far behind the theoretical schedule, but timing will always be somewhat opportunistic. The key is to keep your eye on duration and
  prevent any element falling too far behind.
- *Pace:* Pace has two tactical aspects, and is the key tactical variable. Firstly, pace is
  the key distinction between a revolutionary transformation, which in principle
  can succeed, and piecemeal reform, which will usually fail to achieve more than
  the trend rate of technological change. Average pace, or duration must be such as
  to defeat the adaptive processes of the old system. Secondly and more importantly, control of pace permits choice of the ground, and dictation of the terms
  of battle. In the early stages, in particular, when your own resources are slim, excessive destabilisation will cause a thousand bushfires to break out, or to turn
  them back on the enemy. Instead you moderate the pace on most fronts and
  press forward with maximum speed on one or a few, depending on your capabilities. As your resources expand, overall pace can be increased, and mainforce en-
  gagements become possible first on one, then on more fronts. You must at all
  costs avoid overloading yourself, while purposely overloading the selected point
  of attack. If a reactionary element appears to be failing under pressure, accelerate
  the pace and complete the destruction.
- *Scouting:* Scouting for recruits never ceases. A variety of means should be employed. Talk to as many people as you can. Watch how people relate to others;
  they give themselves away in many cases, and show unsuspected strengths in others. A highly motivated work group probably indicates native managerial talent in
  the supervisor. Discover those whose judgment is sound and rely on them.
  Search particularly for the legion of the damned; they are always there to be
  found, but may need careful reconstruction. Increase the pace in a work area and
  see who responds well. Cross-check the opinions of as many people as possible on
  any potential recruit. In each case you learn something about the potential recruit and something about the respondent.

- *Selection:* Few will rush to join; most will want to judge you, and will sit on the fence, reserving judgment until the scales tilt your way. Those that join early are particularly to be valued, though they will include some misfits. Each victory over the system, no matter how small, will change the inclination of some fence sitters. Any defeat will frighten the worriers, and more seriously, reduce confidence among your followers. Most defeats are to be avoided for this reason; they reduce the field for selection. Where it is necessary to sacrifice a pawn to capture a queen, make sure that your cadres understand your tactics. During a period of revolutionary change, waves of emotion sweep through the organisation daily. The fields for selection will quickly dry up even after minor reverses, and major reverse can produce desertions. Provided things go well, the time will come when selection must be almost entirely delegated. Formal selection procedures of a bureaucratic type must then be employed, so your cadres must be trained in selection. They must be procedurally beyond reproach, or reverses will occur. The forces of reaction must have no effective role in appointments and promotions.
- *Education and Training:* Large deficits of skills exist in all traditional bureaucracies, since system maintenance is threatened by acknowledgement of competence. Ultimately between five and ten per cent of working hours should be directed to education, training, and team-building activities. At the outset, however, the organisation will not be able to absorb anything like this amount of effort. Education and training at the outset is a tactical instrument, but as reconstruction becomes ubiquitous, so will education and training become continuous and universal. Developmental effort is largely counter-productive if administered in a traditional framework, if false expectations are aroused or if the old system is sufficiently strong to nullify the expression of newly acquired skills.
- *Industrial Relations* is both the most and the least important aspect of tactics. It is *most* important in that many aspects of malaise find their expression in industrial conflict, and while this malaise continues, so will conflict. That conflict, if poorly managed, can stop the process of reconstruction and reinstate the old system, with which unions generally have held a symbiotic relationship. It is *least* important in that if sound personnel practice, effective management, and democratic participation in the pursuit of shared goals emerge through the revolutionary process, the role of unions is enhanced but the traditional battle lines are completely redrawn. The correct tactical stance is to act *as if* the future position already exists. However, when conflict breaks out along traditional lines, it should be dealt with by maximum pace, sufficient concentration of forces, and complete technical competence. It should always be remembered that the union's members are one's own colleagues, and one's own view of the position should be able to be worked out by negotiation, conditioned by the revolutionary setting. Accidents of personality can either advance or retard the process. Any loss of pace through industrial action automatically benefits the old system.
- *Client Relations* is ultimately the most important final objective of any organisation. Make the client your ally: you have common objectives. The traditional bureaucracy

generally attaches little significance to external objectives, being totally self-absorbed. At the outset client relations are usually bad. Performance standards are usually low in a service providing organisation. External relations are often good but statutory objectives are often displaced in a regulatory organisation. The problems are different here, and will be disregarded in the present discussion. Level of service can only be increased as productivity is increased. Demands of clients will generally exceed output due to inefficient resource allocation policies. In the face of an exasperated public, the organisation will usually exhibit a hostile and defensive face to the outside world. Pricing and investment policy should be reformed immediately. Public complaints are a vital information source in an environment where information is systematically obliterated. Such complaints will often be the trigger for particular tactical responses. Properly mobilised, external pressures can be turned in on centres of resistance. Ensure that you are recognised as the friend of the public, and not as the defender of the system. This will take time, and some reverses can be expected and tolerated.

WAR AND PEACE

It may have become apparent that revolutionary transformation of bureaucracy calls for an outlook and mode of operations more akin to revolutionary war than to group therapy. This is the key point of departure from the OD orthodoxy. Unbridled aggression is not, in itself, more than a fraction of the regimen either of conventional military doctrine, or of the technique of revolutionary or "peoples" war. Clausewitz (1832) defined war as a continuation of politics by other means, one end of a continuum, not a discrete phenomenon. In peacetime diplomacy, the possibility, the likely terms and probable outcome of war conditions every peaceful act. Conversely the objectives of national policy must condition every military act.

The OD orthodoxy places the reformer in the position of a new and unarmed settler in territory occupied by armed irregular units. If the settlement is to survive at all, it will be necessary to negotiate terms, but the terms will be distinctly unfavourable if not backed by the possibility of equivalent force. This is the real position, but the orthodoxy suggests that the settlement can be secured and expanded by showing an organisation chart to randomly selected individuals from the bands of the local warlords.

The objective is to capture territory, though it is the territory of the mind. The objective and the play resemble the Japanese game of Go, not chess. There is no single focus of play. Rather, battle is joined at many points on the board. At any move the point of attack can change. Major objectives can be approached quite indirectly. The initiative can be lost at any move, and pace is the vital factor in maintaining the initiative.

The Go methaphor takes us only so far; each local fight is far more complex than the simple placement of a stone on the board. However, as in Go, and as in the simple Clauswitzian metaphor, an objective may be gained by threat, or by latent potential for conflict, rather than by actual combat. This is the cheaper way, but will not be possible without the latent threat.

Similarly, when diplomatic means fail and war breaks out, the immediate and ultimate costs should be the minimum required to achieve a decision. There will be casualties, but production of enemy casualties has never been the objective of sound military operations. Clausewitz clearly recognised that, even in narrow military terms, the decisive result lies in the taking of prisoners after there is a decision, rather than in the number of casualties on the field of battle itself. Indeed, in the centuries preceding the appearance of Napoleonic war, clash of arms was often entirely absent; the result was determined by manoeuvre and the victory acknowledged (Fuller 1970). When battle is joined, a very small difference in losses, or even a *smaller* proportion of losses, often precedes the demoralisation of the ultimate loser. A demoralised army in flight is easily rounded up, and materiel captured. The military resources of the opponent are then eliminated from contention at little or no cost. The similarity of the process to the formal propositions of "catastrophe theory" should be noted.

In organisational revolution there are only two objectives. On the part of "the system", the object of winning is to nullify your initiatives, to render you impotent, and to drive you from the organisation. On your part, the objective is to avoid those results, to take prisoners, and to capture territory. Note the essential assymetry of objectives. They strongly condition the range of tactics available and the choice from that range.

Peace becomes possible when you have captured all the territory, re-educated all the prisoners who are willing to become loyal citizens, and put to the sword those who remain unreconstructed. It is vital to know when you are at peace, since the methods of war immediately become counterproductive. Martial law must be lifted and democratic civil government established. Only at this stage does received doctrine on organisational development become applicable.

At this stage the battle is won but all that has been achieved is some small productivity gains, and a total realignment of the culture of the organisation. The latter is the vital result. All positions of authority are occupied by people with a commitment to the external objectives of the organisation as a whole. Piecemeal reforms will then be reinforced rather than negated. Resources invested in education and training will be confirmed and enhanced in operation, so the warranted level of investment increases dramatically. Management will be active by selection, reinforced by the legitimacy bestowed in the new culture. Conflict is present in any social system, and will certainly exist, but it will be conflict about means rather than ends. These are the preconditions for the next finite leap, from an organisation which suffices, to one which is demonstrably excellent. These are not utopian fantasies, since excellent organisations do exist, at least fleetingly.

REFERENCES

Carl von Clausewitz (1832), *On War*, Pelican, 1968.
Peter F Drucker (1946), *The Concepts of the Corporation*, Mentor, 1964.
J F C Fuller (1970), *The Decisive Battles of the Western World 480 BC–1747 AD*, Grenada, 1981.

Mao Tse-Tung (1936), *Problems of Strategy in China's Revolutionary War*, Peking, Foreign Language Press, 1968.

E Mayo (1933), *The Human Problems of an Industrial Civilisation*, Macmillan, 1933.

E Mayo (1946), *The Social Problems of an Industrial Civilisation*, Harvard, 1946.

Miyamoto Musashi (1645), *The Book of Five Rings*, Bantam, 1982.

William G Ouchi (1981), *Theory Z*, Addison-Wesley, 1981.

R T Pascale and A G Athos (1981), *The Art of Japanese Management*, Allen Lane, 1981.

H A Simon (1947), *Administrative Behaviour*, 2nd ed, The Free Press, 1965.

Sun Tzu (490 BC), *The Art of War*, ed Clavell, Hodder & Stoughton, 1981.

F W Taylor (1911), *Principles of Scientific Management*, Harper & Rowe, 1911.

E C Trist & K W Bamforth (1951), "Some Social and Psychological Consequences of the Long-wall Method of Coal Getting", *Human Relations*.

Max Weber (various), *Essays in Sociology from Max Weber*, trans by H H Gerth and C Wright Mills, RKP, 1947.

Peter Wilenski (1977), *Directions for Change*, Interim Report of the Review of NSW Government Administration (Commissioner: Peter Wilenski), Sydney, 1977.

Peter Wilenski (1982), *Unfinished Agenda*, Further Report of the Review of New South Wales Government Administration (Commissioner: Peter Wilenski,) Sydney, 1982.

POSTSCRIPT TO

John Paterson

"BUREAUCRATIC REFORM BY CULTURAL REVOLUTION, THEN AND NOW—CHANGE IN CONTEXT"

When Bill Russell called to ask about republishing "Bureaucratic Reform by Cultural Revolution," I objected, *"Surely it is out of time?"* Australia was a very different place in their early 'eighties.' Most Australian organizations were managed from top to bottom relative to our contemporary norms. Newcastle [where the Hunter District Water Board, which inspired this article, was located] was recognized as among the worst 'industrial' sites in eastern Australia. The Hunter District Water Board was renowned as the dog of the 'Water Industry.'

When I started at the Hunter District Water Board in March 1982, I was a committed adherent of the Organizational Development (OD) school. Within weeks it had been brought home to me, by word and deed, that any proposal *even to discuss* changes to established ways would be massively resisted. Were I to persist I would share the fate of my predecessor, and be destroyed.

I was too young to die. The tool kit of the OD school had no answer to the situation, and I had been sent to Newcastle by the Government to *"Fix the bloody place up."* "Bureaucratic Reform by Cultural Revolution" makes a harsh and bloodthirsty statement against most reasonable standards in organizational life, but it was a quick and effective response to a kill or be killed situation. In 1989 the Hunter District Water Board was rated by the Economic Planning Advisory Council as the best water utility in Australia.

20

Marvin R. Weisbord

TRANSFORMING TEAMWORK: WORK RELATIONSHIPS IN A FAST-CHANGING WORLD

Teamwork has been a contradiction in American society clear back to Alexis de Tocqueville, that astute French observer who coined the phrase "habits of the heart" to describe our folkways. "Each man is forever thrown back on himself alone," wrote de Tocqueville in the 1830s, "and there is danger that he may be shut up in the solitude of his own heart." He called this tendency—lest you wonder where we got that word—"individualism" (de Tocqueville, in Bellah and others, 1985. p. 37). It is our great strength, the bedrock of the entrepreneurial spirit and innovation. Overused, it becomes our strongest weakness.

Productive workplaces need both individual effort and teamwork. And teams get much lip service. We call every work group a team even if they rarely see each other. "Team" rivals "quality" as a business cliché. "I have to see my team about that," says a company president. "Individually, of course," she adds. "I don't want to open a can of worms."

Sometimes people develop teamwork spontaneously, like schoolyard kids in a basketball game. That's what my self-managing teams did in the 1960s. Serving customers, rather than a boss, drove them to cooperate. Sometimes teams need help. In third-wave managing I think this help must include two perspectives: (1), unlearning deeply ingrained, self-limiting assumptions about individualism, authority, and responsibility that defeat cooperation and, paradoxically, individual success; (2), looking outward toward the wider social and business networks that shape their mutual effort. People need both perspectives—relationships *and* environment—to make sense of the workplace. Integrating both to move from competition and individualism toward cooperation and wholeness is what I mean by transforming teamwork. There is no more important task for third-wave managers.

TEAMS AND TEAM BUILDING

Teamwork can be transformed using a particular learning structure a few times a year. It derives from the most widely used and predictably helpful tool in the OD kit: team building. There is no standard procedure. Team building evolved in the early 1960s as a solution to the transfer-of-training dilemma—how to use workshop learning in real life.

Developing self-awareness remains an essential but not sufficient activity for changing companies. . . . To transform team building requires inquiry into the team's open system—personal, companywide, global, past, present, and future. It takes in every agenda.

Not everyone defines it that way. Team building has come to mean everything from interpersonal encounter among co-workers (a format I do not recommend), to joint work on tasks of mutual importance for the future (a format I strongly support). The earliest modes used an exchange of interpersonal feedback as the key building block. In my practice now I am more committed to helping each team member take a public stand on critical issues the team faces, the ones most likely to shape the future. The most powerful team building occurs in the mutual revisiting of an organization's future, its central tasks, the design of its jobs, policies, and systems—and how people move toward or away from these tasks.

Many Methods. Modern methods are available from many sources—everything from self-guided workbooks and cassette tapes to facilitators and consultants. Team building remains durable, flexible, and broadly useful in a wide range of situations: starting new teams and task forces, reorganizing, untangling conflict between departments, setting goals, strategy planning, cultural change—any activity people cannot do alone. In such team meetings well-motivated groups routinely learn how to manage with less frustration and higher output. They usually report more openness, more mutual respect, higher trust and cooperation over time.

I stress well-motivated because that is the building block for all constructive change. You can't play winning football if half the team doesn't give a hoot. The same is true for producing, selling, or managing. That's not to say it takes no work. Even the best-intentioned groups find they must flounder for a while the first time they endeavor to have this sort of meeting. . . .

Conditions for Success. Team building succeeds under four conditions.

1. Interdependence. The team is working on important problems in which each person has a stake. In other words, teamwork is central to future success, not an expression of ideology or some misplaced "ought-to."
2. Leadership. The boss wants so strongly to improve group performance that he or she will take risks.
3. Joint decision. All members agree to participate.
4. Equal influence. Each person has a chance to influence the agenda.

In one typical scenario, the boss calls a meeting, states some personal goals, and asks for discussion. When (as is common) a consultant has been asked to help, the parties need a get-acquainted meeting. (I will describe the meeting from both consultant's and manger's perspectives. I think you will find them often interchangeable.) Often the consultant interviews team members to discover their concerns and wishes. Questions might include each person's objectives, tasks, problems, and the extent of help needed from others. Responses always encompass costs, markets, innovation, and other business-related issues.

Clients (some consultant too) often treat interviews as if their main purpose is for the consultant (doctor) to learn enough to prescribe the right cure. An experienced team-building consultant, however, knows that the prescription is voluntary dialogue. Interviews have two other purposes more important than the consultant's education. One, they help team members collect their thoughts and feelings, zero in on what they really want to say. Two, they reduce the fantasy about the consultant's motives and working methods. The consultant will learn about the organization in any case. What the consultant wants most to know is how much each team member will take responsibility for the meeting's success.

Deciding to Proceed. The consultant presents a summary of interview themes to the team, inviting discussion of the pros and cons of continuing. If the team decides to proceed, it schedules a two- or three-day offsite event. This meeting has a dual focus that makes it different from typical staff meetings. The team works directly on an important task identified by members: strategy formation, reorganizing, dealing with technologies, costs, or markets, quality or customer problems. Here a future scenario—"X Corporation Five Years Hence"—can be a powerful lightning rod for attracting constructive dialogue. Team members also specify what it is about their own processes they wish to improve. This makes it possible for them to periodically step back and observe what they are doing that helps or hinders progress. This discussion can be helped by process-analysis forms like that in "Rating Teamwork," a grandchild of early group dynamics.

Such forms are easily constructed. You can spend days in the library tracking down the issues that decades of research have shown go hand in hand with output and satisfaction. Or you can ask the team members, and get roughly the same list in ten minutes. Nine times out of ten one item on the list will be "trust"—a validation of Jack Gibb's contention (1978) that without it nothing else of consequence is likely to happen.

Making such a list is a focusing device, a learning tool. It is useful when used once or twice to help people internalize key processes. Done by rote, it becomes a meaningless ritual, the social analogy to turning out reams of numbers in a quarterly rollout nobody pays attention to.

A more powerful way to help people experience their own processes is with videotape. Reviewing ten minutes of a meeting and asking people to recall what they were thinking or feeling is probably the simplest way to facilitate team learning (the same way sports teams, tennis players, skiers learn by watching themselves on tape).

The dual focus on task *and* process is the team-building meeting's unique contribution to productive workplaces. I have three success criteria:

1. The team resolves important dilemmas, often ones on which little progress was made before.
2. People emerge more confident of their ability to influence the future.
3. Members learn the extent to which output is linked to their own candor, responsibility for themselves, and willingness to cooperate with others.

PRACTICAL THEORY

I want to describe the underlying theory in business terms, borrowing from an extraordinary consultant, the late Mike Blansfield, who pioneered the method years ago with TRW and other companies. He called his concept "Team Effectiveness Theory." . . . I think it is a major contribution to the transformation of teamwork, fitting in with any agenda you can name. The key to team building, I believe, is its *dual* focus on task and process under conditions of rapid external change, not a narrowly interpersonal focus.

Blansfield's concept highlights universal processes that work teams rarely connect to results. . . . Most managers define positive results as higher productivity, better quality, more profits, and lower costs.

When something on that list goes wrong, people often feel out of control and (secretly) incompetent. They initiate a search for mistakes in techniques, policies, systems, plans. . . , or they seek to finger a villain. In extreme cases, if they have the power, they may fire somebody. Few consider the impact of their own behavior on the *key processes* affected by the situation. These are the three factors on the top list.

From Taylor to Lewis to McGregor to Emery and Trist, observers have identified management's own behavior as *the* starting place for improving anything—systems, labor-management relations, output, work satisfaction, culture, whatever. Blansfield's model highlights the differences between managing a problem one on one and managing a group in which people depend on one another. To do the latter requires an appreciation of task and process applied to teamwork in an unpredictable world. . . .

ADDING TEAMWORK TO EFFECTIVENESS

. . . . Each person in a work group continually struggles with three questions that are never answered "once and for all." They are in jeopardy at every turning point, and must be resolved over and over again.

1. Am I in or out?
2. Do I have any power and control?
3. Can I use, develop, and be appreciated for my skills and resources?

In or Out. Most of us want to belong, to be valued, to have task that matter, and to be recognized as insiders by others. The more "in" we feel, the better we cooperate. The more we feel "out," the more with withdraw, work alone, daydream, defeat ourselves and other people. When I sought single-handedly to patch up the computer system, I drove everybody else out.

Power and Control. Power and control need little explaining after Taylor, McGregor, and the astronauts. We all want power. Faced with changes we can't influence, we feel impotent and in turn, lose self-esteem. It doesn't matter how smart we are, how skilled, or how far up the ladder of success we have climbed. Faced with something we can't influence, we may work harder and do worse, losing self-esteem until we gain control again. That happened to me in the 1960s, and I made it worse for everybody else.

Skills and Resources. Tremendous skills, experience, and common sense exist in every workplace. What keep us from tapping them are outdated assumptions about who can and should do what. Often, jobs are defined so narrowly people can't use the brains they were born with, or even the training they have received. . . . The three team process issues can be resolved only when the tasks are seen as team tasks, not the boss's problem to be solved. That is not to say they automatically *will* be resolved. They won't—unless two things occur. We need to learn how to be open about what's on our minds, and responsive to others. We need to give and get feedback.

Candor and Feedback. These two processes, openness and feedback, link team issues with results. We need a place where we can talk over what each person needs to do and our anxiety about doing it. We need a chance to own up to uncertainty and express differences of opinion constructively. We need to discover that others are in the same boat. We need one thing more. I've been in dozens of these meetings. Sooner or later somebody *always* brings up the importance of trust. Commitment is built on a foundation of mutual trust, and everybody knows it. Trusting one another is the most secure way to manage through tough times. The teambuilding meeting is one way people learn how to develop trust.

Feelings about membership, control, and skills influence our motivation, which in turn determines the quality of our work. If we talk *only* about results, tasks, and plans, without observing our ability to listen and hear, to discuss differences, to solve problems and decide in a way that builds commitment, we ultimately defeat the results we claim to value. It's all one system. Pull on any thread and you untangle the whole net—the task of a dual-focus meeting.

Structure. Such a meeting is helped along by structure. Usually a team-building meeting starts with a discussion of goals and agenda. Often there is considerable discussion just to get a meeting of the minds about the major agenda: why, how, what, who. Sometimes there are prearranged "stop-action" points when people fill out a process observation form or review the videotape. Sometimes a consultant will call time out if people are fighting or running away from the task. Usually a short process discussion is enough to get things tracking again. Sometimes it takes several hours of dialogue. Each team's *own* process requirements should be kept front and center.

If people identify interpersonal conflicts or difficulty in communicating as sources of frustration, some device on personal style (maybe a self-report paper-and-pencil survey) may trigger half a day's discussion. In such exercises people learn to value their differences, to accept their strengths, and to express themselves more clearly.

Sometimes teams engage in role negotiation, a procedure devised by consultant Roger Harrison (1972). Each team member writes down what he or she wants each of the others to do less or more of, and what to keep doing the same. These requests are posted and negotiated. For example, "I'll give you at least a week's notice of schedule changes, if you'll refer customer complaints directly to me." There's no deal unless both parties agree.

Another useful format, responsibility charting, is indicated if the team's self-diagnosis is that important tasks are falling between the cracks. An "R" chart. . . lists who makes which decisions, who must be informed, who must support, and who has the power to veto (Galbraith, 1977). All these activities increase communication, provide feedback, take account of each person's needs, more equitably distribute influence, and promote orderly procedures for managing interdependence.

Leadership and Consensus. Nearly every team gets around to how the boss makes decisions—the authority-dependency issue high-lighted.

The boss laments, "They act like children, bucking everything to me." The team members echo, "He treats us like children and does too much himself." The commonest discovery on both sides is how each acts to reinforce the others' perceptions—unconsciously accepting (even relishing) their roles in this age-old parent/child drama. Inevitably this triggers talk about the meaning of individual versus group decisions, when each is appropriate, what the practical limits of formal power really are, what the risks and payoffs can be when acting without consulting others, and whether consensus means "doing what the group wants."

I find consensus decision making the least understood and most useful dimension of teamwork. Consensus means support derived when each person feels heard and understood. Unanimous decision is a desirable goal. With or without it, a boss has the responsibility to decide. This task is made easier if each team member feels free to speak openly on important matters. Indeed, the simplest team-building technique is the "go-around," where all participants have a chance to say how they see it and what they would do. Bosses can facilitate this task by openly sharing their own dilemmas and willingness to hear people out. To maintain team cohesiveness, all should be satisfied that they had a chance to influence the decision and declare their willingness to support it. When any team member can't do that, the team has a serious problem.

THE FUTURE OF TEAM BUILDING

A team-building meeting can become a procedural nightmare of consultant-orchestrated exercises. It also can be run simply, directly, and to the point. . . . The consultant's role is to help people talk constructively about their work, to learn, and to act. . . . Most folks can discuss, learn, and act as readily with a little structure as with a lot. If you consider the "right" answer the best one that is implementable, this less-is-more approach will be welcome in many situations where participation and commitment are important to success.

Teamwork is essential to large system success. Team building is useful at some point in any change program. Most team members come away feeling more "in," more influential, more competent, more supported, and more committed to their common enterprise. They may also have solved some problems, devised a new strategy, moved toward a new structure, consolidated a future vision.

REFERENCES

Bellah, R. N., and others. *Habits of the Heart: Individualism and Commitment in American Life.* Berkeley and Los Angeles: University of California Press, 1985.

Galbraith, J. R. *Organization Design.* Reading, Mass.: Addison-Wesley, 1977.

Gibb, J. R. *Trust: A New View of Personal and Organizational Development.* Los Angeles: Guild of Tutors Press, 1978.

Harrison, R. "Role Negotiation: A Tough-Minded Approach to Team Development." In W. W. Burke and H. A. Hornstein (eds.), *The Social Technology of Organizational Development.* La Jolla, Calif.: University Associates, 1972.

Tocqueville, A. de. *Democracy in America.* 2 vols. (J. P. Mayer and A. P. Kerr, eds.) New York: Doubleday, 1969. (Originally published 1835.)

8

MANAGERIALISM AND PERFORMANCE MANAGEMENT

The central theme of *managerialism* is: public administrators should be business-like, entrepreneurial, customer-oriented, managers. Public managers should be given the freedom to define organizational objectives, select strategies from among a variety of alternatives, turn activities over to private contractors[1] or "empowered"[2] lower managers, hold contractors and managers responsible for achieving the objectives, measure the quantity and quality of performance, reward those who perform, and punish (or terminate) those who do not perform satisfactorily. Proponents argue persuasively that managerialism offers the only reasonable hope for ever having well-run, purposeful, government agencies—agencies that are flexible, effective, and responsive to the needs of the people they serve.

Managerialism stands in stark contrast to the widely-held view of public management that had prevailed in the U. S. Up through the 1970s. Public management in the U.S. had always given highest priority to the values of fairness, equity, consistency, and political neutrality. These values could be achieved best through systems of uniformly applied rules and procedures, and upward accountability through layers of organizational supervisors who ensured that the rules and procedures were followed. Thus, public managers were largely "overseers" of activities that were defined by written rules and procedures.

In 1937, Luther Gulick defined the job or role of the "traditional" public manager by the acronym POSDCORB.[3] According to Gulick, the seven core functions of management are encompassed in the POSDCORB acronym. The manager's first role, *planning,* means "working out in broad outline the things that need to be done and the methods for doing them to accomplish the purpose" of the organization. *Organizing* is the establishment of "the formal structure of authority through which work subdivisions are arranged, defined and coordinated for the [organization's] defined objective." *Staffing* includes "the

---

Jared C. Bennett, University of Utah, contributed greatly to this chapter essay.

whole personnel function of bringing in and training the staff and maintaining favorable conditions of work." *Directing* "is the continuous task of making decisions and embodying them in specific and general orders and instructions and serving as the leader" of the organization. *Coordinating* is the "the all important duty of interrelating the various parts of the work" to produce the most efficient result. Managers should use the *reporting* process to make "those to whom the executive is responsible informed as to what is going on, which includes keeping himself and his subordinates informed through records, research and inspection." Finally, *budgeting* is the process managers use to ensure that their organizations have the resources they need to achieve their objectives through "fiscal planning, accounting, and control."

Under managerialism, the duty of a public administrator extends well beyond the execution of laws by bureaucratic government agencies that are managed according to POSDCORB principles. Public managers should be activists who influence public policy formation. "Modern public managers are expected to be policy entrepreneurs who forcefully develop, argue for, and yes, sell, creative solutions to vexing problems."[4]

In recent years, the courts also seem to be agreeing that public mangers should take active roles in shaping the laws they will be asked to execute. In *Association of National Advertisers, Inc. v. FTC,* for example, the D.C. Circuit Court of Appeals held: "Agencies are created to maintain or to restructure certain areas of private activity in light of expressed statutory policies. Thus, unlike courts, agencies should be positive actors, not passive adjudicators. . . . If an agency official is to be effective he must engage in debate and discussion about the policy matters before him."[5] Managerialism is thus receiving wide general acceptance at the turn of the millennium. The notion of public administrators as strong, risk-taking, politically involved, entrepreneurial, public managers is in vogue.

Although many of the same POSDCORB activities or roles are performed in today's world of managerialism, the words and phrases mean quite different things than they did to Luther Gulick. *Planning,* for example, for Gulick meant short-term operational planning to achieve specific objectives. For managerialists, planning means long-term strategic-type planning that often changes the organization's objectives to meet changing circumstances and opportunities. For Gulick, *delegating* and *coordinating* meant assigning tasks or projects to subordinates and working closely with them to be certain that their activities meshed with the work of other employees. Under managerialism, *delegating* means turning over activities and decision authority to teams of employees or private contractors who are empowered to exercise considerable discretion in accomplishing their tasks. Most of the *coordinating* role is done by the work teams or the contractors who have access to whatever information is needed to coordinate their work—through networked PCs.

The "tools" used to get work done by "traditional" public managers were organization charts, policies and procedures manuals, directives, and close oversight of subordinates' activities. The "tools of managerialism" that are used most often are *empowerment, reengineering, privatization,*[6] *performance mea-*

surement, benchmarking, and *entrepreneurialism.* Although there are differences among these "tools" of managerialism, they all share a common vision for public agencies including: the need for public organizations to be more flexible and innovative; recognition that the managers and employees who actually do the work are the most knowledgeable about it and usually have the best ideas about how to improve it; and an unwavering conviction that major productivity gains cannot be achieved in "traditional" bureaucratic agencies that are top-heavy with rules and administrators.[7]

EMPOWERMENT

Robert Dahl defined power as: "A has power over B to the extent that he can get B to do something B would not otherwise do."[8] For an agency manager, power means being able to get the members of the organization to do what they otherwise would not do of their own volition. Many studies conducted over the decades have concluded that a manager actually accumulates power by sharing power with others. In other words, power is not a "zero sum game." When others believe that they are "empowered" to increase their effectiveness and can contribute to the success of the organization, the leader that shared power with them gains legitimacy as a leader—and thus power—in the eyes of others.[9] This premise is the central theme of the *empowerment* movement.

Empowerment is a process, not an event. It is "a process of enhancing feelings of self-efficacy among organizational members through the identification of conditions that foster powerlessness and through their removal by both formal organizational practices and informal techniques of providing efficacy information."[10] Empowerment usually is implemented in five steps. First, the organization identifies the conditions in the organization that cause managers and employees to feel powerless. For example, organizational members may feel powerless because of poor communications, authoritarian managers, goals and objectives appear to be unattainable, and the rewards for meeting goals are small or the penalties for not meeting goals are harsh.[11] Second, using the diagnostic information, strategies are implemented to replace "powerless factors" with "empowering factors." For example, goal-setting programs may be implemented with merit-pay systems, job enrichment training seminars, and participative management approaches so that employees have more ability to influence decisions. Third, the implementation strategies used to introduce the "empowering factors" are carefully designed to remove the barriers to empowerment. A key factor here is making certain that employees have access to the data they need to make well-informed decisions. Fourth, as empowerment factors are implemented, organizational members begin to feel effective and more able to make decisions and perform their work. Finally, an empowered work force leads to higher productivity for individuals, work teams, and for the organization.[12]

Self-directed work teams are an interesting approach to empowerment. A self-directed work team is a, "highly trained group of employees, from 6 to 18, on average, fully responsible for turning out a well-defined segment of finished work."[13] Each member of the team is responsible for performing multiple tasks, so members cannot be narrow specialists.

Most importantly, self-directed work teams are semi-autonomous bodies. They alone are responsible for producing quality results on schedule. The team is its own management. They govern themselves. If a member is not performing, the team is responsible for changing the behavior or disciplining the offender. Self-directed work teams often are rewarded with a share of profits or of cost savings. Individual members may receive bonuses for mastering new skills.

When teams manage themselves, higher executives are freed from concerns about day-to-day organizational activities.[14] They can focus their energies on strategic leadership functions, legislative relations, and the organization's alignment with its environment.[15]

REENGINEERING

Reengineering is the opposite of incrementalism. It is an approach that requires rethinking an organization's purposes, products, and processes—starting the organization all over again from "ground zero."[16] According to the "original architects" of reengineering, Michael Hammer and James Champy, reengineering is the "fundamental rethinking and radical redesign of business processes to achieve dramatic improvements in critical, contemporary measures of performance," in a relatively short period of time[17]—starting over.

Reengineering usually involves three phases. First, *process mapping* is the means that an organization uses to "map" how it currently conducts business, how it makes its products or services, and how it delivers to its customers or clients. Second, *customer assessment* involves evaluating the needs of the organization's customers. For example, customers are asked to respond to surveys and questionnaires about the organization's performance. Organizational representatives conduct face-to-face interviews with the customers in order to evaluate how well—or how poorly—the needs of customers are being met. Third, the organization uses the data collected in the first two steps to completely redesign the structure and flow of its business in order to meet customer or client needs in the quickest and least expensive ways possible.

Reengineering is not without risks, however. "Organizations must be made aware of the high failure rate of reengineering efforts. Estimates of failure range from 50 to 60 percent."[18] The difference between success and failure in reengineering is communication. Communication is essential during the conversion from the old to the new organization and during the implementation of new business processes. Even with good communication and a sincere desire to improve operations, reengineering carries a risk of failure.

Suppose that you have worked for the Municipal Department of Public Utilities for 15 years, and you have become highly proficient in your work. You have received regular merit increases and several awards for exceptional performance. The newly appointed Department Director thinks that customer satisfaction is not high enough and has decided to reengineer the department. When the consultant team's analysis was completed, you were instructed to learn a new work procedure that is radically different from the one you have been using. Also, the City Council listened carefully to the reengineering consultants' recommendations and has decided to downsize your department—along with many other departments in City Hall. You will be expected to do considerably more work with less help than you had before. If you do not, you will be downgraded or terminated. How would you and your coworkers feel about reengineering? About the Department Director and the City Council?

ENTREPRENEURIALISM

Simply put, entrepreneurialism means running government more like a hungry business.

> The fundamental point is that the current Zeitgeist of reform in government is to use the market and to accept the assumption that private-sector methods for managing activities (regardless of what they are) are almost inherently superior to the methods of the traditional public sector. . . . In the market view, the principal problem with traditional bureaucracies is that they do not provide sufficient incentive for individuals working within them to perform their jobs as efficiently as they might.[19]

Entrepreneurial public administrators are expected to create a vision for their organizations and to strategically lead their agencies to the vision. This approach requires the use of market-based models for delivering public services.[20] For example, NASA Director Daniel Golding used entrepreneurial principles to reinvent his troubled agency in the years following the ill-fated flight of the Challenger. Using a variety of reengineering and market based management principles, Golding transformed NASA from an agency that was too often behind schedule and significantly over budget into an organization that delivered on time and usually under budget. In 1976, construction of two Viking Mars mission spacecraft cost $3 billion (in 1997 dollars) whereas two Pathfinder Mars mission spacecraft cost $500 million in 1997 dollars—which included the Sojourner rover and a robotic vehicle used to investigate the surface of Mars.[21] Goldin appears to have used entrepreneurialism to effectuate a modern miracle of public administration.

PERFORMANCE MANAGEMENT

Performance Management consists of six phases. (1) The organization specifies clear and measurable objectives. (2) Management selects and uses performance indicators to measure the organization's progress in attaining its objectives. (3) The performance of each employee (or team) is evaluated regularly. (4) Performance incentives are used to help motivate employees to meet the organization's objectives. (5) Financial and human resources are coordinated and budgeted in a manner that focuses resources on organizational objectives. (6) The organization's progress is assessed at the end of each budget cycle, and goals are re-set to continuously improve performance over successive budget cycles.[22]

READINGS REPRINTED IN THIS CHAPTER

In **"Comprehensive Improvement,"**[23] **Marc Holzer and Kathe Callahan** report on the activities of a variety of successful public organizations around the United States. These successful organizations have been able to improve their public services by being innovative. Holzer and Callahan use these success stories to support their *Comprehensive Public Sector Productivity Improvement Model,* a model that uses managerialism and performance management to achieve better results with greater customer satisfaction. The Comprehensive Public Sector Productivity Improvement Model involves five elements: Management for Quality, Development of Human Resources, Adapting Technologies, Promoting Partnerships, Performance Measurement, and Evaluation. Each element contains sub-elements which, when integrated with the financial, human, and energy resources of the organization, yield more output and higher customer satisfaction.

Steven Cohen and William Eimicke "describe strategies for bringing management innovation into public sector organizations and present ideas about how and when to deploy several specific strategies," in **"Understanding and Applying Innovation Strategies in the Public Sector."**[24] Cohen and Eimicke do not agree with the reengineering approach. "Successful innovation is often incremental and small scale," because of the numerous factors and forces that affect government agencies. Public sector innovation requires innovation in both the *design* and the *management* of policies and programs. The *management* innovations that Cohen and Eimicke describe and evaluate are based on the principles of Total Quality Management (TQM).[25] However, TQM by itself is not enough to bring about meaningful change in the organization. Innovative policy *design* approaches must be used in conjunction with the TQM methods to achieve positive change in public organizations.

"Towards a Competitive Public Administration," by **Arie Halachmi and Marc Holzer,**[26] explains that many public agencies in the United States have had to become more competitive with private businesses and other public organizations. The public is demanding more efficiency from public organizations but also do not want to lose the advantages of dealing with government agencies. Halachmi and Holzer warn against blindly pursuing privatization across a wide range of government services. Finally, more research is needed before it will be possible to answer questions about the general applicability of privatizing government services.

NOTES

1. See Chapter 4, "Reinventing the Machinery of Government."
2. See Chapter 7, "Organizational Behavior."
3. Gulick, Luther. (1937). "Notes on the Theory of Organization." *Papers on the Science of Administration.* New York: Institute of Public Administration, pp. 3–13.

4. Shafritz, Jay M., and E. W. Russell. (2000). *Introducing Public Administration* (2nd ed.). New York: Addison-Wesley Longman, p. 263.
5. *Association of National Advertisers, Inc. v. FTC,* 627 F.2d 1151, 1168–1169 (D.C. Circuit 1979).
6. Privatization is discussed extensively in Chapter 4.
7. Ott, J. Steven. (1996). "Teamwork and Empowerment," in J. S. Ott (Ed.), *Classic Readings in Organizational Behavior* (2nd ed.) (pp. 244–302). Fort Worth, TX: Harcourt Brace.
8. Dahl, Robert. (July 1957). "The Concept of Power." *Behavioral Science, 2*(3), 202–203.
9. Ott, J. Steven. (1996). "Power and Influence," in J. S. Ott (Ed.), *Classic Readings in Organizational Behavior* (2nd ed.) (pp. 379–434). Fort Worth, TX: Harcourt Brace.
10. Conger, Jay A., and Rabindra K. Kanungo. (July 1988). "The Empowerment Process: Integrating Theory and Practice." *Academy of Management Review, 13*(3), p. 474.
11. See, for example, Peter Scholtes, Brian Joiner, and Barbara Streibel. (1996). *The Team Handbook* (2nd ed.). Madison, Wisc.: Joiner and Associates: and, Jon R. Katzenbach, and Douglas K. Smith. (1993). *The Wisdom of Teams: Creating the High-Performance Organization.* Boston, Mass.: Harvard Business School Press.
12. Ivancevich, John M., and Michael T. Matteson. (1999). *Organizational Behavior and Management* (4th ed.). New York: Irwin McGraw-Hill. P. 378.
13. Orsburn, Jack D., Linda Moran, Ed Musselwhite, John H. Zenger, and Craig Perrin. (1990). *Self-Directed Work Teams: The New American Challenge.* Homewood, Ill.: Business One Irwin.
14. Shafritz, Jay M., and E. W. Russell. (2000). *Introducing Public Administration* (2nd ed.). New York: Addison-Wesley Longman. 267–68.
15. See Chapter 9, "Strategic Management."
16. Cohen, Steven, and William Eimicke. (1998). "Reengineering," in S. Cohen and W. Eimicke, *Tools for Innovators: Creative Strategies for Managing Public Sector Organizations* (pp. 30–48). San Francisco: Jossey-Bass.
17. Shafritz, Jay M., and E. W. Russell. (2000). *Introducing Public Administration* (2nd ed.). New York: Addison-Wesley Longman, p. 264.
18. Hyde, Albert C. (1998). "Reengineering," in J. M. Shafritz (Ed.), *International Encyclopedia of Public Policy and Administration.* Boulder, Colo.: Westview p. 1928.
19. Peters, B. Guy. (1996). *The Future of Governing: Four Emerging Models.* Lawrence, Kans.: University Press of Kansas, p. 21.
20. Peters, B. Guy. (1996). "Market Models for Reforming Government," in B. G. Peters, *The Future of Governing: Four Emerging Models* (pp. 21–46). Lawrence, Kans.: University Press of Kansas.
21. In Steven Cohen, and William Eimicke. (1998). *Understanding and Applying Innovation Strategies in the Public Sector.* San Francisco, Calif.: Jossey-Bass. P. 1. Both craft, however, were lost!!
22. Shafritz, Jay M., and E. W. Russell. (2000). *Introducing Public Administration* (2nd ed.). New York: Addison-Wesley Longman, pp. 273–74.
23. Holzer, Marc, and Kathe Callahan. (1998). "Comprehensive Improvement," in M. Holzer and K. Callahan, *Government at Work: Best Practices and Model Programs* (pp. 133–146). Thousand Oaks, Calif.: Sage.
24. Cohen, Steven, and William Eimicke. (1998). *Understanding and Applying Innovation Strategies in the Public Sector.* San Francisco, Calif.: Jossey-Bass.

25. Swiss, James E. (July/August 1992). "Adapting Total Quality Management (TQM) to Government." *Public Administration Review, 52,* 356–362.
26. Halachmi, Arie, and Marc Holzer. (March 1993). "Towards a Competitive Public Administration." *International Review of Administrative Sciences, 59,* 1.

21

Marc Holzer and Kathe Callahan

GOVERNMENT AT WORK: BEST PRACTICES AND MODEL PROGRAMS

Cases of exemplary progress often result from multiple approaches to the improvement of public performance integrating several major approaches (Figure 21.1).

Public sector improvement programs operate under many labels. The program's name, however, is less important than its substance: comprehensive productivity improvement in an environment of increasing demands and reduced resources. Such programs improve performance systematically, by integrating advanced management techniques and, in the best cases, institutionalizing productivity improvement initiatives. Some cases offer such comprehensive models. Some examples follow.

Managing Productively. In the late 1980s, Hillsborough County, Florida, confronted an accelerated rate of growth; on average, 20,000 people a year were moving into the county. Such rapid growth led to increased demands for county services, which in turn posed new problems. The provision of quality services to all residents, new and old, was complicated not only by the growth in population, but also by a lack of continuity in leadership. The position of county administrator had been "turning over" every 2 years, straining relationships with both the Board of County Commissioners and county employees. Top administrators in the county, as well as members of the Board of County Commissioners, agreed that dramatic organizational changes would have to be made in order to "provide quality public service second to none." The overall goal of the newly established *Operations Improvement and Development Department* was to enhance public service delivery, reduce the cost of public service, and improve the quality of services to the residents of the county.

The creation of the department was one of several changes that included the restructuring of the county organization to flatten the layers of decision making, and the creation of a new professional ladder in which compensation is based on performance. The department is staffed by a team of professionals who are experts in process consulting, organizational development, management development, strategic planning, and operation planning. It is part of the Productivity and Service Team, which includes Public Information, Cable Services, Information Technology, Legisla-

FIGURE 21.1   *Comprehensive Public Sector Productivity Improvement*

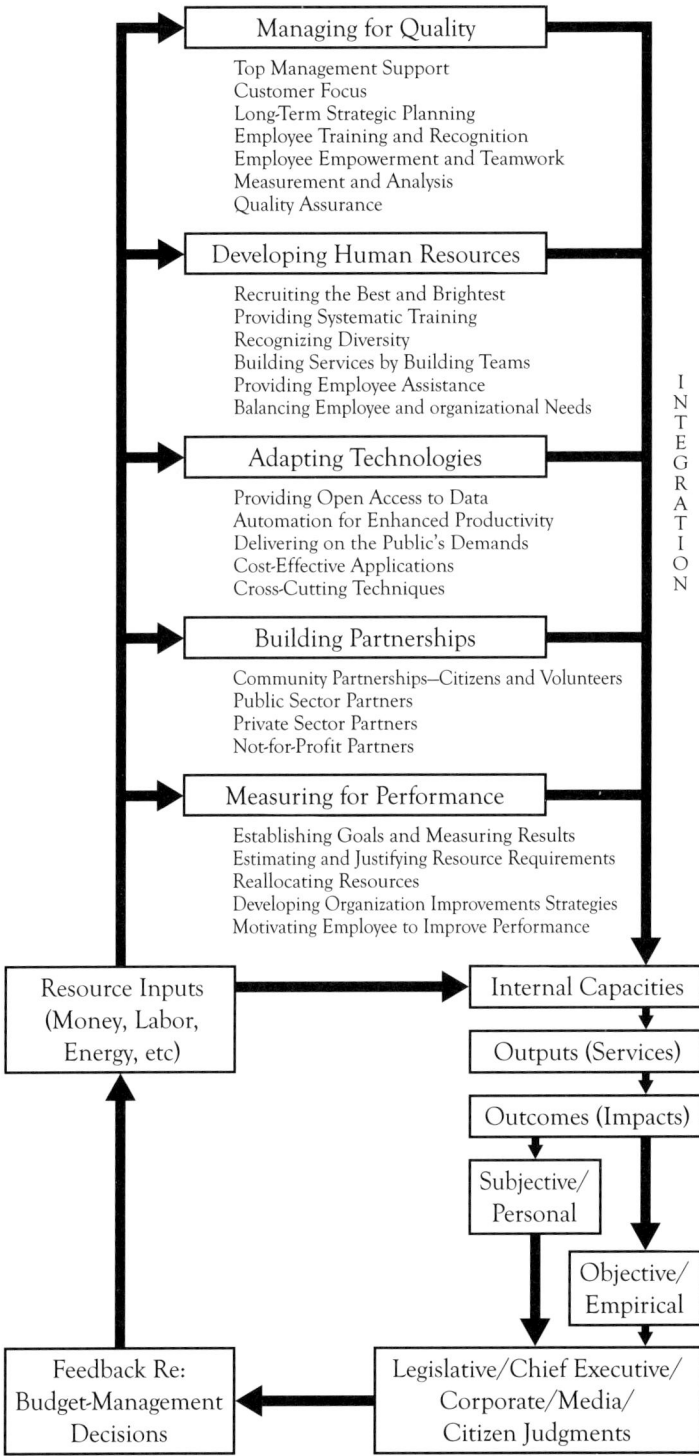

Managing for Quality

Top Management Support
Customer Focus
Long-Term Strategic Planning
Employee Training and Recognition
Employee Empowerment and Teamwork
Measurement and Analysis
Quality Assurance

Developing Human Resources

Recruiting the Best and Brightest
Providing Systematic Training
Recognizing Diversity
Building Services by Building Teams
Providing Employee Assistance
Balancing Employee and organizational Needs

Adapting Technologies

Providing Open Access to Data
Automation for Enhanced Productivity
Delivering on the Public's Demands
Cost-Effective Applications
Cross-Cutting Techniques

Building Partnerships

Community Partnerships—Citizens and Volunteers
Public Sector Partners
Private Sector Partners
Not-for-Profit Partners

Measuring for Performance

Establishing Goals and Measuring Results
Estimating and Justifying Resource Requirements
Reallocating Resources
Developing Organization Improvements Strategies
Motivating Employee to Improve Performance

INTEGRATION

Resource Inputs (Money, Labor, Energy, etc)

Internal Capacities

Outputs (Services)

Outcomes (Impacts)

Subjective/Personal

Objective/Empirical

Feedback Re: Budget-Management Decisions

Legislative/Chief Executive/Corporate/Media/Citizen Judgments

tive Liaison, and Human Resources. These departments share the common goal of improving overall productivity through such actions as the hiring and retaining of competent and committed staff and keeping up with the latest technology. This mission is accomplished through supporting and developing the following:

1. Employee involvement improvement teams
2. Work simplification teams
3. InterSolve teams
4. Management training
5. Employee and trade skills training
6. Strategic planning
7. Technology transfer

An overall emphasis has been on measurable results. Documented cost savings and cost avoidances totalled $3.59 million in the first year. Through 1995, documented cost savings and cost avoidances totaled more than $20 million. One indication of the success of the program is the broad spectrum of departments that have documented savings. The program works not only in those easily measured departments that have "hard" service savings, such as Solid Waste and Public Utilities but also in the "softer" delivery areas such as Social Services and Aging Services. Another indicator of the success of the program is found in the results of the Employee Survey. This survey measured employee satisfaction on a broad range of job components. The results indicated that employees who participate on employee teams or in training and development programs were more satisfied overall than those employees who did not participate in these programs.

Emphasizing Service. Despite cuts following voter approval of California's Proposition 13 in 1978, a comprehensive emphasis on management for quality has helped San Diego improve services through its *Service Enhancement Program.*

At the beginning, under the pressures of Proposition 13, the attitude of many employees at the City of San Diego reflected the resentment of having to increase their productivity without the resources—the personnel, training, equipment, and office space—they perceived as necessary to do their work.

The city manager wanted to change the attitude of employees at all levels of the organization, training them to act as "if our customers had a choice, they'd choose us." This motto and the City Mission Statement became the foundation for 1988—The Year of Service. In February of that year, the city manager's office requested proposals from all department directors for programs designed to enhance citywide services to customers, citizens, and employees. Three departments—Building Inspection, Parks and Recreation, and Fire—were selected to participate in the first phase of such a program. The experiment has been successful, and key components of a comprehensive program that has developed from that initiative include the following:

1. Development of performance measures to assist each department in monitoring the effectiveness of their service
2. Development and administration of pre and post citizen surveys
3. Development of a quarterly service-oriented employee newsletter

4. Citywide training in customer service philosophy and techniques
5. Inclusion of a customer service function and standards in each employee's performance evaluation
6. Revision of citywide polices and procedures to streamline them for service to the customer
7. The development of a telecommunications system to improve communication to city customers

Planning Productivity Improvement. The South Florida Water Management District (SFWMD) received an award for the *Water Management Productivity Improvement Program* (PIP). PIP is a comprehensive design that addresses widespread public demands for optimal utilization of scarce governmental resources. It enhances overall district performance, while at the same time encouraging widespread public commitment and support. Under PIP productivity improvement is defined as a centralized effort to control the yield of resources put into a public agency. District resource expenditures are clearly linked to strategic initiatives based on current mission priorities.

The five main components of the district PIP are:

1. Department/program designed productivity plans
2. A productivity improvement advisory council
3. A districtwide steering committee
4. Departmental PIP task forces
5. A central coordinating unit

These components were established as a result of an exercise that integrates administrative structure with a management planning system. This is an activity that defines a holistic districtwide productivity improvement program in a continuous quality improvement environment. The program equates to an overall enhancement of the quality of work like at the district while improving quality of services in meeting public demands.

CHEATING DETENTION ALTERNATIVES: COOPERATION, NOT INCARCERATION

The McLean County (Illinois) *Extended Day Program (EDP)* is designed for the purpose of providing the county court system with an alternative to secure detention. Due to a change in judicial ordinances, which called for the removal of all juveniles from adult jails, McLean County lost the ability to detain minors locally. The county's options were to detain minors outside the county at a cost of $75.00 per day, or develop an alternative solution. The EDP was developed as a cost-saving option. The program is designed for the purpose of providing the county court system with an alternative to secure detention. The EDP targeted a specific population of minors, aged 11 to 17, who were involved with the juvenile justice system. The program allows minors who should be in secure custody an opportunity to remain in the community by providing the structure that a detention center provides, but in a nonsecure setting. Minors are offered the following services on a daily basis: tutoring, group therapy, and basic life skills. Each minor must provide a service to the community.

The program produces swift consequences for violations of probation. Rather than wait for court hearings on the violations, with the probable outcome being some type of dispositional detention, the minor is immediately ordered into the program. The program further allows for minors who have been charged with a serious offense to be detained initially, but then allowed home confinement, with the restrictions that they attend the program on a daily basis.

The EDP, which was originally unique in the state of Illinois, is innovative in that it is an alternative to detention. It offers avenues other than detention for juvenile delinquents, although detention is often the easier option. This program permits juveniles to function in a very structured, but unlocked, setting and provides those minors with the community resources that are important for shaping and challenging youth. One of the positive outcomes of EDP is that minors do not mind being in the program. Many of the "graduates" drop by to see the staff or other providers. They typically view their service projects as a positive contribution to the community, not just something that an adult tells them "needs to be done." Minors have taken pride in the program and see themselves as being a "part" of it rather than just a "body."

With similar objectives, in the late 1970s the state of California moved to address the pressing needs of 17- to 21-year-old undereducated at-risk urban youth through a highly structured 6-week education and job preparation model, the *Innovative Military Programs and Civilian Training (IMPACT)* program. In particular, IMPACT is designed as an alternative to incarceration. In response to the problem of high youth unemployment, IMPACT's highly structured, short-term education and job-placement curriculum encompasses basic, premilitary, and preemployment skills. Training is provided by a combination of National Guard and civilian instructors who apply the military's highly disciplined approach to teaching/learning techniques, coupled with traditional education methods and philosophies. From 1977 to 1995, IMPACT enrolled 7,017 participants and successfully placed 5,405: 28% entered military service, 57% were employed, and 15% returned to accredited schools. The cost was approximately $1,900 per participant, compared to $25,000 per year for incarceration.

In 1983, in response to the prison overcrowding crisis of the late seventies, the state of New Jersey developed the *Intensive Supervision Program* to prevent prison overcrowding and to improve the screening of nonviolent offenders who are eligible for early release into the community. It is a highly structured program encompassing electronic and substance abuse monitoring, full-time employment, community service, and repayment of court-ordered fines and penalties. By diverting hundreds of prisoners from the system, the high cost of building an additional correctional facility for more serious offenders was avoided.

The program involves intensive screening of inmates who are a minimal threat to the community. They are released into an extremely restrictive but supportive environment where they are monitored by staff and electronic surveillance, must comply with a curfew, maintain fulltime employment, perform community service, satisfy financial obligations, and undergo substance abuse monitoring and counseling. In 1995, the cost of supervising an ISP participant was about $7,500, compared to estimates of $35,000 to incarcerate an offender. The program has achieved cumulative savings (i.e., cost avoidances) of approximately $70 million for the state.

HOUSING: IMPROVING TENANTS' LIVES

A New Lease on Life, a program of the State of Colorado, focuses on the ambitious outcome of enhancing clients' quality of life rather than the more limited, but more easily achieved, workload measures such as tenant occupancy.

In keeping with the movement toward deinstitutionalizing the mentally disabled, the Colorado Department of Institutions established this program in 1977–long before *quality* was a buzzword in either the public or private sector–specifically to meet the public housing needs of person with mental disabilities. This program has been successful on two dimensions: It offers alternatives to institutional living, and it rehabilitates existing housing stock.

A New Lease on Life, in conjunction with subsidies from the federal Department of Housing and Urban Development, provides housing assistance for more than 1,200 disabled persons. Before receiving this assistance, most tenants resided in substandard housing units, were homeless, or were institutionalized. Under the program, the tenant pays approximately 30% of his or her income toward rent, with the average client paying around $96 dollars per month for a $325 per month apartment. Unlike other housing programs, this program offers support services to the client, including case management, mental health counseling, and job training and skills development. Program coordinators, who are specifically trained to evaluate the participants, monitor the services provided to the client population. The direct impact of the program can be measured in terms of the quality-of-life enhancements realized by the clients served: They are afforded clean housing and myriad support mechanisms, as well as the opportunity to live as independently as possible.

A New Lease on Life relies heavily on the cooperation of a number of state and local agencies whose combined resources enable the program to offer decent, affordable housing to mentally disabled individuals. The program has been at the forefront of recognizing the linkage between support services and housing, which ultimately helps the client to become more self-sufficient. This "bootstrap" approach has now become part of the federal government's effort to supply housing to the mentally disabled. The program also facilitates an individual's integration into the community, which stresses the importance of access to basic community-based and real-world services such as banks, churches, shops, and mental health support agencies.

MULTIPLE SOURCES OF COOPERATION

Cooperative via Committee. In Seattle, recognizing the increasing number of incarcerated persons who suffer from mental illness, the Kings County Department of Adult Detention established the *Kings County Correctional Facility Mental Health Committee* program, which addresses the different needs of mentally ill offenders in public prisons.

Working to better understand and satisfy the special needs of such offenders in county jails, the Correctional Department joined forced with the Department of Human Resources to form the Mental Health Committee. It is charged with enhancing the availability of mental health services to prisoners while incarcerated and upon their release. The committee is also involved in generating greater community involvement in addressing the problem of mentally ill offenders. By increasing public awareness and developing strategies to bring appropriate services to the community, the program relies heavily on existing resources and expertise and is therefore cost-effective.

The committee has brought together mental health advocates, judicial representatives, police, and corrections and clinical experts to analyze the growing mental health problem among the correctional population, and to propose workable, coordinated solutions. Specifically, the program has improved the quality of life of mentally ill offenders by establishing support mechanisms, by de-emphasizing the punitive nature of incarceration, and by promising the offender continuation of care upon release from a county prison. It has increased the number of intensive community treatment care centers in King County, and has more than doubled the number of mentally ill offenders served. It offers a model for other municipalities with regard to cooperative efforts among agencies and the ability to put forth solutions to the growing problem of mentally ill offenders in a timely and cost-effective manner.

A STEP-BY-STEP STRATEGY

Complementing the improvement factors of Figure 21.1, public sector performance improvement programs typically follow a multiple-step strategy (Holzer, 1995):

> *Step 1. Clarifying Goals and Obtaining Support.* Productivity programs must agree upon, and have commitments to, reasonable goals and objectives, adequate staff and resource support, and organizational visibility. The full cooperation of top management and elected officials is a prerequisite to success.

> *Step 2. Locating Models.* Because productivity is an increasing priority of government, existing projects can suggest both successful paths and ways to avoid potential mistakes. Models are available from computer networks, the professional literature, and at conferences.

> *Step 3. Identifying Promising Areas.* As a means of building a successful track record, new productivity programs might select as targets those functions continually faced with large backlogs, slipping deadlines, high turnover, or many complaints. Because personnel costs are the largest expenditure for most public agencies, improved morale, training, or working conditions might offer a high payoff. Organizations might also target functions in which new techniques, procedures, or emerging technologies seem to offer promising paybacks.

> *Step 4. Building a Team.* Productivity programs are much more likely to succeed as bottom-up, rather than top-down or externally directed, entities. Productivity project teams should include middle management, supervisors, employees, and union representatives. They might also include consultants, clients, and representatives of advocacy groups. If employees are involved in looking for opportunities, then they are likely to suggest which barriers or obstacles need to be overcome; what tasks can be done more efficiently, dropped, or simplified; which workloads are unrealistically high or low.

Step 5.   Planning the Project. Team members should agree on a specific statement of scope, objectives, tasks, responsibilities, and time frames. This agreement should be detailed as a project management plan, which should then be updated and discussed on a regular basis.

Step 6.   Collecting Program Data. Potentially relevant information should be defined broadly and might include reviews of existing databases, interviews, budgets, and studies by consultants or client groups. A measurement system should be developed to collect data on a regular basis, and all data should be supplied to the team for regular analysis. The validity and usefulness of such information should be constantly monitored.

Step 7.   Modifying Project Plans. Realistic decisions, based on continuing team discussions of alternative approaches and data, must be made about program problems, opportunities, modifications, and priorities. For instance, would a problem be solved best through the more intensive use of technology, improved training, better supervision, or improved incentives?

Step 8.   Expecting Problems. Projects are more likely to succeed if they openly confront and then discuss potential misunderstandings, misconceptions, slippages, resource shortages, client and employee resistance, and so on. Any such problem, if unaddressed, can cause a project to fail.

Step 9.   Implementing Improvement Actions. Implementation should be phased in on a modest basis and without great fanfare. Projects that are highly touted, but then do not deliver as expected, are more likely to embarrass top management (and political supporters), with predictable consequences. Projects that adopt a low profile are less likely to threaten key actors, especially middle management and labor.

Step 10.   Evaluating and Publicizing Results. Measurable success, rather than vague claims, is important. Elected officials, the press, and citizen groups are more likely to accept claims of success if they are backed up by hard data. "Softer" feedback can then support such claims. Particularly important in providing evidence of progress are timely data that reflect cost savings, additional services, independent evaluations of service levels, client satisfaction, and reductions in waiting or processing times.

As with any other "generic recipe," this model should be modified and adapted to specific organizational contexts. Real cases will always be slightly different than the model; in some cases one or two steps might be missing because of the organizational and cultural assumptions of the situation; in other cases several steps can be combined into one. Still, because the steps of the model are analytically distinguishable, the model is useful for analyzing real organizations and programs to highlight the strengths and illuminate the weaknesses of cases under discussion.

CONCLUSION

Overall, then, the most innovative and productive public agencies do not simply execute one good program. Rather, they integrate advanced management techniques into a comprehensive approach to productivity improvement. They institutionalize productivity improvements by identifying, implementing, measuring, and rewarding major cost savings and performance enhancements in their agencies. They benchmark their efforts against similar organizations across the nation. They have a client orientation. Perhaps most important, productive programs are built on the dedication, imagination, teamwork, and diligence of public servants.

REFERENCE

Holzer, M. (1995). Building capacity for productivity improvement. In A. Halachmi & M. Holzer (Eds.), *Competent government: Theory and practice* (pp. 457–467). Burke, VA: Chatelaine.

22

Steven Cohen and William Eimicke

UNDERSTANDING AND APPLYING INNOVATION STRATEGIES IN THE PUBLIC SECTOR

In July 1997, a marvel of scientific and management innovation landed on Mars. The Pathfinder mission was a tremendous success—the result of a series of pathbreaking management innovations brought to the National Aeronautics and Space Administration (NASA) by its administrator, Daniel Goldin. One news account at the time noted: "In the past several years NASA has been quietly reinventing itself. The slow and swollen agency that grew so fat in the post-Apollo years has been painstakingly downsizing itself to something approaching the agency it was first designed to be when it was founded in the late 1950s: a crew of garage engineers cobbling spacecraft from simple parts and getting the job done both on budget and on deadline." (Kluger, 1997, p. 32).

Goldin led a major effort in strategic planning, benchmarking, Total Quality Management (TQM), and reengineering. Under his guidance, NASA totally rethought its standard operating procedures (SOPs) and approach to space travel. Goldin radically revised NASA's organizational culture. The evidence of this transformation can be found by comparing the 1976 Viking Mars missions to the 1997 Pathfinder program—two Viking spacecraft cost $3 billion in 1997 dollars, while two Pathfinder ships cost $500 million, and Pathfinder included the Sojourner rover, a two-foot-long robotic vehicle that conducted a scientific investigation of Mars—and in the fact that Goldin was one of the few senior managers from the Bush administration who held his job into the Clinton administration. Goldin infused NASA with a new sense of strategic purpose.

Goldin's use of a wide variety of management innovation techniques resulted in a new approach to space travel—one that fits within the political and budgetary parameters of the late 1990s. In our view, nothing presents the possibilities of innovation management more graphically than the accomplishments of the Pathfinder program in summer 1997. Can these lessons be applied to management issues on Earth? We think they can.

THE CONCEPT OF PUBLIC SECTOR MANAGEMENT INNOVATION

For us, public sector management innovation is best defined as *the development and implementation of new policy designs and new standard operating procedures by public organizations to address public policy problems.* It is important to emphasize that we are dealing with both the *design* and the *management* of policies and programs. Bureaucracy was created to provide stable, *preformed decisions* (to use the classic formulation of Kaufman, 1960) about specific, relatively stable phenomena and stimuli. These SOPs were designed to be longstanding and unchanging.

As the world enters the twenty-first century, societies and economies are rapidly changing in response to new technologies that have facilitated greater exchange and economic and social interdependency. This accelerated rate of change has challenged the traditional bureaucratic form of organization and thus requires the development of new methods for rapidly modifying organizational strategies and the procedures used to implement those strategies.

Several studies of successful public management innovation illustrate the nature of management change processes in the public sector. Olivia Golden (1990) studied innovation in public sector human service organizations and "the implications of innovation by groping along" (p. 219). She studied the winners of the 1986 Ford Foundation Awards program for innovation in public management and tested the use of the two models of innovation in the public sector. The *policy planning model* emphasizes innovation through creative policy design. In this framework, innovation is the task performed by policy analysts, and line bureaucrats oppose innovation as they defend their traditional SOPs. The *groping-along model* emphasizes field-level experimentation with new ideas. According to Golden, "We cannot know ahead of time what the results of our ideas will be, because the complexities of the real world cannot be anticipated and because ideas divorced from rich operational experience are so general that they are likely to be systematically wrong. Because we cannot know the results of our ideas, we need to try them out in action and learn from experience; based on that learning, we may need to modify not only our actions but also the policy idea and the original objectives" (1990, p. 226).

Mary Bryna Sanger and Martin Levin (1992) built on Golden's analysis in their study of more than twenty-five successful public sector innovations. They concluded that public management innovation is rarely characterized by revolutionary breakthroughs. Instead, it typically involves rearranging old practices in new ways. In organizational learning, rational analysis of options before implementation seems to be less useful than evaluation, and subsequent modification, of programs already under way.

Both of these studies indicate that innovative programs and effective program outcomes seem to be a function of a spirit of experimentation and a willingness to adopt and discard practices rapidly in the face of evidence about the effectiveness of those practices. Although this research does not distinguish the design of organizational routines from the design of programs and policies, we believe that these findings are applicable to both.

Successful innovation is often incremental and small scale because the factors that condition the success of innovative practices vary according to the organization's internal capacity, external environment, and goals or mission. Each organization is different and faces varied situations at particular points in time. The techniques required to promote organizational innovation must therefore be determined situationally. Furthermore, the stability of the organization's environment changes over time, requiring varied degrees of innovation. Finally, the internal social structure and the capacity of an organization to support and carry out changed SOPs will also vary. When considering the application of management change techniques, one size does not fit all.

In our own efforts to adapt TQM to specific government situations, we developed a *project-oriented* approach (Cohen and Eimicke, 1994a). This approach represents an explicit recognition that the specific shape that TQM should take varies in each and every work situation. The general principles of TQM could be taught in two or three hours, but the actual application would evolve over time in individual organizational units.

Our TQM work taught us several other things about bringing innovative practices into organizations. First, TQM in isolation was not a sufficient approach to making organizations agile and effective in rapidly changing conditions. If the organization's overall strategy was faulty, or if its basic agencywide systems were in massive disrepair—for example, a personnel system that prevented hiring and retaining quality staff—TQM would have the same effect as rearranging deck chairs on the Titanic. Through TQM, an effective practice for posting jobs or providing promotional opportunities might have been designed, but if no one got hired or promoted because the overall system was flawed, the newly designed processes would have no real impact on the organization's performance. An example of the type of system failure we refer to here might be a hiring process with so many approval steps that excellent candidates attracted through a newly redesigned posting and advertising process would take jobs with other organizations because of delays in getting hired.

Our TQM experiences started us thinking about how and when to utilize other organizational reform strategies:

- Under what conditions is imagination dry and the need to benchmark other organizational practices acute?
- When should the high organizational cost of top-down, large-scale system reengineering be accepted?
- When should an organization substitute a contractor's work for its own?
- When has the organization's environment changed sufficiently to warrant a revision of it mission, focus, and strategy?
- To what degree should team processes replace individual assignments?

THE PURPOSE OF MANAGEMENT INNOVATION

The first question that public managers face is, *What aspect of the organization are we trying to change?* The answer to this question can lead to the use of a particular innovation technique or sequence of techniques.

The first step in addressing this question involves identifying the potential arenas of organizational change. In our view there are three arenas, each calling for different organization change techniques.

1. *External:* The arena that comprises the organization's environment. Issues addressed here include the organization's mission, resource base, market niche, political support and opposition.
2. *Macro-internal:* The arena of organizational behavior dealing with large-scale, organizationwide systems and infrastructure that support the activities of individual organizational units. This includes the organization's budget, purchasing, personnel, information, security, and communication systems, as well as other similar support systems and structures.
3. *Micro-internal:* The arena of organizational behavior that takes place within individual organizational units as SOPs are developed, implemented, and analyzed. It also includes behavioral incentives or motivation and the entire realm of individual and group interpersonal relations at work.

An organization can have needs in all three arenas, and every technique we discuss in subsequent chapters can have some utility in each arena, but different techniques tend to have greater usefulness in particular arenas. For example, strategic planning is the best method for dealing with issues that appear in the external arena, reengineering is well suited for some macro-internal issues, and TQM is an excellent method for addressing issues in the micro-internal arena.

A FRAMEWORK FOR ANALYZING THE USE OF MANAGEMENT INNOVATION TOOLS

The metaphors of tool and craft are essential to understanding the process of bringing change into organizational settings. We begin with the assumption that organizational management and change is a craft, not a science; and we consciously label the innovation techniques *tools*. The effective public manager applies these tools in an iterative process to build solutions to management problems. With experience, the craftsperson notices patterns and tendencies that allow the tools to be deployed more effectively. The millionth time the carpenter places the nail on the wood, he or she knows where and when to strike the nail with maximum effect.

What conditions affect the use of innovation tools? When do we use the saw? When do we take out the drill? When do we need to hammer a nail? When do we need a strategy? When do we need to benchmark? When must we reengineer? At what point might TQM be introduced? The management craftsperson must learn to identify the proper conditions and the likely impact of a specific tool in a particular situation in a given environment.

Organizational change is a modification of the way an organization responds to specific stimuli. It includes the specific changes brought about, as well as the process by which change takes place. In other words, organizational change may result in changed organizational outputs or outcomes, or in an increased capacity to produce new outputs or outcomes. Another possible goal of organizational change is to create a more agile organization.

Managers have at their disposal a broad range of tools that can be used to bring about organizational change. They have *traditional functional tools,* such as budgets, financial control systems, and information systems. They have *human resources management tools,* such as merit reward systems, competitive hiring procedures, and affirmative action. They have *organizational structure tools,* such as reorganization or decentralization. Managers can also use the media, customers, and other external parties to change the behavior of members of the organization. We discussed these traditional tools in detail in *The New Effective Public Manager* (Cohen and Eimicke, 1995).

In addition to these tools, managers also have available the range of innovation tools: reengineering, TQM, benchmarking, team processes, strategic planning, and privatization. All of these techniques have as their aim influencing the behavior of the people who implement public programs. In the case of privatization and public and private partnerships, public managers may be trying to change the behavior of nongovernmental players. But public managers typically focus their change efforts on government employees. As they progress through the work of innovative change, it is essential to bear in mind the dependent variable in this relationship: the behavior of public implementors.

THE TOOLS

The first factor that the management innovator must consider is the nature of the tool itself: What does the technique do? What kind of organizational learning does it facilitate? How much does it cost to do? Many innovation techniques require investment in teachers or consultants. Most require investment of staff time. Some require investment in computers or communication equipment. Benchmarking frequently involves travel costs. Privatization requires substantial transaction costs if contracts are let and monitored. It is wise to project the potential costs and benefits of deploying a tool before it is utilized.

Each tool has proponents who would like people to believe that their favorite tool is the management silver bullet. We have found that each of these tools has value, but none is a cure-all. Sometimes a reengineered solution will be a disaster, destroying a functioning system within an organization and replacing it with a nonfunctioning system. At times, political conditions do not allow a government organization to engage in benchmarking. Similarly, employing TQM in an organization that has not developed a coherent strategy can result in people doing the wrong thing more effectively.

The first job of the innovator is to learn about the inherent strengths and weaknesses of the tool that derive from the tool's definition. With that understanding in place, the organizational innovator must ask some questions about the organization it-self and about its environment.

The Organization

Organizations are complex social systems built on patterns of human interaction developed over time in the performance of tasks. An innovator must learn about the organization's culture: How are things done around here? What is the informal organization? Who makes things happen? What types of change have been successfully brought about here in the past? What types of change have failed? By studying the development and demise of SOPs in specific organizations, a manager can learn about the organization's patterns and capabilities. This can help the manager to develop a feel for which tool is most appropriate for the specific changes being sought.

We deliberately use the word *feel* in this context. We are convinced that a large number of complex, interconnected variables must be understood in order to determine appropriate change strategies. Tools must be applied gently to test their effect before their use is attempted throughout an organization. In some cases the tool should never be used in certain parts of the organization.

One of the reasons that much real change is gradual, incremental, and "organic" is that its success often depends on the manager's in-depth understanding and intuitive craftlike feel for the vagaries of the organization's life. An effective change agent must either have this knowledge from personal experience or be skilled at drawing it out of others. In any event, attempting to innovate without deep organizational knowledge is like trying to repair a delicate stopwatch with a sledgehammer. Any change that occurs without an understanding of the internal social system of the organization should be treated as a lucky guess and nothing more.

The Environment

Public organizations operate in a media fishbowl and must function in a manner circumscribed by laws and regulations. Laws authorize, shape, and constrain the actions of public organizations. The ability to respond to external stimuli is modified by the political process that creates these rules. Therefore, the use of innovation tools within an organization must be sensitive to the rules governing an organization's behavior. You might find a great program idea by benchmarking an organization in another jurisdiction, and then learn that the practice is illegal in your state.

The organization's strategy is the tool most dependent on an accurate reading of the organization's environment. The goals of a public organization must be designed to elicit both political support and resources from the organization's environment. An effective strategist must understand the politics and the array of social and economic forces related to the organization's work. He or she must be able to project the likely impact of changes in the organization's goals, programs, and activities on its customers, enemies, and friends.

The organization's environment also affects the views and behaviors of those within the organization. If the economy is bad and budgets are being cut, the members or the organization may react by being scared, defensive, and resistant to change. Or they may embrace change as a survival strategy, recognizing that their best defense in a cutback environment is enhanced productivity. They may even offer to take on additional functions as a way of enhancing job security.

Management experts with a private sector orientation often see political factors as illegitimate, exogenous factors in the process of organizational change. In our view, in the case of public organizations such political factors should be conceptualized as central determinants of the ultimate parameters of oranizational change. Politics sets the boundaries for what is feasible in the public sector. To ignore that is to disregard the public in *public sector.*

THE RISKS

To bring about change in an organization a manager must be willing to gamble. The change you are hoping to bring about might not work. If you are careful, the setback will not be catastrophic. We generally suggest small steps and hedging your bets. When using an innovation tool, plan for its possible failure as well as for its possible success. Be ready with a plan B if plan A fails. Being willing to try something new need not require recklessness.

Top managers must be willing to take risks and to tolerate risk taking among middle management and staff. That means that well-conceived experiments that fail must be rewarded from time to time, and whenever possible, not punished.

APPLICATIONS OF THE INNOVATION FRAMEWORK

Our approach to these techniques as tools rather than as all-encompassing answers is designed to encourage you to develop your own analysis of where and when to apply each tool. You will need to decide whether to apply several tools in combination or in a particular sequence as part of an overall effort to bring new ways of thinking and operating into your organization.

Organizational change is not an easy process. There are no shortcuts, technological fixes, or magic bullets. You end up doing a lot of slogging through the mud because in the end you are trying to influence the behavior of people. Many people resist change because they are comfortable with how things are: "If it's not broken, why fix it?"

The contemporary world is characterized by rapid changes in technology, society, politics, communications, and culture. The pace of change is accelerating and effective organizations have little choice but to keep up.

REFERENCES

Cohen, S., and Eimicke, W. "Project-Focused Total Quality Management in the New York City Department of Parks and Recreation." *Public Administration Review,* 5(4). 1994a, 450–456.

Golden, O. "Innovation in Public Sector Human Service Programs: The Innovation by Groping Along." *Journal of Policy Analysis and Man 9,* 219–248.

Kluger, J. "Uncovering the Secrets of Mars." *Time,* July 14, 1997, pp. 27

Sanger, M. B., and Levin, M. A. "Using Old Stuff in New Ways: Innovation as a Case of Evolutionary Tinkering." *Journal of Policy Analysis and Management,* 1992, *11*(1), 88–115.

23

Arie Halachmi and Marc Holzer

TOWARDS A COMPETITIVE PUBLIC ADMINISTRATION

The thesis of this article is that, due to environmental forces (e.g. changes in information technology or the collapse of geopolitical institutions that mitigated against free-market competition in the European theater), public agencies in the United States will be forced to assume a more competitive posture vis à vis other public and private providers of services. The article suggests that the public is going to demand such a stance to preserve the advantages of dealing with a government agency while insisting on better efficiency through competition. The emergence of a competitive public sector, one consisting of government agencies that vie for contracts from other agencies by competing with private (for-profit and non-profit) as well as other public providers is a real possibility. Prospects for such developments will increase in the USA as the European Community creates the necessary conditions for competition to provide selected services (e.g. data processing, programming or public transportation) to its member countries. Specifically, current moves to standardize economic and employment policies, tax codes and other related policies across the board will encourage contracting out some (or parts) of a governmental function to an agency of another member of the Community. In the United States, development in this direction will challenge the longstanding policy of the Federal government to rely on the private sector for the provision of commercial goods and services so that government would not compete with private industry (Naff, 1991: 24).

POLITICS AND THE IMPERFECT WORLD OF PRIVATIZATION

Halachmi points out that 'the debate about the merit of privatization has to do with ideology and political considerations as much as it has to do with questions of effectiveness, efficiency and equity in the delivery of services' (Halachmi, 1989: 625). Proponents of privatization like Savas (1987) argue that private enterprise should replace government whenever possible for pragmatic consideration (e.g. privatization leads to more cost effective public services). Many supporters of privatization embrace the position of the public-choice school of thinking that public agencies are inherently inefficient because they face no competition (Rehfuss, 1991: 239). According to

Savas (1992: 81), 'constitution, achieved by prudent privatization, is the key to improving the productivity of public agencies, more broadly, of public programs and public services.' Other supporters of privatization point out that there are no guards against over-production by government because budgets and staffing levels of agencies are used for projecting images of power and influence rather than for satisfying consumers' demands for services (Wolf, 1979; Niskanen, 1971). Other arguments in favor of using non-governmental providers echo ideological positions (e.g. government is too intrusive; the less government the better: business is inherently more efficient than government) that promote the more efficient use of national resources by private agencies or urge the reform of society through voluntarism on the level of family, church, neighborhood and community (Savas, 1987: 5). According to Jennings (1986), supporters of privatization believe that government is doing more than it should or can handle, that government cannot act effectively or efficiently, that public officials and agencies are not sufficiently responsive and that government makes excessive resource demands that threaten economic growth and diminish individual economic well being. In contrast, some detractors of privatization argue that the practice has a potential for impacting negatively on career public employees: eroding hard-won merit systems; harming or interrupting service quality through work stoppages; creaming practices; losing tax revenues because of private-sector service-delivery incentives; and encouraging bankruptcies, fraud and corruption (Morgan and England, 1988). Others are concerned about the erosion of constitutional protections (Sullivan, 1987), the impact on local government budgets, regressive local taxes and insufficient social services for the poor (Oates and Schwab, 1991: 127).

Typically, articles on privatization do not address some basic realities, namely:

1. that government often gets involved because of shortcomings with private arrangements and private markets or because of ideological reasons that have to do with the welfare of citizens (Graham and Hays, 1986: 9–13; Darr, 1987: 43; Naff, 1991: 24);
2. that privatization suggests competition but may not facilitate or sustain it (National Academy of Public Administration, 1989; Darr, 1987: 48);
3. that competition may lead to waste of resources (Thayer, 1987); or
4. that privatization and contracting out may not be synonymous.

From the public administrator's point of view, some of these issues manifest themselves in connection with the following three issues:

How can short- and long-term liabilities be balanced?
Privatization is promoted as a way to reduce the number of public employees and, thus, the cost of government operations (Brudney, 1987). However, the use of a proxy does not relieve government of its responsibility under the law to ensure the availability of services, such as water treatment or corrections. Thus, it is not always true that using a private contractor results in net savings to government, service recipients or the tax payer. For example, contracting out the management of water treatment or correction facilitates does not absolve state and local authorities from

their responsibility or liability if something goes wrong. The direct and indirect costs for managing such contracts may deprive a local authority of some of the fiscal savings in the short run without shielding it from various legal and fiscal liabilities in the long run. A recent evaluation of the out-sourcing of garbage collection for a small city in the South East illustrates the point. The official purpose of the contract was to reduce direct costs for salaries, benefits and the city's liability for workers' compensation claims for lower-back injuries. The study computed the immediate savings to the city after the first year. However, the evaluation also pointed out that the city acquired a possible liability and had no way to estimate or plan for it in advance. The city, it was found, could not escape its workers' compensation liability if the contractor defaulted on its obligations as an employer of individuals assigned to work alongside city employees (Twilla, 1991).

How to reduce the sunk cost

When a government agency stops delivering a service, it generates a sunk cost to the public. One part of the cost results from the liquidation of tangible assets such as buildings, equipment and inventories. Another part of the sunk cost results from lost intangibles, such as special expertise and common but valuable know-how. Governments have several options for reducing the tangible part of the sunk cost, and these can produce a net saving to the public in the short term. Reducing the sunk cost to the public for the intangibles of a government service is not as simple. As governments divest themselves of services, they generate the conditions that allow individuals trained at the public expense to offer their government experience to private industry, perhaps becoming entrepreneurs themselves. In other words, governments pursuing privatization may deprive their citizens of a fair return on their past investment in the formal or on-the-job training of employees.

The difficulty of asserting a clear-cut dichotomy between efficient and inefficient organizations (or employees) solely on the basis of ownership was illustrated in a comparative study of urban transit systems. According to Perry and Babitsky (1986), privately owned and managed transit systems were found to perform significantly better, as measured by output per dollar, than four other types of organizations. However, the same study shows that the efficiency of contract-managed systems is no better than those publicly managed. Perry and Babitsky go on to suggest that 'forces in the environments of private organizations encourage efficiency, and analogous forces for public organizations discourage efficiency' (1986: 61). They support this possible interpretation of their findings by pointing out that 'costs are held down by private systems by running older, possibly more accident-prone buses for longer periods of time' (Perry and Babitsky, 1986: 63).

Business practices, such as the ones used by the private transportation system in this study, may not be a viable option for a public transportation system. Public managers cannot afford an audit finding that they take chances with the safety of the public, nor can they risk being the subject of letters to the editor or editorials on the looks or cleanliness of their aging fleet. Though private business may also want to avoid negative images, concern for sales figures and the bottom line is a potent pressure not properly relevant to or as clearly measured by the public manager. Commenting on such contrasting approaches, one observer points out that 'the private sector obtains cost advantages by purchasing more effective equipment better suited to perform specific tasks. Public Agencies . . . purchase equipment to match the budget' (Darr, 1987: 47).

For public managers, the need to anticipate public opinion (e.g. 'buy American') is a constraint as much as the politics involving the development and the execution of an agency's programs. Expressions such as 'to get what you want you have to ask for more' or 'what you do not spend this year will reduce your budget for next year' depict some scenarios typical of the political implementation process in government. Both expressions sum up one of the reasons why public administrators end up making decisions on the basis of a criterion that has to do with the bureaucratic context rather than with the substance of the issue at stake. Indeed, the finding of Perry and Babitsky (1986) support the thesis that efficiency is not solely a function of the legal provision under which an organizational entity operates or the framework for the relationships between its managers and its employees. Efficiency, as they suggest, may have to do more with the organizational context, i.e. with the different environmental forces at work in public and private organizations. Thus, as will be pointed out later, changing the nature of these forces may affect the performance of both private and public agencies.

Public accountability versus contractual obligations

Privatization implies that public accountability for the quality of the service is replaced by a contractual relationship. Such relationships are established when a user becomes eligible (or pays a provider) for a service. Such a relationship moves issues of government accountability from the ballot box to the courthouse. It replaces the democratic process that implies responsiveness to emerging need with a legal competence that jealously monitors the cost of existing services. In the process, considerations of public will and public welfare may be displaced as lawyers put more emphasis on the integrity of the contract, as a legal instrument, than on the essence of the service(s) at stake. Contracts are appropriate for dealing with commercial transactions but may not be the optimal instrument for dealing with issues involving the provision of vital public goods. In such cases the public expects the spirit, not just the letter of the 'contract', to be used for reference. The built-in provision for an appeal addresses this expectation in the public sector. Contractual relations with private providers, on the other hand, may serve the desire for greater managerial competence and net profit at the expense of other cherished public values such as fairness or social justice (Morgan and England, 1988: 984).

The problem, as some writers see it, is not with the paring of expenses form the public budget but with the abdication of the government's responsibility for the welfare of its citizens (Abramovitz, 1986; Darr, 1987: 47). To use the terminology that was offered by Brudney (1987), provision (i.e. public policy-making) can be separated from production of services. Once separated, however, the actual determination of the policy is made by the provider and not by the official that contracted out the service. The contractor assumes the policy-making capacity to become the real policy-maker, like one of Lipsky's (1980) 'street level bureaucrats'. The 'what, how and when' of the service are determined by their implications for the bottom line rather than the public welfare. We are back again to the looming specter of the 'hollow state' with agencies out-sourcing the provisions of the service they are expected to administer under the law.

The attractiveness of a 'hollow state' should be weighed against the odds that an agency that contracts out or provides no direct services at all may, over time, lose the expertise it once brought to policy issues (Rehfuss, 1991: 242). A case in point is the use of GEO\Resource Consultants Inc. to operate a Superfund hotline. Answering questions from government agencies, industry and the public, the contractor ends up interpreting federal statutes on behalf of the Environmental Protection Agency (EPA) (Goldstein, 1990: 31), thus becoming the actual policy-maker. By out-sourcing the service, the EPA became a little closer to the 'hollow corporation' model but in the process lost its own input into the policy-making process.

Dahl and Glassman (1991) suggest a topology of privatization. The topology uses a continuum to depict the degree to which essential elements of a public agency's mission are contracted to private firms. Figure 23.1 describes the way they envision their topology.

It is not hard to see, looking at this topology, that the move toward the right end of the continuum, i.e. toward 'contracting aspects of mission determination', establishes a change in policy by departing from the 'old' practices rather than using an alternative means for achieving the same end. To be sure, carrying court decisions by the use of private facilities has the potential of reversing the expectation that if a service is an important one it should be provided by government. Ironically, this expectation was generated when services such as elementary education, delivery of mail, fire protection or mass transportation were shifted from private to public hands. The purpose of the shift was to ensure minimum quality, the dependability and affordability of the services that were critical to the welfare of the community.

The point here is that as government reduces its direct involvement in various aspects of service delivery, it relinquishes, willingly or not, its public policy making duties. Allowing private entrepreneurs to have a greater say about how services should be provided is not much different from allowing business interests to decide what should be provided, a procedure that can stifle rather than encourage competition.

Since government is the sole consumer of many goods and services, for example those involved with the space program, reliance on a single private vendor may increase costs and result in inherent inefficiencies or corruption and waste (Morgan and England, 1988: 979). As pointed out by Darr (1987: 48), 'in many cases the service providers were created in response to the state's need for services. They were private, but not really private because their only client was the commonwealth. That doesn't create competition if the state is the sole service purchaser.' For our purposes here, the implication is that the option of privatization (which excludes contracting out to other public agencies) is not necessarily to be accepted as a preferred strategy for productivity improvement.

Elected officials should also be aware that contracting out to reduce taxes and attract prospective businesses may have predictable negative consequences. According to Fosler (1991), the increasing economic importance of state and local government services has tended to blur the lines and conceptual distinctions between the economic roles of the public and private sectors. In the conventional model, the private sector, for all intents and purposes, is the economy. Government's role is limited to interventions to correct market failures and to provide a limited menu of public goods. The

FIGURE 23.1   *Degrees of Public-Sector Contracting*

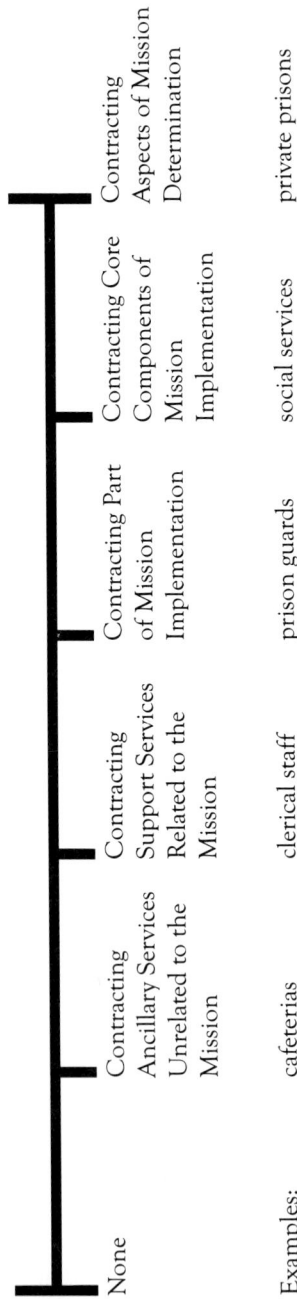

new strategies conceive of a state or local jurisdiction as a far more complex unit of production. Such a conception not only accepts the blurred line between public and private sectors but also views the relationship between the two sectors less as a set of distinct responsibilities—sometimes supportive sometimes antagonistic—and more as a web of interdependent and mutually reinforcing functions (Fosler, 1991: 249). Viewed in this way, it is not important who provides the service, government or a private contractor, as long as the service is available to the community. By privatizing and leaving the provision of services to the forces of the free market, government reduces the certainty of their availability. This, in turn, may make a given locality a less desirable place for living or for business. The State of Tennessee, for example, has learned, albeit too late for influencing an important federal decision, that leaving matters to the forces of the free market, or assuming that private entrepreneurs are present where government is absent, can be an expensive proposition. Tennessee officials discovered after losing the atom smasher project to Texas in 1988 that one of the reasons for the decision had to do with the quality of the education system. Thus the alleged savings to Tennesseans through lower taxes and little government involvement in the direct provision of services in areas such public education, the arts and other public goods produced some unexpected costs when the state lost this important project. Tennessee can only speculate on the number of other endeavors it lost to other states that had higher taxes but offered more or better public services to prospective employers.

TOWARD A COMPETITIVE PUBLIC ADMINISTRATION

In the private sector, being competitive means being able to match or surpass the performance of a rival in a given market. Competitiveness in the public sector implies, therefore, the ability of an agency to meet the level of performance of other providers in a given market. Such providers may come from the private sector and operate a service for (or not for) profit. However, from an economic or societal point of view, there is no reason to rule out providers from the public sector. Indeed, if competition implies greater choices, elected officials and the public are likely to have more alternatives to choose from by cultivating public-sector options. These options would not only supplement those that are available from the private sector but would prevent the emergence of either public or private monopolies.

For a government agency, the universe of alternative providers consists of private contractors and vendors from the public sector. The latter may be counterpart units of other government entities with capacity to spare. Such government entities may not be able to reduce the spare capacity without loss to their own productivity due to technical, financial or legal reasons. These agencies may lease out their excess capacities to offset some of the fixed costs of maintaining the full capacity needed for carrying out their primary mission. In theory, it means that the Government Printing Office could compete with private and other public printing services (e.g. a state university's print shop) for the contract to print the telephone directory. In fact, local governments have practiced this principle for many years. The practice allows one local government to get from another services such as fire or police protection, garbage collection, solid waste disposal, library services, high-school enrollment privileges, cemetery space and other public services at a fraction of the cost of maintaining its own in-house capacity. In many cases, it is not difficult to calculate the costs and benefits of securing such services from another public agency. Once the calculation model is established, comparisons can be made among the alternatives—another public agency, a private vendor or an in-house solution. A widespread practice among school districts is to offer their school buses for charter, during the summer or after hours, to private groups on an hourly or daily basis. In many cases this practice involves direct competition with commercial enterprises. Even more significant is the trend for public universities to cancel summer sessions that do not generate enough revenue in order to sublet university facilities to groups and individuals. The trend illustrates not only the existence, but the public's willingness to accept competition between public and private entities in certain markets.

The attractiveness of a competitive public agency that manages to secure a service contract from another government entity is twofold. First, such a contract may allow the bidding agency to spread the fixed cost over a larger number of service recipients, thus reducing its relative weight to each recipient. This benefits, in particular, service recipients in the base territory (or jurisdiction) of the contracted government entity. Service recipients outside that base would not have to shoulder part of the fixed costs if a cheaper service could be obtained from other public or private sources. Second, concerns about vendor accountability, ethics, the quality of service and maintaining the proper balance of profit motivation with compassion could be put to rest. That is because complaints from outside the base territory/jurisdiction of a public vendor are still likely to have political ramifications for elected or appointed officials of the contracted agency. Since agencies are more concerned about media reports and/or public hearings than private corporations, they are likely to be more responsive to all service recipients than a private provider. It would not take long for the managers and employees of a controversial agency to realize that failing to meet service demands in terms of efficiency, effectiveness or consumer satisfaction may result in the out-sourcing of their own operation.

THE POSSIBLE NEW FACES OF PUBLIC-SECTOR COMPETITION

Using market prices to compare various options is not unusual. In Phoenix the five garbage collection districts are divided among two competing private contractors and city forces. The service contract for each district is awarded in a competitive bid. The city claims that after losing four or five solid waste bids, it has won the last two (Rehfuss, 1991: 224).

The city of Phoenix has not seen bids from outside contractors (public or private) with capacity to spare. A spare capacity results when a contractor is required by contractual obligation to maintain a reserve capacity as a safety margin for meeting peak hour demand for a given service, e.g. snow removal. Or it may be the result of technical characteristics of the machinery used for providing the service. To cover some of the fixed costs and recover their investment in machines or personnel, contractors may be willing to mobilize the spare capacity and sell it for the variable cost plus a fraction of the fixed cost. Clients who are willing to accept that their demand for service is a second priority may get the service even below cost. This practice is common among local governments that keep their prisoners in the jailhouse of other jurisdictions. The local authority that out-sources the housing of prisoners saves the cost of building, rebuilding or planning a fully fledged jail to meet a sporadic demand for such a service. The authority may have such agreements with several other localities. This way, if there is no vacancy in one jail they can take a prisoner to the jail of yet another locality. When a prisoner is brought in, the host jail recovers all of the variable cost and some of the fixed cost by using the idle capacity. Because of the fixed cost, the host facility is better off even when it charges the other local authority less than the true (variable plus fixed) cost to keep its own prisoners.

There is every reason to assume that bids involving the mobilization of idle capacity at or even below cost will be common in the not so distant future. Against this backdrop, is it inconceivable to think about out-sourcing various services in one country to public or private contractors from another country?

Maintaining a public-sector option when an agency engages the service of a private-sector contractor is not a new idea. In many instances nervous public administrators insist that they must retain a residual capacity to move in and take over if and when the commercial provider fails to perform as expected. As an executive of a city-owned public utility explained to us, he could not take the chance of not having a mechanic on hand when there was a need to restore service in the middle of the night in severe weather conditions. Indeed, the alternative to having such a mechanic on the payroll just for emergency situations was to request such support from other units of government. The problem with this option, as that executive saw it, was that under such extreme weather conditions other units of government may need to use such resources themselves and may not be able to help. The problem could be aggravated further if other government units in the region contract out the same service. Thus, even though the said utility contracted out the maintenance function, some in-house capacity would be retained for dealing with emergency situations. As this executive saw it, the public is not going to accept the explanation that a contractor failed to deliver. He thought that it was bad politics to be left with such an excuse as the only responsive option. The implication is clear: if governments are to retain the residual capacity to respond when private contractors fail to deliver, why not develop this capacity as a full-blown alternative?

Another alternative for the use of public employees in a competitive manner involves the use of ad-hocracy. According to Halachmi (1989), the use of matrix organizations and project management techniques allows the configuration of ad hoc work groups to carry out many of the tasks government is expected to perform. Such work groups possess the necessary skills for performing a specific task during a given period of time. The combination of skills, the size of the group, and many other aspects of its performance can be tailored to meet a given target. The resulting flexibility, like that enjoyed by similar groups in the private sector, is likely to yield the same levels of performance. Halachmi's concept of ad-hocracy replaces the guarantee of civil service protection with an option for a career in the public sector through ad hoc contractual arrangements. Such arrangements may provide for some civil service like conditions of employment (e.g. handling of grievances) but not for others (e.g. a ceiling on compensation). A public-sector career without civil service status may ensue from a series of consecutive ad hoc assignments to task-specific working groups. Each assignment is likely to result from the reputation and performance of the individual (and/or the performance of their group) on the previous assignment (Halachmi, 1989: 646).

Another approach to retaining a public-sector capacity to provide services that are usually obtained from the private sector is the rediscovery of governmental corporations. The decision of the IRS to establish a non-profit organization that would assist in the agency's massive tax-system modernization is a case in point. The purpose of the new organization is to facilitate productivity improvement without developing an undesired dependency on outside sources (Anthes, 1991a). The Federally Funded Research and Development Center (FFRDC) will specialize in computer/Management Information System related issues, have a staff of thirty to ninety employees, and will operate for five years with a renewable option. The original proposal for the establishment of the Center prohibits it from performing services for any government agency other than the IRS. However, its establishment signals a new era in the relationship between government and those private vendors that enjoy a monopolistic status as a sole source for specialized services.

Government corporations with their own sources of revenue are likely to enjoy greater flexibility in mobilizing resources for the accomplishment of a given task. Being free of some of the constraints that reduce the ability of regular government agencies, they can reach private-sector-like efficiencies. If allowed to solicit contracts from other units of government, the use of government corporations can facilitate a competitive spirit that does not involve relinquishing accountability or policy-making roles. The availability of alternatives in the private sector may force government corporations to remain highly efficient in order to receive service contracts from other agencies and generate revenues for survival. The competition of government-owned and private airlines for government contracts in some European countries is a case in point.

NEEDED RESEARCH

At this time we do not have a theory for a competitive public administration or models to describe and prescribe the behavior of clients and providers in various markets where government agencies participate. In order to assess the competitive potential of government agencies we need a better understanding of the dynamics and behavior of public markets—the markets where government, not-for-profit and private organizations offer their services for a fee. Some of the questions that need to be researched are as follows:

1. What happens when a government agency provides services in an area that is under the jurisdiction of another government. Is there a difference between the case when the service is provided to another agency and the case where the service is provided directly to the public?

Contracting out aspects of the service to other government agencies and giving citizens a choice between private or public providers represent different competitive situations. At this time we do not have enough data to assess the relative advantage of either approach under various circumstances.

A related question has to do with the relative advantages of contracting out the management of a service for an adjacent unit of government versus the creation of a new special district. The ability of one water/sewer system to use slack capacity for managing an adjacent water/sewer system does not imply that the creation of a unified service district will be as beneficial to residents of either locality. There is reason to believe that in the past the attractiveness of special districts had to do with the notion that it was inconceivable to think about a public or private contractor as a common provider of the same service for several government units in a given geographical area.

2. What are the implications of new information technology? The use of common data banks, remote processing and networking allows job sharing. A system which monitors general trends, like the one used by Employment Security agencies in the USA to monitor the labor market, may consist of two components. One component may be operated by one government for the benefit of several other government units. This component may include the development of models and all analytical work. The other component involves the inputting of data and keying in the requests for specific reports. Centralization of selected functions and cost sharing on the basis of a formula that takes into consideration the complexity or the volume of the service that is provided to each 'customer' can reduce the operational cost to each government unit. At the same time such arrangements may facilitate the hiring and retention of highly qualified personnel that none of the participating governments can attract or afford should they try to do it in a unilateral fashion.

3. One important set of research questions involves the assessment of the relative advantages of alternative organizational solutions. Such alternatives may include, for example, the creation of a government corporation or an authority that is run jointly by several government entities. Or, in the absence of a dedicated unit, such as a public authority, the out-sourcing of all or part of the service an agency is expected to provide or produce to other government entities. Under what conditions would the creation of a special district or special authority to provide a needed service to the residents of several localities constitute a preferred solution? And, when should officials seek an external provider rather than foster a pact with other government entities?

4. Out-sourcing of services in the public sector goes beyond the mere provision of a service. Whenever a service is contracted out there are implications due to the political economy of data sharing. Unlike the sharing of an airport or a snow plough, sharing a database can give one party of a service contract an advantage over the other. At a time when state and local authorities are competing with each other to attract investments and jobs, a shared data base has a value that is independent of the one that is derived from the need to implement existing policies.

The research questions about this issue need to be examined in connection with the question about the relative advantage of creating a joint pact or contracting the service out. Being part of an intergovernmental pact (e.g. one that involves the collection and analysis of data for an area that is larger than the one under the jurisdiction of any one government) gives each member of the pact an advantage over other units of governments that are not members of the same or similar pacts. The advantage is both operational and functional. It gives each member a functional capacity that may not be feasible otherwise at an affordable cost. Yet government units that could not provide certain services without being a member of the pact (e.g. a joint authority or a government corporation) can now enter other markets as competitors. As governments race each other to attract new investments, a joint effort with another entity to increase efficiency in the short run may be at the cost of losing such investments. The loss of new investments to governments that could provide the service, though inefficiently, before the pact may be greater than the gains from reducing the cost or improving the quality of the service under the new 'intergovernmental' pact.

5. Even though governments may privatize the provision of certain services they may have to retain some capacity to move in and resume the provision of the service under a variety of emergency conditions. Such conditions range from situations where the private vendor unexpectedly defaults or under emergency situations when it is impossible for a non-governmental entity to carry out its mission, e.g. to collect the garbage in an area where two gangs fight each other for control. The cost of maintaining the residual capacity and the need to utilize and test this capacity from time to time to ensure its readiness justifies the involvement of a government entity in the provision of the service on a small scale. The research question here involves the development of models for determining the optimal size of the residual capacity. In other words: what is the capacity that should be retained for being able to respond to various contingencies and can the cost of maintaining this capacity be minimized?

6. What must be done to ensure that government corporations are more responsive than private corporations whose stocks are being held by the public. Government corporations can be unresponsive and unaccountable.

Government corporations are supposed to retain the public interest and to hold it above the profit motive. Yet, as illustrated by the case of NES, government corporations can become less responsive than private ones because they are shielded from the effects of some market forces. The research question here is how to balance the need for responsibility and accountability with the need to ensure immunity from undue political pressures. To be competitive, public agencies should be free from the constraints of parochial considerations. However at the same time they should be responsive to the wishes the public express directly or through its elected officials. The need to balance short- and long-term considerations (i.e. the general will and the general welfare) creates a special problem in the case of public agencies that need to compete with other agencies or private entities.

Private organizations that opt to be responsive and give more weight to short-term considerations over long-range ones may have to go out of business. The cost, in real terms, for a public entity may be prohibitive. Yet, giving too much attention to the long-run implications of alternative options for action may foster a public feeling that a given public agency is unaccountable.

REFERENCES

Abramovitz, M. (1986) 'The Privatization of the Welfare State: A Review'. *Social Work* 31 (July/Aug): 257–64.

Anthes, G. H. (1991a) 'IRS Proposal Worries Governmental Bidders', *Computerworld* (19 August): 8.

Anthes, G. H. (1991b) 'Offshore Software Crews Save Labor Costs', *Computerworld* (28 October): 89.

Brudney, J. L. (1987) 'Coproduction and Privatization: Exploring the Relationship and Its Implications', *Journal of Voluntary Action Research* 16(3): 11–21.

Cobb, R. W. and Elder, C. D. (1975) *Participation in American Politics*. Baltimore: The Johns Hopkins University Press.

Dahl, J. G. And Glassman, A. M. (1991) 'Public Sector Contracting: The Next Growth Industry for Organization Development?', *Public Administration Quarterly* 14(4): 483–97.

Darr, T. B. (1987) 'Pondering Privatization May Be Good for Your Government', *Governing* 1(2): 42–50.

Fosler, S. R. (1991) 'Does Economic Theory Capture the Effects of New and Traditional State Policies on Economic Development?', in D. A. Kanyon and J. Kincaid (eds) *Competition Among States and Local Governments*, pp. 247–58. Washington, DC: The Urban Institute.

Goldstein, M. L. (1990) 'The Shadow Government', *Government Executive* 22(5): 30–1, 34, 36–7, 56–7.

Graham, C. B. And Hays, S. W. (1986) *Managing the Public Organization*. Washington, DC: CQ Press.

Halachmi, A. (1989) 'Ad-hocracy and the Future of the Civil Service', *International Journal of Public Administration* 12(4): 617–50.

Jennings, E. T. (1986) 'Public Choice and the Privatization of Government: Implications for Public Administration', in J. S. Ott et al. (eds) *Public Management: The Essential Readings*, pp. 113–29. Chicago: Lyceum Books.

Lipsky, M. (1980) *Street Level Bureaucrats*. New York: Russell Sage.

Morgan, D. R. And England, R. E. (1988) 'The Two Faces of Privatization', *Public Administration Review* 48(6): 483–97.

Naff, K. C. (1991) 'Labor-Management Relations and Privatization: A Federal Perspective', *Public Administration Review* 51(1): 23–9.

National Academy of Management (1989) *Privatization: The Challenge to Public Management*, Report No. 89.04. Washington, DC: National Academy of Management.

Niskanen, W. (1971) *Bureaucracy and Representative Government*. Chicago: Aldine-Atherton.

Oates, W. E. and Schwab, R. M. (1991) 'The Allocative and Distributive Implications of Local Fiscal Competition', in D. A. Kanyon and J. Kincaid (eds) *Competition Among States and Local Governments*, pp. 127–45. Washington, DC: The Urban Institute.

Perry, J. L. And Babitsky, T. T. (1986) 'Comparative Performance in Urban Bus Transit: Assessing Privatization Strategies', *Public Administration Review* 46(1): 57–66.

Rehfuss, J. (1991) 'A Leaner, Tougher Public Management? Public Agency Competition with Private Contractors', *Public Administration Quarterly* 51(2): 239–52.

Savas, E. S. (1987) *Privatization: The Key to Better Government.* Chatham, NJ: Chatham House.

Savas, E. S. (1992) 'Privatization and Productivity', in M. Holzer (ed.) *Handbook of Public Productivity*, pp. 79–98. New York: Marcel Dekker.

Stenberg, C. W. (1985) 'States under the Spotlight: An Intergovernmental View', *Public Administration Review* 45(2): 319–26.

Stenberg, C. W. (1991) 'Preliminary Results of Past Presidents' Survey', memorandum to the president and members of the national council of ASPA, Washington, DC.

Sullivan, H. J. (1987) 'Privatization of Public Services: A Growing Threat to Constitutional Rights', *Public Administration Review* 47(6): 461–7.

Thayer, F. C. (1987) 'Privatization, Carnage, Chaos and Corruption', in J. S. Ott et al. (eds) *Public Management: The Essential Readings*, pp. 154–68. Chicago: Lyceum Books.

Twilla, G. T. (1991) 'Out Sourcing Services: An Evaluation of a Contract Employee Program', unpublished seminar paper. Institute of Government at Tennessee State University, Nashville.

Wolf, C. (1979) 'A Theory of Nonmarket Failure', *Public Interest* 55: 114–33.

Wysocki, B., Jr (1991) 'American Firms Send Office Work Abroad to Use Cheaper Labor', *The Wall Street Journal* (14 August): 1.

STRATEGIC PLANNING AND MANAGEMENT IN PUBLIC ADMINISTRATION

9

Strategic management is an approach to managing an organization that emphasizes long-term thinking and, as the term states, managing "strategically" instead of reactively or intuitively. It also differs in the public sector context from approaches to public administration that emphasize the importance of carrying out legislative obligations with only limited regard for strategic issues.

Strategic planning is the all-important first step in strategic management. Strategic plans identify the effects of current decisions on future operations.[1] Because strategic planning is comprehensive in its scope and approach, the processes used to develop strategic plans usually involve a wide array of insiders and outsiders such as, for example, members of legislative committees, clients, public interest groups, and public administrators from other jurisdictions and levels of government.

Strategic planning and *strategic management* both imply the anticipation of future trends and events, and developing comprehensive, proactive approaches for influencing the environment or coping with an environment that will change, often quite unpredictably. Thus, *strategic planning* is a holistic, long-term, direction-setting process for organizations. *Strategic management* is the collection of management techniques, tools, and approaches that are used to turn a strategic plan into reality. Strategic management is effective, coordinated action.

BRIEF HISTORY OF STRATEGIC MANAGEMENT

Strategic management became a "household term" in corporate America in the 1970s. One of the earliest statements of the strategic management concept was in H. Igor Ansoff's 1972 article, "The Concept of Strategic Management." Ansoff noted that managers should use strategic planning and strategic management approaches to guide their organizations creatively toward a discontinuous and turbulent future.[2] Several large corporations that were early adopters of strategic management include General Electric and Lockheed Aircraft. Large corporations have particular need to re-position their businesses periodically on the basis of strategic thinking.

Strategic management has been linked closely with business policy and strategic marketing, both in practice and in most MBA programs. Corporations that think and act strategically are more likely to prosper and survive; those that cannot are likely to be overtaken by more dynamic corporations or left with shrinking markets and growing losses. Tombstones in the grave-yards of corporate America provide numerous examples that support this belief.

EVOLUTION OF STRATEGIC PLANNING AND MANAGEMENT IN THE PUBLIC SECTOR

Although President Johnson's "Planning, Programming & Budgeting System"[3] (PPBS), a budgeting approach that Johnson mandated all U.S. government agencies to begin using in 1968, had some similarities to strategic management, PPBS and strategic management are quite different. The two approaches are similar in that they focus on rational planning, defining the objectives of programs, and measuring the attainment of objectives through performance indicators. However PPBS was not as comprehensive or as sophisticated as strategic management, and it never evolved into strategic management. Instead, strategic management in the public sector mostly resulted from the transfer of ideas from the private sector in the 1970s and 1980s. By the mid-1980s, it had become common to see strategic management concepts being used in the public sector, especially in city government and larger nonprofit organizations.

Publication of the first edition of John Bryson's book, *Strategic Management for Public and Nonprofit Organizations* in 1988,[4] was an important milestone for strategic management in government.[5] The appearance of publications such as Bryson's and Paul Nutt and Robert Backoff's 1987 article, "A Strategic Management Process for Public and Third Sector Organizations," [6] coincided with the growing popularity of *managerialism* and *the new public management* in the second half of the 1980s. (See Chapters 4 and 8.) Strategic management thus developed into a "hot item" in the public sector during the last decade of the century.

CHARACTERISTICS OF STRATEGIC PLANNING AND MANAGEMENT

The pursuit of organizational purpose is the core concept of *strategic management.* Typical activities used in strategic management include:

- The identification and articulation of a *vision* and longer term *objectives* that define what the organization wishes to achieve, both in general and in specifics;
- the adoption of a time frame or *planning horizon* within which these objectives are to be achieved;
- a systematic analysis of the organization's current *capabilities*—strengths and weaknesses—to ascertain what capabilities it must add or develop in order to achieve its objectives;
- an assessment of current and emerging *environmental factors* that will affect its path to the achievement of its objectives;
- the identification of alternative strategies and selection of a preferred *strategy* for achieving the objectives; and
- the *integration of organizational efforts* around this strategy.

As Henry Mintzberg has pointed out, "one single set of concepts underlies virtually all the proposals to formalize the process of strategy formation"[7]— comparisons between the organization's internal strengths and weaknesses *and* the threats and opportunities that exist (or may exist soon) in its external environment.

APPLYING STRATEGIC PLANNING AND MANAGEMENT IN PUBLIC ORGANIZATIONS

Strategic management in the public sector is necessarily a more open and political process than its private sector equivalent. Unlike executives in most private corporations, public administrators cannot conduct the strategic management process in secret.[8] Instead, most public organizations are legally and morally required to develop and implement their strategies "out in the sunlight" of public oversight. In addition, public sector strategic management must be consistent and compatible with the policy programs of elected officials. Nancy Roberts[9] has summarized the difficulties of using strategic management in public agencies: bureau managers must share their power; operate in a political rather than a rational environment; operate with less autonomy than their private sector counterparts and thus face a potentially complex and difficult environment for strategic decision making.

Not all public sector organizations pose equally serious challenges for strategic management. Clearly, the highly charged politics of departmental administration in Washington, DC is a difficult setting for managing strategically. By contrast, a small, self-contained, self-funded organization or special district that has a degree of autonomy, independence, and clearly defined goals, will find the strategic management task more straightforward. It is not surprising, therefore, that strategic management has been used extensively in nonprofit organizations, local government departments, and in the health care industry.

ADAPTING TO THE LIMITATIONS OF STRATEGIC PLANNING AND MANAGEMENT

Early strategic management efforts usually started with the development of voluminous "strategic plans." Although the task of producing such plans often took considerable effort, they could be very worthwhile. Strategic planning requires an organization to take stock of its position and to articulate its goals, options, responses to stakeholder needs, and chosen directions. Every organization should rethink its strengths, weaknesses, opportunities and threats and develop conscious strategies periodically. The strategic planning process, however, can become an end in itself, causing considerable effort and resources to be used for the production of thick documents that are read by no one.

Public agencies can avoid some of the commonly encountered problems or "fallacies" associated with strategic planning and management by using three approaches. First, distinguish between strategic management and strategic planning. As Mintzberg observed, it is possible to think and manage strategically without having strategic planners or a strategic plan. The problems of the weighty plan, read and acted on by nobody, is overcome in this way. So too are the fallacies of formalization and pre-determination. The manager thinks strategically, and acts strategically, but is not dominated by planners nor encumbered by a formal strategic planning process.[10] Richard David Hames has described this process as 'strategic navigation'.[11]

Second, if strategic planning and management would be too burdensome for an organization, instead use "business planning," a planning process that uses plans and targets, but the plans are less weighty, the targets more short term, and the process less formal than strategic planning. Public organizations have turned to business planning for two primary reasons. For some organizations, the speed of change in the social, political, economic, or technological environment make it unable to predict future conditions with enough confidence to permit useful strategic planning. Other agencies have decided they could not afford to engage in strategic planning and have divided themselves into smaller, "business unit structures" to develop tight, highly focused, shorter term plans. These "business plans" may add together to form a comprehensive plan for the agency—or they may not. Thus, business planning is a shorter term, more pragmatic approach to planning that is suited to an age of very rapid technological and social change, where comprehensiveness and a longer term planning horizon preclude the use of strategic planning.

The third approach is a reassertion of traditional incrementalist skepticism about "excessive planning" in government. Charles Lindblom's article "The Science of Muddling Through" (reprinted in Chapter 3), remains the classic statement of this position. Henry Mintzberg's early writings on the role of managers as intuitive interactive people who are not premeditated rational decision makers[12] and his more recent writings on the shortcomings of strategic planning,[13] together represent a plea for a return to thinking strategically in organizations—and de-emphasizing the use of formal strategic planning and strategic management processes.

STRATEGIC PLANNING AND MANAGEMENT CONTINUE TO BE VITAL

Although Mintzberg and others have identified important limitations of strategic planning and management, many government constituents or "stakeholders" (and sometimes statutes) expect or require public agencies to prepare and provide strategic plans. A public agency with relatively clear and discrete purposes can reasonably be expected to manage strategically: in local government, for example, street repairs ("public works"), emergency medical services ("EMS"), and trash removal ("sanitation"). Public agencies with relatively clear purposes can—and should—plan ahead, set objectives, articulate and communicate their plans, choose the best available strategies from among alternatives, explain how and why the chosen strategies suit the situation, and report back on how well the objectives have been achieved.

In most circumstances, strategic management should be undertaken by public organizations. Mintzberg's three fallacies of strategic planning, however, serve as reminders to avoid pitfalls: do not permit the strategic plan to become an obsession; when the environment is too volatile for the future to be forecast realistically, avoid undue attempts at forecasting; and do not let the strategic planning process become too formalized or too dependent on planners. Foresight and judgment should characterize strategic management—in addition to intelligent, respectful relationships between administrators of a public agency and the citizens it exists to serve.

READINGS REPRINTED IN THIS CHAPTER

John Bryson bases his rationale for strategic planning, **"Why Strategic Planning in Public and Nonprofit Organizations Is More Important Than Ever,"**[14] on three phenomena: the extent and rapidity of environmental and organizational change; the interconnectedness of the public, private and nonprofit sectors; and the blurring of distinctions between policy boundaries. In Bryson's view, these developments require public and nonprofit agencies to think and act strategically as never before.

Bryson identifies four categories of benefits that are derived from the strategic planning process. Strategic planning should:

1. cause organizations to think and acting strategically. It leads organizations to gather information more carefully; to pay attention to internal and external environments and to organizational learning; to clarify the organization's priorities and directions for future action;

2. produce better decision making by helping organizations make decisions in light of their future consequences and on the basis of coherent and defensible reasons;

3. improve organizational responsiveness and performance by introducing better methods for identifying internal and external demands, influences, and pressures; and

4. promote teamwork and better utilization of the organization's employees.

Bryson presents examples of strategic planning in a school district, a public library, a federal program, and a church. These examples illustrate four different approaches to strategic planning and thereby allow readers to identify common success factors. The chapter ends on a confident note, predicting that strategic planning in public and nonprofit agencies will persist—if the plans accept and build on political decision making. Without question, this is one of the most interesting and important issues in the debate about the usefulness of strategic planning in the public sector: Strategic planning may work well in the confidential confines of private corporations' board rooms, but can it survive in the political world of government agencies? Bryson says it can, and his arguments are convincing.

In **"The Fall and Rise of Strategic Planning"**[15] **Henry Mintzberg** analyzes and critiques the arguments for strategic planning and management that had been put forward in several earlier books and articles. Mintzberg reviews the history of strategic planning in the U. S. in the last three decades of the 20th century and argue that several fundamental fallacies have been associated with it. They include:

- The *fallacy of predetermination*—an unwarranted reliance on forecasting, the performance of which has not been good;
- The *fallacy of detachment*—an assumption that strategy making can be detached from operations, a fallacy that Mintzberg claims has been "terribly costly to many organizations"; and
- The *fallacy of formalization*—the belief that planning systems can detect discontinuities, provide creativity, and inject program intuition. Mintzberg refers to the fallacy of formalization as "the grand fallacy."

Mintzberg's argument is extensive, detailed, and thought-provoking. It has profound implications for how public sector organizations attempt to plan and manage strategically.

If strategic management is an approach which asks managers to focus on specifying the objectives towards which their work is directed, it follows that they must think clearly about what those aims are. **Mark Moore's** chapter, **"Defining Public Value,"**[16] examines the overall aim of managerial work in the public sector. Moore's "simple proposition" is that the aim of managerial work in the public sector is to create public value . . . for government managers, this is "the whole point of their work".[17] Moore's analysis of the different standards which may be used to measure the creation of public value is an important starting point for a strategic approach to public sector management.

Moore begins from the problem a public administrator, such as a sanitation commissioner, might face in demonstrating that the work for which she is responsible creates public value within democratically set mandates. Strategic management in the public sector can help create a framework which clearly links democratic mandates to the creation of public value, showing how the managerial and operational work undertaken is justified and may be measured against appropriate standards. Most public managers face similar issues.

NOTES

1. Bryson, John M. (1988). "Strategic Planning," in Jay M. Shafritz (Ed.), *International Encyclopedia of Public Policy and Administration* (pp. 2160–2167). Boulder, Colo.: Westview.

2. Ansoff, H. Igor. (1990). "General Management in Turbulent Environments", *The Practicing Manager, 11*(1), 6–27.

3. Jones, L. R. (1998). "Planning, Programming, Budgeting System (PPBS)," in Jay M. Shafritz (Ed.), *International Encyclopedia of Public Policy and Administration* (pp. 1670–1674). Boulder, Colo.: Westview.

4. Bryson, John M. (1988). *Strategic Planning for Public and Nonprofit Organizations: A Guide to Strengthening and Sustaining Organizational Achievement.* San Francisco: Jossey-Bass. (A revised edition was published in 1995.)

5. An earlier and important contribution to this area was Jean Ruffat's 1983 article, "Strategic Management of Public and Non-Market Corporations," in *Long Range Planning, 16* (2), 74–83.

6. For example, Paul Nutt and Robert W. Backoff (1987), "A Strategic Management Process for Public and Third Sector Organizations." *Journal of the American Planning Association, 53,* 44–57.

7. Mintzberg, Henry. (1994). *The Rise and Fall of Strategic Planning.* New York: Free Press, p. 36.

8. Except in quite unusual circumstances. For example, when national security or a pending sale of public property is involved.

9. Roberts, Nancy C. (1993). "Limitations of Strategic Action in Bureaus," in Barry Bozeman (Ed.), *Public Management: The State of the Art* (pp. 153–172). San Francisco: Jossey-Bass.

10. Mintzberg, Henry. (1994). *The Rise and Fall of Strategic Planning.* New York: Free Press.

11. Hames, Richard David. (1994). *The Management Myth: Exploring the Essence of Future Organizations.* Chatswood, NSW : Business & Professional Publishing.

12. Mintzberg, Henry. (1973). *The Nature of Managerial Work.* New York: Harper and Row.

13. Mintzberg, Henry. (1994). *The Rise and Fall of Strategic Planning.* New York: Free Press, p. 36.

14. Bryson, John M. (1995), *Strategic Planning for Public and Nonprofit Organizations: A Guide to Strengthening and Sustaining Organizational Achievement* (rev. ed.). San Francisco: Jossey-Bass.

15. Mintzberg, Henry. (January-February 1994), "The Fall and Rise of Strategic Planning." *Harvard Business Review,* 107–113.

16. Moore, Mark H. (1995). "Defining Public Value," in M. Moore, *Creating Public Value: Strategic Management in Government* (pp. 27–56). Cambridge, Mass: Harvard University Press.
17. Moore, Mark H. (1995). "Defining Public Value," in M. Moore, *Creating Public Value: Strategic Management in Government.* Cambridge, Mass.: Harvard University Press, p. 29.

24

John M. Bryson

WHY STRATEGIC PLANNING IN PUBLIC AND NONPROFIT ORGANIZATIONS IS MORE IMPORTANT THAN EVER

Leaders and managers of governments, public agencies of all sorts, nonprofit organizations, and communities face difficult challenges in the years ahead. Upheaval and change surround them. Consider, for example, several events and trends of the past two decades: demographic changes, shifts in values, increased interest-group activism, the privatization of public services, tax levy limits, tax indexing, unfunded federal and state mandates, shifts in federal and state responsibilities and funding priorities, a volatile global economy, and the increased importance of the nonprofit sector. Organizations that want to survive and prosper must respond to these changes. Their response may be to do what they have always done, only better; it may also involve important shifts in organizational focus and action. While organizations typically experience long periods of relative stability, they also typically encounter periods of rapid change (Gersick, 1991; Land and Jarman, 1992; Mintzberg, 1994a, 1994b). These periods of organizational change can be exciting, but they can also be anxiety-producing—or even terrifying. As paleontologist Stephen Jay Gould notes, "Life seems to be characterized by long stretches of boredom punctuated by periods of intense terror."

These environmental and organizational changes are aggravated by the increased interconnectedness of the world. Changes anywhere typically result in changes elsewhere (Luke, 1989, 1991). This increased interconnectedness is perhaps most apparent in the blurring of three traditionally important distinctions—between domestic and international spheres; between policy areas; and between public, private, and nonprofit sectors (Cleveland, 1973, 1985; Nutt and Backoff, 1992; Osborne and Gaebler, 1992). These changes have become dramatically apparent since the mid seventies. During the 1973 and 1978 oil embargoes, it became obvious that the U.S. economy is part of a world economy and that events abroad have domestic repercussions. The completion of the General Agreement of Tariffs and Trade (GATT) in 1992 will eventually further integrate the U.S. economy with the rest of the world. And in a stunning about-face for those of us who grew up in the shadow of *Sputnik,* key elements of our current economic policy—reducing the national debt and converting the U.S. away from military production—have become tied not to *countering* Russia but to *cooperating* with her and other former communist states. If these nations fail in their attempts to convert to democracy and a free market economy, we may have no choice but to rebuild our arms budget and scale back our domestic ambitions.

Distinctions between policy areas are also hard to maintain. For example, educational reform is touted as a type of industrial policy, to help U.S. firms cope more effectively with foreign competition. Strengthening the economy will not eliminate government human service costs, but letting it falter will certainly increase them. The connections between national industrial or full employment policies and local economic development are obvious. Finally, the boundaries between public, private, and nonprofit sectors have eroded. Sovereignty, for example, is increasingly "farmed out." Taxes are not collected by government tax collectors but are withheld by private and nonprofit organizations from their employees and turned over to the government. The nation's health, education, and welfare are a public responsibility, yet increasingly, we rely on private and nonprofit organizations for the production of services in these areas. Weapons systems are not produced in government arsenals but by private industry. When such fundamental public functions as tax collection; health, education, and welfare services; and weapons production are handled by the private and nonprofit sectors, then surely the boundaries between public, private, and nonprofit sectors are irretrievably blurred.

The blurring of these boundaries means that we have moved to a world in which no one organization or institution is fully in charge, and yet many are involved or affected or have a partial responsibility to act (Bryson and Einsweiler, 1991; Bryson and Crosby, 1992). This increased jurisdictional ambiguity requires public and nonprofit organizations (and communities) to think and act strategically as never before. Strategic planning is designed to help them do so. The extensive experience of public, nonprofit, and private organizations with strategic planning in recent decades yields a rich storehouse of advice on how to apply strategic planning.

PURPOSE AND BENEFITS OF STRATEGIC PLANNING

What is strategic planning? Drawing on Olsen and Eadie (1982), I define strategic planning as a disciplined effort to produce fundamental decisions and actions that shape and guide what an organization is, what it does, and why it does it. To deliver the best results, strategic planning requires broad yet effective information gathering, development and exploration of strategic alternatives, and an emphasis on future implications of present decisions. Strategic planning can help facilitate communication and participation, accommodate divergent interests and values, foster wise and reasonably analytic decision making, and promote successful implementation. In short, as its best strategic planning can prompt in organizations the kind of imagination— and commitment—that psychotherapist and theologian Thomas Moore thinks are necessary to deal with individuals' life conundrums.

Most work on strategic planning in this century has focused on for-profit organizations. Until the early 1980s, strategic planning in the public sector was applied primarily to military organizations and the practice of statecraft on a grand scale (Quinn, 1980; Bracker, 1980).

It can be applied, however, to a number of public and nonprofit organizations as well, as we shall see throughout this book. Specifically, strategic planning can be applied to

- Public agencies and their departments or other major organizational divisions
- General-purpose governments, such as city, county, state, or tribal governments
- Nonprofit organizations that provide what are essentially public services
- Organizations providing specific services—such as transportation, health, or education—which bridge organizational and governmental boundaries
- Interorganizational networks in the public and nonprofit sectors
- Entire communities, urban or metropolitan areas, or regions or states

Organizations engage in strategic planning for many reasons. Proponents of strategic planning typically try to persuade their colleagues with one or more of the following kinds of statements (Barry, 1986; Nutt and Backoff, 1992):

"We face so many conflicting demands, we need a process for figuring out our priorities."

"We need to clarify what we do well so that we can do it better, and we also need to figure out what we should be doing that is new."

"We have a total quality management program under way, and now we are being asked to 'reinvent' and 'reengineer' ourselves as well. How can we make sure all of this effort is headed in the right direction?"

"We can expect a severe budget deficit next year unless we drastically rethink the way we do business."

"A number of private-sector competitors are going after our clients; we have to figure out a way to meet the competition."

"Issue x is staring us in the face. We need some way to help us think about its resolution, or else we will be badly hurt."

"Our funders [or board of directors] have asked us to prepare a strategic plan."

"We need to integrate or coordinate better the services we provide with those of other organizations."

"We know a leadership change is coming, and we want to prepare for it."

"We want to use strategic planning to educate, involve, and revitalize our board and staff."

"Our organizations has an embarrassment of riches, but we still need to figure out how we can have the biggest impact; we owe it to our stakeholders."

"Everyone is doing strategic planning these days; we'd better do it, too."

Regardless of why public and nonprofit organizations engage in strategic planning, similar benefits are likely to result. Many authors have argued that strategic planning can produce a number of different benefits for organizations (Steiner, 1979; Barry, 1986; Koteen, 1989; Mercer, 1991; Nutt and Backoff, 1992; Berry and Wechsler, 1995). The first and perhaps most obvious potential benefit is the promotion of strategic thought and action. This in turn leads to more systematic information gathering about the organization's external and internal environment and various actors' interests, heightened attention to organizational learning, clarification of the organization's future direction, and the establishment of organizational priorities for action.

The second benefit is improved decision making. Strategic planning focuses attention on the crucial issues and challenges an organization faces, and it helps key decision makers figure out what they should do about them. Strategic planning thus can help organizations formulate and clearly communicate their strategic intentions. It can help them make today's decisions in light of their future consequences. It can help them develop a coherent and defensible basis for decision making and then coordinate the resulting decisions across levels and functions. And finally, it can help them exercise maximum discretion in those areas under their organization's control.

The third benefit—enhanced organizational responsiveness and improved performance—flows from the first two. Organizations engaging in strategic planning are encouraged to clarify and address major organizational issues, respond wisely to internal and external demands and pressures, and deal effectively with rapidly changing circumstances. Strategic thinking *and* acting are what count, not just thinking alone.

Finally, strategic planning can directly benefit the organization's people. Policy makers and key decision makers can better fulfill their roles and meet their responsibilities, and teamwork and expertise are likely to be strengthened among organizational members.

Although strategic planning *can* provide all these benefits, there is no guarantee it will. Indeed, it is highly unlikely that any organization will experience all or even most of the benefits of strategic planning the first time through—or even after many cycles of strategic planning. For one thing, strategic planning is simply a set of concepts, procedures, and tools. Leaders, managers, and planners need to be very careful about how they engage in strategic planning because their success will depend at least in part on how they tailor the process to their specific situation.

There are two compelling reasons for some organizations to hold off on a formal strategic planning effort. First, as Mitroff and Pearson (1993) point out, strategic planning may not be the best first step for an organization whose roof has fallen (keeping in mind, of course, that every crisis should be *managed* strategically). For example, an organization may need to remedy a cash flow problem before undertaking strategic planning. Or it may need to postpone strategic planning until it fills a key leadership position. Second, if an organization lacks the skills, resources, or commitment by key decision makers to produce a good plan, strategic planning will be a waste of time. Such a situation embodies what Bill Roering and I have called "the paradox of strategic planning": it is most needed where it is least likely to work and least needed where it is most likely to work (Bryson and Roering, 1988, 1989). If strategic planning is undertaken in such a situation, it should probably be a focused, limited effort aimed at developing the necessary skills, resources, and commitment.

A number of other reasons can be offered for not engaging in strategic planning. Too often, however, these "reasons" are actually excuses, used to avoid doing what should be done.

Many organizations prefer to rely on the intuition and vision of extremely gifted leaders instead of on formal strategic planning processes. If these leaders are strategically minded and experienced, there may be no need for strategic planning for the purpose of developing strategies. It is rare, however, for any one leader to have all the information necessary to develop an effective strategy, and rarer still for any strategy developed by a single person to engender the kind of commitment that is necessary for effective implementation. A reasonably structured and formalized strategic planning process helps organizations gather the information necessary for effective strategy formulation. It also provides the discipline and commitment necessary to effectively implement strategies.

In addition, many organizations—particularly those that have enormous difficulty reaching decisions that cut across levels, functions, or programs—find that incremental decision making and mutual adjustments of various sorts among interested partisans is the only process that will work. "Muddling" of this sort, as Charles Lindblom (1959) describes it, legitimizes the existing distribution of power and resources in an organization and allows its separate parts to pursue opportunities as they arise. Interesting and useful innovations can result from muddling, enhancing learning, and promoting useful adaptations to changing circumstances. In fact, if the muddling occurs within the context of a general agreement on the organization's overall direction, everyone may be better off (Lindblom, 1959, 1965, 1977; Braybrook and Lindblom, 1963; Quinn, 1980). Unfortunately, muddling typically results in a chronic organizational underperformance, and therefore, key external and internal constituencies may be badly served.

Strategic planning also probably should not be undertaken if implementation is extremely unlikely. Engaging in strategic planning when effective implementation will not follow is the organizational equivalent of the average New Year's resolution. On the other hand, when armed with the knowledge that implementation will be difficult, key decision makers and planners can focus extra attention on ensuring implementation success.

Finally, organizations simply may not know where to start the process. The good news is that strategic planning can begin almost anywhere—the process is so interconnected that you end up covering most phases via conversation and dialogue, no matter where you start.

WHAT STRATEGIC PLANNING IS NOT

Clearly, strategic planning is no panacea. As noted, strategic planning is simply a set of concepts, procedures, and tools designed to help leaders, managers, and planners think and act strategically. Used in wise and skillful ways by a "coalition of the willing" (Cleveland, 1993), strategic planning can help organizations focus on producing effective decisions and actions that further the organization's mission, meet its mandates, and satisfy key stakeholders. But strategic planning is not a substitute for strategic thinking and acting. Only caring and committed people can do that. And when used thoughtlessly, strategic planning can actually drive out precisely the kind of strategic thought and action it is supposed to promote.

Furthermore, strategic planning is not a substitute for leadership. In my experience there is simply *no* substitute for leadership when it comes to using strategic planning to enhance organizational performance. At least some key decision makers and process champions must be committed to the strategic planning process, or any attempts to use it are bound to fail.

In addition, strategic planning is not synonymous with creating an organizational strategy. Organizational strategies have numerous sources, both planned and unplanned. Strategic planning is likely to result in a statement of organizational *intentions*, but what is *realized* in practice will be some combination of what is intended and what emerges along the way (Mintzberg, 1987, 1994a, 1994b; Mintzberg and Waters, 1985; Mintzberg and Westley, 1992). Strategic planning can help organizations develop and implement effective strategies, but they should also remain open to unforeseen opportunities. Too much attention to strategic planning and excessive reverence for strategic plans can blind organizations to other unplanned and unexpected—yet incredibly useful—sources of information, insight, and action.

It should now be clear that the *discipline* necessary for strategic planning can be of two sorts. The first harkens back to the Latin root of the word *discipline*, emphasizing instruction, training, education, and learning. The second embodies later interpretations of the word, emphasizing order, control, and punishment. I personally prefer the emphasis on education and learning, although there clearly are occasions when imposing order, taking control, and enforcing appropriate sanctions are appropriate.

WHY STRATEGIC PLANNING IS HERE TO STAY

Many leaders and managers are likely to groan at the prospect of having yet another new management technique foisted upon them. They have seen cost-benefit analysis, planning-programming-budgeting systems, zero-based budgeting, management by objectives, Total Quality Management, reinvention, reengineering, and a host of other techniques trumpeted by a cadre of authors and management consultants. They have also, all too often, seen such techniques fall by the wayside after a burst of initial enthusiasm. Managers in particular frequently, and justifiably, feel like victims of some sort of perverse management hazing or "status degradation ritual" (Schein, 1987, pp. 84-86).

But strategic planning is not just a passing fad, at least not the sort of strategic planning proposed in this book. The reason is that the strategic planning process presented here builds on the nature of *political* decision making. So many other management techniques fail because they ignore, try to circumvent, or even try to *counter* the political nature of life in private, public, and nonprofit organizations. Too many planners and managers, at least in my experience, just do not understand that such a quest is almost guaranteed to be quixotic.

Most of these new management innovations have tried to improve government decision making and operations by imposing a formal rationality on systems that are not rational, at least in the conventional meaning of the word. Public and nonprofit organizations (and communities) are *politically rational*. Thus, any technique that is likely to work well in such organizations must accept and build on the nature of political rationality (Wildavsky, 1979; March and Olsen, 1989).

Let us pursue this point further by contrasting two different kinds of decision making: the "rational" planning model and political decision making. It represents a rational-deductive approach to decision making. It begins with goals; policies, programs, and actions are then deduced to achieve those goals. If there is such a thing as a traditional planning theology, this model is one of its icons.

Let us now examine the fundamental assumption of the rational planning model— that in the fragmented, shared-power settings that characterize many public and nonprofit organizations, networks, and communities, there will either be a *consensus* on goals, policies, programs, and actions necessary to achieve organizational aims, or there will be someone with enough power and authority that consensus does not matter. This assumption just does not hold true in most circumstances. Only in fairly centralized, authoritarian, or quasimilitary bureaucracies will the assumption hold—maybe.

Let us now examine a model that contrasts sharply with the rational planning model—the political decision making model. This model is inductive, not rational-deductive. It begins with issues, which by definition involve conflict, not consensus. The conflicts may be over ends, means, timing, location, political advantage, reasons for change, or philosophy, and the conflicts may be severe. As efforts proceed to resolve these issues, policies and programs emerge to address them that are politically rational; that is, they are politically acceptable to involved or affected parties. Over time, more general policies may be formulated to capture, frame, shape, guide, or interpret the policies and programs developed to deal with the issues. The various policies and programs are, in effect, treaties among the various stakeholder groups. And while they may not exactly record a consensus, at least they represent a reasonable level of agreement among stakeholders (Lindblom, 1965, 1980; Pfeffer and Salancik, 1978; March and Olsen, 1989).

Now, the heart of the strategic planning process discussed in Chapter Two is the identification and resolution of strategic—that is, very important—issues. The process, in other words, accepts political decision making's emphasis on issues and seeks to inform the formulation and resolution of those issues. Effective strategic planning, therefore, should make political decision makers more effective; and if it is practiced consistently, it might even make their professional lives easier (Janis, 1989). Since every key decision maker in a large public or nonprofit organization is, in effect, a political decision maker (Mintzberg, 1983; Pfeffer, 1992; Fesler and Kettl, 1994; Herman, 1994; Peters, 1995), strategic planning can help these organizations. Strategic planning, therefore, will last in government and nonprofit organizations because it accepts and builds on the nature of political decision making. If done well, strategic planning can actually improve the political decisions made within these organizations, as well as their programs and policies.

Having drawn a sharp distinction between the rational planning model and political decision making, I must now emphasize that the two models are not inherently antithetical. They simply need to be relied upon appropriately. This may mean, for example, sequencing them properly. The political decision-making model is thus necessary to work out consensual agreements on what programs and policies will best resolve key issues. The rational planning model can then be used to recast that consensus into the form of goals, policies, programs, and actions. While the planning and decision making that goes into the formulation of a strategic plan may look fairly sloppy to an outsider, once a consensus is reached on what to do, the resulting strategic plan can be rewritten in a form that is in fact quite rational by ordinary definitions of the term.

Furthermore, the rational planning model may be used to sort out and address any minor (and perhaps major) inconsistencies embedded in the political outcome.

To use another example, in many organizations and communities there already exists a broad-based consensus on basic purposes and values—and often on many policies, programs, and actions as well. There may even be a consensus on the organization's or community's "vision." This consensus can be recast using the rational planning model. The political model can then be used to address remaining issues on which there is no agreement. In particular, these issues are likely to revolve around what needs to be done in order to achieve the agreed-upon goals or vision.

To summarize: a great advantage of the strategic planning process outlined in this book is that it does not presume consensus where consensus does not exist, but it can accommodate consensus where it does exist. Because there is no presumption of consensus, the process is more suitable for politicized circumstances than are purely "rational" approaches. An intense attention to stakeholders and their interests, external and internal environments, and strategic issues means that the actions that are ultimately agreed upon are more likely to be *politically* rational, and that organizational survival and prosperity are, therefore, more likely to be assured. Furthermore, by gathering relevant information, asking probing questions, and focusing on how best to raise issues, the process can be used to inform political decision making in such a way that virtuous public and nonprofit purposes are better served than they would be if only the rawest forms of political decision making prevailed. The process, in other words, provides a way of blending substantive *and* political rationality—content *and* process—in wise ways, to the betterment of the organizations and communities that use the process (see March and Simon, 1958; Lynn, 1987; Stone, 1988; Benveniste, 1989; March and Olsen, 1989; Bryson and Crosby, 1992).

SUMMARY

[The] importance of strategic planning stems from its ability to help public and nonprofit organizations and communities respond effectively to the dramatically changed circumstances that now confront them.

Not only have the environments of public and nonprofit organizations and communities changed dramatically in the recent past, more upheaval is likely in the future. Those of us who grew up in the 1950s and 1960s came to think that continuous progress was the norm, that everything would always continue to get steadily better. How wrong we all were! The norm is not continuous progress, but periods of stability interrupted by significant change, uncertainty, and surprise. The period prior to the 1950s saw two world wars, big booms, big busts, and the development of major new roles for government. The period after the 1950s brought the civil rights movement, the women's movement, major student disruptions, the disastrous war in Vietnam, the environmental movement, dramatic shifts in the dominant political ideology in the United States, plus all of the other changes noted in the opening paragraphs of this chapter.

Strategic planning is one way to help organizations and communities deal with changed circumstances. Strategic planning is intended to enhance an organization's ability to think and act strategically. It can help organizations formulate and resolve the most important issues they face. It can help them build on their strengths and take advantage of major opportunities, while they overcome or minimize their weaknesses and serious threats to their existence. It can help them be much more effective in a hostile world. If it does not do that, it probably was not worth the effort, even though it may have satisfied certain legal mandates or symbolic needs.

Strategic planning is a leadership and management innovation that is likely to persist because, unlike many other recent innovations, it accepts and builds on the nature of *political* decision making. The raising and resolving of important issues is at the heart of political decision making, just as it is at the heart of strategic planning. Strategic planning seeks to improve on raw political decision making, however, by helping ensure that issues are raised and resolved in ways that benefit the organization, its key stakeholders, and society.

REFERENCES

Barry, B. W. *Strategic Planning Workshop for Nonprofit Organizations.* St. Paul, Minn.: Amherst H. Wilder Foundation, 1986.

Benveniste, G. *Mastering the Politics of Planning: Crafting Credible Plans and Policies That Make a Difference.* San Francisco: Jossey-Bass, 1989.

Berry, F. S., and Wechsler, B. "State Agencies' Experience with Strategic Planning: Findings from a National Survey." *Public Administration Review,* 1995, 55(2), pp. 159–168.

Bracker, J. "The Historical Development of the Strategic Management Concepts." *Academy of Management Review,* 1980, 5, 219–224.

Braybrooke, D., and Lindblom, C. E. *A Strategy of Decision: Policy Evaluation as a Social Process.* New York: Free Press, 1963.

Bryson, J. M., and Crosby, B. C. *Leadership for the Common Good: Tackling Public Problems in a Shared Power World.* San Francisco: Jossey-Bass, 1992.

Bryson, J. M., and Einsweiler, R. C. (eds.). *Shared Power: What Is It? How Does It Work? How Can We Make It Work Better?* Lanham, Md.: University Press of America, 1991.

Bryson, J. M., King, P. J., Roering, W. D., and Van de Ven, A. H. "Strategic Management at the Amherst H. Wilder Foundation." *Journal of Management Case Studies,* 1986, 2. 118–138.

Bryson, J. M., and Roering, W. D. "Initiation of Strategic Planning by Governments." *Public Administration Review,* 1988, 48, 995–1004.

Bryson, J. M., and Roering, W. D. "Mobilizing Innovation Efforts: The Case of Government Strategic Planning." In A. Van de Ven, H. Angle, and M. S. Poole (eds.). *Research on the Management of Innovation.* New York: Harper Business, 1989.

Cleveland, H. *The Future Executive.* New York: HarperCollins, 1973.

Cleveland, H. *The Knowledge Executive.* New York: Dutton, 1985.

Cleveland, H. *Birth of a New World: An Open Moment for International Leadership.* San Francisco: Jossey-Bass, 1993.

Fesler, J., and Kettl, D. *The Politics of the Administrative Process.* (2nd ed.) Chatham, N.J.: Chatham House, 1994.

Gersick, C. "Revolutionary Change Theories: A Multilevel Exploration of the Punctuated Equilibrium Paradigm." *Academy of Management Review,* 1991, 16, 10–36.

Herman, R. D., and Associates. *The Jossey-Bass Handbook of Nonprofit Leadership and Management.* San Francisco: Jossey-Bass, 1994.

Janis, I. L. *Crucial Decisions: Leadership in Policymaking and Crisis Management.* New York: Free Press, 1989.

Koteen, J. *Strategic Management in Public and Nonprofit Organizations.* New York: Praeger, 1989.

Land, G., and Jarman, B. *Breaking Point and Beyond.* New York: Harper Business, 1992.

Lindblom, C. E. "The Science of Muddling Through." *Public Administration Review,* 1959, *19,* 79–88.

Lindblom, C. E. *The Intelligence of Democracy.* New York: Free Press, 1965.

Lindblom, C. E. *Politics and Markets.* New York: Free Press, 1977.

Lindblom, C. E. *The Policy-Making Process.* (2nd ed.) Englewood Cliffs, N.J.: Prentice-Hall 1980.

Luke, J. S., and Caiden, G. E. "Coping with Global Interdependence." In J. L. Perry (ed.) *Handbook of Public Administration.* San Francisco: Jossey-Bass, 1989, pp. 83–93.

Luke, J. "Managing Interconnectedness: The Challenge of Shared Power." In J. M. Bryson and R. C. Einsweiler (eds.), *Shared Power: What Is It? How Does It Work? How Can We Make It Work Better?* Lanham, Md.: University Press of America, 1991, pp. 25–50.

Luttwak, E. *The Grand Strategy of the Roman Empire.* Baltimore, Md.: Johns Hopkins University Press, 1977.

Lynn, L. E., Jr. *Managing Public Policy.* Boston: Little, Brown, 1987.

March, J. G., and Olsen, J. P. *Rediscovering Institutions: The Organizational Basis of Politics.* New York: Free Press, 1989.

March, J. G., and Simon, H. A. *Organizations.* New York: Wiley, 1958.

Mercer, J. L. *Strategic Planning for Public Managers.* Westport, Conn.: Quorum, 1991.

Mintzberg, H. "Crafting Strategy." *Harvard Business Review,* July/Aug. 1987, pp. 66–75.

Mintzberg, H. "The Fall and Rise of Strategic Planning." *Harvard Business Review,* 1994a, Jan./Feb., pp. 107–114.

Mintzberg, H. *The Rise and Fall of Strategic Planning.* New York: Free Press, 1994b.

Mintzberg, H., and Waters, J. A. "Of Strategies, Deliberate and Emergent." *Strategic Management Journal,* 1985, *6*(3), 257–272.

Mintzberg, H., and Westley, F. "Cycles of Organizational Change." *Strategic Management Journal,* 1992, *13,* 39–59.

Mitroff, I. I. "Systemic Problem Solving." In M. W. McCall, Jr., and M. M. Lombardo (eds.), *Leadership: Where Else Can We Go?* Durham, N.C.: Duke University Press, 1978.

Mitroff, I. I., and Pearson, C. M. *Crisis Management: A Diagnostic Guide for Improving Your Organization's Crisis-Preparedness.* San Francisco: Jossey-Bass, 1993.

Nutt, P. C., and Backoff, R. W. *Strategic Management for Public and Third Sector Organizations: A Handbook for Leaders.* San Francisco: Jossey-Bass, 1992.

Osborne, D., and Gaebler, T. *Reinventing Government.* Reading, Mass.: Addison-Wesley, 1992.

Peters, G. *The Politics of Bureaucracy.* (4th ed.) White Plains, N.Y.: Longman, 1995.

Pfeffer, J. *Managing with Power: Politics and Influence in Organizations.* Boston: Harvard Business School Press, 1992.

Pfeffer, J., and Moore, W. "Power in University Budgeting: A Replication and Extension." *Administrative Science Quarterly,* 1980, *25,* 637–653.

Pfeffer, J., and Salancik, R. *The External Control of Organizations: A Resource Dependence Perspective.* New York: HarperCollins, 1978.

Quinn, J. B. *Strategies for Change: Logical Incrementalism.* Homewood, Ill.: Richard D. Irwin, 1980.

Schein, E. H. *Process Consultation: Lessons for Managers and Consultants,* Vol. 2. Reading, Mass.: Addison-Wesley, 1987.

Steiner, G. A. *Strategic Planning: What Every Manager Must Know.* New York: Free Press, 1979.

Stone, D. A. *Policy Paradox and Political Reason.* Glenview, Ill.: Scott, Foresman, 1988.

Wildavsky, A. *Speaking Truth to Power.* Boston: Little, Brown, 1979.

25

Henry Mintzberg

THE FALL AND RISE OF STRATEGIC PLANNING

When strategic planning arrived on the scene in the mid-1960s, corporate leaders embraced it as "the one best way" to devise and implement strategies that would enhance the competitiveness of each business unit. True to the scientific management pioneered by Frederick Taylor, this one best way involved separating thinking from doing and creating a new function staffed by specialists: strategic planners. Planning systems were expected to produce the best strategies as well as step-by-step instructions for carrying out those strategies so that the doers, the managers of businesses, could not get them wrong. As we now know, planning has not exactly worked out that way.

While certainly not dead, strategic planning has long since fallen from its pedestal. But even now, few people fully understand the reason: *strategic planning* is not *strategic thinking*. Indeed, strategic planning often spoils strategic thinking, causing managers to confuse real vision with the manipulation of numbers. And this confusion lies at the heart of the issue: the most successful strategies are visions, not plans.

Strategic planning, as it has been practiced, has really been *strategic programming*, the articulation and elaboration of strategies, or visions, that already exist.

Organizations disenchanted with strategic planning should not get rid of their planners or conclude that there is no need for programming. Rather, organizations should transform the conventional planning job. Planners should make their contribution *around* the strategy-making process rather than *inside* it. They should supply the formal analyses or hard data that strategic thinking requires, as long as they do it to broaden the consideration of issues rather than to discover the one right answer. They should act as catalysts who support strategy making by aiding and encouraging managers to think strategically. And, finally, they can be programmers of a strategy, helping to specify the series of concrete steps needed to carry out the vision.

The label "strategic planning" has been applied to all kinds of activities, such as going off to an informal retreat in the mountains to talk about strategy. But call that activity "planning," let conventional planners organize it, and watch how quickly the event becomes formalized (mission statements in the morning, assessment of corporate strengths and weaknesses in the afternoon, strategies carefully articulated by 5 P.M.).

Strategic thinking, in contrast, is about *synthesis*. It involves intuition and creativity. The outcome of strategic thinking is an integrated perspective of the enterprise, a not-too-precisely articulated vision of direction.

Such strategies often cannot be developed on schedule and immaculately conceived. They must be free to appear at any time and at any place in the organization, typically through messy processes of informal learning that must necessarily be carried out by people at various levels who are deeply involved with the specific issues at hand.

Formal planning, by its very analytical nature, has been and always will be dependent on the preservation and rearrangement of established categories—the existing levels of strategy (corporate, business, functional), the established types of products (defined as "strategic business units"), overlaid on the current units of structure (divisions, departments, etc.). But real strategic change requires not merely rearranging the established categories, but inventing new ones.

Search all those strategic planning diagrams, all those interconnected boxes that supposedly give you strategies, and nowhere will you find a single one that explains the creative act of synthesizing experiences into a novel strategy.

Strategy making needs to function beyond the boxes, to encourage the informal learning that produces new perspectives and new combinations. As the saying goes, life is larger than our categories. Planning's failure to transcend the categories explains why it has discouraged serious organizational change. This failure is why formal planning has promoted strategies that are extrapolated from the past or copied from others. Strategic planning has not only never amounted to strategic thinking but has, in fact, often impeded it. Once managers understand this, they can avoid other costly misadventures caused by applying formal technique, without judgment and intuition, to problem solving.

THE PITFALLS OF PLANNING

If you ask conventional planners what went wrong, they will inevitably point to a series of pitfalls for which they, of course, are not responsible. Planners would have people believe that planning fails when it does not receive the support it deserves from top management or when it encounters resistance to change in the organization. But surely no technique ever received more top management support than strategic planning did in its heyday. Strategic planning itself has discouraged the commitment of top managers and has tended to create the very climates its proponents have found so uncongenial to its practice.

The problem is that planning represents a *calculating* style of management, not a *committing* style. Managers with a committing style engage people in a journey. They lead in such a way that everyone on the journey helps shape its course. As a result, enthusiasm inevitably builds along the way. Those with a calculating style fix on a destination and calculate what the group must do to get there, with no concern for the members' preferences. But calculated strategies have no value in and of themselves; to paraphrase the words of sociologist Philip Selznick, strategies take on value only as committed people infuse them with energy.

At lower levels in the hierarchy, the problem becomes more severe because planning has often been used to exercise blatant control over business managers. No wonder so many middle managers have welcomed the overthrow of strategic planning. All they wanted was a commitment to their own business strategies without having to fight the planners to get it!

THE FALLACIES OF STRATEGIC PLANNING

An expert has been defined as someone who avoids the many pitfalls on his or her way to the grand fallacy. For strategic planning, the grand fallacy is this: because analysis encompasses synthesis, strategic planning is strategy making. This fallacy itself rests on three fallacious assumptions: that prediction is possible, that strategists can be detached from the subjects of their strategies, and, above all, that the strategy-making process can be formalized.

The Fallacy of Prediction. According to the premises of strategic planning, the world is supposed to hold still while a plan is being developed and then stay on the predicted course while that plan is being implemented. How else to explain those lockstep schedules that have strategies appearing on the first of June, to be approved by the board of directors on the fifteenth.

In 1965, Igor Ansoff wrote in his influential book *Corporate Strategy*, "We shall refer to the period for which the firm is able to construct forecasts with an accuracy of, say, plus or minus 20 percent as the *planning horizon* of the firm. What an extraordinary statement! How in the world can any company know the period for which it can forecast with a given accuracy?

The evidence, in fact, points to the contrary. While certain repetitive patterns, such as seasons, may be predictable, the forecasting of discontinuities, such as a technological innovation or a price increase, is virtually impossible. Of course, some people sometimes "see" such things coming. That is why we call them "visionaries." But they create their strategies in much more personalized and intuitive ways.

The Fallacy of Detachment. In her book *Institutionalizing Innovation*, Mariann Jelinek developed the interesting point that strategic planning is to the executive suite what Taylor's work-study methods were to the factory floor—a way to circumvent human idiosyncrasies in order to systematize behavior. "It is through administrative systems that planning and policy are made possible, because the systems capture knowledge *about* the task." Thus "true management by exception, and true policy direction are now possible, solely because management is no longer wholly immersed in the details of the task itself."[1]

According to this viewpoint, if the system does the thinking, then strategies must be detached from operations (or "tactics"), formulation from implementation, thinkers from doers, and so strategists from the objects of their strategies.

The trick, of course, is to get the relevant information up there, so that senior managers on high can be informed about the details down below without having to immerse themselves in them. Planners' favored solution has been "hard data," quantitative aggregates of the detailed "facts" about the organization and its context, neatly packaged and regularly delivered. With such information, senior managers need never leave their executive suites or planners their staff offices. Together they can formulate—work with their heads—so that the hands can get on with implementation.

All of this is dangerously fallacious. Innovation has never been institutionalized. Systems have never been able to reproduce the synthesis created by the genius entrepreneur or even the ordinary competent strategist, and they likely never will.

Ironically, strategic planning has missed one of Taylor's most important messages: work processes must be fully understood before they can be formally programmed.

But where in the planning literature is there a shred of evidence that anyone has ever bothered to find out how it is that managers really do make strategies? Instead many practitioners and theorists have wrongly assumed that strategic planning, strategic thinking, and strategy making are all synonymous, at least in best practice.

The problem with the hard data that are supposed to inform the senior manager is they can have a decidedly soft underbelly. Such data take time to harden, which often makes them late. They tend to lack richness; for example they often exclude the qualitative. And they tend to be overly aggregated, missing important nuances. These are the reasons managers who rely on formalized information, such as market-research reports or accounting statements in business and opinion polls in government, tend to be detached in more ways than one. Study after study has shown that the most effective managers rely on some of the softest forms of information, including gossip, hearsay, and various other intangible scraps of information.

My research and that of many others demonstrates that strategy making is an immensely complex process, which involves the most sophisticated, subtle, and, at times, subconscious elements of human thinking.

A strategy can be deliberate. It can realize the specific intentions of senior management, for example, to attack and conquer a new market. But a strategy can also be emergent, meaning that a convergent pattern has formed among the different actions taken by the organization one at a time.

In other words, strategies can develop inadvertently, without the conscious intention of senior management, often through a process of learning. A salesperson convinces a different kind of customer to try a product. Other salespeople follow up with their customers, and the next thing management knows, its products have penetrated a new market. When it takes the form of fits and starts, discoveries based on serendipitous events, and the recognition of unexpected patterns, learning inevitably plays *a*, if not *the*, crucial role in the development of novel strategies.

Contrary to what traditional planning would have us believe, deliberate strategies are not necessarily good, nor are emergent strategies necessarily bad. I believe that all viable strategies have emergent and deliberate qualities, since all must combine some degree of flexible learning with some degree of cerebral control.

Vision is unavailable to those who cannot "see" with their own eyes. Real strategists get their hands dirty digging for ideas, and real strategies are built from the occasional nuggets they uncover. These are not people who abstract themselves from the daily details; they are the ones who immerse themselves in them while being able to abstract the strategic messages from them. The big picture is painted with little strokes.

The Fallacy of Formalization. The failure of strategic planning is the failure of systems to do better than, or even nearly as well as, human beings. Formal systems, mechanical or otherwise, have offered no improved means of dealing with the information overload of human brains; indeed, they have often made matters worse. All the promises about artificial intelligence, expert systems, and the like improving if not replacing human intuition never materialized at the strategy level. Formal systems could certainly process more information, at least hard information. But they could never *internalize* it, *comprehend* it, *synthesize* it. In a literal sense, planning could not learn.

Formalization implies a rational sequence, from analysis through administrative procedure to eventual action. But strategy making as a learning process can proceed in the other direction too. We think in order to act, to be sure, but we also act in order to think. We try things, and those experiments that work converge gradually into viable patterns that become strategies. This is the very essence of strategy making as a learning process.

Formal procedures will never be able to forecast discontinuities, inform detached managers, or create novel strategies. Far from providing strategies, planning could not proceed without their prior existence. All this time, therefore, strategic planning has been misnamed. It should have been called strategic programming, distinguished from other useful things that planners can do, and promoted as a process to formalize, when necessary, the consequences of strategies that have already been developed. In short, we should drop the label "strategic planning" altogether.

PLANNING, PLANS, AND PLANNERS

Two important messages have been conveyed through all the difficulties encountered by strategic planning. But only one of them has been widely accepted in the planning community: business-unit managers must take full and effective charge of the strategy-making process. The lesson that has still not been accepted is that managers will never be able to take charge through a formalized process. What then can be the roles for planning, for plans, and for planners in organizations?

Planners and managers have different advantages. Planners lack managers' authority to make commitments, and, more important, managers' access to soft information critical to strategy making. But because of their time pressures, managers tend to favor action over reflection and the oral over the written, which can cause them to overlook important analytical information. Strategies cannot be created by analysis, but their development can be helped by it.

Planners, on the other hand, have the time and, most important, the inclination to analyze. They have critical roles to play alongside line managers, but not as conventionally conceived. They should work in the spirit of what I like to call a "soft analyst," whose intent is to pose the right questions rather than to find the right answers. That way, complex issues get opened up to thoughtful consideration instead of being closed down prematurely by snap decisions.

Planning as Strategic Programming. Planning cannot generate strategies. But given viable strategies, it can program them; it can make them operational. For one supermarket chain that a colleague and I studied, planning was the articulation, justification, and elaboration of the strategic vision that the company's leader already had. Planning was not deciding to expand into shopping centers, but explicating to what extent and when, with how many stores, and on what schedule.

An appropriate image for the planner might be that person left behind in a meeting, together with the chief executive, after everyone else has departed. All of the strategic decisions that were made are symbolically strewn about the table. The CEO turns to the planner and says, "There they all are; clean them up. Package them neatly so that we can tell everyone about them and get things going." In more formal language, strategic programming involves three steps: codification, elaboration, and conversion of strategies.

Codification means clarifying and expressing the strategies in terms sufficiently clear to render them formally operational, so that their consequences can be worked out in detail. This requires a good deal of interpretation and careful attention to what might be lost in articulation: nuance, subtlety, qualification. A broad vision, like capturing the market for a new technology, is one thing, but a specific plan—35% market share, focusing on the high end—is quite another.

Elaboration means breaking down the codified strategies into substrategies and ad hoc programs as well as overall action plans specifying what must be done to realize each strategy: build four new factories and hire 200 new workers, for example.

And conversion means considering the effects of the changes on the organization's operations—effects on budgets and performance controls, for example. Here a kind of great divide must be crossed from the nonroutine world of strategies and programs to the routine world of budgets and objectives. Objectives have to be restated and budgets reworked, and policies and standard operating procedures reconsidered, to take into account the consequences of the specific changes.

One point must be emphasized. Strategic programming is not "the one best way" or even necessarily a good way. Managers don't always need to program their strategies formally. Sometimes they must leave their strategies flexible, as broad visions, to adapt to a changing environment. Only when an organization is sure of the relative stability of its environment and is in need of the tight coordination of a myriad of intricate operations (as is typically the case of airlines with their needs for complicated scheduling), does such strategic programming make sense.

Plans as Tools to Communicate and Control. Why program strategy? The most obvious reason is for coordination, to ensure that everyone in the organization pulls in the same direction. Plans in the form of programs—schedules, budgets, and so on—can be prime media to communicate strategic intentions and to control the individual pursuit of them, in so far, of course, as common direction is considered to be more important than individual discretion.

Plans can also be used to gain the tangible as well as moral support of influential outsiders. Written plans inform financiers, suppliers, government agencies, and others about the intentions of the organization so that these groups can help it achieve its plans.

Planners as Strategy Finders. As noted, some of the most important strategies in organizations emerge without the intention or sometimes even the awareness of top managers. Fully exploiting these strategies, though, often requires that they be recognized and then broadened in their impact, like taking a new use for a product accidentally discovered by a salesperson and turning it into a major new business. It is obviously the responsibility of managers to discover and anoint these strategies. But planners can assist managers in finding these fledgling strategies in their organizations' activities or in those of competing organizations.

Planners can snoop around places they might not normally visit to find patterns amid the noise of failed experiments, seemingly random activities, and messy learning.

They can discover new ways of doing or perceiving things, for example, spotting newly uncovered markets and understanding their implied new products.

Planners as Analysts. In-depth examinations of what planners actually do suggests that the effective ones spend a good deal of time not so much doing or even encouraging planning as carrying out analyses of specific issues. Planners are obvious candidates for the job of studying the hard data and ensuring that managers consider the results in the strategy-making process.

Much of this analysis will necessarily be quick and dirty, that is, in the time frame and on the ad hoc basis required by managers. It may include industry or competitive analyses as well as internal studies, including the use of computer models to analyze trends in the organization.

But some of the best models that planners can offer managers are simply alternative conceptual interpretations of their world, such as a new way to view the organization's distribution system. As Arie de Geus, the one-time head of planning at Royal Dutch/Shell, wrote in his HBR article "Planning as Learning" (March-April 1988), "The real purpose of effective planning is not to make plans but to change the . . . mental models that . . . decision makers carry in their heads."

Planners as Catalysts. The planning literature has long promoted the role of catalyst for the planner, but not as I will describe it here. It is not planning that planners should be urging on their organizations so much as any form of behavior that can lead to effective performance in a given situation.

26

Mark H. Moore

DEFINING PUBLIC VALUE

On the day he was appointed, the sanitation commissioner drove through the city.[1] Everywhere he saw signs of public and private neglect. Trash barrels left too long at the curb were now overflowing. Back alleys hid huge, overflowing bins that had never made it to the curbs. Emptied bins were ringed by trash spilled during the emptying. In the poorer sections of town, rats scurried among the cans.

Perhaps because he was newly appointed, the commissioner felt his public accountability quite keenly. The city spent a great deal of money each year to sustain the organization's activities. Hundreds of employees earned their pay and made their careers in his organization, and scores of trucks were garaged, maintained, and deployed under his supervision. Most important, millions of people relied on his organization to keep the city clean and healthy.

Happily, as he drove through the city, he saw evidence of his organization at work. Huge trucks, painted in distinctive colors, rumbled by, trailed by sanitation workers who tipped garbage pails into their gaping maws. Street-cleaning machines trundled along the gutters in the wake of the tow trucks that removed illegally parked cars from their path. An occasional street sweeper appeared with broom and dustbin, emptying the cans that had been set out to hold the public's litter.

Still, he could not help thinking that his organization could do more. As the newly appointed commissioner, he wanted to make a difference. He wanted his organization to have an impact on the conditions he could see around him. He wanted to create value for the citizens of the city. But how?

The question seemed particularly urgent because the newly elected mayor had asked him to define and set out his management objectives for the Department of Sanitation. As part of that strategic plan, the mayor wanted to know whether it would be advisable to privatize some or all of the operations of the Department of Sanitation.

THE AIM OF MANAGERIAL WORK

The sanitation commissioner is a manager at work. The question is: At work on what? What is the point of his efforts?

We know the aim of managerial work in the private sector: to make money for the shareholders of the firm.[2] Moreover, we know the ways in which that goal can be achieved: by producing products (including services) that can be sold to customers at prices that earn revenues above the costs of production.[3] And we know how managerial accomplishments can be gauged: through financial measures of profit and loss and changes in the firm's stock price.[4] If private managers can conceive and make products that earn profits, and if the companies they lead can do this continually over time, then a strong presumption is established that the managers have created value.[5]

In the public sector, the overall aim of managerial work seems less clear; what managers need to do to produce value far more ambiguous; and how to measure whether value has been created far more difficult. Yet, to develop a theory of how public managers should behave, one must resolve these basic issues. Without knowing the point of managerial work, we cannot determine whether any particular managerial action is good or bad. Public management is, after all, a normative as well as technical enterprise.

As a starting point, let me propose a simple idea: the aim of managerial work in the public sector is to create *public* value just as the aim of managerial work in the private sector is to create *private* value.

This simple idea is often greeted with indignation—even outrage. A liberal society like ours tends to view government as an "unproductive sector." In this view government cannot create value. At best, it is a necessary evil: a kind of referee that sets out the rules within which a civil society and a market economy can operate successfully, or an institution that fills in some of the gaps in free market capitalism. While such activities may be necessary, they can hardly be viewed as value creating. But this view denies a reality that public managers experience daily. From their perspective it is government, acting through its managers, that shields the country from foreign enemies, keeps the streets safe and clean, educates the children, and insulates citizens from many man-made and natural disasters that have impoverished the lives of previous human generations. To them it seems obvious that government creates value for the society. That is the whole point of their work.

Of course, this account is not entirely satisfactory; it looks only at the benefits of governmental activity, not at the costs. In reality public managers cannot produce the desirable results without using resources that have value in alternative uses. To keep the streets clean; to insulate the disadvantaged from the ravages of poverty, ignorance, and joblessness; even to collect the taxes that society has agreed are owed, public managers must have money to purchase equipment, pay their workers, and provide mandated benefits to clients. The money they use is raised through the coercive power of taxation. That money is lost to other uses—principally, private consumption. That loss must be laid against the putative benefits of public enterprises.

Moreover, to achieve their goals, public managers often use a resource other than money: they use the authority of the state to compel individuals to contribute directly to the achievement of public objectives.[6] Litterers are fined to help keep the cities clean; welfare recipients are sometimes obliged to find work; and every citizen is made to feel the weight of the obligation to pay taxes to help the society achieve its collective goals.[7]

In a society that celebrates private consumption more than the achievement of collective goals, values individual liberty greatly, and sees private entrepreneurship as a far more important engine of social and economic development than governmental effort, the resources required by public managers are only grudgingly surrendered. So, it is not enough to say that public managers create results that are valued; they must be able to show that the results obtained are worth the cost of private consumption and unrestrained liberty forgone in producing the desirable results. Only then can we be sure that some public value has been created.

The Political Marketplace: "We Citizens" as a Collective Consumer

But to whom should such a demonstration be made? And how could anyone know whether the demonstration is convincing?

In the private sector these key questions are answered when individual consumers stake their hard-earned cash on the purchase of a product, and when the price paid exceeds the costs of making what is sold. These facts establish the presumptive value of the enterprise. If individuals do not value the products or service enough to pay for them, they will not buy them; and if they do not buy them, the goods will not be produced.[8]

In the public sector, however, the money used to finance value-creating enterprises is not derived from the individual, voluntary choices of consumers. It comes to public enterprises through the coercive power of taxation. It is precisely that fact that creates a problem in valuing the activities of government (at least from one point of view).[9]

The problem (from this point of view) is that the use of the state's coercive power undermines "consumer sovereignty"—the crucial link between the individual judgments of value on the one hand and control over what is to be produced on the other, which provides the normative justification for private sector enterprises.[10] The coercion blots out the opportunity for individuals to express their individual preferences and to have those preferences control what is to be produced. Because individuals do not choose individually to purchase or contribute to discrete governmental activities, we cannot be sure that they want what the government supplies. And if we cannot be sure that individuals want what the government produces, then, by some reckoning at least, we cannot be sure that the government produces anything of value.

What this account overlooks, however, is that the resources made available to public sector managers *are* made through a process of voluntary choice—namely, the process of representative government. To be sure, *individual,* voluntary choice does not control this system. But the institutions and processes of representative democracy come as close as we now can to creating the conditions under which individuals can voluntarily assemble and decide collectively what they would like to achieve together without sacrificing their individual desires. It is the only way we know how to create a "we" from a collection of free individuals.[11] That "we," in turn, can decide to make common cause, to raise resources, and to organize to achieve its goals—all the activities that go into the policy-making and implementation roles associated with government.

Indeed, it is the explicit recognition of the power of politics to establish normatively compelling collective purposes that makes legislative and political mandates central to traditional conceptions of public administration. Those legislative mandates properly guide public sector production specifically because they define collective aspirations. The collective aspirations, in turn, establish a presumption of public value as strong as the presumption of private value created by market mechanisms—at least if they can be achieved within the terms of the mandate. So, we should evaluate the efforts of public sector managers not in the economic marketplace of individual consumers but in the political marketplace of citizens and the collective decisions of representative democratic institutions.[12]

Precisely to make such demonstrations the sanitation commissioner prepares a plan to present to the newly elected mayor. In doing so, he tries to satisfy representatives of the public that his organization responds to the public's aspirations. Once he presents the plan, he will be accountable for producing measures to show that the goals and objectives of the plan have, in fact, been achieved.[13]

The claim that public managers can presume that public value is created if they meet the test of the political marketplace is also often greeted by derision. We have all become painfully aware of the folly and corruption that can beset the deliberations and choices of representative democratic institutions.[14]

Practicing public managers, however, have no choice but to trust (at least to some degree) in the normative power of the preferences that emerge from the representative processes. Those choices establish the justification for managerial action in the public sector. Because public managers spend public resources in the enterprises they lead, they must act as though a coherent and normatively compelling "we" existed even if they have their doubts. Otherwise, their enterprises are ill-founded.

DIFFERENT STANDARDS FOR RECKONING PUBLIC VALUE

Reconciling the tension between the desire to have democratic politics determine what is worth producing in the public sector and the recognition that democratic politics is vulnerable to corruption of various kinds has been the persistent challenge to those who would offer a theory of public management in a democracy.[15] Over time, we have relied on different concepts as standards for defining managerial purposes.

Achieving Mandated Objectives Efficiently and Effectively

For most of our recent history, the predominant conception has been that public managers should work to achieve the legislatively mandated goals and objectives of their organizations as efficiently and effectively as they can. Thus, the sanitation commissioner's job is to clean the streets as efficiently and effectively as possible.

It is quite easy to agree with this conception. Yet, reflection reveals an important feature of this common standard that is often overlooked or taken for granted: namely, this standard establishes the preeminence of *political*—primarily legislative—processes in determining what is valuable for the public sector to produce. To those who value politics as a way of creating a collective will, and who see democratic politics as the best answer we have to the problem of reconciling individual and collective interests, it is hardly surprising that the political process would be allowed to determine what is worth producing with public resources.[16] No other procedure is consistent with the principles of democracy.

But to those who distrust the integrity or utility of political processes, the idea that public value would be defined politically is a little hard to stomach. They have seen too much corruption to trust the determination of public value to political processes. At a minimum these critics want assurances that the political processes. At a minimum these critics want assurances that the political process is a principled one that accepts the proper limits of governmental action or meets some minimal standards of fairness and competence in the deliberations that produce the mandates.[17] Alternatively, they would prefer some more objective ways of ascertaining the value of public sector enterprises and some platform for confronting political processes with this objective information.[18]

Politically Neutral Competence

At the turn of the century Woodrow Wilson offered a solution: separate politics from administration and perfect each activity in its own sphere.[19] Thus, public administrators were to imagine that political mandates came to them in the form of coherent, well-defined policies. As the hard-won products of intense political processes, the policies would have all the moral weight that effective democratic politics could give them.

Given this accomplishment of politics, public administrators could then safely turn their attention to finding the most efficient and effective way to achieve the mandated purposes. To meet these responsibilities, the public administrators were assumed to have knowledge about both the substance of the fields in which they were operating and the arts of administration.[20] By knowing what could be produced and how organizations could be made to produce what was desirable public administrators earned their keep.

However, this traditional conception failed to consider what would happen if the political reality fell short of the ideal. Often, political mandates came loaded down with special interests that were hard to reconcile with the desire to guard the general public interest.[21] Other times, managers received incoherent mandates: they were expected to produce several different things that were inconsistent with one another and were given no useful instructions about which goals and objectives should take precedence over others when conflicts arose.[22] Still other times, political mandates shifted in arbitrary and unpredictable ways, destroying investments and draining momentum that had previously been built up and would be needed again once the political balance was restored to its original position.[23]

Facing this political reality, even Wilsonian public administrators sometimes found it necessary to challenge the wisdom of politically expressed policy mandates. They did so on the basis of their moral obligations to defend the general public interest and preserve the continuity of important public enterprises.[24] In their minds their substantive and administrative expertise gave them the right to stand up to the misguided vagaries of politics. In the pantheon of bureaucratic heroes, the image of a civil servant who challenged badly motivated politicians to defend the long-term public interest stands right alongside the dutiful, responsive servant.

Once revealed, this sort of bureaucratic resistance to political mandates could not stand in a democracy such as ours. Indeed, a favorite target of our populist politics is the bureaucratic mandarin. As a result, much of this bureaucratic resistance went underground. It became a covert but legitimate rationale for bureaucrats of all political stripes to conduct guerrilla warfare against political demands for change on the grounds that the politicians were ill-informed, short-sighted, or badly motivated.

Analytic Techniques for Assessing Public Value

Yet politics, too, is mistrusted in our political culture, and soon a new platform for disciplining and rationalizing democratic politics emerged. This new platform was established on a new kind of expertise. Whereas the traditional theory of public administration acknowledged the substantive and administrative expertise of professionals (developed through professional experience and education), the new formulation held that special analytic techniques, drawn from the fields of economics, statistics, and operations research, could be used objectively to gauge in advance—or to learn after the fact—whether public enterprises were valuable or not.[25] The new techniques included policy analysis, program evaluation, cost-effectiveness analysis, and benefit-cost analysis. Reformers hoped that use of these techniques could infuse policy deliberations with objective facts about the extent to which proposed initiatives could be expected to work and the extent to which the costs of government efforts could be justified by general benefits to society.

There is much to be said about whether these techniques have lived up to their promise—much more than can be said here. From the perspective of someone analyzing their overall impact on policy-making, one can fairly say that the techniques are neither routinely used nor invariably powerful when they are.[26] Still, they have succeeded in changing the political discourse about governmental programs. They have increased the appetite of the political process for fact-based arguments about the extent to which government programs achieve their stated objectives to serve the general interest.[27]

In discussing the utility of these techniques to managers' efforts to define and measure the value of what they are achieving, however, three points seem key. First, for reasons that are not entirely obvious, these techniques seem to be more valuable in estimating the value of particular programs or policies than the overall value of an organization's efforts. One reason, I suspect, is that to deploy these techniques successfully, managers must have narrowly specified objectives and narrowly specified means for achieving the objectives. Specific objectives and specific means are precisely what define governmental policies and programs.

In contrast, an organization is rarely easily conceptualized as a single program or policy. Often, organizations incorporate bundles of programs and policies. The different programs and policies may have been combined to achieve some larger coherent purpose, but the achievement of that larger purpose is often exceedingly difficult to measure and even harder to attribute to the overall operations of any single organization.

It may also be important that, as already mentioned, public organizations have some kind of capital value rooted in their ability to adapt and meet new tasks and challenges. To the extent that they do, an evaluation of their performance in existing tasks and programs would not capture their full benefit to the society. In any case, use of these techniques to evaluate programs and policies have been far more common than their use in assessing the overall value produced by public organizations.

Second, we should distinguish between the use of these techniques to estimate in advance of action whether a particular governmental initiative will prove valuable or not and the use of these techniques after a program has been tried to determine whether it was successful. Policy analysis often focuses on the first, program evaluation on the second. The distinction is particularly important when one uses comparisons with private sector management to offer guidance to public sector managers about how they could better reckon the value of their enterprises.

As noted above, the private sector seems to have a far more reliable way of measuring the value of its production than the public sector. The revenues and profits earned from selling particular products and services—that is, the famed bottom line—provides a direct measure of a private sector enterprise's success. What is interesting about profitability, however, is that it measures what happened in the past. That piece of information is taken very seriously in the private sector, partly because it can be used to hold managers accountable and give them incentives for performance, but also because it gives private sector managers an advantage in thinking about the future. Indeed, many private sector firms have been advised to reduce their reliance on strategic planning efforts designed to produce more accurate predictions about the future and, instead, to rely on their ability to react quickly to the market conditions they encounter through their current operations.

Thus, the lesson from the private sector seems to be that it is extremely valuable to develop accurate information about performance in the past rather than concentrate all one's efforts on guessing about the future. To the extent this is true, it follows that public sector agencies should be focusing more on program evaluation and less on policy analysis. My impression, however, is that they do the opposite. This is unfortunate, for the inconsistent attention given to program evaluation deprives the public sector of the kind of accountability, incentives for action, and capacity to react quickly that the private sector has gained by paying close attention to its bottom line.

Third, we need to look at what sorts of preferences public enterprises are designed to satisfy. Most often, analytic techniques are presented as though they were all useful tools designed to help government learn whether its efforts are valuable or not. Among them, benefit-cost analysis is usually presented as the superior technique, the one that is most general and most reliably linked to value. The only reason not to rely on benefit-cost analyses is that they are more difficult to complete. Thus, program evaluation and cost-effectiveness analysis are presented as poor second cousins to benefit-cost analysis.

Yet I see an important conceptual distinction among the techniques and would agree that for most public purposes, program evaluation and cost-effectiveness analysis are the conceptually as well as practically superior approaches. Benefit-cost analysis, taking guidance from the principles of welfare economics, assumes that public sector activities should be valued by individuals sizing up the (positive or negative) consequences for them as individuals. In contrast, the techniques of program evaluation and cost-effectiveness analysis find their standard of value not in the way that individuals value the consequences of government policy but instead in terms of how well the program or policy achieves particular objectives set by the government itself. Thus, program evaluation measures how well the program achieves its intended purposes, and those purposes are inferred from the language of the statutes or policies that authorized it. Cost-effectiveness analysis measures how well a particular governmental effort scored with respect to a particular set of purposes that had been defined for that particular effort—probably with the help of professionals who could help government policymakers define what constituted a valuable kind of "effectiveness."

In short, both program evaluation and cost-effectiveness analysis define public value in terms of collectively defined objectives that emerge from a process of collective decision-making, whereas benefit-cost analysis defines value in terms of what individuals desire without reference to any collective decision-making process. The reliance of benefit-cost analysis on pure individual preferences is, of course, what makes it a conceptually superior approach to welfare economists. But to those who believe in the capacity of a political process to establish an articulate collective aspiration, and who believe that this is the most appropriate guide to public action, program evaluation and cost-effectiveness analysis seem the better techniques precisely because they look away from individual preferences and toward collectively established purposes.

Focusing on Customer Service and Client Satisfaction

More recently still, public administrators have developed a new conception of how to gauge the value of their enterprises: borrowing from the private sector, they have embraced the goal of customer service, and committed themselves to finding the value of their efforts in the satisfaction of their "customers."[28] This idea has some important virtues. Insofar as it encourages government managers to think about the quality of the interactions that government agencies have with citizens whom they encounter as clients, and to make those encounters more satisfactory, much good will come of adopting this perspective. We have all had our fill of rude bureaucrats and badly designed governmental operations and procedures.

Yet, this idea, too, has flaws. It is by no means clear who the customers of a government agency are. One naturally assumes that they are the *clients* of government organizations—the citizens the organizations encounters at its "business end" through individual encounters or transactions.

Insofar as government provides services and benefits to citizens, that model seems to work fairly well. But government is not simply a service provider. Often it is in the business of imposing *obligations,* not providing services.[29] This is true for police departments, environmental protection agencies, commissions against discrimination, and tax collectors among others. These organizations meet individual clients not as service providers but as representatives of the state obliging clients to absorb a loss on behalf of the society at large.

Of course, it may be valuable for regulatory and law enforcement organizations to think of the citizens whom they regulate as customers and to design their "obligation encounters" with as much care as "service encounters" now are.[30] Nevertheless, it is unreasonable to imagine that regulatory and enforcement agencies find their justification in the satisfactions of those whom they compel to contribute to public purposes. More likely, the justification comes from the generally attractive consequences for others of imposing particular obligations on a few. Moreover, there may be many others than those obliged who are interested in the justice or fairness with which the obligations are imposed, the fairness they would wish for themselves if they were similarly obliged.

The point is important because it reminds us that service-providing agencies, too, are judged and evaluated by citizens as well as by those who are clients of the organization. Consider welfare departments, for example. In evaluating the performance of the welfare department, we need to know how clients feel about the services they receive. But we cannot rely on their evaluation as the only or even the most important way of judging the value of the services provided. Citizens and their representatives want to be sure that the total cost of the program remains low, that no one steals from the program (even if it costs more to prevent the stealing than would have been lost if the stealing occurred), and even that the clients experience some degree of stigmatization in enrolling in the welfare program (to mark the distinction between those who can be independent and those who must rely on the state).

In short, it is important to distinguish the evaluation that *citizens* and their representatives give to governmental activities from the evaluation that would be given by *clients.* The arrested offender is not in a particularly good position to judge the value of the police department's operations. And the welfare client might not be either. The ultimate consumer of government operations is not the individuals who are served or obliged in individual encounters (the clients of the enterprise) but citizens and their representatives in government who have more general ideas about how a police department should be organized or welfare support delivered. They decide what is worth producing in the public sector, and their values ultimately matter in judging whether a governmental program is valuable or not.

In the end none of the concepts of "politically neutral competence," "policy analysis" and "program evaluation," or "customer service" can finally banish politics from its preeminent place in defining what is valuable to produce in the public sector. Politics remains the final arbiter of public value just as private consumption decisions remain the final arbiter of private value. Public mangers can proceed only by finding a way to improve politics and to make it a firmer guide as to what is publicly valuable. That is why political management must be part of our conception of what public managers should do.

To see how these general considerations might affect the perceptions and calculations of public sector managers, let us return to the problem faced by the sanitation commissioner at the beginning of the chapter. How ought he to think about the question of what value he is creating, for whom, and how?

Justifications for Public Intervention

As a matter of political philosophy, most members of a liberal society generally prefer to leave the organization of its productive enterprises to markets and private institutions rather than to public mandates and governmental bureaucracies. Consequently, for a public enterprise to be judged worthwhile, it must pass a test beyond the mere demonstration that the value of its products exceeds the value of the resources used in producing the results: it must explain why the enterprise should be public rather than private.[31]

This preference stems from three ideological pillars that define a proper ordering of institutions in a liberal society: first, deep respect for the power of markets to ensure that productive activities respond to individual desires; second, a belief that private institutions are better able to cultivate and exploit individual initiative and are therefore more adaptable and efficient than public bureaucracies; third, confidence that private institutions become an important bulwark of freedom against the power of government.

To a degree, the sanitation commissioner could treat these ideas as mere abstractions that have little to do with the day-to-day running of the organization he leads. Alternatively, he could think of them as important philosophical principles that he endorses and seeks to realize in his organization's operations. Or, he could recognize that, even if these principles are not important to him, they might be important to the citizens and representatives who superintend his enterprise, and that their concerns about these matters should be accommodated.

Indeed, this last perspective would come quite naturally as these ideas gained concrete political force in his city's political processes, or as cities around the country began privatizing their sanitation departments. To satisfy those interested in ensuring proper institutional relations in a liberal society, then, a manager of a public enterprise must show that there is some special reason why government, and its authority, should be used to finance and supply the service.

In general, two different justifications for public intervention carry weight. One is that there is a technical problem in the organization of a market to supply the good in question—some reason why free exchanges among producers and consumers will not result in the proper level of production.[32] Government must intervene to correct the defect in the market.

A second justification is that there is some crucial issue of justice or fairness at stake in the provision of the service—some right or claim of an individual against the society that others agree must be honored.[33] Government must intervene to ensure that the claim is honored—not only for the current individual who has a claim but generally for all.

Note that the first justification leaves undisturbed the primacy of individual preferences as the arbiter of social value. Ideally, both the quantity and the distribution of a particular good will be determined solely by individual preferences.

The second justification, by contrast, substitutes a different standard for establishing social value. A collective judgment is made about the value of the proposed public enterprise. Citizens acting through politics, rather than consumers acting through markets, establish both the level and the distribution of production. It is the combined preferences of citizens for an aggregate social condition that must be satisfied.

These different justifications correspond more or less closely to the two different frames for establishing the value of garbage collection: the production of tidiness and the production of public health. In one frame, public sector garbage collection provides an amenity much like any other consumer good—a tidy urban environment. One thinks principally in terms of technical problems in the organization of markets as the justification for public sector intervention.

In the second frame, public collection produces something more fundamental—the protection of public health. Here one thinks more in terms of guaranteeing a socially valuable condition, fairly distributing its benefits and accepting some social obligation to help meet the required condition.

These distinct frames express the different statuses that the two values—cleanliness and health—have in our politics. Tidiness is an amenity rather than a necessity; therefore, its production and distribution can be comfortably left to markets unless some technical problem makes this impossible. Health makes a claim as a "primary good" with strong connections to common aspirations; therefore, its production and distribution become an appropriate focus of a society acting through government to assure justice.[34]

Within the frame of efficiently producing and distributing an amenity to those who really value it, public intervention is justified by three specific arguments. First, substantial economies of scale in garbage collection could justify public intervention.[35] This occurs either because the technology of garbage collection shows declining costs across the relevant range of production, or because the value associated with garbage collection is concentrated in the last few increments of performance, when the municipal environment is transformed from a bit untidy to pristine, or from pretty safe to entirely safe.

To take advantage of these economies of scale without leaving the citizens vulnerable to exploitation by a private monopoly, the society has two choices: it can establish a regulatory agency to oversee the natural monopoly that will arise in the private sector, or it can choose to supply the service itself. In the case of garbage collection, the society has often decided to have the government supply the service itself.

Second, although clean streets, fragrant air, and the absence of vermin in alleyways are all things citizens value, they are currently unowned and unpriced.[36] As a result, individual citizens have no incentive to "produce" these goods by disposing of their garbage somewhere other than in the common streets and alleyways.

To deal with this problem, the society might reasonably decide to assert common ownership of these public spaces. Having asserted ownership, it could then either establish a market for the use of these spaces by charging citizens for the privilege of dumping, or, relying on its authority, it can require private citizens to keep these areas clean on pain of both fines and the stigmatization of violating public ordinances.[37] Alternatively, the society might simply decide to supply the service itself through governmental operations and make it unnecessary for citizens to litter. In the case of garbage collection, the society has often relied on a mix of these approaches, with an emphasis on public sector provision.

Third, because the aesthetic and health benefits of collecting garbage are generally available to all citizens of the city, it is hard to exclude citizens from enjoying these benefits even if they refuse to pay for them.[38] Thus all citizens have an incentive to conceal their true interests in having clean streets. If they don't contribute to the cleanup, maybe someone else will, and they can enjoy the benefit without having to do the work. Or, even if they are willing to make the appropriate contribution, they might be reluctant to do so for fear that they would be exploited and thought foolish by their more cynical fellow citizens. In either case the city will end up dirtier than individual citizens would desire because everyone would hang back from making the appropriate contributions. To avoid this result, the society can oblige everyone to make financial and other contributions to the solution of what is, in the end, a common problem.

All these justifications for public intervention begin with the assumption that individual preferences properly establish the value of such efforts but that some technical problems in the organization of markets for the service justify public intervention. As noted above, however, one can consider garbage collection from an entirely different perspective. Instead of viewing the problem as one of organizing efficiently to meet individual desires for clean streets and alleyways, one can see the issue as a case of fairly distributing the benefits and burdens of meeting a public health need that has been recognized by individuals in the society as a collective aspiration and responsibility.

This language, and the analytic frame it invokes, changes a great deal in our view of the public value of garbage collection. Instead of seeing the value of the effort in terms of its impact on the desire of individual consumers for cleanliness and health, the value seems to be established exogenously by a public health imperative. Sanitary streets are a public necessity! Citizens have a right to be protected! Such pronouncements replace—even "trump"—individual preferences in establishing the value of the enterprise.[39]

Viewed from this vantage point, public sector garbage collection is justified by a shared social aspiration for a healthy (and clean) environment and by the necessity of fairly distributing the benefits and burdens of producing that result through a governmental enterprise. Its value registers partly in terms of the satisfactions of individuals who now enjoy clean streets (balanced by the pain of paying taxes and accepting obligations to assist in the garbage collection enterprise), and partly in terms of the satisfactions of citizens who have seen a collective need, fashioned a public response to that need, and thereby participated in the construction of a community (balanced by worries on their part that they have threatened a proper ordering of social institutions by making something public that might more usefully have remained private).

These views are often considered separate and inconsistent. One sees the problem either from the perspective of efficient production and distribution or from the perspective of justice and a fair distribution of burdens and benefits. My view, however, is that public managers must always see public sector enterprises from *both* perspectives. They cannot shrug off the question of efficient production and delivery of a service. Nor can they ignore the question of a fair distribution of privileges and burdens. Once public authority is engaged, issues of fairness are always present. And public authority is *always* engaged when tax dollars are being spent.

The Value of the Authorizing Process

The fact that public authority is always engaged in public sector enterprises changes who must be satisfied with the performance of an enterprise and what characteristics constitute a satisfactory performance. Because authority is engaged, and authority can only be spent by citizens and their representatives, its use must be guided by *political* agreements rather than by individual market transactions. Individual citizens thinking about what is good for the society (rather than just what is good for themselves as clients) must be satisfied with the conduct of the public enterprise as well as the clients who are directly affected by the enterprise; so must those in representative institutions who authorize the enterprise.

Consensus rarely arises in political discussions of the value of public sector enterprises. More often, debate ensues over whether and how the enterprise should be conducted. In an important sense this political dialogue is to public sector enterprises what the market is to private efforts—the place where consumers with money to spend decide what they want to buy. But three differences apply: (1) these consumers are spending their freedom as well as their money by authorizing the government to act on their behalf; (2) they are buying the product for everyone's benefit according to a political view of what is desirable for the society as a whole; and (3) they are buying whole enterprises rather than individual products of the enterprise. In short, what citizens (as opposed to clients) want is their particular conception of a fair and efficient garbage collection effort.

These apparently abstract issues often become quite concrete in the politics surrounding a sanitation department. The most common issue concerns the proper distribution of the available service across geographic areas, ethnic groups, social classes, and members of political parties.[40] Distribution provokes political debate not only because there are competing interests but also because there are quite different principles which might reasonably be used to decide how to distribute the services.

When one thinks about the distribution of the service in terms of market efficiency or welfare maximization, one is tempted by a principle that directs garbage collection efforts to areas where they will do the most good, that is, where the efforts will produce the largest gains in terms of aesthetics and public health outcomes per unit of effort expended.[41] An alternative concept would be to allocate public services toward those areas that already do a lot privately, partly as an incentive to maintain (or increase) private contributions and partly because the elevated levels of private effort indicate a stronger desire for cleanliness and therefore a more valuable place to spend public cleanup resources.[42]

When one thinks of distributing the benefits of the enterprise in terms of meeting social needs, quite different principles become salient. One is to allocate garbage collection efforts to those areas most in need.[43] This approach will establish a minimum level of cleanliness throughout the city. A second principle, linked closely to fairness, is to supply the same amount of public effort to all areas of the city and let the differences in actual levels of cleanliness reflect differences in private desires and capabilities to keep the areas clean.[44]

In the end none of these principles can stand as the proper basis for allocating services, though at any given moment each will have its advocate. Instead, as a practical matter, the distributional issue is resolved by a continuing political and administrative process that holds these competing principles in tension and adapts to changes in political demands or policy fashion.

Issues of administrative efficiency and program effectiveness are usually debated in terms of effectiveness and costs rather than fairness and justice. Rarely do these concerns arise as a result of reports issued by government agencies revealing shortfalls in performance. Instead, they arise from external sources: some dramatic (but temporary) performance failure such as an inability to clear the streets after an unexpected snowfall; or a newspaper story about corruption, waste, and inefficiency in a sanitation department; or the initiation of a broad effort to increase productivity by an incoming administration; or the initiation of a new project by a new commissioner (for example, a rat extermination program in vacant lots); or the encouragement of block parties to clean up a neighborhood.[45] Such debates about performance will generally be resolved by reports, studies, and the creation of new policies and procedures designed to rectify the problem.

The political debates surrounding the fairness and efficiency of garbage collection are important for at least two reasons. First, they renew the authorization of the enterprise, which maintains the flow of resources that the organizations deploys to keep the streets clean. Second, they provide a continuing occasion for the society to reconsider the question of whether the resources committed to the enterprise are being used well. Like the annual meetings with stockholders in the private sector, the irregular but frequent meetings of the sanitation commissioner with public interest groups, the media, and elected representatives of the people give the commissioner an opportunity to account for his enterprise and to use that account to sustain old—and attract new—investment.

This ongoing political process authorizing the garbage collection efforts to continue (perhaps on some new terms) can have many different attributes. It can be more or less open, more or less fair, more or less well-informed about past performance and future opportunities, and more or less reasonable in its decisions. The particular qualities of this authorizing process are important since it is this process that links the enterprise of garbage collection to those who consume the enterprise as an institution of a well-ordered society.[46]

Since the process can satisfy or disappoint citizens who desire a fair, efficient, and effective public sanitation effort, and since their satisfaction is an important part of the success or failure of a public enterprise, one must view that political process as creating a kind of value. If the ongoing process of authorization is managed well, if citizens feel that their common aspirations are satisfied through a process of consultation and review, the enterprise will be more valuable than if they are not. And this aspect of public value exists independently of the difference between the value of cleanliness and the cost of the resources used to produce it.

The Capital Value of the Institution

There is one last thing to observe about garbage collection. Typically an existing organization—generally, a municipal sanitation department—carries out the activity. Over time that organization develops significant expertise in collecting the garbage.[47] It has operating procedures that accomplish the extraordinary task of gathering workers and equipment from all over a city and sending them out to collect the garbage. It sustains a staff of employees who know where they should go and what they should do to produce this result. It utilizes some accounting systems to show the managers and overseers of the enterprise how much it costs to collect the garbage and how much of the budget has already been spent. And it employs some managers who make sure that everyone in the organization plays his or her assigned role. All this operational capability represents an investment that the society has made in the municipal sanitation department.

Many would say that this cumulative experience and operating capability is an important asset that should be protected, or at least not casually abandoned. Those who express this view see in the competence of public sector organizations a broad, long-term perspective that is useful in balancing the narrow, short-term perspective of political representatives.[48]

To a degree, this view has merit. There *is* value in the cumulative experience of the organization. It would be very costly to have to replace it. And even though much of the productivity gains associated with its accumulating experience have probably been appropriated by its managers in terms of organizational slack that reduces their uncertainty and increases their ability to respond to crises (and by its workers in the form of less pressure in the job), the organization is still likely to be much more productive in its current activities than any alternative.[49]

The problem is that respect for institutional continuity can become an excuse for resisting change. Even something as apparently routine as garbage collection is not static. The world changes. Neighborhoods gain or lose population. Private efforts wax and wane. New technologies for picking up the garbage become available. New problems (such as toxic wastes) make new claims on the organization's sorting and disposal capabilities. New labor contracts change staffing patterns. All these changes affect the basic operations of garbage collection.

In addition, the political demands on the Sanitation Department might change. Perhaps a scandal will force important changes in the geographic allocation of services or the level of supervision. Or, the Sanitation Department might suddenly be directed to become an employer and route of upward mobility for ghetto teenagers rather that simply an agency that picks up the garbage. Alternatively, the sanitation commissioner might see an opportunity to use his force of street cleaners as a device for encouraging the development of block groups that could restore pride and stimulate investment in declining city neighborhoods.

The point is that the organization's value is not necessarily limited to its operating value in its current mission. It also has a kind of capital value rooted in both its ability to adapt its specific methods to new aspects of garbage collection and its ability to produce new things potentially valuable to the society. To the extent that the organization can exploit opportunities to perform its traditional mission more efficiently or more fairly, to the extent that it can adapt to changing circumstances, and to the extent that an organization can exploit its distinctive competence to produce other things that would be valuable to citizens, the enterprise will be more valuable than it seems from observing its current performance. Indeed, it is precisely the *adaptability* of organizations that determines the long-run value of private sector firms.[50] Perhaps the same should be true of public sector firms.

TOWARD A MANAGERIAL VIEW OF PUBLIC VALUE

What does this particular discussion of the public value of garbage collection tell us more generally about how public managers and all the rest of us citizens who rely on them should analyze the value of public sector enterprises? Six points seem key.

First, an axiom: value is rooted in the desires and perceptions of individuals—not necessarily in physical transformations, and not in abstractions called societies. Consequently, public sector managers must satisfy some kinds of desires and operate in accord with some kinds of perceptions.

Second, there are different kinds of desires to be satisfied. Some are for goods and services that can be produced and distributed through markets. These are the focus of private management and need not concern us. Others are for things produced by public organizations and are (more or less imperfect) reflections of the desires that citizens express through the institutions of representative government. Citizens' aspirations, expressed through representative government, are the central concerns of public managers.

At first glance, citizens' aspirations seem to be of two types. One type concerns collective things that are individually desired and consumed but cannot be provided through market mechanisms because the product cannot be divided up and sold to individual consumers. A second type involves political aspirations that attach to aggregate social conditions such as a proper distribution of rights and responsibilities between public and private organizations, a fair distribution of economic opportunities or social obligations, and a suitable desire to economize on the use of tax monies invested in public sector organizations.

In practice, these two different kinds of desires collapse into one for a very important reason: whenever public authority is invoked to solve the technical problems in the market, the enterprise takes on public characteristics. Every time the organization deploys public authority directly to oblige individuals to contribute to the public good, or uses money raised through the coercive power of taxation to pursue a purpose that has been authorized by citizens and representative government, the value of that enterprise must be judged against citizens' expectations for justice and fairness as well as efficiency and effectiveness. Once the public starts producing something with public resources raised through state authority, it can no longer be viewed independently of citizens' political preferences and desires. The capacity of a public enterprise to satisfy these preferences is, therefore, an important part of its value-creating capabilities.

Third, it follows that managers of public sector enterprises can create value (in the sense of satisfying the desires of citizens and clients) through two different activities directed at two different markets. The most obvious way is to deploy the money and authority entrusted to them to produce things of value to particular clients and beneficiaries: they can establish clean parks to be used by families; they can provide treatment to heroin addicts; they can deploy military forces to make individuals secure and confident in the future. We can call this creating value through public sector production, even though what is being produced and valued is not always a physical product or service consumed by individual beneficiaries.

Public managers can also create value by establishing and operating an institution that meets citizens' (and their representatives') desires for properly ordered and productive public institutions. They satisfy these desires when they represent the past and future performance of their organization to citizens and representatives for continued authorization through established mechanisms of accountability. We might think of this activity as helping to define rather than create public value. But this activity also creates value since it satisfies the desires of citizens for a well-ordered society in which fair, efficient, and accountable public enterprises exist. The demands of citizens, rather than of clients or beneficiaries, are being met.

This dual nature of public sector value creation might seem odd. But an approximate analogue exists in the private sector. Private sector managers have two different groups they must satisfy: they must produce a product or service that customers will buy at a price that pays for the costs of production; and they must sell their ongoing capacity to produce valuable products to their shareholders and creditors. A similar situation confronts public managers: they must produce something whose benefits to specific clients outweigh the costs of production; and they must do so in a way that assures citizens and their representatives that something of value has been produced. In short, in both cases, both customers and owners must be satisfied with what the manager does.

Fourth, since governmental activities always engage political authority, the relative importance of these two different parts of management shifts. Because authority is involved, the importance of reassuring the "owners" that their resources are being used well gains relative to satisfying the "clients" or "beneficiaries" of the program.

Fifth, what citizens and their representatives (as opposed to clients and beneficiaries of programs) "buy" from public managers is an account of the public enterprise— a story contained in a policy. In this sense, a policy is to the public sector manager what a prospectus is to a private entrepreneur. Viewed from the manager's side of this transaction, the manager receives an authorization to use resources to accomplish public purposes through specified means. Viewed from the citizen side of this transaction, the authorization is the purchase of an aggregate enterprise that promises to create value. It is a collective, political agreement to meet a problem (or exploit an opportunity) in a particular way. Politics is the answer that a liberal democratic society has given to the (analytically unresolvable) question of what things should be produced for collective purposes with public resources.

If public managers are to create value over the long run, then, an important part of their job consists of strengthening the policies that are sold to their authorizers. Specifically, the policies that guide an organization's activities must reflect the proper interests and concerns of the citizens and their representatives; the story about the value to be produced must be rooted in accurate reasoning and real experience; and the real operating experience of the organization must be available to the political overseers through the development of appropriate accounting systems that measure the performance and costs of the organization's performance. It is here that the analytic techniques of policy analysis, program evaluation, cost-effectiveness analysis, and benefit-cost analysis make their major contributions.[51] Otherwise, the strengths of the political process will not be exploited, the knowledge and experience of the operating managers will not be utilized, and the acknowledged weaknesses of the process will not be challenged.

Sixth, the world in which a public manager operates will change. Citizens' aspirations will change, as will methods for accomplishing old tasks. So might the organization's task environment shift: new problems may crop up to which the organization may propose a useful solution, much as the problem of latchkey children arose as a problem for public libraries to solve. It is not enough, then, that managers simply maintain the continuity of their organizations, or even that the organizations become efficient in current tasks. It is also important that the enterprise be adaptable to new purposes and that it be innovative and experimental.

This, then, is the aim of managerial work in the public sector. Like private sector managers, managers in the public sector must work hard at the task of defining publicly valuable enterprises as well as producing that value. Moreover, they must be prepared to adapt and reposition their organizations in their political and task environments in addition to simply ensuring their continuity.

NOTES

1. This case, like the case of the librarian, is a hypothetical one based on an common story. It comes generally from the experience of public managers but is not the precise history of any particular manager. I use it to illustrate the kinds of problems that managers do face and the ways in which they might think.

2. Richard A. Brealey and Stewart C. Myers, *Principles of Corporate Finance*, 4th ed. (New York: McGraw-Hill, 1991), p. 22.

3. It may not be strictly true that *managers* in the private sector are responsible for *conceiving* products or services. More often, it seems that they are responsible for producing products that have been conceived by others—the chief executive officers of the firm and the marketing people. Yet, if we think of the chief executive officers and marketing people as "managers" as well, then it is true that the managers of a firm are responsible for conceiving as well as producing products. Moreover, it is increasingly true that private sector firms are structuring themselves to encourage entrepreneurship among midlevel managers.

4. These are the criteria Thomas J. Peters and Robert H. Waterman use to identify the firms that embody "excellence"; and it is the creation of organizations that are capable of maintaining profitability over the long run that they take to be the key managerial challenge in the private sector. See Peters and Waterman, *In Search of Excellence: Lessons from America's Best-Run Companies* (New York: Warner, 1982), pp. 121–125.

5. Of course, it is not strictly true that the profitability of a firm in either the short or long run gives certain evidence of the firm's ability to create value. Insofar as the firm uses unowned and unpriced resources valuable to others in its productive activities, such as air or water, or unidentified risks to workers, it financial success may give a distorted view of its overall activity. Still, as a first approximation, the financial success of a firm does create a presumption that some value has been created for consumers and, therefore, for society at large.

6. James W. Fesler and Donald F. Kettl also treat authority as a key resource for public managers in *The Politics of the Administrative Process*. (Chatham, N.J.: Chatham House, 1991), p. 9.

7. For a discussion of how "obligations" to pay taxes might be mobilized, see Mark H. Moore, "On the Office of Taxpayer and the Social Process of Taxpaying," in Phillip Sawicki, ed., *Income Tax Compliance* (Reston, Va.: American Bar Association, 1983), pp. 275-291.

8. Interestingly, the economics profession no longer seems to feel as though it has to defend markets philosophically as an appropriate way to allocate goods in the society. Reading through several microeconomics texts in search of a ringing philosophical endorsement of market mechanisms, I came up empty. To find the philosophical justification, one must go back to earlier writers who thought they were producing a normative political theory as well as a technical discussion of how economies functioned.

9. The point of view I am alluding to here is one associated with "welfare economics." For a very good summary of these ideas and how they relate to social decision processes, see Edith Stokey and Richard Zeckhauser, *A Primer for Policy Analysis* (New York: Norton, 1978), pp. 257-290.

10. Rhoads, *The Economist's View of the World*, pp. 62-63.

11. In proposing the existence of a coherent "we," I am departing from a prevailing commitment to "liberal" political and economic philosophies that emphasize the importance of individuals, and the difficulty or impossibility of assembling individuals into coherent wholes that can have preferences, formed within the group through a political process, to develop a meaningful collective aspiration. I am entering the realm of "communitarian" philosophies that take a more optimistic view of the possibility (and desirability) of forging individuals into citizens of communities that can have collective aspirations.

12. What that marketplace looks like, and what it is trying to purchase, is, as a positive matter, the focus of political science. As a normative matter, it is something that all citizens, elected representatives, and public managers have to be concerned about. For one "hopeful" view of how this market now functions, see Kelman, *Making Public Policy*.

13. William F. Willoughby emphasized the importance of providing accurate information about how plans have been carried out by public administrators in 1918: "The popular will cannot be intelligently formulated nor expressed unless the public has adequate means for knowing currently how governmental affairs have been conducted in the past, what are present conditions, and what program for work in the future is under consideration." Willoughby, *The Movement for Budgetary Reform in the States* (New York: D. Appleton, for the Institute for Government Research, 1918); Jay M. Shafritz and Albert C. Hyde, eds., *Classics in Public Administration*, 2d ed. (Chicago: Dorsey Press, 1987), reprint Willoughby's text.

14. Kenneth A. Shepsle, "Positive Theories of Congressional Institutions," occasional paper 92-18, Center for American Political Studies, Harvard University, 1992.

15. John Chubb and Paul Peterson make this point succinctly: "The problem of governance in the United States is mainly one of creating institutions or governing arrangements that can pursue policies of sufficient coherence, consistency, foresight and stability that the national welfare is not sacrificed for narrow or temporary gains." See Chubb and Peterson, eds., *Can the Government Govern?* (Washington, D.C.: Brookings Institution, 1989), p. 4.

16. For a defense of this position, see Kelman, *Making Public Policy*.

17. Woodrow Wilson, for example, thought that the crucial question politics had to resolve in committing the government to action was to "discover, first, what government can properly and successfully do." Wilson, "The Study of Administration," *Political Science Quarterly*, 2 (June 1887), reprinted in Shafritz and Hyde, *Classics*, p. 10. Modern economists also prefer that the processes that engage governmental action meet these conditions. See, for example, Stokey and Zeckhauser, *Primer*, pp. 283-285, 292-293, 310-319.

18. Richard Zeckhauser and Derek Leebaert observe: "Our governmental structure requires only that beliefs and values be expressed through the electoral process, whether those beliefs are well- or ill-informed, whether those values are self-serving or public spirited. In practice, our nation has taken minimal steps—most significantly through the support of public education—to encourage a more informed outcome of the political process. Zeckhauser and Leebaert, *What Role for Government: Lessons from Policy Research* (Durham, N.C.: Duke University Press, 1983), pp. 10–11.

19. Woodrow Wilson, "A Study of Administration." For the imagery of perfection in each sphere, see Frank J. Goodnow, *Politics and Administration: A Study in Government* (New York: Russell and Russell, 1900), reprinted in Shafritz and Hyde, *Classics*, pp. 26–29.

20. Edward Banfield makes the distinction between substantive knowledge and administrative knowledge. See Banfield, "The Training of the Executive," *Public Policy: A Yearbook of the Graduate School of Public Administration*, vol. 10 (1960): 20–23.

21. E. Pendelton Herring is most insistent about this fact. See Herring, *Public Administration and the Public Interest* (New York: McGraw-Hill, 1936).

22. This problem continues today and is one of the reasons that public management is so difficult. See Erwin C. Hargrove and John C. Glidewell, eds., *Impossible Jobs in Public Management* (Lawrence: Unversity of Kansas Press, 1990).

23. On the problem of "fickle mandates," see Martha Derthick, *Agency under Stress: The Social Security Administration in American Government* (Washington, D.C.: Brookings Institution, 1990), p. 4.

24. According to Dwight Waldo, "It can be argued with some persuasiveness that the proper role of a bureaucracy is to act as a stabilizing force in the midst of vertiginous change, and that this is what it is doing when it seems to be unresponsive and stupid. In this view it has a balance wheel or gyroscopic function." It is significant, however, that Waldo goes on to reject this view in favor of increased responsiveness or leadership from public managers. See Waldo, "Public Administration in a Time of Revolution," *Public Administration Review*, 28 (July-August 1968), reprinted in Shafritz and Hyde, *Classics*, p. 367.

25. There is, now a large literature that describes the techniques, gives representative examples of their application, assesses their impact on policy-making processes within and outside organizations, and offers critiques of their utility or appropriateness.

26. See preceding note, particularly Lynn, Meltsner, Wildavsky, Forester, and Lindblom.

27. The literature on the utility of techniques of policy analysis and program evaluation is more limited than the literature on it successes. It consists mostly of examples of good pieces of policy analysis or program evaluation, not a demonstration that the work had much impact on policy-making processes.

28. See David Osborne and Ted Gaebler, *Reinventing Government: How the Entreprenuerial Spirit Is Transforming the Public Sector from Schoolhouse to Statehouse, City Hall to the Pentagon* (Reading, Mass.: Addison-Wesley, 1992), pp. 166–194; and Michael Barzelay with Babak Armajani, *Breaking through Bureaucracy: A New Vision for Managing in Government* (Berkeley: University of California Press, 1987), pp. 8–9.

29. Malcolm Sparrow, *Imposing Duties: Government's Changing Approach to Compliance* (Westport, Conn.: Praeger, 1994).

30. On the concept of a service encounter in the private sector, see John A. Czepiel, Michael R. Solomon, and Carol F. Surprenant, eds., *The Service Encounter: Managing Employee/Customer Interaction in Service Businesses* (Lexington, Mass.: D.C. Heath, 1985); and James L. Heskett, W. Earl Sasser, and Christopher W. L. Hart, *Service Breakthroughs: Breaking the Rules of the Game* (New York: Free Press, 1990).

31. Some important justifications for public intervention are presented in Stokey and Zeck-hauser, *Primer*, pp. 291–319.
32. Ibid.
33. Ibid.
34. Rawls makes the distinction between "primary goods," which must be the concerns of justice, and natural goods in *Theory of Justice*, p. 62. He also cautions against doing what I am doing in this section: using his ideas about how to define justice at the broadest social level to also define justice in particular policy contexts. See pp. 9–10.
35. Zeckhauser and Leebaert, *Role for Government*, pp. 3–15.
36. Ibid.
37. Robert Stavins has developed these ideas extensivley in the domain of environmental policy. See Stavins, *Project 88: Harnessing Market Forces to Protect Our Environment* (Washington, D.C.: U.S. Senate, 1988).
38. This idea, too, appears in Zeckhauser and Leebaert, *Role for Government*, pp. 3–15.
39. Dworkin, *Taking Rights Seriously*, pp. 82–100.
40. Doug Yates, *The Ungovernable City: The Politics of Urban Problems and Policy-Making* (Cambridge, Mass.: MIT Press, 1977).
41. For an in-depth discussion of this efficiency criterion, see Stokey and Zeckhauser, *Primer*, pp. 155–158.
42. Ibid., pp. 312–315.
43. This is a natural idea about distributional justice. For a discussion of the idea of need, its role in a theory of justice, and how it relates to governmental institutions, see Rawls, *Theory of Justice*, pp. 274–284. For an interesting empirical exploration of citizens' views of justice in contemporary America, see Jennifer L. Hochschild, *What's Fair: American Beliefs about Distributive Justice* (Cambridge, Mass.: Harvard University Press, 1981).
44. This is a principle of "horizontal equity": everyone gets treated the same by the public regardless of their status. For a discussion in the context of taxation, see Richard A. Musgrave and Peggy B. Musgrave, *Public Finance in Theory and Practice*, 5th ed. (New York: McGraw-Hill, 1989), pp. 218–219, 223–228. For a discussion in the context of law and justice, see Winston, "On Treating Like Cases Alike."
45. To many people, it is a little bit disappointing that the accounting systems of public sector organizations do not necessarily trigger political discussions about the cost-effectiveness of public sector organizations the way that they do in the private sector. Perhaps this difference occurs because the measurement systems for public sector organizations are weaker in revealing the value-producing capability of the organizations. But it may also signify that the political marketplace seems to be much less interested in "numbers" that in "stories" that seem to indicate something about how the organization is important.
46. For a discussion of some of the desirable qualities of a political deliberative process, see Kelman, *Making Public Policy*, pp. 248–270; and Robert Reich, "Policy Making in a Democracy," in Reich, *The Power of Public Ideas*, pp. 123–156.
47. Allison, *Essence of Decision*, pp. 67–100. For examples of organizations whose continuity has been remarkable and important to their overall effectiveness (and difficulties!), see Herbert Kaufman, *The Forest Ranger* (Baltimore: John Hopkins University Press, 1960); and Arthur Maas, *Muddy Waters: The Army Engineers and the Nation's Rivers* (New York: Da Capo Press, 1974).
48. Hugh Heclo states succinctly: "Paradoxically, civil servants can provide some of their most valuable service [to political executives interested in change] by resisting." Heclo, *A Govern-*

ment of Strangers: Executive Politics in Washington (Washington, D.C.: Brookings Institution, 1977), p. 176.

49. Jay R. Galbraith discusses the useful role of "organizational slack" in enhancing the flexibility of organizations in *Designing Complex Organizations* (Reading, Mass.: Addison-Wesley, 1973).

50. Peters and Waterman, *In Search of Excellence,* pp. 121–125.

51. Giandomenico Majone, "Policy Analysis and Public Deliberation," in Reich, *The Power of Public Ideas.*

10

LEADERSHIP AND ACCOUNTABILITY

LEADERSHIP[1]

For a term that is used as commonly as *leadership,* it is a surprisingly complex topic. When leadership is put in the context of permanent organizations, another dimension of complexity is added; and leadership in public administration adds innumerable additional confounding variables and factors. This chapter: explains why leadership and leadership in public administration are complex topics; sorts through some of the more difficult issues involving leadership in government organizations; and, introduces a closely related issue, establishing and maintaining government accountability.

Why then is a topic that is used as often and freely as *leadership,* so complex? First, and perhaps surprisingly, there is not clear-cut agreement about what leadership is.

> Although leadership is important and has been studied by behavioral scientists for decades, it remains something of a mystery. Even after thousands of studies, the experts still lack consensus on exactly what leadership is and how it should be analyzed.[2]

> "Leadership" is one of the most magnetic words in the English language. Mention it, and a perceptible aura of excitement, almost mystical in nature appears. . . . [Yet] if leadership is bright orange, leadership research is slate gray.[3]

Frederick Gibson and Fred Fiedler define *leadership* as: "The actions of a person who, whether elected, appointed, or emerging by group consensus, directs, coordinates, and supervises the work of others for the purpose of accomplishing a given task. . . . It has been said that there are as many definitions of leadership as people who write about it."[4]

Is *leadership* an attribute—a *trait* that some individuals possess but others do not? Is it some*thing* that some people are born with? Can individuals who possess leadership exercise it widely in a variety of situations and in different groups? This line of thinking is usually known as *trait theory* of leadership. A *trait* is a "personality attribute or a way of interacting with others which is independent of the situation, that is, a characteristic of the person rather than of the situation."[5] The trait theory approach assumes that leaders possess traits that are fundamentally different from followers. "The view of trait theorists is that 'great men' rise to leadership positions because of their superior abilities and attributes."[6]

Or is *leadership* the ability to use specific interpersonal skills effectively? Whereas the trait theory approach views leadership as something(s) inherent in a leader, the *transactional theory* approach views leadership as a set of functions and roles that develop from an interaction between two or more people. Although there are enormous differences among the many transactional theories, they all focus on the interaction (or "transaction")—what happens and why as two or more people interact. They also focus on the factors that directly and indirectly influence or shape the nature and quality of the transaction. And, because the transactional theories assume that leadership is the application of skills, they also assume that leadership *behavior* can be learned and acquired.

There is, though, general agreement about some things related to leadership. First, leadership cannot exist unless others are willing to follow. Leadership also involves a relationship between people in which influence and power are unevenly distributed. Thus, most observers of leadership agree that leadership requires *legitimacy*. *Legitimacy* is, in essence, the "fuel" of leadership. It is the reason why some people will follow another or allow themselves to be influenced by another. Legitimacy has many sources, including among others, *charisma*[7] and *technical expertise*.[8]

LEADERSHIP AND MANAGEMENT

When legitimacy is "bestowed" by an organization, yet another set of important but confounding distinctions is introduced: *authority* and the difference between *leadership* and *management*. Although these two functions and roles overlap substantially, *manager* implies that authority has been formally granted to an individual by an organization, and *authority* is thus another source of legitimacy.

Management involves authority bestowed on the occupant of a position by a higher organizational authority. With the power of management come responsibility and accountability for the use of organizational resources. Managers in formal organizations are responsible for and entrusted with such functions as planning, organizing, and controlling. In contrast, *leadership* implies effective use of influence that is rather independent of the authority granted because of organizational position. It is a role and set of functions that are exercised through informal channels.[9] *Management* is a role that is "given" to an individual by higher-ups in the organization. When *leadership* is defined as a transaction, it cannot be "bestowed" upon a person by a higher authority.

Effective managers also must be leaders, and many leaders become managers, but the two sets of roles and functions differ. According to Abraham Zaleznik,[10] leaders in organizations have the ability to handle ambiguity, work with less structure, and do not need to rush to decisions. Managers prefer order, stability, and control and thus will tend to make decisions rapidly, sometimes before they understand the importance of the underlying issues.

LEADERSHIP IN GOVERNMENT

If asked a question about leaders in government, most of us would conjure up images of great presidents, prime ministers, senators, governors, and military leaders: examples might include John F. Kennedy, Ronald Reagan, Nelson Mandela, Winston Churchill, Margaret Thatcher, Dwight Eisenhower, and Douglas MacArthur. With the notable exception of military leaders in wartime, most of the leaders in government that we can identify have been elected officials or their highest-ranking appointees, such as perhaps George Marshall, Henry Kissinger or C. Everett Koop.

In Chapter 4, we discuss the separation of powers between branches of government and between levels of government in the U. S. As a nation, we have not wanted any individual or group in government to have "too much" power or unchecked powers. Thus, the powers of the president are carefully limited by the Constitution-based powers of the legislative branch, the judicial branch, and the states. At other psychological levels, though, we want strong, effective, trustworthy national and state leaders. As a nation, we seem to have loving-but-suspicious feelings toward our elected leaders. We expect them to lead, to be visionary in seeking solutions to deep problems, to propose bold policy initiatives, and to convince the legislature to support and fund their programs—but within carefully prescribed limits.

Elected and appointed public officials are directly accountable to the electorate. Every several years we decide at the ballot box whether we want them to remain in their leadership position. If we decide that they have not been effective leaders, not led in directions that we support, or perhaps even that they have accumulated too much power or remained in office too long, we vote them and their administration out of office. Thus, in addition to the Constitutional "checks and balances" on public leaders, we also have a direct check on their power through the election process.

LEADERSHIP AND PUBLIC ADMINISTRATION

Leadership requires flexibility or *discretion*. A leader must have room to act with some freedom. What discretion—and thus ability to lead—should be available to public administrators, especially administrators who are in the civil service? Civil servants essentially have permanent positions. They do not stand for re-election and are not directly accountable to the electorate. They may be accountable "in theory" up through the bureaucracy to elected officials, but realistically, elected officials have only limited control over the hundreds of thousands of "nameless and faceless bureaucrats." What checks are in place to hold public administrators accountable to whom and for what?

The questions are numerous and important. Should career civil servants indeed be "leaders," or should they be followers who dutifully implement policy directives and who account to offices above them in the bureaucracy? Should public administrators with high levels of technical expertise be expected to defer to elected officials with high levels of political expertise or should they also be public policy leaders?

These questions are not hypothetical, and they are extraordinarily difficult to answer with certainty and clarity. They are laced with both practical and normative uncertainties. Is it possible for a bureaucrat to be a leader? Is it desirable for a bureaucrat to be a leader? In what sense of the word "leader"? Under what circumstances? Within what limits? How can we protect against unaccountable bureaucrats acquiring too much power and leading government unchecked? How can government possibly work if bureaucrats are not allowed to exercise leadership?

ACCOUNTABILITY

Accountability is *answerability* for one's actions. In organizations, accountability is "to higher authorities including elected and appointed officials who sit at the apex of institutional chains of command and to directly involved stakeholders, for performance involves delegation of authority to act."[11] Accountability thus is an integral part of bureaucracy, and leadership, bureaucracy, and accountability are intertwined. Accountability "flows" upward through hierarchical layers of public administrators to elected public officials who "are theoretically accountable to the political sovereignty of the voters."[12]

As the provision of human services by contracted nonprofit organizations became the norm in the 1980s and 1990s (see Chapter 4), a replacement for bureaucratic accountability had to be found. "The state is responsible for actions committed in its name, and those who exercise the power of the state are answerable for their actions."[13] Nonprofit organizations that contract with government to provide services for, for example, people with autism, mental retardation, chronic mental illness, and at-risk youth, are accountable to the government agency. The agency remains accountable for the use of public funds and for the services provided by the nonprofit organizations. When services are contracted out, accountability cannot simply flow up the chain of command. It also has to cross organizational and sectoral boundaries. As government continues to rely more and more heavily on contracted services, public administration, accountability, and leadership within bureaucracies also continue to become more and more challenging tasks.[14]

READINGS REPRINTED IN THIS CHAPTER

"Leadership of Public Bureaucracies: The Administrator as Conservator,"[15] **by Larry Terry** opens the readings in this chapter. Terry argues thoughtfully that scholars and practitioners in the U. S. have largely neglected the topic of leadership in public bureaucracies for many of the long-standing reasons discussed above: "Americans' deeply rooted fear of bureaucracy, the myopia created by Progressive Era reforms [see Chapter 11 in this book], scientific management [see Chapter 6 in this book], and the unintended consequences of scholarly attempts to reconcile bureaucracy with democracy." Terry also adds that "influential scholars, most notably Herbert Kaufman,[16] have perpetuated the belief that public bureaucracies are guided by powerful forces beyond the control of individual leaders."

From Kaufman's point of view, career government executives have only limited effects on the performance of their agencies. But, Terry argues, "it is time to put leadership back into the administration of public bureaucracies." The difficulty, though, is building an argument that un-elected career civil servants *should* exercise leadership and influence. Terry's solution is to define leadership in the civil service in a special way: A leader in a government bureaucracy should be a conservator—not a policy visionary. "The primary function of bureaucratic leaders is to protect and maintain administrative institutions in a manner that promotes or is consistent with constitutional processes, values, and beliefs." This form of leadership is based on legitimate authority and concerned first with stability based "based upon the recognized beliefs, values, and interest of the community."[17] A leader-as-a-conservator takes an active role in "strengthening and preserving an institution's special capabilities, its proficiency, and thereby its integrity so that it may perform a desired social function." As leader-conservators, career civil servants are responsible for the perpetuation and conservation of the values that framed the Constitution and that continue to serve as the foundation of this society. When public administrators take an oath to uphold the Constitution, they are making a moral commitment to the continuance of constitutional processes that encompass particular values, beliefs, and interests.

Public administrators thus must be responsive and responsible to numerous stakeholders and "at the same time must preserve the integrity of public bureaucracies. Public administrators must not be weak or subservient, nor must they be empire builders or public entrepreneurs." This is a tall order. It requires a well developed, internalized, sense of ethics and honor. (See Chapter 15.) "Leadership of Public Bureaucracies," though, provides a useful perspective on leadership in public administration. It also provides an interesting basis for defining leadership effectiveness.

Norma Riccucci's, "Execucrats, Politics, and Public Policy,"[18] is a chapter from her book, *Unsung Heroes: Federal Execucrats Making A Difference.* As the title suggests, "Execucrats" is about U. S. federal civil servants who have "made a difference" without attracting headlines. "The American people often overlook the fact that it is not just the people we elect to government office who make social and political decisions about how this country is run. There is also a layer of high-level civil servants in the federal bureaucracy who are responsible for decisions and policies that affect our lives in vital ways. They are the 'execucrats,' the career *execu*tives/bureau*crats*. . . ." Riccucci explains that effective execucrats do indeed exercise leadership and influence public policy. "Execucrats are delegated the power needed to make high-level decisions and public policy."

Riccucci's execucrats are the leaders in the career service that Larry Terry argues should be conservator-leaders. Execucrats are individuals who have chosen careers in government bureaucracies and worked their way up through the ranks to high levels. Unlike appointed officials, execucrats are not loyal to specific elected leaders and their motives for being in government differ markedly from political appointees. "There is an ethos among the vast majority of execucrats that is characterized by a desire not for monetary rewards but to serve as change agents, fighting for positive change in specific policy spheres—a clean environment, the public health, safe and efficient sources of energy, global harmony."

Although execucrats often shape public policy, they do not work alone or in a vacuum. They participate in the formulation of public policy with leaders of congressional committees, committee staffs, appointed executives, interest groups, and a host of other players. They also participate in the formulation of public policy in a variety of other ways: they provide advice to presidents, congressional leaders, and congressional staff; draft bills for Congress, interpret laws after they have been passed by Congress through the rule-making process; develop and implement specific programs to enact laws; and through the conduct of executive branch adjudicatory and regulatory processes. Riccucci concludes that effective execucrats are leaders who also possess technical expertise, political skills, personality, experience in government, and the ability to strategize.

"Accountability in the Public Sector: Lessons from the Challenger Tragedy," by Barbara Romzek and Melvin Dubnick,[19] bridges between the two topics addresses in this chapter: leadership and accountability. Why did the launch of the space shuttle Challenger proceed on January 28, 1986, even though there was a clear and present danger? To what extent was the Challenger accident the result of technical problems, leadership failures, and/or institutional pressures?

Who was accountable? In a bureaucracy such as NASA, contractors are accountable to NASA project personnel who are accountable to higher level "execucrats," to highest level executive branch officials, and to Congress and the public. Where and why did leadership and accountability fail? Romzek and Dubnick identify four types of accountability that are commonly used by public agencies to manage expectations of them within and outside the organization: bureaucratic accountability, legal accountability, professional accountability, and political accountability. They argue that NASA had been an organization in which professional accountability prevailed. "Over time, the pressures to develop a politically responsive agency became dominant. . . . This reliance on bureaucratic and political accountability systems [over professional accountability systems] produced circumstances which made the agency ill-equipped to contend with the problems that eventually led to the Challenger disaster. . . . In the late 1960s, NASA faced a leveling off of both its political and financial support."

The Vietnam War, President Johnson's "War on Poverty," and declining interest in space exploration meant that NASA no longer took priority. In effect, circumstances largely outside of NASA caused NASA's leadership and accountability systems to gradually change from their professional orientation to political and bureaucratic orientations. "It was under these conditions that decisions . . . were being made when the Challenger lifted from its Kennedy Space Center pad on January 28, 1986."

NOTES

1. Portions of this essay on leadership are adapted from J. Steven Ott. (1996). "Leadership," Chapter III in J. S. Ott (Ed.), *Classic Readings in Organizational Behavior* (2nd ed.) (pp. 163–174). Fort Worth, TX: Harcourt Brace.
2. Ivancevich, John M., and Michael T. Matteson. (1996). *Organizational Behavior and Management* (4th ed.). New York: Irwin McGraw-Hill, p. 411.
3. Lombardo, Michael M., and Morgan W. McCall, Jr. (1978). "Leadership," in M. W. McCall and M. M. Lombardo (Eds.), *Leadership: Where Else Can We Go?* Durham, NC: Duke University Press, p. 3.
4. Gibson, Frederick W., and Fred E. Fiedler. (1998). "Leadership," in Jay M. Shafritz (Ed.), *International Encyclopedia of Public Policy and Administration*. Boulder, Colo.: Westview, p. 1264.
5. Fiedler, Fred E., and Martin M. Chemers. (1974). *Leadership Style and Effective Management*. Glenview, IL: Scott, Foresman, p. 22.
6. Gibson, Frederick W., and Fred E. Fiedler. (1998). "Leadership," in Jay M. Shafritz (Ed.), *International Encyclopedia of Public Policy and Administration*. Boulder, Colo.: Westview, p. 1265.
7. Shafritz, Jay M. (1988). "Charisma," in J. M. Shafritz (Ed.), *The Dorsey Dictionary of Politics and Government*. Chicago: Dorsey Press, p. 89.
8. For the "all-time classic" on the sources of legitimacy and thus influence, see John R. P. French and Bertram Raven. (1959). "The Bases of Social Power," in Dorwin Cartwright and Alvin Zander (Eds.), *Studies in Social Power* (pp. 150–167). Ann Arbor, Mich.: University of Michigan, Institute for Social Research.
9. See Chapter 6, "Organizational Behavior."
10. Zaleznik, Abraham. (March–April 1992). "Managers and Leaders: Are They Different?" *Harvard Business Review*, 126–135.
11. Kearns, Kevin P. (1996). *Managing for Accountability: Preserving the Public Trust in Public and Nonprofit Organizations*. San Francisco: Jossey-Bass, p. 11.
12. Shafritz, Jay M. (1992). *The HarperCollins Dictionary of American Government and Politics*. New York: HarperCollins, p. 4.
13. Dwivedi, O. P., and Joseph G. Jabbra. (1988). "Public Service Responsibility and Accountability," in J. G. Jabbra and O. P. Dwivedi (Eds.), *Public Service Accountability* (p. 3).
14. Ott, J. Steven, and Lisa A. Dicke. "Important but Largely Unanswered Questions about Accountability in Contracted Public Human Services." *International Journal of Organization Theory & Behavior*, 3(3 & 4), Summer 2000, 283-317.
15. Terry, Larry D. (1995). "Bureaucratic Leadership in a Democratic Republic," in L. D. Terry, *Leadership of Public Bureaucracies: The Administrator as Conservator* (pp. 1–31). Thousand Oaks, Calif.: Sage.

16. Kaufman, Herbert. (1981). *The Administrative Behavior of Federal Bureau Chiefs.* Washington, D.C.: Brookings; and, Herbert Kaufman. (1981). "The Fear of Bureaucracy: A Raging Pandemic." *Public Administration Review, 41*, 1–9.
17. Friedrich, Carl J. (1961). "Political Leadership and the Problem of the Charismatic Power." *The Journal of Politics, 23*, 21.
18. Riccucci, Norma M. (1995). "Execucrats, Politics, and Public Policy," in N. M. Riccucci, *Unsung Heroes: Federal Execucrats Making a Difference* (pp. 1–21). Washington, D.C.: Georgetown University Press.
19. Romzek, Barbara S., and Melvin J. Dubnick. (1987). "Accountability in the Public Sector: Lessons from the Challenger Tragedy." *Public Administration Review, 47*(3), 227–238.

27

Larry D. Terry

LEADERSHIP OF PUBLIC BUREAUCRACIES: THE ADMINISTRATOR AS CONSERVATOR

At century's end, the United States is confronted with a host of complex problems that tough every segment of society. The nation's urban communities are in crisis as homelessness, crime, and severe poverty continue to take their toll. Once again, our public education system is under attack. The embarrassing discovery that millions of adults are illiterate has stoked the fires of education reformers who believe that massive changes are needed for America to compete successfully in a rapidly changing, increasingly interdependent world. The number of Americans who lack adequate health care because of prolonged unemployment or underemployment has become a national disgrace as U.S. corporations continue to move manufacturing operations abroad. Although labor officials and the general public have expressed outrage over the loss of well-paying jobs and the displacement of thousands of blue-collar and white-collar workers, they seem virtually helpless in dissuading corporations from pursuing this "competitive" cost-saving strategy.

The nature and scope of these and countless other problems and the perception that public and private institutions are ineffective in solving them have sparked a renewed interest in leadership. Americans from Wall Street to Main Street are expressing dissatisfaction with the performance of leaders in government, business, and labor. In fact, it seems that the United States is in the midst of a leadership reform movement. From all indications, this movement is gaining momentum and has turned into a referendum on the quality of leadership in this country. A consensus is emerging that more effective leadership is needed to rescue the United States from the valleys of decline. There is a perception that if only leaders were up to the challenges, our complex problems would somehow disappear.

THE NEGLECT OF BUREAUCRATIC LEADERSHIP

In all of this talk about more effective leadership, the topic of *bureaucratic leadership* is conspicuously absent. By bureaucratic leadership, I mean institutional leadership in the administration of public bureaucracies within the executive branch of all levels of government.[1] More specifically, bureaucratic leadership is an active process that emanates from the executive branch and entails the exercise of power, authority, and strategic discretion in pursuit of the public interest.

Why has there been so little scholarly interest in the role and function of bureaucratic leaders?

The neglect of bureaucratic leadership may arise from a combination of related factors, including Americans' deeply rooted fear of bureaucracy, the myopia created by Progressive Era reforms and scientific management, and the unintended consequences of scholarly attempts to reconcile bureaucracy with democracy.

THE FEAR OF BUREAUCRATIC POWER

The rise and expansion of public bureaucracies, especially at the national level, have generated a great deal of hostility toward public bureaucracies and career civil servants. Although such growth has been in response to a complex mixture of socioeconomic and political conditions, the expansion of public bureaucracies is nevertheless viewed by many as a threat to democracy. Public bureaucracies have been aggressively attacked by segments of the general public, the news media, the academic and business community, the judiciary, and the political establishment. These attacks have contributed to a legitimacy crisis for public bureaucracies. James O. Freedman (1978) goes straight to the heart of the matter when he says that "the growth of the administrative process has raised troubling questions concerning its implications for the character of American democracy, the nature of American justice and the quality of American life" (p. 260).

Although critics offer different arguments to substantiate their attacks, the fear of bureaucratic power is a common theme. Public bureaucracies are perceived as wielding too much power. Critics charge that career civil servants have accumulated vast amounts of power and thus are no longer responsive and accountable to elected political authorities. This so-called unaccountable power is regarded as incongruent with the values of the American democratic system.

The fear of governmental power is inextricably interwoven into the fabric of our society. Critics of bureaucracy quickly point out that the enormous power exercised by bureaucrats in the so-called fourth branch of government is incompatible with the constitutional design envisioned by the founders. They suggest that the founders did not anticipate nor would they approve of a powerful, largely autonomous political institution controlled by nonelected and nonpolitically appointed public officials. The founders were deeply concerned, so the argument goes, about the possibility of substantial power residing in one person or political institution. This explains their rejection of the notion of the president as "leader" as well as their preoccupation with the need to check the exercise of political power.[2]

Kenneth J. Meier (1987), a leading critic of bureaucratic power, expresses many of the aforementioned concerns. According to Meier, the bureaucracy has been transformed into a "political institution" (p. 134).

Meier is not alone in his fear of bureaucratic power. The ominous specter of a powerful, imperial bureaucracy controlled by a cadre of unaccountable technocrats has also heightened the concerns of many other Americans as well. The fear of bureaucracy has become so pervasive in recent years that Herbert Kaufman (1981) describes the situation as a "raging pandemic" (p. 1). Antibureaucratic forces have responded to such fears by devising strategies to strip public bureaucracies of their power. These strategies include, among others, extensive politicization of bureaucracy; constant reorganization; extensive use of deregulation and budget, program, and personnel cuts to reduce the size of government; the exclusion of career executives from policy discussions and formal processes; and expansion of the size of both executive and legislative staffs to reduce the expertise gap between these branches of government and public bureaucracies. These strategies are guided by the assumption that bureaucratic power can be curtailed by severely reducing and tightly controlling the discretion and authority of administrative officials.

Supporters of public bureaucracies contend that the aforementioned power-stripping strategies have caused serious long-term damage and have undermined the capacity of administrative institutions of government to serve the public good. Supporters argue that such strategies not only have weakened public institutions but also have relegated the notion of bureaucratic leadership to a meaningless status. Critics respond that the concept of bureaucratic leadership is a contradiction in terms and thus deserves the dubious status of oxymoron. Why should anyone be concerned about bureaucratic leaders if there is no need for them? After all, the weakening of public bureaucracies is intended to limit the power, authority, and strategic discretion of career executives. Moreover, because the founders were reluctant to use the term *leader* when referring to the president, an elected political official, it stands to reason that the notion of bureaucratic leadership would have little intellectual currency.

I draw the following conclusions with respect to the problem of legitimizing the role of public bureaucracies in the American political system:

1. The role of public bureaucracies in the structure of American government is compatible with original constitutional principles.
2. The role of both public bureaucracies and career civil servants is to sustain and preserve constitutional principles. Public administrators have a moral obligation to sustain such principles because they took an oath to uphold the Constitution of the United States.
3. Although public bureaucracies must occupy a subordinate yet autonomous role with respect to other democratic institutions and processes, the performance of this role does not mean that career civil servants should become passive participants in governance. Guided by classical constitutional theory and, in turn, the logic of a constitution, public administrators have a legitimate right to check the power of elected political leaders.

4. Public bureaucracies heal the constitutional defect with respect to representation. They also serve as a representative institution that participates in and ensures reasoned deliberations on public policy issues.

5. Although public bureaucracies exercise combined executive, legislative, and judicial powers, the exercise of such powers in a subordinate capacity is consistent with the framers' relaxed interpretation of the separation-of-powers doctrine. Public bureaucracies also fulfill the constitutional design with respect to separation of powers because of their permanency and stability; they are equipped to give priority to "steady administration of law" (Cook, 1992, p. 422).

6. Public bureaucracies play an important role by helping form the character of citizens by contributing to the ongoing process of making the American regime what it is.

With these conclusions in mind, it is now possible to make some statement of theory about leadership in the administration of public bureaucracies. I argue that public bureaucracies must be preserved so that they can serve the public good. Thus, the *primary function of bureaucratic leaders is to protect and maintain administrative institutions in a manner that promotes or is consistent with constitutional processes, values, and beliefs*. If this is indeed the case, then leadership in administration of public bureaucracies is similar to what Carl J. Friedrich (1961) describes as "maintaining leadership," a type of political leadership concerned with stability of the regime and based on authority—authority defined as the "capacity for reasoned elaboration based upon the recognized beliefs, values, and interest of the community" (p. 21). According to Friedrich, the maintaining leader is a *conservator* because his or her primary function is to protect and preserve the existing government and its traditions.

The concept of maintaining leadership, when applied to public bureaucracies, sheds some light on the notion of bureaucratic leadership. Grounded in this concept, then, public administrators are administrative conservators. As such, they are actively engaged in a special type of leadership: *administrative conservatorship*.

THE CONCEPT OF ADMINISTRATIVE CONSERVATORSHIP

The concept of administrative conservatorship is consistent with the American constitutional tradition and provides a perspective for conceptualizing the leadership role of career executives in governance. Administrative conservatorship is statesmanship in the tradition of Edmund Burke, the 18th-century British politician and philosopher, because it requires a "disposition to preserve and an ability to improve." Administrative conservatorship is also an intellectual progeny of the institutional leadership school in sociology, particularly as manifest in the work of Philip Selznick (1957).

The term *conservatorship* was coined to characterize an active leadership role for public administrators in governance. The term is derived from the Latin word *conservare*, meaning to preserve. Someone who engages in the act of preserving is defined as a conservator. More specific, a conservator is a guardian, someone who conserves or preserves from injury, violation, or infraction. From an institutional perceptive, administrative conservatorship is an active and dynamic process of strengthening and preserving an institution's special capabilities, its proficiency, and thereby its integrity so that it may perform a desired social function.

Administrative conservatorship is not an attempt to preserve a comfortable or static state and should not be confused with administrative *conservership* as described by Anthony Downs (1967, chap. 8 & 9). Rather, controlled adaptation to changing circumstances is obviously an ongoing necessity. As prudently stated by Selznick (1957), "To the essentially conservative posture of the responsible leader we must add a concern for change and reconstruction" (p. 149).

Because it is linked to much broader considerations, administrative conservatorship concentrates on more than solely fulfilling the needs of organizational members. Properly conceptualized, administrative conservatorship is the willingness of *administrative elites*, out of traditional loyalty and moral principles, to preserve authority and distribution of power with regard to the propriety of an *institution's* existence, its functional niche, and its collective institutional goals. In the final analysis, administrative conservatorship is concerned with the preservation of *institutional integrity*.

The significance and meaning of the terms *institution*, *institutional integrity*, and *administrative elites* used in the above definition of administrative conservatorship must be clarified. The term *institution* as conceptualized here is consistent with the definition offered by theorists of the institutional school in sociology and is best represented by the works of Selznick. For analytical purposes, the institution is differentiated from an organization, which is a rational, means-oriented instrument guided by the "cult" of efficiency. In contrast, the institution is considered a creation of social needs and aspirations; it is an adaptive, responsive, cooperative system that embodies cultural values. The cultural values and moral commitments of a society are implanted in its institutions. In short, institutions represent the "ethos of the culture, its particular way of self fulfillment" (Selznick, 1952, p. 295).

The next term, *institutional integrity*, is central to the concept of administrative conservatorship. The idea of institutional integrity has not received the scholarly attention it deserves. Chester I. Barnard (1948) alludes to this:

> The primary efforts of leaders need to be directed to the *maintenance* and guidance of organizations as whole systems. I believe this to be the most distinctive characteristic sector of leadership behavior, but it is the least obvious and least understood. The leader has to guide all in such a way to *preserve* organization as the instrument of action. (p. 89; italics added)

Institutional integrity is related to the notion of "distinctive competence" (Selznick, 1957, p. 139), the special capacities, abilities, and proficiencies possessed by an agency in the performance of particular functions. An institution's distinctive competence is developed by a combination of value commitments made by administrative conservators. Value commitments are decisions that obligate and bind institutional activities and processes to specific course of action. They are "choices that fix the assumptions of policymakers as to the nature of the enterprise" (p. 55). Administrative decisions relating to institutional purpose, the means for its accomplishment, and the social composition of the members are examples of areas bound by value commitments. Value commitments vary in terms of their importance to the formation and maintenance of an institution's distinctive competence. Because they provide the foundation of an institution's distinctive competence, some value commitments may be considered hypersensitive.

The notion of distinctive competence is the heart of *institutional integrity*. The word *integrity* refers to the completeness, wholeness, and intact quality of an entity. In the context of administrative conservatorship, institutional integrity refers to the completeness, wholeness, soundness, and persistence of administrative processes, value commitments, and unifying principles that determine an institution's distinctive competence. The preservation of institutional integrity is an important area of administrative concern. As noted by Selznick (1957), "the protection of integrity is more than an aesthetic or expressive exercise, more than an attempt to preserve a comforting, familiar environment. It is a practical concern of the first importance because the defense of integrity is also a defense of the organization's *distinctive competence*" (p. 139).

The final term, *administrative elites*, does not necessarily mean or imply aristocrats in the traditional sense; rather, it refers to those individuals or groups who are responsible for the promotion and conservation of social values. Although egalitarians may find the term *elite* somewhat unsettling, I advocate that elites are essential to the perpetuation and preservation of society because they are the bearers and conservators of cultural values.

In the context of administrative conservatorship, elites are public officials who are neither elected nor politically appointed but who hold administrative positions by virtue of a merit system. These officials influence public policy by exercising their administrative discretion. Administrative elites are *bureaucrats* as honorably defined by Rohr (1978). As administrative elites, career civil servants are responsible for the perpetuation and conservation of "regime values," that is, "values of the political entity that [was] brought into being by ratification of the Constitution that created the present American republic" (p. 59). The Constitution is the foundation of our society and symbolizes the society's frame of mind. According to George Will (1983):

> The Constitution does not just distribute power, it does so in a cultural context of principles and beliefs and expectations about appropriate social outcome of the exercise of those powers. . . . A Constitution not only presupposes a consensus of "views" on fundamentals; it also presupposes concern for its own continuance. Therefore, it presupposes efforts to predispose rising generations to the "views" and habits and dispositions that underlie institutional arrangements. In this sense, a constitution is not only an allocator of power; it is also the polity's frame of mind. (p. 79)

When public administrators take an oath to uphold the Constitution, they are making a moral commitment to the continuance of constitutional processes that encompass particular values, beliefs, and interests. This commitment is expressed in practical terms through their fidelity to duty in the administration of governmental institutions, including the values embodied in the Constitution. Through such institutions, the authoritative allocation of resources is made to sustain the Republic's cohesion and moral balance. As a repository of regime values, governmental institutions must be conserved especially because the strength of cultural values is contingent on the capacity of primary institutions to transmit them without serious distortion.

The perpetuation of cultural values depends on the security of key institutions. Security in this context implies stability, strength, and overall integrity. Ensuring security of governmental institutions is, to a large extent, the responsibility of public administrators because they are vital in providing continuity and stability. This role is especially important in a democratic system in which political appointees are merely temporary custodians of governmental institutions (see Heclo, 1977).

The efforts of administrative executives to preserve the integrity of public bureaucracies afford them the distinction of being called administrative conservators. As conservators of public bureaucracies, administrative executives are active and legitimate participants in "statecraft." Statecraft, as coined by Will (1983), is "soulcraft" in that it involves the "conversation of values and arrangements that are not subjects of day-to-day debate" (p. 156). Soulcraft does not imply the conservation of values espoused by a particular political party, nor does it suggest the preservation of passing whims. Rather, soulcraft entails the conservation of regime values, which is a moral obligation. The preservation of public bureaucracies and, in turn, regime values reflects the normative quality of administrative conservatorship.

If a regime is fundamentally unjust and even immoral, it will be difficult for the public administrator to be a "good human being and a good citizen [of that regime] at the same time" (Rohr, 1978, p. 61). Nazi Germany's Third Reich was an extreme case. Not all regimes are so unjust. It is also possible for administrative executives to circumvent regime values, as illustrated by the actions of J. Edgar Hoover at the end of his reign and of Anne Burford during her tenure as administrator of the U.S. Environmental Protection Agency. Their actions did not constitute administrative conservatorship.

Administrative conservatorship may be regarded as a type of statesmanship. It requires balancing the inherent tension in the political system between the need to *serve* and the need to *preserve*. Public administrators must be responsive to the demands of political elites, the courts, interest groups, and the citizenry and at the same time must preserve the integrity of public bureaucracies. Public administrators must not be weak or subservient, nor must they be empire builders or public entrepreneurs conceptualized in a pejorative sense. Rather, public administrators must honorably hold up the administrative side of the governance equation. Paul Appelby (1949) said it best:

> Administrators share with all others in places of special responsibility the special obligation of *leadership*. They can, in all innocence, contribute to organizational practices and form elements that are inimical to popular government. They can help "take things out of politics"—or take themselves too far out of politics. They, like citizens and legislators, are capable of yielding too much to the prestige of military or other experts, too little to the politician who is the central factor in civilian control and popular government. By dealing with the legislature too directly, they may undermine and confuse executive responsibility; by the same tactics they may inadvertently substitute control by members of Congress for control by Congress as a body. By failing to be imaginative about legislative needs, attitudes, and prerogatives, they

may overburden, and thus degrade the legislature. Their *special duty* is in part to help clear the way so that other parts of government and the other political processes may function well. (p. 199; italics added)

The concept of administrative conservatorship provides a valuable perspective in which public administrators and others may view their administrative leadership role in the American political system. It is offered as a means of restoring respectability to public administrators and the public service. The concept of administrative conservatorship is also offered as a framework for measuring administrative leadership effectiveness.

NOTES

1. The term *institutional leadership* is used in the manner suggested by Philip Selznick (1957, 1992). According to Selznick (1992), "institutional leadership" is concerned with governance. The institutional leader is responsible for "the whole life of the institution" and "takes account of all the interests that affect the viability, competence, and moral character of an enterprise" (p. 290). Quotations from Selznick (1992), *The moral commonwealth; Social theory and the promise of community* are reprinted by permission of the University of California Press, Berkeley.
2. As noted by Rohr (1986), the Federalists used the term *leadership* in a pejorative manner. The term was closely associated with *favorite* or *demagogue*.

REFERENCES

Appelby, P. (1949). *Policy and administration.* University: University of Alabama Press.
Barnard, C. I. (1948). *Organization and management.* Cambridge, MA: Harvard University Press.
Burke, E. (1987). *Reflections on the revolution in France* (J. G. A. Pocock, Ed.). Indianapolis: Hackett. (Original work published 1789)
Cook, B. J. (1992). The representative function of bureaucracy: Public administration in a constitutive perspective. *Administration & Society, 23,* 403–429.
Downs, A. (1967). *Inside bureaucracy.* Boston: Little, Brown.
Freedman, J. O. (1978). *Crisis and legitimacy: The administrative process and American government.* New York: Cambridge University Press.
Friedrich, C. J. (1961). Political leadership and the problem of the charismatic power. *The Journal of Politics, 23,* 3–24.
Friedrich, C. J. (1963). *Man and his government.* New York: McGraw-Hill.
Friedrich, C. J. (1972). *Tradition and authority.* New York: Praeger.
Heclo, H. (1977). *A government of strangers: Executive politics in Washington.* Washington, DC: Brookings Institution.
Kaufman, H. (1981). The fear of bureaucracy: A raging pandemic. *Public Administration Review, 41,* 1–9.
Meier, K. J. (1987). *Politics and the bureaucracy: Policymaking in the fourth branch of government* (2nd ed.). Monterey, CA: Brooks/Cole.
Meier, K. J. (1989). Bureaucratic leadership in public organizations. In B. D. Jones (Ed.), *Leadership and politics* (pp. 267–286). Lawrence: University Press of Kansas.
Rohr, J. A. (1978). *Ethics for bureaucrats.* New York: Marcel Dekker.

Rohr, J. A. (1986). *To run a constitution: The legitimacy of the administrative state*. Lawrence: University Press of Kansas.

Selznick, P. (1949). *TVA and the grass roots*. Berkeley: University of California Press.

Selznick, P. (1952). *The organizational weapon: A study of the Bolshevik strategy and tactics*. New York: McGraw-Hill.

Selznick, P. (1957). *Leadership in administration: A sociological interpretation*. Evanston, IL: Row, Peterson.

Selznick, P. (1987). The idea of a communitarian morality. *California Law Review, 75*, 445–468.

Selznick, P. (1992). *The moral commonwealth: Social theory and the promise of community*. Berkeley: University of California Press.

Will, G. (1983). *Statecraft as soulcraft: What government does*. New York: Simon & Schuster.

28

Norma M. Riccucci

UNSUNG HEROES: FEDERAL EXECUCRATS MAKING A DIFFERENCE

bureaucrat—a government official who follows a narrow, rigid, formal routine, without exercising intelligent judgment.

> *Webster's Ninth New Collegiate Dictionary*
> and *Random House Dictionary of the English Language*

"Ozone friendly, no fluorocarbons," read the message on the instant whipped-cream can in bold red letters. As I continued to shop for groceries, I began to think about the ozone war, embodied right here on a 7 oz. can of whipped cream. It's comforting to know, I thought, that the government was still working to make our environment cleaner, healthier, and safer and that at the same time, we could continue to enjoy the modern conveniences of aerosol-type products. But who are the people in government, I asked myself, that are actually on the front line of the ozone war? Would I recognize their names and faces? Do they get adequate praise and accolades for their hard work in and commitment to such an important yet relatively understated area of public policy as the environment? I then reflected, such profound thoughts brought forth from a $1.49 can of fake cream!

Most people would not ruminate over their groceries in this fashion. Likewise, the average citizen gives little thought to the government workers who devote their lives to improving our quality of life by making our environment healthier and cleaner, our streets safer, our housing more affordable, and our nation free from the terrorism that pervades so many other countries. Although we learn about U.S. presidents and members of Congress in our high-school history and American government textbooks, we don't hear about the nonelected government workers who are also influential players in the governing of America. We then learn as adults, by reading the newspaper, going to a movie, or waiting in a long line at the DMV for a driver's license, about "lazy, inefficient bureaucrats," who do nothing but waste taxpayers' hard-earned dollars.[1]

This book seeks to present a more complete and accurate picture of the work performed by high-level civil servants (a.k.a. Senior Executive Servants or SESers) and the factors that contribute to their effectiveness in a setting that is immensely political. These civil servants are rarely if ever placed in the limelight for their contributions to advancing the well-being of the American people. You will not recognize their names, because they don't tend to appear in *Time*, *Newsweek*, or your local newspapers. They seldom receive praise or recognition for their hard work and commitment to promoting the public good. They are the "unsung heroes"—the people who are behind the scenes and whom we rarely learn about.

EXECUCRATS AND THE BUREAUCRACY

The American people often overlook the fact that it is not just the people we elect to government office who make social and political decisions about how this country is run. There is also a layer of high-level civil servants in the federal bureaucracy who are responsible for decisions and policies that affect our lives in vital ways. They are the "execucrats," the career *executives/bureaucrats*, who are neither elected nor appointed to office.

It is no small wonder that the average American knows little about execucrats, because on the grander scale of politics and policy, these individuals are often misjudged or underestimated. This is in large part due to intentional efforts to characterize them as being powerless and unable to influence public policy. There has indeed been a tendency to view execucrats as the "cogs" who merely implement the decisions of elected officials.

But because of the nature of the American political system, it has become more apparent that execucrats not only possess the skills and resources to formulate policy decisions but are explicitly relied upon to do so.[2] That is to say, because elected leaders lack the necessary technical expertise and are politically reluctant to make choices that may undermine their standing with their constituencies, execucrats are delegated the power needed to make high-level decisions and public policy. As political scientist David Rosenbloom points out, "public employees have emerged as a major—perhaps in some policy areas, *the* major—power center in complex political systems such as the United States.[3]

Perhaps the best evidence that execucrats do in fact possess the power to influence public policy is seen in the intentional efforts by presidents and their political staffs to block execucrats from using that power. While it was less blatant under the Clinton and Bush administrations, President Reagan and many of his appointees were notorious for doing this as they sought to push through the administration's ideology and policies. Anne Gorsuch (now Burford), whom Reagan appointed to head the EPA, will be well remembered for her contemptible treatment of execucrats. Gorsuch, like many of Reagan's appointees, was very suspicious and mistrustful of execucrats. EPA execucrats who worked for Gorsuch at the time described her as "a manager who did not trust the agency's career civil servants"[4] and would not make "a major yes-no decision based on recommendations [from them]."[5] She was simply not interested in the advice or input of people she presumed to be at odds with Reagan-Gorsuch policy directions. So, instead, Gorsuch totally trusted and relied on the policy advice of not only her political staff but also industry representatives, the very people the EPA is supposed to regulate for environmental abuse.[6]

Gorsuch's success in excluding EPA execucrats from policy making was short-lived, however, since it soon became apparent that her political staff did not possess the knowledge or expertise needed to formulate and execute environmental policy. As one EPA official observed, "Most of Gorsuch's . . . staff [were] second-rate industry lawyers, lobbyists and public relations people."[7] One execucrat went even further to say that President Reagan's political appointees to the EPA "had the lowest IQ's I have ever encountered."[8] So, in the end, Gorsuch really had no other choice but to turn to the execucrats.

In short, execucrats are relied upon to make high-level decisions and public policy. Moreover, sometimes the decisions they make represent invaluable contributions and improvements to our quality of life, from the creation of new jobs to the discovery of new preventive measures for such fatal diseases as AIDS. This, too, is not widely known or understood beyond academic circles because of the politics that pervade the congressional and White House establishments, politics that reflect the efforts by politicians to get reelected. Execucrats may make important policy decisions, but it is the elected leaders who will assume credit when the policy decisions and choices that execucrats make are perceived as "good" by the general public. When they are seen as poor decisions, the American people are usually told that those "damn bureaucrats" are to blame.

While this may help politicians get reelected, it certainly doesn't help the image of execucrats, who are brought into the limelight only when someone or something is to be blamed for waste, fraud, corruption, and inefficiency.

This book will show not only that federal execucrats possess the power to make high-level decisions and public policy but also that contrary to popular belief, these decisions and policies represent important contributions to our society in a host of policy domains.

This task is difficult but essential because, if the work of the public service is to be carried out effectively, the American public must have a better understanding of what execucrats do as well as the constraints they face. In addition, by providing positive role models, this work could encourage young persons to consider careers in government and could also boost the morale and self-esteem of those currently working in government.

EXACTLY WHO ARE THESE EXECUCRATS?

Execucrats, as noted earlier, are those persons who have chosen to make a career out of government service. They are not elected to office, nor are they appointed by an elected leader, such as the president. Rather, they enter government service as a result of their performance either on a civil service test or in an interview, the latter being much like what one would encounter in private enterprise.[9] Moreover, many have worked their way up the ranks of government, just as one would in any career. In short, they represent the permanent corps of the public service.

Execucrats and political appointees are often lumped into one category, even by the media. But there are notable differences between the two. First, execucrats, unlike political appointees, do not serve at the pleasure of elected officials and hence are not indebted (or indentured!) to them. Admittedly, political appointees will sometimes break rank with their superiors, but this is generally the exception to the rule. Execucrats, on the other hand, "have a responsibility that is institutional and enduring, whoever the political figures in charge might be."[10] Indeed, this is the raison d'être of a civil service: "To institute a civil service system is to accept the idea that competent personnel [staffing] the government machinery should be available for use by—but not at the absolute disposal of—any political group arriving in office through legitimate means."[11]

Execucrats, then, unlike political appointees, do not have specific loyalties to elected leaders. To be sure, many execucrats do develop strong professional linkages with congressional leaders, since Congress is the body that is empowered to fund their agencies and programs. In general, execucrats work with and sometimes must maneuver around politicians, but they are not "held hostage" by them. As for their loyalties? It would appear that execucrats tend to enter into the public service to promote the interests of the American people. They certainly cannot be in it for the money, because the pay in the public sector is typically not commensurate with that in private business. On average, federal execucrats earn almost 25 percent less than their counterparts in the private sector.[12] Why, then, would one—especially at the upper, executive level—choose a profession in government over business, when the latter clearly pays more? There is an ethos among the vast majority of execucrats that is characterized by a desire not for monetary rewards but to serve as change agents, fighting for positive change in specific policy spheres—a clean environment, the public health, safe and efficient sources of energy, global harmony.

It would be naive to think, however, that some execucrats are not motivated by self-interest. As prominent economist Anthony Downs has claimed, government does have its share of "climbers," those "bureaucrats motivated solely by the desire to maximize their own personal power, income and prestige."[13] Yet even Downs, who, overall, holds a rather Hobbesian view of government workers, points out that "even [those] who usually behave like climbers are also sometimes moved by charity, anger, patriotism, loyalty to superiors . . . and myriad additional goals."[14]

There are also those execucrats who, given the nature of their agencies, may be working on behalf of small, circumscribed constituencies. We often hear about members of Congress working to advance the goals of special interest groups, sometimes at the expense of the general public. Farming, banking, insurance, and firearms interests are but a few that represent important voting blocs to elected officials. Once Congress is able to appropriate public monies to accommodate their interests, execucrats are then relied upon to divvy up the monies among the respective groups. One political scientist explains it in this fashion: "[Execucrats] are heavily engaged in policy and politics a good share of their time . . . . It is controversy, competition and negotiation among different factions within the bureaucracy itself. It consists in dealing with, responding to, or [sometimes] resisting clienteles and other interest groups outside the bureaucracy, and dealing with Congressional groups and other individual congress [persons]."[15] It has been pointed out, however, that "[f]rom this melee . . . will emerge a degree of order and balance roughly responsive to the *people* expressing themselves through organized groups."[16] In other words, over time, it is often the case that everyone benefits, particularly when we take into account the various *public*-interest groups working on behalf of all Americans to improve such social conditions as the environment and public health.[17] For example, when the Natural Resources Defense Council (NRDC), a prominent environmental group, works with Congress and execucrats from the Environmental Protection Agency (EPA) to combat air and water pollution, all of us ultimately benefit.

There are forces operating in our society that further ensure that the general public does not go unrepresented under this political system of pluralism. For example, the president of the United States is expected to act on behalf of the *whole* people.[18] In addition, there is "the somewhat hopeful concept that conscientious, educated and well-disposed public servants will behave in the general *public interest*."[19] In fact, there are instances when execucrats and the bureaucracy serve as advocates not for the power brokers in our society but for the disenfranchised. As one student of bureaucratic politics points out:

> One of the historic functions of bureaucracy in American society has been to provide a means of effective expression in policy deliberations for community groups that are inarticulate, poorly organized, or for some other reason unable to speak for themselves. With administrative help, these stepchildren of the political system may acquire a political equality with other groups that they could never hope to attain through the ordinary processes of politics alone.[20]

Finally, there is the concept of "representative bureaucracy," whereby the recruitment and hiring processes of the civil service result in the representation of both women and men with a wide variety of backgrounds, education, training, race, and ethnicity. It is then the expectation that execucrats, to the extent they are in positions of power, will represent and respond to the needs and interests of their counterparts in the general population, to ensure ultimately the democratic representation of the broader society.[21] Representative bureaucracy holds, for example, that African-American execucrats would make policy choices reflecting the needs of African Americans in the general population.

Sometimes we also find execucrats working to advance their own "elite" professions such as medicine or law.[22] Devices built into the American political system, however, prevent professional groups from advancing their own parochial interests at the expense of the public's.

There are other important differences between execucrats and political executives that go beyond the issues of loyalty and self-interest. One is that political appointees are "strangers" to government and, hence, are relatively naive about its inner workings. Hugh Heclo, author of the well-known book *A Government of Strangers*, has pointed out that "the top political layers are filled with newcomers to government—politically important outsiders credited by defenders with introducing a fresh view of government operations and labeled by detractors as ignorant intruders . . . they are the 'in-and-outers,' that is, people who periodically interrupt their private careers to move in and out of the public service."[23]

A good example can be seen in the political appointments made by President Reagan. Many of Reagan's political appointees were much more Republican and conservative than Nixon's and perhaps even Bush's. The Reagan administration made a concerted effort to appoint people who would be "loyal" to the president and his "political program" rather than people who were knowledgeable in Washington ways or were experts in a specific policy area.[24] The upshot was that the ability of many of Reagan's political appointees to operate in a government rather than business setting was extremely deficient compared to that of execucrats. They simply were not prepared for how Washington works.

Indeed, Reagan himself entered the presidency as an inexperienced Washington hand.[25] President Bush, on the other hand, whether we agree or not with his politics, appointed persons familiar with the Washington establishment, although, in the words of presidential reporter Burt Solomon, they were "mainly affable white men in their 30s and 40s"[26] and, as such, not representative of the broad social spectrum of American society.

Unlike execucrats, who remain with government for the duration of their careers, political appointees are transients who serve in their positions for a very short period of time. On average, top political appointees stay on their jobs for about two years.[27] This, too, prevents political appointees from acquiring work experience in government. Execucrats acquire expertise "through the concentrated attention they give to specific problems. Dealing day in and day out with the same tasks gives [execucrats] an invaluable kind of practical knowledge that comes from experience. . . . The sustained attention that [they] can devote to specific problems gives them a decided advantage over political officials who deal with . . . public policy only at sporadic intervals."[28]

The ephemeral presence of political appointees also prevents them from developing strong working relationships among themselves. Ultimately, there is no sense of community, unity, stability, or cohesion among this group, as witnessed by the tensions among top presidential appointments. While any administration could provide examples, the most recent can be seen in the warfare between John Sununu, former White House chief of staff under President Bush, and just about any of Bush's cabinet heads, who unaffectionately referred to him as "King John." Resentment and hostility were surely the end products when Sununu bellowed at you in open meetings, "Come back when you know what you're talking about."[29]

We now see that there are notable differences between execucrats and political appointees. The distinctions between the two underscore differences in the roles they play in public policy making and in policy outcomes as well.

WHAT EXACTLY DO EXECUCRATS DO?

Lower-level government workers are the housekeepers and custodians of government, ensuring that the day-to-day routines run smoothly. They are the people who process our social-security checks, issue our educational loans, patrol our neighborhoods, clean our streets, and pick up our garbage. The execucrats are responsible for fulfilling the higher-order needs of the American people by making and implementing public policy. It goes without saying that public policy making is an extremely complex process, characterized by uncertainty, ambiguity, conflict, and, above all, politics. In essence, it is not a formula-driven, predictable process. Let us enter into the world of bureaucratic politics to get a better idea of execucratic involvement in high-level decision and policy making.

First and foremost, it must be recognized that execucrats and administrative agencies do not make policy in a vacuum. Rather, depending upon the policy environment and the agency, they must interact with a host of actors, including the president, Congress, political appointees, interest groups, members of the media, and the general public. In addition, courts and other administrative agencies are tacit partners in shaping public policy insofar as they exert pressures on, and create constraints for, execucrats and government agencies. The process is unpredictable and ambiguous because of these vast competing interests, all of which have some stake in the outcome of policy decisions. The task of addressing and responding to the divergent demands and desires of the various players is a monumental one; execucrats are at the center of this melee.

In some cases, such as foreign affairs and policy, execucrats are typically in a position to shape public policy with less involvement from the general public and interest groups.[30] Moreover, in this area there are greater incentives, if not pressures, for execucrats and political appointees to cooperate, since the policies being addressed are usually quite sensitive to such concerns as national security and global harmony. For example, the common goal—for the State Department's execucrats and political appointees—of resolving (or at least easing) the Arab-Israeli conflict precludes either group from acting arbitrarily or unilaterally.

In short, depending upon the agency and the policy domain, execucrats participate with a host of different actors in the development of public policy in an environment that is highly politically charged. But how and when do they actually participate? And what do they actually do? One way execucrats make policy is through direct participation in the policy process. Here execucrats work directly with leaders of congressional committees, interest groups, and other players in the formulation of public policy. (This policy environment is referred to by the students of bureaucratic politics as the "iron triangle," or, more recently, "issue networks.")[31] For example, public policy on clean air is formulated as a result of the interaction among execucrats of the EPA, members of the House Committee on Energy and Commerce (and its Subcommittee on Health and the Environment), members of the Senate Committee on Environment and Public Works (and its Subcommittee on Environmental Protection), and such environmental groups as the NRDC and Friends of the Earth.[32]

Some execucrats also affect policy by drafting laws for Congress. Such "agency bills" obviously result from interactions with the president, congressional leaders, interest groups, and other relevant participants. The volume of legislation formulated by execucrats is quite formidable. For example, in a single legislative year, most of the three hundred bills in the area of housing and urban development were initiated by execucrats from the Department of Housing and Urban Development (HUD).[33]

Execucrats also participate in formulating and shaping public policy by interpreting laws once they are passed by Congress. These mandates are often quite broad and vague; in order to execute these laws—a major responsibility of public agencies—

execucrats must interpret and operationalize them. One way they do this is through rule making, a process whereby execucrats issue agency statements or rules on a particular law passed by Congress. Agency rules carry the force and effect of statutory law and guide the application of public policy.[34] Through rule making, execucrats shape and create public policy. Continuing with our earlier example, federal execucrats, congressional leaders, and interest groups might work together to enact a clean-air bill. But what exactly are the standards for clean air? How will this broad mandate be operationalized? Execucrats are, in large part, responsible for determining exactly how clean air will be realized, by developing and issuing rules, regulations, and standards for industry on acceptable thresholds for the emission of pollutants into the atmosphere.[35]

Carrying out laws through the development and implementation of programs is another way in which execucrats influence public policy. Again, execucrats are in a position to use their discretion in interpreting vague mandates and translating them into concrete programs and services. The programs created to fight poverty in this nation, for example, represented execucratic interpretations of the broad war-on-poverty mandate.

Execucrats also participate in public policy making through adjudication. Here one or more execucrats form an administrative tribunal, which charges and tries individuals or groups believed to have violated an existing law or rule. This function enables execucrats to shape public policy through their interpretation and application of rules and statutes. An example can be seen in the Mine Safety and Health Administration's (MSHA's) prosecution of industries that have exposed workers to unsafe or unhealthy working conditions, such as illegal levels of coal dust while they were working in coal mines. Another example is when the Federal Trade Commission (FTC) adjudicates alleged violations of those consumer protection laws that seek to prevent industries from engaging in false or misleading advertising.

Another way in which execucrats participate in policy making, albeit at a lower level, is through law enforcement, that is, by securing compliance with existing laws and statutes. For example, the EPA, the Occupational Safety and Health Administration (OSHA), and the Nuclear Regulatory Commission (NRC) maintain a cadre of investigators and inspectors who police industries for violations of the laws and rules encompassed by their respective policy spheres. If violations are found, citations are issued and fines imposed. Sometimes the penalties are much more severe. For example, nuclear power plants can be completely shut down by the NRC.[36]

Execucrats also participate in policy making indirectly by providing advice to the president, political executives, and congressional leaders. Because of their technical expertise and knowledge, they are heavily relied upon by political leaders to assist in the formulation of high-level decisions and policies.

> It is clear that the ability to channel information into policy deliberations provides substantial leverage with which [exec]ucrats can affect the shape of decisions. If there are cases in which administrators appear only to be telling political officials what they want to hear, there are equally striking illustrations of situations in which staff members of executive agencies have substantially reshaped the attitudes of political leaders in both Congress and the executive.[37]

For example, former Secretary of Defense Clark Clifford (appointed in 1968) initially supported America's involvement in the Vietnam War. He later changed his position, however, as a result of briefings by civilian execucrats. Clifford's critical advice to President Johnson about the war helped push the president to accept one idea of a negotiated settlement.[38]

Execucrats serve a vital role in policy formulation and implementation. As direct or indirect participants, they shape and influence high-level decisions and policies in a host of domains. And contrary to popular belief, their contributions to public policy have often been very significant. Not only can their contributions be of major consequence to the American people; in a more pragmatic sense, they "help make policy sensible while serving as a bulwark against corruption."[39]

In studying execucratic effectiveness and innovation through an analysis of the behaviors and political environments of federal execucrats, it would not be unreasonable or implausible to begin with the premise that federal execucrats do influence public policy. Moreover, we know that execucrats can be successful and effective in performing their duties.[40] But what exactly accounts for effective execucratic performance? What exactly are the ingredients for execucratic success?

If we begin by identifying an outcome or implemented policy that is perceived, at first glance, as successful, we can then examine the factors that account for the success. Lynn has identified four factors that can influence effective executive performance. Drawing on these, I offer seven factors that can influence execucratic effectiveness:[41]

1. *political skills*
2. *management and leadership skills*
3. *situational factors*
4. *experience in government*
5. *technical expertise*
6. *strategy*
7. *personality*

Political skills are an essential ingredient for execucratic success. As we have already seen, execucrats do not make policy in a vacuum. Their ability to maneuver in political environments, building support from relevant coalitions such as Congress, the president, political appointees, interest groups, government agencies, the media, and the public, could spell success or failure in their efforts. Political skills also mean that execucrats know the policy process ascribed to their agency and, importantly, how to operate in it.

In addition to political skills, there are a host of other factors that can influence the performance of execucrats. For instance, an effective execucrat must have *management and leadership skills*,[42] which, as many have pointed out, include the ability to plan, organize, communicate clearly, and set realistic goals.[43] A "good" manager or leader is also someone who can motivate agency staff and "appreciate[s] and use[s the] organization to good effect."[44] Effective leaders must also be fair, understanding, knowledgeable about agency politics, and expert in their fields. They must also be able to adapt their leadership styles and behaviors to the particular circumstances and situations at hand.[45]

Situational factors, such as political and structural environments, create challenges and opportunities for execucrats to achieve their goals effectively. For example, the resources available, legal mandates, rules and regulations bearing on execucrats, and the policy domain in which they operate will make it easier or harder for them to effect change. The characteristics of bureaucracy itself pose serious constraints on execucrats. Rigid hierarchies and civil service rules operate to reduce execucratic flexibility and discretion. A federal execucrat, for example, unlike a private-sector executive, cannot simply hire and fire staff at will. This certainly limits execucrats' ability to surround themselves with the most suitable employees or support staff. All of these factors encroach upon execucratic behaviors, actions, and, ultimately, effectiveness.

The effectiveness of execucrats depends upon their *experience in government*. As discussed earlier, execucrats operate in a politically charged setting, characterized by uncertainty and ambiguity. Experience in this setting is a tremendous asset. It could spell success or failure to the execucrats in Health and Human Services (HHS), for example, in their efforts to improve Medicare and Medicaid benefits as they apply to nursing homes, a complex and polemical policy area, to say the least. As Lynn astutely notes, "Knowing what to anticipate and how to act can greatly shorten the time needed to master the specific demands of the job."[46]

Technical expertise, which stems in part from experience, is also an important ingredient for effective execucratic performance. The noted sociologist Max Weber saw this as a critical attribute. "The political master," he writes, "finds himself in a position of the 'dilettante' who stands opposite the 'expert,' . . . the trained official who stands within the management of administration."[47] Technical competence certainly influences how effective an execucrat is in her or his job.

The specific *strategy* employed by execucrats can affect their performance. Strategy refers to what the execucrats do and how—in other words, the goals they set for themselves and the means they employ to accomplish the task. It is the execucrat's plan or mode of action under environmental conditions that are typically marked by turbulence, conflict, and uncertainty. In more sophisticated terms, it is "a set of premises or propositions deliberately chosen by public executives to provide direction to their thinking, choices and administrative behavior."[48] What is the strategy of the execucrat in the Drug Enforcement Administration, for example, who is responsible for strengthening antidrug operations in the United States and abroad? Should it include cooperative linkages with local, state, and foreign counterparts? A sound strategy, appropriate for the prevailing circumstances, can lead to effective execucratic performance.

Finally, the *personality* of the career official impinges upon her or his success. Personal attributes and style would lead us to conclude, for example, that an execucrat is cooperative or adversarial, honest or deceitful, fair or unfair, aggressive or passive, reserved or outgoing, flexible or rigid, modest or egotistical. Although the personal attributes of an execucrat are a critical ingredient for success, they are certainly conditioned by situational factors. In this sense, an execucrat's personal style may be more effective in some situations than in others.[49]

NOTES

1. See Frank J. Thompson, "Critical Challenges to State and Local Public Service," in Frank J. Thompson, ed., *Revitalizing State and Local Public Service*, Publication of the National

(Winter) Commission on the State and Local Public Service (San Francisco: Jossey-Bass, 1993), 1–38, which discusses the negative responses citizens have toward public workers in such regulatory agencies as motor vehicles and police. Also see Daniel Katz et al., *Bureaucratic Encounters* (Ann Arbor: Institute for Social Research, University of Michigan, 1975); and Charles T. Goodsell, *The Case for Bureaucracy: A Public Administration Polemic*, 2d ed. (Chatham, N.J.: Chatham House, 1985).

2. See David Nachmias and David H. Rosenbloom, *Bureaucratic Government, USA* (New York: St. Martin's Press, 1980); Michael Lipsky, *Street-Level Bureaucracy: Dilemmas of the Individual in Public Services* (New York: Russell Sage Foundation, 1980); Kenneth J. Meier, *Politics and the Bureaucracy*, 3d ed. (Pacific Grove, Calif.: Brooks-Cole, 1993); B. Guy Peters, *The Politics of Bureaucracy*, 3d ed. (New York: Longman, 1989); Francis E. Rourke, *Bureaucracy, Politics, and Public Policy*, 2d ed. (Boston: Little, Brown 1976); and Peter Woll, *American Bureaucracy*, 2d ed. (New York: Norton, 1977). But also see Joel D. Aberbach, "Public Service and Administrative Reform in the United States: The Volcker Commission and the Bush Administration," *International Review of Administrative Sciences* 57 (1991): 403–19, whose interviews with high-level career executives reveal a diminishing of execucratic power over public policy, beginning with the final years of the Reagan administration.

3. David H. Rosenbloom, *Public Administration: Understanding Management, Politics, and Law in the Public Sector*, 2d ed. (New York: Random House, 1989), p. 48; emphasis added.

4. Lawrence Mosher, "Move Over, Jim Watt, Anne Gorsuch Is the Latest Target of Environmentalists," *National Journal*, October 24, 1981, 1901.

5. Ibid., 1902.

6. Ibid.

7. Ibid.

8. As told to author. Source wishes to remain anonymous.

9. Civil service exams are rarely required at the upper levels of government.

10. Hugh Heclo, *A Government of Strangers* (Washington: Brookings Institution, 1977), 21.

11. Ibid.

12. U.S. General Accounting Office, *Recruitment and Retention: Inadequate Federal Pay Cited as Primary Problem by Agency Officials* (Washington: USGAO, September 1990).

13. Anthony Downs, *Inside Bureaucracy* (Boston: Little, Brown, 1967), 4.

14. Ibid.

15. Frederick Mosher, *Democracy and the Public Service*, 2d ed. (New York: Oxford University Press, 1982), 95.

16. Ibid.; emphasis added.

17. But see the discussion of interest groups by Theodore Lowi, *The End of Liberalism* (New York: W. W. Norton, 1969).

18. For a discussion, see Mosher, *Democracy and the Public Service*.

19. Ibid., 97; emphasis in original.

20. Rourke, *Bureaucracy*, 3.

21. It must be noted, however, that women and persons of color are not well represented in the upper, policy-making levels of government service.

22. For an excellent article on the compatibility of professionalism and bureaucratic responsiveness, see Richard C. Kearney and Chandan Sinha, "Professionalism and Bureaucratic Responsiveness: Conflict of Compatibility," *Public Administration Review* (January-February 1988): 571–79.

23. Heclo, *A Government of Strangers*, 100.

24. See Aberbach, "Public Service"; and Carolyn Ban and Patrician W. Ingraham, "Short-Timers: Political Appointee Mobility and Its Impact on Political-Career Relations in the Reagan Administration," *Administration and Society* 22 (May 1990): 106–24.

25. Ibid.

26. Burt Solomon, "In Bush's Image," *National Journal*, July 7, 1990, 1644.
27. C. Brauer, "Tenure, Turnover, and Postgovernment Employment Trends of Presidential Appointees," in G. C. Mackenzie, ed., *The In-and-Outers: Presidential Appointees and Transient Government in Washington* (Baltimore: Johns Hopkins University Press, 1987), 175.
28. Rourke, *Bureaucracy*, 15.
29. Larry, Martz, "The 'Air Sununu' Flap," *Newsweek*, May 6, 1991, 33.
30. Yet private-interest groups sometimes organize and exert pressure even in the domain of foreign affairs and policy, which further muddies the waters. A notable example is the efforts, several years ago, of private groups that were dissatisfied with the government's policy on economic aid to the contras, the insurgents seeking to overthrow the communist regime of Nicaragua. Civilians flew over Central America to deliver private aid, in the form of military hardware and other supplies to the contras.
31. Other terms, including "cozy relationships," "cozy triangles," and "subgovernments," have been used to describe iron triangles. See Nachmias and Rosenbloom, *Bureaucratic Government, USA*. "Issue networks," on the other hand, is a more voguish term, and it implies that there is greater openness to policy-making configurations than is allowed by iron triangles. I make no effort to prove or disprove this notion. Rather, I use the terms interchangeably, because I accept the fact that with any public administrative phenomena, there will always be new twists to old concepts, given the ever-growing complexity of government and its decision-making apparatus. For a further discussion of issue networks, see Charles H. Levine, B. Guy Peters, and Frank J. Thompson, *Public Administration: Challenges, Choices, and Consequences* (Glenview, Ill.: Scott, Foresman, 1990); and Hugh Heclo, "Issue Networks and the Executive Establishment," in Anthony King, ed., *The New American Political System* (Washington: American Enterprise Institute, 1978), 87–124.
32. The original legislation on clean air, e.g., the Air Pollution Control Act of 1955 and the Clean Air Act of 1963, preceded the existence of the EPA. Also, the congressional committees and subcommittees operated under different names, and different environmental groups existed at the time.
33. Rourke, *Bureaucracy*, 26.
34. For a discussion of rule making in one administrative agency, see William F. West, "The Politics of Administrative Rulemaking," *Public Administration Review* (September-October 1982): 420–26.
35. But Congress sets emission standards for automobiles.
36. But see Meier, *Politics*, for a discussion of how selective enforcement of certain laws has become intentional policy.
37. Rourke, *Bureaucracy*, 20.
38. Ibid.
39. Goodsell, *The Case for Bureaucracy*, 154.
40. See Goodsell, *The Case for Bureaucracy*; Doig and Hargrove, *Leadership and Innovation*; Terry L. Cooper and N. Dale Wright, eds., *Exemplary Public Administrators* (San Francisco: Jossey-Bass, 1992); and Robert L. Haught, ed., *Giants in Management* (Washington: National Academy of Public Administration, 1985).
41. I also draw on other bodies of literature that address effective public administrative performance. See James L. Perry, "The Effective Public Administrator," in James L. Perry, ed., *Handbook of Public Administration* (San Francisco: Jossey-Bass, 1989), 619–27; N. Joseph Cayer, "Qualities of Successful Program Managers," in Robert E. Cleary and Nicholas Henry, eds., *Managing Public Programs* (San Francisco: Jossey-Bass, 1989), 121–42; and Robert B. Denhardt, *The Pursuit of Significance: Strategies for Managerial Success in Public Organizations* (Belmont, Calif.: Wadsworth, 1993).

42. A distinction is sometimes drawn between management and leadership, but for the purposes of this book, no such distinction is made. For discussions of both approaches, see Bernard M. Bass, *Bass and Stogdill's Handbook of Leadership,* 3d ed. (New York: Free Press, 1990); Sue R. Faerman, "Organizational Change and Leadership Styles, *"Journal of Library Administration* 19 (1993): 55–79; and John P. Kotter, A *Force for Change: How Leadership Differs from Management* (New York: Free Press, 1990).

43. Theories abound on effective leadership and management styles, and there is, as in most academic discourse, no consensus (nor should there be) on what the "best" approach is. Nonetheless, from this discourse emerges a plethora of research on effective management and leadership styles. See Lynn, *Managing Public Policy;* Lynn, "The Reagan Administration"; Perry, "The Effective Public Administrator"; Cayer, "Qualities of Successful Program Managers"; Denhardt, *The Pursuit of Significance;* Debra W. Stewart and G. David Garson, *Organizational Behavior and Public Management* (New York: Marcel Dekker, 1983); Grover Starling, *Managing the Public Sector* (Belmont, Calif.: Wadsworth, 1993); Sue R. Faerman et al., A *Framework for Excellence* (Albany, N.Y.: Governor's Office of Employee Relations, 1990); and Richard E. Boyatzis, *The Competent Manager* (New York: Wiley, 1982).

44. Lynn, "The Reagan Administration," 362.

45. Stewart and Garson, *Organizational Behavior,* 63. For additional attributes, the reader may wish to consult the works cited in note 48.

46. Lynn, "The Reagan Administration," 341–42.

47. H. H. Gerth and C. Wright Mills, *From Max Weber: Essays in Sociology* (New York: Oxford University Press, 1946), 232.

48. Lynn, *Managing Public Policy,* 131.

49. See Lynn, "The Reagan Administration"; Fred I. Greenstein, *Personality and Politics* (New York: W. W. Norton, 1975); Aaron Wildavsky, "The Analysis of Issue-Contexts in the Study of Decision-Making" *Journal of Politics* 24 (1962): 717–32; Edward A. Shils, "Authoritarianism: 'Right' and 'Left,'" in Richard Christie and Marie Jahoda, eds., *Studies in the Scope and Method of "The Authoritarian Personality"* (Glencoe, Ill.: Free Press, 1954), 24–49; and Sidney Verba, "Assumptions of Rationality and Non-Rationality in Models of the International Systems," *World Politics* 14 (1961): 93–117.

29

Barbara S. Romzek and Melvin J. Dubnick

ACCOUNTABILITY IN THE PUBLIC SECTOR: LESSONS FROM THE CHALLENGER TRAGEDY

On January 28, 1986, the space shuttle Challenger exploded in mid-flight and seven crew members lost their lives. The widely known details of that tragic event need not be retraced here. Opinion is growing, however, that the official explanations offered by the Presidential Commission on the Space Shuttle Challenger Accident (the Rogers Commission) fail to provide full answers to why the disaster occurred. We offer an alternative explanation which addresses institutional factors contributing to the shuttle accident.

1. Seeking an Institutional Perspective

Two common threads ran through public discussions of the Challenger incident. First was the urge to pinpoint the technical problems contributing directly to the booster rocket explosion on the shuttle. Second was the desire to uncover human and managerial errors that might have caused National Aeronautics and Space Administration (NASA) officials to overlook or ignore those technical flaws. By the time the Rogers Commission issued its findings on June 9, 1986, those technical and managerial issues dominated its conclusions.

More interesting, however, is the untravelled investigative path which asks if the problems at NASA and in the space shuttle program were institutional as well as technical or managerial. The institutional perspective is familiar to students of organizational theory who, following the lead of Talcott Parsons and James D. Thompson, note three levels of organization responsibility and control: technical, managerial, and institutional.[1]

At the *technical level,* organizations focus on the effective performance of specialized and detailed functions. At the *managerial level,* an organization provides for mediation among its technical components and between its technical functionaries and those "customers" and "suppliers" in the organization's "task environment." At the *institutional level,* the organization deals with the need for being part of the "wider social system which is the source of the 'meaning,' legitimation, or higher-level support which makes implementation of the organization's goals possible."[2]

Applying this framework to the study of specific program or project failures such as the Challenger, one can argue that critical problems can arise at any or all three levels. Thus, an investigation of such events would be incomplete without considering the possible implications of activity at each level. The fact that NASA and other public agencies must constantly contend with the institutional forces that surround them (i.e., the "wider social system" of which they are part) is worthy of attention because agency efforts to deal with those forces may contribute to shaping the outcomes of agency action.

Investigators might ignore the role of institutional factors for several reasons. Attention to such factors might raise questions that are too basic and too dangerous for the organization or its supporters. Thus, a commission composed of individuals committed to the enterprise under investigation[3] and to the political system in general[4] is unlikely to open up the Pandora's Box of institutional factors. In contrast, institutional factors might be overlooked because analysts lack a conceptual framework that facilitates such considerations. Assuming the latter explanation, we offer a framework useful for highlighting the institutional factors that might have contributed to the Challenger disaster.

2. An "Accountability" Perspective

While often regarded as a unique public organization,[5] NASA has institutional characteristics similar in very important respects to other public sector agencies. As such, NASA has to deal with the diversity of legitimate and occasionally conflicting expectations emanating from the democratic political system of which it is a part (its institutional context). In the following pages we present a framework of public accountability as a means for examining NASA's management of its institutional pressure and its implications.

Managing Expectations

Accountability is a fundamental but underdeveloped concept in American public administration. Scholars and practitioners freely use the term to refer to answerability for one's actions or behavior. Administrators and agencies are accountable to the extent that they are required to answer for their actions. Beyond this basic notion of answerability, there has been little refinement of the term. Most of the discussion in the literature centers on the "best" strategy for achieving accountability, with the Friedrich-Finer exchange of the 1940s being the most cited example.[6]

From an alternative perspective, accountability plays a greater role in the processes of public administration than indicated by the idea of answerability. In its simplest form, answerability implies that accountability involves limited, direct, and mostly formalistic responses to demands generated by specific institutions or groups in the public agency's task environment. More broadly conceived, *public administration accountability involves the means by which public agencies and their workers manage the diverse expectations generated within and outside the organization.*[7]

Viewed as a strategy for managing expectations, public administration accountability takes a variety of forms. The focus here is on four alternative systems of public accountability, each based on variations involving two critical factors: (1) whether the ability to define and control expectations is held by some specified entity inside or outside the agency; and (2) the degree of control that entity is given over defining those agency's expectations. The interplay of these two dimensions generates the four types of accountability systems illustrated in Figure 29.1.

Regarding the first dimension, the management of agency expectations through accountability mechanisms calls for the establishment of some authoritative source of

FIGURE 29.1   *Types of Accountability Systems*

		Source of Agency Control	
		Internal	External
Degree of Control Over Agency Actions	High	1. Bureaucratic	2. Legal
	Low	3. Professional	4. Political

control. Internal sources of control rely on the authority inherent in either formal hierarchical relationships or informal social relationships within the agency. External sources of control reflect a similar distinction, for their authority can be derived from either formalized arrangements set forth in laws or legal contracts or the informal exercise of power by interests located outside the agency.

A second ingredient in any accountability system is the degree of control over agency choices and operations exercised by those sources of control. A high degree of control reflects the controller's ability to determine both the range and depth of actions which a public agency and its members can take. A low degree of control, in contrast, provides for considerable discretion on the part of agency operatives.

Bureaucratic accountability systems (cell 1) are widely used mechanisms for managing public agency expectations.[8] Under this approach, the expectations of public administrators are managed through focusing attention on the priorities of those at the top of the bureaucratic hierarchy. At the same time, supervisory control is applied intensively to a wide range of agency activities. The functioning of a bureaucratic accountability system involves two simple ingredients: an organized and legitimate relationship between a superior and a subordinate in which the need to follow "orders" is unquestioned; and close supervision or a surrogate system of standard operating procedures or clearly stated rules and regulations.[9]

Legal accountability[10] (cell 2) is similar to the bureaucratic form in that it involves the frequent application of control to a wide range of public administration activities. In contrast to bureaucratic accountability, however, legal accountability is based on relationships between a controlling party outside the agency and members of the organization. That outside party is not just anyone; it is the individual or group in a position to impose legal sanctions or assert formal contractual obligations. Typically, these outsiders make the laws and other policy mandates which the public administrator is obligated to enforce or implement. In policymaking terms, the outsider is the "lawmaker" while the public administrator has the role of "executor."

The legal accountability relationship between controller and the controlled also differs from that found between supervisor and subordinate in bureaucratic accountability forms. In the bureaucratic system, the relationship is hierarchical and based on the ability of supervisors to reward or punish subordinates. In legal accountability, however, the relationship is between two relatively autonomous parties and involves a formal or implied fiduciary (principal/agent) agreement between the public agency and its legal overseer.[11] For example, Congress passes laws and monitors a federal agency's implementation of those laws; a federal district court orders a school board to desegregate its classrooms and oversees the implementation of that order; the local city commission contracts with a private firm to operate the city refuse dump. In each case the implementors are legally or contractually obliged to carry out their duties, and the enforcement of such obligations are very different from those found in situations where bureaucratic accountability systems are applied.[12]

Professional accountability[13] (cell 3) occurs with greater frequency as governments deal increasingly with technically difficult and complex problems. Under those circumstances, public officials must rely on skilled and expert employees to provide appropriate solutions. Those employees expect to be held fully accountable for their actions and insist that agency leaders trust them to do the best job possible. If they fail to meet job performance expectations, it is assumed they can be reprimanded or fired. Otherwise they expect to be given sufficient discretion to get the job done. Thus, professional accountability is characterized by placement of control over organizational activities in the hands of the employee with the expertise or special skills to get the job done. The key to the professional accountability system, therefore, is deference to expertise within the agency. While outside professional associations may indirectly influence the decision making of the in-house expert (through education and professional standards), the source of authority is essentially internal to the agency.

Typically the professional accountability organization will look like any other public agency with a manager in charge of a set of workers, but the relationships among them are much different. Under a bureaucratic accountability system, the key relationship would be that of close supervision. In contrast, under professional accountability the central relationship is similar to that found between a layperson and an expert, with the agency manager taking the role of the layperson and the workers making the important decisions that require their expertise.[14]

Political accountability (cell 4) is central to the democratic pressures imposed on American public administrators. If "deference" characterizes professional accountability, "reponsiveness" characterizes political accountability systems (cell 4).[15] The key relationship under these systems resembles that between a representative (in this case, the public administrator) and his or her constituents (those to whom he or she is accountable). Under political accountability, the primary question becomes, "Whom does the public administrator represent?" The potential constituencies include the general public, elected officials, agency heads, agency clientele, other special interest groups, and future generations. Regardless of which definition of constituency is adopted, the administrator is expected to be responsive to their policy priorities and programmatic needs.

While political accountability systems might seem to promote favoritism and even corruption in the administration of government programs, they also serve as the basis for a more open and representative government. The urge for political accountability, for example, is reflected in open meetings laws, freedom of information acts, and "government in the sunshine" statutes passed by many state and local governments.

Table 29.1 summarizes the principal features of the four general types of accountability systems. Under the bureaucratic system, expectations are managed through a hierarchical arrangement based on supervisory relationships; the legal accountability system manages agency expectations through a contractual relationship; the professional system relies on deference to expertise; while the political accountability system promotes responsiveness to constituents as the central means of managing the multiple expectations.

Preferences for Accountability Systems

Given these alternative means for managing expectations, what determines the preference for one accountability approach over others in any particular situation? The appropriateness of a specific accountability system to an agency is linked to three factors: the nature of the agency's task (technical level accountability); the management strategy adopted by those heading the agency (management level accountability); and the institutional context of agency operations (institutional level accountability.)[16] Ideally, a public sector organization should establish accountability mechanisms which "fit" at all three levels simultaneously.

In the American political system, all four accountability types offer potentially legitimate means for managing *institutional level expectations*.[17] Under current institutional norms, no single type of accountability system is inherently more acceptable or legitimate than another. *In theory*, each of the four accountability systems can insure agency responsibility at the institutional level. Thus, in theory an agency might manage its expectations using the accountability system most appropriate in light of relevant institutional considerations. The same potential flexibility may not exist at the technical or managerial levels where the appropriateness of accountability mechanisms is more closely tied to specific tasks or the strategic orientations or idiosyncrasies of individual managers.

In reality, most U.S. public agencies tend to adopt two or more types of accountability systems at any time depending on the nature of existing environmental (institutional) conditions as well as their technical tasks and management orientations. We argue, however, that institutional pressures generated by the American political system are often the salient factor and frequently take precedence over technical and managerial considerations.[18] If this is the case, the challenge of managing expectations changes as institutional conditions change. If the environmental changes are drastic enough, they may trigger a different type of accountability system, one which attempts to reflect those new institutional conditions.

3. ACCOUNTABILITY UNDER DIFFERENT CHALLENGES: THE CASE OF NASA

NASA was an organizational initiative born in the midst of a national crisis and nurtured in the relatively protective shelter of an institutional consensus that lasted until at least 1970. That nurturing consensus focused attention on President Kennedy's mandate to land an American on the moon by the end of the 1960s. In addition, it

TABLE 29.1
Relationships Within Accountability Systems

Type of Accountability System	Analogous Relationship (Controller/Administrator)	Basis of Relationship
1. Bureaucratic	Superior/subordinate	Supervision
2. Legal	Lawmaker/law executor Principal/agent	Fiduciary
3. Professional	Layperson/expert	Deference to expertise
4. Political	Constituent/representative	Responsiveness to constituents

fostered the belief that achieving that objective required complete deference to those experts who could get the job done. In short, it was a consensus which supported a professional accountability system.

Over time, the pressures to develop a politically responsive agency strategy became dominant. Even before the successful lunar landing of Apollo 11, changing institutional conditions were creating an organizational setting that encouraged more reliance on bureaucratic and political accountability mechanisms. This reliance on bureaucratic and political accountability systems produced circumstances which made the agency ill-equipped to contend with the problems that eventually led to the Challenger disaster. Furthermore, institutional reactions to the Challenger tragedy itself may be creating new pressures that are moving the agency toward a greater reliance on legal and bureaucratic accountability methods for managing expectations.

The Professionalization of the Space Program

NASA's earliest programs had three important characteristics: they involved clearly defined outcome objectives, highly technical methodologies for achieving those goals, and almost unqualified political (and therefore budgetary) support.[19] The task of overcoming the technical barriers to space exploration was central to the agency's mission, and NASA was able to invest its expenditures primarily in research and development projects associated with its missions.[20]

Those early conditions had a significant impact on the development and management of NASA. The agency's structure and recruiting practices reflected an institutional willingness to respect the technical nature of NASA's programmatic tasks. NASA's form of organization emphasized deference to expertise and minimized the number of political appointments at the top of the administrative structure (in this case, two political appointees with extensive professional expertise in public management).[21] NASA's initial staff consisted almost entirely of individuals with the relevant substantive knowledge, primarily aeronautical engineers.

These circumstances afforded NASA the opportunity to become among the most innovative organizations (public or private) in recent American history and a classic example of an agency operating under a professional accountability system. The locus of control over agency activities was internal; NASA's relationship to outside sources (including Congress, the President, and the general public) was that of expert to layperson. Internally, NASA developed a matrix structure in which managers and technicians were assigned to project teams based on the expertise they could offer to the particular task at hand. Technical experts in NASA were expected to make decisions based upon their expertise. Thus, within the agency the degree of control exercised over NASA technical personnel was relatively low. Much of this deference to NASA's technical experts was based on trust in their judgment as well as their expertise. The early mangers at NASA "were highly technical people, who knew the spacecraft from the ground up, and they were all very conservative." If "an order to launch came down from on high, they wouldn't do it without first giving everybody the bottom line."[22]

In 1967, however, a major long-term effort was made to reduce the autonomy of the manned space flight centers in light of the agency's first major budget constraints and the launch pad fire that killed three astronauts.[23]

The Politicization and Bureaucratization of Accountability

Although many of the technical tasks facing NASA did not change significantly over the past 30 years, institutional pressures on the agency have undergone considerable change. In the late 1960s, NASA faced a leveling off of both its political and financial support. Beginning in the early 1970s there was more concern about the managerial challenges inherent in making NASA into an operational agency—a concern arising from pressures to make the shuttle system a fully operational program.[24] The result of these pressures was a reconfiguration of the accountability systems used by some of the agency's key units. Ironically, the very success of NASA's early programs generated those changes.

NASA's apparent victory in the "space race" coincided with an end to the nurturing consensus that permitted the agency to rely almost exclusively on professional accountability for managing expectations. With America's attention turned increasingly toward Vietnam and economic issues, the space program no longer took priority. A new consensus had to be constructed around some new programmatic mission, and in the late 1960s the idea of a space shuttle began to take form.

The effort to gain presidential endorsement for the space shuttle program made NASA more aware of and responsive to key actors in the political system. Building the necessary consensus was not easy in the highly volatile and competitive institutional context of the early 1970s. Most of the opposition to the shuttle came from the Office of Management and Budget which was supported by negative assessments of the program by a presidential scientific advisory committee and the RAND Corporation.[25]

During this period NASA entered into political coalitions with groups that it had previously ignored or fought in the policy-making arena, as well as with its traditional supporters in government and among its contractors. The shuttle program, for example, was designed to attract the support of those who might take advantage of its capacity to launch satellites and conduct unique scientific and technological experiments in space. Aided by the military, the scientific community, and parts of the business community, NASA was able to get President Nixon's backing for the program in 1972 despite OMB's opposition. Political accountability was no longer secondary or peripheral to NASA.[26] It became a critical ingredient in guaranteeing its maintenance as a viable agency. In more recent years, that urge for public and political support was implicit in NASA's widely publicized efforts to include members of Congress and non-agency civilians on its shuttle flights. These programs represented NASA's efforts to cultivate or maintain general support for its activities.

Another important (and related) set of institutional constraints emerged in the form of major budget cutbacks and (in the late 1970s) greater pressures for privatization. From the height of its support in the late 1960s to the mid–1970s, NASA's budget was cut in half (in constant dollars). Recent estimates indicate that NASA went through a staff cut off 40 percent from the big-budget days of Apollo and that NASA's safety and quality control staff alone were cut by 71 percent between 1970 and 1986.[27] Operating with fewer resources, the agency had to economize; it became just like most other agencies in Washington. NASA experienced a new-found interest in efficiency and thus became more willing to use bureaucratic means for dealing with its financial problems.

NASA officials intended to accommodate these new institutional pressures by reducing the organizational costs that characterized NASA in the "old days" when external support and availability of resources were not major concerns. NASA has "had to pinch pennies to protect the shuttle, accepting lower-cost technologies and making what seem to have been extravagant claims for its economic potential.[28] Agency decentralization and field center specializations continued, and decentralization brought with it increasing reliance on bureaucratic accountability mechanisms. The shift allowed for economies due to a careful division of labor and compartmentalization of authority based on position. While professional accountability systems survived *within* some of the field centers, for the agency as a whole professional accountability patterns characteristic of the early NASA nearly disappeared. With decentralization in NASA came an isolation and competition among field centers.[29]

NASA's use of contractors was, to a certain extent, a manifestation of its efforts to manage changing institutional expectations. In addition to any technical and financial benefits they provided NASA, contractors had always proved very helpful politically in establishing support for the agency's programs and annual funding requests. During the 1970s the link between contract decision and political support became increasingly critical to NASA.[30]

Bureaucratically, contracting out established the ultimate superordinate/subordinate relationship between NASA's top managers and those carrying out the specific parts of the shuttle program. A contract establishes clear responsibilities and gives top management considerable leverage to apply pressures for better performance. It also allows top management to avoid the problems and costs associated with directly maintaining professional accountability mechanisms. Thus, contracting out not only enhanced the bureaucratization process at NASA; it also reduced reliance on deference to expertise characteristic of professional accountability systems.

Changing institutional conditions altered the locus of control over NASA's activities as well as the degree of control over agency activities. The result was a shift in the types of accountability systems relevant to NASA's operations. In place of the dominant professional accountability systems of the pre-Apollo 11 era, NASA created an elaborate mixture of accountability mechanisms that stressed the political and bureaucratic. It was under these conditions that decisions regarding the general schedule of space shuttle flights and specific launch times were being made when the Challenger lifted from its Kennedy Space Center pad on January 28, 1986.

The Case of the Challenger

Evidence gathered by the Rogers Commission Report and through the mass media illustrate the various forms of accountability in operation in NASA before the launch of the Challenger. The principal question is whether (and to what extent) the Challenger accident resulted from the efforts by NASA's leadership to manage changing institutional expectations through political and bureaucratic forms of accountability. Did

NASA's emphasis on these accountability mechanisms eventually take precedence over the professional system of accountability that characterized NASA in the early 1960s? Were the problems that eventually led to the Challenger accident linked at all to the poor fit between agency tasks and agency accountability mechanisms? In our view, the answer to both questions is "yes."

Political pressures. The contention that NASA was feeling considerable political pressure to launch the Challenger on January 28 was widely rumored just after the Challenger accident, particularly stories about direct pressure emanating from the White House. The Rogers Commission emphatically denied the truth of those rumors.[31] Nonetheless, similar pressures existed and came from a variety of sources outside of NASA, including the White House.

On the official policy level, President Reagan announced in July 1982 that the first priority of the shuttle program was "to make the system fully operational." Given the costs involved in supporting the program, additional pressures emanated from an increasingly budget-conscious Congress.[32] Other pressures on NASA were due to widespread reporting of shuttle delays in the mass media. One top agency official argued that the press, in giving major coverage to numerous shuttle delays over the previous year, had "pressured" the agency to jeopardize flight safety. "I don't think it caused us to do anything foolish," he said. "But that's where the pressure is. It's not from anywhere else."[33]

These external pressures were easily translated into internal decisions that set an overly ambitious launch schedule.[34] In short, NASA set that schedule for the purposes of reducing the program's cost factors and appeasing various attentive publics, including the White House, Congress, the media, and the agency's military and private sector "customers" who were important actors in NASA's supportive political coalition.

These political pressures may not have been specifically addressed to the Challenger launch, but there is little doubt they were felt throughout the agency. The increasing emphasis on political accountability was bound to cause attitudinal as well as operational problems. "The pressure on NASA to achieve planned flight rates was so pervasive," concluded a congressional report, "that it undoubtedly adversely affected attitudes regarding safety."[35] An agency official noted that NASA's organization culture changed "when NASA felt itself under pressure to demonstrate that the shuttles were operational vehicles in a 'routine' transportation system."[36] Part of that "routinization" took the form of "streamlining" the reporting requirements for safety concerns. Less documentation and fewer reporting requirements replaced previous directives that all safety problems and responses were to be reported to higher levels in NASA's hierarchy. The "old requirements," it was argued, "were not productive for the operational phase of the Shuttle program."[37]

The same political accountability pressures had an impact on NASA's key shuttle program contractor, Morton Thiokol. The assent of Morton Thiokol management (and the silence of their engineers) to the Challenger launch recommendation was influenced in part by NASA's importance as a primary customer—a customer who was in the process of reviewing its contracts with the firm. The company's management did not want to jeopardize their relationships with NASA. As a result, rather than emphasizing deference to the experts who worked for them, Morton Thiokol deferred to the demands of NASA's top managers who, in turn, were under a self-imposed, politically derived launch schedule.

Bureaucratic Pressures. Indications of preference for bureaucratic rather than professional forms of accountability in NASA are evident in the agency's shuttle program operations. By the early 1980s, NASA's managers were having difficulty coordinating their projects.[38] They came to rely increasingly on hierarchical reporting relationships, a clear manifestation of bureaucratic accountability. This had two effects. First, it increased the potential for "bureaupathological" behavior which the professional accountability system attempted to minimize.[39] Second, it reduced the cross-cutting communications channels which once characterized the less hierarchical and flexible matrix structure at NASA.

The failure of NASA's management system is a fundamental theme of the Rogers Commission. But what the Rogers Commission perceived as a failure of the agency's management system was, in fact, an inherent characteristic of the bureaucratic accountability system adopted by NASA in order to meet the institutional expectations of the post-Apollo 11 era.

Under NASA's shuttle program, responsibility for specific aspects of the overall program was allocated to supervisors at lower levels in the reporting hierarchy, and the burden for giving the go ahead to launch decision makers shifted from the engineers and experts toward those supervisory personnel. As scheduling and other pressures increased, so did the reluctance of those supervisors to be the individual who threw a monkey wrench into the shuttle program machinery. Thus it is not surprising that lower-level managers tried to cope on their own instead of communicating their problems upward.[40]

The relevance of this problem to the Challenger disaster was illustrated time and time again in the testimony given before the Rogers Commission. NASA officials noted that individuals higher up in the agency had not been informed about the Rockwell engineers' reservations about ice on the launch pad nor the concerns of Morton Thiokol's personnel about weather conditions and the O-rings.[41] In another instance, when asked why he had not communicated the Thiokol engineers' concerns about the O-ring seals to the Program Manager of the National Space Transportation System, the manger of the Solid Rocket Booster Project (based at the Marshall center) answered that he believed it was an issue that had been resolved at his level in the organization.[42] As one reporter observed, "no one at Marshall saw any reason to bother the managers at the top of NASA's chain of command—the normal procedure in the face of disturbing new evidence." This bureaupathological behavior reflects an attitude among employees at Marshall who feel they are competing with Johnson and the other centers. "Nothing [sic] was ever allowed to leave Marshall that would suggest that Marshall was not doing its job. . . ."[43]

The impact of the bureaucratic accountability system is also evident in testimony about discussions between NASA representatives and Thiokol engineers on the night before the Challenger launch. During an "off-line" caucus between Morton Thiokol management and their engineers (while NASA prelaunch review officials were "on hold"), a member of management asked one of his colleagues *to take off his engineering hat and put on his management hat.* From that point on, management formulated the points to base their decision on. There was never one comment in favor . . . of launching by any engineer or other nonmanagement person in the room before or after the caucus. . . . [The engineers were] never asked nor polled, and it was clearly a management decision from that point. . . . This was a meeting where the determination was to launch, and it was up to [the Thiokol engineers] to prove beyond a shadow of a doubt [to Thiokol management and NASA] that it was not safe to do so. This is in total reverse to what the position usually is in a preflight conversation or a flight readiness review. It is usually exactly opposite that.[44] (emphasis added)

A final example of the bureaucratic accountability system's relevance to the failure of the Challenger focuses on an incident occurring in 1984. Problems with the O-rings were noticed and noted by Morton Thiokol engineers in February that year after the tenth Shuttle mission had been completed, and a report on the problem was ordered by the Office of the Associate Administrator for Space Flight before the launch of the eleventh flight in late March. A decision was made to launch the shuttle, but not before it was determined by the Associate Administrator, James Abrahamson, and NASA's Deputy Administrator, Hans Mark, that the O-ring problem had to be solved. A meeting to discuss the problem with relevant officials from the different NASA centers was called for May 30. It was a meeting that would have drawn attention to the technical factor that would later cause the shuttle tragedy; it was a meeting that never took place. By May 30, Abrahamson had left the agency to work on President Reagan's Strategic Defense Initiative, and Deputy Administrator Mark cancelled the meeting to visit Austin, Texas, where he was being considered for the position of University Chancellor. Abrahamson's successor, Jesse A. Moore, was never informed of the problem, and Mark's successor was not appointed for a full year. Thus, the O-ring problem was never communicated to the relevant experts for action. In Mark's words, it was "a classic example of having something fall between the 'cracks.'"[45] In our terms, it was another instance of bureaucratic accountability applied in inappropriate circumstances.

4. A Post-Commission Era: The New Institutional Pressures

Given the technical and managerial focus of the Rogers Commission Report and other investigations of the Challenger accident, it is not surprising that calls for changes in the space program tend to favor two objectives: punishing those in NASA who were to blame for the tragedy and instituting reforms that would guarantee that a similar event would not occur in the future. In both form and content, these efforts represented increased institutional pressures for NASA, pressures likely to lead the agency to develop new legal accountability mechanisms as well as increase its reliance on bureaucratic accountability mechanisms.

The search for scapegoats and legal responsibility for the Challenger ac   cident are unsavory but perhaps unavoidable by-products of the Rogers Commission's focus on technical and managerial problems.

On less personal levels, suggestions for reforms in the space agency have proliferated. On the surface many of these seem to signal a return to professional accountability. Some recommendations call for improving the role and voice of certain classes of individuals within NASA with special or unique insight into the risks associated with space exploration. There is, for example, a proposal for placing ex-astronauts in management positions at NASA.[46] At first glance, this looks like an attempt to reinvigorate the role of experts and professionals in the agency, but bringing former astronauts into NASA does not guarantee improvement in technical expertise and actually looks more like a thinly veiled attempt to use highly visible symbols of the space program to enhance the agency's damaged credibility.

Another proposal that at first seems to involve a return to professional accountability calls for establishment of explicit guidelines and criteria for use in making launch decisions. Supposedly these criteria would represent the accumulated wisdom of many experts in the field, but they can just as easily be regarded as another step away from deference to professional engineering judgments and toward imposing accountability that carries with it threats of legal liability if such checklists are not properly followed.

Legal accountability mechanisms are also manifested in the emphases in many other proposed reforms on establishing independent or external oversight bodies capable of vetoing decisions by agency personnel regarding safety issues. Actors outside the normal lines of the agency hierarchy would oversee key decision-making points within NASA dealing with the design and launch of future manned space flights.[47] While these bodies are not intended to exercise direct control over the day-to-day operations of NASA's space shuttle program, such bodies would have jurisdiction over a wide range of agency actions.

It is also evident that congressional oversight of NASA activities is likely to focus a great deal more on details of technical and managerial matters than in the past.[48] In the past, Congress' role regarding NASA was that of patron rather than overseer. For the most part, congressional concerns about NASA were limited to the general priorities of the agency and its potential as a source of pork-barrel projects. In the near future, at least, members of relevant congressional committees and their staffs will become more involved in the details of NASA's operations.[49]

Other suggested reforms (some already being implemented) attempt internal changes in NASA that would complement this movement toward changing accountability. For example, recommendations for reorganizing the shuttle management structure include redefining the program manager's responsibilities to enhance that official's decision-making role.

It was inevitable that the Challenger disaster would generate strong institutional pressures for NASA, and those pressures are creating new demands and expectations for the agency. Ironically, the direction of those pressures has been toward enhanced bureaucratic structures and growing reliance on legal accountability mechanisms which stress NASA's formal responsibilities for the safety of its astronauts. There is little likelihood that Challenger-related reforms will reflect the need for NASA to reestablish the priority of professional accountability systems which held sway in the agency during pre-Apollo 11 heydays.

5. Conclusion

The primary contention of this paper is that the Rogers Commission was shortsighted in focusing exclusively on the failure of NASA's technological or management systems. The problem was not necessarily in the *failure* of those systems, but rather in the *inappropriateness* of the political and bureaucratic accountability mechanisms which characterized NASA's management approach in recent years. The agency's emphasis on political and bureaucratic accountability was a relevant response to changing institutional expectations in NASA's environment, but they were inappropriate for the technical tasks at hand. To the extent that these accountability mechanisms were ill-suited to the technical nature of NASA's agency task, they comprised a major factor in the Challenger tragedy.

In more prescriptive terms, if the professional accountability system had been given at least equal weight in the decision-making process, the decision to launch would probably not have been made on that cold January morning. Had NASA relied exclusively on a professional system of accountability in making the decision to launch the Challenger space shuttle, perhaps deference would have been given to the technical expertise of the engineers. Their recommendation against launch might never have been challenged by the Project Manager for the Solid Rocket Booster.[50] Instead, the Thiokol engineers' initial recommendation against launch was ignored by their hierarchical superiors. Decision makers relied upon supervisors to make the decision rather than deferring to professional experts.

If this assessment of the role of institutional factors in the success and failure of NASA's programs is correct, then the proposals for reform increase the chances of other failures. This conclusion is consistent with the thesis that adding safety mechanisms to already complex systems in fact may increase the chances that something can go wrong.[51] As NASA gets drawn further away from what it can do best—namely, mobilizing the expert resources needed to solve the technical challenges of space exploration—its chances for organizational success are diluted. Ideally, NASA needs to return to what it does best, using the form of accountability that best suits its organizational mission, i.e., a professional accountability based on deference to expertise.[52] The reality of NASA's institutional context, however, makes achievement of this ideal highly improbable. NASA no longer enjoys a nurturing institutional context; instead it faces increased environmental pressures calling for the adoption of political, bureaucratic, and legal accountability mechanisms. Such is the dilemma facing NASA and the challenge confronting all American public administrators.

Notes

1. See James D. Thompson, *Organizations in Action: Social Science Bases of Administrative Theory* (New York: McGraw-Hill Book Co., 1967). pp. 10–11.
2. Thompson, *Organizations in Action*, p. 11.
3. Besides current astronaut Sally Ride and former astronaut Neil Armstrong, the commission membership included: Eugene Covert, an MIT professor and frequent consultant to NASA who received the agency's "Public Service Award" in 1980; Robert W. Rummel, an aerospace engineer and private consultant who was also a recipient of a

NASA public service award; and Major General Donald J. Kutyna, director of the U.S. Air Force's Space Systems program and former manager of the Defense Department's space shuttle program.

4. For example, Commission Chair Rogers was Attorney General for President Eisenhower and Secretary of State for Richard Nixon. David C. Acheson, a well-known Washington lawyer, had previously served as a U.S. Attorney, counsel for the Atomic Energy Commission, and Senior Vice President of COMSAT. Other members of the Commission were: two physicists, Richard P. Feynman and Albert D. Wheelan (Executive Vice President, Hughes Aircraft); astronomer, Arthur B. C. Walker, Jr.; test pilot, Charles E. Yeager; aeronautical engineer, Joseph F. Sutter; and Robert B. Hotz, former editor of *Aviation Week and Space Technology Magazine*.

5. See Paul R. Schulman, *Large-Scale Policy Making* (New York: Elsevier North Holland, Inc., 1980), pp. 22–41; James E. Webb, *Space Age Management* (New York: McGraw-Hill Book Co., 1968); Leonard R. Sayles and Margaret K. Chandler, *Managing Large Systems* (New York: Harper and Row, 1971); and Peter F. Drucker, *Management: Tasks, Responsibilities, and Practices* (New York: Harper and Row, 1974), chapter 47.

6. See discussion in Herbert A. Simon, Donald W. Smithburg, and Victor A. Thompson, *Public Administration* (New York: Alfred A. Knopf, Inc., 1950), especially chapters 24 and 25. Also, Carl Joachim Friedrich, "Public Policy and the Nature of Administrative Responsibility," in C. J. Friedrich and Edward S. Mason, eds., *Public Policy, 1940* (Cambridge: Harvard University Press, 1940), pp. 3–24; and Herman Finer, "Administrative Responsibility and Democratic Government," *Public Administration Review*, vol. 1 (Summer 1941), pp. 335–350.

7. This view of accountability is developed more fully in Barbara Romzek and Mei Dubnick, "Accountability and the Management of Expectations: The Challenger Tragedy and the Costs of Democracy," presented at the annual meeting of the American Political Science Association, the Washington Hilton, August 28–31, 1986.

8. See Max Weber, *Economy and Society; An Outline of Interpretive Sociology*, edited by Guenther Roth and Claus Wittich (Berkeley: University of California Press, 1987), chapter XI.

9. See Alvin Gouldner, *Patterns of Industrial Bureaucracy* (New York: The Free Press, 1954), pp. 159–162.

10. Philosophically and ideologically, the basis of legal accountability is found in the "rule of law" concept; see Friedrich A. Hayek, *The Road to Serfdom* (Chicago: University of Chicago Press, 1944), chapter VI; also see Theodore J. Lowi's call for "juridical democracy" in *The End of Liberalism: The Second Republic of the United States*, 2d ed. (New York: W. W. Norton and Co., 1979), chapter 11.

11. For a comprehensive application of the theory of agency, see Barry M. Mitnick, *The Political Economy of Regulation: Creating, Designing, and Removing Regulatory Forms* (New York: Columbia University Press, 1980).

12. While bureaucratic accountability relies on methods available to members, such as close supervision and rules and regulations, legal accountability is limited to the tools available to outsiders, such as monitoring, investigating, auditing, and other forms of "oversight" and evaluation.

13. See Carl Joachim Friedrich, "Public Policy and the Nature of Administrative Responsibility."

14. For an example of a professional accountability system, see the story of the Manhattan Project offered in Peter Wyden, *Day One: Before Hiroshima and After* (New York: Warner Books, 1985), Book One.

15. See Emmette S. Redford, *Democracy in the Administrative State* (New York: Oxford University Press, 1969); also set works by Paul Appleby and Herman Finer.

16. See James Thompson, *Organizations in Action*.

17. See Robert C. Fried, *Performance in American Bureaucracy* (Boston: Little, Brown and Co., 1976).

18. It is possible (at least theoretically) for different accountability mechanisms to operate within one agency at different levels of the organization. For example, a professional accountability mechanism may be in operation at the technical level of an organization while a legal accountability mechanism may be used to manage external expectations at the institutional or boundary-spanning level. See Thompson, *Organizations in Action.* For an application of this notion in a related area, see Donald Klingner and John Nalbandian, "Values and Conflict in Public Personnel Administration," *Public Administration Quarterly* (forthcoming).

19. See Hans Mark and Arnold Levine, *The Management of Research Institutions: A Look at Government Laboratories* (Washington: National Aeronautics and Space Administration, 1984), pp. 117–118. On the political support for NASA in those early years, see Don K. Price, *The Scientific Estate* (Cambridge, MA: The Belknap Press, 1965), pp. 222–223. On the effects of its budgetary support through 1966, see Paul R. Schulman, *Large-Scale Policy Making* (New York: Elsevier North Holland, Inc., 1980), pp. 87–88.

20. Through the Apollo program, NASA spent over 80 percent of its funding on research and development (R&D) efforts. See Philip N. Whittaker, "Joint Decisions in Aerospace," in Matthew Tuite, Roger Chisolm, and Michael Radnor, eds., *Interorganizational Decision Making* (Chicago: Aldine Publishing Co., 1972), p. 272.

21. On the early history of NASA by an "insider," see John D. Young, "Organizing the Nation's Civilian Space Capabilities: Selected Reflections," in Theodore W. Taylor, ed., *Federal Public Policy: Personal Accounts of Ten Senior Civil Service Executives* (Mt. Airy, MD: Lomond Publications, Inc., 1984), pp. 45–80. Some analysts have defined that "nurturing consensus" as little more than a "political vacuum" in which the agency got to define its own programmatic objectives. See John Logsdon, *The Decision to Go to the Moon,* cited in Lambright, *Governing Science and Technology* (New York: Oxford University Press, 1976), pp. 41–42.

22. Henry S. F. Cooper, Jr., "Letter from the Space Center," in *The New Yorker* (November 10, 1986), p. 93.

23. Mark and Levine, *The Management of Research Institutions,* pp. 60, 200–202.

24. Schulman, *Large-Scale Policy Making,* pp. 62–74. Also Cooper, "Letter from the Space Center," p. 99.

25. Lambright, *Governing Science and Technology,* p. 43. Also see Wayne Biddle, "NASA: What's Needed To Put It On Its Feet?" *Discover,* vol. 8 (January 1987), pp. 36, 40.

26. It is incorrect to think that NASA was apolitical even during its early years. Tom Wolfe describes a heated argument between John Glenn and NASA Administrator James Webb when Glenn bitterly complained of the number of trips he had to take at the request of members of Congress or the White House. See Wolfe's *The Right Stuff* (New York: Bantam Books, 1979), p. 331. See also Mark and Levine, *The Management of Research Institutions,* p. 82, for a discussion of the importance of generating "new business" for the agency. The politics surrounding the shuttle are reflected in investigations of the role Fletcher played in awarding contracts for the shuttle project in 1973; see William J. Broad, "NASA Chief Might Not Take Part in Decisions on Booster Contracts," *The New York Times* (December 7, 1986), pp. 1, 14.

27. W. Henry Lambright, *Governing Science and Technology,* pp. 21–22; and U.S. Congress, House, Committee on Science and Technology, *Investigation of the Challenger Accident,* Report, 99th Congress, 2d Session (Washington: U.S. Government Printing Office, 1986), pp. 176–177.

28. John Noble Wilford, "NASA May Be a Victim of Defects in Its Own Bureaucracy," *The New York Times* (February 16, 1986), p. 18E.

29. See Cooper, "Letter from the Space Center," especially pp. 85–96.

30. See Mark and Levine, *The Management of Research Institutions*, pp. 122–123, on NASA contracting. NASA's use of "pork barrel" politics dates to the agency's earliest years; see Amitai Etzioni, *The Moon Doggle* (Garden City, NY: Doubleday and Co., 1964), and Price, *The Scientific Estate*, pp. 21–23. The continuation of political considerations in NASA's contracting practices during the 1970s is demonstrated by the circumstances surrounding the competition for the shuttle's booster rocket contract which was eventually awarded to Thiokol in 1973; see Broad, "NASA Chief May Not Take Part in Decisions on Booster Contracts."

31. *Report on the Presidential Commission on the Space Shuttle Challenger Accident* (Washington: June 6, 1986), p. 176j hereafter cited as *Rogers Commission Report*.

32. *Rogers Commission Report*, pp. 176, 201. Also Cooper, "Letter from the Space Center," pp. 99–100, and U.S. Congress, House, *Investigation of the Challenger Accident*, pp. 119–120.

33. William J. Broad, "NASA Aide Assails Panel Investigating Explosion of Shuttle," *The New York Times* (March 16, 1986), p. 23.

34. U.S. Congress, House, *Investigation of the Challenger Accident*, p. 120.

35. U.S. Congress, House, *Investigation of the Challenger Accident*, p. 122. Richard P. Feynman, a member of the Rogers Commission, speculated about agency attitudes regarding safety. He believed the agency might have downplayed the riskiness of the shuttle launching to "assure" Congress of the agency's "perfection and success in order to ensure the supply of funds." See David E. Sanger, "Looking Over NASA's Shoulder," *The New York Times* (September 28, 1986), p. 26E.

36. John Noble Wilford, "NASA Chief Vows to Fix Problems," *The New York Times* (June 10, 1986), p. 22.

37. *Rogers Commission Report*, pp. 153–54.

38. Laurie McGinley and Bryan Burrough, "Backbiting in NASA Worsens the Damage from Shuttle Disaster," *The Wall Street Journal* (April 2, 1986), p. 1.

39. See Victor A. Thompson, *Modern Organizations*, 2d ed. (University: University of Alabama Press, 1977), chapter 8.

40. On the factors which make it difficult for employees to pass bad news to upper levels of the organization, see Chris Argyris and Donald A. Schon, *Organizational Learning: A Theory of Action Perspective* (Reading, MA: Addison-Wesley Publishing Co., 1978).

41. *Rogers Commission Report*, p. 82.

42. Testimony of Lawrence Mulloy, *Rogers Commission Report*, p. 98.

43. Cooper, "Letter from the Space Center," pp. 89, 96.

44. Testimony of Roger Boisjoly, *Rogers Commission Report*, p. 93. Also see testimony of R. K. Lund, *Rogers Commission Report*, p. 94.

45. David E. Sanger, "Top NASA Aides Knew of Shuttle Flaw in '84," *The New York Times* (December 21, 1986), pp. 1, 22.

46. *Rogers Commission Report*, pp. 199–201.

47. *Rogers Commission Report*, pp. 198–199.

48. Members of Congress criticized the Commission for not going deeply enough into the question of which individuals bore direct responsibility for the accident. See Philip M. Boffey, "Shuttle Panel is Faulted for Not Naming Names," *The New York Times* (June 11, 1986), p. 16.

49. Philip M. Boffey, "NASA Challenged on Modification That Rockets Met Requirements," *The New York Times* (June 12, 1986), p. 18.

50. *Rogers Commission Report*, p. 96.
51. See Charles Perrow, *Normal Accidents: Living With High Risk Technologies* (New York: Basic Books, Inc., 1984).
52. Our suggestion that a professional system of accountability is the most appropriate to NASA should not be construed as an endorsement of professional accountability under all circumstances. Rather, our point is to indicate that the type of accountability system needs to suit the agency task.

11

PERSONNEL
MANAGEMENT

Public personnel management is "the management of a system whereby public agencies recruit, compensate, and discipline their employees. The system is normally characterized by a watchdog differentiation between the structures that perform personnel tasks and structures that protect employee rights and insulate the process from politics."[1] As several prominent observers of public personnel systems have noted, however, "the essential difference between personnel management in the private sector and personnel management in the public sector can probably be summed up in one word—politics. The public personnel process is a political process. Frankly, that is what makes it so interesting as an area of study."[2]

THREE COMPETING VALUES

Why are public personnel systems so "political"? Because they play a central role in helping government agencies maintain a careful balance among three competing political values: strong executive leadership, politically neutral competence, and representativeness.[3] We will use these three values to help explain some of the ins-and-outs of public personnel management.

- *Strong Executive Leadership* gives primary value to the right of elected and appointed public officials to run government as they see fit. When someone is elected (or appointed by an elected official) to office, they should have the authority and flexibility to lead—to run—government. This includes particularly the right of leaders to choose their trusted "lieutenants"—the people who will loyally help them implement the policies that got them elected. "Strong executive leadership" thus reflects the belief that government will be most efficient and effective when leaders are given the flexibility and power to choose their subordinates who will implement their policies, with as little interference as possible.
- *Politically neutral competence* gives greatest value to the belief that people should be hired, selected for advancement, and terminated on the basis of

their *job-related* knowledge and skills. Government efficiency and effectiveness are maximized by keeping politics, "old boy networks," and "cronyism" out of government hiring and firing—by hiring and retaining the best qualified employees that can be found.

- Finally, *representativeness* places highest priority on the value of the government work force resembling the population that it governs. Unless citizens (or groups of citizens) believe that government is "connected" to them—that government employees understand and empathize with them—they will be reluctant to "consent" to being governed. Representativeness thus reflects the belief that government efficiency and effectiveness can be increased by consciously hiring and retaining people who "represent" the population governed.

The effort to maintain a balance among these three competing values is, in essence, the history of public personnel management.

From the founding of the U.S. as a nation almost until 1900, virtually all positions in the executive branch of governments were filled by *patronage,* the long-established practice of rewarding the political party "faithful" with government jobs, without regard for qualifications. During this era, the value "strong executive leadership"—essentially, the right of public leaders to lead as they saw fit—had higher standing than "politically neutral competence" and "representativeness." Popular pressure began mounting in the early-1880s to eliminate the spoils system, however, at least partially because of high media attention and public outrage during and following the administration of President Andrew Jackson. The 1881 assassination of President James A. Garfield by a disgruntled office seeker became the "trigger event," the occurrence that created a climate of public urgency and eventually resulted in passage of the first significant civil service reform legislation in the U.S.—the Pendleton Act of 1883. The "civil service reform movement" of the late 1880s thus reflected the ascendance of "politically neutral competence as the dominant value that shaped public personnel policy in the U.S. for many decades thereafter " (and the decline of "strong executive leadership"). At various times in the second half of the 20th century, each of these values had periods when it "dominated." The administration of President Ronald Reagan, for example, valued "strong executive leadership," President Jimmy Carter's administration gave priority to "politically neutral competence," and Presidents John Kennedy and Lyndon Johnson gave priority to "representativeness."

What we have been discussing has been historical "public policy of personnel management." Readers who want to know about the "practical" side of public personnel management should see any of many good public personnel management texts listed in the Chapter References. We will only introduce a few realities here. For example: What does "public personnel management" mean in practice—what does it do? What are the important, current, practical, public personnel management questions or controversies? What difference does public personnel management make—to public employees, to public administrators, and to the general public?

THE FUNCTIONS OF PUBLIC PERSONNEL MANAGEMENT

Public personnel management involves many "people-related" functions, including:[4]

- Recruiting and selecting government employees;
- Developing and maintaining a system for classifying government positions (jobs) and establishing equitable pay and benefit ranges for each position classification;
- Developing and supporting the employee performance appraisal system;
- Managing employee-labor relations, including collective bargaining with public unions and contract maintenance;
- Disciplining and terminating employees who violate rules or who do not perform at expected levels, including maintaining the grievance system;
- Coordinating training programs for employees and managers.

Public personnel departments, or as they usually are labeled now, "human resource management departments" or "HRM departments," are "staff" departments that serve the needs of "line" managers and employees. In practice, this means that HRM departments *do not make decisions* about individual hirings, advancements, and terminations. Instead, HRM departments *work with* other managers to make certain that hiring, advancement, and termination decisions are handled legally, ethically, responsibly, according to personnel policy, and as expeditiously as possible. HRM departments are staffed by experts who, for example: know the laws governing the advertisement of government position openings, have studied comparable wages in other government units and industries in the area, are able to construct examinations that can accurately identify people with the skills needed to perform specific tasks (or who know where to find already-constructed examinations), and who know what overtime pay and scheduling practices are required and prohibited by law. Thus HRM departments establish and oversee policy guidelines and requirements that line managers must follow *and* they also serve as "consultants" to line managers as they go about the task of recruiting, selecting, promoting, paying, disciplining, evaluating, training, and terminating employees. A city's HRM department therefore cannot decide that "Joan Smith" will be hired to fill a vacant position as a night shift Police Department dispatcher. That decision can only be made by the supervisor or manager of the dispatchers. The HRM department may: verify that the Police Department is authorized to fill the vacant position, arrange to advertise the opening in local newspapers, notify the supervisor how much the city will pay the person who is hired and what benefits the city will offer, conduct preliminary "screening" of applicants to make certain they have necessary skills, and provide the dispatch supervisor with a list of applicants who meet the qualifications that are included in the position description.

The "personnel administration functions" or "human resources management functions" thus are joint responsibilities of all government managers—the people who make the final decisions about their employees—and of the HRM department staff that both assists and regulates the line managers in the performance of the HRM functions.

THE POLITICS OF PUBLIC PERSONNEL MANAGEMENT

Why is public personnel management "so political"? A few of the reasons should be becoming evident. First, public administrators must have enough qualified employees to get the work done—and well. If the personnel system doesn't work as well as its should, or if it favors (or disadvantages) some managers over others, it can help or hurt some departments' ability to perform, and it can directly help or hurt the career prospects of some public administrators. Second, elected public officials usually want the freedom to select and promote many of the middle managers and employees who will work in their administration. Also, government jobs can be important political "paybacks" for help (including large contributions) or loyalty during political campaigns—and an important way to keep key political aides available for future campaigns. On the other side of the coin, using government jobs to reward political loyalty does not necessarily lead to hiring well-qualified employees. HRM departments and other advocates for "good government" argue instead for the use of fair, open, valid, processes whereby the individuals who are best able to perform a job are selected or permitted to advance into it—free from political considerations. Public personnel management is marked by an ongoing tension between the principles of strong executive leadership on the one hand and of politically neutral competence on the other. Policy and practice need to balance these principles wisely.

CURRENT PUBLIC HRM QUESTIONS AND CONTROVERSIES

We have already addressed a few of the political issues that swirl around public personnel administration. Here, we introduce four other current controversies that reflect widely divergent views about how to achieve efficient and effective government and that involve public HRM policies, practices, statutes, case law, and ethics.

- A pervasive belief has taken hold in many counties (including Great Britain, New Zealand, and Australia as well as the United States) that the best decisions are made by people and organizations closest to those who will be most directly affected by the decisions.[5] It does not matter if the question is whether a decision should be made in Washington, DC or in state houses; in a state house or in city halls; or by higher-level public managers or the employees who work with the recipients of services. This belief is having major effects on public HRM. As this *wave of reform* has swept through governments around the world and across the U.S., public organizations have been *downsized* and their services *"devolved"* to lower levels of government and *"diffused"* out of government to nonprofit organizations and businesses, employee morale has suffered. Fears and insecurities have destroyed government organizational cultures.[6] Attempts to *empower* employees—to give employees the power to make decisions that used to be made by higher level officials—and to *redesign jobs* often are seen as nothing more than manipulative schemes by management to get employees to "do more with less." HRM departments are being called upon to institute a variety of *empowerment programs,* most particularly during the 1990s, such as total quality management (TQM) and *self-directing work teams.* These attempts to empower employees offer many opportunities to improve operations and improve the quality of work life for employees. They also, however, raise serious questions about accountability for government programs and services, the Constitutional legitimacy of many such programs,[7] and employer manipulation of employees.

- Government personnel (HRM) departments, and their policies and practices are the recipients of considerable criticism. Often they are viewed as "part of the 'government problem'"—as impediments to "getting the job done"—instead of an aid to managing government agencies. Thus the institutions, rules, and practices of public personnel management have persistently bred discontent. They have fueled an interest in finding alternatives to traditional civil service or merit systems. "For many state and local government managers, civil service systems and unions often are seen primarily as constraints, as something that gets in the way of their ability to manage the organizations and thus limits performance."[8] In 1948, Wallace Sayre put a label on public personnel administration that has "stuck" ever since—"the triumph of techniques over purpose."[9] In sum, "civil service . . . is now clearly associated with inefficiency, rigidity, and indifference to performance."10 The current issue for the profession of public HRM, then, is whether it can "reinvent itself" and once again become an efficient and effective facilitator of government agency improvement.

- This introductory essay has so far addressed the values of "strong executive leadership" and "politically neutral competence." But, what about *"representativeness"*? Equity, and thus representativeness, is—and always has been—a central issue for public HRM. Although women have been more successful in securing jobs in government than in private industry, they remain under-represented in the higher management levels. And, isn't government likely to be more effective when there are minorities working in the police and fire departments who can respond to calls in predominately minority neighborhoods (as well as non-minority neighborhoods)? What should be done, however, if there are not "qualified" minority (or women) applicants for vacant positions? Should white males be the only people hired, or should special efforts be made to find and develop qualified minority and women applicants? These types of questions are merely the "tip of" the huge and highly emotional controversies in the "iceberg" of representativeness. Collectively they are best known as *equal employment opportunity (EEO) and affirmative action (AA)* issues.

- *Labor relations* are an integral part of public HRM, and public sector unions, contract negotiations, and strikes have always been highly controversial. Are unions of government employees "part of government's problem," or "part of the solution"? City garbage collectors strike, district schoolteachers demand smaller classes, police officers all contract a mysterious "blue flue" on the same day. Should government employees be permitted to join labor unions or to strike for better wages or working conditions? Should they have the same right of association as employees in private businesses? Should government agency managers be required to meet with union representatives—to recognize and negotiate with them? These are difficult questions, and the answers complex and controversial—more so than in the private sector.

READINGS REPRINTED IN THIS CHAPTER

The readings that are reprinted in this chapter highlight two of these current controversies in public personnel management: The implications of the world-wide "reinventing government" movement for public HRM; and the extent to which public HRM is seen "part of government's problem" and thus in need of "reinventing" itself. Social equity in the public workplace is the sole topic of Chapter 12.

"Whither the Senior Executive Service?" by Mark Huddleston and William Boyer is a search for reasons why the Senior Executive Service (SES) has not become a well-accepted institution in the U.S. At a different level, however, "Whither the Senior Executive Service?" is an examination of the reasons why the U.S. civil service system is not an "elite corps" in comparison with civil service systems in European and Asian nations. "The SES almost wholly lacks prestige, esprit de corps, closed career paths, domination of top managerial, positions, and so forth."

The SES has not been particularly successful for the same reasons that an "elite" civil service system has not developed in the U.S., and the reasons are numerous and long-standing. Several of which most people would consider to be favorable turns for democracy, such as "the timing of the emergence of widespread political participation relative to the development of strong state institutions."

Huddleston and Boyer assert that "no nation can prosper in the modern world without a neutrally competent higher civil service at the core of its government. . . . The United States needs a government that is as sagacious, steady, and responsible as we can possibly get." They offer four sets of proposals to help accomplish this end: (1) eliminate all political appointments below that of assistant secretary; (2) establish clear career tracks for senior executives; (3) put specialists and generalists in separate tracks; and (4) treat senior administrators as public officials as well as public servants.

"Reinventing Government, The New Public Management and Civil Service Systems in International Perspective," by Richard Kearney and Steven

Hays describes the ideologies behind the "reinventing government movement" and the underlying reasons why it has been initiated—in various forms—in countries around the world (including the U.S.). Kearney and Hays conclude that reinventing government movement's potential impacts on democratic governments and for civil service systems could be harmful. Thus, Kearney and Hays address both the first and the second of our "current controversies." The authors assert that the reinventing government movement represents in part an attack on bureaucratic power and on career civil servants. They argue that contrary to the pronouncements made by "reinventing government's proponents," the movement "threatens to undermine the important role played by public servants in modern democratic governments." Evidence of the movement's world-wide influence is provided through examples from developed as well as developing nations including, for example, Australia, Brazil, Canada, Great Britain, Japan, Malaysia, Mexico, New Zealand, Nigeria, the Philippines, Portugal, Sweden, and Turkey. But Hays and Kearney urge caution.

> Despite their many blemishes, the professional personnel systems of most industrialized nations have served them extraordinarily well. In exchange, reinventing government proponents offer the unsure promise of greater efficiency, customer satisfaction, and responsiveness to political authority. As the politicians' grasp over the civil service system tightens, however, one wonders whose interests will ultimately be served. . . . Reinventing government . . . involves . . . assumptions, values, and practices that are shaking, and threatening to destroy, the foundations of effective and accountable public administration. . . .

Thus, "public employees must understand that their administrative landscape is being altered significantly, and that it will never look the same."

"Reinventing Public Administration: Reform in the Georgia Civil Service," by **Rex L. Facer II,** also addresses the first two of the current controversies identified above—"reinventing government" and "reinventing public HRM"—as "reinventing government" is being implemented in Georgia state government. For many years, Georgia has been a leader in trying new management approaches to improve government. In the 1970s, for example, then-Governor Jimmy Carter lured Peter Pyhrr, a Texas Instrument executive, to Georgia to implement outcomes-oriented "Zero Base Budgeting" (ZBB) across state government. (In 1976, presidential-candidate Carter made ZBB a campaign promise, and as President in 1977, he ordered its adoption across the U.S. government.) In 1993, Governor Zell Miller introduced two broad personnel reforms that were key pieces in his overall program to reform ("reinvent") Georgia state government: the dismantling of merit (civil service) protections for new employees, and "GeorgiaGain," a performance-based compensation system. These pioneering reforms are being watched closely by other states and by public administration scholars. Do the Georgia reforms represent the future of "good government" that should be adopted elsewhere, or are they just another well-intentioned but faddish government reform that will land in the trash heap of failed reinvention approaches? Facer's article presents one of the first comprehensive overviews of the Georgia reform initiatives.

NOTES

1. Sylvia, Ronald D. (1998). "Public Personnel Administration," in Jay M. Shafritz (Ed.), *International Encyclopedia of Public Policy and Administration.* Boulder, Colo. Westview Press, p. 1843.
2. Shafritz, Jay M., Norma M. Riccucci, David H. Rosenbloom, and Albert C. Hyde. (1992). *Personnel Management in Government: Politics and Process* (4th ed.). New York: Marcel Dekker, p. viii.
3. Kaufman, Herbert. (January/February 1969). "Administrative Decentralization and Political Power." *Public Administration Review, 29,* 3–15.
4. Donald Klingner and John Nalbandian group these public personnel management functions into four major categories: planning, acquisition, development, and sanction, in *Public Personnel Management: Contexts and Strategies* (3rd ed.). Upper Saddle River, NJ: Prentice Hall, 1993, p. 2.
5. Ott, J. Steven, and Lisa A. Dicke. (2001). "Challenges Facing Public Sector HRM in an Era of Downsizing, Devolution, Diffusion and Empowerment . . . and Accountability?" in Ali Farazmand (Ed.). *Strategic Public Personnel Administration/HRM: Building Human Capital for the New Century.* Westport, Conn.: Greenwood.
6. Ott, J. Steven. (1998). "Understanding Organizational Climate and Culture," in Stephen E. Condrey (Ed.), *Handbook of Human Resource Management in Government* (pp. 116–140). San Francisco: Jossey-Bass.
7. David H. Rosenbloom, "Constitutional Problems for the New Public Management in the United States," a Colloquium in Current Public Policy, School of Public Administration, Florida Atlantic University, Ft. Lauderdale, Florida, November 17, 1997.
8. Ban, Carolyn, and Norma M. Riccucci. (1993). "Personnel Systems and Labor Relations: Steps Toward a Quiet Revitalization," in Frank J. Thompson (Ed.), *Revitalizing State and Local Public Service.* San Francisco: Jossey-Bass, p. 71.
9. This was the title of an article by Wallace Sayre. (Spring 1948). "The Triumph of Techniques Over Purpose." *Public Administration Review, 8,* p. 134.
10. Ukeles, J. B. (1982). *Doing More with Less: Turning Public Management Around.* New York: AMACOM, p. 17.
11. Pyhrr, Peter A. (January/February 1977). "The Zero-Base Approach to Government Budgeting." *Public Administration Review, 37,* 1–8.

30

Mark W. Huddleston and William W. Boyer

WHITHER THE SENIOR EXECUTIVE SERVICE?

WHY HAS THE UNITED STATES FAILED TO DEVELOP A HIGHER CIVIL SERVICE?

Some might object that even to pose this first question is to assume a fact not in evidence. The Senior Executive Service (SES) may not be perfect, it may be argued, but certainly it *is* a higher civil service. We believe, however, that such an argument is true only in terms of the narrowest of definitions. The SES is a *higher* civil service only in contrast to the *lower* civil service, a distinction of dubious utility. Most of the structures that political scientists and other close observers refer to as higher civil services in the rest of the world have in common a set of characteristics that the SES almost wholly lacks: prestige, esprit de corps, closed career paths, domination of top managerial positions, and so forth. Indeed, we define a higher civil service as *an elite corps of career public officials who fill key positions in governmental administration.* By this definition, which we believe captures general usage quite well, the SES is simply not a higher civil service.[1]

The real U.S. counterparts of the mandarins of Britain, France, Germany, and Japan are political appointees, not civil servants. Nor are Britain, France, Germany, and Japan the only countries that provide such contrast with the United States. Virtually every other nation in the world—certainly every other nation in the developed world—has created a higher civil service. It is the striking singularity of the American experience that makes this question—Why not the United States?—so compelling.

This is not to say, by the way, that these higher civil services are somehow better across the board than what the United States has produced. Indeed, Milton Esman believes "the growing complexity of government favors the U.S. pattern," which encourages the movement of program specialists into senior civil service posts.[2] Moreover, the United States may well tap men and women to manage its public institutions who are brighter, more competent, more ethical, more representative, and more responsible and accountable than those who occupy similar positions in some other countries. Furthermore, all top public managers, whether nominally civil servants or political appointees, are by the nature of their work political actors. Indeed, it is undoubtedly true that top civil servants in some nations exhibit less neutral competence and more bald partisanship than many political appointees in the United States. These caveats notwithstanding, the fact remains that the United States has walked a markedly different administrative path from the rest of the world. Why?

The answer reflects both history and ideas, or—better—the interplay between history and ideas. Unlike those in European states, the U.S. bureaucracy was not wrought from long-standing legacies. To begin with, public administration in America started with a fairly clean slate, or at least as clean a slate as any nation is ever likely to find. As European states began in the late eighteenth and early nineteenth centuries, and Japan in the late nineteenth century, to construct what we now know as their higher civil services, they were mindful of existing structures and often built on top of them, propelled as they were by conflicts, forces, and ideas centuries in the making. It is not coincidental that Japan's elite bureaucrats are deemed latter-day samurai or that members of France's *grand corps* trace their lineage past Napoleon to Colbert. Americans, on the other hand, had no state-building Frederick the Great or Louis the XIV in their past, no Colbertian minions of kings to build an apparatus of control, no established church to provide a template for hierarchy and centralized administrative management.[3]

The United States became a nation (and began building its administrative structures) at a time when the model that Americans might logically have used—Great Britain, the former colonial power—was scarcely in a position to teach sound administrative lessons to anyone else. British institutions of public administration were rightly regarded, at home and abroad, as corrupt and inefficient.

If Americans had anything at all written on their otherwise blank administrative page, it was ringing "self-evident truths" from the Declaration of Independence about equality, rights, and consent of the governed and a litany of abuses committed by King George III. Our oft noted distrust of executive authority and disdain for officialdom were not simply present at our creation; they were *reasons* for our creation. Alexis de Tocqueville, that peripatetic and perspicacious Frenchman, observed that Americans' natural inclination is to diffuse and decentralize power: an administrative function concentrated in one powerful official in France, he noted, is spread over nineteen minor—and publicly accountable—magistrates in America.[4] There seemed little basis for a higher civil service in a system that generally deconcentrates power and distributes most governmental functions over a multiplicity of states and localities.

Founding ideals aside, perhaps the most crucial historical factor that explains the failure of the United States to develop a higher civil service is the timing of the emergence of widespread political participation relative to the development of strong state institutions. Simply put, in Europe and Japan administration preceded participation. In the United States participation preceded administration. In those different sequences lay tremendous variation in administrative development.

In the United States participation was widespread from the outset, at least relatively speaking. The winds blew strong before the seeds could even take root. America's administrative structures—and administrative outcomes—were thus bent to popular participation to an extent unparalleled in Europe or anywhere else in the world. Not only could virtually all white males vote but, as Tocqueville pointed out, virtually all were, in a sense, administrators.

> In America the power that conducts the administration is far less regular, less enlightened, and less skillful, but a hundredfold greater than in Europe. In no country in the world do the citizens make such exertions for the common weal. I know of no people who have established schools so numerous and efficacious, places of public worship better suited to the wants of the inhabitants, or roads kept in better repair.[5]

One practical effect of this early and widespread participation was to create a self-perpetuating civic assumption: government, at all levels and in all its institutional manifestations, can and should be in the hands of those who are governed. Why suffer the ministrations of separate and self-inflated elites? Government is not complicated. It does nothing beyond the reach and ken of the common man. Or to use Andrew Jackson's more eloquent words, "The duties of all public officers are, or at least admit of being made, so plain and simple that men of intelligence may readily qualify themselves for their performance; and I can not but believe that more is lost by the long continuance of men in office than is generally to be gained by their experience."[6] Indeed, throughout the early years of the Republic, the duties of administrators *were* plain and simple.

This civic assumption maintains, furthermore, that those public officials whom American democracy simply cannot do without—elected or otherwise—need constant reminding that they are no higher and no better than anyone else. Americans maintain this system, Tocqueville averred, by refusing to elevate officials over the citizenry. Public officials here are accessible, "uniformly simple in manner," without airs or robes of office. They are also attentive, obliging, and open. And by offering only "drudgery and subsistence . . . to those entrusted with . . . administration," Americans have, in Jefferson's words, taken "a wise and necessary precaution against the degeneracy of the public servants."[7]

Self-interest bolstered this ethic, of course. Throughout the nineteenth century, public contracts and public jobs were viewed as a sort of booty to be claimed by privateers who, with each election, swept in on the not particularly fat but nonetheless undefended ship of state. Patronage was the order of the day, with rotation its great principle and corruption its great result.

And whatever selfishness failed to stimulate, partisanship provided. President John Adams arguably set the cycle in motion with a series of "midnight appointments" shortly before leaving office in 1801. As the first non-Federalist to take office, Thomas Jefferson, Adams's successor, felt bound to undo these and to appoint loyal Republicans as further vacancies arose.[8] Although the threat from Federalists faded through the terms of Presidents Madison and Monroe, the practice of appointing loyalists became accepted. With the election of Jackson and the simultaneous reflowering of a serious partisan opposition in the Whigs the practice became a principle.[9]

Deterioration of urban life in the late nineteenth century, moral revulsion toward corruption, and fear of the rising power of immigrant-based political machines touched off a wave of administrative and political reform.

The political ethos of the times ordained that civil servants—higher or otherwise—have no role in government except as executors of policy made by elected officials or their appointees. Why bother building elaborate systems on the European model which would socialize elite administrators and inculcate appropriate republican values? We need only keep our bureaucrats on a short political leash and subject them to close checks by legislators and elected executives. And certainly we did not need to encourage the development of a *generalist* class of higher administrators.

Thus, by the time the U.S. national government began in the late nineteenth century to take on those functions that require a significant administrative infrastructure—economic and social regulation, broad internal improvements, active foreign polity—U.S. "higher" administration looked substantially different from that found anywhere else in the world. Riddled with politics, uninsulated from legislative interference, and viewed with little or no respect by the public, the federal service was dominated—where there were careerists at all—by specialists and was seemingly dedicated to the proposition that anything smacking of an elite, including adequate pay, appropriate training, and a closed, bottom-up system of recruitment, would contaminate democracy's blood. With all this as prolegomenon, it is little wonder that the Senior Civil Service foundered, the Federal Executive Service failed, and the Senior Executive Service fizzled.

WHERE DO WE GO FROM HERE?

An obvious conclusion to draw from the above analysis is that a genuine higher civil service is not in the American future. The burden of U.S. history and the weight of U.S. culture are fundamentally at odds with the notion of elite public administration.

Even if some such system were to be foisted on the federal government, it would soon be reshaped to conform to existing biases. The SES is a case in point.

This conclusion is obvious but, in our judgment, dubious. It suffers, to begin with, from a kind of simple-minded historicism. Although the past certainly conditions the public policy choices of the present and the future, it does not determine them. Nothing is already scripted. Political and administrative institutions are the product of collective human decisions made and remade constantly. As anemic as the Senior Civil Service, Federal Executive Service, and SES were and are, their existence provides unmistakable markers of change.

And what does reason suggest? First and most important, reason suggests that no nation can prosper in the modern world without a neutrally competent higher civil service at the core of its government. The day of a public service filled with Cincinnatuses leaving for a turn plow and farm has passed. So, too, has the day of the canny partisan who changes overnight from speech writing or managing literature drops to managing major federal programs. Both images are romantic. Both resonate with basic chords of American democracy. But neither is realistic. Continuity, steadiness, experience, expertise: these are the values that higher administrators need especially to embody in an age of complexity—along with virtue and a sense of responsibility, which all public officials, elected or otherwise, ought to share.

To move us farther in this direction, we offer here four sets of specific proposals. Some of them are modest and may easily be accommodated within the structure of the SES. Others require more fundamental change.

Eliminate All Political Appointments Below That of Assistant Secretary

In 1991, approximately 3,000 federal jobs encompassing everything from cabinet secretary to cook were subject to the vagaries of the political appointment process.

The need in a republic for certain of these jobs to be filled by political appointment is beyond serious dispute. Cabinet secretaries and their chief deputies need to have the absolute confidence of the president and to be prepared to advance the president's agenda with partisan enthusiasm. Somewhere around the level of assistant secretary, however, the balance of required skills shifts. More time is spent on the pith of day-to-day management, less on strategy, speechmaking, and consultation with partisan movers and shakers. Needed here are the talents of the experienced professional: rationality, substantive expertise, disinterested judgment.

The ironic fact is that presidents would be better served if they did not put their "own people" in place. They, like the American people at large, benefit most when wise decisions are made and programs run smoothly.[10] Who, then, gains from the present system, and who would lose most through reform? Individual members of Congress, to begin with. Their ability to get themselves re-elected is a function of their ability to dispense favors and largesse, which in turn is a function, at least in part, of the wheels they can turn and buttons they can push in the bureaucracy. And administrative appointments are themselves favors, of course. It was Congress, after all, that created the spoils system, and it was Congress that had to be dragged kicking and screaming into making even minor modifications in it.[11] Lobbyists, think tank scribes and consultants, representatives of interest groups of various sorts—including those from self-described public interest groups[12]—and even some academics—often have a vested interest in the prevailing system as well and would stand to lose from reform. The revolving door pivots past their offices too. How else can the Sierra Club get its man in the Environmental Protection Agency or the coal industry its woman in Interior? How would the Heritage Foundation have done without the Reagan administration? The Kennedy School without Clinton?

Some may object that our proposal to eliminate most political appointees resurrects and leans on the timeworn dichotomy between politics and administration. Perhaps it does. But in response we would say two things. First, anyone who doesn't advocate turning all administrators into political appointees (or vice versa) leans on this dichotomy to some extent. The question for most people is not whether, but where, the line should be drawn. Second, we find some attacks on this distinction too epistemologically slippery by half. To observe correctly, for example, that high civil servants do make policy and then conclude that *therefore* there is no difference between policy and administration is to strip two perfectly good and useful words—*policy* and *administration*—of meaning and distinction. Such tortuous logic exemplifies much of the destructive nonsense known as post-modern analysis.[13]

Establish Clear Career Tracks for Senior Executives

Where are the dedicated and talented senior administrators of tomorrow going to come from? So far the federal government has assumed, like the baseball-loving farmer in *Field of Dreams*, "that if we need them, they will come." And so far that has worked fairly well. Sufficient numbers of qualified GS-14s and -15s have been interested in entering the senior ranks to satisfy demand. But levels of satisfaction with federal service have been declining. And alternatives for midcareer managers, especially given a new pension system, have been looking brighter. In any event, while this system often promotes excellent people, it does so ultimately as a result of serendipity. Why wait until individuals have reached the top rung of the General Schedule and are perhaps in their late forties or early fifties to begin considering and grooming them for senior positions?

What is needed is a system that identifies potential senior executives early, preferably at the point of college graduation, and then move them along through progressively more responsible positions, providing further education and training at regular intervals. Ideally, this program of career development would involve considerable rotation of assignments, both within and outside the primary agency.[14] Indeed, a structured system of postings to nonfederal and even nongovernmental organizations has considerable merit, as the French have discovered. An expanded version of the Presidential Management Intern Program would be a good first step in this direction. Loosening the iron bands of rank-in-job classification in the middle levels of the civil service would be a good second step.

Another measure would be to follow the lead of the military services and create an academy for civilian officers, an idea that has surfaced occasionally over the years.[15] We believe this idea makes eminent good sense. At one level the military academies exist to provide training in certain technical skills that each service needs. Far more important, though, they *socialize* our future senior commanders. They use their uniquely intense and insulated atmospheres to inculcate a set of values—honor, commitment, responsibility—that the services themselves, and U.S. society as a whole, consider useful. By what logic do we assume that our civilian administrators are less important to the nation's future and can be left to their own devices or to those of the general culture to imbibe appropriate values?[16]

Put Specialists and Generalists in Separate Tracks

American bureaucracy has long been dominated by technical specialists, men and women who, first and foremost, are capable chemists, economists, virologists, accountants, and so forth. In this regard our public service is at the opposite end of the spectrum from the British, which, as we have seen, has traditionally prized the generalist. Long and ultimately fruitless debates have taken place as to which system is better.[17]

It is clear to us that upper reaches of administration need specialists *and* generalists. It is equally clear, however, that a single personnel system cannot accommodate the needs of both groups. A system that rewards broad management skills tends to undervalue, and thus to discourage, good science. A system built wholly of technical experts is ineffective and undirected.

Although the SES tried, in effect, to meld the two by putting the same sorts of people (specialists) into a putatively more generalist-oriented, rank-in-person structure, it wound up with the worst of both worlds. Because the SES is the only route upward for talented people at top levels of the General Schedule, excellent bench scientists (and their equivalents in other disciplines) are forced to choose between promotion and better pay, on the one hand, and what they do best, on the other. By the same token, because the SES has done nothing to encourage the cultivation of generalist talents at the front end of the process (see the preceding section), the best that can be done is to take middle-aged men and women who are good specialists, give them a course or two at the Federal Executive Institute, and hope that they become good general managers in the SES. In operation this is not quite the so-called Peter Principle, but it is close.

We believe that is makes more sense to adopt a two-track system. Parallel to (and equal with, in terms of pay and status) a generalist-oriented SES, a senior specialist corps is needed, modeled perhaps on the Department of Health and Human Service's Senior Scientific Service.[18] This would keep experts on tap and at least next to the top. It would meet the needs of specialists and the organizations they serve while allowing the SES or a similar system to develop its generalist potential more fully.

Treat Senior Administrators as Public Officials as Well as Public Servants

American administrators have never had a well-defined role in our system of governance. American political theory does not accommodate them. The Constitution neither anticipates nor mentions public administration, as many political science professors tell their students.

The logic that seems to be operating here is that because elections are the only way to confer legitimacy in a democratic system, appointed administrators cannot be given anything important to do, at least not without being watched closely and checked by legislators, elected executives, political appointees, and assorted others. It follows, then, that certainly such administrators cannot be allowed (again, in theory) broad discretionary power, or have the status of official conferred upon them. To do so would violate the precepts of popular sovereignty, and hence the essence of the Constitution. Or at least such is the argument.[19]

Can the existence of an active higher civil service be reconciled with the Constitution? John Rohr, for one, seems to think so and has done some especially creative and useful analysis on this point. He begins by pointing out that while the Constitution omits mention of the word *administration* specifically, administration was nevertheless among the framers' foremost concerns, at least if *Publius* is any guide: "The word *administration* and its cognates appear 124 times through the *Federalist Papers*; more frequently than *Congress*, *President*, or *Supreme Court*."[20] Rohr argues very persuasively that our administrative state *is* fundamentally compatible with the plan of the founders; that the higher civil service today fulfills executive functions originally intended for but relinquished by the Senate; and that public administration further "heals a defect" in our body politic by overcoming the inadequate representation in the House of Representatives.[21]

We agree with Rohr's analysis and would add that a strong case can be made that the founders envisaged an administrative system that looked far more like what we recommend here than that which exists.

To treat senior administrators as public *officials* as well as public *servants*, then, is to accept them as a legitimate part of government. It implies recognizing the constitutionality as well as the reasonableness of broad, though bounded, grants of administrative discretion. The three principal branches of the U.S. government—Congress, President, and Supreme Court—ought to return to their primary constitutional functions and leave administration to administrators. Congress needs to quit trying to micromanage federal programs; the president needs to forgo his army of political appointees; and the courts need to hew to the old principle that administrators are the best judges of matters in their own domain.

But what about administrative responsibility? How could a democracy regard bureaucrats with such equanimity? Who would make them accountable to the public interest?

Bureaucracy can be regulated with checks that are internal as well as controls that are external. Internal checks can be more effective and efficient. Careful training is always better than a stout leash. In the opening salvo of his famous exchange with Herman Finer, Carl Friedrich wrote:

> Responsible conduct of administrative functions is not so much enforced as it is elicited. . . . Even under the most tyrannical despot administrative officials will escape effective control. . . . The problem of how to bring about responsible conduct of the administrative staff of a large organization is, particularly in a democratic society, very largely a question of sound work rules and effective morale.[22]

In the final analysis the most compelling argument in favor of our vision of an American higher civil service is neither historical nor constitutional. It is an argument from necessity: In an increasingly complex, competitive, and interdependent world, the United States needs a government that is as sagacious, steady, and responsible as it can possibly get. We can no longer afford the costs attendant upon an apparatus that looks as though it were cooked up by Mr. Dooley in the smoke-filled back room of a nineteenth-century political club. Although the connection is seldom made, virtually every major government scandal and policy disaster of recent years can be traced to the system of political administration that suppresses the wisdom and values of career professionals and gives free rein to the lightly toasted ideas and short-term interests of political appointees. How many Watergates, Irangates, Challenger disasters, and Department of Housing and Urban Development scandals do we have to suffer before we recognize the ineptitude and corruption this system encourages? Not many, we hope.

Opposition to these proposals will come from many of the same quarters that opposed the spirit of the Senior Civil Service, the Federal Executive Service, and the SES; from congressional micromanagers, members and staff, who see electoral advantage in being able to influence appointment and direct the outcome of particular administrative cases, from denizens of the think tanks and Beltway bandits who furnish so many of the in-and-outers who prosper under the current arrangements; from interest groups and lobbyists fearful of losing access. Indeed, even to cite these sources of opposition is to remind ourselves that meaningful administrative reform, as always, requires broader political reform. Changes in campaign finance, the structure of congressional committees, and ethics legislation are crucial.

Do we as a people have the political will to make these changes? If will can spring from despair, perhaps so. But those who looked to the return of a Democrat in the White House in 1993 were to be disappointed. By the middle of 1993, Bill Clinton's first year as president, public disgust with governmental performance had reached historic proportions. Spending was seen as out of control, the deficit nearly beyond reckoning. Government as in gridlock, to use the popular phrase. To paraphrase columnist George Will, government was not just going through another of its bad patches. Rather it had settled into a deep trough and lacked the strength to lift itself out.[23]

Although conditions improved by the end of Clinton's first year as president, with the economy recovering, gridlock seemingly broken, and Clinton's popularity rising, the SES continued to falter. On February 10, 1993, in the second month of his presidency, Clinton took executive action to "reduce the federal bureaucracy by at least 100,000 positions." Whereas each executive department and agency with over 100 employees was ordered to eliminate not less than 4 percent of its civilian positions over the next three years, Clinton stipulated that "at least 10 percent of the reductions shall come from the Senior Executive Service, GS-15 and GS-14 levels or equivalent."[24]

At the same time, President Clinton announced that there would be no pay increases for federal employees in 1994, and increases would be 1 percent less than current law for each of the three years after that. "It is time for government to demonstrate in the condition we're in," said Clinton, "that we can be as frugal as any household in America."[25] By freezing federal pay for his first two years at the level fixed by President Bush for 1993 and promising reduced increases thereafter, President Clinton effectively assured that the gap in pay between the SES and the private sector would widen still more.

Finally, neither Clinton's promise to "reinvent government" nor the resulting Gore Report included any proposal to improve the SES.[26] Indeed, by calling for a massive decrease in management positions, the Gore Report would accelerate the long-term trend toward a higher ratio of political appointees to career executives.[27]

NOTES

1. For a more detailed discussion of this issue, see Mark W. Huddleston, "The SES: A Higher Civil Service?" *Policy Studies Journal* 17 (Winter 1998–89): 406–19.
2. Milton J. Esman, *Management Dimensions of Development: Perspectives and Strategies* (West Hartford, Conn.: Kumarian Press, 1991), 46.
3. For a broad review of European administrative history, see Ernest Barker, *The Development of Public Services in Western Europe 1600–1930* (London: Oxford University Press, 1944); on Japan see Edwin Dowdy, *Japanese Bureaucracy: Its Development and Modernization* (Melbourne, Australia: Cheshire, 1972). Two works that encompass both Europe and Asia are Gladden, *History of Public Administration*, and Reinhard Bendix, *Kings or People: Power and the Mandate to Rule* (Berkeley and Los Angeles: University of California Press, 1973). Bendix's work, which is the more sophisticated of the two, uses a Weberian framework and places a heavy emphasis on the role of bureaucratic officialdom in the process of historical transformation.
4. Alexis de Tocqueville, *Democracy in America* (New York: Vintage, 1990), 72.
5. Tocqueville, *Democracy in American*, 92.
6. From President Andrew Jackson's first address to Congress, December 8, 1829, quoted in Leonard D. White, *The Jacksonians: A Study in Administrative History, 1829–1861* (New York: Macmillan Co., 1954), 318. See also Arthur M. Schlesinger Jr., *The Age of Jackson* (Boston: Little, Brown & Co., 1945), 46–48, esp. 46.
7. Leonard D. White, *The Federalists: A Study in Administrative History* (New York: Macmillan Co., 1948), 211–12, 293.
8. See Leonard D. White, *The Jeffersonians: A Study in Administrative History, 1801–1829* (New York: Macmillan Co., 1951), 352–54. White notes, in Jefferson's defense, that our third president forswore *removing* officers for political reasons. It is interesting to speculate in this vein what might have happened had the Federalists held the presidency for another term or had Jefferson been less inclined to bow to partisan pressure in making appointments. Certainly the Federalist legacy in administration was extraordinary: moral and intellectual standards were higher than the nation would see again for generations; assuming good performance, continuity in office was assured. In these circumstances, it is plausible that we would have seen a career service much earlier than the 1880s. An even more intriguing "What if?" is to ponder the effects of a Hamilton presidency—or even a continued Hamiltonian influence on the course of administrative development. Alexander Hamilton was arguably the country's greatest public administrator and institution builder. He not only created and ran the Treasury Department, which at the time exercised nearly all the domestic functions of government, but he also took a leading role in every other area of federal affairs as well—much to Jefferson's dismay at the State Department, one might add. Hamilton's early departure from government (he left Washington's second administration in January 1795 to pursue business interests in New York, though he continued to advise and dabble behind the scenes) and his untimely demise by the pistol of Aaron Burr were tragic for the course of U.S. public administration. For a classic and still fascinating consideration of Hamilton's impact on public administration, see Lynton K. Caldwell,

The Administrative Theories of Hamilton and Jefferson: Their Contributions to Thought and Public Administration, 2d ed. (New York: Holmes & Meier, 1988).

9. See White, *Jacksonians,* esp. chs. 8, 16–18, and 21.

10. Among those making a similar argument is James Pfiffner, who has written: "The argument here is not to discard the in-and-outer system that has served government well. The argument is that the capacity of the White House is being strained and the effectiveness of the government is being undermined by the present trend toward increasing numbers of political appointees. Reversing this direction would increase the capacity of the government to function efficiently and effectively without sacrificing political accountability or responsiveness" (James P. Pfiffner, "Political Appointees and Career Executives: The Democracy-Bureaucracy Nexus," in Ingraham and Kettl, *Agenda for Excellence,* 62).

11. See, e.g., White, *Jeffersonians,* ch. 9.

12. Curiously, Ralph Nader was one of the loudest critics of the SES, on the grounds that it would *inhibit* the use of political appointees.

13. For a general review of the postmodern and deconstructionist turn in social science analysis, with some attention to public administration in particular, see Pauline Marie Rosenau, *Post-Modernism and the Social Sciences* (Princeton, N.J.: Princeton University Press, 1992).

14. Both the Federal Employees Training Act of 1958 and the Intergovernmental Personnel Act of 1970 provided for such assignments to foster mobility.

15. See, for instance, Senior Executives Association, "Proposal for a National Civil Service Academy," mimeographed document, October 21, 1985.

16. Our various university-affiliated schools of public administration may raise objections, of course, fearing a usurpation of their functions. But by restricting such an academy to post-graduate or even post-postgraduate education, on the model perhaps of the French École National d'Administartion, such anxieties might be eased.

17. See, for instance, Frederick F. Ridley, *Specialists and Generalists: A Comparative Study of the Professional Civil Servant at Home and Abroad* (London: George Allen & Unwin, 1968).

18. This proposal is elaborated in Huddleston, "To Track or Not Two Track."

19. See Huddleston, "Carter Civil Service Reforms" for an elaboration of this argument.

20. See John Rohr, *To Run a Constitution, The Legitimacy of the Administrative State* (Lawrence: University of Kansas Press, 1986), 1.

21. Ibid. esp. chs. 2–4.

22. Carl J. Friedrich. "Public Policy and the Nature of Administrative Responsibility," in Carl J. Friedrich and Edward S. Mason, eds., *Public Policy: A Yearbook of the Graduate School of Public Administration, Harvard University* (Cambridge: Harvard University Press, 1940), 19.

23. George Will, *Restoration: Congress, Term Limits, and the Recovery of Deliberative Democracy* (New York: Free Press, 1992), 3. Will was actually referring to Congress alone here, but we suspect he wouldn't disagree with the spirit of our emendation. The actual quotation is: "By the beginning of the 1990s it was beginning to seem that Congress was not just going through another of its bad patches. Rather, Congress seemed to have settled into a deep trough, and it lacked the strength to lift itself out."

24. Executive Order 12389, February 10, 1993, sec. 1.

25. President Bill Clinton, Address to Joint Session of Congress, February 17, 1993.

26. See Press release, "A Revolution in Government," Office of Domestic Policy, White House, March 3, 1993; Vice President Al Gore, *Creating a Government That Works Better and Costs Less: Report of the National Performance Review* (Washington, D.C.: Government Printing Office, September 7, 1993). Though no reference is made in the text of the Gore Report to improving the SES, buried in its appendix C without elaboration is this recommendation (HRM11): "Create and reinforce a corporate perspective within the Senior

Executive Service that supports governmentwide culture change. Promote a corporate succession planning model to use to select and develop senior staff. Enhance voluntary mobility within and between agencies for top senior executive positions in government" (163). The practice of the Office of Personnel Management under the Bush administration of issuing annual reports on the status of the SES was not continued under the Clinton administration. On Clinton's first year, the *Economist* (January 15, 1994, 24) commented, "Often—as with the programme to 'reinvent government'—the fanfare is not matched by the follow-up."

27. See Ronald C. Moe, "The 'Reinventing Government' Exercise: Misinterpreting the Problem, Misjudging the Consequences," *Public Administration Review* 54 (March–April 1994): 116; Robert Garcia, "Growth in Number of Political Appointee Positions as Ratio of Total Full-Time Federal Employees," Congressional Research Service Report, September 1993.

31

Richard C. Kearney and Steven W. Hays

REINVENTING GOVERNMENT, THE NEW PUBLIC MANAGEMENT AND CIVIL SERVICE SYSTEMS IN INTERNATIONAL PERSPECTIVE

THE DANGER OF THROWING THE BABY OUT WITH THE BATHWATER

The reinventing government movement that has so dominated scholarly and practitioner literature and debate in the United States during the past several years has its roots in the American governmental settings but it is anything but another example of American exceptionalism. Rather, it is a movement of international importance that has swept across Europe, permeated Latin America, entered Asia, and most recently penetrated Africa. And reinventing government is not simply the latest management fad to bloom as a panacea for the conventional litany of management ills, only to wither, fade, and be dumped unceremoniously into the trash bin with *zero-based budgeting, program budgeting, one minute management*, and, possibly *total quality management.*

The reinventing government movement, known as *administrative reform, new public management,* and a variety of other names in other national contexts, has gradually evolved from a complex web of political and economic developments over the past fifteen years into an expansive holistic approach to public administration and to government in general. In many respects, reinventing government represents a "paradigm shift" of major proportions (Lan & Rosenbloom 1992; Moe & Gilmour 1995), and possibly one of the most important historical developments in public administration will occur during our own lifetimes.

This essay argues that the reinventing government movement represents a pervasive and potentially pernicious attack on bureaucracy that may ultimately undermine the professional public service. The resulting "disempowerment" of the career civil service is not occurring from a full frontal assault, but from a much more subtle and sanitized process. Although wrapped in a blanket of reform and bolstered by a plethora of positive motives, reinventing government's progress may bring with it a weakening of neutral competence, merit, professionalism, and related values—even though the movement's rhetoric emphasizes "worker empowerment" while putatively enabling civil servants to exercise discretion and perform more efficiently. When the most likely immediate outcomes of reinventing government strategies are considered, one need not be an alarmist to discern that bureaucracy is often the primary target of change and that the career public service is the most seriously affected victim of reform.

THE RISE OF THE REINVENTING GOVERNMENT MOVEMENT

No precise chain of events can be linked causally to the rise of reinventing government, but several factors clearly have played a role. In industrialized countries, World War II was followed by a prolonged period of growth in government expenditures and almost unparalleled prosperity. Accompanying these expansive times were rising levels of citizen education, political participation, and expectations concerning the role of government. Citizens were becoming both more sophisticated and more demanding in terms of policy and program expectations. But the growing scope of government activities soon ran headlong into a parade of seemingly intractable problems, including environmental pollution, the urban and energy crises, illicit drug use and trade, economic and budgetary problems, and an array of other domestic and international conundrums that produced great expenditures of taxpayers' dollars to little apparent positive effect.

It did not take a great leap of imagination to make government the scapegoat for the persistence of such problems. Public bureaucracy was faulted by citizens and politicians alike for such failings as "the daily annoyances of irksome restrictions, cumbrous red tape, unpleasant officials, poor service, and corrupt practice" (Caiden, 1991, p. 367). Disillusionment with government fertilized the political field for those espousing anti-bureaucratic, non-statist philosophies. Conservative politicians such as Reagan in the United States, Mulroney in Canada, and Thatcher in Great Britain honed "attack campaign" techniques to spotlight the blemishes of government and to further defame it in the eyes of the electorate (Hood, 1991, p. 7). The "public" or "rational choice" school of economic theory provided intellectual sustenance to the attack on bureaucracy and "budget-maximizing bureaucrats" (Niskanan, 1971; Dubnick, 1994), and helped foster the notion that government is a burden that diverts resources from the more productive private sector (Mascarenhas, 1993).

In the less developed countries, fiscal stress and public dissatisfaction with government performance were joined by more instrumental concerns in creating a political climate conducive to reinventing government efforts. Colonial administrative systems, originally designed primarily to extract resources and maintain order, were highly legalistic and ill-suited for coping with the demands for rapid social and economic change. The administrative legacies for newly-independent states were extreme centralization, inadequate capacity, scarce resources, and self-serving elites (Caiden, 1991). Ossified bureaucracies became bloated playpens of patronage and employers of last resort, unable to satisfy post-independence popular expectations for development.

According to a World Bank report (Nunberg & Nellis, 1995, p. 1), these civil service institutions were "too large, too expensive, and insufficiently productive." They were also paradoxical (with surplus numbers of employees yet an incapacity for instrumental actions and economic development achievements) and ironic (with excessive public sector wage bills but pay structures too low and inequitable to keep most employees out of dire poverty) (Nunberg, 1995, pp. 2–3). Bad situations in the less developed countries became much worse with a series of "oil shocks" and international recessions that resulted in massive borrowing of money for immediate consumption rather than for development projects (Baker, 1991, p. 362).

THE ATTACK ON BUREAUCRACY

Reinventing government launched an attack on a phenomenon that is nearly universally distrusted and feared: bureaucratic power. There is a rich literature on bureaucratic power (see, for example, Rourke, 1984; Rainey, 1991), which need not be explored here. The important point is that much of the power that arrogates to large government organizations is embodied in, or exercises through, the career civil service. A highly articulated career service protects bureaucrats from political retribution by elected officials, promotes neutral competence and professionalism in the delivery of programs and services, and functions as the state's administrative arm and driving force for economic and social development. Despite being an essential ingredient in the maturation of a nation's political and social systems, however, career civil service institutions tend to suffer from some chronic diseases. Insularity, insensitivity to the wishes of the public, inefficiency, and self-serving motives are traits that are commonly attributed to bureaucracies in both developed and underdeveloped nations throughout the world.

Perhaps for this reason the contemporary attack on public bureaucracy and the career civil service is strikingly similar across nations. Among the prevalent themes of reinventing government are decentralization of administrative authority (heretofore, administrative reform usually implied the centralization of power and authority), increased managerial flexibility, downsizing of government agencies, and increased reliance on market-based approaches to service delivery. Among the buzzwords in vogue are *reorganization, load-shedding, prioritizing, user fees* and *putting customers first* (Peters, 1991a, pp. 386–394). Insofar as the civil service is specifically concerned, common reinvention goals include: expanded managerial discretion over the assignment and utilization of civil servants, decentralized selection, and enhanced agency control over reward and punishment. These objectives are apparent in the National Performance Review program in the United States (Gore, 1993), and in similar efforts throughout much of the English-speaking world (Hood, 1990). Much of the remaining reinventing government agenda is less directly aimed at the professional public service, yet its potential negative impact upon the civil service is self-evident. Although any number of categorizations could be applied to investigate the many reinventing government themes, we employ the three that appear to be most pervasive: *debureaucratization* and *decentralization, privatization,* and *managerialism.*

Deburaucratization and decentralization are related themes that are intended to alter the way public organizations operate.

Debureaucratization and decentralization can entail several different strategies. Perhaps most conventionally, decision-making authority is delegated to units that are organizationally or physically removed from the bureaucratic power center. This approach in federal systems such as the United States and Canada involves increasing territorial decentralization to states or provinces. It is also increasingly evident in federal and unitary systems in Latin America and Europe (Hood & Jackson, 1991).

Functional decentralization can also erode the influence of centralized bureaucracies. For example, government power in Italy is dispersed among over 40,000 autonomous and semiautonomous public agencies (Hine, 1993, p. 229). Reinventing government proponents in many other industrialized countries have advocated the segmentation of agency functions and the farming out of agency activities to semiautonomous units. Thatcherite leaders, for instance advocated "the breakup of traditional public bureaucratic structures into quasi-autonomous units that deal with each other increasingly on a supplier-user basis" (Christoph, 1992, p. 174).

Another broad approach to debureaucratization that has been much heralded by reinventing government advocates is worker empowerment, which is concerned with granting employees the authority they require to perform their tasks with a minimum of top-down interference. The assumption, when worded positively, is that civil servants are good people trapped in bad systems. Reform should thus focus on liberating public workers from the restrictive embrace of unnecessary controls, procedures, and red tape. Moreover, civil service systems should be redesigned to permit suitable rewards to be provided to workers whose performance warrants recognition.

Debureacratization's dark side emerges from the many reinventing government champions who perceive bureaucracy and those who toil within it to be "the problem." Subtle and not-so-subtle evidence of this perception pervades the literature on administrative reform in the United States.

In Great Britain, the negative view of the civil service may be seen in criticisms of "bloated bureaucracy" that produced proposals to "deprivilege" the civil service (Christoph, 1992, pp. 166–167) by limiting job security and promotional opportunities. New Zealand, meanwhile, embarked on a program that threatens to virtually "abolish a unified permanent career service for public servants through contractual appointments and agency hiring by chief executives" (Gregory, 1991).

Less direct assaults on bureaucrats involve edicts to cut unnecessary rules and regulations. In 1994, for instance, the Canadian government instructed agencies to reduce all regulations by 25 percent and to "significantly change" another 25 percent (U.S. General Accounting Office, 1994, p. 34). In Brazil, the longstanding debureaucratization campaign aims to "reduce unnecessary restrictions on individual liberty and to eliminate needless bureaucracy that people have been forced to endure" (Caiden, 1991a, p. 371). Similar goals have preoccupied many other governments across the globe.

Privatization is used generically to describe the variety of means for shifting public services and activities to the private or nonprofit sectors, and for replacing government processes with market mechanisms. Privatization has spread across nations like a highly contagious rash with a variety of names attached to the process in various national settings. In the 1980s, some countries "denationalized" public or parastatal organizations by selling them to corporations and private investors. Examples include such diverse nations as Turkey, Malaysia, Nigeria, and the Philippines (Moussios & Legge, 1991). Mexico reduced its number of state-owned enterprises from 1200 to 300 during a ten-year period ending in 1992 (Cothran, 1993).

Another variation of the privatization initiative is *corporatization*, whereby public and quasi-public enterprises are required to operate according to the rules of the marketplace. For instance, in Australia, Japan and New Zealand numerous state-owned businesses such as utilities and airlines are expected to fund their operations entirely from revenues generated from their customers (Caiden, 1994; Wolferen, 1993). Related reforms are underway in many less developed countries, where state subsidies for consumption are being phased out.

A popular reinventing government term in the United States that implies privatization is *downsizing*. Efforts to trim overhead costs frequently mean reducing the size of government bureaucracy. A Canadian report issued during the Mulroney government, entitled *Structural Reform: A Blueprint for Change*, is strikingly similar to the National Performance Review. It recommends a 50 percent reduction in federal departments and a 25 percent cut in cabinet ministers (Fulton, 1993).

Another dominant theme in reinventing government is managerialism, which represents the triumph of the value of efficiency as embodied in business ideology and practice. Its major assumptions are that business management practices applied to government will solve a wide variety of economic and social problems (Pollitt, 1990), and that corporate-style management is good because it is efficient and apolitical. The concept is warmly embraced by the National Performance Review (Hays & Kearney, 1997).

Managerialism dominates the practice of public management in the world today. Key components emerge in such trends as performance measurement, merit pay, productivity incentives, and increased supervisory discretion over subordinates. These and other strategies have been employed in Australia, Great Britain, Canada, Japan, New Zealand, Portugal, France, Japan, Sweden, an array of less developed countries (Holmes, 1992; Dunsire & Hood, 1989; *Economist*, 1992; Rocha, 1998). In Europe the reinventing government movement is generally known as the *new public management*, and it has been endorsed by labor and conservative governments alike (Hood, 1991; Rocha, 1998).

In all fairness it must be noted that the reinventing government movement has chalked up some impressive achievements, many of which have been reported in the scholarly and professional literature. Major structural changes have occurred in the nexus between the public and private sectors. Because the political and economic forces that unleashed reinventing government continue to prevail, further changes are likely to occur. However, the meaning of reinventing government's conquests remain poorly understood. As the reinvention process unfolds, it seems worthwhile to take a critical look at how the reforms might affect the professional public service, and how traditional perceptions of bureaucratic power might be altered.

POWER (AND EMPOWERMENT)

One need not be very perceptive to identify an excruciating inconsistency in reinventing government dogma. The movement is, at heart, an assault on bureaucratic power, yet one of its chief principles is the empowerment of the very individuals who are often blamed for government's shortcomings. Proponents argue that application of reinventing government principles will empower public employees by increasing their authority and flexibility, cutting constricting red tape, and giving them more control over their work. Cautious bureaucrats will be transformed into entrepreneurial risk takers in the private-sector mold, and will be held accountable for results. This is a marvelous proposition in principle, but is seriously flawed in philosophic underpinnings and in practice (see Kettl, 1994, pp. 11-12).

Philosophically, empowerment assumes that politicians and the general public will consent to loosening the reins on bureaucrats and to tolerating the occasional well-intended plan or action gone awry. As already noted, however, the public is rarely tolerant of bureaucratic mistakes, and often views the civil service as more of a problem than a solution to government ills. Granting bureaucrats more authority—even if this is accomplished merely by lifting the veil of rules and procedures that putatively ensure "accountability"—contradicts this distrusting attitude and assumes that politicians are willing to accept errors benignly and patiently explain them to the press when they are inevitably brought to public attention. If public managers are truly liberated and blessed with the authority of their private-sector counterparts, they will be permitted to hire and fire with a minimum of procedural constraints, negotiate and abrogate contracts, and abandon unprofitable enterprises and activities, among other things (Caiden, 1991, p. 237). Clearly, these notions of bureaucratic empowerment and risk-taking inevitably clash with the desire for bureaucratic *accountability*. It is something of "a stretch" to envision political leaders who won't yield to the temptation to blame the civil servants—and to retaliate in some fashion—when embarrassing failures surface.

This prompts another important question. What is supposed to convince public employees to become risk takers? What sorts of incentives will be effective in persuading them to climb out on the proverbially limb? The practical difficulties of structuring incentive systems in government are illustrated by the repeated frustrations and failures of the popular pay-for-performance plans in the United States, Australia, New Zealand, Canada, and at least twelve nations of Europe (Ingraham & Eisenberg. 1995). The history in the United States and elsewhere of structural flaws and political intrusions is sufficient to cast doubt on any empowerment strategy. In this respect, public employee cynicism might be a logical and even rational response to reinventing government.

A great deal of administrative reform in the 1980s (which is simply reinventing government by a different rubric) was aimed at fundamentally changing the prevailing administrative culture of public organizations to comport with many of the principles of reinventing government as we know it today. Perhaps Gerald Caiden (1991, pp. 236-237) explains best why such efforts largely failed. They were concerned with replacing the old guard with outsiders who had better attitudes by

> . . . retraining and reeducating the savable, the ambitious, and the amenable, by browbeating, threatening and cajoling the unbending, by organizing, restructuring, reequipping and rearranging to give insiders no option than going along with the new . . . by advancing a new generation of upward mobile "with it" opportunists . . . by employing shock tactics. . . . The trouble was that irrespective of the methods used, the objective itself had not been properly thought out. It seemed to have been stumbled onto rather than deliberately planned. . . .

Caiden's analysis implies that reinventing government as theory is no more than half-baked. At its most innocuous level, the movement resembles the "good government" efforts in which progressive ideals were encouraged through administrative reforms. At its most troublesome level, in contrast, reinventing government "puts an acceptable face" on neo-conservative efforts to eviscerate public employee unions, shrink government, and punish public servants (Hood, 1991). If, as the old saying goes, "the devil is in the details," then reinventing government can be **either** a boon or a bane to civil servants.

If we assume the worst, then reinventing government as political ideology suggests the disempowerment of public employees and the career civil service. Privatization, debureaucratization, and decentralization reduce the size and scope of government; managerialism makes public servants more like corporate workers (a goal that, admittedly, resonates with much of the public) and reinstates the politics/administration dichotomy. When central government is downsized and load shedding shifts government activities to the private or non-profit sectors, public employees and organizations that represent them lose numbers standing, influence, and power.

With these *caveats* duly noted, let us now speculate concerning the possible power redistributions that may occur within a reinvented system.

Whichever group absorbs the hardest punch from reinventing government, civil servants will collectively suffer in similar ways. There is an obvious risk that high-quality employees in government may be inclined to bail out for the private sector, thereby driving down the overall quality of the public work force. Contributing to this risk are declining relative wages, benefits and working conditions; a general disaffection with the status of public employment; a drop in employee morale; and the unequivocal message from politicians and a large segment of the general public that public workers are unappreciated and even disdained (Peters, 1991b). Writers on several continents have recorded how public servants have been insulted, lied to, and otherwise abused during reinventing government reforms (Christoph, 1992; Caiden, 1994; Leemans, 1987). In the United States, reinventing government as represented in the National Performance Review has been condemned as a "put down" to "an already demoralized and disillusioned career service" (Jasper & Alpern, 1994) "about to be 'rolled over' by the NPR bandwagon" (Kam & Shaw, 1993-94).

Similarly, politicians may turn less and less to career policy experts for advice because careerists are not trusted and their actions are perceived to be self-serving. As a consequence, the traditional sense of job satisfaction that comes from "making a difference" in peoples' lives becomes problematic, and turnover among dedicated public servants—particularly those whose talents are in high demand within the Beltway—is likely to increase (Stahl, 1995).

The business sector clearly benefits from reconceptualization and change in the content of public policy to reflect business outlooks and concerns.

Implementation of reinventing government principles may tend to increase the power and authority of central executive branch agencies, contrary to the pronouncements by proponents of reinvention who extol the virtues of debureaucratization and empowerment. Broad discretionary power clashes with the need for political control and responsibility over government policy. As Peters (1991a, pp. 430–431) observes, reinventing government's emphasis on economy and efficiency favors central controls, especially through the financial function. In less developed countries, decentralization and debureaucratization reforms quickly run headlong into the lack of bureaucratic capacity in local governments or in the field offices of the national government, resulting eventually in reconcentration of power at the central agency level.

Meaningful decentralization of decision-making power to lower levels of organizations or governments is further stifled by the desire of elected and appointed officials to sever bureaucratic influence over public policy and to assume more political control and authority themselves. When reinventing government programs threaten their power and authority, political officials have been known to quietly detail them (Caiden 1991b, p. 1). An untold story of the reinventing government movement is that it is not infrequently accompanied by growth in the number of political appointees in government and is the politicization of bureaucratic decision making. Arrogation of power from the legislature often swells the number of appointive positions available to executive officials, leading potentially to a politicization of the appointment process. Most recently, for instance, the National Performance Review implicitly calls for an increase in political appointees as a means of restoring accountability to bureaucracy. Similar politicization moves have been underway in various other nations, many of them with long traditions of insular civil service systems. Perhaps the most surprising case is that of Japan, where the all-powerful central government bureaucracy is gradually being opened to "outside" (i.e. political) influences (Sakamoto, 1991), a process that is also becoming increasingly evident in the current government within Great Britain.

THE IMPLICATIONS OF DISEMPOWERMENT

Debureaucratization, privatization, a managerialism have profound implications for the theory and practice of public administration. One of the most obvious, as noted above, is a loss of political accountability. Privatization in particular weakens accountaiblity by restructuring the delivery of various services from a single public provider to parastatal, corporate, or nonprofit entities.

Another oft-cited complaint is that reinventing government reforms open the back door to reinstitutionalization of the politics/administration dichotomy. The managerial focus on business ideology and techniques at the expense of bureaucratic participation throughout the policy process runs as a deep current through reinventing government activities in many countries. The business model in government implies that political officials who are the "bosses" who make policy and are to be obeyed in their policy directives by civil servants.

Another widespread dilemma is that the principal strategies of reinventing government ignore the problems of politics. The question, of course, is where the problem resides: is it in the bureaucracy or in the poorly designed and misguided policies of elected and appointed officials? Simply stated, reinventing government many sometimes be the product of problem misidentification.

Finally, reinventing government's attack on public employees and public bureaucracy to a considerable extent weakens the traditional career public service, and even weakens the foundations of merit-based bureaucracy. Continual increases in the number of political appointees, the growing reluctance to rely upon the expertise of bureaucrats in molding public policy (Rourke, 1992), the rise of contract employees and the decline of career protections in civil service systems, the downsizing of public organizations, the virtual elimination of "merit systems" in many locations, and the growth industry for nongovernmental advisors all imply the rejection of some fundamental values in civil service systems specifically, and public administration generally. Merit, neutral competence, and professionalism all stand to lose ground under the wholesale rush toward such values as marketplace efficiency, managerial accountability for results, and executive leadership.

Much of the professional community—both practitioner and academic—seems to ignore the inherent tradeoffs that reinventing government occasions. Our collective backs are being turned on more than 100 years of experience with merit-based bureaucracy, an era marked by unprecedented government accomplishments and astounding advances in public management values and operations. Despite their many blemishes, the professional personnel systems of most industrialized nations have served them extraordinarily well. In exchange, reinventing government proponents offer the unsure promise of greater efficiency, customer satisfaction, and responsiveness to political authority. As the politicians' grasp over the civil service system tightens, however, one wonders whose interests will ultimately be served.

If current trends continue, the benefits of a professional public service "characterized by independence of judgment and indifference to political pressures" (Rourke, 1992, p. 542) may gradually dissipate. The reinvented public service, in contrast, is likely to be more servile, more specialized, more responsive to political direction, yet lacking in the continuity, competence, and fortitude of its predecessors.

Until quite recently, the need for governments to establish and maintain stable, career-based public administration grounded in the values of neutrality, competence, accountability, and attention to the public interest was taken as conventional wisdom. Efficiency alone is not a sufficient substitute for these traditional values of public management.

Reinventing government surely embraces some valuable and useful ideals and practices. But reinventing government also involves other assumptions, values, and practices that are shaking, and threatening to destroy, the foundations of effective and accountable public administration.

In the current international dialogue, few individuals or groups have risen to counter the antigovernment, antibureaucratic rhetoric of reinventing government. Public employee unions have occasionally weighed in against reinventing government initiatives in the nations of Western Europe, Australia, and North America, but their voices have been muted by effective counterattacks from political officials and the sheer force of the reinventing government tidal surge.

What, if anything, will stem the tide of reinventing government and protect the career civil service and traditional values of public administration? Constitutional protections may suffice to prevent truly harmful abuses in some nations, and statutory provisions may play the same saving role in others. In a Hegelian dialectic, the thesis of reinventing government will eventually spawn an antithesis, or counteraction. However, public employees must understand that their administrative landscape is being altered significantly, and that it will never look the same. Those reinventing government components and innovations that further the traditional and still relevant values and principles of the merit-based career service while making government more efficient and customer oriented should be welcomed, adopted, and incorporated within the new civil service of 2000 and beyond. But meanwhile, public employees and the organizations that represent them have the responsibility to speak out and articulate the values of a merit-based, career civil service in order to inform and convince the public and political officials of its importance.

REFERENCES

Baker, R. (1991). The role of the state and the bureaucracy in developing countries since World War II. In A. Farazmand (Ed.), Handbook of comparative and development administration (pp. 353-363). New York: Marcel Dekker.

Caiden, G. (1991a). Administrative reform. In A. Farazmand (Ed.), Handbook of comparative and development administration (pp. 367-380). New York: Marcel Dekker.

Caiden, G. (1991b). Administrative reform comes of age. New York: Walter de Gruyter.

Caiden, G. (1994, March-April). Administrative reform—American style. Public Administration Review 54, 123-128.

Cristoph, J. (1992, August). The remaking of British administrative culture. Administration and Society 24, 163-181.

Cothran, D. (1993, September-October). Entrepreneurial budgeting: An emerging reform? Public Administration Review, 53, 445-454.

Dubnick, M. (1994). A coup against king bureaucracy? In J. DiIulio (Ed.), Deregulating the public service (pp. 249-287). Washington, D.C.: Brookings.

Dunshire, A. & Hood, C.C. (1989). Cutback management in public bureaucracies. Cambridge: Cambridge University Press.

Economist (1992, October 31). Reshaping Britain's civil service. Economist, 19-21.

Fulton, E. K. (1993, March 31). Gathering dust. Maclean's, 10-11.

Gore, A. (1993). From red tape to results: Creating a government that works better and costs less. Washington, D.C.: U.S. Government Printing Office.

Gregory, R.J. (1991, July 1). The attitudes of senior public servants in Australia and New Zealand: Administrative reform and technocratic consequences? Governance, 4, 295-331.

Hays, S. & Kearney, R. (1997). Riding the crest of a wave: The National Performance Review and public management reform. International Journal of Public Administration 20 (1), 11-40.

Hine, D. (1993). Governing Italy, Oxford: Clarendon Press.

Holmes, M. (1992, October). Public sector management reform: Convergence or divergence? Governance, 5, 472-483.

Hood, C. & Jackson, M. W. (1991). Administration argument. Brookfield, Vermont: Dartmouth.

Hood, C. (1991, Spring). A public management for all seasons. Public Administration, 69, 3-19.

Hood, C. (1990). Beyond the bureaucratic state: Public administration in the 1990s. London: School of Economics.

Ingraham, P. & Eisenberg, E. (1995). Comparative examination of national civil service and personnel reforms. In J. Rabin (Ed.), *Handbook of public personnel administration.* New York: Marcel Dekker.

Jasper, H. & Alpern, A. (1994, Spring). National Performance Review: The good, the bad, the indifferent. *The Public Manager, 27–34.*

Kam, A. & Shaw, G.J. (1993-94. Winter). Managers and top professionals band together. *The Public Manager, 7–10.*

Kettl, D. (1994). *Reinventing government? Appraising the National Performance Review.* Washington, D.C.: U.S. Government Printing Office.

Lan, Z. & Rosenbloom, D. (1992, November–December). Public administration in transition? *Public Administration Review, 52,* 535–537.

Leemans, A. (1987). Recent trends: The career service in European countries. *International Review of Administrative Sciences, 53* (1), 63–88.

Mascarenhas, R.C. (1993, July–August). Building an enterprise culture in the public sector in Australia, Britain, and New Zealand. *Public Administration Review, 53,* 319–328.

Moe, R. & Gilmour, R. (1995, March–April). Rediscovering principles of public administration: The neglected foundation of public law. *Public Administration Review, 55,* 135–140.

Moussios, A. & Legge, J. (1991). Implementing the denationalization options: Great Britain and the United States. In A. Farzmand (Ed.). *Handbook of comparative and development administration* (pp. 41–52). New York: Marcel Dekker.

Niskanan, W. (1971). *Bureaucracy and representative government.* Chicago: Aldine Atherton.

Nunberg, B. (1995). *Managing the civil service: Lessons from advanced industrialized countries.* Washington, D.C.: The World Bank.

Peters, G. (1991a). Government reform and reorganization in an era of retrenchment and conviction politics. In A. Farazmand (Ed.), *Handbook of comparative and development administration* (pp. 381–403). New York: Marcel Dekker.

Peters, G. (1991b). Morale in the public service: A comparative inquiry. *International Review of Administrative Sciences 57,* 421–440.

Pollitt, C. (1990). *Managerialism and the public service. The Anglo-American experience.* Oxford Basil Blackwell.

Rainey, H. (1991). *Understanding and managing public organizations.* San Francisco.: Jossey-Bass.

Rocha, J.A.O. (1998, Spring). The new public management and it consequences in the public personnel system. *Review of Public Personnel Administration, 18,* 82–87.

Rourke, F. (1992, November–December). Responsiveness and neutral competence in American bureaucracy. *Public Administration Review, 52,* 539–546.

Rourke, F. (1984). *Bureaucracy, politics, and public policy.* Boston: Little, Brown.

Sakamoto, M. (1991). Public administration in Japan: Past and present in the higher civil service. In A. Farazman (Ed.), *Handbook of comparative and development administration* (pp. 101–125). New York: Marcel Dekker.

Stahl, O. (1995). A retrospective and prospective: The moral dimension. In S. Hays and R. Kearney (Eds.), *Public personnel administration: Problems and prospects* (pp. 331–344). Englewood Cliffs, NJ: Prentice Hall.

U.S. General Accounting Office (1994). *Management reforms.* Washington, D.C.: U.S. Government Printing Office.

Wolferen, K. (1993, September–October). Japan's non-revolution. *Foreign Affairs, 72,* 54–65.

32

Rex L. Facer II

REINVENTING PUBLIC ADMINISTRATION: REFORM IN THE GEORGIA CIVIL SERVICE

INTRODUCTION

Several of the philosophical principles from the reinventing movement have direct bearing on the civil service reforms that have occurred in Georgia. The leading voices of the reinvention movement, Osborne and Gaebler (1992), argue that the current strategies used by governments throughout the United States were hampering the efficient and effective provision of public services. They claim that one of the major obstacles to "good" government is the way in which personnel systems are managed. Specifically, they argue that "we must change the basic incentives that drive our governments" (*Ibid.* 23).

Osborne and Gaebler suggest that the bureaucratic system is keeping governments from ameliorating many of the intractable problems of modern society (this is their assertion and clearly debatable). Most of the reinventing government discussion focuses on government as a system and how the principles of entrepreneurial government can improve the public sector. There are several ways in which these principles can be applied. For example, the principle of decentralized government suggests that the personnel function would be most effective if individual agencies and departments had full decision authority over personnel issues. This would range from recruitment and selection to retention or dismissal efforts. Following the reinventing paradigms, personnel functions should be able to change the incentive structures and be more flexible in using alternative staffing solutions.

Another reinventing government principle with direct bearing on the personnel function in government is mission-driven government. Mission-driven government seeks to move away from rules as the driving force to a more "ends" perspective focusing on the desired outcomes of government. Personnel policy and practice in public agencies are frequently cited as being very rule-bound and inflexible (for example, see Rainey, Facer, and Bozeman, 1995).

Letting goals drive the decision process is in harmony with the principle of mission-driven government. Personnel policy would be radically different under this approach. Managers would find the possibility of greater flexibility liberating in many senses but confining in others. Personnel rules have developed over time usually in response to specific abuse or incompetence. Many managers find solace in being able to "hide" behind these rules. A mission-driven personnel system, that minimized rules, would force many managers into a role of increased discretion.

It is sufficient to say that following the principles professed within the reinvention movement, the personnel function could be changed radically.

There have been efforts in other states to adopt reinventing philosophies into the state's personnel system. Perhaps one of the most notable cases was the state of Florida. This is notable for two reasons. First, Osborne and Gaebler (1992: 128) use this reform effort as an example of a government moving in the right direction. Second, Governor Chiles explicitly espoused the reinvention philosophies as the guiding framework. Unfortunately, this reform effort has not had any real impact on personnel in Florida's state agencies (Wechsler, 1994).

Following many of the themes of reinventing government, the reforms in Georgia have sought to use approaches that are seen as innovative and effective from the private sector and apply them to the public sector. However, as many scholars have cautioned, reform efforts must be done very carefully and must consider a wide range of issues if the reforms are to be successful.

Two major personnel reforms that have recently been implemented in Georgia state agencies are GeorgiaGain, which is a performance-based compensation system and the dismantling of "merit" protections for new employees hired after July 1, 1996. Both of these reforms were the result of Governor Zell Miller's desire to change the way state government operates in Georgia.

LOOKING TO REFORM STATE GOVERNMENT

Given the widespread attention to reinvention and other efforts to improve government, it is not surprising that Georgia has engaged in reform efforts. The "bureaucracy" has become an easy target for criticism in recent years. It is not the only government institution that is criticized by opponents of government but it is perhaps the most frequently attacked. Yet, with this propensity to attack and criticize the bureaucracy and the bureaucrats, reformers often lost sight of the causes of many of the inefficiencies that are targeted.

Much of government red tape is the direct result of legislative direction to prevent or bring resolution to corruption that has occurred in the government. Much of this corruption was the result of spoil systems and political machines that rewarded political friends while not recognizing the value of technical competence. As a result, public bureaucracies have become characterized as being very rule-oriented and inattentive to the needs of the citizenry. Even while these criticisms are being raised, there is a substantial body of literature, both scholarly and popular, that suggests that governmental organizations do things well and that the citizenry is generally very happy with the services they receive (see Goodsell, 1994, for an excellent discussion of this point). Georgia's elected officials sought to capitalize on the criticisms targeted at the bureaucracy to marshal the necessary resources for reform.

In 1993, Governor Zell Miller established a multi-agency task force to consider personnel issues in state government. By early 1994, the task force was moving ahead with two related projects. The first was the restructuring the job information/job evaluation system and, second, developing and implementing a new pay and performance management system (Georgia State Merit System of Personnel Administration [GSMSPA], 1994a). These reform efforts have become known as GeorgiaGain.

Governor Miller became committed to reforming state government early in his first term. This commitment helped create an environment that was conducive to change and reform.

The Governor announced his intention to introduce legislation that would remove merit protections for anyone employed after July 1, 1996 (Miller, 1995). The Governor's interest in reform helped set the tone and continued to foster an environment that was conducive to reform.

The Governor through executive order initiated the GeorgiaGain program. Then, later working with the legislature, eliminated merit protections for employees hired after July 1, 1996. The political environment allowed Governor Miller to move ahead full steam with both pay for performance and the elimination of the merit system.

CIVIL SERVICE BEFORE REFORMS

Prior to imitating reforms in the civil service system, Georgia used a traditional approach to public-sector personnel. An organization named the Merit System of Personnel Administration was in charge of overseeing the civil service in state government. It was the central clearinghouse for recruitment and was responsible for ensuring that merit protections were upheld. The compensation system was primarily based on grade and longevity in position. The original merit system was established to create a system that would protect public employees from many of the ills of political patronage. In addition, the system was supposed to attract and retain qualified individuals who would provide good public service to the citizens of Georgia.

CIVIL SERVICE REFORMS

As part of the reform efforts, there were some significant changes in both the guiding legal framework for the merit system and the compensation used in state agencies. Most of the reforms were done through executive orders and through the current rulemaking structure available to state agencies. Some changes, such as the elimination of merit protections for new hires, required the passage of legislation.

Implementing dramatic changes, such as restructuring the classification and pay systems and elimination of merit protections to new employees, has required a major effort by state officials to guide a difficult and comprehensive process. The changes in the merit system, for example, were swift and direct. By legislative action the merit protections were abolished during the 1996 legislative session and went into effect on July 1, 1998. While the merit changes are altering the nature of public-sector employment in Georgia, the process creating these changes were simple and straightforward. The changes associated with GeorgiaGain, however, were much more involved.

GeorgiaGain. GeorgiaGain began through a task force appointed by Governor Miller. Since 1993 (Figure 1 displays a brief time line of the implementation of the GeorgiaGain program), the task force has sought to accomplish a major restructuring of the job classification system[1] and the pay and performance management systems of the state. The first major task was to assess how employees felt about the systems in place.

FIGURE 32.1   *Time Line for GeorgiaGain*

1993	Initial development of ideas around altering the current compensation and evaluation system in state government.
1993	Initial assessment of employee perceptions.
1994	Begin data collection for the new job classification scheme.
1994	Develop a job classification plan.
1994	Implement pilot projects of the job evaluation plan.
1995	Complete new descriptions, link employees to new jobs, refine new job structure (with employee feedback) and complete pay structure (1/95-9/96).
1995	May–September, 16,000 state managers participate in a four-day training session on performance management.
1995	August–October, employee group meetings to explain the transition to the new GeorgiaGain Performance Management Process.
1995	First performance management cycle. Implement test run of evaluation plans in all state agencies with no links between performance plan and compensation (10/95-9/96).
1996	April–September, train managers on new job and pay structures.
1996	Effective July 1, new hires are no longer under the "merit" system.
1996	Notify all employees of their new job classification.
1996	Second performance management cycle. Evaluate all jobs based on new position descriptions and the new job classification scheme. This evaluation will be tied to compensation (10/96-9/97).
1997	Base compensation adjustments on the job performance from 10/96-9/97.

In 1993 the task force developed a guiding philosophy for compensation, agreed on concepts associated with how to design pay for performance, selected potential compensation factors, and began the development of an automated database for job descriptions and evaluations. One of the major accomplishments of 1993 was the completion of an assessment of employee perceptions.

In 1993, with the assistance of an outside consulting firm, the state mailed out survey questionnaires to 10,000 randomly selected state employees. The survey had a response rate of 62 percent. There was widespread agreement among the employees around pay for performance issues. Ninety-nine percent of employees surveyed believed they should be held accountable for their performance; 93 percent felt that appraisals were a valuable tool for understanding their performance.

However, 36 percent of respondents said that appraisals were not conducted fairly. In addition, 68 percent said that supervisors gave the same rating regardless of performance. This sentiment was widely shared. Even among those respondents who said appraisals are done fairly, about half agreed that supervisors gave the same ratings regardless of performace.

In addition, the employees surveyed held contradictory views about pay for performance. For example, 89 percent responded that they would work harder if pay were linked to performance. Yet 73 percent said they would work their best without pay for performance. In addition, 77 percent of employees agreed that favoritism and low morale would result from pay for performance (GSMSPA, 1994a). Yet, as reform efforts proceeded, they ignored these large negative responses.

These survey responses helped the task force design an implementation plan that would help employees adjust to the changes associated with a new personnel system and also provide sufficient training to supervisors so they would be able to assess performance adequately. Throughout the remainder of the GeorgiaGain process, several work teams in addition to the task force have focused on different aspects of the project. The task force developed six key objectives for GeorgiaGain:

1. Improve responsiveness of the compensation program to the outside job market to help the state to remain competitive in attracting and retaining employees.
2. Establish an effective rewards program to recognize employees' achievements.
3. Motivate high levels of performance to enable state government to function more effectively and economically.
4. Establish standards of performance to help employees know what is expected of them on the job and to help supervisors better manage employees' performance.
5. Automate job information to make it easier to keep job information current and accurate.
6. Automate administration of the compensation program to improve its responsiveness to agencies' business needs (GSMSPA, 1997).

To accomplish these objectives, the implementation of GeorgiaGain was divided into two phases.

Phase I focused on collecting the data that would allow for the mapping of the new job classification system. The second phase was a statewide trial implementation of the performance management system. Thirteen agencies agreed to participate in Phase I. The major task for Phase I was to collect information on all of the jobs in the participating agencies and then to arrange those jobs in a new classification system as part of an automated computer system (GSMSPA, 1994b, 1994c). The classification system would be based on a set of compensable factors as are most compensation systems.

The Job Evaluation Work Team, made up of employees from 14 different agencies, selected and defined the compensable factors that would be used for the evaluation of jobs. These factors were then approved by a series of other project groups and finally the task force. There were four different factors serving as the basis for the analysis of the jobs. These included knowledge/education, complexity, fundamental job skills, and dangerous working conditions (Figure 2 details the criteria under each category) (GSMSPA, 1994c). These categories have minimums and maximums, and employee's performance then impacts how much an employee is paid within the pay bands.

In an effort to address many of the concerns that were raised through the organizational assessment, training is a central focus of GeorgiaGain. This has been done through several different media. For example, roughly 16,000 managers, statewide, have received at least two practical hands-on training on how to do the performance management system. These training sessions focused on: how to link performance plans to organizational goals; interpersonal communication skills; the role of the supervisor/manager in the performance management process; and other topics (GSMSPA, 1995a).

The second phase was officially underway in the fall of 1995. The new performance management system was used for one year with the old job classification and pay struc-

FIGURE 32.2   *Compensable Factors Under GeorgiaGain*

Knowledge/Education

Education Required
Field of Study Required
Certification/Licensure
Diversity of Knowledge

Complexity

Freedom of Action
Innovation/Creativity
Planning
Problem Solving/Analytical Skills
Policies and Procedures
Supervisory Responsibilities

Fundamental Job Skills

Design and Art Skills
Computer Skills
Equipment Use, Inspection or Repair
Interpersonal Communication Skills
Mathematical Skills
Observation Skills
Research/Information Collection Skills
Writing Skills
Reading Skills

Dangerous Working Conditions

---

tures still in place to give employees and managers a chance to get used to the new system prior to linking pay and performance with the new system. The Governor led the way in championing the second phase and the GeorgiaGain project in general. Governor Miller said that the performance management process of GeorgiaGain are "steps toward shaping State Government for a more competitive environment" (GSMSPA, 1995a:1, 2).

In order to prepare for the second phase implementation, managers were required to participate in a four-day workshop on performance management occurring from May to September of 1995. These training sessions focused on different aspects of the performance management process.

On October 1995, the statewide implementation of the performance management process began. The first year of the statewide implementation, there was no formal linkage between the pay increases and performance. This implementation was designed to allow employees to adjust to the four new evaluation categories which include: does not meet expectations; meets expectations; exceeds expectations; far exceeds expectations (GSMSPA, 1995k). When performance is linked, those who perform at the meets expectations level and above will be rewarded with increased pay. Previously, the state had a performance appraisal system but pay was not linked to performance.

These new evaluation criteria were a critical issue for the new system. Under the old evaluation system, the state used a 5-point scale and over half of the state's employees scored a 4.0 or above. The state hopes that this new program will bring evaluations more in line with the "general rule" in private industry that 15 percent of employees will fall in the exceeds expectations category. Merit System Commissioner Bennett stressed that "if managers properly establish performance standards up front, we would expect only three to five percent of state employees to be rated at the Far Exceeds Expectations level. The Task Force has not yet set a policy that managers be given set percentages of employees that can be rated at each level. However, the reality is that agencies do not have unlimited funds to devote to salary increases" (GSMSPA, 1995k:1, 5). Instead of being limited on the number of employees that are in each category, agencies will be limited to a certain percentage of their overall salary budget that can be used to award performance-based increases (GSMSPA, 1995l).

Starting in the spring of 1996, managers were trained on the new job classification structure and the new pay structure. These finalized systems would then begin to be linked to the new performance management cycle that began in the fall of 1996. After making adjustments based on the feedback from managers and employees, GeorgiaGain was ready to begin its first year of "real" implementation.

In October 1996, the state started its second performance cycle and linked pay to the performance evaluations given to employees. The outcome of the personnel reforms in Georgia will begin their full impact as the performance management cycle progresses. Nevertheless, it is clear that GeorgiaGain is a radical departure from the personnel systems traditionally used in Georgia state government.

CONCLUSION

State merit system Commissioner Bobbie Jean Bennett summed up the scope and challenges of these reforms when she said, "GeorgiaGain is a massive undertaking. It's going to affect everything we do. It is a cultural change, reinventing government" (GSMSPA, 1994b:1, 3). GeorgiaGain and the elimination of the merit system have been efforts to emulate and implement many of the reforms suggested by the reinventing government movement. It is still too early to assess the final impact of these reforms but a preliminary assessment suggests that these reforms will have mixed results.

GeorgiaGain is another manifestation of a merit play plan that is subject to all of the same problems that have plagued such systems. Unfortunately, in designing this system, there were not any explicit attempts to avoid the problems that have generally been associated with merit pay—probably the reformers' biggest failure. The reinventing government paradigm, in ignoring the scholarly literature on government reform efforts, has missed several critical lessons that could be learned.

For merit or pay for performance systems the biggest problem is the systemic belief that there is no link between pay and performance in public agencies (Rainey, Facer, and Bozeman, 1995). The National Performance Review (NPR), ascribed very closely to the reinventing philosophy of Osborne and Gaebler, recognized that there is "insufficient empirical evidence that pay for performance programs are effective"

(Gore, 1993: 36). The GeorgiaGain pay for performance effort was theoretically bankrupt.

However, as a large change effort, there have been several positive aspects of the GeorgiaGain effort. As Rainey (1997b, 1996, 1997a) suggests, there are several elements that are necessary for a large-scale organizational change to be successful, including:

- Widespread belief in the need for change;
- Clear, sustained leadership, including support from top executives;
- Broad participation in diagnosing problems and planning the change; and
- Flexible, incremental implementation, involving experimentation, feedback, adaptation, and building on prior success to institutionalize change.

All of these elements have been present in the GeorgiaGain reforms efforts. From the first survey that was done as part of the reform effort, employees, managers, and political executives shared a belief that positive changes in the personnel system could occur. The Governor and the task force gave consistent leadership that emphasized the broad inclusiveness of the process and gave substantial commitment to the reforms. Early in the GeorgiaGain effort, input was sought from large groups of employees, most importantly by staffing the permanent work teams of the task force with "regular" employees. Finally, GeorgiaGain has been a very incremental process. The process has sought to build into the implementation process by staggering the implementation of the pay for performance linkage.

The most interesting stages in GeorgiaGain are yet to come. Personnel managers have expressed hope that the final outcome of these reforms will be positive. However, at the same time, managers have reported doubts that there will be real changes.

Notes

1. Under the old job classification system, there were approximately 50 different grades for state employees. Under the GeorgiaGain restructuring there are now only 26 grades.

References

Georgia State Merit System of Personnel Administration (1994a), "Assessment: GeorgiaGain Gains Support." *State Personnel News: A News Quarterly for and About Georgia State Employees* 18 (January):1, 3.

_____. (1994c). "Q & A on GeorgiaGain." *State Personnel News: A News Quarterly for and About Georgia State Employees* 18 (April):1, 3.

_____. (1994d). "GeorgiaGain: Employees will See Scope as Teams Move Forward." *State Personnel News: A News Quarterly for and About Georgia State Employees* 18 (July):1, 2.

_____. (1995a). "Executive Briefings: Held on GeorgiaGain." *State Personnel News: A News Quarterly for and About Georgia State Employees* 19 (January):1, 2.

_____. (1994b). "GeorgiaGain: Data Collection on Jobs Begins." *State Personnel News: A News Quarterly for and About Georgia State Employees* 18 (April):1, 3.

_____. (1994e). "GeorgiaGain: Compensable Factors are Key Ingredients to Set Pay." *State Personnel News: A News Quarterly for and About Georgia State Employees* 18 (July):6.

Georgia State Merit System of Personnel Administration (1995b). "GeorgiaGain: Responses to Employee Q & A." *State Personnel News: A News Quarterly for and About Georgia State Employees* 19 (January):4.

_____. (1995c). *Georgian Questions and Answers*. (March).

_____. (1995d). "GeorgiaGain Master Trainer: Views on Hopes and Challenges Ahead." *State Personnel News: A News Quarterly for and About Georgia State Employees* 19 (April):3.

_____. (1995e). "Accountability: Key Issue of PMP." *State Personnel News: A News Quarterly for and About Georgia State Employees* 19 (April):3.

_____. (1995f). "GeorgiaGain: "Responses to Employee Q & A." *State Personnel News: A News Quarterly for and About Georgia State Employees* 19 (April): 4

_____. (1995g). "Employee Meetings Will be Held to Introduce GeorgiaGain Performance Management Program." *State Personnel News: A News Quarterly for and About Georgia State Employees* 19 (July):3

_____. (1995h). "GeorgiaGain: Responses to Employee Q & A." *Georgia Personnel News: A News Quarterly for and About Georgia State Employees* 19 (July):4.

_____. (1995j). GeorgiaGain: *Employees Video Transcript*. (September).

_____. (1995k). "GeorgiaGain: Performance Management Process Transition Begins." *State Personnel News: A News Quarterly for and About Georgia State Employees* 19 (October):1, 5.

_____. (1995l). "GeorgiaGain: Responses to Employee Q & A." *State Personnel News: A News Quarterly for and About Georgia State Employees* 19 (October):4–5.

_____. (1997). Official Agency Website: http://www.State/Ga.US/SMS/.

Goodsell, Charles F. (1994). *The Case for Bureaucracy*. Chatham, NJ: Chatham House.

Gore, Al (1993). *Reinventing Human Resource Management*. Washington, D.C.: Office of the Vice President.

Miller, Zell (1995). Governor of Georgia. Memorandum to all agency heads. Office of the Governor, Atlanta. November 27. Duplicated.

Osborne, David and Ted Gaebler (1992). *Reinventing Government: How the Enterpreneurial Spirit is Transforming the Public Sector*. Reading, MA: Addison-Wesley.

Rainey, Hal G. (1997a). *Understanding and Managing Public Organizations*, 2nd ed. San Francisco: Jossey-Bass.

_____. (1997b). "Analyzing Administrative Reform from an Organizational Change Perspective: The Case of the National Performance Review," in Patricia W. Ingraham, Ronald P. Sanders, and James R. Thompson (eds.). *Transforming Management, Managing Transformation*, forthcoming. San Francisco: Jossey-Bass.

_____. (1996). "Assessing Past and Current Personnel Reforms: The Pursuit of Flexibility, Pay-for-Performance, and the Management of Reform Initiatives." Paper prepared for the Canadian Center for Management Development "Taking Stock" Project, Ottawa, May 9–12, fourth draft, November 14.

Rainey, Hal G., Rex L. Facer II, and Barry Bozeman (1995). "Repeated Finding of Sharp Differences Between Public and Private Managers' Perceptions of Personnel Rules." A paper presented at the Annual Meeting of the American Political Science Association, Chicago, August 31–September 3.

Wechsler, Barton (1994). "Reinventing Florida's Civil Service System: The Failure of Reform." *Review of Public Personnel Administration* 9 (Spring): 64–76.

12

SOCIAL EQUITY

BRIEF HISTORY

Social equity is a dynamic term that has had panoply of meanings at different times in the history of the United States. In 1776 *social equity* was defined by the Declaration of Independence as, ". . . all men are created equal, that they are endowed by their Creator with certain unalienable Rights . . ."[1] What Thomas Jefferson and the rest of the Continental Congress really meant, however, was "all *white men*" have "certain unalienable rights . . ." In 1789, the U.S. Constitution defined *social equity* as: all white men were whole citizens while all African slaves were three-fifths of a person for purposes of taxation.[2] Once again, women were excluded from the definition. With the adoption of the "Civil War Amendments, in the mid-1860s, social equity was redefined to include African Americans as whole citizens."[3] African American men received the right to vote, but women of all races remained second class citizens. The definition of *social equity* was changed again 31 years later, in the case of *Plessy v. Furguson* (1896)[4] when the U.S. Supreme Court decided that social equity meant "separate but equal." The previous, hard fought gains made by African Americans during the Civil War were destroyed by one Supreme Court opinion. Finally, in 1920 the definition of *social equity* was expanded to include women when the 19th Amendment[5] granted them suffrage.

1954 proved to be a redefining year for social equity pertaining to race when the Supreme Court handed down its landmark decision in *Brown v. Board of Education of Topeka*. Supported by a unanimous Court, Chief Justice Earl Warren declared that "the doctrine of separate but equal has no place in the field of public education"[6] and integration was to begin "with all deliberate speed."[7] The long and bloody process of integrating U.S. society began with

Jared C. Bennett, University of Utah made major contributions to this chapter. We are grateful for his able research, uniformly useful suggestions about readings to include, and for his writing of major portions of this introductory essay.

these words. The integration process spawned civil unrest, assassinations and significant political bloodshed in the halls of Congress and state legislatures around the nation.

The 1960s and 1970s provided important legislation that redefined social equity for minorities and women in the workplace and in other places of "public accommodation."[8] The foundation for current public policy pertaining to race and gender, the Civil Rights Act of 1964, stated that discrimination based on race, religion, color, age or gender was a violation of federal law. However, the passage of the Civil Rights Act of 1964 and its 1972 amendment were only the beginning of a new struggle to redefine social equity. Gays and lesbians, left out by the act, began to organize and demand protection against discrimination based on sexual orientation. Controversial programs such as affirmative action (AA) and Equal Employment Opportunity (EEO) began to cause white males to fear that they would become victims of reverse discrimination. Law suits and subsequent court rulings under sexual harassment laws began to redefine interpersonal relationships at work.

Modern Social Equity

This process of constant change begs the question: What is *social equity* today? George Frederickson defines it as, "The need or requirement to deliver public services fairly or equitably . . . to connote the value of fairness in the use of administrative discretion . . . [and] government programs designed to help minorities, women, the poor, or others who may have limited political power."[9] Other scholars define *social equity* as the principle that each citizen has a right to equal treatment by the political system.[10] On its face this definition seems reasonable, but are there situations that justify unequal treatment in order to ensure social equity?

Social Equity as Public Policy: Affirmative Action

Many proponents of affirmative action have argued for the unequal treatment of some to ensure equity for others. In a speech at Howard University, President Lyndon B. Johnson stated: "You do not take a person who, for years, has been hobbled by chains and liberate him, bring him up to the starting line of a race and then say, 'you are free to compete with others' and still justly believe you have been completely fair."[11] Whereas EEO was intended to create a "level playing field" by giving everyone an equal chance at education and employment, affirmative action was created to give certain groupings of people preference over others in order to compensate for past discriminations.

Opponents of affirmative action disagree with proponents of affirmative action on several grounds. First, opponents contend that affirmative action violates the Civil Rights Act of 1964. If there is to be no racial discrimination, there cannot be discrimination against whites. Second, affirmative action has not furthered the cause of protected groups, but instead has caused members of protected groups to appear as though they received opportunities through an informal quota, not because of individual merit. Finally, should an African American student whose father earns over $100,000 per year have preference over a white student whose single parent earns a wage below the poverty line?

If the question of affirmative action is difficult for you, you are not alone. The U.S. Supreme Court has struggled with it as well. In *Regents of University of California v. Baake* (1978)[12] the Court handed down a 5–4 decision saying that formal racial quotas are unconstitutional. However, a careful reading of the opinions indicates that the decision was really 4 1/2 to 4 1/2. The Court decided that although formal racial quotas are unconstitutional, race and gender may be *considered* when selecting applicants. The Court drew a very fine line for employers and admissions boards to follow. Race and gender are not to be *determinative factors* in the selection process—but they may be factors. The question the court left unanswered is the significance that race and gender may have in the selection process.

In 1996 the 5th Circuit Court of Appeals answered part of the question left unanswered by *Baake* when it declared that the University of Texas School of Law could not use race as a factor in deciding who to admit. In *Hopwood v. Texas* (1996)[13] four white students who were denied admission to the University of Texas Law School sued the University and Board of Regents because of the disparate admission policy the school used in admitting African-American and Hispanic students. The University used an admission index score. The score that African Americans and Hispanics needed for admission was 10 to 12 points lower than whites. The U.S. Supreme Court declined to hear the case on appeal in 1996, thus permitting the appellate court's opinion to stand as the law in the 5th Circuit. The *Hopwood* case rekindled a debate that has spread into other Circuit Courts of Appeal. If the Circuit Courts make different rulings on affirmative action, the U.S. Supreme Court eventually will have to decide if and in what form affirmative action will survive.

Affirmative action inevitably will come before the Court again because of affirmative action-killing initiatives that voters passed in California and Washington in 1996 and 1998 respectively and that are moving forward in several other states. Opponents of the California and Washington initiatives have challenged the constitutionality of the anti-affirmative action laws. Will the Court decide to protect affirmative action as it is now? With the conservative lean of the Court, probably not. However, the political balance of the Court could change if a Democratic president were to make one new appointment.

Although the courts continue to struggle with affirmative action, public administrators at all levels of government must deal with it. If you were hiring a street dispatcher for your public utilities department and you had a Hispanic and a white candidate tied for the highest score on the municipal civil service exam, who would you select? How would you justify your selection if the person who was turned down for the job brought a lawsuit for racial discrimination against your department under the Civil Rights Act of 1964?

GENDER EQUITY

Gender relations in the work place also has evolved into a salient social equity issue that affects the work of public administrators and the agencies they manage. *Causes of action*, or statutory permission to bring a lawsuit, for sexual harassment were created by a 1972 amendment to Title VII of the Civil Rights Act of 1964. The courts have interpreted Title VII to include two basic forms of sexual harassment; *quid pro quo* and *hostile environment sexual harassment.*[14] Translated literally from Latin, *quid pro quo* means, "this for that." In other words, a person is guilty of *quid pro quo sexual harassment* if sexual favors are solicited or demanded in exchange for a promotion, a good review, continued employment or other economic gain. This is the most blatant form of sexual harassment, and once proven, courts and juries usually have awarded large judgments against offending persons and organizations.

Hostile environment is the more common of the two forms of sexual harassment. The U.S. Supreme Court has defined *hostile environment* as "harassment, while not affecting economic benefits, creates a hostile or offensive working environment."[15] A victim of *hostile environment sexual harassment* may sue both the offending person and the employer if "uninvited, unwanted sexual attention" is given to a co-worker. Sexual jokes, teasing and innuendo, whether of the opposite sex or not, may be an actionable hostile environment sexual harassment claim. A male calling a female secretary "honey," "sweetheart," or "doll," asking a female executive to take notes at meetings, or to fetch coffee or perform other tasks below her position *after the female worker has objected*, may also be actionable grounds for sexual harassment.

As a public manager, how would you deal with an employee whose steady stream of jokes always involves sexual innuendoes or who sends e-mails containing messages of double entente under the guise of humor? Do you allow such activity at all, or just until someone notifies you that they are offended? What will a policy limiting "jokes" do for the morale, collegiality and employee confidence in your department?

Women also face pregnancy discrimination. Many employers have been reluctant to hire women, especially married women, because of the possibility of pregnancy and subsequent maternity leave. In 1978, Congress amended Title VII of the Civil Rights Act of 1964 to protect women from this type of employer discrimination. For example, employers are not allowed to ask a woman applicant whether she has children, is married, or plans to have children. In spite of these protections many women still feel that their marital status puts them at a hiring disadvantage because of the potential of a pregnancy.

What would you do in the following situation? Because of tight budgets, you are only able to hire one network engineer who will be solely responsible for the maintenance of your entire computer network throughout the year. One finalist for the job is a man who is slightly less qualified than the other finalist, a woman who is visibly pregnant. Can your department bear the risk of having no computer failures during the 12-week maternity leave the female applicant could take, under Title VII? The female applicant may not take the full 12 weeks of maternity leave but you are not allowed to ask her how much leave she plans to take. If she takes the full 12 weeks, could you find or reassign a worker who could immediately learn your entire network system and administer it effectively for 12 weeks?

Although women and minorities have made significant gains in public sector employment, women are still paid less for doing the same work as men, and both women and minorities are under-represented in the management levels. This has caused many scholars to conclude that a "glass ceiling"[16] exists over women and minorities that allows them to think they can advance into management levels where in reality they are discriminated against. Thus, only a disproportionate, small percentage of women and minorities make it into management roles.

SEXUAL ORIENTATION

While women and ethnic minorities are protected by the Civil Rights Act of 1964, gays and lesbians do not have protected status under federal law. In *Bowers v. Hardwick* (1986),[17] a homosexual man challenged a Georgia sodomy statute as a violation of the U.S. Constitution that was written to encompass both hetero- and homo-sexual relationships. The U.S. Supreme Court held that homosexual relations are not protected under the Constitution. Although the Constitution does not protect homosexual acts, federal courts have held that a homosexual may not be terminated from public employment solely on the basis of sexual orientation. Instead, the government must show that a "rational nexus"[18] exists between a person's sexual orientation and the reason why he or she was terminated. Many homosexuals feel that this "test" provides little protection against discrimination. Instead, gay and lesbian groups have been lobbying for protection under the Civil Rights Act of 1964 by the addition of "sexual orientation" to the list of federally protected categories.

Attempts to provide social equity for homosexuals has proven to be extremely controversial. President Clinton discovered how heated the topic was when he tried to implement his campaign promise to allow gays in the military in 1993. Because of the intense political forces that were against his proposal, the military settled for the "don't ask, don't tell" policy—a policy that is highly unsatisfactory to all parties. The future of gay and lesbian equity is difficult to predict considering the intense moral, policy and political issues involved.

Suppose a well-known and highly able person in the agency you manage began to take an active part in the local gay rights movement and publicly expressed his homosexuality on television at a gay rights rally. Other employees in the organization now refuse to work with this employee, and work in this agency has almost ground to a halt. Upper-level administrative and elected officials direct you to fire this individual because many constituents have called expressing their disapproval for the government allowing its employees to be involved in such "immoral" behavior. The elected officials let you know, very clearly, that your agency is losing credibility in the eyes of the elected officials and that unless something is done quickly, it will face severe budget cutbacks. What would you do? What are your rights as an employer under the law? What does your definition of "social equity" say the outcome should be?

Disabled Americans and Social Equity

Over the past decade, people with disabilities have been added to the definition of "social equity." With the passage of the Americans with Disabilities Act (ADA)[19] in 1990, employers can no longer discriminate against people because of physical or mental disabilities that "impair one or more major life activities."[20] Employers must also make "reasonable accommodations"[21] in order to help people with disabilities perform their jobs. An employer may not need to accommodate an employee's disability if the employer can show that the accommodations would place an "undue burden"[22] on the employer. What constitutes "reasonable accommodation" remains unclear. How much of a cost does the accommodation have to be before it changes from "reasonable" to an "undue burden?"

Suppose a person in the agency you manage suffers from a diagnosed mental disability called "panic disorder" in which the person feels constant stress regardless of whether there are any demands upon her. Your agency is entering a time of year where this employee's workload will increase dramatically. What "reasonable accommodations" will you need to satisfy the ADA but still assure that your department completes its assignments on time? What effect will your treatment of the employee with disabilities have on the other employees in your department? If you believe that the accommodations to meet the needs of the disabled employee would be an "undue burden" and you therefore had to decide to let the disabled employee go, what would you use to show a court that the accommodations presented an "undue burden?"

The Future of Social Equity

The definition of "social equity" is still evolving. Have we reached a point in society where all people will be treated equally or do we still need to protect certain groups and treat them differently from other groups in the name of "equality"? Has affirmative action outlived its usefulness? Will the "glass ceiling" be removed so that women and minorities can move into upper-management positions in government? Will women and minorities be paid the same as white males for doing the same work? Will gays and lesbians be included as a protected minority class under federal law? What long-term effects will the ADA have on the costs of government? The answers to these questions will change the current definition of "social equity" and will ultimately raise new questions about how government benefits, rights and privileges should be distributed—which will raise new questions about what "social equity" means.

READINGS REPRINTED IN THIS CHAPTER

In the first reading, **"Public Administration and Social Equity,"**[23] **George Frederickson** argues that the criteria for judging the worth of public administration should not be limited to efficiency and economy but should also include social equity. If public administration focuses only on neutrality in policy making and efficiency and economy in carrying out the will of the legislature, social equity concerns will be ignored. Social equity competes with the values of neutrality, economy and efficiency.

Social equity is defined as the application of three factors that Frederickson calls "equalities": simple individual equalities, segmented equality and block equality. The concept of *individual equality* "consists of one class of equals," such as "one person-one vote." *Segmented equality* is the result of society's complex division of labor. Equality may exist in one segment of society while there may be disparities of treatment between different segments of society. For example, all private practice lawyers within a jurisdiction are regulated by the same laws of professional conduct whereas medical doctors are not regulated by the same laws of professional conduct as lawyers. *Block equality* calls for equality between groups. Women lawyers seeking equal pay as male lawyers would be an example of block equality.

It would be ludicrous to apply block equity to lawyers, accountants and doctors. Therefore, Frederickson suggests that each of the three equalities has a certain "domain." If one of the equalities is applied outside of its domain, the concept of equity as a whole is harmed. Frederickson then analyzes the applications of this concept of equity by the courts and Congress to different situations in which government confronts questions of economy, efficiency and social equity.

Gregory Lewis recounts the federal government's treatment of gays and lesbians in, **"Lifting the Ban on Gays in the Civil Service: Federal Policy Toward Gay and Lesbian Employees since the Cold War."**[24] The federal government has always required that its employees be of "good moral character." After World War II, the federal government became consumed with the threat of communist infiltration into the government and homosexuals as well. Homosexuals were deemed to be security risks because they could be blackmailed into telling government secrets to prevent public exposure. The U.S. Senate and executive branch went to great lengths to identify and expel all homosexuals from government service. Lewis documents government activities with respect to homosexuals from the beginning of the Cold War in 1945 to the late 1990s.

The final reading in this chapter, by **James Slack**, proposes a change from affirmative action to "full spectrum diversity," in **"From Affirmative Action to Full Spectrum Diversity in the American Workplace."**[25] The original intent of affirmative action was to establish a representative bureaucracy. Slack argues that current affirmative action policies help only certain groups of Americans and therefore cannot possibly achieve a truly representative bureaucracy. For example, current affirmative action policies exclude European Americans and Canadian Americans from adding to the diversity equation of an organization. Affirmative action also fails to take into consideration religious diversity. U.S. policy should take into account all factors of diversity.

Unfortunately, the current system of affirmative action pits merit against diversity in hiring decisions. Slack's model for "full spectrum diversity" attempts to balance considerations of merit with diversity. The five steps in Slack's model are: job description, job advertisement, job pool analysis, interviewing top candidates, and hiring one of the top candidates. Steps (1) and (3) focus solely on merit; step (4), interviewing top candidates, focuses on full spectrum diversity. Finally, hiring one of the top candidates, step (5), should enhance the organization's decision-making ability and avoid competition between merit and diversity. "Full spectrum diversity" will better serve the policy goals of affirmative action by creating a truly diverse public sector through balancing merit and diversity.

NOTES

1. See DECLARATION OF INDEPENDENCE, (1776).
2. See U.S. CONSTITUTION, ART. I §2, (1789).
3. See U.S. CONSTITUTION, AMEND. 13, 14, 15 (1865, 1868, 1870).
4. See Plessy v. Furguson, 163 U.S. 537, 547 (1896).
5. See U.S. CONSTITUTION, AMEND. 19 (1920).
6. See Brown v. Board of Education of Topeka, 347 U.S. 483, 495 (1954).
7. See Brown v. Board of Education of Topeka, 349 U.S. 294, 301 (1955).
8. See 78 Stat 241 §201 (a)(b)(c)(e); §§203–207.
9. Frederickson, H. George. (1998). "Social Equity," in Jay M. Shafritz (Ed.), International Encyclopedia of Public Policy and Administration. Boulder, Colo.: Westview, p. 2073.
10. Shafritz, Jay M., and E.W. Russell. (2000). Introducing Public Administration (2nd ed). New York: Addison-Wesley Longman, p. 449.
11. Shafritz, Jay M., and E.W. Russell. (2000). Introducing Public Administration (2nd ed). New York: Addison-Wesley Longman, p. 449.
12. See Regents of University of California v. Baake, 438 U.S. 265 (1978).
13. See Hopwood v. Texas, 21 F.3d 603 (1994).
14. See Meritor Savings Bank v. Vinson, 477 U.S. 57, 65 (1986); See also Harris v. Forklift Systems, 510 U.S. 17 (1993); 42 USCS §2000e Et seq. (1999).
15. See Meritor Savings Bank v. Vinson, 477 U.S. 57, 65 (1986); See also Harris v. Forklift Systems, 510 U.S. 17 (1993); 42 USCS §2000e Et seq. (1999).
16. Naff, Katherine C. (1994). "Through the Glass Ceiling: Prospects for the Advancement of Women in the Federal Civil Service." Public Administration Review, 54(6): 507–514.
17. See Bowers v. Hardwick, 478 U.S. 186 (1986).
18. See Norton v. Macy, 417 F.2d 1161, 1164 (D.C. Circuit 1969).
19. See 42 USC §§12112–14 (1999).
20. See 42 USC §12102(2)(A) (1999).
21. See 42 USC §12111 (1999).
22. Id. at §12111 (1999).

23. Frederickson, H. George. (March-April 1990). "Public Administration and Social Equity." *Public Administration Review, 50*(2): 228–237.
24. Lewis, Gregory B. (September-October 1997). "Lifting the Ban on Gays in the Civil Service: Federal Policy Toward Gay and Lesbian Employees since the Cold War." *Public Administration Review, 57*(5): 387–395.
25. Slack, James D. (Fall 1997). "From Affirmative Action to Full Spectrum Diversity in the American Workplace." *Review of Public Personnel Administration, 17*(4): 75–87.

33

H. George Frederickson

PUBLIC ADMINISTRATION AND SOCIAL EQUITY

It was 1968. Inequality and injustice, especially based on race, was pervasive. A government built on a Constitution claiming the equal protection of the laws had failed in that promise. Public administrators, those who daily operate the government, were not without responsibility. Both in theory and practice public administration had, beginning in the 1940s, emphasized concepts of decision making, systems analysis, operations research or management science, and rationality. In running the government the administrator's job was to be efficient (getting the most service possible for available dollars) or economical (providing an agreed-upon level of services for the fewest possible dollars). It should be no surprise, therefore, that issues of inequity and injustice were not central to public servants or to public administration theorists.

Social equity began as a challenge to the adequacy of concepts of efficiency and economy as guides for public administration. In time social equity took on a broader meaning.

> Social equity is a phrase that comprehends an array of value preferences, organizational design preferences, and management style preferences. Social equity emphasizes equality in government services. Social equity emphasizes responsibility for decisions and program implementation for public manager. Social equity emphasizes change in public management. Social equity emphasizes responsiveness to the needs of citizens rather than the needs of public organizations. Social equity emphasizes an approach to the study of and education for public administration that is interdisciplinary, applied, problem solving in character, and sound theoretically.[1]

The development of the concept of social equity was followed by a considerable literature both pro and con. Philosophically the views ranged from social equity as providing the proper normative basis for a new public administration on the one hand to social equity as an attempt by some to "steal popular sovereignty" on the other.[2] Researchers, especially in the public policy fields, began to analyze variations in the distribution of public policy fields, began to analyze variations in the distribution of public service by income, race, and neighborhood, and eventually by gender. The concept of equity was included in the first adopted Principles for the American Society for Public Administration (ASPA), which later became the Code of Ethics. In 1981, the ASPA *Professional Standards and Ethics Workbook and Study Guide for Public Administrators*, in the section on professional ethics, listed as the first two Principles to be the pursuit of equality, which is to say citizen A being equal to citizen B, and equity, which is to say adjusting shares to that citizen A is made equal with citizen B.[3]

PHILOSOPHICAL AND THEORETICAL DEVELOPMENTS

Public administration, it has been said, is the marriage of the arts and sciences of government to the arts and sciences of management.[4] Efficiency and economy are primarily theories of management while social equity is primarily a theory of government. In the early years of modern American public administration the marriage, particularly in the conceptions of Woodrow Wilson, was balanced.[5] Theories of business efficiency were routinely mixed with theories of democratic government, the argument being that a government can and should be efficient and fair. However, by the 1950s the marriage was dominated by management theories and issues, having begged questions of equity and fairness. Even though it was and is generally agreed that public administration is part of the political process, there was little interest in developing specifics regarding the ends to which politics and public administration could be put.

In the early years it was also the conventional wisdom that public administration was neutral and only marginally involved in policy making. Under those conditions it is possible to ignore social equity. Now the theology holds that public administration is a part or form of politics, that it often exercises leadership in the policy process, and that neutrality is next to impossible. If that is the case, then it is not logically possible to dismiss social equity as a suggested guide for administrative action, equal to economy and efficiency.

Initial attempts to return to the marriage questions of equity and fairness were simplistic and superficial. Willbern, in his splendid review of the early literature on social equity and the so-called new public administration, observed that critics were "not very precise in defining the goals or values toward which administration and knowledge must be arrived."[6]

So the task was clear, social equity needed flesh on its bones if it was to be taken seriously as a third pillar for public administration. The process was begun with a symposium on "Social Equity and Public Administration," which appeared in the *Public Administration Review* in 1974. In an especially important way, that symposium is illustrative of theory building in public administration.

First, the subject is parsed, in this case, into considerations of social equity: (1) as the basis for a just, democratic society; (2) as influencing the behavior of organization man; (3) as the legal basis for distributing public services; (4) as the practical basis for distributing public services; (5) as operationalized in compound federalism; and, (6) as a challenge for research and analysis.[7]

Second, the subject having been taken apart, good theory building suggests putting it back together. Looking back, it is now clear that considerable progress has been made in thinking about, understanding, and applying various parts of the subject. But it has yet to be put back together.

Third is the arduous task of definition. In this case, it was appropriate to turn to the theories of distributive justice for definition. The phrase social equity and the word equality were essentially without definition in the field. As Rae and his associates have said: "Equality is the simplest and most abstract of notions, yet the practices of the world are irremediably concrete and complex. How, imaginably, could the former govern the latter?"[8] Yet, society equity was advanced in the 1960s and the 1970s as an essential third pillar of public administration.

When ideas such as social equity or the public interest or liberty are suggested as guides for public action, the most compelling definitions are often the most abstract. And so it was in this case. The initial attempts to define social equity as it applies to public administration were fastened to John Rawls' *A Theory of Justice*.[9] The Rawlsian construct is an ideal type addresses the distribution of rights, duties, and advantages in a just society. Justice, to Rawls, is fairness. To achieve fairness the first principle is that each person is guaranteed equal basic liberties consistent with an extensive system of liberty for all. The second principle calls for social and economic inequalities to be managed so that they are of greatest benefit to the least advantaged (the difference principle); it seeks to make offices and positions open to all under conditions of *fair* equality of opportunity.

This analysis turns, then, to a more descriptive theory for both greater definition and more likely applicability to the theories and practices of public administration. Following Douglas Rae and associates, a rudimentary language and a road map are set forth for the notion of equality, with attendant definitions and examples.[10] I label this the Compound Theory of Social Equity. This Compound Theory serves as the basis for later considerations of legal and research perspectives on social equity in public administration.

Simple Individual Equalities

Individual equality consists of one class of equals, and one relationship of equality holds among them. The best examples would be one person-one vote and the price mechanism of the market, which offers a Big Mac or a Whopper at a specific price to whomever wishes to buy. The Golden Rule or Immanuel Kant's Categorical Imperative are formulas for individual equalities.

Segmented Equality

Any complex society with a division of labor tends to practice segmented equality. Farmers have a different system of taxation than do business owners, and both differ from wage earners. In segmented equality, one assumes that equality exists within the category (e.g., farmers) and that inequality exists between the segments. All forms of hierarchy use the concept of segmented equality. All five-star generals are equal to each other as are all privates first-class. Equal pay for equal work is segmented equality. Segmented equality is, in fact, systematic or structured inequality. Segmented equality is critically important for public policy and administration because virtually every public service is delivered on a segmented basis and always by segmented hierarchies.

Block Equalities

Both simple individual and segmented equalities are in fact individual equalities. Block equalities, on the other hand, call for equality *between* groups or subclasses. The railroad accommodations for Blacks and whites could be separate, so long as they were equal in *Plessy v. Ferguson* (1889).[11] *Brown v. Board of Education* (1954)[12] later concluded that separation by race meant inequality; therefore, the U.S. Supreme Court required school services to be based upon simple individual equality rather than block equality, using race to define blocks. The claims for comparable worth systems of pay for women are, interestingly, block egalitarianism mixed with equal pay for equal work, which is segmented equality.

The Domain of Equality

How does one decide what is to be distributed equally? The domain of equality marks off the goods, services, or benefits being distributed. If schools and fire protection are to be provided, why not golf courses or recreational facilities? Domains of equality can be narrowly or broadly defined, and they can have to do with *allocations* based on a public agency's resources or they can be based on *claims*–claimants' demands for equality. Domains of equality constantly shift, aggregate, and disaggregate. Certain domains are largely controlled by the market such as jobs, wages, and investments, while others are controlled primarily by government. It is often the case that the governmental domain seeks equality to correct inequalities resulting from the market or from previous governmental policies. Unemployment compensation, Aid to Families with Dependent Children, college tuition grants, and food stamps are all kinds of government compensatory inequality to offset other inequalities outside of the governmental domain of allocation but within a broader domain of claims.

Domains can also be intergenerational, as in the determination of whether present taxpayers or their children pay for the federal debt built up by current deficits.

Equalities of Opportunity

Equalities of opportunity are divided into *prospect* and *means* opportunity. Two people have equal opportunity for a job if each has the same probability for attaining the job under conditions of prospect equality of opportunity. Two people have equal opportunity for a job if each has the same talents or qualifications for the job under conditions of means-equal opportunity. Examples of pure prospect equality of opportunity are few, but the draft lottery for the Vietnam War is very close. In means equality of opportunity, *equal rules*, such as Intelligent Quotient (I.Q.) tests, Standard Achievement Test (SAT) scores, equal starting and finishing points for footraces, and so forth define opportunity. "The purpose and effect of these equal means is not equal prospect of success, but legitimately unequal prospects of success."[13] Aristotle's notion that equals are to be treated equally would constitute means-based equality of opportunity.

In any given society not all talent can be equally developed. Following John Schaar: "Every society has a set of values, and these are arranged in a more or less tidy hierarchy. . . . The equality of opportunity formula must be revised to read: equality of opportunity for all to develop those talents which are highly valued by a given people at a given time."[14] How else, for example, can one explain the status of rock musicians in popular culture?

The Value of Equality

The value of equality begins with the concept of *lot equality* in which shares are identical (similar housing, one vote, etc.) or equal. The advantage of lot equality is that only the individual can judge what pleases or displeases him or her. Lots can also be easily measured and distributed, and they imply nothing about equal well-being. The problem, of course, is that lot equality is insensitive to significant variations in need. To remedy this, Rae and associates suggest a "person equality" in which there is nonarbitrary rule-based distribution of shares based on nonneutral judgments about individuals' needs. A threatened person may require more protection (and police officials may so decide) merely to make that person equal to the nonthreatened person. The same can be said for the crippled as against the healthy child, the mentally retarded as against the bright. Person-regarding equality is often practiced in public administration to "make the rules humane."

It is clear that any universal scope for equality is both impossible and undesirable. Rather than a simple piece of rhetoric or a slogan, the Compound Theory of Social Equity is a complex of definitions and concepts. Equality then changes from one thing to many things—equalities. If public administration is to be inclined toward social equity, at least this level of explication of the subject is required. In the policy process, any justification of policy choices claiming to enhance social equity needs to be analyzed in terms of such questions as: (1) Is this equality individual, segmented, or block? (2) Is this equality direct, or is it means-equal opportunity or prospect-equal opportunity? What forms of social equity can be advanced so as to improve the lot of the least advantaged, yet sustain democratic government and a viable market economy? The Compound Theory of Social Equity would serve as the language of the framework for attempts in both theory building and practice, and it would serve to answer these questions.

SOCIAL EQUITY AND THE LAW

Marshal Dimock made this dicta famous: "public administration is the law in action." It should be no surprise, then, that the most significant developments in social equity have their genesis in the law. "Local, state and national legislators—and their counterparts in the executive branches—too often have ignored, abdicated or traded away their responsibilities. . . . By default, then, if for no other reason, the courts would often have the final say."[15] The courts are the last resort for those claiming unequal treatment in either the protection of the law or the provision of service. Elected officials—both legislators and executives—are naturally inclined to the views and interests of the majority. Appointed officials—the public administrators—have until recent years been primarily concerned with efficiency and economy, although effectiveness was also an early concern, as noted by Dwight Waldo in *The Administrative State*.[16]

Employment

The most important legal influences resulting in more equitable government are in the field of employment, both public and nonpublic. The legal (not to mention administrative) questions are: who ought to be entitled to a job, what are the criteria, and how ought they to be applied?

The Civil Rights Act of 1964 as amended and the Equal Employment Act of 1972 were designed to guarantee equal access to public and private employment. This was done by a combination of block equalities (whereby persons in different racial categories could be compared and, if found subject to different treatment, a finding of violation of law would be made) and a means-equal opportunities logic (whereby fair measurements of talent, skill, and ability would determine who gets jobs). The landmark case was *Griggs v. Duke Power*, in which the U.S. Supreme Court held that job qualifications that were not relevant to a specific job and that on their face favored whites over blacks were a violation of the law.[17] The Court clearly rejected the idea of prospect equality, but because it upheld the idea of equality by blocks or, to use the words of the law, "protected groups," a strong social equity signal was sent. Race-consciousness as an affirmative action was to be based upon equality between Blacks and whites both in the work cohort and between the work cohort and the labor market—a kind of double application of equality.

John Nalbandian, in a recent review of case law on affirmative action in employment, observed that cases subsequent to *Griggs* have systematically limited "affirmative action tightly within the scope of the problem it was supposed to solve." The case law has sought to limit negative effects, such as unwanted inequality befalling nonminorities as a result of these programs.[18] *The University of California Regents v. Bakke* was the most celebrated example of judicial support for block equality to bring Blacks up to an enrollment level equal to whites, while at the same time protecting a nonminority claimant who would likely have qualified for admissions in the absence of a protected class.[19]

The affirmative action laws, and the Court's interpretations of them, have had a significant effect on equalizing employment opportunities, first between minorities and nonminorities and more recently by gender.[20] Nalbandian predicts, however, that the values of social equity may decline in a shift toward a new balance in employment practices, giving greater emphasis to efficiency.[21]

Contracting

In the 1977 Public Works Employment Act the national government established a minority-business-enterprise 10-percent setaside, requiring that 10 percent of all public works contracts be reserved for firms and owned by minorities. The 10-percent set-aside was tested and affirmed in *Fullilove v. Klutznik* (1980).

In a 1989 affirmation of the 10-percent set-aside provisions of the 1977 Federal Public Works Employment Act, the U.S. Supreme Court struck down a 30-percent set-aside for minority construction firms on contracts with the city of Richmond, Virginia. This was immediately regarded as a significant setback for the affirmative action programs of 33 states and over 200 municipalities. The *Richmond* decision reasoned that

the 14th Amendment was violated by the set-aside because it denied *whites* equal protection of the law.[22] No doubt the set-aside provision has enhanced social equity. It is
clear, however, that the law has used inequality to achieve equality.

Government Service

In 1968 Andrew Hawkins, a Black handyman living in a neighborhood called the
Promised Land, an all-Black section of Shaw, Mississippi, gathered significant data to
show that municipal services such as paved streets, sewers, and gutters were unequally
distributed. Because these services were available in the white section of Shaw,
Hawkins charged that he and his class were deprived of the 14th Amendment guarantee of equal protection of the law. The U.S. District Court disagreed, saying that such a
distribution had to do with issues of "municipal administration" that were "resolved at
the ballot box."[23] On appeal, the decision of the District Court was overturned by the
U.S. Court of Appeals, in part based on this amicus curiae brief from the Harvard-MIT
(Massachusetts Institute of Technology) Joint Center for Urban Studies:

> . . . invidious discrimination in the qualitative and quantitative rendition of basic
> governmental services violates an unyielding principle . . . that a trial court may not
> permit a defendant local government to rebut substantial statistical evidence of dis-
> crimination on the basis of race by entering a general disclaimer of illicit motive or by
> a loose and undocumented plea of administrative convenience. No such defense can
> be accepted as an adequate rebuttal of a prima facie case established by uncontro-
> verted statistical evidence of an overwhelming disparity in the level and kind of pub-
> lic services rendered to citizens who differ neither in terms of desire nor need, but
> only in the color of their skin.[24]

While the appellate court ruled in Hawkins' favor, it construed the issue of equal
protection so narrowly as to all but preclude significant court intervention in service allocation decisions where *intent* to discriminate cannot be conclusively demonstrated.

Desegregation of public schools following *Brown v. Board of Education* has resulted
in varied and creative ways to define and achieve equality. Busing is a means of achieving
at least the appearance of block equality. Bussing has, however, been primarily from the
inner city out. Magnet schools are an attempt to equalize the racial mix via busing in the
other direction. Building schools at the margins of primarily white and primarily Black
(or Hispanic) neighborhoods preserves the concept of the neighborhood school while
achieving integration. The major problem has been jurisdictional or to use the language
of equality, domain. The familiar inner city, primarily non-white school district surrounded by suburban, primarily white school districts significantly limits the possible
equalizing effects of *Brown v. Board of Education*. This is especially the case when wealth
and tax base follow white movement to the suburbs. State courts have in many places interpreted the equality clauses of state constitutions to bring about greater equality. Beginning with *Serrano v. Priest* in California, state equalization formulas for school
funding have in many states required the augmentation of funding in poor districts.[25]
Ordinarily this is done on a dollar-per-student basis. This procedure broadens the domain of the issue to the state, and it is also a simple formula for individual equality. It
does, of course, bring about this equality by race-based inequality.

From the point of view of competing concepts of equality, the Kansas City Missouri School District desegregation cases may be the most interesting. After *Brown v. Board of Education* determined that separate but equal schooling was in fact unequal and unconstitutional, two questions remained. Was it sufficient for school districts and state departments of education to stop segregating? Or, was it necessary to repair the damage done by a century of racially separate school systems? In *United States v. Jefferson City Board of Education* the Court of Appeals declared that school officials: "have an affirmative duty under the Fourteenth Amendment to bring about an integrated unitary school system in which there are no Negro schools and no white schools—just schools. . . . In fulfilling this duty it is not enough for school authorities to offer Negro children the opportunity to attend formerly all-white schools. The necessity of overcoming the effects of the dual school system in this circuit requires integration of faculties, facilities and activities as well as students."[26]

Later in *Swann v. Charlotte-Mecklenburg Board of Education* the U.S. Supreme Court stated that "the objective today remains to eliminate from the public schools all vestiges of state imposed segregation."[27]

Two conditions pertain in Kansas City, Missouri. First is a dual housing market resulting from an interaction between private and governmental parties in the real estate industry, resulting in racially segregated residential areas. This has resulted in racially segregated school roughly mirroring the segregated neighborhoods. Originally segregated all-Black schools are now schools of mostly Black students and teachers. The 11 suburban school districts surrounding Kansas City have almost all white students and teachers.

In *Jenkins v. Missouri* in 1984 the trial court under Judge Clark found the Kansas City Missouri School District and the State of Missouri liable for the unconstitutional segregation of the public schools.[28] The problem, of course, was the remedy. It is one thing to identify inequality; it is another to achieve equality. The School District tried and failed to secure passage of tax levies and bond issues to comply with Judge Clark's order.

Following the *Liddell* and *Griffin* cases, Judge Clark ordered both tax increases and bond issuances to cover the remedies sought in 1986.[29] The court also held that 75 percent of the cost of the plan was allocated to the State of Missouri for funding. The appellate court sustained all of Judge Clark's remedies with the exception of a 1.5-percent surcharge on incomes earned in Kansas City by nonresidents and instructed the state and the district to proceed with the remedies.[30]

If the majority of the citizens had turned down bond issues and had refused higher taxation to enable the school district to meet its desegregation objectives, how could the judge justify imposing those taxes as a matter of law? He said,

> A majority has no right to deny others the constitutional guarantees to which they are entitled. This court, having found that vestiges of unconstitutional discrimination still exist in the KCMSD is not so callous as to accept the proposition that it is helpless to enforce a remedy to correct the past violations. . . . The court must weigh the constitutional rights of the taxpayers against the constitutional rights of the plaintiff students in this case. The court is of the opinion that the balance is clearly in favor of the students who are helpless without the aid of this court.[31]

From an equality point of view, there are several examples of competing views of fairness. *First,* with the individual definition of equality, each vote is equal to each other vote, and the majority wins in a representative democracy. The court here clearly said that a majority cannot vote away the constitutional rights of a minority to equal schooling. *Second* is the dimension of time or intergenerational equality. The century of inequality in schools for Black children was to be remedied by a period of inequality toward nonminorities to correct for the past. *Third* is the question of domain. To what extent should the issue be confined to one school district? Because schools are constitutionally established in the State of Missouri, Judge Clark concluded that the funding solutions for desegregation were ultimately the responsibility of the state. Indeed, Arthur A. Bensen II, an attorney for the plaintiff, argued persuasively that it was fully within the authority of Judge Clark not only to impose either state or areawide financing to solve school desegregation but also to reorganize the school districts to eliminate the vestiges of prior discrimination.[32] The judge chose not to go that far.

Many more examples of equality can be traced to the courts, including equalizing funding for male and female student athletes in schools and colleges.

SOCIAL EQUITY AND ANALYSIS

Both the ideological and methodological perspectives in policy analysis have been dominated by economics. While the economic model has been a powerful influence on policy analysis, it has been tempered, especially in recent years, by use of measures of both general and individual well-being that are more compatible with governmental goals. Long-standing and powerful governmental concepts, such as justice, fairness, individual rights, and equality, are now being measured and used in analysis. Broad collective measures, the so-called social indicators such as unemployment and homelessness, are now more often used in policy analysis. Measurements of variations in the distribution of public services by age, race, gender, income, and the like are relatively routine. Social equity concepts are used not only as theory or as legal standards but as measures or variables in research. The problem, of course, in social equity analysis, as in the use of social equity in law or theory, is the compound character of equality.

At the level of the individual, data and findings are now available that map, in at least a rudimentary way, personal views and preferences regarding equality. Jennifer Hochschild has determined that people have contradictory views of equality.[33]

In the social domain people hold strongly to norms of equal shares and equal procedures. Equal treatment of children, one spouse, equal sacrifice for the family, and equal treatment in the neighborhood mark the general views of the poor, the middle class, and the rich. In schools, equal or fair procedures are important to just determination of grades. In schools, families tend to move somewhat away from strict individual equality toward a differentiation based upon investment, such as the handicapped child's needing more, an example of Rawlsian justice. And there is evidence of a differentiation of investment for the more gifted or those with greater potential. People are not, however, equally happy with the egalitarian character of social life. If they feel they have some control over their fate and are able to act on the principles of equality, they are more happy. If not, they are bitter and unhappy.

These same people endorse differentiation or means-based equality in the economic domain. People, in other words, want an equal chance to become unequal. Productivity should be rewarded, the poor feeling this would produce more equal incomes, the rich believing it would result in less equal incomes. Private property is deeply supported. Accumulated wealth is not generally opposed by poor or rich, and both strongly oppose inheritance taxes. And both partially abandon their different views when it comes to poverty, feeling that "something should be done."

In the political domain these people are egalitarian again. Political and civil rights should be distributed equally to all. "They want tax and social welfare policies mainly to take from the rich and give to the poor and middle classes. Their vision of utopia always includes more equality. . . . [34] There is deep resentment over perceived unfairness resulting from loopholes in the graduated income tax because it treats people unequally. Many people endorse tuition subsidies for the poor, housing subsidies, and even a national health insurance.

Yet, with all of this, Hochschild found ambivalence. People recognize that their views are sometimes inconsistent or that they are confused. And there is some helplessness and anger over whom to blame for inequality or how to make things better.

As the different domains of people's lives best explain how they feel about equality, they also generally conform to the compound conception of social equity set out in Section II. Both in the theoretical model and in people's outlooks, equality splits into equalities depending on domains, dimensions of time, jurisdictions, abilities, effort, and luck.

Field research on the distribution of local government service is filled with implications for social equity and public administration. Much of this research tests the "underclass hypothesis." If one accepts that hypothesis, it follows that the distribution of libraries, parks, fire protection, water, sewers, policy protection, and education services follows power, wealth, and racial variations. The findings of research on municipal services generally indicate that the underclass hypothesis does not hold.[35] Fixed services such as parks and libraries exhibit "unpatterned inequalities" that are not correlated with power, wealth, or race. These inequalities are more a function of the age of the neighborhood and the condition of housing. Mobile services such as police and fire protection tend to be distributed relatively equally, and such variation as can be determined is not associated with race or wealth. On the burden side, evidence indicates that property tax assessments are unequal in the direction of lower proportionate assessments for minorities and the poor and higher proportionate assessments for the rich and the white.[36]

Both interdistrict and intradistrict school funding variations have tended, on the other hand, to confirm the underclass hypothesis. In the past 20 years, primarily as a result of court cases, more than half of the states have undertaken school-finance reforms designed to equalize funding between schools within districts or between districts. When compared to nonschool-finance reform states, the reform states now evidence greater equity in per-student funding.[37]

Why has the underclass hypothesis not been demonstrated in field research, except in the case of schools? Robert Lineberry and others argue persuasively that urban and state bureaucracies, following patterned decision rules or service delivery rules, have distributed public services in such a way as to ameliorate the effects of poverty and race. The effects of municipal reform, including city managers, merit-based bureaucracies, at-large elections, nonpartisan elections, and the like, have strengthened the public services at the local level. The public services are routinized, patterned, incremental, and predictable, following understood or accepted decision rules or service delivery rules. Police and fire rules require decentralization and wide discretion in deployment of staff and equipment. Social services tend to respond to stated demands. Each service has some basis for its service delivery rules.[38]

What is most significant here is that it is bureaucracy, professional public administration, particularly in larger cities, that distributes public services either generally equally or in the direction of those especially in need. The point is that public administration understands and practices social equity. Social equity is understood or given, in the same way as efficiency or economy, in general public administration practice.

What explains school funding inequities? School bureaucracies have virtually no control over interdistrict funding levels. What explains Shaw, Mississippi, and other glaring examples of race-based service inequity? Often it is the lack of a genuinely professional public service.

It is a great irony of these times that all of this has occurred during a period referred to as the "age of the new individualism" or the "age of narcissism."[39] The dominant political ethos of the last 12 years has been pro-business and anti-government, anti-tax, anti-welfare, and particularly anti-bureaucracy. This ideological consensus seems to indicate that the majority share this ethos. In addition, this has been a lengthy period of sustained economic growth. Yet, under the surface of majoritarian consensus, one sees a significant adjustment of the workforce from primary production to information and service at net lower wages, a sharp increase in two-worker families, a profound discontinuity in income and ability to acquire housing, transportation, and food, an increase in homelessness, and an increase in poverty.[40] Thus, while social equity has undergone development as a theory—and while public administrators have, following a social equity ethic, ameliorated the effects of inequality—still inequality has increased as a fact.[41]

Most important in these conclusions is the research which indicates that public administration tends to practice social equity. This is no surprise to those who are in public management at the local level. Public administrators solve problems, ameliorate inequalities, exercise judgment in service allocation matters, and use discretion in the application of generalized policy. Fairness and equity have always been commonsense guides for action. Some are concerned that this seems to put bureaucracy in a political role.[42] No doubt exists that public administration is a form of politics. The issue is, what theories and beliefs guide public administrators' actions? As it has evolved in the last 20 years, social equity has served to order the understanding of public administration and to inform the judgment necessary to be both effective and fair.

NOTES

1. *Ibid.*, p. 6.
2. George Berkeley, *The Administrative Revolution: Notes on the Passing of Organization Man* (Englewood Cliffs, NJ: Prentice-Hall, 1971); Victor Thompson, *Without Sympathy or Enthusiasm* (University: The University of Alabama Press, 1975).

3. Herman Mertins, Jr., and Patrick J. Hennigan, eds. ASPA *Professional Standards and Ethics Workbook and Study Guide for Public Administration* (Washington: The American Society for Public Administration, 1981), pp. 22–23.

4. Dwight Waldo, *The Administrative State* (San Francisco: The Ronald Press, 1948).

5. Woodrow Wilson, "The Study of Administration," *Political Science Quarterly,* vol. 56 (December 1941; originally copyrighted in 1887).

6. York Willbern, "Is the New Public Administration Still With Us?" *Public Administration Review,* vol. 33 (July/August 1973), p. 376.

7. David K. Hart, "Social Equity, Justice and the Equitable Administrator;" Michael M. Harmon, "Social Equity and Organization Man: Motivation and Organizational Democracy"; Eugene B. McGregor, Jr., "Social Equity and the Public Service;" Steven R. Chitwood, "Social Equity and Social Service Productivity;" David O. Porter and Teddie Wood Porter, "Social Equity and Fiscal Federalism;" Orion J. White, Jr., and Burce L. Gates, "Statistical Theory and Equity in the Delivery of Social Services," vol. 34, *Public Administration Review* (January/February 1974), pp. 3–51.

8. Douglas Rae and Associates, *Equalities* (Cambridge, MA: Harvard University Press, 1981), p. 3.

9. John A. Rawls, *A Theory of Justice* (Cambridge, MA: Harvard University Press, 1971).

10. Much of what appears in the following page is taken from Rae and Associates, *Equalities* (Cambridge, MA: Harvard University Press, 1981).

11. *Plessy v. Ferguson,* 163 U.S. 537 (1896).

12. *Brown v. Board of Education of Topeka* (I) 3/4/47 U.S. 483 (1954).

13. Rae, *op. cit.,* p. 66.

14. John Scharr, "Equality of Opportunity and Beyond," in NOMOS IX: *Equality,* J. Rowland Pennock and John W. Chapman, eds. (New York: Atherton Press, 1967), pp. 231. See also Scharr, "Some Ways of Thinking About Equality," *Journal of Politics,* vol. 26 (November 1964), pp. 867–895.

15. Charles M. Haar and Daniel W. Fessler, *Fairness and Justice: Law in the Service of Equality* (New York: Simon and Schuster, 1986), p. 18.

16. Waldo, *op. cit.*

17. *Griggs v. Duke Power Company,* 401 U.S. 424 (1971). The U.S. Supreme Court in 1989 stepped considerably back from the Duke Power requirement that employees must demonstrate that the hiring requirements do not discriminate. In *Wards Grove Packing v. Antonio,* in a five-to-four decision, the U.S. Supreme Court now requires a plaintiff to prove employment discrimination. See *The New York Times* (June 7, 1989), pp. 1 and 11. *Wards Grove Packing v. Antonio,* Doc. No. 87-1387, 5 June 1989.

18. John Nalbandian, "The U.S. Supreme Court's 'Consensus' on Affirmative Action," vol. 49, *Public Administration Review* (January/February 1989), pp. 38–45.

19. *University of California Regents v. Bakke,* 438 U.S. 265 (1978).

20. Patricia W. Ingraham and David H. Rosenbloom, "The New Public Personnel and the New Public Service," vol. 49, *Public Administration Review* (March/April 1989), pp. 116–125.

21. Nalbandian, *op. cit.,* p. 44.

22. From *The New York Times* (January 24, 2989), pp. 1 and 12. See *City of Richmond v. Crosan,* 98 LE2d 976, 108 SCT 1010 (1989).

23. *Hawkins v. Town of Shaw,* 303 F. Supp. 1162, 1171 (N.D. MISS. 1969).

24. Haar and Fessler, *op. cit.,* p. 14.

25. *John Serrano, Jr., et al. v. Ivy Baker Priest,* 5 Cal. 3d584. See also Richard Lehane, *The Quest for Justice: The Politics of School Finance Reform* (New York: Longman, 1978).

26. *Green v. School Board,* 391 U.S. 430, 437–38 (1968).

27. *Swann v. Charlotte-Mecklenburg Board of Education,* 402 U.S. 1 (1971).

28. *Jenkins v. Missouri*, 593 F. Supp. 1485 (W. D. MO 1984).

29. *Liddell v. State of Missouri*, 731 F. 2D 1294, 1323 (8 Cir. 1984) and *Griffin v. School Board of Prince Edward County*, 377 U.S. 218, 233, 84 S. Cp. 1226, 1234, 12 L. Ed. 2d256 (1964).

30. *Jenkins v. State of Missouri*, 855 Fed. R. 8th Circuit 1297–1319.

31. *Jenkins v. State of Missouri*, 672 F. Supp. 412.

32. Arthur A. Bensen II. "The Liability of Missouri Suburban School Districts for the Unconstitutional Segregation of Neighboring Urban School Districts, University of Missouri at Kansas City Law Review*, vol. 53 (Spring 1985), pp. 349–375. Bensen's argument was counter to case law based on *Milliken v. Bradley*, 418 U.S. 717 (1974), in which the U.S. Supreme Court found that jurisdictional boundaries are not barriers to effective segregation, except desegregation under certain conditions. Bensen claims that the Kansas City case satisfies those conditions.

33. Jennifer L. Hochschild, *What's Fair? American Beliefs About Distributive Justice* (Cambridge, MA: Harvard University Press, 1981). Much of this page summarizes *What's Fair?*

34. *Ibid.*, p. 181.

35. See Robert L. Lineberry, *Equality and Urban Policy: The Distribution of Municipal Services* (Beverly Hills, CA: SAGE Publications, 1977) for a thorough review of the literature as well as a full presentation of the "decision rules" hypothesis.

36. *Idem.*

37. Leanna Stiefel and Robert Berne, "The Equity Effects of State School Finance Reform: A Methodological Critique and New Evidence," *Policy Sciences*, vol. 13 (February 1981), pp. 75–98.

38. Lineberry, *op. cit.*, and Bryan D. Jones, Saadia R. Greenberg, Clifford Kaufman, and Joseph Drew, "Service Delivery Rules and the Distribution of Local Government Services: Three Detroit Bureaucracies," *Journal of Politics*, vol. 40 (May 1978), pp. 333–368.

39. Christopher Lasch, *The Culture of Narcissism: American Life in an Age of Diminishing Expectations* (New York: Norton, 1978).

40. Frank Levy, *Dollars and Dreams: The Changing American Income Distribution* (New York: Russell Sage Foundation, 1987).

41. William Julius Wilson, *The Truly Disadvantaged: The Inner City, the Underclass and Public Policy* (Chicago: The University of Chicago Press, 1987).

42. Rodney E. Hero, "The Urban Service Delivery Literature: Some Questions and Considerations," *Policy*, vol. 18 (Summer 1986), pp. 659–677.

34

Gregory B. Lewis

LIFTING THE BAN ON GAYS IN THE CIVIL SERVICE: FEDERAL POLICY TOWARD GAY AND LESBIAN EMPLOYEES SINCE THE COLD WAR

The federal government has traditionally required that its employees be of good moral character, a standard that historically excluded known homosexuals. Regulations have long instructed the bureaucracy to deny examinations to applicants, refuse appointments to eligibles, and remove incumbent employees from their jobs for "criminal, infamous, dishonest, immoral, or notoriously disgraceful conduct" (U.S. Civil Service Commission, 1941, 37). We know of isolated dismissals for homosexuality long before the Cold War. (The Interior Department fired Walt Whitman in 1865 and the Post Office discharged the founder of the country's first homosexual political organization in 1925. See Katz, 1976).

It is not clear how actively civil servants attempted to prevent the employment of lesbians and gay men. By 1950, however, many in the Senate were impatient with "the false premise that what a Government employee did outside of the office on his own time, particularly if his actions did not involve his fellow employees or his work, was his own business" (U.S. Senate, 1950, 10). The problem began with a list of "admitted homosexuals and suspected perverts" sent by a Senate Appropriations subcommittee to the State Department in 1947 (Wherry, 1950, 1). In early 1950, a State Department official testified before that subcommittee that 91 "sex perverts" had been allowed to resign in the previous three years, and that some had subsequently been reemployed by other federal agencies. The Republicans launched blistering attacks on the Truman administration both for employing these people and for allowing them to resign without permanent blots on their records (although taboos on discussing homosexuality severely limited the publicity). The chairman of the Republican National Committee sent an open letter charging that "the sexual perverts who have infiltrated our Government in recent years . . . [were] perhaps as dangerous as the actual Communists" ("Perverts," 1950).

Republican Senators Wherry and Hill formed a subcommittee to study the issue and called in the experts—military investigators and the Washington, DC, morals squad. These experts "testified that moral perverts are bad national security risks . . . because of their susceptibility to blackmail on threat of exposure of their moral weakness" (Wherry, 1950, 2).

Wherry complained that there were inadequate safeguards to prevent reemployement of "moral weaklings" forced out of one agency, and that agencies made inadequate use of these lists of homosexuals. The Civil Service Commission responded with instructions to the agencies requiring them to submit detailed reasons for removals or resignations when those reasons could affect employees' suitability for reemployment so that the commission could prevent it if necessary. Commission Chairman Harry Mitchell also suggested that if local police departments would report all morals arrests with sufficient detail to the FBI, then the FBI could give the information to the Civil Service Commission. The commission could then pass the information on to relevant agencies to remove current employees, and the FBI could maintain the lists so that job applicants could be screened against them. Indeed, Blick testified that he was already furnishing names and fingerprints of all moral arrests to the FBI (Wherry, 1950, 9–10).

The Senate followed with a full-scale inquiry by the Hoey Committee to discover "the reasons why their [homosexuals'] employment by the Government is undesirable" (U.S. Senate, 1950, 1). The committee found several reasons. The behavior of homosexuals was criminal and immoral; they lacked emotional stability because "indulgence in acts of sex perversion weakens the moral fiber;" they frequently attempted to seduce normal people, especially the young and impressionable; and they had a "tendency to gather other perverts" around them (U.S. Senate, 1950, 4).

Probably most importantly, homosexuals were seen as security risks. On the one hand, their emotional instability and moral weakness made them "vulnerable to interrogation by a skilled questioner and they seldom refuse to talk about themselves" (U.S.

Senate, 1950, 5). (Bérubé [1990] notes that the skilled questioners had typically been military investigators in positions of authority over suspected homosexuals in the military.) On the other hand, "the pervert is easy prey to the blackmailer" (5). Although the Hoey Committee referred to rings of blackmailers exploiting homosexuals for money, it presented only one example of a homosexual betraying state secrets as a result of blackmail: Colonel Raedl in Austria in 1912. Military intelligence may have presented this as a clear case of homosexual blackmail, but most accounts of the Raedl case suggest that his motive was not blackmail but "money, which he needed to pay for a sybaritic homosexual life" (Buranelli and Buranelli, 1982, 261; see also Rowan, 1939; Dulles, 1963; Ind, 1963; Sith, 1975; and Maclean, 1978). The Hoey Committee also noted several other attempts by "Nazi and Communist agents . . . to obtain information from employees of our Government by threatening to expose their abnormal sex activities," but their language implies that these attempts were unsuccessful (U.S. Senate, 1950, 5).

The Hoey Committee was able to report marked progress since the Wherry-Hill inquiry in April 1950. Federal agencies had handled only 192 homosexual cases in the 38 months before the hearings, but they had processed 382 in the next seven months. Two-thirds of the early cases had involved international agencies (the State Department and Economic Cooperation Administration), but efforts to weed out perverts had spread well into domestic agencies after the Senate investigation. FBI checks had also prevented employment for 1700 homosexual applicants between January 1947 and August 1950 (U.S. Senate, 1950, 9).

Still, the Hoey Committee called on agencies to do more to eliminate homosexuals among current employees by aggressively investigating every reasonable complaint. Arrest records were the best starting point for investigations, but there had been inadequate liaison between police and the FBI; not until the Wherry-Hill inquiry had the Civil Service Commission learned the names of 457 homosexual federal employees arrested in the nation's capitol during the previous three years.

> Adequate procedures have now been established to correct this regrettable situation . . . The FBI [has] obtained all available police records in the District of Columbia of persons who had been charged with perverted sex offenses and this information was furnished promptly to the Civil Service Commission and the other agencies of Government. The FBI also began furnishing to the Civil Service Commission the criminal records of persons currently arrested by the police throughout the country on charges of sex perversion who were known to be Government employees. Upon receipt of that information the Civil Service Commission transmits the data to the employing agency and later checks up with the agency to determine what, if any, action has been taken in each case (U.S. Senate, 1950, 13).

In September 1946, the secretary of the navy had rejected a proposal to turn the navy's list of homosexuals over to the FBI and other government agencies (Bérubé, 1990, 264), but that decision was apparently taken out of military hands in 1950.

The use of arrest records was no small problem for gay men. In the postwar years, Bérubé (1990, 259) reports substantial increases in arrests of lesbians and, especially, gay men for "consensual sodomy, sexual perversion, . . . public indecency, patronizing a gay bar, touching in public, or wearing the clothing of the other gender." Washington police averaged 1,000 gay-related arrests per year in the early 1950s, and Philadelphia perhaps 1,200 arrests per year (D'Emilio, 1983a). A single jurisdiction within Los Angeles

County arrested 1,000 gay men a year in the early 1960s ("Consenting," 1966). In one large sample of gay men in the early 1970s, one-fourth had been arrested on sex-related charges (Weinberg and Williams, 1974, 185).

The situation for lesbian and gay employees worsened during the first 100 days of the Eisenhower administration. President Truman had instituted a loyalty program for federal employees in 1947. In 1951, he changed the standards for dismissal from "reasonable grounds for belief that the person is disloyal" (Executive Order 9835) to "reasonable doubt as to the loyalty of the person involved" (Executive Order 10241; see U.S. Civil Service Commision, 1952, 33). In 1953, Eisenhower ordered that the government could employ and retain employees only when "clearly consistent with the interests of national security" and for the first time listed sexual perversion as a condition demanding removal from the federal service (Executive Order 10450). Similar regulations applied to private sector employees needing security clearances. During the same period, state and local governments were passing similar regulations. Licensing boards restricted homosexuals from many occupations, and private employers banned homosexuals officially or unofficially. Overall, lesbians and gay men were officially barred from at least 20 percent of the nation's jobs (Bérubé, 1990, 269-270).

Why Did the Crackdown on Gays Occur?

The fall of Eastern Europe to the Soviet Union and of China to the Communists, the explosion of the Soviet atom bomb, and the conviction of Alger Hiss made Americans warier about their national security, but why did that focus so much attention on homosexuals? D'Emilio (1989) suggests a fear that homosexuals, like Communists, hid their true natures, allowing them to "infiltrate" government in a way other out-groups could not. (One right-wing columnist, cited by Johnson (1994-1995, 50), charged that "an all-powerful, supersecret inner circle of highly educated, socially highly placed sexual misfits in the State Department" controlled foreign policy. Homosexuals were also easier to catch than Communists (they comprised 54 of 66 State Department employees fired under the security regulations in 1950, 119 of 154 in 1951, and 134 of 204 in 1952 (Shilts, 1993, 106)) and were so unpopular that even the American Civil Liberties Union (ACLU) supported prohibitions on their employment.

The extremity of the language used to depict homosexuals suggests that more than national security was at stake, however. A 1950 White House staff memo stated that "the country is more concerned about the charges of homosexuals in the Government than about Communists" (D'Emilio, 1983b, 13). Johnson argues that publicity about its dismissals of homosexuals "rendered the State Department a dirty joke" and presents a New Yorker cartoon in which a job applicant assures a potential employer, "It's true, sir, that the State Department let me go, but that was solely because of incompetence" (1994-95, 47). The government fired many employees with little conceivable link to national security; the vast majority of dismissals of employees and rejections of applicants were on the basis of suitability rather than national security.

Johnson (1994-95, 46) argues that the ban on gay employees "reflected an underlying anxiety over the bureaucratization and urbanization of Washington, changes largely precipitated by the New Deal and World War II." The great increases in the size of the federal bureaucracy "offered a haven for deviants. . . . Like Communism itself, bureaucracy raised the specter of a face-less, gender-less, family-less welfare state. Homosexual civil servants were seen as the natural conclusion of this frightening trend" (51).

The dramatic social changes brought on by World War II helped build the gay community and increased the general society's perception of it (D'Emilio, 1983a; Bérubé, 1990). After the war, Americans had to deal with "deep anxieties . . . about the disruptive effects of World War II on family life, sexual mores, and gender norms" (Chauncey, 1993, 175). D'Emilio describes a new "politics of personal life tailored to restore a different form of domestic tranquillity": a generous GI Bill of Rights, federal home mortgages, and a propaganda campaign pressuring women out of the workforce, "and extolling the virtues of marriage and childrearing" (1989, 236).

The Role of the Civil Service Commission

The crackdown against homosexuals began in the Senate and was stoked by the political rhetoric of the 1952 election campaigns. The Civil Service Commission and the FBI expanded their efforts to purge homosexual employees in response to political demands, and the agencies dismissed gay employees when the pressure was high. When homosexual civil servants ceased to be a political issue, the commission stopped gathering information on gay dismissals leaving us with little information about the bureaucracy's continued response.

The public administration community cannot entirely escape responsibility for this period, however. No loud voices arose arguing that homosexuality had nothing to do with merit or neutral competence. Even those who attacked the loyalty-security programs had little to say about homosexuals (e.g., Brown, 1958; Bontecou, 1953). FBI Director J. Edgar Hoover played a leading role in justifying the crackdown and pursued homophile and gay liberation organizations for decades (perhaps in response to a fear that a small homophile magazine, One, would "out" him as a homosexual; see Shilts, 1993, 110).

Efforts to organize homosexuals to fight federal policy proved unsuccessful in the 1950s because of fear of the consequences (D'Emilio, 1983a, 62). A campaign began in the early 1960s after Frank Kameny, an astronomer with a Harvard Ph.D., lost a three-year court battle to retain his job with the U.S. Army Mapping Service. With Bruce Scott, he formed the Mattachine Society of Washington and launched efforts to meet with top government officials to discuss the employment ban (D'Emilio, 1983a, 154). The society argued that homosexuals were a minority group and that federal employment policies toward gays were equivalent to racial discrimination. Kameny testified before a congressional committee in August 1963, and the society picketed the White House repeatedly in the summer of 1965 (Johnson, 1994-95, 57, 59-60).

The Mattachine Society finally achieved a meeting with a committee from the Civil Service Commission in the fall of 1965, prompting the first full justification of the policy.[1] After the meeting, Commission Chairman John W. Macy, Jr., wrote to the Mattachine Society completely rejecting their contention that the exclusion of homosexuals constituted discrimination against an oppressed minority, and claiming that there was no such thing as a homosexual. Instead, there were only homosexual acts, and the attempt to define people with homosexual inclinations as a minority group was an attempt to excuse them from taking responsibility for their immoral actions (Macy, 1966).

Since the concern was with homosexual acts, the Civil Service Commission needed to investigate the acts in detail to determine whether the "deviate sexual behavior" was "isolated, intermittent or continuing . . . aggressive or passive," and to investigate as well a variety of aggravating and mitigating circumstances. They also sought to determine "the extent or effect of rehabilitative efforts, if any, and the admitted acceptance of , or preference for homosexual relations" (Macy, 1966, 44). Since commission policy seems to have been that *any* homosexual conduct disqualified an individual for federal employment, it is unclear why this level of detail was needed, but civil service investigators wanted to know names, dates, and locations of sexual contacts as well as the specific sex acts performed (Ridgeway, 1964).

According to Macy, employment of homosexuals impeded "the efficiency of the service" because of:

> the revulsion of other employees by homosexual conduct and consequent disruption of service efficiency, the apprehension caused other employees by homosexual advances, solicitations or assaults, the unavoidable subjection of the sexual deviate to erotic stimulation through on-the-job use of common toilet, shower, and living facilities, the offense to members of the public who are required to deal with a known or admitted sexual deviate to transact Government business, the hazard that the prestige and authority of a Government position will be used to foster homosexual activity, particularly among the youth, and the use of Government funds and authority in furtherance of conduct offensive both to the mores and the law of our society (Macy, 1966, 44).

As with the military's justification for its exclusionary policy, Macy did not contend that homosexuals lacked the competence to perform their work successfully. The threats to the efficiency of the service arose from the perceptions and prejudices of coworkers and the public (revulsion, apprehension, and offense). As gay employees cannot control those perceptions, the policy punishes them for others' prejudices. Macy's letter shows that he shared those prejudices and viewed homosexuals as uncontrollably driven by their perverted desires.

In an interview three years later, the Civil Service Commission's Director of Personnel Investigations admitted that homosexual employees were no less efficient than heterosexuals, but argued that since the public still viewed homosexuals as repugnant, the commission should continue to disqualify them "in order to retain public confidence" ("Government-created," 1969, 1742).

The Role of the Courts

Few homosexuals fought their dismissals in court in the 1950s; those who did had little success. The courts at that time adhered to what Rosenbloom and Carroll (1995) call the "doctrine of privilege." This doctrine states that since federal employment was not a right, the government could impose essentially any conditions it chose on that employment. The one relevant protection veterans had was that they could not be dismissed unless the dismissal promoted "the efficiency of the service." However, the courts generally showed great deference to administrators in determining what affected efficiency." In *Dew v. Halaby*, 317 F.2d 582 (DC Cir. 1963), cert. dismissed, 379 U.S. 951 (1964), an air traffic controller with veterans' preference was fired when evidence emerged that he had "committ[ed] at least four unnatural acts with males . . . when he was 18 or 19," eight years prior to his firing (*Dew*, 583). A psychiatric evaluation showed that Dew was now happily married with a child, was emotionally stable, did not have a "homosexuality personality disorder," and was performing successfully on his job. However, his appeals examiner concluded that to "require employees to work with persons who have committed acts that are repugnant to established and accepted standards of decency and morality can only have a disrupting effect upon the morals and efficiency of any organization" (*Dew*, 587). The appellate court saw nothing arbitrary and capricious in firing a competent employee because the civil service demanded "character as well as fitness" and his homosexual conduct, no matter how far in the past, showed a lack of character (*Dew*, 588).[2]

By the mid-1960s, many courts had begun consitutionalizing public employment cases (Rosenbloom and Carroll, 1995), a trend the *Harvard Law Review* calls a move from a "private sector" to an "individual rights" vision ("Developments," 1984). Gays were a beneficiary of this trend. When Mattachine Society cofounder and federal job applicant Bruce Scott refused to answer unspecified evidence that he was a homosexual, claiming his sexual orientation was irrelevant to his job performance, the Civil Service Commission disqualified him from federal employment based on "immoral conduct." In *Scott v. Macy*, 349 F.2d 192 (DC Cir. 1965), the Washington DC court of appeals ruled that the immoral conduct charge stigmatized Scott by disqualifying him from federal employment and jeopardizing his chance of finding employment elsewhere. This damaged his liberty interests and required the government to make a more compelling case for its actions. The court ruled for Scott, with Judge Bazelon arguing that the Civil Service Commission had to state how the alleged immoral conduct was "related to 'occupational competence or fitness'" (*Scott*, 184–185). However, the concurring opinion only called for greater specification of the immoral conduct charge, and future Chief Justice Warren Burger dissented, arguing that Congress and the executive branch had already decided that homosexual conduct established unsuitability—the Civil Service Commission need not prove it in each case. While the case pointed the direction for the future, it provided a very weak precedent.

Four years later, the Washington DC court of appeals decided the landmark case, *Norton v. Macy*, 417 F.2d 1161 (DC Cir. 1969). DC morals squad officers arrested Norton, a NASA budget analyst, for picking up another man in a gay cruising area. Police called the NASA security chief to secretly monitor the lengthy police interrogations, then released Norton to several more hours of questioning at NASA headquarters. Although Norton denied being a homosexual, NASA fired him.

In an opinion written by Judge Bazelon, the court ruled that Norton's sexual conduct was largely irrelevant because "the notion that it could be an appropriate function of the federal bureaucracy to enforce the majority's conventional code of conduct in the private lives of its employees is at war with elementary concepts of liberty, privacy, and diversity" (*Norton*, 1165). To justify his dismissal, the government must be able to "demonstrate some 'rational basis' for its conclusions that a discharge 'will promote the efficiency of the service'" (1164).

This came to be known as the "rational nexus" text for determining whether an employee could be dismissed for homosexual or other immoral conduct. Although it was a massive step forward, it did not provide unqualified support for gay employment rights. The *Norton* decision went to great lengths to state that homosexual conduct might be grounds for dismissal in certain circumstances—blackmail risk, personal instability, offensive overtures, or notorious conduct. "Whether or not such potential consequences would justify removal, they are at least broadly relevant to 'the efficiency of the service'" (*Norton*, 1166).

In this case, however, Norton was a competent employee, there were no security concerns, his coworkers were unaware of his conduct, and he did not work with the public. The only justification his supervisor gave for firing Norton was that a repeat episode might "turn out to be embarrassing to the agency" (*Norton*, 1167). Possible embarrassment was not sufficient justification, however. "A reviewing court must at least be able to discern some reasonably foreseeable, specific connection between an employee's potentially embarrassing conduct and the efficiency of the service" (*Norton*, 1167).

In the short run, the *Norton* decision had little apparent impact on the Civil Service Commission or the courts. Both continued to find a rational nexus between homosexual conduct and the efficiency of the service based on the weakest evidence. In *Vigil v. Post Office Department*, 406 F.2d 921 (10th Cir. 1969), the court upheld the firing of an assistant janitor, ignoring the *Norton* decision because Vigil had been convicted while Norton had not. In *Schlegel v. United States*, 416 F.2d 1372 (Ct. Cl. 1969), the court found the impact of homosexuality on the efficiency of the service to be self-evident: "Any schoolboy knows that a homosexual act is immoral, indecent, lewd, and obscene. . . . If activities of this kind are allowed to be practiced in a government department, it is inevitable that the efficiency of the service will in time be adversely affected" (*Schlegel*, 1378). The concurring opinion launched an even sharper attack on the notion that potential embarrassment to the agency should not be grounds for dismissal: "In this context, the word 'embarrassment' may appear to some the understatement of 1969. . . . The presence of a known homosexual in an executive agency will bring the agency into hatred, ridicule, and contempt, to the grave detriment of its ability to perform its mission" (*Schlegel*, 1382).

The Courts and the Civil Service Commission

In the early 1970s, changing attitudes began to make the Civil Service Commission's exclusion of homosexuals less acceptable. In the wake of the sexual revolution, the Stonewall riots, and the gay liberation movement, more gays were open about their sexuality; homosexuality was no longer a taboo topic that could be dismissed without discussion. The *Washington Post* criticized the policy of the Civil Service Commission, arguing that if homosexuals possessed the necessary skills and "if they conduct themselves like other employees with reasonable circumspection and decorum, their private sexual behavior is their own business" ("Fairness," 1971). A gay rights plank was debated before the 1972 Democratic National Convention, with one speaker attacking injustices against gays, such as the $12 million the Civil Service Commission spent annually investigating gay civil servants (Shilts, 1993, 169).

The commission reluctantly recognized the change in the moral climate of the nation. In its 1971 annual report, it bemoaned "the passing of the day when 'living in sin' meant just that to most people," and regretted a recent set of court cases that limited its ability to consider the morality of the private lives of both homosexuals and heterosexuals. "This does not mean that indiscreet, promiscuous, notorious, criminal, or illegal conduct will not support disciplinary actions. It will and does" (U.S. Civil Service Commission, 1972, 49). The report indicated that the courts were upholding the principle that the government could not fire employees for being gay, but it also emphasized circumstances that would justify not hiring them.

The definitive change in commission policy came as the result of a class action suit brought in San Francisco (*Society for Individual Rights, Inc. v. Hampton*, 63 F.R.D. 399 [1973]). A supply clerk, fired because his army discharge papers revealed he was gay, brought suit against the government's blanket exclusion of homosexuals. The court found that the only reason for the dismissal was "the [commission's] view that the employment of such persons will bring the government service into "public contempt'" (400). The *Norton* decision had already found that ground to be arbitrary and capricious, and the court required the commission to demonstrate a rational connection between homosexual conduct and the efficiency of the service. "The Commission has not met—indeed, it has not even tried to meet—this standard" (*Society for Individual Rights, Inc.*, 401). The court granted class action relief because this was the only way to prohibit the commission "from continuing to ignore the plain holding of *Norton*" (401). It therefore ordered the commission to "forthwith cease excluding or discharging from government service any homosexual person whom the Commission would deem unfit for government employment solely because the employment of such a person in the government service might bring that service into contempt" (*Society for Individual Rights, Inc.*, 402).

On December 21, 1973, the commission issued a bulletin to all agencies stating that they could not "find a person unsuitable for Federal employment merely because that person is a homosexual," but that they could dismiss or refuse to hire a person whose "homosexual conduct affects job fitness—excluding from such considerations, however, unsubstantiated conclusions concerning possible embarrassment to the Federal service." On July 3, 1975, a press release from the Civil Service Commission announced that a "significant change from past policy—resulting from court decisions and injunction [sic]—provides for applying the same standard in evaluating sexual conduct, whether heterosexual or homosexual." It continued to stress, however, that certain circumstances might justify dismissing a homosexual. The policy did not apply to the FBI or the intelligence agencies.

A major case decided the next year, however, suggested the limits of the Norton decision and the commission's policy change (*Singer v. U.S. Civil Service Commission*, 429 U.S. 1034 [1977]). Singer, a gay clerk-typist with the Seattle EEOC, was fired in 1972 for "flaunting" his homosexuality by being active in the gay rights movement, kissing a man in public, and applying for a marriage license. The Civil Service Commission upheld the firing because, among other reasons, "You have flaunted and broadcast your homosexual activities . . . [and] advocated for a socially repugnant concept" (*Singer*, 250).

The appellate court found that neither the *Norton* nor the *Society of Individual Rights, Inc.* decisions prevented the use of homosexual conduct as a basis for dismissal in all cases. Applying a balancing test, the court ruled that "the interest of the Government as an employer 'in promoting the efficiency of the service' outweighed the interest of its employee in exercising his First Amendment Rights through publicly flaunting and broadcasting his homosexuality" (*Singer*, 256). The Supreme Court vacated the decision the following year but, because the government then dropped the case, the Court did not issue a decision explaining its logic. Subsequent cases suggest that the free speech rights of gay public employees are protected (e.g., *Van Ooteghem v. Gray*, 628 F.2d 488 [5th Cir. 1980], cert. denied, 455 U.S. 909 [1982]).

Action by Gay and Employee Groups

Given this level of protection, the next focus was on obtaining an executive order prohibiting discrimination on the grounds of sexual preference or orientation. In December 1979, Carter aide Anne Wexler told gay leaders that such an executive order was "under active consideration" but, according to Shilts (1993, 333), Wexler and domestic policy advisor Stuart Eisenstadt then recommended against it as politically unwise. No executive order was issued.

Instead, Eisenstadt approached Alan Campbell, the director of the U.S. Office of Personnel Management, about issuing a memorandum in place of an executive order (Campbell, 1993). Campbell's memo was essentially a gloss on 5 U.S.C. §2302(b)(10) (prohibited personnel practice 10),which prohibits federal employees from discriminating for or against other employees or applicants "on the basis of conduct which does not adversely affect either the employee's own job performance or the performance of others." According to Campbell's memo, this meant that "applicants and employees are to be protected against inquiries into, or actions based upon, non-job-related conduct, such as religious, community or social affiliations, or sexual orientation" (Campbell, 1980). Theoretically, gay employees could fight against an adverse action that they felt was discriminatory by claiming it was a prohibited personnel practice. In practice, few cases have raised this issue.

Pressure continues for an executive order prohibiting discrimination on the basis of sexual orientation in federal employment. In the 1984 presidential campaign, several Democratic candidates discussed such an order favorably (Shilts, 1993, 453). In 1992, Vice President Quayle stated that "that Bush-Quayle administration has a good record in implementing nondiscrimination against gays and lesbians" (Freeland, 1992, A19). Many expected President Clinton to issue an executive order on nondiscrimination in the civil service. Indeed, the first page of briefing books Clinton's cabinet appointees received asked them to consider what steps they would take to protect gay and lesbian employees in their agencies from discrimination (Hattoy, 1993). The debacle of the gays in the military issue, however, indicated the political danger of an executive order.

In November 1993, openly gay congressman Barney Frank wrote to OPM Director James King requesting both clarification on "federal laws and personnel procedures regarding discrimination based on sexual orientation," and a formal notification to all federal agencies about "the state of these rules and procedures." Instead, OPM Director King responded in a letter to Frank. Rather than issuing guidance to other agencies, King states, "I like to view OPM as a model agency and see my role as working with all of our employees to assure that we conduct ourselves in such a way that other agencies choose to adopt our methods of operation" (King, 1994). He reiterated the Campbell memo, noting that "OPM has long taken the position that [prohibited personnel practice 10] applies directly to discrimination on the basis of sexual orientation." Gay victims of discrimination could appeal through the Merit Systems Protection Board or file a grievance but could not file a complaint through the Equal Employment Opportunity Commission. Though the letter provides guidance to the courts that federal policy prohibits discrimination on the basis of sexual orientation, it was not a stirring condemnation of the practice.

Although a more explicit, government-wide nondiscrimination policy may still be years in the future, federal employee groups have been pushing for such a policy on an agency-by-agency basis. In 1988, the negotiations of the National Treasury Employees Union (NTEU) with the Department of Health and Human Services allowed union members to bring grievances charging discrimination based on sexual orientation. In 1990, the American Federation of Government Employees (AFGE) negotiated a similar agreement with the Department of Housing and Urban Development, which also extended certain benefits to domestic partners of gay and lesbian employees. Department secretary Jack Kemp refused to sign the agreement arguing that the nondiscrimination policy exceeded federal law, but the Federal Labor Relations Authority (FLRA) upheld the agreement, and a federal court upheld the FLRA on appeal. Unions have also extended some protections to gay and lesbian employees in the Internal Revenue Service, the Bureau of Alcohol, Tobacco, and Firearms, the U.S. Customs Service, and the Pension Benefit Guaranty Corporation (Freeland, 1992, A19).

Partly as a result of employee pressure and partly due to sympathetic managers and department heads, several agencies now list sexual orientation in their nondiscrimination policies. These agencies include: the Department of Agriculture, the Bonneville Power Administration, the General Services Administration, Housing and Urban Development, the National Academy of Sciences, the Department of State, the Department of Transportation, the U.S. Information Agency, the White House, the Departments of Justice, Interior, and Commerce, the international Trade Commission, the Small Business Administration, Merit Systems Protection Board, and some regions of the Forest Service and the Park Service. Negotiations are ongoing in several agencies and the situation is changing rapidly. In addition, at least 18 states have policies protecting gay and lesbian employees in state and local government including: California, Connecticut, Hawaii, Illinois, Louisiana, Maine, Maryland, Massachusetts, Michigan, New Jersey, New Mexico, New York, Ohio, Pennsylvania, Rhode Island, Vermont, Washington, and Wisconsin.

CONCLUSION: WHERE DO WE STAND? WHAT'S AHEAD?

At the national level, gay men and lesbians have fared poorly when their employment rights have become political issues. When the Republicans attacked the Democrats for being soft on Communism in the 1950s, homosexuals became an easy target for both parties because "sex perverts" were so widely despised that not even the American Civil Liberties Union would stand up for them. The politicians strengthened laws and pushed the bureaucracy to enforce them, and the bureaucratic structure—especially the Civil Service Commission and the FBI—continued to enforce the exclusion of gay employees long after the political issue had died down.

Likewise, when the military's ban on gay service members became a political issue in 1993, gays were severely routed by conservative forces. This occurred despite polls suggesting that the issue would be far less controversial than it proved to be. Four Gallup polls from 1977 through 1989, for instance, showed approval for hiring gays into the armed forces rising steadily from 51 to 60 percent. Polls in 1992 generally showed a plurality of the public in favor of lifting the ban. However, polls also showed that large majorities consider homosexual acts to be immoral and that the public is less willing to allow gay people to have homosexual sex than to have equal employment rights. In that context, political support for gay employment rights is likely to be tepid and theoretical, while opposition can be both vocal and fanatic.

Gay and lesbian federal employees have had more success within the court system. While the judiciary was reluctant to infringe on administrative discretion in hiring and firing decisions in the 1950s and 1960s, their decision that administrators needed to show a rational connection between homosexual conduct and the efficiently of the service effectively ended the blanket exclusion of gays from the civil service. To date, however, no court has ruled that homosexuality or homosexual conduct is necessarily irrelevant to employment decisions. Even the key pro-gay cases (*Norton* and *Society for Individual Rights, Inc.*) have emphasized that there may be legitimate reasons for denying employment to gay men and lesbians, Most courts continue to uphold the exclusion of gays from the military and the denial of security clearances for homosexuals (or at least the courts uphold practices that make it more difficult for gays to achieve them). The Supreme Court has clearly ruled that there is no fundamental right to homosexual sodomy (*Bowers v. Hardwick*, 478 U.S. 186 [1987]). The occasional court has ruled that gays are a suspect or quasi-suspect class (*Watkins v. U.S. Army*, 875 F.2d 699 [9th Cir. 1988]; *High Tech Gays v. Defense Industrial Security Clearance Office*, 895 F.2d 563 [9th Cir. 1990]) and that laws or regulations having an adverse impact on them require heightened scrutiny. Those decisions have been quickly overturned, however. The Court's recent decision overturning Colorado's Amendment Two (*Romer v. Evans*, 116 S. Ct. 1620 [1996]) creates more hope for equal protection cases, but gay legal activists remain skeptical about how sympathetic the Court is to gay causes (Keen, 1996).[3]

Recent progress has come about largely through the bureaucracy. The Civil Service Commission fought implementation of the *Norton* decision for years, but its change in regulations in response to *Society for Individual Rights, Inc. v. Hampton* and OPM Director Campbell's 1980 memo probably provide the strongest protection that most gay federal employees enjoy. Those with stronger protections have obtained them largely through labor contracts or nondiscrimination policies for single agencies or single divisions within agencies. These protections have generally arisen out of negotiations between unions or gay employee groups and federal bureaucrats. (Civil servants are significantly more likely than the general public to support civil rights for gays and lesbians and less likely to feel that homosexual acts are always wrong; see Lewis, 1990). Department heads appointed by President Bush generally opposed the policy changes, while some Clinton appointees have productively supported them. These piecemeal, agency-by-agency negotiations and policy changes may eventually provide a strong enough framework, making a presidential executive order prohibiting discrimination on the basis of sexual orientation on a government-wide basis seem a trivial policy change not worth fighting against. In the absence of clear statutory protection for gay employees, these agreements plus a general belief among federal employees that discrimination against lesbians and gay men is wrong are probably the strongest protection.

Notes

1. I found this letter in the OMP library card catalog under "Homosexuality," but it was clear from the way it was marked that it had originally been filed under "Moral Perverts."
2. The Supreme Court agreed to hear the appeal, which suggested that there were limits to the government's power to fire homosexuals, and the government dropped its case, making this the first victory of its sort. However, the Court did not clarify what employment rights homosexuals had.
3. The Court remains headed by a man who once argued that whether gay students should be allowed to organize is "akin to whether those suffering from measles have a constitutional right, in violation of quarantine regulations, to associate together and with others who do no presently have measles, in order to urge the repeal of a state law providing that measles sufferers be quarantined" (*Gay Lib v. University of Missouri*, 558 F.2d 848 [8th Cir. 1977], cert. denied, 434 U.S. 1080 [1978], 1084).

References

Bérubé, Allan (1990). *Coming Out Under Fire: The History of Gay Men and Women in World War II.* New York: Free Press.

Bérubé, Allan, and John D'Emilio (1984). "The Military and Lesbians during the McCarthy Years." *Signs* 9 (Summer): 759–785.

Bontecou, Eleanor (1953). *The Federal Loyalty-Security Program.* Ithaca, NY: Cornell University Press.

Brown, Ralph S., Jr. (1958). *Loyalty and Security: Employment Tests in the United States.* New Haven: Yale University Press.

Buranelli, Vincent, and Nan Buranelli (1982). *Spy/Counterspy: An Encyclopedia of Espionage.* New York: McGraw-Hill.

Campbell, Alan K. (1980). "Memorandum: Policy Statement on Discrimination on the Basis of Conduct Which Does Not Adversely Affect the Performance of Employees or Applicants for Employment." 12 May.

_____. (1993). Telephone interview, 17 June.

Chauncey, George, Jr. (1993). "The Postwar Sex Crime Panic." In William Graebner, ed., *True Stories from the American Past.* New York: McGraw-Hill, 160–178.

"The Consenting Adult Homosexual and the Law: An Empirical Analysis of Enforcement and Administration in Los Angeles" (1966). *UCLA Law Review* 13: 643–832.

D'Emilio, John (1983a). *Sexual Politics, Sexual Communities: The Making of a Homosexual Minority in the United States, 1940–1970.* Chicago: University of Chicago Press.

————. (1983b). "The Evolution and Impact of Federal Antihomosexual Policies during the 1950s." Unpublished manuscript.

————. (1989). "The Homosexual Menace: The Politics of Sexuality in Cold War America." In Kathy Peiss and Christina Simmons, eds., *Passion and Power: Sexuality in History.* Philadelphia, PA: Temple University Press, 226–240.

"Developments in the Law: Public Employment" (1984). *Harvard Law Review* 97: 1611–1900.

Dulles, Allen (1963). *The Craft of Intelligence.* New York: Harper & Row.

Executive Order 9835, 12 Fed. Reg. 1935 (1947).

Executive Order 10241, 16 Fed. Reg. 3690 (1951).

Executive Order 10450 "Security Requirements for Government Employment." (1953)

"Fairness for Homosexuals." (1971). *Washington Post,* 2 February, A14.

Frank, Barney (1993). Letter to OPM Director James King, 29 November.

Freedland, Jonathan (1992). "Agencies Balk at Gay Rights Policy: Park Service Limits Employment Protection to San Francisco Region." *Washington Post,* 18 September, A19.

"Government-created Employment Disabilities of the Homosexual" (1969). *Harvard Law Review* 82: 1738–1751.

Hattoy, Robert (1993). Speech to Federal GLOBE, Washington, DC, 6 January.

Ind, Colonel Alison (1963). *A Short History of Espionage.* New York: David McKay.

Johnson, David K. (1994–1995). "Homosexual Citizens: Washington's Gay Community Confronts the Civil Service." *Washington History* 6 (Fall/Winter): 44–63.

Kameny, Frank (1993). Personal interview, 17 August.

Katz, Jonathon (1976). *Gay American History: Lesbians and Gay Men in the U.S.A.* New York: Harper & Row.

Keen, Lisa (1996). "Gay Legal Activists Still Wary of Supreme Court: Lawyers Admit the Court's 'Favorable Record' Is Not Long." *The Washington Blade* 27 (August 2): 1, 21.

King, James B. (1994). Letter to Congressman Barney Frank, 26 January.

Lewis, Gregory B. (1990). "In Search of the Machiavellian Milquetoasts: Comparing Attitudes of Bureaucrats and Ordinary People." *Public Administration Review* 50 (2): 220–227.

Maclean, Fitzroy (1978). *Take Nine Spies.* New York: Atheneum.

Macy, John W., Jr. (1966). "The Issue of Homosexuality and Government Employment." Department of State Newsletter (April): 44–45.

"Perverts Called National Peril" (1950). *New York Times,* 19 April.

Ridgeway, James (1964). "The Snoops: Private Lives and Public Service." *New Republic* (December 19): 13–18.

Rosenbloom, David H., and James D. Carroll (1995). "Public Personnel Administration and Law." In Jack Rabin, Thomas Vocino, W. Bartley Hildreth, and Gerald J. Miller, eds., *Handbook of Public Personnel Administration.* New York: Marcel Dekker, 71–113.

Rowan, Richard Wilmer (1939). *The Story of the Secret Service.* Garden City, NY: Garden City Publishing Co., Inc.

Shilts, Randy (1993). *Conduct Unbecoming: Gays & Lesbians in the U.S. Military.* New York: St. Martin's Press.

Sith, Ronald (1975). *Encyclopedia of Espionage.* London: New English Library.

U.S. Civil Service Commission (1941). *Civil Service Act, Rules, Statutes, Executive Orders, and Regulations.* Washington, DC: U.S. Government Printing Office.

————. (1952). *68th Annual Report.* Washington, DC: U.S. Government Printing Office.

————. (1972). *A Pace-Setting Year for Personnel Management: 88th Annual Report.* Washington, DC: U.S. Government Printing Office.

_____. (1973). Mandate for Merit: 1972 Annual Report. Washington D.C.: U.S. Government Printing Office

_____. (1975). Press Release. 3 July.

U.S. General Accounting Office (1974). *Personnel Security Investigations: Inconsistent Standards and Procedures.* B-132376. Washington, DC: U.S. Government Printing Office.

U.S. Navy (1957). "Report of the Board Appointed to Prepare and Submit Recommendations to the Secretary of the Navy for the Revision of Policies, Procedures and Directive Dealing with Homosexuals, 21 December 1956-15 March 1957." (The Crittenden Report).

U.S. Senate (1950). Committee on Expenditures in the Executive Departments. Subcommittee on Investigations. *Employment of Homosexuals and Other Sex Perverts in Government.* 81st Cong., 2d sess. Document No. 241. Washington, DC: U.S. Government Printing Office.

Weinberg, Martin S. and Colin J. Williams (1974). *Male Homosexuals: Their Problems and Adaptations.* New York: Oxford University Press.

Wherry, Kenneth S. (1950). Report of the Investigations of the Junior Senator of Nebraska, A Member of the Subcommittee Appointed by the Subcommittee on Appropriations for the District of Columbia, on the Infiltration of Subversives and Moral Perverts into the Executive Branch of the United States Government. 81st Cong., 2d sess. Washington, DC: U.S. Government Printing Office.

35

James D. Slack

FROM AFFIRMATIVE ACTION TO FULL SPECTRUM DIVERSITY IN THE AMERICAN WORKPLACE

SHIFTING THE ORGANIZATIONAL PARADIGM

More so than any other cultural attribute, diversity is the cornerstone of the American experience. There are currently over 50 distinctive ethnic groups in the U.S. All strive to acquire economic and political power.

Perhaps because it is so central to our common experience, diversity has also been the focal point of some of our most perplexing challenges over the past two centuries. The crux of the matter is really two-fold. On the one hand, certain groups have never been accepted fully due to the antecedents of prejudice and ignorance. And consequently, while all groups have had to struggle to be included within the political mainstream of American life, some groups have had to wage more costly battles than others. Sadly, some battles remain unwon.

On the other hand, there remains a cultural desire to regard everyone as "Americans," despite the persistence of ignorance and prejudice. But the fact that diversity ultimately means a recognition of distinctiveness can easily convert the hope of commonality into a feeling of unease among many people within the mainstream. Not surprisingly, the uneasiness felt about diversity seems to transcend racial, ethnic and gender differences among those who are already in the mainstream. For some, there is a tendency to resent those who rebuff the invitation to "be like us." For others, there is a likelihood to suspect people who press to maintain a distinct and separate ethnic, linguistic, religious or lifestyle identity. Moreover, philosophical tensions always exist between the American demand for its *raison d'etre*, individualism, and the American need for the concomitant value of equality that is fundamental to ensuring individual rights.

The quandary over diversity has led government to take many and often contradictory actions, including conducting armed conflict during the 1860s and imposing Jim Crow laws and implementing "separate but equal" doctrines in the decades that followed. In perhaps more rational times we have experimented with a wide array of employment strategies, ranging from patronage practices to equal employment opportunity policies, designed with the dual hope of opening further the doors of opportunity to members of additional, underutilized groups while ensuring the right of every individual, regardless of group identification, to walk through those same doors. During the last part of the twentieth century, we have relied heavily on affirmative action principles in our efforts to accomplish this two-fold objective.

This article addresses the need to enhance both group diversity and individualism in the workplace by shifting attention away from affirmative action principles and strategies, as they are commonly implemented, and focusing more on securing a comprehensive, or full spectrum version of diversity in the workplace. To do so, an accompanying shift in organizational paradigm must also occur. By affirmative action, I mean the development and implementation of reactive workplace practices designed to redress the adverse ramifications of past discrimination against people holding protected-class status: women, African Americans, Hispanic Americans, Asian Americans, Native Americans, and Pacific Islanders. By full spectrum diversity, I mean having work settings reflect proactively the gender, cultural and ethnic complexity of each local community as well as the American society.

AFFIRMATIVE ACTION AND CONSTRAINTS ON DIVERSITY

Despite much evidence about the political (Riccucci, 1997) and employment (Hale, 1996; Naff, 1997) limitations of affirmative action, it remains true that members of protected groups have benefitted from such policies over the past several decades. In comparison to just a generation ago, there are more minorities (Murray & Terry, 1994; Page, 1994) and women (Guy, 1993; Kelly, Guy & Bayes, 1991) in government now, although still too few are at the upper echelons of management. Some agencies are less successful than others in accomplishing affirmative action outcomes (Kellough, 1989) but there is a growing number of public sector organizations which excel in the processes of including more members of protected groups in the work force (Chamber & Riccucci, 1997). Certainly American society, and its workplace, has benefitted greatly from the implementation of affirmative action strategies in the public and private sectors.

Yet the outcomes of current affirmative action policies is a product of externally-driven forces. For many workplace managers, the primary incentives to develop and implement affirmative action plans are three-fold: compliance with federal laws, fear of adverse court rulings in response to non-compliant practices, and concern over potential political consequences within the outside community or the larger organizational structure for either defiant non-compliance or zealous over-compliance with the law. The philosophical rationale behind affirmative action, that it is a means to realize a truly representative bureaucracy, as well as the organizational rationale, that a representative bureaucracy is good for the health and effectiveness of the organization, all become lost to the intergovernmental, legal and political dimensions of the process. Therefore, current affirmative action practices offer workplace managers few internally-based, organizational incentives to pursue work force diversity actively and aggressively.

Three consequences tend to follow from this situation. First, exclusively focusing on some groups which historically have experienced workplace discrimination, current affirmative action strategies limit the utilization of the vast, full spectrum of American diversity. In terms of the workplace diversity equation, therefore, externally-driven factors designate some groups as irrelevant, while earmarking others as being obstructive. The vast majority of cultural and ethnic groups in America do not enjoy protected-class status and, therefore, are excluded from diversity calculations. One side-effect is that people in these groups can fall prey to subtle and unchecked discrimination in employment decisions. Gay Americans also remain unprotected by federal affirmative action guidelines. They, too, are deemed irrelevant to diversity considerations and can be discriminated against legally in many work settings.

Moreover, current affirmative action policies prevent Europeans Americans and Canadian Americans from contributing in a positive way to the workplace diversity equation. The same is true of men who, in comparison to women, are not regarded as meaningful weights in that equation. As a result of externally-driven forces, current affirmative action programs also deem religious and linguistic diversity as being irrelevant to the American workplace composition.

Second, current affirmative action policies also have a tendency to involve a substantial degree of stereotyping, or oversimplification, of the many attributes of diversity. Consequently, externally-driven factors not only prevent a recognition of the full spectrum of diversity in society, but they also lend credence to ignoring the complete diversity within individuals who are members of protected groups. Complex cultural and ethnic considerations are melted down and poured into denotative boxes on pre-employment documents. Complex individual identities are easily assigned to these oversimplified categories in the minds of employers and coworkers alike. One is "thought of" as being primarily African American, overriding perhaps more important personal experiences, religious beliefs and family attributes. One is "viewed" simply as being Latino, regardless of national and cultural origin, or as Native American without thought to tribal ancestry or geographical identity.

Third, there is the omnipresent possibility that, throughout the hiring and promotion processes within each workplace, an artificial tension will be created between the value of merit and the value of diversity. The artificial tension tends to send misleading and confusing signals to well-intentioned workplace managers. This phenomenon, too, is the result of externally-driven forces because it is the seemingly contradictory nature of federal guidelines and court decisions which permits the tension to emerge in the first place. On the one hand, equal employment opportunity (EEO) guidelines require employers to remain color- and gender-blind in making hiring and promotion decision. Managers are supposed to take into consideration only the issues of merit and performance. Yet current affirmative action guidelines call for color- and gender-consciousness. Employers are required to take into consideration the oversimplified categories of human characteristics, or ethnic and cultural stereotypes, as discussed above. The dilemma is that workplace managers must comply simultaneously with both sets of guidelines, representing two distinct sets of values.

In this quagmire, managers can conclude mistakenly that they must either be "blind but to merit" or be "conscious only of color and gender." For some workplace managers, implementation of affirmative action strategies can become the overriding goal in the hiring and promotion processes rather than simply one of several important objectives in the workplace equation. For other managers, the fact that it is far too easy to pit unnecessarily the value of merit against the value of diversity is welcome ammunition. They use it to underscore "tokenism" in the selection and promotion processes. For the vast majority of well-intentioned managers, perceived or real pressures to give priority to the value of affirmative action can leave a foul taste in the mouth of merit. Yet this group of professionals also tends to want to distance itself from bigot-driven arguments about tokenism. Unfortunately, this conflict can also lead to a vastly diminished self-view for some members of protected-groups, even though the overwhelming majority are hired and promoted under the principle of merit.

TOWARD FULL SPECTRUM DIVERSITY

Certainly the solution of the dilemma of enhancing workplace diversity does not lie in dismantling affirmative action results; it may not even lie in the dismantling of affirmative action programs. The original intent of affirmative action, that of establishing a truly representative bureaucracy, must remain a sacred principle to the public service regardless of what workplace strategies are adopted.

It is for this one common mission, the realization of a representative bureaucracy, that the concept of affirmative action becomes the antecedent to the concept of full spectrum diversity. The objective of full spectrum diversity, however, is more than a singular focus on protecting members of selected groups which have a long and painful history of being victims of workplace discrimination. In addition, a focus on full spectrum diversity ensures that contributions of members of all groups, however they define themselves, are viewed as having important value in the human resource equation.

A shift in organizational paradigm is required to accomplish the transition from affirmative action to full spectrum diversity. We must move from a focus that reacts primarily to externally-driven factors to one that is more proactive and inward-looking about shaping the future of the organization.

Managers who think primarily in terms of externally-driven factors—compliance with federal guidelines, avoidance of court mandates, and accommodation to local political pressures—fall prey to ignoring other diversity considerations and stereotyping members of protected groups. In far too many instances, they also find themselves pitting the value of merit against the value of diversity.

In order to accomplish full spectrum diversity in the workplace, and to avoid the pitfalls of current affirmative action practices, managers need to think selfishly about what is best for their organizations and even their own careers. They need to consider an internally-based rationale for taking proactive measures to enhance the mix of human resources. From this perspective, diversity means bringing qualified professionals to the organization's "table" because these people not only possess prerequisite technical knowledge and work-related expertise, but they also have unique backgrounds and intangible insights which are quintessential to addressing organizational needs and solving public problems.

The greater numbers of diverse people with technical merit at this table, the more likely the organization will be successful in accomplishing its mission and be effective in responding to the citizenry. Consequently, there is a greater chance that the manager will be successful in her own career. Rather than being responsive to externalities, therefore, the manager has internally-based incentives to seek out independently and aggressively a work force characterized by full spectrum diversity. The side-effects of doing so can also be enormously beneficial to the health and well-being of all employees. Not only will pursuing such a strategy actually accomplish the goals of current federal affirmative action regulations, the participation of nonprotected group members will also become truly meaningful in the workplace diversity equation.

In summary, the concepts of affirmative action and full spectrum diversity are similar in that both share the goal of building a representative bureaucracy. As outlined in Figure 35.1, however, there are several substantive and procedural differences between the practice of affirmative action in many organizations and an effort to realize full spectrum of diversity in any workplace. Affirmative action strategies represent a historically reactive process that is designed to correct the consequences of past discrimination. Full spectrum diversity, on the other hand, entails a more proactive outlook. It attempts to gauge and assess the nature and composition of the current work force with a constant eye toward changes which might occur in the community.

Only specific groups are protected in the case of affirmative action, whereas full spectrum diversity considers all groups to be important in the workplace equation.

FIGURE 35.1   *Differences Between Full Spectrum Diversity and Affirmative Action*

Full Spectrum Diversity	Affirmative Action
• Proactive	• Reactive
• Concern about all groups in the community, including members of underutilized groups	• Concern for members of underutilized groups
• Recognition of diversity within the individual	• Simplification and stereotyping
• Value of merit and the value of diversity: competitive	• Value of merit and the value of diversity: noncompetitive
• Internally-driven factors	• Externally-driven factors

While affirmative action tends to result in the stereotyping of individuals, a concern for full spectrum diversity encourages the realization that each individual is a complex, diverse entity who cannot be placed into over-simplified categories. Whereas a concern for affirmative action sometimes results in an artificial conflict between the values of diversity and merit, a concern for full spectrum diversity facilitates a better understanding about the non-competitive nature of the relationship between these two values.

A WORKPLACE PROCEDURE FOR IMPLEMENTING FULL SPECTRUM DIVERSITY

The shift in paradigm does not necessarily entail radical changes in the selection and promotion processes as found in many affirmative action policies. It does, however, assume much more clarity and rationality in the various stages in those processes in order to avoid the pitfalls commonly associated with many current affirmative action practices. The model, presented in Figure 35.2, illustrates how the shift to an internally-based paradigm might be implemented. It breaks the hiring (or promotion) process into five distinct steps: (1) creating the job description; (2) advertising the position; (3) creating a pool of applicants; (4) interviewing finalists; and, (5) the hiring decision.

The first step entails developing the job description. At this step, managers remain focused on the issue of technical merit. Duties are written strictly in terms of work-related skills. All discussions, even informal conversations, exclude the expression of hopes, concerns or expectations about hiring members of protected or non-protected groups. Doing so would only lead to some of the pitfalls of current affirmative action practices entailing confusion over the value of merit and the value of diversity, as well as permitting externally-based factors to take priority over the internal needs of the organization.

The second step entails advertising the position. As in the first step, the manager selfishly does what is in the best interest of the organization. This means that she now focuses on the diversity question, not because of existing and externally-driven affir-

FIGURE 35.2   *A Model For Full Spectrum Diversity Recruitment*

Step 1: Job Description
    Focus = Merit
Step 2: Job Advertisement
    Focus = Agressive action (AA)
Step 3: Job Pool Analysis
    Focus = Merit
Step 4: Interviewing Top Candidates
    Foci = Full spectrum diversity
    Other job-related considerations
Step 5: Hiring one of Top Candidates
    Result-Enhancement of the organization's table
    Technical merit not in competition with full spectrum diversity

---

mative action policies, but because it is in the best interest of the organization to have the largest possible pool of technically qualified candidates emerge from the search.

Hence, managers now have an internally-based rationale to switch from a reactive routine of complying with affirmative action procedures to a more proactive mode of taking "aggressive action" to ensure that the widest net is used to capture a pool of applicants which adds to the organization's technical expertise.

The third step involves the review and narrowing of the pool of job applicants. As in each of the other steps, the manager has internally-based incentives to do what is best for the organization. At this point, however, attention returns strictly to matters of technical merit because workplace competency must be the primary goal of any organization. Discussions about diversity at the stage of reviewing resumes and job applications, therefore, encourage the seamy side of affirmative action politics—that is, the emergence of the artificial tension between merit and diversity, as well as allegations and innuendoes of tokenism.

Let us assume that this process results in selecting the top five applicants who are all technically qualified for the position. The manager invites the five individuals to interview with the organization, which is step four in the model. At this point, attention is directed to a wide array of job related issues which extend beyond technical merit. Included here are concerns about effective oral communication skills, ability to work well in team settings, motivation, personality traits which might help or hinder job performance. Verification of technical merit might also occur, but this is certainly not the focus of step four. Since the previous step established that each of the five finalists is technically qualified to perform the job tasks, merit is not longer a primary consideration.

It is at this step that full spectrum diversity becomes an issue. The manager looks at who is not at the organization's table and, more importantly, who needs to be at the table based on the demographics of the local community. The fulfillment of this assessment will, in all likelihood, result in compliance with current affirmative action guidelines.

Step 5 entails the hiring of one applicant to fill the position. The selection of this person is based on a number of job-related factors. First, she or he is one of a handful of technically competent finalists and, therefore, the concern about merit is satisfied. Two, the successful applicant demonstrated competency in a number of other job-related areas during the interview. Third, he or she brings some intangible and underrepresented trait to the table.

ANALYSIS

From the perspective of diversity, a shift to an internally-based paradigm does not guarantee desired results. For instance, five European American males might be finalists for the position of police chief in a community that is 75 percent African American. Or, five Latinos might be finalists for that position in a community that is overwhelmingly Italian American. There may be an absence of homosexuals who are police chief finalists in communities like San Francisco, California or Lakewood, Ohio which have significant concentrations of gay Americans.

While the results may not always reach our hopes, the process can certainly meet our expectations. Contrary to reactive affirmative action strategies, the approach described here prevents the value of merit from competing with the value of diversity. Hence, it also eliminates the chance of tokenism. Unlike current affirmative action policies, the model also reduces the chance of stereotyping by de-emphasizing the need to comply with federal regulations. The probability of achieving the original intent of affirmative action policies, however, is enhanced since managers will less likely think in terms of simply filling over-simplified boxes on annual Equal Employment Opportunity (EEO) reports. Embracing the concept of full spectrum diversity, moreover, limits the chance of adverse reactions toward personnel decisions throughout the entire work force.

The fact that this model relies on internally-based incentives means that management will investigate proactively to ensure that hopes and expectations are accomplished. The clarity and distinctiveness of each step helps in this search. If the person hired does not meet diversity expectations, then management may decide to invest more time and resources in Step 2 during the next round of hiring. If the pool does not produce a sufficient number of technically meritous finalists, then management has an additional reason to make greater investments in Step 2. It might also want to revisit the job description process in Step 1 in order to assure that expectations of competency are reasonable and achievable.

Given the rapidly changing complexity of American society, it may be far easier for managers to determine expectations of competency and merit than it is for them to gauge diversity within the local community and among job applicants. Some individuals do not identify with specific groups, even though they may ostensibly "fit" into a particular category. Moreover, most individuals "fit" into several categories of diversity. Hence, one question arises: How should managers determine and assess the ethnic, religious, and linguistic attributes, as well as the sexual preference, of a job applicant and a community?

The answer may lie in the development of more elaborate EEO forms which encourage people to identify with a myriad of ethnic, religious and lifestyle categories. In terms of cultural stereotyping, however, over-specification on pre-employment documents could easily result in an much damage as the current practice of oversimplification. While people may identify with several categories, these categories are always evolving due to their unique life experiences. For instance, a Mexican American in Ohio or Minnesota may have a completely different self-identity than a Mexican American in California or Texas. A Prussian American may identify more with being a Christian than with any particular Junker quality. The sudden infliction of a physical disability, such as heart disease or arthritis, may alter drastically the self-identity and life priorities of a lesbian. In essence, the pre-determined categories are the product of a paradigm driven by external factors and, therefore, they do not necessarily reflect the evolving self-views of the specific job applicant, the changing nature of a particular community, or the special needs of each organization.

The nature of life itself necessitates more open-endedness to gauge the self-identity of the individual. From the point of view of the what is best for the organization, what matters is not which pre-determined box on the pre-employment form is checked by the job applicant. The checked box merely represents a superficial snapshot of a complex, evolving human being. The task of the workplace manager in an increasingly diverse society is to rely less on the forced-choice response categories required by externally-driven considerations. Rather, the challenge for management is to assess holistically the additional perspectives and intangible skills, information, and expertise each meritous job applicant can bring to the organization's table.

The shift in paradigms places a much greater burden on the organization. No longer willing to rely solely on predetermined forced-choice responses, workplace managers and selection committees must accept the responsibility of acquiring a better, holistic "feel" for the cultural dynamics of the communities in which they live and work. They may be assisted in this process with a variety of external devices, such as becoming involved in nonwork-related community and neighborhood groups, establishing community advisory boards to keep the organization informed about local concerns, and placing community members on selection and promotion committees. Modifications in internal processes will also be needed, such as devising a greater degree of open-endedness on pre-employment forms and integrating more subjectivity, perhaps in the form of essay-oriented material, into application practices. Managers must engage in cultural conversations in the interview stage in order to better gauge the potential contributions of each meritous candidate. While fear of litigation currently prevents such conversations from occurring in earnest, the paradigmatic change will help place these conversations in the proper context and, thereby, reduce the chance of using responses for discriminatory purposes.

One final question remains: How can organizations get every manager, especially those who do not share an authentic appreciation for diversity, to embrace wholeheartedly the new paradigm?

A shift to an internally-based paradigm provides no inherent guarantees that past practices and current prejudices will not contaminate new procedures. Zealot advocates of protected groups might still find ways to insert diversity issues at inappropriate stages of the process. Bigoted members of hiring committees might still find ways of justifying the hiring the "same-type" people, or in spreading rumors about tokenism when the organization hires otherwise. Unfortunately, the motives of individuals can always bastardize the best intentions of organizations.

Yet leadership in any organization begins at the top, and leadership in every organization has the responsibility to monitor and evaluate the behavior of its staff, as well as the outcomes of its processes. Managers can be held accountable to the organization, and this is very much part of the shift to an internally-based rationale. Internal incentives, perhaps in the form of raises or other organizational benefits, must be provided for managers who engage in the dual processes of acquiring a better "feel" for the cultural dynamics of the community and securing full spectrum diversity in the workplace. Penalties must be incurred by those who try to thwart those processes.

Public organizations are also accountable to the citizenry. It is ironic, therefore, that a new set of external factors might be required to encourage the leadership of public organizations to accept and implement an internally-based paradigm. Citizens may have to be re-educated to understand the importance of having public organizations functioning effectively and responsively without regard to external preferences and politics and, consequently, striving to build a work force that truly represents the entire community. The history of our field reminds us that managers are not only responsible for leadership within the public organization, but they must also exert leadership among the public-at-large. Similar to what occurred toward the end of last century, therefore, another public service reform movement may be needed prior to the close of the present century.

CONCLUSION

Diversity has always represented America's greatest asset, in addition to being its most common attribute. Through the successive and incremental inclusion of many different groups over the past two centuries, diversity has helped shape and refine our democratic traditions and sociopolitical processes. This evolution will certainly continue well into the next millennium.

To the American workplace, the twenty-first century will present an increasingly complex layering of diversity that will demand much more thought and insight than is provided by the singular denotations of today. This will be demonstrated by the number of new groups which will be defined as "American" and, hence, will have the right to be seated at the organization's table. It will also be seen in how each individual—every "new" and "old" American—redefines him- or herself within the ever changing context of both macro and micro cultures.

As a result, the challenges placed before the public service will be greater than at any other time in our history. A shift away from the traditional view of affirmative action, to one more concerned with the full spectrum of diversity, will enable public servants to address more effectively and responsively the many, and as yet unknown, needs of a very new and different America. A shift in organizational paradigm, from one externally-driven to one that is internally-centered, will help the public service in preparing to meet these new challenges.

REFERENCES

Chambers, T. & Riccucci, N. M. (1997). Models of excellence in workplace diversity. In C. Ban and N. M. Riccucci (Eds.), *Public personnel management: Current concerns, future challenges* (pp. 73–90). New York: Longman.

Guy, M. E. (1993). Three steps forward, two steps backward: The status of women's integration into public management. *Public Administration Review, 53* (4), 285–292.

Hale, M. M. (1996). Gender equality in organizations. *Review of Public Personnel Administration, 16* (1), 7–18.

Kellough, J. E. (1989). *Federal equal employment opportunity policy and numerical goals and timetables: An impact assessment.* New York: Praeger.

Kelly, R. M., Guy, M. E. & Bayes, J. (1991). Public managers in the states: A comparison of career advancement by sex. *Public Administration Review, 51* (5), 402–412.

Mosher, F. C. (1982). *Democracy and the public service.* New York: Oxford University Press.

Murray, S. & Terry, L. D. (1994). The role demands and dilemmas of minority public administrators: The Herbert thesis revisited. *Public Administration Review, 54* (5), 409–417.

Naff, K. C. (1997). Colliding with a glass ceiling: Barriers to the advancement of women and minorities. In C. Ban and N. M. Riccucci (Eds.), *Public personnel management: Current concerns, future challenges* (pp. 91–108). New York: Longman.

Page, P. (1994). African Americans in executive branch agencies. *Review of Public Personnel Administration, 16* (1), 24–51.

Riccucci, N. M. (1997). Will affirmative action survive into the 21st century? In C. Ban and N. M. Riccucci (Eds.), *Public personnel management: Current concerns, future challenges* (pp. 57–72). New York: Longman.

13

Public Budgeting

At all levels of government, the flow and management of financial resources define the scope and capability of action and often establish the authorization for public activity. In many respects, public budgeting is a definitive management action, by which resources are set into a preferred pattern of allocation embodying the policies of those in power. In the budgeting process, any particular program or initiative may receive increased funding while another program may have its funds terminated, held to the present level, or decreased. Such are budgetary decisions, whether made at the national level and concerning trillions of dollars, or made locally by a body such as a school board or sewer district, perhaps involving only a few thousand dollars.

BUDGET PURPOSES

Budgetary allocation is a process which chooses the public programs that will be supported and to what extent. Thus it is a process for managing a multiplicity of requests and competing visions from all over a jurisdiction. When they are making a budget, legislators "horse-trade" on our behalf or on behalf of other constituencies they are supporting. From this great market place, a somewhat democratic or pluralist outcome may result. Such is our hope as constituents, that the public budgeting process is in the hands of democratically elected representatives who will fight budgetary battles in a publicly visible, "above the table," and responsible way. The Boston Tea Party symbolized America's resentment of taxation and spending being implemented without the consent of the governed. The tyranny being rejected back in 1773 was primarily a tyrannical public finance process! Consent of the governed is a key ingredient of public budgeting, and as much now as back then, we expect an open and responsible process. A legislator who appears to work only for a few special interest groups without general consent is soon likely to be exposed and reviled.

The public budget process is not just about allocating resources. It is also the centerpiece of economic and financial management. At the national level, budgets embody and represent the government's view of the balance of taxing and spending (and borrowing) which will put the national economy on the soundest footing possible. A "balanced' budget" would be one in which revenues and expenditures for the coming year are equal, without the need to borrow to make up for a deficit or a funds shortfall. Today, it is common for governments to pursue balanced budgets or budgets that are in surplus, with revenue exceeding spending. It is not uncommon, however, for governments to legislate budget deficits, sometimes to boost economic activity, or simply to finance the programs and promises to which they feel committed.

BUDGETARY REFORM

Because of the importance of the budgetary process, it has been the subject of numerous reform measures over the decades and remains the subject of a range of reform proposals now at the turn of the century. Indeed, the very idea of a national budget was itself a reform when first recommended by the Taft Commission in 1912. To us, an annual budget seems as natural as apple pie, but governments in the past did without them, voting revenue and spending measures on an item-by-item basis.

William F. Willoughby (a member of the Taft Commission), argued that a regular formal budget process would: (1) allow popular control of spending and taxing (as the executive would have to clearly articulate and gain the approval of the legislature for financial plans); (2) enhance legislative and executive co-operation (by providing a focus for discussion and approvals of what was proposed for the coming year); and, (3) improve efficiency (by imposing rules on the legislature that made the process more regular). The Budget and Accounting Act of 1921 put these recommendations into effect, requiring the President to submit an annual budget to Congress. Many years later, Aaron Wildavsky identified the following as the key purposes of the budgetary process: (1) control over public money and accountability to public authority; (2) predictability and planning; (3) relating expenditure to revenue; (4) varying spending to suit the economy; and, (5) using the budget as a lever for efficiency.[1]

Many other waves of "budgetary reform" have followed over the decades. An important area of reform endeavor has been the attempt to make budgets more meaningful (to legislators and the public) by changing their format. Early budgets were in "line-item" format. Proposed items for spending were listed under functional headings or "lines" such as "salaries," "administrative costs," and "travel." This simple format was proven and reliable, but often its headings were so broad that legislators had difficulty knowing just what the money was to be spent for and what an expenditure would produce. Because the "line item" approach to budgeting is simple, however, it endures still in many public organizations, especially in smaller ones where the functional headings aren't as likely to mislead or conceal information as they may in a larger organization.

The famous budget theorist Aaron Wildavsky paid tribute to the traditional "line-item" budget format in his famous 1978 article, "A Budget for all Seasons: Why the Traditional Budget Lasts" (reprinted in this chapter). In larger organizations, a number of attempts have been made since World War II to make budget definitions and categories sharper and more suited to legislators who may want to question, or change, a pattern of proposed resource allocations. First came the *performance budget*, a type of budgeting that originated in New York City government and was promoted nationwide by the Hoover Commission in 1949. "Performance budgets" seek to couple budget allocations with efficiency measures for each spending area. Performance budgets recognize that legislators who are asked to fund a program might want information about the agency performance they are "buying." If the legislature allocates funds to a program it should have a right to know what it can expect for its "investment." Thus, many governments, especially local governments, furnish some performance information in their budget papers.

PROGRAM BUDGETING

The next huge and lasting contribution to budget theory, *program budgeting*, started with a 1954 RAND Corporation paper. In essence, program budgeting gathers expenditures into large, purpose-oriented groupings called *programs*. Instead of being asked to decide whether line-items such as "salaries" should be increased, or "administration" should be decreased, legislators are given discrete "blocks of activities"—*programs*—to fund. The blocks of activities are aimed at particular objectives, so that legislators and interested onlookers in the press and among the public could think in terms of choices between, for example, "submarines" and "missiles."

Program budgeting was a great step forward. Indeed, it looked so good that in 1965 President Lyndon B. Johnson rather hastily mandated its implementation across all federal agencies. Hasty implementation and inadequate training and development led to many problems for program budgeting, and the Nixon administration "unadopted" it in 1971. Many critics[2] welcomed the abandonment. Despite the setbacks, program budgets have endured as a permanent building block for many (perhaps most) government agencies.

EXECUTIVE AND CONGRESSIONAL ROLES

William F. Willoughby, one of the founders of the federal budget process in the U.S., had hoped that the budget process would enhance co-operation between the legislative and executive branches of government—between Congress and the White House. Instead, the budget process has been a focus for each branch of government to exert its intentions forcefully. At times, there has been co-operation, but there also has been conflict and at times gridlock. For many years, the White House held a special advantage because it was advised by the in-house Bureau of the Budget[3] which was created in 1939 at the recommendation of the Brownlow Committee to provide detailed professional budgetary and financial expertise to the President.[4] Congress finally acquired its own in-house equivalent in 1974 with the creation of the Congressional Budget Office.

The Congressional Budget and Impoundment Control Act of 1974, which created the Congressional Budget Office, was not necessarily aimed at reducing public spending. Its purpose instead was to create the capability for Congress to analyze and thus compete with the President and the Office of Management and Budget. The Act established a process through which Congress could make comprehensive decisions on the entire budget package and thereby avoid piecemeal decisions that had resulted in "a chronic failure to consider revenues and expenditures in relation to each other."[5]

EXPENDITURE REDUCTION AND DEFICIT LIMITATION

The budgetary reform process is a continuing one. Through the 1980s and 1990s, considerable emphasis was placed on expenditure limitations and deficit reduction. Collectively, the Budget and Deficit Reduction Act of 1985 (often referred to as the Gramm-Rudman-Hollings Act)[6], the Budget Enforcement Act of 1990, and the Omnibus Budget Reconciliation Act of 1993 refocused the budget process on spending limitations. Together, these measures imposed real reductions in spending in successive fiscal years through the 1990s.[7] They also created a complex budgeting process that is biased toward expenditure reductions. As Joyce points out in an article reprinted in this chapter, a good budget process does not have a single purpose. It combines several purposes, such as preventing insolvency, making efficient allocations of government's resources, achieving inter-generational equity, contributing to fiscal stabilization, and responding to public demands. A good budget process must identify these goals and prioritize them.[8]

READINGS REPRINTED IN THIS CHAPTER

The late **Aaron Wildavsky** was perhaps the foremost American budget theorist, and we have chosen to reprint here a classic piece that was first published in *Public Administration Review* in 1978: **"A Budget for all Seasons: Why the Traditional Budget Lasts."**[9] This article epitomizes Wildavsky's critique of program budgeting as an unworkable system that embodies a contradiction between its built-in planning and analytical requirements and the political nature of the budgetary process. "A Budget for All Seasons" reminds us that there can be a large gap between what theorists might want the budget process to be like, and what it is likely to happen in the hothouse of budget negotiations in Washington, D.C. or a state capital.

"Congressional Budget Reform: the Unanticipated Implications for Federal Policy Making," by **Philip Joyce** focuses on budget reforms in Congress.[10] During the budgetary process in Washington, interplay between Congress and the

White House is a key theme. Joyce traces the evolution of legislation and policies surrounding Congress's role in this process since the creation of the Congressional Budget Office in 1974. More recently, Joyce points out, Congressional budget reforms have been dominated by expenditure reduction and deficit containment objectives. The budget has other objectives as well, however, such as the prevention of insolvency, achieving inter-generational equity, meeting constituency demands, and contributing to economic stability. Joyce asks whether current budget processes give these other budgetary purposes sufficient weight.

James J. Gosling's chapter, **"Budgetary Decision Making,"**[11] provides a recent, in-depth analysis of budgetary theories. Gosling outlines the classic battles between the "incrementalists," such as Lindblom and Wildavsky, who believe that incremental budgeting has "a rationality of its own," and the ideas of rational, analytic decision making which can be traced back to the work of Herbert Simon. Gosling argues for the central role of *decision items* in budgetary processes, "institutionally supported initiatives to increase, reduce or reallocate the expenditure authority of an agency's budget whether they occur across appropriations within the same program, across programs, or even across agencies."[12]

Gosling also discusses the interplay between the tendency of decision makers to focus on "decision items" that are often *micro* in nature, with related *macro* decisions such as impacts on budget balances; tax levels, and spending levels. Gosling points to various balanced budget and deficit control acts (referred to above) and concludes that more attention is paid to these issues now than when Wildavsky and his colleagues conducted their research on federal budgeting. And, the federal government is not alone in experiencing the emergence of macro-budgeting—similar trends are apparent at state and local government levels as well.

Numerous attempts have been made over the years to incorporate analysis into the budgetary process, including program budgeting and zero-based budgeting (ZBB). Gosling notes, however, that "budgetary choice is in reality political choice."[13] Although analysis can influence budgetary choices, the choices are made by decision makers who will use the analysis to support decisions "shaped by other factors such as normative values, preconceived notions, or views of what is politically feasible." "Budgetary Decision Making" concludes with five key factors influencing contemporary budgetary decisions: 1) *Decision cues*, such as the extent to which recommendations depart from the budgetary base; 2) *Reactions* to other participants' expected choices; 3) characteristics of *individual decision items*, including their policy significance; 4) the persuasive power of *analysis*; and, 5) the influence of *macro level parameters*, such as overall tax and spending levels.[14] The key to understanding budgetary decisions is to systematically identify the factors that apply in particular cases.

The budgetary process is central to public administration and to the shaping of public programs. Not surprisingly, the process has been subject to continuing scrutiny and reform proposals. It has also been the center of a continuing debate about the nature of political decision making and the extent to which political processes may be influenced by analytical processes.

NOTES

1. Wildavsky, Aaron. (1991). *The New Politics of the Budgetary Process* (2nd ed.). New York: HarperCollins, pp. 425–426.
2. Including Aaron Wildavsky, who had written a devastating critique in 1969 titled "No one can do PPBS."
3. Later renamed the Office of Management and Budget.
4. Shafritz, Jay M., and E. W. Russell. (2000). *Introducing Public Administration* (2nd ed.). New York: Addison Wesley Longman, p.102.
5. Joyce, Philip G. (July-August 1996). "Congressional Budget Reform: The Unanticipated Implications for Federal Policy Making." *Public Administration Review, 56*(4), 318.
6. Wildavsky, Aaron. (1991). *The New Politics of the Budgetary Process* (2nd ed.). New York: HarperCollins, 248–249.
7. Joyce, Philip G. (July-August 1996). "Congressional Budget Reform: The Unanticipated Implications for Federal Policy Making." *Public Administration Review, 56*(4), 320.
8. Joyce, Philip G. (July-August 1996). "Congressional Budget Reform: The Unanticipated Implications for Federal Policy Making." *Public Administration Review, 56*(4), 324.
9. Wildavsky, Aaron. (November/December 1978). "A Budget for all Seasons: Why the Traditional Budget Lasts." *Public Administration Review, 38*(6), 501–509.
10. Joyce, Philip G. (July-August 1996). "Congressional Budget Reform: The Unanticipated Implications for Federal Policy Making." *Public Administration Review, 56*(4), 317–324.
11. Gosling, James J. (1997). "Budgetary Decision Making," in J. J. Gosling, *Budgetary Decision Making in American Governments* (2nd ed.) (pp. 31–58). New York: Garland.
12. Gosling, James J. (1997). "Budgetary Decision Making," in J. J. Gosling, *Budgetary Decision Making in American Governments* (2nd ed.). New York: Garland, p. 39.
13. Gosling, James J. (1997). "Budgetary Decision Making," in J. J. Gosling, *Budgetary Decision Making in American Governments* (2nd ed.). New York: Garland, p. 55.
14. Gosling, James J. (1997). "Budgetary Decision Making," in J. J. Gosling, *Budgetary Decision Making in American Governments* (2nd ed.). New York: Garland, pp. 56–57.

36

Aaron Wildavsky

A BUDGET FOR ALL SEASONS? WHY THE TRADITIONAL BUDGET LASTS

Almost from the time the caterpillar of budgetary evolution became the butterfly of budgetary reform, the line-item budget has been condemned as a reactionary throwback to its primitive larva. Budgeting, its critics claim, has been metamorphosed in reverse, an example of retrogression instead of progress. Over the last century, the traditional annual cash budget has been condemned as mindless, because its lines do not match programs, irrational, because they deal with inputs instead of outputs, short-sighted, because they cover one year instead of many, fragmented, because as a rule only changes are reviewed, conservative, because these changes tend to be small, and worse. Yet despite these faults, real and alleged, the traditional budget reigns supreme virtually everywhere, in practice if not in theory. Why?

The usual answer, if it can be dignified as such, is bureaucratic inertia. The forces of conservatism within government resist change. Presumably the same explanation fits all cases past and present. How, then, explain why countries like Britain departed from tradition in recent years only to return to it? It is hard to credit institutional inertia in virtually all countries for a century. Has nothing happened over time to entrench the line-item budget?

The line-item budget is a product of history, not of logic. It was not so much created as evolved. Its procedures and its purposes represent accretions over time rather than propositions postulated at a moment in time. Hence we should not expect to find them either consistent or complementary.

Control over public money and accountability to public authority were among the earliest purposes of budgeting. Predictability and planning—knowing what there will be to spend over time—was not far behind. From the beginning, relating expenditure to revenue was of prime importance. In our day we have added macro-economic management to moderate inflation and unemployment. Spending is varied to suit the economy. In time the need for money came to be used as a level to enhance the efficiency or effectiveness of policies. He who pays the piper hopes to call the tune. Here we have it: Budgeting is supposed to contribute to continuity (for planning), to change (for policy evaluation), to flexibility (for the economy), and to provide rigidity (for limiting spending).

These different and (to some extent) opposed purposes contain a clue to the perennial dissatisfaction with budgeting. Obviously, no process can simultaneously provide continuity and change, rigidity and flexibility. And no one should be surprised that those who concentrate on one purpose or the other should find budgeting unsatisfactory or that, as purposes change, these criticisms should become constant. The real surprise is that traditional budgeting has not been replaced by any of its outstanding competitors in this century.

If traditional budgeting is so bad, why are there no better alternatives? Appropriate answers are unobtainable, I believe, so long as we proceed on this high level of aggregation. So far as I know, the traditional budget has never been compared systematically, characteristic for characteristic, with the leading alternatives.[1] By doing so we can see better which characteristics of budgetary processes suit different purposes under a variety of conditions. Why, again, if traditional budgeting does have defects, which I do not doubt, has it not been replaced? Perhaps the complaints are the clue: What is it that is inferior for the most purposes and yet superior over all?

The availability of a process to score high on one criterion may increase the likelihood of its scoring low on another. Planning requires predictability and economic management requires reversibility. Thus, there may well be no ideal mode of budgeting. If so, this is the question: Do we choose a budgetary process that does splendidly on one criterion but terribly on others, or a process that satisfies all these demands even though it does not score brilliantly on any single one?

THE TRADITIONAL BUDGET

Traditional budgeting is annual (repeated yearly) and incremental (departing marginally from the year before). It is conducted on a cash basis (in current dollars). Its content comes in the form of line-items (such as personnel or maintenance). Alternatives to all these characteristics have been developed and tried, though never, so far as I know, with success. Why this should be so, despite the obvious and admitted defects of tradition, will emerge if we consider the criteria each type of budgetary process has to meet.

What purpose is a public sector budget supposed to serve? Certainly one purpose is accountability. By associating government publicly with certain expenditures, opponent can ask questions or contribute criticisms. Here the clarity of the budget presentation in linking expenditures to activities and to responsible officials is crucial. Close to accountability is control: Are the funds which are authorized and appropriated being spent for the designated activities? Control (or its antonym "out of control") can be used in several senses. Are expenditures within the limits (a) stipulated or (b) desired. While a budget (or item) might be "out of control" to a critic who desires it to be different, in our terms "control" is lacking only when limits are stipulated and exceeded.

Budgets may be mechanisms of efficiency—doing whatever is done at least cost or getting the most out of a given level of expenditure—and/or of effectiveness—achieving certain results in public policy like improving the health of children or reducing crime.

In modern times, budgeting has also become an instrument of economic management and of planning. With the advent of Keynesian economics efforts have been made to vary the rate of spending so as to increase employment in slack times or to reduce inflation when prices are deemed to be rising too quickly. Here (leaving out alternative tax policies), the ability to increase and decrease spending in the short run is of paramount importance. For budgeting to serve planning, however, predictability (not variability) is critical. The ability to maintain a course of behavior over time is essential.

Now, as everyone knows, budgeting is not only an economic but a political instrument. Since inability to implement decisions nullifies them, the ability to mobilize support is as important as making the right choice. So is the capacity to figure out what to do—that is, to make choices. Thus, the effect of budgeting on conflict and calculation—the capacity to make and support decisions—has to be considered.

UNIT OF MEASUREMENT: CASH OR VOLUME

Budgeting can be done not only in cash but by volume. Instead of promising to pay so much in the next year or years, the commitment can be made in terms of operations performed or services provided. Why might anyone want to budget in volume (or constant currency) terms? One reason, obviously, is to aid planning. If public agencies know they can count not on variable currency but on what the currency can buy, that is, on a volume of activity, they can plan ahead as far as the budget runs. Indeed, if one wishes to make decisions now that could be made at future periods, so as to help assure consistency over time, stability in the unit of effort—so many applications processed or such a level of services provided—is the very consideration to be desired.

So long as purchasing power remains constant, budgeting in cash or by volume remains a distinction without a difference. However, should the value of money fluctuate (and, in our time, this means inflation), the public budget must absorb additional amounts so as to provide the designated volume of activity. Budgeters lose control of money because they have to supply whatever is needed. Evidently, given large and unexpected changes in prices, the size of the budget in cash terms would fluctuate wildly. Evidently, also, no government could permit itself to be so far out of control. Hence, the very stability budgeting by volume is designed to achieve turns out to be its major unarticulated premise.

Who pays the price for budgeting by volume? The private sector and the central controller. Budgeting by volume is, first of all, an effort by elements of the public sector to invade the private sector. What budgeting by volume says, in effect, is that the public sector will be protected against inflation by getting its agreed level of services before other needs are met. The real resources necessary to make up the gap between projected and current prices must come from the private sector in the form of taxation or interest for borrowing. In other words, for the public sector volume budgeting is a form of indexing against inflation.

Given an irreducible amount of uncertainty in the system, not every element can be stabilized at one and the same time. Who, then, will be kept stable and who will bear the costs of change? Within the government the obvious answer is that spending by agencies will be kept whole. The central budget office (the Treasury, Ministry of Finance or the Office of Management and Budget, as it is variously called) bears the brunt of covering larger expenditures and takes the blame when the budget goes out of control, i.e., rises faster and in different directions than predicted. In Britain, where budgeting by volume went under the name of the Public Expenditure Survey, the Treasury finally responded to years of severe inflation by imposing cash limits, otherwise known as the traditional cold-cash budget. Of course, departmental cash limits include an amount for price changes, but this is not necessarily what the Treasury expects but the amount it desires. The point is that the spending departments have to make up deficits caused by inflation. Instead of the Treasury forking over the money automatically, as in the volume budget, departments have to ask and may be denied. The local spenders, not the central controllers, have to pay the price of monetary instability.[2]

Inflation has become not only an evil to be avoided but a (perhaps *the*) major instrument of modern public policy. Taxes are hard to increase and benefits are virtually impossible to decrease. Similar results may be obtained through inflation, which artificially elevates the tax brackets in which people find themselves and decreases their purchasing power. Wage increases that cannot be directly contested may be indirectly nullified (and the real burden of the national debt reduced) without changing the ostensible amount, all by inflation. The sensitivity of budgetary forms to inflation is a crucial consideration.

From all this, it follows that budgeting by volume is counter-productive in fighting inflation because it accommodates price increases rather than struggling against them. Volume budgeting may maintain public sector employment at the expense of taking resources from the private sector, thus possibly reducing employment there. There can be no doubt, however, that volume budgeting is for counter-cyclical purposes because the whole point is that the amount and quality of service do not vary over time; if they go up or down to suit short-run economic needs they are bound to be out of kilter over the long run.

How does volume budgeting stack up as a source of policy information? It should enable departments to understand better what they are doing, since they are presumably doing the same thing over the period of the budget, but volume budgeting does poorly as a method of instigating change. For one thing, the money is guaranteed against price changes, so there is less need to please outsiders. For another, volume budgeting necessarily leads to interest in internal affairs—how to do what one wishes—not to external advice—whether there are better things one might be doing. British departments that are unwilling to let outsiders evaluate their activities are hardly going to be motivated by guarantees against price fluctuations.

TIME SPAN: MONTHS, ONE YEAR, MANY YEARS

Multi-year budgeting has long been proposed as a reform to enhance rational choice by viewing resource allocation in a long-term perspective. Considering one year, it has been argued, leads to short-sightedness—only the next year's expenditures are reviewed; over-spending—because huge disbursements in future years are hidden; conservatism—incremental changes do not open up larger future vistas; and parochialism—programs tend to be viewed in isolation rather than in comparison to their future costs in relation to expected revenue. Extending the time-span of budgeting to three or five years, it is argued, would enable long-range planning to overtake short-term reaction and substitute financial control for merely muddling through. Moreover, it is argued, the practice of rushing spending to use up resources by the end of the year would decline in frequency.

Much depends, to be sure, on how long budgetary commitments last. The seemingly arcane question of whether budgeting should be done on a cash or a volume basis will assume importance if a nation adopts multi-year budgeting. The longer the term of the budget, the more important inflation becomes. To the degree that price changes are automatically absorbed into budgets, a certain volume of activity is guaranteed. To the degree agencies have to absorb inflation, their real level of activity declines. Multi-year budgeting in cash terms diminishes the relative size of the public sector, leaving the private sector larger. Behind discussions of the span of the budget, the real debate is over the relative shares of the public and private sectors—which one will be asked to absorb inflation and which one will be allowed to expand into the other.

A similar issue of relative shares is created within government by proposals to budget in some sectors for several years, and, in others, for only one. Which sectors of policy will be free from the vicissitudes of life in the short term, the question becomes, and which will be protected from them? Like any other device, multi-year budgeting is not neutral but distributes indulgences differently among the affected interests.

Of course, multi-year budgeting has its positive parts. If control of expenditure is desired, for instance, a multi-year budget makes it necessary to estimate expenditures far into the future. The old tactic of the camel's nose—beginning with small expenditures while hiding larger ones later on—is rendered more difficult. Still, hard-in, as the British learned, often implied harder-out. Once an expenditure gets in a multi-year projection it is likely to stay in because it has become part of an interrelated set of proposals that could be expensive to disrupt. Besides, part of the bargain struck when agencies are persuaded to estimate as accurately as they can, is that they will gain stability, i.e., not be subject to sudden reductions according to the needs of the moment. Thus, control in a single year may have to be sacrificed to maintaining limits over the multi-year period; and, should the call come for cuts to meet a particular problem, British experience shows that reductions in future years, (which are always "iffy") are easily traded for maintenance of spending in the all-important present. By making prices more prominent due to the larger time period involved, moreover, large sums may have to be supplied in order to meet commitments for a given volume of services in a volatile world.[3]

Suppose, however, that is were deemed desirable to reduce significantly some expenditures in order to increase others. Due to the built-in pressure of continuing commitments, what can be done in a single year is extremely limited. Making arrangements over a three to five year period (with constant prices, five percent a year for five years compounded would bring about a one third change in the budget) would permit larger changes in amount in a more orderly way. This may be true, of course, but other things—prices, priorities, politicians—seldom remain equal. While the British were working under a five year budget projection, prices and production could hardly be predicted for five months at a time.

As Robert Hartman put it, "there is no absolutely right way to devise a long-run budget strategy."[4] No one knows how the private economy will be doing or what the consequences will be of a fairly wide range of targets for budget totals. There is no political or economic agreement on whether budget targets should be expressed in terms of levels required for full employment, for price stability, or for budget balancing. Nor is it self-evidently desirable either to estimate where the economy is going and devise a governmental spending target to complement that estimate or to decide what the economy should be doing and get the government to encourage that direction.

In any event, given economic volatility and theoretical poverty, the ability to outguess the future is extremely limited. Responsiveness to changing economic conditions, therefore, if that were the main purpose of budgeting, would be facilitated best with a budget calculated in months or weeks rather than years. If it is immediate responsiveness that is desired, as in economic management, the shorter the span the better.

Just as the annual budget on a cash basis is integral to the traditional process, so is the budgetary base—the expectation that most expenditures will be continued. Normally, only increases or decreases to the existing base are considered in any one period. If budgetary practices may be described as incremental, the main alternative to the traditional budget is one that emphasizes comprehensive calculation.

CALCULATION: INCREMENTAL OR COMPREHENSIVE

Let us think of PPB as embodying horizontal comprehensiveness—comparing alternative expenditure packages to decide which best contributes to larger programmatic objectives. ZBB, by contrast, might be thought of as manifesting vertical comprehensiveness—every year alternative expenditures from base zero are considered for all governmental activities or objectives treated as discrete entities. In a word, PPB compares programs and ZBB compares alternative funding.

The strength of PPB lies in its emphasis on policy analysis to increase effectiveness. Programs are evaluated, found wanting, and presumably replaced with alternatives designed to produce superior results. Unfortunately, PPB engenders a conflict between error recognition and error correction. There is little point in designing better policies so as to minimize their prospects of implementation. But why should a process devoted to policy evaluation end up stultifying policy execution? Because PPB's policy rationality is countered by its organizational irrationality.

If error is to be altered, it must be relatively easy to correct,"[5] but PPB makes it hard. The "systems" in PPB are characterized by their proponents as highly differentiated and tightly linked. The rationale for program budgeting lies in its connectedness—like-programs are grouped together. Program structures are meant to replace the confused concatenations of line-items with clearly differentiated, non-overlapping boundaries; only one set of programs to a structure. This means that a change in one element or structure must result in change reverberating throughout every element in the same system. Instead of alerting only neighboring units or central control units, which would make change feasible, all are, so to speak, wired together so the choice is effectively all or none.

Imagine one of us deciding whether to buy a tie or a kerchief. A simple task, one might think. Suppose, however, that organizational rules require us to keep our entire wardrobe as a unit. If everything must be rearranged when one item is altered, the probability we will do anything is low. The more tightly linked the elements, and the more highly differentiated they are, the greater the probability of error (because the tolerances are so small), and the less the likelihood the error will be corrected (because with change, every element has to be recalibrated with every other one that was previously adjusted). Being caught between revolution (change in everything) and resignation (change in nothing) has little to recommend it.

Program budgeting increases rather than decreases the cost of correcting error. The great complaint about bureaucracies is their rigidity. As things stand, the object of organizational affection is the bureau as serviced by the usual line-item categories from which people, money, and facilities flow. Viewed from the standpoint of bureau interests, programs, to some extent, are negotiable; some can be increased and others decreased while keeping the agency on an even keel or, if necessary, adjusting it to less happy times without calling into question its very existence. Line-item budgeting, precisely because its categories (personnel, maintenance, supplies) do not relate directly to programs, is easier to change. Budgeting by programs, precisely because money flows to objectives, makes it difficult to abandon objectives without abandoning the organization that gets its money from them. It is better that non-programmatic rubrics be used as formal budget categories, thus permitting a diversity of analytical perspectives, than that a temporary analytic insight be made the permanent perspective through which money is funneled.

The good organization is interested in discovering and correcting its own mistakes. The higher the cost of error—not only in terms of money but also in personnel, programs, and prerogatives—the less the chance anything will be done about them.

Organizations should be designed, therefore, to make errors visible and correctable—that is, noticeable and reversible—which, in turn, is to say, cheap and affordable.

The ideal, a-historical information system is zero-base budgeting. The past, as reflected in the budgetary base (common expectations as to amounts and types of funding), is explicitly rejected. There is no yesterday. Nothing is to be taken for granted. Everything at every period is subject to searching scrutiny. As a result, calculations become unmanageable. The same is true of PPB, which requires comparisons of all or most programs that might contribute to common objectives. To say that a budgetary process is a-historical is to conclude that it increases the sources of error while decreasing the chances of correcting mistakes. If history is abolished, nothing is settled. Old quarrels become new conflicts. Both calculation and conflict increase exponentially, the former worsening selection, and the latter, correction of error. As the number of independent variables grows, because the past is assumed not to limit the future, ability to control the future declines. As mistrust grows with conflict, willingness to admit and, hence, to correct error diminishes. Doing without history is a little like abolishing memory—momentarily convenient, perhaps, but ultimately embarrassing.

ZBB and PPB share an emphasis on the virtue of objectives. Program budgeting is designed to relate larger to smaller objectives among different programs, and zero base budgeting promises to do the same within a single program. The policy implications of these methods of budgeting, which distinguish them from existing approaches, derive from their overwhelming concern with ranking objectives. Thinking about objectives is one thing, however, and making budget categories out of them is quite another. Of course, if one wants the objectives of today to be the objectives of tomorrow, which is to say if one wants no change in objectives, then building the budget around objectives is a brilliant idea. However, if one wants flexibility in objectives (sometimes known as learning from experience) it must be possible to change them without simultaneously destroying the organization by withdrawing financial support.

Both PPB and ZBB are expressions of the prevailing paradigm of rationality in which reason is rendered equivalent to ranking objectives. Alas, an efficient mode of presenting results in research papers—find objectives, order them, choose the highest valued—has been confused with proper processes of social inquiry. For purposes of resource allocation, which is what budgeting is about, ranking objectives without consideration of resources is irrational. The question can not be "what do you want?" as if there were no limits, but should be "what do you want compared to what you can get?" (Ignoring resources is as bad as neglecting objectives as if one were not interested in the question "what do I want to do this for?"). After all, an agency with a billion dollars would not only do more than it would with a million dollars but might well wish to do different things. Resources affect objectives as well as the other way around, and budgeting should not separate what reason tells us belongs together.

For purposes of economic management, comprehensive calculations stressing efficiency (ZBB) and effectiveness (PPB) leave much to be desired. For one thing, comprehensiveness takes time and this is no asset in responding to fast-moving events. For another, devices that stress the intrinsic merits of their methods—this is (in)efficient and that is (in)effective—rub raw when good cannot be done for external reasons, i.e., the state of the economy. Cooperation will be compromised when virtue in passing one test becomes vice in failing another.

I have already said that conflict is increased by a-historical methods of budgeting. Here I wish to observe that efforts to reduce conflict only make things worse by vitiating the essential character of comprehensiveness. The cutting edge of competition among programs lies in postulating a range of policy objectives small enough to be encompassed and large enough to overlap so there are choices (trade-offs in the jargon of the trade) among them. Instead, PPB generated a tendency either to have only a few objectives, so anything and everything fit under them, or a multitude of objectives, so that each organizational unit had its own home and did not have to compete with any other.[6] ZBB worked it this way: Since a zero base was too threatening or too absurd, zero moved up until it reached, say 80 per cent of the base. To be sure, the burden of conflict and calculation declined, but so did any real difference with traditional incremental budgeting.

Insofar as financial control is concerned, ZBB and PPB raise the question of control over what? Is it control over the content of programs or the efficiency of a given program or the total costs of government or just the legality of expenditures? In theory, ZBB would be better for efficiency, PPB for effectiveness, and traditional budgeting for legality. Whether control extends to total costs, however, depends on the form of financing, a matter to which we now turn.

Appropriations or Treasury Budgeting

A traditional budget, without saying much about it, depends on traditional practice— authorization and appropriation followed by expenditure post-audited by external authorities. In many countries traditional budgeting is not, in fact, the main form of public spending. Close to half of public spending in the United States as well as in other countries does not take the form of appropriations budgeting, but what I shall call treasury budgeting. I find this nomenclature useful in avoiding the pejorative connotations of what would otherwise by called "backdoor" spending, because it avoids the appropriations committees in favor of automatic disbursement of funds through the treasury.

For present purposes, the two forms of treasury budgeting that constitute alternatives to traditional appropriations are tax expenditures and mandatory entitlements. When concessions are granted in the form of tax reductions for home ownership or college tuition or medical expenses these are equivalent to budgetary expenditures except that the money is deflected at the source. In the United States, tax expenditures now amount to more than $100 billion a year. In one sense this is a way of avoiding budgeting before there is a budget. Whether one accepts this view is a matter of philosophy. It is said, for instance, that the United States government has a progressive income tax. Is that the real tax system or is it a would-be progressive tax as modified by innumerable exceptions? The budgetary process is usually described as resource allocation by the president and Congress through its appropriations committees. Is that the real budgetary process or is it that process together with numerous provisions for "backdoor" spending, low interest loans, and other devices? From a behavioral or descriptive point-of-view actual practices constitute the real system. Then the exceptions are part of the rule. Indeed, since less than half of the budget passes through the appropriations committees, the exceptions must be greater than the rule, and some would say the same could be said about taxation. If the exceptions are part of the rule, however, tax expenditures stand in a better light. Then the government is not contributing or losing income but legitimately excluding certain private activities from being considered as income. There is no question of equity—people are just disposing of their own income as they see fit in a free society. Unless whatever is, is right, tax and budget reformers will object to sanctifying regrettable lapses as operating principles. To them the real systems are the ones which we ought to perfect—a progressive tax on income whose revenues are allocated at the same time through the same public mechanism. Tax expenditures interfere with both these ideals.

Mandatory, open-ended entitlements, our second category of treasury budgeting, provide that anyone eligible for certain benefits must be paid regardless of the total. Until the legislation is changed or a "cap" limits total expenditure, entitlements constitute obligations of the state through direct drafts on the treasury. Were I asked to give an operational definition of the end of budgeting, I would say "indexed, open-ended entitlements". Budgeting would no longer involve allocation within limited resources but only addition of one entitlement to another, all guarded against fluctuation in prices.

Obviously, treasury budgeting leaves a great deal to be desired in controlling costs of programs, which depend on such variables as levels of benefits set in prior years, rate of application, and severity of administration. Legal control is possible but difficult because of the large number of individual cases and the innumerable provisions governing eligibility. If the guiding principle is that no one who is eligible should be denied even if some who are ineligible must be included, expenditures will rise. They will decline if the opposite principle—no ineligibles even if some eligibles suffer—prevails.

Whether or not entitlement programs are efficient or effective, the budgetary process will neither add to nor subtract from that result simply because it plays no part. To the extent that efficiency or effectiveness are spurred by the need to convince others to provide funds, such incentives are much weakened or altogether absent. The political difficulties of reducing benefits or eliminating beneficiaries speak eloquently on this subject. No doubt benefits may be eroded by inflation. Protecting against this possibility is the purpose of indexing benefits against inflation (thus doing for the individual what volume budgeting does for the bureaucracy).

Why, then, in view of its anti-budgetary character, is treasury budgeting so popular? Because of its value in coping with conflict, calculation, and economic management. After a number of entitlements and tax expenditures have been decided upon at different times, usually without full awareness of the others, implicit priorities are produced *ipso-facto*, untouched as it were, by human hands. Conflict is reduced, for the time being at least, because no explicit decisions giving more to this group and less to another are necessary. Ultimately, to be sure, resource limits will have to be considered, but even then only a few rather than all expenditures will be directly involved, since the others go on, as it were, automatically. Similarly, calculation is contracted as treasury budgeting produces figures, allowing a large part of the budget to be taken for granted. Ultimately, of course, days of reckoning come in which there is a loss of flexibility due to the implicit pre-programming of so large a proportion of available funds. For the moment, however, the attitude appears to be "sufficient unto the day is the (financial) evil thereof."

For purposes of economic management, treasury budgeting is a mixed bag. It is useful in providing what are called automatic stabilizers. When it is deemed desirable not to make new decisions every time conditions change, as pertains to unemployment benefits, an entitlement enables funds to flow according to the size of the problem. The difficulty is that not all entitlements are counter-cyclical (child benefits, for example, may rise independently of economic conditions) and the loss in financial flexibility generated by entitlements may hurt when the time comes to do less.

Nevertheless, treasury budgeting has one significant advantage over appropriations budgeting, namely, time. Changes in policy are manifested quickly in changes in spending. In order to bring considerations of economic management to bear on budgeting, these factors must be introduced early in the process of shaping the appropriations budget. Otherwise, last-minute changes of large magnitude will cause chaos by unhinging all sorts of prior understandings. Then the money must be voted and preparations made for spending. In the United States under this process—from the spring previews in the Office of Management and Budget, to the president's budget in January, to congressional action by the following summer and fall, to spending, in the winter and spring—18 to 24 months have elapsed. This is not control but remote control.

"Fine-tuning expenditures," attempting to make small adjustments to speed up or slow down the economy, do not work well anywhere. Efforts to increase expenditures are as likely to decrease the expenditure in the short-run due to the effort required to expand operations. Efforts to reduce spending in the short run are as likely to increase spending due to severence pay, penalties for breaking contracts, and so on. Hence, even as efforts continue to make expenditures more responsive, the attractiveness of more immediate tax and entitlement increases is apparent.

The recalcitrance of all forms of budgeting to economic management is not so surprising; both spending programs and economic management cannot be made more predictable if one is to vary to serve the other. In an age profoundly influenced by Keynesian economic doctrines, with their emphasis on the power of government spending, however, continued efforts to link macro-economics with micro-spending are to be expected.

THE STRUCTURAL BUDGET MARGIN

One such effort is the "Structural Budget Margin" developed in the Netherlands. Due to dissatisfaction with the Keynesian approach to economic stabilization, as well as disillusionment with its short-term fine-tuning, the Dutch sought to develop a longer-term relationship between the growth of public spending and the size of the national economy. Economic management was to rely less on sudden starts and stops of taxation and expenditure, and greater effort was to be devoted to controlling public spending. (The closest the United States has come is through the doctrine of balancing the budget at the level of full employment which almost always would mean a deficit). The Dutch were particularly interested in a control device because of the difficulty of getting agreement to hold down expenditures in coalition governments. Thus, spending was to be related not to actual growth but to desired growth, with only the designated margin available for new expenditure.[7]

Needless to say there are differences in definition of the appropriate structural growth rate and it has been revised up and down. Since the year used as a base makes a difference, that has also been in dispute. As we would also expect, there are disagreements over calculation of cash or volume of services with rising inflation propelling a move toward cash. Moreover, since people learn to play any game, conservative governments used the structural budget margin to hold down spending and socialists used it to increase it, for then the margin became a mechanism for figuring out the necessary increases in taxation. Every way one turns, it appears, budgetary devices are good for some purposes and not for others.

Why the Traditional Budget Lasts

Every criticism of traditional budgeting is undoubtedly correct. It is incremental rather than comprehensive; it does fragment decisions, usually making them piecemeal; it is heavily historical looking backward more than forward; it is indifferent about objectives. Why, then, has traditional budgeting lasted so long? Because it has the virtue of its defects.

Traditional budgeting makes calculations easy precisely because it is not comprehensive. History provides a strong base on which to rest a case. The present is appropriated to the past which may be known, instead of the future, which cannot be comprehended. Choices that might cause conflict are fragmented so that not all difficulties need be faced at one time. Budgeters may have objectives, but the budget itself is organized around activities or functions. One can change objectives, then, without challenging organizational survival. Traditional budgeting does not demand analysis of policy but neither does it inhibit it. Because it is neutral in regard to policy, traditional budgeting is comparable with a variety of policies, all of which can be converted into line-items. Budgeting for one year at a time has no special virtue (two years, for instance might be as good or better) except in comparison to more extreme alternatives. Budgeting several times a year aids economic adjustment but also creates chaos in departments, disorders calculations, and worsens conflict. Multi-year budgeting enhances planning at the expense of adjustment, accountability, and possible price volatility. Budgeting by volume and entitlement also aid planning and efficiency in government at the cost of control and effectiveness. Budgeting becomes spending. Traditional budgeting lasts, then, because it is simpler, easier, more controllable, more flexible than modern alternatives like PPB, ZBB, and indexed entitlements.

A final criterion has not been mentioned because it is inherent in the multiplicity of others, namely, adaptability. To be useful a budgetary process should perform tolerably well under all conditions. It must perform under the unexpected—deficits and surpluses, inflation and deflation, economic growth and economic stagnation. Because budgets are contracts within governments signifying agreed understandings, and signals outside of government informing others of what government is likely to do so they can adapt to it, budgets must be good (though not necessarily great) for all seasons. It is not so much that traditional budgeting succeeds brilliantly on every criterion, but that it does not entirely fail on any one that is responsible for its longevity.

Needless to say, traditional budgeting also has the defects of its virtues. No instrument of policy is equally good for every purpose. Though budgets look back, they may not look back far enough to understand how (or why) they got where they are. Comparing this year with last year may not mean much if the past was a mistake and the future is likely to be a bigger one. Quick calculation may be worse than none if it is grossly in error. There is an incremental road to disaster as well as faster roads to perdition; simplicity may become simple-mindedness. Policy neutrality may degenerate into disinterest in programs. So why has it lasted? So far, no one has come up with another budgetary procedure that has the virtues of traditional budgeting but lacks its defects.

At once one is disposed to ask why it is necessary to settle for second or third best: Why not combine the best features of the various processes, specially selected to work under prevailing conditions? Why not multi-year volume entitlements for this and annual cash zero base budgeting for that? The question answers itself; there can only be one budgetary process at a time: Therefore, the luxury of picking different ones for different purposes is unobtainable. Again, the necessity of choosing the least worst, or the most widely applicable over the largest number of cases is made evident.

Yet almost a diametrically opposite conclusion also is obvious to students of budgeting. Observation reveals that a number of different processes do, in fact, co-exist right now. Some programs are single year but others are multi-year, some have cash limits while others are open-ended or even indexed, some are investigated in increments but others (where repetitive operations are involved) receive, in effect, a zero-base review. Beneath the facade of unity, there is, in fact, diversity.

How, then, are we to choose among truths that are self-evident (there can be only one form of budgeting at a time and there are many)? Both cannot be correct when applied to the same sphere but I think they are when applied to different spheres. The critical difference is between the financial form in which the budget is voted on in the legislature, and the different ways of thinking about budgeting. It is possible to analyze expenditures in terms of programs, over long periods of time, and in many other ways without requiring that the form of analysis be the same as the form of appropriation. Indeed, as we have seen, there are persuasive reasons for insisting that form and function be different. All this can be summarized: The more neutral the form of presenting appropriations, the easier to translate other changes—in program, direction, organizational structure—into the desired amount without making the categories into additional forms of rigidity, which will become barriers to future changes.

Nonetheless, traditional budgeting must be lacking in some respects or it would not be replaced so often by entitlements or multi-year accounts. Put another way, treasury budgeting must reflect strong social forces. These are not mechanisms to control spending but to increase it. "The Budget" may be annual, but tax expenditures and budget entitlements go on until changed. With a will to spend there is a way.

Social forces ultimately get their way, but while there is a struggle for supremacy, the form of budgeting can make a modest difference. It is difficult to say, for instance, whether the concept of a balanced budget declined due to social pressure or whether the concept of a unified budget, including almost all transactions in and out of the economy, such as trust funds, makes it even less likely. In days of old when cash was cash, and perpetual deficits were not yet invented, a deficit meant more cash out than came in. Today, with a much larger total, estimating plays a much more important part, and it's anyone's guess within $50 billion as to the actual state of affairs. The lesson is that for purposes of accountability, and control, the simpler the budget the better.

Taking as large a view as I know how, the suitability of a budgetary process under varied conditions depends on how well diverse concerns can be translated into its forms. For sheer transparency, traditional budgeting is hard to beat.

NOTES

1. But, for a beginning, see Allen Schick, "The Road to PPB: The Stages of Budget Reform," *Public Administration Review*, (Dec. 1966) pp 243-258.
2. Hugh Heclo, Aaron Wildavsky, *The Private Government of Public Money: Community and Policy Inside British Political Administration*, London, Macmillan; Berkeley and Los Angeles, University of California Press, (2nd edition forthcoming).
3. *Idem.*
4. Robert A. Hartman, "Multiyear Budget Planning," in Joseph A. Pechman, ed. *Setting National Priorities: The 1979 Budget.* (The Brookings Institution, Washington, D.C. 1978) p. 312.
5. This and the next eight paragraphs are taken from my "Policy Analysis is What Information Systems are Not," *New York Affairs*, Vol. 4, No. 2 Spring 1977.
6. See Jeanne Nienaber, and A. Wildavsky, *The Budgeting and Evaluation of Federal Recreation Programs, or Money Doesn't Grow on Trees*, New York, Basic Books, 1973.
7. J. Diamond, "The New Orthodoxy in Budgetary Planning: A Critical Review of Dutch Experience," In *Public Finance*, Vol. XXXII, No. 1 (1977) pp 56-76.

37

Philip G. Joyce

CONGRESSIONAL BUDGET REFORM: THE UNANTICIPATED IMPLICATIONS FOR FEDERAL POLICY MAKING

The Congressional Budget and Impoundment Control Act of 1974, the landmark piece of legislation that created the congressional budget process, is now more than 20 years old. The budget process has undergone substantial revisions since its inception, largely the result of a change in the focus of the process from priority setting to controlling the size of the federal budget and federal budget deficits. Many of these changes have had consequences (some of them unanticipated) that have fundamentally changed federal policy making.

The Congressional Budget Process—Original and Subsequent Aims

The process of developing a budget was relatively uncoordinated in both the legislative and executive branches before 1921, when the Budget and Accounting Act made the President a central player in the process by requiring that he submit a unified budget to the Congress. This gave the executive branch the responsibility for defining the structure and the details of the federal budget. Prior to the passage of the Congressional Budget Act of 1974 "(c)urious and uncoordinated legislative procedure hid the implicit tradeoffs involved in fiscal legislation from both the Congress and the public, and there was a chronic failure to consider revenues and expenditures in relation to each other" (Stith, 1988; 515). Early each year, the President proposed a budget, which was considered by the Congress, primarily through the fragmented or uncoordinated committee process. The congressional "budget" was the cumulative (and somewhat accidental), result of legislation affecting annual discretionary appropriations, mandatory programs, and revenues. The Congress never examined or voted on over all spending or revenues or the appropriate stance of fiscal policy. Many members of Congress and observers of congressional budgeting were concerned that this failure to consider the whole was leading to irresponsible results, particularly given the increase in the proportion of the budget financed outside of the appropriations process—so-called backdoor spending. Irresponsible or not, however, members of Congress generally agreed that this piecemeal approach to the budget constrained Congress's ability to make comprehensive policy. At the same time, Congress was faced with a fundamental challenge to its spending priorities when President Nixon refused to spend funds appropriated by Congress for programs with which he did not agree.

These concerns prompted Congress in 1973 to create the Joint Study Committee on Budget Control. This process ultimately resulted in the enactment of the Congressional Budget and Impoundment Control Act of 1974. The act created a process by which budget decisions could be made comprehensively and could be protected from the normal parliamentary hurdles faced by other legislation. The process was neutral as to budget outcomes but could "be deployed in favor of higher or lower spending, bigger or smaller deficits" (Schick, 1980; 73). Although some members of Congress voted for the subsequent Congressional Budget Act because they believed that it would control spending or the deficit (some subsequent evaluations [Fisher, 1985] have deemed it a failure because it has not), the act itself contained no provisions which biased it one way or the other. It would have been biased, for example, if it had required supermajorities (such as two-thirds of the members in each house) to exact a tax increase. The act was outcome neutral, truly a *process* reform.

The act also embodied certain other principles, including preserving the ability of the Congress to act according to its budgetary preferences (hence, no points of order requiring supermajorities); substituting information for control (the Budget Act opted to make the Congress aware of what they were doing, rather than preventing them from doing it through spending limitations); preserving the participation of members in the budget process (rather than stacking the deck in favor of particular committees); allowing Congress to consider budget priorities comprehensively; and establishing a process to control presidential impoundments (Schick, 1980).

As the budget deficit grew substantially in the wake of the passage of the Reagan economic program in 1981, the Congress became increasingly aware that the budget process could not (nor, as noted above, was it intended to) serve as a constraint against these large deficits. Frustration with large deficits and the inability to contain them ultimately led to the passage in 1985 of the Balanced Budget and Emergency Deficit Control Act of 1985, popularly known as Gramm-Rudman-Hollings (GRH). GRH attempted to control the deficit through setting gradually declining deficit targets and was supposed to result in a balanced budget by fiscal year 1991. If the deficit targets were not met, automatic across-the-board spending reductions, or sequestrations, were to take effect.

The passage of GRH represented a fundamental change in the focus of the budget process. For the first time, the budget process was used to specify the end result to be achieved, rather than simply the rules to be followed that might lead to any number of different budget outcomes. As such, it was a switch from what Hanushek (1986; 6) has described as "process rules" (that is, rules governing decisions, timing, and priority setting) to "allocation rules" (which specify particular budget results, such as levels of spending and the deficit). According to Kate Stith (1988; 597), "[b]y establishing binding deficit limitations enforced outside of the legislative budget process, GRH sought to . . . amend our 'fiscal constitution,' which for over two centuries had permitted prevailing legislative minorities to spend without limitation."

The deficit, of course, did not come down as promised by the Gramm-Rudman-Hollings legislation. In fact, the fiscal year 1993 deficit (which would have been zero if the law, as revised in 1987, had met its goal) was actually $255 billion (Congressional Budget Office, 1994b). The act put a premium on short-term budgeting; under GRH, all that mattered was the single year for which the projections were being made. These annual targets were met through short-term fixes and budget gimmickry, including basing the budget on optimistic economic and technical assumptions, selling assets, and shifting costs between fiscal years.

The successor to Gramm-Rudman-Hollings, the Budget Enforcement Act (BEA), was passed in 1990 and was designed to enforce the five-year deficit reduction agreement reached between the President and Congress in that year. The BEA effectively eliminated annual deficit targets, placed limits on the level of discretionary spending through fiscal year 1995, and established the pay-as-you-go (PAYGO) process to ensure that any tax or mandatory spending changes were deficit neutral. The original Budget Enforcement Act would have expired in 1995; the Omnibus Budget Reconciliation Act of 1993 extended both the discretionary spending limits and PAYGO until 1998. The BEA shifted the process away from deficit targets to controls on legislative changes in spending or revenues. By so doing, it focused attention on those actions that Congress and the President could directly control (spending and revenue actions), rather than holding them accountable for the size of the annual deficit, which can be influenced by the performance of the economy and other factors not controlled through the annual budget process (Joyce and Reischauer, 1992). As such, it has been described as a no-fault budget process. As long as budget rules are followed, the deficit can grow substantially without anyone being held responsible for the increase (Doyle and McCaffrey, 1991).

HOW HAVE THE CHANGES SINCE 1974 AFFECTED POLICY MAKING?

Unquestionably, the process that exists today is different in many important ways from the process that was designed in 1974. The budget process has reasserted the congressional role in budgeting, has increased the information available to Congress on the budget and economy, and has curbed the President's impoundment powers. The process has not been viewed as an overwhelming success in other respects. The most frequent criticism is that it has not brought the order and timeliness to congressional budget action for which advocates had hoped. Deadlines for enacting budget resolutions and the passing of appropriation bills have routinely been missed.

Rather than comment further on issues such as these, this article focuses on three important changes to the budget process that have received less scrutiny, yet have fundamentally influenced the way budget policy is made. First reconciliation, almost an afterthought in 1974, has become in many ways the most important part of the process. It has been used to make major policy shifts, most recently embodied in omnibus, multi-year, deficit-reduction packages. Second, while the Budget Act was policy neutral by design, this neutrality has been undone by subsequent reforms that sought to use the budget process to limit government spending or the size of the deficit. The failures (some real and some imagined) of GRH and the BEA to control spending and the deficit, coupled with the increasing complexity of the process, have contributed to widespread disillusionment, not only with the budget process but with government in general. Third, the increasing importance of budget enforcement has had important implications for policy making by forcing policy makers to take budgetary effects into account. The manner in which information provided for enforcement purposes is used has sometimes caused distortions, as policies are designed with enforcement in mind. Budget enforcement has also further empowered a minority of legislators who can often use budget rules to block policies.

Reconciliation—A Powerful New Tool for Centralized Control

In establishing its own budget process in 1974 and in the changes that have been made in that process since, Congress has been bucking its general trend toward decentralized decision making. While the Congress is generally viewed as an institution that has been moving away from centralized control—the declining influence of parties and the reduced influence of the congressional leadership are often presented as evidence of this—the congressional budget process attempts to move toward greater centralization of decision making (Ellwood, 1985; Schick, 1980). Nowhere is that centralizing trend more apparent than in reconciliation, where the Congress as a whole (through the budget resolution) is empowered to give instructions concerning changes in law to congressional committees. The centralizing tendency of the budget process in the face of the increasing fragmentation of the Congress has certainly contributed to the dissatisfaction of members with the state of congressional budgeting. In short, members of Congress and congressional committees do not like to be told what to do, but the budget process—and particularly reconciliation—is designed to allow the whole Congress to control its committees and members.

The framers of the Budget Act viewed reconciliation as unimportant; it was an optional process for tying the ceilings enacted in the second concurrent budget resolution (since eliminated) to the changes in laws governing taxes and spending (mainly appropriations) necessary to achieve them. Because the changes in the second resolution were only designed to accommodate revisions in political or economic circumstances since the passage of the first, and in any event came very late in the budgeting cycle, Schick wrote that "the reconciliation process is not likely to offer much opportunity for reconsideration of past actions" (Schick, 1980; 321).

Enter the Reagan revolution. President Reagan had proposed a radical budget restructuring that included large income tax cuts, increases in defense spending, and reductions in domestic spending. Amid a concern that the tax cut might not be enacted without first passing the budget cuts that made them appear affordable, the Reagan administration, led by Budget Director David Stockman, attempted to use reconciliation as a means to use the budget resolution to carry out the Reagan spending program by subjecting the program to a single up-or-down vote, thus paving the way for the tax cut. Although the tax cuts themselves were not enacted through reconciliation, the argument, as articulated by Stockman, was that the tax cuts might not have survived politically without first moving to cut spending (Stockman, 1986).

1981 was the second time that reconciliation had been used in concert with the first budget resolution—President Carter and the Congress had agreed to a small deficit reduction package enacted through the reconciliation process only a year earlier—but the use of reconciliation in 1981 was a watershed "because of the size and scope of the changes made and the threat they pose to hallowed congressional procedures" (Hartman, 1982; 389). Many analysts have argued that the large changes that took place in 1981—changes that resulted in a legacy of large deficits—would not have been possible under the previously decentralized budget process (Fisher, 1990; Rivlin, 1986; Penner and Abramson, 1988). The use of reconciliation to drive the spending cuts on the front end in anticipation of the tax cuts was certainly an important part of that story.

Reconciliation has also proved to be an important part of the solution to the problem of large deficits. This was anticipated by Hartman, writing in 1982 about the results of the 1981 budgetary process (Hartman, 1982; 397).

> Procedural changes directed toward strengthening budget control . . . make the most sense if one envisions the environment of the future as one of heightened attention to solving expenditure growth and cutting deficits. The crucial procedural innovation of the last few years—reconciliation early in the budget process—seems essential to any move to strengthen control. Because the predominant message for the congressional committees in this austerity scenario is that spending be cut and taxes raised, it is unrealistic to expect such measures to be put into effect unless committees are forced to act. This is the primary function of reconciliation: it allows Congress as a whole to order its committees to take actions.

In fact, while 1981 is remembered as a year when the congressional budget process was used to promote what are in retrospect viewed as irresponsible, deficit-exploding changes to the budget, the use of reconciliation in subsequent years has been for the opposite reason. Omnibus budget reconciliation acts (OBRAs) became commonplace in the 1980s, with the enactment of OBRAs in 1982, 1983, 1984, 1986, 1987, and 1989. The three most recent multi-year deficit reduction packages to pass Congress—the five-year agreements of 1990 and 1993 and the seven-year package passed in 1995—were each implemented through use of the reconciliation process.

Reconciliation is so important for policy making because it permits actions to be taken in tandem that would arguably never survive separately, for two main reasons. First, combining spending and tax changes as part of one large package can communicate to members of Congress and the public that unpopular policies are part of an overall package intended to achieve some larger (and more popular) objective. In 1990 and 1993, the strategy focused on the argument that everyone's ox was being gored simultaneously (or, to use a less colorful phrase made popular during the legislative battles over OBRA-1993, they are engaged in shared sacrifice). In 1995, the spending reductions induced through the reconciliation process were marketed as necessary to fulfill the twin Republican promises of balancing the budget and cutting taxes.

Second, when done through the reconciliation process, the required changes in law are mandated. Under reconciliation, the details of legislation are fair game, but committees are required to report legislation that results in changes of the magnitude required by the budget resolution. If each change were considered without such a mandate, many of them would be picked off in committee and never see the light of day. In addition, bills considered outside of reconciliation could be filibustered in the Senate, whereas the Budget Act establishes a specific time limit for debating reconciliation legislation.

An End to Policy Neutrality

As noted above, the drafters of the Congressional Budget Act viewed it as very important that the process not be biased in the direction of particular budget outcomes. For this reason, they designed a process that could be used to increase or decrease spending (or revenues), or for increased or decreased deficits. (Recall that they wanted the Congress to play a role in the setting of short-run macroeconomic policy, a function of the budget that has all but disappeared today.) Beginning with Gramm-Rudman in 1985 and continuing through the Budget Enforcement Act, the focus of the process has changed markedly from a policy-neutral process to a process that is designed to be used to achieve particular policy objectives.

Relative to the original goals of the Budget Act, the important distinction to make is one of control over the *budget*—that is, over total taxes and spending—versus control over only spending or control leading to a prescribed deficit number. The Budget Act was designed to foster control over the former—to permit a comprehensive evaluation of taxing and spending. GRH and the BEA created norms for budget outcomes concerning either the deficit (GRH), spending (the discretionary caps), or deficit neutrality (PAYGO).

Beyond the important implications of this shift for the budget process itself is the effect that this change in emphasis has had over the credibility of the process. After 1985, observers and participants were justified in judging the process according to budgetary outcomes, regardless of whether the process should have ever been expected to force those outcomes or not (Joyce, 1993). Seen in this light, the inability of GRH to re-duce the deficit to the levels specified by the legislation was an indictment not only of Congress and the President (or the public's conflicting demands that they balance the budget without raising taxes or cutting spending) but of the budget process itself. The public wonders how elected officials can judge a budget process to be successful if, in enforcing a deficit *reduction* agreement, it permits $200 billion deficits to be replaced with $300 billion deficits. In short, the continued large deficits are viewed by many as evidence that the budget process itself is broken and needs to be overhauled.

Aside from whether the outcomes promised by these budget reforms were achieved or not, there is the issue of the complexity of the process. The Congressional Budget Act layered a new process on top of existing authorization and appropriations processes. The budget changes that have occurred since 1974 have either expanded the use of procedures (like reconciliation) that were not used much prior to the 1980s, or have created new procedures, reports, and rules on top of the old ones. GRH added deficit targets, sequestration, and sequestration reports. The BEA gave us spending caps and PAYGO, so that the possibility existed for not one sequestration, but three. Imagine the plight of the large number of freshman members of Congress elected in 1992 and 1994 when they first confronted a budget process which seemed to be written in a foreign language. And this is nothing compared to the confusion that the general public must feel.

The Increasing Importance of Enforcement in the Budget Process— The Ascendancy of Scorekeeping

Unquestionably, the framers of the Budget Act wanted congressional budgeters to take into account the consequences of their actions. For this reason, they not only created the budget committees and the concurrent budget resolution devices for coor-dinating congressional attention to the whole budget, but they also created enforce-ment mechanisms designed to discourage the Congress from breaching the discipline offered by the budget resolution. Congressional Budget Office cost estimates were de-signed early on to play this role—to answer the question "what does it cost?" when the Congress was debating a piece of legislation.

Cost estimating and scorekeeping played a somewhat limited role in influencing the policy process from 1974 to 1985 compared to what has happened since GRH and BEA. This is primarily because the consequences of failing to adhere to the re-quirements of the budget process have become more real. After the passage of GRH, enacting legislation that would cause the deficit targets to be breached became an event that could trigger across-the-board cuts in spending. Note that this gets the attention of the whole Congress, because actions under the jurisdiction of one com-mittee can lead to cuts in programs under the jurisdiction of others. Since the BEA was enacted, the existence of explicit spending limits (the discretionary caps) and ex-plicit assumptions of deficit neutrality (PAYGO) has made the question., "How will you pay for it?" the first one asked of proponents of costly new spending. How much they will have to pay is tied up in the enforcement mechanisms established as part of the budget process.

This development was undoubtedly necessary given the change in the focus of the process. Once the decision was made to use the budget process to return the budget to (or closer to) balance through enacting deficit limits and spending limits, it was necessary to have some kind of mechanism in place to enforce those strictures. This has given rise to a complex set of administrative rules and procedures that govern the "scorability" of various policy changes. In response to these rules, advocates of particular policies sometimes adjust the parameters of their policy proposals to reflect how OMB and CBO will score them. This allegedly happened in the design of President Clinton's health reform plan, where caps on insurance premiums were included not because the administration thought they were a good idea, but because they believed that the Congressional Budget Office would score them as reducing spending.

A discussion of budget enforcement carries with it some natural bias, depending on the actor, since the world of federal budgeting is generally divided into enforcers and victims. Those who participate in enforcing the rules—primarily the budget committees, CBO, and OMB—are constantly defending their decisions against attack from those who feel aggrieved by them—primarily other congressional committees and federal agencies. For this reason, rather than discuss whether enforcement is inherently good or bad (which seems a moot point since, in the current environment, the option of abandoning enforcement seems neither desirable nor likely), I would like to discuss several limitations of the current emphasis on enforcement that might be considered either when applying the current budget law or considering its revision.

Narrow Scope of Budget Enforcement. By design, the enforcement procedures created as a part of the budget process have a narrow focus. The question that is asked under the BEA, for example, is, "What is the effect of this policy (bill) on federal taxes and spending for each of the next five (or fewer) fiscal years?" This is the right question in many cases, although it does create incentives to push costs beyond the five-year enforcement window in others. Relying solely on the information created as a result of these rules may distort decision making in cases where the important effects on the federal budget occur many years in the future, or where the more important effects to be considered are the overall economic effects, independent of the federal budgetary effects. In other words, because enforcement focuses on short-term federal budget effects and ignores cost and benefits to nonfederal actors, there is some danger of over-emphasizing only one part of the story.

Artificial Division of Spending Discourages Tradeoffs. Because the Budget Enforcement Act, for the first time, divided the budget into three categories—Social Security (which has its own budget rules), PAYGO (including other mandatory spending and revenues), and discretionary spending—it also created walls between them. The divisions were set up with good reason. The drafters of the act wanted to hold congressional committees accountable for their own actions. Therefore, an overage on the PAYGO scorecard results in a sequestration of mandatory spending (which affects authorizing committees), while a breach of the discretionary spending caps results in an across-the-board cut in appropriated spending (which affects appropriations committees). The exclusion of Social Security from PAYGO was for a separate reason—the myth that Social Security, as a "self-financed" program, should be walled off from the rest of the budget.

However good the reason, this kind of a process has one major drawback from the perspective of setting overall budgetary priorities. It does not permit, without changes in law, tradeoffs that would cross the divide between the categories. There-fore, revenue increases can be used to finance increases in mandatory spending, but cannot be used (without increasing the caps) for increases in discretionary spending, even if there is substantial agreement that these increases would have positive effects that more than offset the cost of raising taxes. Take well-chosen public investment pro-grams as an example. A President or a Congress seeking to increase spending on in-frastructure or other "investment" spending, even if there was general agreement concerning the worthiness of such spending (and a corresponding willingness to ante up new taxes to pay for it), could not do so under the existing budget process without recommending corresponding decreases in other discretionary programs. Indeed, this is the dilemma that has faced the Clinton administration in getting the President's in-vestment programs funded, given a shrinking discretionary pie.

The purpose of the buyout legislation was to save money associated with the salaries of federal workers—a savings that would affect the discretionary portion of the budget. But the bill created costs as well, mainly in the form of earlier retirement pay-ments made to bought-out workers. This cost showed up in the mandatory portion of the budget. The savings to be gained from salary savings could not be counted as an offset against the increase in retirement payments, therefore, the bill had to include offsets to make up for the overage on the PAYGO scorecard. This was almost enough to scuttle a bill that was widely supported and that everyone agreed would lead to a net reduction in federal spending.

Proliferation of Points of Order Expands Use of Budget Rules to Block Legislation. An-other area where the evolution of the budget process has led to substantial changes in policy making concerns the use of points of order to block legislation, particularly in the Senate. Points of order, which are procedural devices that can be used to block leg-islation if all or part of that legislation would violate the law or congressional rules, have become more important with the use of the budget process for deficit reduction and enforcement. Not only have new points of order been created but, beginning with GRH in 1985, a three-fifths requirement was established in the Senate for the first time to waive many Budget Act points of order. This requirement was expanded and extended by the BEA, both in the 1990 act and when it was renewed in 1993. In fact, while only 10 Budget Act points of order were considered in the Senate in the 12 years between 1975 and 1986, more than 120 were considered between 1987 and 1994. (Bach, 1989; Congressional Research Service, 1995).

The proliferation of points of order has provided more tools to a minority that can be used to change or block legislation. This has the effect of both altering the drafting of legislation to attempt to eliminate possible sources of points of order and providing opportunities to kill bills once they have come to the floor.

CONCLUSION—WHAT DOES THE FUTURE HOLD?

The point of the preceding discussion is not to suggest that the deficit-driven changes that have occurred in the budget process were unnecessary or even, on balance, for the worse. The point is that they have fundamentally changed the process from what was intended in 1974. Perhaps this was inevitable following the explosion of the deficit after 1981. But it is worth considering that the damage that has been done—in terms of the credibility of the process, its complexity, and the opportunities that it presents to influence or block policy—is a byproduct of the use of the process to control federal deficits and spending.

Someday, the problem of large federal deficits may be behind us. At that point, it will be worth reconsidering what we have done to the budget process and evaluating whether the procedures established under the 1974 act were fundamentally correct and should be reestablished. Agreement is certainly not universal on that point. For example, Fisher has argued forcefully that the 1974 budget process has fundamentally damaged budget policy making by allowing the President to escape responsibility for budget outcomes (Fisher, 1990). Regardless of whether the 1974 budget process was an improvement over what preceded it or not, it is clear that the changes that have occurred since 1985, even if necessary, have had effects that would need to be reconsidered if, as the 104th Congress desires, there is to be a return to equality between federal spending and taxes.

Acknowledging the limitations of the current budget process is not the same as prescribing a new one. Many budget observers would agree that the current process is necessarily too complex, too rule-bound, and too biased. The question, however, of what constitutes a good budget process has continued to elude budget scholars. This in part stems from precisely the problem, as noted by Roy Meyers, that the budget process is expected to achieve a large number of diverse (and sometimes contradictory) goals simultaneously, including "preventing insolvency, making efficient allocations of the government's limited financial resources, approaching intergenerational equity, contributing to fiscal stabilization, and being responsive to public demands" (Meyers, 1995). Establishing a good budget process requires not only defining these goals but prioritizing them. Further, the priorities set, as reflected by the experience of the last 20 years in the federal process, do affect budget outcomes and budget decision making in important ways.

References

Bach, Stanley, 1989. "Points of Order and Appeals in the Senate." Congressional Research Service.

Congressional Research Service, 1995, *Waivers of the Budget Act Considered in the Senate.* Unpublished.

Doyle, Richard and Jerry McCaffery, 1991. "The Budget Enforcement Act of 1990: The Path to No-Fault Budgeting." *Public Budgeting and Finance,* vol. 11 (1), 25–40.

Ellwood, John, 1985. "The Great Exception: The Congressional Budget Process in an Age of Decentralization." In Lawrence Dodd and Bruce L. Oppenheimer, eds., *Congress Reconsidered,* 3rd ed. Washington: Congressional Quarterly, pp. 315–342.

_____. 1988. "The Politics of the Enactment and Implementation of Gramm-Rudman-Hollings: Why Congress Cannot Address the Deficit Dilemma." *Harvard Journal of Legislation,* vol. 25, 553–575.

Fisher, Louis, 1985. "Ten Years of the Budget Act: Still Searching for Controls." *Public Budgeting and Finance,* vol. 5 (Autumn), 3–28.

_____. 1990. "Federal Budget Doldrums: A Vacuum in Presidential Leadership." *Public Administration Review,* vol. 50 (November/December), 693–700.

Haem, Sung Duek, Mark S. Kamlet, David C. Mowery, and Tsai-Tsu Su, 1992. "The Influence of the Gramm-Rudman-Hollings Act on Federal Budgetary Outcomes, 1986–1989." *Journal of Policy Analysis and Management,* vol. 11 (2), 207–232.

Hanushek, Eric, 1986. "Formula Budgeting: The Economics and Analytics of Fiscal Policy Under Rules." *Journal of Policy Analysis and Management*, vol. 6 (1), 3–19.

Hartman, Robert, 1982. "Congress and Budget-Making." *Political Science Quarterly*, vol. 97 (Fall), 381–402.

Joyce, Philip G., 1993. "The Reiterative Nature of Budget Reform: Is There Anything New in Federal Budgeting?" *Public Budgeting and Finance*, vol. 13 (Fall), 36–48.

Joyce, Philip G. and Robert D. Reischauer, 1992. "Deficit Budgeting: The Federal Budget Process and Budget Reform." *Harvard Journal on Legislation*, vol. 29, 429–453.

Meyers, Roy T., 1996. "Is There a Key to the Normative Budgeting Lock?" *Policy Sciences* (forthcoming).

Penner, Rudolph and Alan Abramson, 1988. *Broken Purse Strings: Congressional Budgeting 1974–1988*. Washington, DC: The Urban Institute.

Reischauer, Robert D., 1990. "Taxes and Spending Under Gramm-Rudman-Hollings." *National Tax Journal*, vol. 63 (September), 223–232.

_____. 1993. Testimony before the Joint Committee on the Organization of Congress. March 4.

Rivlin, Alice, 1986. "The Need for a Better Budget Process." *Brookings Review* (Summer), 3–10.

Schick, Allen, 1980. *Congress and Money*. Washington, DC: The Urban Institute.

_____. 1991. Testimony before the House Committee on the Budget. October 10.

Stith, Kate, 1988. "Rewriting the Fiscal Constitution: The Case of Gramm-Rudman-Hollings." *California Law Review*, vol. 76 (May), 593–668.

Stockman, David, 1986. *The Triumph of Politics: Why the Reagan Revolution Failed*. New York: Harper and Row.

United States Congressional Budget Office, 1994a. *An Analysis of the Administration's Health Proposal*. Washington, DC: U.S. Government Printing Office.

_____. 1994b. *The Economic and Budget Outlook, An Update*. Washington, DC: U.S. Government Printing Office.

38

James J. Gosling

BUDGETARY DECISION MAKING

FACING THE CONSTRAINTS ON BUDGETARY CHOICE

Budgetary choices are made in an environment characterized by greatly compressed time lines, information overload, complex technical issues, competing values (leading to different definitions of the problems requiring government action), and alternative ways of addressing those problems. All these factors contribute to the efforts of budget makers to simplify budgetary choice.

In his classic study, *Administrative Behavior*, Herbert Simon observes that decision makers simplify choice by making decisions within a closed system of "givens." Cues inconsistent with those givens are screened out as prospective influences on decision making. Thus the search for solutions to problems is undertaken only within the confines of a restricted set of options that are in harmony with the givens. Decision makers need not compare the means and ends of an indefinite number of alternatives in making choices; they "statisfice," instead, by restricting their search to options consistent with the established givens, selecting the first alternative that appears to meet their objectives.[1]

In characterizing decision making as an activity characterized by statisficing, Simon takes issue with the classical model of rational decision making. According to that model, rational decisions require that decision makers

1. identify their objectives and rank them in order of priority.
2. identify all alternatives that might realize those objectives.
3. select criteria by which to evaluate each alternative.
4. choose the alternative that best satisfies the criteria and attains the objectives.

For advocates of rational decision making, this model was advance as the way rational decisions should be made; doing less would be something other than rational choice. Simon, the empiricist, argues that decisions are, in fact, not made that way, suggesting that his model more closely represents the way complex choices are made in practice.

Charles Lindblom, building on the work of Simon, also takes issue with the rational-choice model. In Lindblom's view, decision makers do not approach problems in the comprehensive fashion dictated by the rational model; instead, they focus on piecemeal, adjustive choice. They focus on the increments of change, first by examining only limited alternatives that involve small changes from existing policies and second by adjusting their choices on those increments to the choices of prior actors.[2] In this way, reminiscent of Simon, they engage in a form of satisficing.

For Lindblom, incremental adjustment sidesteps problems posed by disagreement on values and objectives. Decision makers do not begin by clarifying their values and then ranking their objectives, consistent with those values, in priority order. To the contrary, the values underlying the objectives of preexisting choices remain essentially intact; only adjustments on the margin become the subject of inquiry. The inheritance of prior choice remains largely undisturbed. In focusing on increments of change rather than objectives, individuals can often either agree on actions to be taken even if they hold conflicting values or permit their values to become clarified or changed in application.

With mutual adjustment, decision makers choose ends and means simultaneously, something the rational model does not allow. The prior or expected choices of others provide signals about the likely political success of different means; and in the politics of accommodation, these cues may often prompt modifications in the sought-after ends themselves. Procedurally, the flexibility inherent in adjustive choice allows complex problems to be broken down into their simpler components, so that subgroups can deal with each, ultimately putting together a solution through mutual adjustment.

As choices on the margin are adjusted to choices of other decision makers, values neglected by some decision makers may be represented by others. For Lindblom, public policies achieved through adjustive, piecemeal choice generally embody a broader community of values than is possible under the top-down rational model. To Lindblom, that is the way decisions should be made in a democratic society. Given mankind's limited intellect, the incrementalism of adjustive choice is not only a way in which decision makers cope with complexity; it also reflects a certain "intelligence of democracy."[3]

Aaron Wildavsky, commonly recognized as the father of budgetary incremental-ism, was greatly influenced in his early work by the theories of both Herbert Simon and Charles Lindblom. On the basis of his early research on the politics of the federal budgetary process, Wildavsky concluded that budget makers treat the budgetary base as a given of sorts, freeing their attention to the budgetary increments of change re-quests and recommendations that depart from the base. For Wildavsky, budget mak-ers do not make such choices in isolation; they do so in relation to the anticipated decisions of other institutional participants. Like Lindblom, Wildavsky observes that participants adjust their budgetary choices to what they expect other participants will do. The institutional roles of participants in the budgetary process serve as the basis for that anticipated choice.

It is clear to Wildavsky that in adjusting their choices to the expected behavior of other institutional actors, budget makers think in terms of percentages as they con-sider incremental departures from the base. Thus central budget officers focus on the percentage increases requested by the agencies. In turn, legislative budget participants look at the percentage increases over the base recommended by the chief executive. In focusing on the percentage increments from the base and on reciprocal expectations of budgetary behavior, budget makers greatly simplify their decisions. They avoid the overwhelming problem of comparing the values of all existing programs with all possi-ble alternatives for each, as the rational decision-making model dictates. For Wil-davsky, then, budgeting is experiential, simplified, satisficing, and incremental.[4]

> Budgeting is incremental, not comprehensive. The beginning wisdom about an agency budget is that it is almost never actively reviewed as a whole every year in the sense of reconsidering the value of all existing programs as compared to all possible alterna-tives. Instead, it is based on last year's budget with special attention given to a narrow range of increases or decreases. Thus, the men who make the budget are concerned with relatively small increments to an existing base. Their attention is focused on a small number of items over which the budgetary battle is fought.[5]

Just as Lindblom sees a certain "intelligence" in mutual adjustive choice, Wil-davsky believes incremental budgeting has a rationality of its own. It uses experience (the budgetary base and the earlier choices of participants), role perceptions and asso-ciated expectations of choice, and a decentralized decision-making process to reduce the complexity of strategic calculations to a manageable level. For Wildavsky, not only does incremental budgeting have a certain rationality, but also it is in line with the re-alities of the democratic political process, in which the politics of mutual adjustment appropriately determine those objectives toward which governments should commit public resources.

THE CRITICS OF INCREMENTALISM

It is one thing to show that linear equations can approximate the outcomes of the budgetary process and quite another to account for that behavior theoretically. Davis, Dempster, and Wildavsky maintain that the results of their models confirm the incremental thesis of budgeting, at least as it operates at the federal level. Crit-ics, on the other hand, take issue both with the validity of the conclusions drawn from the regression models and with the ties back to the theory of budgetary incrementalism itself.[6]

The work of both John Wanat and John Gist supports the first line of criticism. Using the same models as Davis and his associates but substituting randomly generated data, Wanat came up with correlations as high as those found earlier and concluded that the presence of high correlations does not support the existence of budgetary decision rules.[7]

Reanalyzing the data used by Davis, Dempster, and Wildavsky, Gist found that the high correlations in the regression models were the result of a methodological limitation—not controlling for colinearity in the data, where both independent and dependent variables share common components that account for high correlations.[8]

Notwithstanding such criticisms of empirical methodology, other researchers take issue with the theoretical basis of incrementalism. John Bailey and Robert O'Connor find fault with the "descriptive precision" and "explanatory usefulness" of budgetary incrementalism. Findings suggesting that budgets grow stably over time through relatively small changes to their existing base are cited by proponents of incrementalist theory as evidence that decision makers make choices incrementally. Thus "incrementalism in outcomes" is used as support for "incrementalism in the process." But what constitutes incrementalism in outcomes is subject to dispute.

Pointing to findings in which slightly more that half of appropriations reviewed increased by less than 10 percent a year, Wildavsky finds that outcome supports the incremental thesis. Yet, as Bailey and O'Connor note, the same findings also mean that in about half the cases, appropriations exceeded a 10 percent annual rate of growth. Wildavsky adds that three-quarters fell within a 30 percent increase, hardly what would be considered to fall within the rubric of incremental change.[9]

Even if one accepts that budgeting is associated with stable appropriations patterns over time, apparent stability at the agency level may mask instability at the program level. The use of aggregate budget totals at the agency level may represent a netting of choices made by institutional budget participants across programs, thus concealing possible competition and tradeoffs among them.

With access to budget requests and decisions at the subagency, agency, central budget office (OMB), and presidential levels for the Atomic Energy Commission between 1958 and 1972, Peter Natchez and Irving Bupp examined what they believed to be the competition between programs and policies that takes place within what appears to be the stability of incremental decision making. Examining the programs dealing with high-energy physics, nuclear rockets, nuclear weapons, and thermonuclear research, Natchez and Bupp found considerable differences in their respective patterns of budgetary increase and decrease. If their analysis had been confined to agency-level dollar totals, those fluctuations would not have been apparent.

The Natchez and Bupp findings suggest that budget makers may indeed apply different decision rules to guide their choices at the discrete program level. Restricting the analysis to the agency level of aggregation may hide that variation in choice and give the appearance that a unidimensional decision rule is being used.[10] Others studies analyzing the budgets of the Department of Defense, the National Aeronautics and Space Administration, and the State Department came up with similar findings.[11]

MOVING BEYOND INCREMENTALISM

Among the various criticisms of budgetary incrementalism operationalized by researchers, one stands out. It points to the gap between the findings produced by empirical models of incremental decision making and their theoretical underpinnings. The identification and testing of simple decision rules, using total-dollar amounts aggregated at the agency level, produce a picture of budgetary decision making that appears to be oversimplified and even misleading.

The research suggests that budget makers concern themselves primarily with the size of increments in relation to the budgetary base, both in making requests and in acting upon the requests or recommendations of others. We know that agencies tend to pad their requests, expecting that they will be cut back by budget reviewers. The incrementalists further suggest that budget makers apply a limited number of simple incremental decision rules to guide their budgetary choices, irrespective of the program areas in question, the nature of the discrete budget items before them, or the macrolevel constraints facing them whether those be tax or spending limitations at the state and local levels or spending ceilings imposed at the federal level. On the contrary, any theory of budgetary decision making must take such factors into account.

Budget makers at all levels of government are bombarded with innumerable cues that compete to influence budgetary decision making. These cues include the program areas affected, the costs of budget items, the sources of funding involved, the degree of increase of decrease sought or recommended, the relative uncontrollability of the spending, its intergovernmental and constituency effects, views of what constitutes the appropriate role of government in society, different standards of judgment employed in defining problems and in evaluating alternative courses of action to resolve them, a sense of appropriate policy priorities, some sense of the prospective efficiency and effectiveness of what is requested or recommended, partisan influences, some assessment of the political feasibility of different budgetary options, the actual choices of those participants deciding earlier in the serial budgetary process, and expectations about how other decision makers will behave in making their own choices.

Budget participants do no attempt to measure their preferences along each of these dimensions of decision making; to take them all systematically into account in a sort of calculus of decision making would overwhelm participants' cognitive ability. Budget makers, however, do respond selectively to these influences, giving heed to some in preference to others. They draw upon cues selectively, depending on the decisions before them. And if they regularly turn to certain cues in certain situations, they can be said to follow decision rules. The challenge, then, is to identify the factors that prompt institutional budget participants to adopt certain decision rules in certain situations.

Focusing on Decision Items

Pursuing this line of reasoning, we need to look at the major items considered in budgetary decisions, not at the aggregate dollars requested, recommended, or approved for each government agency, or even for programs or subprograms within those agencies. Such items can be thought of as institutionally supported initiatives to increase, reduce, or reallocate the expenditure authority of an agency's budget base whether they occur across appropriations within the same program, across programs, or even across agencies.

Here are two examples of such decision items at the federal level: The first might be a presidential recommendation to provide the Department of Defense with additional funds to procure eight new high-cost B-2 bombers. The second might be initiation by the Senate, in its deliberations on the federal budget, of a program of financial aid to cities to assist them in meeting the rising costs of medical care and social services for the rapidly increasing number of people with acquired immune deficiency syndrome (AIDS).

Decision items can also be recommendations to reduce or eliminate funding for government activities. A presidential recommendation to eliminate federal operating subsidies for mass transit presents the Congress with a discrete item for decision. So does a presidential proposal to reduce significantly the level of agricultural price supports for certain commodities.

Examples are prevalent in state and local budgeting as well. At the state level, a legislative budget committee's action to earmark state funding for special educational programs for disadvantaged children in major metropolitan school districts forces the entire legislature to act on that item. Similarly, a governor's proposal to close a state mental health institution and increase support for community-based treatment centers puts that choice before the entire state legislature.

At the municipal level, a mayor's request for funds to establish a new drug enforcement program in the police department, including the authorization of 20 new positions, confronts the city council with a distinct budgetary choice. Such examples can be multiplied many times over at all levels of government.

The structure of decision items is imposed by budget participants as they organize the budget into discrete items around which they believe decisions should be made. Although the administrative agencies get the first crack at structuring the budget when they develop their requests, the chief executive and the legislature can alter that structure. The chief executive decides what parts of the requests to recommend and how to organize them for presentation to the legislature (except where constrained by law or practice to include all agency requests in the executive budget document). The legislature, in turn, decides how it wants to break down the executive budget for review.

True to the basic tenet of incrementalism, the budget base is taken as a "given" unless an institutional participant proposes to alter it in one of the ways mentioned here. Where they are permitted, initiatives in the budget can also create, change, or repeal statutory law, and thus they too are decision items. To qualify as a decision item in either case, the initiative must be officially endorsed by the institution and not merely proposed by one of its members.

All the items in agency budget requests can be considered as decision items in the sense used above because agency leaders have officially endorsed them. These decision items, in turn, are acted upon by subsequent participants in the serial budgetary process—at least as far down the line as the requests survive. It thus becomes possible to track the fate of decision items throughout the budgetary process. In jurisdictions where agency requests must be included in the executive budget book along with the chief executive's recommendation, it is possible to examine the latter's action on each. Upon receipt of the executive budget, a legislative fiscal or appropriations committee is free to accept, reject, or modify the chief executive's recommendations; and when it rejects a recommendation, it may return the decision item to the form originally requested by the agency. The committee can also initiate budget recommendations of its own for which no requests or recommendations have been made either by an agency or by the chief executive. The legislature as a whole faces similar options; it can concur with its committee's recommendation, modify it, or reject it altogether. The legislature also can initiate recommendations that have not yet been considered by any participant coming earlier in the process.

In some cases, an institutional participant may amend a request or recommendation in a way that greatly changes the essence of the decision item. For example, a state appropriations committee might approve a request from the department of public instruction (supported by the governor) to finance 20 new academic subject-matter consultants to work with local school districts. The committee could then further recommend that the new consultants, as well as all consultants already in the department, be placed on program revenue, to be supported by user fees paid by the local districts. This recommendation would significantly change the nature of the decision item. Not only would it alter the department's relationship with local school districts, but also it would result in a base cut of state funds (substituting program revenue for state general revenue support). In this example, although a major change would be made to the request, the action would not create a new decision item; instead, the item initiated by the department would be changed, albeit significantly. On the other hand, if the whole idea of adding these consultants had been initiated by the legislature itself, another decision item would have been added for consideration.

Decision items differ not only in the ways they are initiated and chosen but also in their characteristics. Some involve the prospective expenditure of hundreds of millions of dollars from the public treasury. This phenomenon, for example, might be seen in a proposal to increase state support for primary and secondary education from 40 to 50 percent of available costs. Other decision items that entail no new expenditure of public funds can nonetheless be of major policy significance.

In addition to knowing the characteristics of decision items budget makers are attentive to the broader context in which these items are considered. Incrementalist theory suggests that budget makers may view a decision item that calls for a large increase over base quite differently from the way they see a decision item that includes only a modest request. It also is conceivable that institutional budget participants react differently to decision items from different sources—cabinet agencies, agencies headed by constitutionally elected officials, boards, or commissions. For example, a chief executive may be more inclined to support the requests of cabinet officials than to advocate those coming from elected officials, who may be political rivals.

Serial Budgeting, Interruptions and Adjustments, and Participant Choice

Budget makers also pay attention to the budgetary decisions of the institutional participants who precede them in the serial budgetary process. Documents prepared by staff often track the decisions of prior participants. Thus, for example, members of a state legislature can see what their budget committee did to the governor's recommendation in light of the governor's earlier recommendation. Such information is important because the legislature might well be more likely to support the governor's recommendation when its own committee concurred with it.

Public budgeting, with its serial decision making, is a product of delegation, initiation, and reactive choice. Delegation can be either conscious or unconscious. Conscious delegation is a decision on the part of a budget participant to accept the version of the budget passed on by the immediately preceding institutional participant. Unconscious delegation is really a nondecision, in which the version sent forward by a participant remains unaltered because the following participants fail to act on it at all. Those participants do not concur with it affirmatively; they simply do not bother to reject or amend it. The budget item may not even come to their attention; it moves along "unflagged" for review. Such a foregone opportunity to exercise conscious choice becomes tantamount to agreement, in that the budget item is sent to the succeeding institutional participants in unaltered form, just as if there had been conscious concurrence.

Budget makers are not willing to delegate their choices across the board. Instead, they are selective about such delegation, relinquishing direct control of that part of the budget that involves little or no policy change or has little or no fiscal effect. Once such a budget item is initiated, chances are good that it will be included in the approved budget. For this relative chaff of the budgetary process, however, a decision by any institutional participant to reject an item altogether just about seals its doom, for it is unlikely that subsequent participants will care enough to reinsert it. Most likely, other participants will not even be aware that the minor decision item had ever been "alive."

Delegation represents a "rational" decision strategy of sorts. It is a way of conserving resources to be invested in budgetary decisions that really matter to budget reviewers. And each institutional participant employs its own criteria in deciding what is important. Because of this selective exercise of delegation and amendatory choice, the final approved budget is a much different product from the document first advanced by the chief executive.

Although there is a distinct seriality to budgeting, budgetary decisions are subject to adjustments based on new and changing information. A certain interdependence exists between identifiable phases of the budgetary process, such as revenue estimating, spending choices, and issues of implementation. New revenue estimates issued by legislative staff well after the legislature has already begun its consideration of the executive's budget recommendations (which were based on earlier executive branch revenue projections) provide important and timely information that most likely would prompt legislators to go back and reconsider the earlier spending recommendations of their fiscal committees. Irene Rubin, a perceptive analyst of budgetary decision making, views this information penetration, and the subsequent adjustments it occasions, as a key feature of what she refers to as real-time budgeting. It disrupts what otherwise appears to be serial, or sequential, decision making, and prompts decision makers to reexamine assumptions and prior choices and adjust them to the new environmental reality.

Therefore, although budget participants do indeed react to the choices of prior institutional participants in the budgetary process, they must continually reassess their budgetary choices in light of new information. That often means revisiting prior choices and delaying other decisions that should follow in sequence. For Rubin, real-time decision making allows the process to be disrupted, interrupted, and repeated.[12]

The Influence of Macrodecision Making on Microchoices

The decision-item approach focuses on what can appropriately be called micro decision making. Microlevel decisions can focus on the individual decision items considered by budget participants on their line items or on the amounts requested or recommended for agencies, their organizational subcomponents, programs, or subprograms. Macrodecision making transcends agency-specific boundaries and involves a priori choices about how much a governmental jurisdiction should spend and how fast that spending should grow; how much taxing the jurisdiction should do; what the appropriate distribution of budget shares among programs should be; and what an appropriate budget balance or deficit (where permitted) should constitute.[13] Both micro- and macrodecisions affect budgetary outcomes, but most students of contemporary budgeting would probably argue that macrolevel decisions today play a more significant role in shaping public budgets than they did nearly three decades ago—the time when Wildavsky and his colleagues conducted their research on federal budgeting. Although this generalization probably applies to all levels of government, it is most apparent at the federal level.

Macrobudgeting has intruded on microbudgeting at the state and local government levels as well. The taxpayer revolt, which started at the local level in the late 1970s and spread to the states, combined with the recession-induced austerity of the early 1980s, created a changed environment for subfederal public budgeting. No longer could agencies count on incremental budgetary growth—the tenor of the times in many state and local government promoted flat budgets and even some decremental budgeting, where expenditures were budgeted to decline from one year to the next. In many state and local governments, tax or spending limitations kept government growth within bounds. The recession created the highest levels of unemployment since the Great Depression and cut significantly into normal state revenue expectations while simultaneously pushing expenditures up for public assistance and social services. The 1990–1991 recession, although less severe than that of a decade earlier, placed new pressures on state and local budgets.

In this environment, protectionism often became the name of the budgetary game—warding off budget cuts, staff reductions, and even program elimination. State and local budget officers put the lid on new program creation and existing program growth, and agencies were characteristically called upon to reallocate existing resources to meet new priorities. Budgeting became a zero-sum game in many jurisdictions, as selective increases had to be offset by decreases elsewhere in an agency's budget base.

Fiscal austerity can conceivably affect budgetary choice in different ways. When it is most severe, budget reviewers may feel they have been given a ready rationale for rejecting all but the most pressing nonentitlement spending. Where budgets must be balanced, at the state and local levels, budgeting can maintain that revenues are merely sufficient, if even that, to cover mandated increases. In this setting, budget reviewers may pay little heed to information offered in support of most requests. Nor are they likely to spend much time analyzing budget alternatives. The expectation of a ready-made "no" invites little analytical effort. Conversely, a competing perspective suggests that budgetary analysis is most highly valued in an austere fiscal environment. As the argument goes, tough choices must be made; priorities must be set; and even existing programs and services may need to be cut. Analysis can serve as a useful tool in helping budget participants make those decisions, by highlighting the implications of alternative choices and assessing the relative efficiency of alternative resource uses.

Several close observers of budgeting argue that the other extreme, steady and significant revenue growth, tends to be more conducive to incremental decision making.[14] Lacking tight fiscal constraints, budget makers are able to avoid the difficult priority choices and more readily rely on nonpolicy decision rules, focusing on requests in relation to the budgetary base. When there are enough revenues to go around, aggregated budgetary choices can be put together through the politics of mutual adjustment.

ANALYSIS IN BUDGETARY DECISION MAKING

There are those who advocate the incorporation of policy analysis into budget making as a means of promoting better-informed budgetary decisions regardless of the fiscal environment.[15] Analysis can help decision makers define the problematic, assess the consequences of alternative courses of action, and become aware of the different criteria by which alternatives can be evaluated. At a minimum, advocates view analysis as a filter of sorts that provides decision makers with a sense of which considerations are significant in making different budgetary choices and which are relatively unimportant. They also see analysis as a means of sensitizing budget participants to the fact that there can be more than one criterion or standard of judgment upon which budget requests or recommendations are based. Knowledge of the underlying criterion of judgment provides important information that helps the reviewer to comprehend why a problem is defined a certain way and why one alternative is preferred over another.

Policy analysis, when used in budgeting, usually does not begin with clearly defined objectives and clarified values, as the rational model dictates; instead, policy analysis often focuses on specific, fairly well defined issues or problems in the short run; and it usually is confined to an examination of a relatively narrow range of alternatives. Budget issue papers, for example, may be produced on a variety of topics. At the federal level, they might examine the appropriateness and implications of existing levels of borrowing and debt, credit programs, and tax expenditures. At the state level, appropriate topics might be the comparative adequacy of public-university faculty salaries, alternative approaches to property tax relief, or the appropriateness of existing public-assistance support levels. Subjects for analysis at the municipal level could include the adequacy of neighborhood police protection, the need for and implications of expanded user fees, or options for increasing operating revenues for mass transit. All these would-be analyses have one feature in common: they attempt to make complex issues more readily understandable to decision makers.

Program Budgeting

One noteworthy attempt, with vestiges that remain today, was the effort to institutionalize program budgeting. Introduced in the Department of Defense in 1961 as the Planning-Programming-Budgeting System (PPBS), it was based on the premise that all elements of the defense budget could be grouped into discrete program categories reflecting the department's various missions, showing how they collectively contribute to the whole and at what cost. These programs could cut across existing organizational boundaries, grouping like activities together and thus modifying the notion that each agency has the exclusive prerogative of delivering the programmatic objectives assigned exclusively to it.

As an illustration, the strategic forces program incorporates nuclear submarines, capable of launching shorter-range nuclear missiles, together with land-based intercontinental ballistics missiles and long-range heavy bombers, capable of carrying nuclear bombs. All three can be said to provide this nation with a nuclear strike force capable of deterring first strikes by other nations. Yet the delivery systems are organizationally assigned to different departments within Defense. With PPBS, then, the objective was to come up with that package of nuclear strike capability that best meets the overarching objective of deterrence at the lowest cost, raising the standard of efficiency as the prime criterion of choice.

Program budgeting starts with the notion of zeroing in on the goals and related objectives of government and then relating government's various activities to those objectives. It is hoped that by doing so alternative ways of realizing those objectives will be more broadly explored by decision makers, regardless of organizational lines. Analysis is directed at the desired outcomes and the best way to achieve them. Therefore, analysis must be devoted to measuring the benefits as well as the costs associated with each alternative.

In order to institutionalize PPBS in the federal government and expand its use beyond the Department of Defense, the Bureau of the Budget (BOB) created a budgeting system that it imposed on all executive departments in 1965. Goals, objectives, programs, subprograms, and program elements had to be identified for all agencies. Base budgets had to be restructured along programmatic lines, and requests had to be justified by showing that they represented the most efficient (and adequately effective) use of resources to achieve the desired objectives and their ultimate goals. The BOB developed forms and formats to structure the agencies' analyses, among them the so-called program memorandum (PM) that was to serve as the analytical justification for each program element request. Accompanying the PM was the program and financial plan (PFP), which was to show the financial implications over five years, associated with support of the request. Finally, special analytical studies (SAS) were to be prepared by the requesting agencies on major issues addressed in the budget. These issues were usually identified by the BOB, and their development occurred under its watchful eye.

The use of policy analysis to evaluate alternative solutions to public problems was nothing new; it had been used to inform policy choice well before PPBS came on the scene. What was new was the attempt to incorporate analysis systematically into the fabric of budgeting through program budgeting to make analysis an inherent part of budget development and review. As Charles Schultze remarked

> Analytical efforts that stay outside of the stream of decisions remain just that—analytical efforts, not instruments for shaping decisions. The crucial element of PPBS is that it operates through the budget process. It seeks to bring analysis to bear on decisions by merging analysis, planning and budgetary allocation. It is a decision structure, and therefore must relate to other elements of the decision process.[16]

The creators of PPBS had great expectations about how it would change decision making in the executive branch and spill over into the congressional arena. Not only would decisions be made in relation to clearly identified goals, but also alternative choices would be evaluated using clearly identified criteria. However, these expectations were never realized in practice. Although forms were created to provide the appearance that analysis was being incorporated into budgetary decision making, beyond its early use within the Department of Defense, where it was promoted by top management, PPBS never really caught on in the federal bureaucracy. By 1969, only three federal department had made substantial progress toward implementing it, according to the General Accounting Office.[17] Nor did it ever become an accepted part of congressional decision making on the budget. At the executive level, PPBS degenerated into a "paper exercise"—a conformance to form rather than to spirit. By the time the Nixon administration came into office, even the attention to form was put aside. In 1971, the Office of Management and Budget (OMB, successor to the BOB) discontinued its requirement that agencies submit PFPs, PMs, and SASs. Except for the continuation of selective special analyses, PPBS as a ubiquitous structure in federal budgeting was allowed a quiet death.[18] Within Congress, Appropriations Committee members, accustomed to line-item budgeting, never became comfortable with program budgeting, retaining their desire for organizationally related "numbers."

Several state and local governments, watching the genesis and growth of program budgeting at the federal level during the 1960s, initiated their own experiments. Help in these efforts came from a Ford Foundation grant, supporting the State-Local Finances Project—an attempt to provide technical assistance to five states (California, Michigan, New York, Vermont, and Wisconsin), five counties (Dade, Los Angeles, Nashville-Davidson, Nassau, and Wayne), and five cities (Dayton, Denver, Detroit, New Haven, and San Diego) in designing and implementing program budgeting systems. Some other governments also implemented their own systems, most notably Hawaii, Pennsylvania, New York City, and Philadelphia.

On the whole, however, the experience of the state and local governments adopting program budgeting systems paralleled that of the federal government. Some of the forms of program budgeting were incorporated into their budget systems, but nowhere did a PPBS-like system survive at the state or local level. Pennsylvania came closest to implementing a "pure" program budgeting system, but program budgeting never fully displaced the traditionally organized budget. The Pennsylvania Legislature, in fact, demanded both forms, along with a "cross-walk" relating the two. Today, the two are merged in a pseudo-program-budget format.

What has remained of the early experiments in most state and local governments is a program structure that parallels departmental organization. Thus program-related numbers are also organization-related numbers. Moreover, as happened at the federal level, several states institutionalized the production of selective policy-issue papers as companions to the executive budget book(s).

Zero-Base Budgeting

While program budgeting was falling out of favor and being abandoned or greatly modified at all levels of government, a "new" form of budgeting was gaining popularity at the state level. That form, called zero-base budgeting (ZBB), originated in the private sector; but within government it was first systematically applied in the state of Georgia, although the U.S. Department of Agriculture experimented with a variant of ZBB in the 1960s. Identified with the Jimmy Carter administration, ZBB received national attention as its alleged successes became a prominent element of Carter's campaign for the presidency. In that campaign, the former governor of Georgia promised, if elected, to bring ZBB to the federal government. As touted, ZBB would force all budgets to be examined and justified from "scratch," including all elements of the base. In practice, it did not work that way.

Upon President Carter's election in 1976, the OMB began developing ZBB into a form that could be used by all federal departments. On April 19, 1977, the OMB issued its formal budgetary instructions. Agencies were to break their budgets down into discrete decision units, the lowest level at which meaningful management decisions are made. But the instructions left it up to each agency to decide what should constitute a decision unit; it could variously be a program, subprogram, program element, or a cost center. Regardless of the budget level selected, managers had to identify and rank decision packages at four hypothetical funding levels for each decision unit: (1) the minimum level, below which the enterprise would no longer be viable; (2) the maintenance level, that which is required to continue the existing level of operations or services without any policy change; (3) the intermediate level, some point between the minimum and maintenance levels; and (4) the improvement level, requiring additional resources to expand operations or services.[19] In the aggregate then, four budgets were to be prepared, one for each funding level.

The response to ZBB was mixed during the Carter administration. The Office of Management and Budget liked the technique and its products largely because it forced the agencies to place priorities on decision packages, giving the OMB the ready opportunity to cut lower-ranked priorities from the request. Anticipating such behavior, agencies, generally attempted to make the case that cuts below current levels would be disastrous to agency programs and that even funding at current levels would result in program erosion through the effects of nonaccommodated inflation. Thus the exercise for agencies became highly guarded and defensive. It also saddled agency budget staffs with much heavier work loads and greatly increased paperwork requirements, all for the purpose, from the agencies' perspective, of giving the OMB ammunition for budget reductions.[20]

Although ZBB is no longer used as a coherent system for federal budgeting, remnants remain today. The Reagan administration retained the requirement that agencies submit alternative budget requests, including one lower than the base, at a percentage decrement prescribed by the OMB.[21] That practice continued under the Bush administration.

As had happened with PPBS, the status of ZBB as the national government's "new" budgetary system prompted a number of state and local governments to give it a try. Yet they frequently adopted only selective elements of ZBB as it was employed at the federal level. Most commonly, state and local governments incorporated some form of alternative budgeting whereby agencies were required to submit requests corresponding to different target levels perhaps at 80, 90, 100, and 105 percent of base so that the tradeoffs among them would be apparent to budget reviewers. This technique fit nicely with the budgetary climate of economic downturn and heightened taxpayer sensitivity in the early 1980s.

Analysis Apart from Budgetary Systems

Analysis outside formal budgetary systems can inform budgetary choice. At a minimum, decision makers use it to support decisions shaped by other factors such as normative values, preconceived notions, or views of what is politically feasible. Analyses prepared by respected staff officers or by trusted personal aides will be used as decision aids much more readily than analyses prepared by those who are ideologically or politically suspect.

Where there is credibility, analysis can influence budgetary choice. Well-reasoned and supported recommendations can sway decision makers, especially when they are premised on a criterion of evaluation prized by the decision makers. For example, a recommendation that defines a budgetary issue largely as a problem of inequity and evaluates budgetary options in terms of the extent to which they improve equity will not go far in swaying a decision maker who sees the problem not in terms of inequity but as an issue of inefficiency.

When preferred options are not premised on shared criteria of evaluation, the analyst faces the considerable challenge of persuading the client that the former's way of viewing the problem and weighing alternatives is better than the latter's.

Such caveats suggest that budgetary choice is in reality political choice. As such, it is significantly influenced by the values and perceptions of political relationships. At the same time, the budget's size and complexity constrain the degree to which analysis can influence budgetary decision making.

MAKING BUDGETARY CHOICES: PUTTING THE PIECES TOGETHER

Faced with the constraints on choice discussed in the previous section, budget participants turn to decision shortcuts. Although they give special attention to the major decision items that more readily catch their attention (because of an item's cost, its exposure in the media, its normative implications, its effects on key constituencies, its political support or opposition from party leaders, or any of several other factors), they do not give the other parts of the budget equal attention. Instead, they may simply defer to the choices of prior institutional participants. They may also adopt incremental decision rules, supporting what they believe to be an acceptable percentage over the base, and move on to other decisions.

Choices on discrete decision items or agency-level budget totals can nevertheless be conditioned by macrolevel decisions, such as those that preordain budget shares as part of an agreed-upon level of aggregate spending. When this occurs, budget participants are forced to make their choices on key budget items conform in order to be consistent with the aggregate framework. But in setting that framework—for instance, as the outcome of a bipartisan executive-legislative budget summit—difficult choices must be made up front on the relative share that should go to the various (or at least major) functional areas of the budget. Those very choices become highly significant political decisions, subject to all the vagaries of political choice already discussed.

Summary and Conclusions

Public budgeting is a complex enterprise. Not only do government budgets represent plans to spend large sums of public money, but also they serve as key vehicles for public policy making. Budgets can be overwhelming in their size, policy and programmatic diversity, process, structure, specialized nomenclature, and politics. Tight timetables for budget development, review, and action make the decision-making task even more formidable.

Budget makers cope with these constraints by simplifying budgetary decision making. Instead of taking carefully considered positions on all budget elements before them, budget participants selectively turn to decision cues to assist them in making choices. One cue appears to be the extent to which requests and recommendations depart from the budgetary base. A second consists of expectations about how participants will react to the expected choices of other participants. A third involves the characteristics of the individual decision items making up the budget, including their relative policy significance and their fiscal and distributive effects. A fourth can be the persuasive power of analysis that supports a given budget alternative in preference to others. A fifth consists of the influence of macrolevel parameters on microlevel budgetary decisions. Macroinfluences can include a priori decisions about aggregate levels of taxing and spending, the existence of tax and spending limitations, and automatic spending mechanisms (such as entitlements and sum-sufficient appropriations) that commit resources outside the normal appropriations process.

All of these factors appear to influence contemporary budgetary decision making, although it appears that macrolevel influences have become more prominent during the last two decades. The key to understanding the budgetary decision making is to be able to identify systematically the factors that prompt budget participants to apply certain decision criteria in certain situations.

Notes

1. Herbert A. Simon, *Administrative Behavior* (New York: Macmillan, 1958).
2. Charles E. Lindblom, "Decision Making in Taxation and Expenditures," in National Bureau of Economic Research, *Public Finances: Needs, Sources, and Utilization* (Princeton, NJ: Princeton University Press, 1961), 295–323.
3. Charles E. Lindblom, *The Intelligence of Democracy: Decision Making through Mutual Adjustment* (New York: Free Press, 1966).
4. Aaron Wildavsky, *The Politics of the Budgetary Process* (Boston: Little, Brown, 1964).
5. Ibid., 15.
6. Lance T. LeLoup provides a nice "roadmap" to the literature critical of incrementalism. "The Myth of Incrementalism: Analytical Choices in Budgetary Theory," *Polity* 10 (Summer 1978): 488–509.
7. John Wanat, "The Bases of Budgetary Incrementalism," *American Political Science Review* 68 (September 1974): 1221–1228.
8. John R. Gist, "Mandatory Expenditures and the Defense Sector: Theory of Budgetary Incrementalism," *Sage Professional Papers in American Politics*, vol. 2, series 04-020 (Beverly Hills, Calif.: Sage Publications, 1976).

9. John J. Bailey and Robert J. O'Connor, "Operationalizing Incrementalism: Measuring the Muddles," *Public Administration Review* 35 (January/February 1975): 64–65.

10. P.B. Natchez and I.C. Bupp, "Policy and Priority in the Budgetary Process," *American Political Science Review* 67 (September 1973): 951–963.

11. John R. Gist, "Mandatory Expenditures"; Arnold Kanter, "Congress and the Defense Budget: 1960–1970," *American Political Science Review* 66 (March 1972): 129–143.

12. Irene S. Rubin, *The Politics of Public Budgeting*, 2nd ed. (Chatham, N.J.: Chatham House Publishers, 1993), 258–273.

13. For a discussion of the concepts of microbudgeting and macrobudgeting, see Lance T. LeLoup, "From Microbudgeting to Macrobudgeting: Evolution in Theory and Practice," in *New Direction in Budget Theory*, ed. Irene S. Rubin (Albany, N.Y.: State University of New York Press, 1988), 19–42. See Gregory W. Fischer and Mark S. Lamlet, "Explaining Presidential Priorities: The Competing Aspiration Levels Model of Macrobudgetary Decision Making," *American Political Science Review* 78 (June 1984): 356–371, for a discussion of the interdependence of defense and nondefense program shares at the federal level.

14. Allen Schick, "The Budget As an Instrument of Presidential Policy," in *The Reagan Presidency and the Governing of America*, ed. Lester M. Salamon and Michael S. Lund (Washington, D.C.: Urban Institute, 1985), 91–125.

15. Barry Bozeman and Jeffrey D. Straussman "Shrinking Budgets and the Shrinkage of Budget Theory," *Public Administration Review* 42 (November/December 1982): 509–515; Allen Schick, "Incremental Budgeting in a Decremental Age," *Policy Sciences* 16 (September 1983): 1–26; Daniel Tarchys, "Curbing Public Expenditures: A Survey of Current Trends" (Paper prepared for the Organization for Economic Cooperation and Development, October 1982); Irene S. Rubin, "Budget Theory and Budget Practice: How Good the Fit?" *Public Administration Review* 50 (March/April 1990): 179–189.

16. S. Kenneth Howard, *Changing State Budgeting* (Lexington, Ky: Council of State Governments, 1973); Arnold J. Meltsner, *Policy Analysts in the Bureaucracy* (Berkeley: University of California Press, 1976); Charles L. Schultze, *The Politics and Economics of Public Spending* (Washington, D.C.: The Brookings Institution, 1968).

17. Schultze, *Politics and Economics*, 77.

18. K.E. Marvin and A.M. Rouse, "The Status of PPB in Federal Agencies: A Comparative Perspective," in United States Congress, Joint Economic Committee, *Analysis and Evaluation of Public Expenditures: The PPB System* (Washington, D.C.: Government Printing Office, 1969), 814.

19. Office of Management and Budget, "Preparation and Submission of Budget Estimates," Circular A–11 (June 1971).

20. Donald Axelrod, *Budgeting for Modern Government* (New York: St. Martin's Press, 1988), p. 296.

21. See Allen Schick, "The Road from ZBB," *Public Administration Review* 38 (March/April 1978): 177–180.

14

EVALUATION AND MEASURING PRODUCTIVITY

A person who owns stock in a corporation will often be found scrutinizing the fine print in the stock exchange reports. Such reports occupy pages in the daily newspapers, and are the subject of on-line inquiries on the Internet, reports in TV news bulletins, and flashing mobile signs above our city skylines. Why? Because stockholders want to know exactly how their investments are doing, and how their corporation is performing. In the private market, share prices, profit and dividend results and the threat of takeover are ever-present concerns. As well, the New York Stock Exchange and the Securities and Exchange Commission are vigilant watchdogs making sure that misleading prospectuses are detected and dirty deals stopped in their tracks.

HOW DO WE KNOW IF A PUBLIC AGENCY IS PERFORMING WELL?

But how do we know if a public agency is performing well? Since private sector markets and sanctions do not apply, can public administrators get away with fraud, waste, poor performance or ineffective programs? In truth, they sometimes can, but to do so they must avoid a comprehensive set of scrutiny mechanisms designed to examine performance and productivity; detect and expose fraud or lack of compliance with financial mandates; and to assess and evaluate broader issues to do with program effectiveness. These are very important topics in public administration, reflecting the force of public and congressional scrutiny under which public administrators operate. And there are developed disciplines and institutions to do this work, including congressional committees, audit bodies such as the General Accounting Office, and program evaluators or consultants who may be engaged by a particular agency to take a close look at some aspect of their work.

COMPLIANCE AUDIT

The *compliance audit* is the simplest and most common form of scrutiny of public agencies. An auditor checks whether financial transactions undertaken by a public agency comply with relevant financial laws and regulations. The auditors undertaking this work need to be "at arm's length," free of direction from management as to what findings they make. Such arm's length auditors are said to be *external auditors.* They are outside the organization and independent of its control. The most prestigious grouping of external auditors in the public sector is the General Accounting Office (GAO), headed by the Comptroller of the United States. The Comptroller of the United States is an important official able to offer "free and frank advice" to the President. Nobody can tell the Comptroller what to investigate and what to put into or leave out of a report. Many public agencies have *internal auditors* on their staff as well. Internal auditors can play an important in-house early warning role, but they lack the independence of external auditors.

Compliance audits go back a long way. The office of Comptroller of the United States was created as part of the 1921 Budget Reform Act that we reviewed in Chapter 13. But reviewing just for financial compliance may not go far enough. A public agency can comply completely with laws and financial regulations but still be inefficient, and still be focusing its attention in the wrong place, or going about its work the wrong way.

EFFICIENCY AND PRODUCTIVITY

The second level of scrutiny looks at the efficiency or productivity of an organization's effort. Productivity in simple terms is the ratio between resources needed to do a job (inputs) and the quantity of results produced (outputs). *Productivity measurement* and efficiency reviews have been key issues for public managers and Congress for many years, and a substantial body of knowledge has been developed in the area. The journal, *Public Productivity & Management Review* is devoted exclusively to this topic. In some fields of government operations, standard measures of productivity have emerged, and organizations often rate themselves against their peers through formal or informal "benchmarking"[1] processes.

Productivity measurement has problems. It is much easier to use where a routine processing activity is involved, and where staff are devoted to a single output—like processing mail. In more complex areas of government work, like policy advice, the measurement of productivity is much more difficult. It's also harder where staff split their time over many diverse activities.[2]

A very useful tool in this area is the *performance indicator,* sometimes termed a *key performance indicator* or *kpi.* A performance indicator is a "surrogate" or "representative" measure that has been accepted as indicative of efficiency in the area studied. Typically, organizations select a variety of tried and tested indicators rather than trying to measure everything. Such an approach may be adequate, but one must remember the human tendency to focus on and reward what can be measured and neglect what cannot. Such neglect can be very much out of place in a complex and sensitive area, for example, such as human services.

PROGRAM EVALUATION

Efficiency and productivity measurement, however, are not the end of the story either. Suppose our agency is extremely efficient, but it isn't attacking the most important problems? Efficiency or productivity numbers alone won't answer the searching questions a good chief executive, congressional committee or citizen might have about a government activity. A much more comprehensive, back-to-basics examination of a government program may be required. This is *program evaluation.* A program evaluator looks at the original aims of a program, and tries to assess how current activities relate to them. Is this really the best way to achieve those aims? Or was it a good way once, but it is out of date now? And what unplanned side effects is the program causing?

Many years ago, the best way to prevent shipwrecks was to have a comprehensive chain of lighthouses. Governments ran ships to bring provisions, including lighting kerosene for the lamps, to the lighthouse keepers on various remote islands and peninsulas. Years later, helicopters emerged as a more effective way to deliver stores to lighthouses. Today a Global Positioning System is in place, and most lighthouses have become museums. A program evaluation at any stage of this evolution would have endorsed the aim of preventing shipwrecks, for it is an enduring aim. Over time, however, the technology, the staffing profile, the stores needed and the kind of organization required, all have changed markedly. Program evaluations identify such changes and propose options so that legislators, public administrators or program watchdogs can observe the emerging patterns and evaluate future options.

SCRUTINY AND ACCOUNTABILITY

In Chapter 10, we looked at *accountability*—answerability for actions taken in public organizations. The topics of this chapter—compliance, productivity, efficiency and effectiveness are closely related to accountability. First, an organization and its management may be held accountable on the basis of the findings of audit studies, productivity assessments or program evaluations. Evaluations and audits are important foundations of accountability. Managers who are to be held accountable will pay close attention to ensuring that their organizations stand up to audit scrutiny, and receive positive program evaluations. A manager who does not may find a need to seek alternative employment!

Second, people and interest groups outside the organization, whether members of congressional oversight committees, other senators and representatives, newspaper reporters, academic commentators or voters tend to rely on these processes to formulate the questions that those who are accountable must answer. Why did this program cost so much? What were the impacts of this spending on employment? Audits and evaluations thus vitally affect both those who are accountable and those to whom they are accountable.

COMMUNICATING AUDIT AND EVALUATION RESULTS

When a public organization is the subject of an investigation, the results of the scrutiny may become widely known or they may be kept secret—at least for a time. Congressional hearings are likely to be widely publicized, perhaps even televised. General Accounting Office reports are often posted on the Internet, where anyone worldwide can download them. On the other hand, internal audit reports or consultants' findings may be kept secret within an organization. Today, there is a high expectation of *public accountability* by public organizations. Indeed high levels of public disclosure are necessary if voters in a democracy are to be sufficiently informed to cast their votes wisely. Today's public administrators need to manage in the expectation of disclosure and to pro-actively initiate reviews in potential problem areas before they are "revealed" in audit findings.

READINGS REPRINTED IN THIS CHAPTER

Susan Paddock's essay, **"Evaluation,"**[3] provides a useful historical review of program evaluation and examines the purposes of program evaluation and its relation to program planning and design. Paddock also discusses the utilization of evaluation findings, noting how political, measurement or usefulness problems may emerge. Evaluators may limit the usefulness of their work if they use too many technical terms and complex statistical analysis. Despite the potential problems, Paddock argues that today's environment of financial constraint and frequent change is one in which program evaluation may be even more important than in the past.[4]

In **"Measuring Productivity,"**[5] **Evan Berman** provides a concise overview of key types of measurement approaches and some important measurement issues. Berman bases the need for productivity measurement in the requirements of accountability. In his view, it also arises from other needs served by productivity measurement including improved planning and budgeting, the need to assess what is working and what is not working, and the need to determine the effectiveness of productivity improvement efforts. Berman systematically moves down the hierarchy of productivity measures, beginning with measures of effectiveness, outcomes and outputs; through measures of efficiency; and on to workload measures and cost-effectiveness measures. Berman also discusses a number of practical requirements in effectiveness measurement including: measurement guidelines, establishing the validity of measures, using comparison groups, and issues relating to data, surveys and focus groups.

The processes of audit, productivity measurement and program evaluation are typical—and crucial—components of effective and accountable public administration. They present both threats and opportunities, however, to the manager whose organization or program is being assessed as well as to those evaluating or holding managers accountable. A competent public administrator today must be familiar with the range of audit, productivity measurement and program evaluation approaches available and the ways in which they can be employed to improve results.

During the 1980s and early 1990s, many units of government at all levels attempted to implement a variety of management approaches or "tools" that utilized performance management systems. These systems usually contained elements of strategic management, performance appraisals at the individual level, and organizational performance assessments as measured by outputs and performance indicators. Too often these custom-built performance management systems failed to survive, however, because they were too complex, required information that was not readily available, and provided insufficient incentives to middle managers to undertake the work needed.

The **"Balanced Scorecard"** approach promoted by Robert S. Kaplan and David P. Norton, has been a breakthrough that has helped performance management move past some of these implementation barriers. The reading that we have included to illustrate these developments is from the website of the **City of Charlotte, North Carolina.**[6] The Charlotte monograph illustrates how the Balanced Scorecard has been used to integrate the performance measures that the city has been collecting for many years with its overall strategies.

The Balanced Scorecard arose from a multi-company study undertaken in 1990 by a research arm of the management consulting firm KPMG. The result was the "Balanced Scorecard" approach that looks not only at the usual financial measures of performance but also at several non-financial measures such as customer service, quality, cycle times and new product development. It is a systematic, strategy-related way of viewing and assessing an organization's performance and results.

The City of Charlotte example illustrates how practical local government managers who are well versed in performance management have applied the Balanced Scorecard. Charlotte's "scorecard" includes the four perspectives of the Balanced Scorecard: customer perspective, financial perspective, internal process perspective, and learning and growth perspective), and the city applies the scorecard to its five focus areas: community safety, city within a city, transportation, economic development, and restructuring government. Unlike some management techniques borrowed from the private sector, this tool can be adapted well to many public sector environments.

The Balanced Scorecard is used in many countries today by public sector organizations at the national, state and local levels. Public sector managers find the scope of the Balanced Scorecard very relevant to their needs, since non-financial outputs for public organizations can be the most important areas of their work. The Balanced Scorecard has already proven to be more durable and adaptable than many of the on again-off again, custom-made, performance management systems of the late 1980s. It is a standardized approach that is well-supported with implementation materials. It provides an attractive way to implement performance management that is able to generate enthusiastic commitment and new applications.

NOTES

1. See, for example, Evan N. Berman's chapter that is reprinted here, "Measuring Productivity" from his 1998 book, *Productivity in Public and Non-Profit Organizations: Strategies and Techniques.* Thousand Oaks, Calif.: Sage, pp. 51–76.
2. For an excellent description of the strengths and limitations of benchmarking, see Steven Cohen and William Eimicke's chapter, "Benchmarking and Performance Management," in their 1998 book, *Tools for Innovators: Creative Strategies for Managing Public Sector Organizations.* San Francisco: Jossey-Bass.
3. Paddock, Susan C. (1998). "Evaluation," in J. M. Shafritz (Ed.), *International Encyclopedia of Public Policy and Administration* (pp. 818–823). Boulder, Colo.: Westview.
4. Paddock, Susan C. (1998). "Evaluation," in J. M. Shafritz (Ed.), *International Encyclopedia of Public Policy and Administration.* Boulder, Colo.: Westview, p. 822.
5. Berman, Evan M. (1998). "Measuring Productivity," in E. M. Berman, *Productivity in Public and Non-Profit Organizations: Strategies and Techniques.* Thousand Oaks, Calif.: Sage, 51–76.
6. City of Charlotte and Mecklenburg County (July 19, 1999), website, Balanced Scorecard, http:\\www.ci.charlotte.nc.us/cicouncil, pp. 1–8.

39

Susan C. Paddock

EVALUATION

Evaluation means to judge the worth or value of a program or activity. Evaluation determines the value or effectiveness of an activity for the purpose of decisionmaking.

The valuing or judging of people, processes, and things is a pervasive daily human activity. As such, most evaluation is informal. Formal evaluation makes the explicit judging process an integral part of program management. Evaluation determines value by weighing costs, both tangible and intangible, against benefits. It determines effectiveness by assessing whether a service or program has met identified needs or objectives, or has made a difference. In this process, evaluation provides information that aids decisionmakers in determining whether to continue, modify, or terminate a funded activity or which of several alternatives to support. Good evaluation improves the quality of those decisions.

In formal evaluation we make explicit (1) the object of our review, (2) the criteria with which value will be assigned and a judgment based, and (3) the behavior or outcomes necessary if the object of the evaluation is to be judged as having met standards or expectation. An evaluation that is not explicit about these three issues will generate fear or frustration among those affected by the evaluation and will mitigate its effect.

HISTORY OF THE DEVELOPMENT OF PROGRAM EVALUATION

Formal evaluation is not new. We find formal evaluation as far back as 2000 B.C.E. when Chinese officials conducted civil service exams (DuBois 1970). Within Western tradition we find evaluation in a number of places, most notably in 1870 during the Age of Reform in England. There, the evaluation of educational achievement led to a call for what today we might term incentive pay or pay for performance (Madaus et al. 1983).

In the United States, the formal evaluation of organizations and their programs and services began in schools. In 1897–1898 Joseph Rice conducted a comparative study of the spelling performance of 33,000 students in a large city school system (DuBois 1970). Originally, formal evaluation in education was closely associated with the measurement tradition of psychology. Robert Thorndike, sometimes called the father of the educational testing movement, was an important influence in encouraging the application of measurement technology to the determination of human abilities (Thorndike and Hagen 1969). His prestige led to the introduction of standardized testing in the 1920s as a means to assess students. Evaluation approaches were next applied to pedagogy, in an effort to improve teaching (Smith and Tyler 1942). The evaluation practices developed for schools were applied to work relief and public housing programs of President F. D. Roosevelt's New Deal.

Evaluation gained in importance and visibility after World War II. In education, the Cold War threat of Soviet preeminence and the concern that American schools were second-class caused evaluators to increase their scrutiny of educational practices and outcomes. This work led to the development of a language, a research process, and a theoretical basis for the evaluation discipline (Cronbach and Suppes 1969; Scriven 1958). By the end of the 1960s the focus of educational evaluation included policy and political questions, especially related to equal education (Coleman et al. 1966; Jencks 1972).

Evaluation in public administration initially focused on programs of the federal government. There were two schools of development. One school focused on the management and allocation of resources for national defense programs. The Program Evaluation Review Technique (PERT), for example, was developed to correlate different contractor management systems in the development of complex weapon systems (Cook 1966). Planning, Programming, and Budgeting System (PPBS) also was developed primarily as a means of applying economic analysis to management systems (Wildavsky 1966). Systems analysis techniques were intended to improve decisionmaking about the development and implementation of military operations (Miser and Quade 1985). These were primarily planning or front-end analysis evaluation approaches.

The other school of public administration evaluation was linked to earlier efforts in education and focused on outputs or outcomes. Evaluation efforts with a foundation in experimental design, for example, were used to judge the relative merits of federally funded agricultural programs and products. The social welfare programs of the

Great Society, which accounted for rapidly increasing federal expenditures, were accompanied by an increase in attention paid to evaluation (Rossi et al. 1979).

In the 1970s the U.S. Office of Management and Budget (OMB) created an Evaluation and Program Implementation Division, a reflection of the growing importance of evaluation. State governments also began to pay attention to evaluation in the mid-1970s, although there it was called productivity measurement rather than program evaluation, and often was linked to sunset legislation. The two schools of evaluation in public administration began to coalesce. Awareness and use of program evaluation grew with the publication of *The Handbook of Evaluation Research* (1975) and the initiation in 1977 of the journal *Evaluation Quarterly.*

In the past decade, evaluations of governmental programs have changed their focus from being dominated by the evaluation of achievement of great objectives, typical of the Great Society and War on Poverty programs, to using multifaceted approaches (Rossi and Freeman 1993). Evaluation continues to be an important part of most federally funded programs. As a result, the federal government plays a central role in the development of evaluation approaches, methodologies, and techniques.

EVALUATION PURPOSES

Evaluation is a process to judge success, assure accountability, and determine more effective resource allocation. It does not simply measure; it also judges, or assigns value. It seeks to assess social utility. It is concerned with both program process and program product. Evaluation serves a variety of purposes. These purposes, and the name of the approach most frequently associated with each purpose, are (1) to inform planning decisions, particularly in the development of policy (front-end analysis); (2) to answer policy execution questions and determine if a full-scale evaluation of the program is useful and feasible (evaluability assessment); (3) to track program progress and identify actual or emerging problems (program and problem monitoring); (4) to determine whether a program has accomplished its goals or met its objectives (impact analysis or product evaluation); (5) to determine if a program has been implemented as planned, regardless of outcomes (process analysis or process evaluation); (6) to measure the effectiveness or efficiency of units or practices (management analysis or context evaluation); (7) to determine if there are unintended consequences from program implementation (goal-free analysis); (8) to assess the degree of public or stakeholder satisfaction with the program (service analysis); and (9) to compare various programs or approaches to determine which might be the best to implement in a new setting (policy analysis). In addition, a branch of evaluation research examines whether evaluation findings are used, or compares evaluation findings (utilization analysis, evaluation synthesis, or meta-evaluation). Program evaluation should result in a good explanation or generalization about why change did or did not take place.

Evaluation differs from the related practices of research and auditing. Research is a test of a theory and represents a more disinterested study, but results are intended to be generalizable to the greater population. Auditing is an attempt to measure the extent to which the procedures of a program are consistent with those intended in original legislation and to identify deficiencies or discrepancies.

RELATION TO PROGRAM PLANNING AND IMPLEMENTATION

To be effective, program evaluation must be integral to the program cycle, from the initial needs assessment to the final formal evaluation stage. Failing to plan for program evaluation from the beginning of a program usually means the data or data sources necessary for making a judgment may not be available. An evaluation conducted under these circumstances can only answer questions for which data are available, which may not be the most important or most interesting questions.

Evaluation can occur in any phase of a program. During needs assessment evaluators ask, "What needs attention? What is the program trying to accomplish?" During planning, evaluators assess the outcomes to be achieved and the courses of action to be taken. During development, evaluators examine the extent to which program execution is taking place as planned. This is formative evaluation and can suggest changes to assure goal achievement or program improvement. Finally, during program delivery, evaluators judge the overall effectiveness of the project or program and recommend future courses of action. This is summative evaluation, which describes a program as a finished work.

DETERMINATION OF EVALUATION FEASIBILITY

The temptation for most evaluators is to spend most of their time planning the design and technical elements of the study. However, it is at least as important to spend time thinking about the purpose of the evaluation and how its findings will be used, and to plan the evaluation with that in mind. Before undertaking any evaluation, three questions about the study's feasibility should be asked. First, can the results of the evaluation influence decisions about the program? If there are strong, preconceived ideas on the part of policymakers about the program, the effect of the evaluation will be limited or nonexistent. In addition, the evaluation schedule must be such as to assure that the study can be completed in time to inform decisions. Second, can the evaluation be carried out? There must be sufficient resources available to support the evaluation, and the program must be stable enough so that it can be studied. Finally, is the program consequential enough to merit evaluation? Programs most eligible for evaluation are those that require significant resources, those that are operating in a marginal or improvable manner, or those that are candidates for expansion or replication. A negative response to any of these questions will bring into question the likelihood that the study will be completed or that its results will be useful.

AUDIENCE AND CONSTRAINTS

It is important to identify the evaluation's audience. Evaluators should ask; Who needs the information to be provided by the study? What kind of information do they require? When will they need it? How will they use it? The early identification and involvement of potential users of evaluation results is critical to the study's success (Chelimsky 1985; Weiss 1982).

After having identified purpose, feasibility, and audience, the evaluator must determine what decisions must be informed by the evaluation and what constraints exist. Constraints exist when there are insufficient materials and equipment, personnel, or funds, or when the political climate is adverse. Because evaluation takes place in a political environment, it is subject to political constraints and pressures. Understanding this political environment is important for the person who must manage the evaluation effort.

APPROACH OR DESIGN

The evaluator must determine the evaluation approach or design. At least twelve kinds of evaluation approaches or models have been identified, many of which can be used at any stage in a program's development or to inform any of the evaluation purposes identified earlier. These approaches are: (1) objectives-based or goal-oriented, in which the evaluation assesses the discrepancy between planned and achieved objectives (Smith and Tyler 1942); (2) consumer-oriented, or goal-free evaluation, which discovers what the program is by what it does, not by what it purports to do (Scriven 1972); (3) testing, or the comparison of performance against norms or preestablished criteria (Thorndike and Hagen 1969); (4) evaluation research, or the identification of causal relationships between variables (Campbell and Stanley 1966); (5) cost assessment or cost-benefit analysis, or the assessment of the costs and benefits of proposed or actual policies (Coleman et al. 1966; Jencks 1972); (6) accreditation or certification, or the determination if programs or people meet established standards; (7) management information systems, which provide information needed to fund, direct, and control programs, but which are not related to program outcomes directly; (8) accountability or performance contracting, which provides information to funding agencies on the extent to which program objectives have been met; (9) client-centered evaluation, which attempts to understand activities from the users' perspectives (Stake 1970; Guba and Lincoln 1989); (10) decision-oriented evaluation, used to provide information specifically to assist legislators or administrators in making or defending decisions (Stufflebeam et al. 1971); (11) adversary evaluation, which provides policymakers with opposing views in a kind of "judicial" framework (Wolf and Arnstein 1975); and (12) just-in-time evaluations, which are geared for smaller, more responsive evaluations of isolated elements of programs.

Although the tools, techniques, and methodologies used by each of these approaches may be the same, the perspective assumed by the evaluator influences the focus of the study, and thus the kind of information provided to decisionmakers.

Decisions about the procedures or methods to be used for gathering data are critical to a study's success. Data collection will be affected by costs associated with various methods, as well as by the availability and accessibility of records, documents, and informed sources, and the willingness of clients, program staff, or other stakeholders to provide accurate, reliable, and honest information. It is tempting to evaluate that which is easy to measure or for which data can be easily obtained. Evaluators should resist that temptation, since the most significant or interesting information may not be quantifiable or easy to access or report.

Data can be obtained from questionnaires (multiple-choice, checklist, ratings, rankings, or open-ended questions), surveys, tests, interviews, observations, performance records, data banks; or organizational documents (ordinances, laws, resolutions, and other public documents). Data should be both quantitative and qualitative (subjective). Information sources include legislators, citizen groups, individuals, program personnel, other executives in government, program clients, and evaluations by other governmental agencies. Multiple measures of the evaluation objects should be obtained whenever possible. Criteria must be valid, reliable, timely, and credible.

DATA ANALYSIS AND REPORTING

Analysis of data begins with the determination that data collected are useful. Data must be relevant, timely, accurate, and understandable. The evaluator, in analyzing data, also must be aware of the effects of attrition, the Hawthorne effect, evaluator bias, or any changes in organizational facilities, personnel, policies, or funding that may have affected the program or the analysis of program data.

The final role for the evaluator is the reporting of findings. The evaluator must decide how and to whom the evidence will be presented. The evaluation report should present information in a way that is useful to policymakers and aids in their decisionmaking. It should be structured so as to inform future decisions. Effective evaluation reports are free of jargon, focus directly and specifically on decisions or problems, provide the basis for setting priorities, and involve program administrators in the recommendations process.

UTILIZATION OF EVALUATION FINDINGS

Recently, critics have argued that the requirement of Total Quality Management (TQM) or of the "new public management" described by Osborne and Gaebler (1993) are antithetical to program evaluation (Behn 1991). These approaches require public managers to move decisionmaking to the lowest level possible, to eliminate unnecessary rules and regulations, and to innovate quickly. By contrast, traditional program evaluation requires time and a more-hierarchical decisionmaking process. "New" program evaluation must, therefore, be "just-in-time," providing smaller packages of evaluation findings for use in assessing innovations. TQM practices, such as statistical process control and the Plan-Do-Check-Act cycle, can be integrated into traditional evaluation practices.

Rapid change increases the requirement to demonstrate that an agency's program is accomplishing something (Behn 1991). Small-scale, timely evaluation can help others understand innovations and, if appropriate, replicate them (Levin and Sanger 1994). Formative evaluations, or evaluations that are process-oriented, that answer the questions of primary stakeholders, and that include qualitative methods that allow a "holistic assessment of relevant phenomena" (Thomas 1995), will be more useful to public managers and policymakers. The application of technological tools such as automated information systems, telephone surveys, and computer-assisted analysis and reporting can increase the possibility of evaluation being timely and useful to public managers. Benchmarking, or the establishing of standards or "best practices," leads not only to evaluation of current programs but also to goal-setting for program improvement.

The problems with evaluations fall into three categories: political, measurement, and usefulness. Political problems result from the tension between those being evaluated and the evaluators, especially when there is a probability of program termination or reduction. In public management, political problems also emerge when the priorities of a legislative of funding body are different from those of the agency. Measurement problems occur because many governmental programs or services are difficult to measure, and evaluators must develop measures for selected objectives. Stakeholders in the evaluation process may not agree as to the appropriateness or accuracy of those measurements. The usefulness of evaluations is compromised if the study is ad hoc or ex post facto rather than an integral and inherent part of the program from its inception. Then, necessary data may be incomplete or absent.

Usefulness is also limited when evaluators issue reports filled with technical terms and complex statistical analyses that confuse and mislead. Evaluation reports that are simple and easy to understand, however, may miss important, more complex elements of the program. Practitioners of the "new" evaluation must be more involved in the program planning and development process, building alliances with public managers so that these problems are avoided or minimized and evaluation findings have an impact on how social services are delivered.

The usefulness, and therefore the utilization of program evaluation, can be improved in a number of ways: (1) Be clear about premises underlying a program and conduct the evaluation in such a way that those premises are addressed; (2) identify objectives and evaluation criteria that are people-oriented; (3) explicitly consider potential unintended consequences of programs, especially negative effects; (4) specify processes inherent in the program that the evaluation ought to investigate; (5) identify potential users of evaluation results early in the process; (6) analyze alternative approaches within the program; (7) consider more than one objective and multiple evaluation criteria; (8) do not reject evaluation criteria because they are difficult to measure; (9) err on the side of too many objectives or criteria, rather than too few; (10) specify client groups on which the analysis should attempt to estimate program impacts; (11) always include dollar costs as one criterion; (12) involve administrators and program practitioners at every step of the evaluation, from planning to the writing of the draft report; (13) involve potential users of the evaluation where possible; (14) complete the evaluation on time and release the results as soon as possible; and (15) use effective teaching and marketing approaches in presenting and disseminating findings. (Chelimsky 1985; Hatry 1987; Weiss 1982).

Evaluation is always a political process, since it involves identifying objectives, selecting measurement criteria, accessing a variety of information sources, analyzing data within a specified environment, and reporting those data in ways that are understandable and useful. The impact of politics on evaluation in the public management setting is even more profound. Evaluations can be used as a political tactic; evaluators who are aware of implicit or explicit politics can minimize this practice. Alternatively, evaluation can be used as a guide in shaping policy or program changes.

The very act of conducting an evaluation may be important, if it encourages members of the organization to examine their work and the structure that supports it (Weiss 1977). Evaluation may help agency administrators and staff, as well as legislators and other important parties, to review program goals and renew their commitment to program outcomes. This review may lead to behavioral and policy changes at a number of levels, regardless of the findings of the evaluation study. Thus effective evaluation may be even more important in today's environment of frequent and rapid changes and increasing fiscal constraints in assuring the success of public management programs and services.

BIBLIOGRAPHY

Behn, Robert D., 1991. *Leadership Counts: Lessons for Public Managers from the Massachusetts Welfare, Training and Employment Program.* Cambridge: Harvard University Press.

Campbell, David T., and Julian C. Stanley, 1966. *Experimental and Quasi-experimental Designs for Research.* Chicago: Rand-McNally.

Chelimsky, Eleanor, (ed.), 1985. *Program Evaluation: Patterns and Directions.* Washington, DC: American Society for Public Administration.

Coleman, James S., et al., 1966. *Equality of Educational Opportunity.* Washington, DC: U.S. Government Printing Office (GPO).

Cook, Desmond L., 1966. *Program Evaluation and Review Technique.* Washington, DC: GPO.

Cronbach, Lee J., and P. Suppes, 1969. *Research for Tomorrow's Schools: Disciplined Inquiry for Education.* New York: Macmillan.

DuBois, P. H., 1970. *A History of Psychological Testing.* Boston: Allyn and Bacon.

Guba, Egon C., and Yvonne Lincoln, 1989. *Fourth Generation Evaluation.* Newbury Park, CA: Sage Publications.

Hatry, Harry, 1987. *Program Analysis for State and Local Government.* Washington, DC: Urban Institute.

Jencks, Christopher, 1972. *Inequality. A Reassessment of the Effect of Family and Schooling in America.* New York: Basic Books.

Levin, Martin A., and Mary Bryna Sanger, 1994. *Making Government Work: How Entrepreneurial Executives Turn Bright Ideas into Real Results.* San Francisco: Jossey-Bass.

Madaus, George F., Michael Scriven, and Daniel Stufflebeam, 1983. *Evaluation Models: Viewpoints on Educational and Human Services Evaluation.* Boston: Kluwer-Nijhoff.

Miser, Hugh J., and Edward S. Quade, eds., 1985. *Handbook of Systems Analysis.* New York: North-Holland.

Osborne, David, and Ted Gaebler, 1993. *Reinventing Government: How the Entrepreneurial Spirit Is Transforming the Public Sector.* New York: Penguin.

Rossi, Peter H., Howard E. Freeman, and Sonia R. Wright, 1979. *Evaluation: A Systematic Approach.* Beverly Hills, CA: Sage Publications.

Rossi, Peter H., and Howard E. Freeman, 1993. *Evaluation: A Systematic Approach.* 5th ed. Newbury Park, CA: Sage Publications.

Scriven, Michael, 1958. "Definitions, Explanations, and Theories." In H. Fiegl, M. Scriven, and G. Maxwell, eds., *Minnesota Studies in the Philosophy of Science,* Vol. 2. Minneapolis: University of Minnesota Press.

_____. 1972. "Prose and Cons About Goal-Free Evaluation." *Evaluation Comment* 3:4.

Smith, E. R., and Ralph W. Tyler, 1942. *Appraising and Recording Student Progress.* New York: Harper & Row.

Stake, Robert E., 1970. "Objectives, Priorities, and Other Judgment Data." *Review of Educational Research* 40: 181–212.

Stufflebeam, Daniel L., et al., 1971. *Educational Evaluation and Decision Making.* Itaska, IL: F. E. Peacock.

Thomas, John Clayton, 1995. "Adapting Program Evaluation to New Realities: The Challenge of the New Public Management." Paper presented at Trinity Symposium, San Antonio, Texas, July 23.

Thorndike, Robert L., and E. Hagen, 1969. *Measurement and Evaluation in Psychology and Education.* New York: Wiley and Sons.

Weiss, Carol H. 1977., "Research for policy's sake: The enlightenment function of social research." *Policy Analysis.* 3: 532–545.

———. 1982. "Measuring the use of evaluation." *Evaluation Studies Review Annual.* 7: 129–145.

Wildavsky, Aaron, 1966. "The political economy of efficiency: Cost-benefit analysis, systems analysis and program budgeting." *Public Administration Review* (December) 293–302.

Wolf, R. L., and G. Arnstein, 1975. "Trial by jury: A new evaluation method." *Phi Delta Kappan,* 57:3 185–190.

40

Evan M. Berman

MEASURING PRODUCTIVITY

THE NEED FOR MEASUREMENT

Funding agencies, elected officials, and citizens want to know what public and nonprofit organizations are accomplishing. Through measurement, public and nonprofit organizations give accountability for their results, show responsiveness to clients and constituents, improve the planning and budgeting of programs by obtaining an objective assessment of what is working and what is needed, and determine the effectiveness of productivity improvement efforts. Measurement is also used to provide cost justification for investment decisions, and it helps with the oversight of contracts by keeping contractors accountable for their results. Measurement is a foundation of productivity improvement. It is consistent with professional norms of accountability, openness, and maintaining high standards, and many organizations need managers and employees with the ability to measure program outcomes.

Productivity measurement can be either a one-time event or an ongoing activity. As a one-time effort, it frequently uses program evaluation strategies that were developed in the 1960s and 1970s, which provide a detailed and comprehensive analysis of outcomes. These approaches also seek to determine the unique effect of program activities on program outcomes. Examples of program evaluation include many assessments of the Head Start program, crisis response programs, and technology development efforts. Although some evaluations are repeated over time, they are nonetheless understood as discrete studies (Rossi & Freeman, 1993). Since the early 1990s, however, productivity measurement is increasingly used as an ongoing activity, called *performance measurement,* and is increasingly demanded by the U.S. Congress, state legislatures, local bodies, and grant agencies. For example, the 1993 Government Performance and Results Act requires federal agencies to establish quantitative performance measures and targets. Agencies are required to submit annual reports that monitor their performance. Usually, performance measurement is not as comprehensive as program evaluations. Only a few key indicators are used. Some cities and organizations provide quarterly performance measurement reports and have developed a detailed infrastructure for generating and analyzing outcome-oriented performance data.[1]

As an ongoing activity, performance measurement is increasingly tied to budgeting and strategic planning in public and nonprofit organizations. Performance measurement allows units to show how they are making progress toward strategic objectives, and this information feeds into the funding decisions of the budget process. In a recent survey, 73% of cities more than 50,000 indicated the use of performance measurement.

MEASURES OF PRODUCTIVITY

Measuring Effectiveness

Effectiveness is vital for productivity in public and nonprofit organizations. Effectiveness is defined as the *level of outcomes* accomplished. For example, the number of clients that are successfully served, the level of satisfaction that clients or citizens experience with program services, or the number of visitors to museum exhibitions. Outcomes are accomplishments, not efforts. Long-term outcomes are distinguished from outputs. Long-term outcomes (or goals) measure the ultimate objectives of organizations and reflect basic rationales for programs and organizations. The time horizon of such goals is often three to five years and sometime even more. For example, some long-term outcomes of museums are to increase the quality of life in cities and increase support and appreciation for local artists. Goals of many teacher improvement programs (which help teachers teach better) are to increase the reputation of school districts and to help students learn more.

Outputs are defined as outcomes that are the direct, immediate consequences of strategies. They are sometimes called short-term outcomes. It is a tenet of productivity measurement that all activities produce short-term outcomes. All activities have consequences. For example, teacher training programs often increase the skills of teachers to communicate difficult material, to conduct classes in an orderly manner, to better prepare lesson plans, and so on.

Productivity measurement efforts begin by (a) specifying the activity that is being evaluated and (b) identifying outcomes and outputs that are to be assessed. An important distinction between ad hoc program evaluation and ongoing performance measurement is that program evaluation attempts to measure all outcomes and outputs, including those that occur but are not intended. Such elaboration is an extensive, but justified, process because program evaluation seeks a complete and comprehensive assessment of the program. By contrast, performance measurement focuses only on key outcomes. Only those outputs and outcomes are measured that are most important to the program and that can be measured within the context of current or slightly expanded management information systems. For example, some easily measured outputs of crime control are the clearance rate of burglary, murder, robbery, rape, and narcotics cases as well as the percentage of cases closed, the timeliness of responses to 911 calls, and the number of arrests. Some outcome measures are the actual burglary and other crime rates, citizen fear of crime, teen participation in gangs, the level of illegal drug use, and death and injury resulting from automobile accidents.

The relationship between long-term outcomes and outputs is not always singular. For example, a reduction in AIDS cases (an outcome) may be caused by campaigns to increase awareness or the use of new drugs, or both. That is, outcomes are affected by program activities as well as other occurring events. Whereas program evaluation designs take great pains to isolate program effects from other effects (see below), performance measurement acknowledges these other effects but focuses on outputs. The reasons for emphasizing outputs over outcomes are (a) that managers have more control over outputs and (b) that program outcomes occur over time horizons that are very long from the vantage point of program development. Program outputs are more relevant for today's decisions. Current program outcomes are shaped by past program activities, not those of the present. However, program outcomes are useful to increase understanding of the salience of current program goals. Program outcomes help assess the relevance of proposed activities and output measures.

Measuring Efficiency

Efficiency is defined as the ratio of outcomes or outputs to inputs (O/I), for example, the number of client problems solved per counselor, the number of crimes solved per police officer, or the number of completed health inspections per health inspector (Halachmi, 1992; Rosen, 1993).[2] Efficiency calculations require that managers have data about outcomes and inputs. It bears repeating that efficiency measures focus on outcomes, not activities; caseloads or service calls per employee are not measures of efficiency. (They are discussed further.)

Efficiency can be measured in many different ways. It is seldom possible to measure the efficiency of an entire public or nonprofit organization. In its simplest approach, conceptually, efficiency is calculated by identifying all outcomes and dividing these by all inputs. This is called *total efficiency.* For example, a measure of total efficiency is the total cost per counselor of solving all client problems, or the total cost per completed health inspection. Total efficiency requires that all costs be taken into account, hence salaries, overhead, materials, and so forth. It also requires enumeration of all outcomes. When multiple outcomes are produced, then these too must be taken into account. For example, when a second outcome is the processing of insurance claims, total efficiency is the average cost for solving X problems and Y insurance claims per counselor. Total efficiency is a simple but impractical measure when multiple outcomes exist that are not readily aggregated in the same units. This is often the case in dealing with public and nonprofit outputs that are not readily expressed dollar or other common units.

For this reason, most efficiency measures focus on single outcomes. These are called *partial efficiency* measures. For example, teacher outputs include student test scores, graduation rates, as well as student counseling and advancing community interests through volunteer efforts. The number of students who pass standardized tests per teacher is a measure of partial efficiency. It does not assess other outcomes, such as counseling or volunteer services. Performance measures are often based on such practical considerations as the availability of data. For example, student test scores may be available but not other measures of student ability or attitude. Other examples, drawn from public safety, are the cost per cleared case, cost (or hours) per arrest, cost per emergency response call that is attended to, number of executed warrants per employee per day, cost per collected traffic citation, average time per completed assist to other agencies, and so on.

Managers must choose in what ways they will measure inputs. The basic efficiency formula assumes that all inputs are taken into consideration, that is, salaries, overhead, materials, and so forth. This approach is complicated by the fact that while such data are often available at the level of organizations, they are seldom readily available for subunits. Also, using such data for lower units requires that managers allocate fractions of overhead and capital expenditures to different units or even individual employees. Lower units of analysis frequently use salary cost or number of personnel as input measures. This is called *labor efficiency*. Such measures are justified because lower level managers often have little control over overhead. In the above examples, a measure of labor efficiency is the number of client problems solved per counselor or the fraction of students who pass tests per teacher. A common problem in calculating labor efficiency is dividing outcomes into labor totals without appropriately allocating the fraction of labor that is responsible for producing the output. This is justifiable only when units that are compared are assumed to have the same labor allocations. For this reason, efficiency measures are often controversial when used to make comparisons across organizations. For example, some schools have higher graduation rates per teacher but also make more use of teacher assistants and computer resources. Efficiency measures are usually used to compare the development of organizations over time.

Efficiency measures also vary to the extent that they consider the quality of inputs and outputs. For example, teachers may have similar student graduation or pass efficiencies but may vary according to the quality of students that they start off with or with regard to their own skills. Experienced teachers may cost more but produce better results. Such differences should be taken into account. Quality should be specified to better compare among organizations or units. Finally, it is common to calculate efficiency indices that assess the development of productivity over time.

Clearly, efficiency can be measured in many different ways. In most areas of public and nonprofit activity, there are few standard, agreed-upon ways of measuring efficiency. Most professional organizations do not recommend or mandate the use of certain measures. Thus organizations must often design their own measures. However, in many instances, relevant measures often suggest themselves. For example, parks departments often measure the cost per acre of lawn care or mowing. Police departments often measure the cost per cleared case. Many productivity improvement efforts suggest additional efficiency measures. For example, the efficiency of a new social service partnership might be measured by its cost of treating patients. To assist in the development effort, this chapter discusses standards for measurement (see below). It is also a good practice to engage stakeholders and employees in a dialogue about the feasibility and relevance of different measures to ensure acceptance. Managers must decide which measures they will use, acknowledging the strengths and weaknesses of each.

It is important to note that many employees experience an excessive emphasis on efficiency as demeaning and demotivating. Employees often measure their job satisfaction by standards of effectiveness (i.e., solving an important problem) rather than by how fast they did it or how many client problems per hour they solved (that is, efficiency). Efficiency measures are therefore seldom used in isolation from other performance measures and are never used in lieu of comprehensive performance appraisals. Nevertheless, measures of efficiency are increasingly important in justifying program costs as well as productivity improvement efforts that require investment: In the world of competing top management priorities, proposals that promise efficiency as well as effectiveness gains are likely to be more favorably viewed than those that only yield effectiveness gains. Hence proposals for productivity improvement frequently provide balanced objectives of both effectiveness and efficiency gains, and productivity improvement efforts are frequently designed to produce both. However, undue emphasis on efficiency may generate perverse behavior that should be avoided. For example, teacher efficiency measures should not draw teachers away from devoting time to students with special needs.

Other Measures

Workloads are defined as the activity levels of departments and organizations, and workload measures assess activities or strategies, such as the number of classes taught, the number of parks maintained, the number of patrols conducted, the number of fire inspections, and so on. Workloads are often related to inputs, for example, the number of classes taught per teacher, the number of full-time equivalent ground maintenance personnel used per acre of park, the number of patrols per police officer or the number of officers per patrol. These are workload ratios, although some authors refer to these measures as efficiency or productivity measures, even though they do not measure outcomes (e.g., Ammons, 1996). A useful feature of workload measures and workload ratios is that often they are readily available from administrative records. Some examples of workload ratio measures in public safety are the average number of bookings per day, the number of emergency calls received per day, the number of hours spent in court per case, the number of citizen volunteer hours used per police unit, the number of minutes per inspection, and the time spent per suspect sketch. Note that none of these concerns outputs or outcomes.

Equity measures are important. Workloads and outcomes are sometimes compared across different target groups, and these measures often have political ramifications. For example, police departments often must show that they serve different neighborhoods in an equal manner. Different arrest rates in black versus other locations must be explained, for example, on the basis of emergency calls, robberies, or substance use rates. Although it is not always possible to explain equity differences, they should be noted. For example, differentials in student test scores must be explained across gender and race divisions, even though it is not always possible to explain why these differences occur.

Benchmarking has also increased in recent years. Benchmarks are standards rather than measures of actual performance. Benchmarks exist for outcomes as well as for workload ratios. For example, a benchmark for fire serve response time is usually

3.5 minutes, and the minimum staffing for trucks and engines is about three fire-fighters. Standards for parks maintenance are 2.0 to 2.8 hours mowing per acre, and there are many detailed standards for tree, lawn, and weed control. Published standards must be adapted to specific local conditions.

Finally, the above efficiency measures are readily transformed into cost-benefit or cost-effectiveness estimates. Cost-benefit measures require that benefits are expressed in monetary values: Because this is often extremely difficult with public and nonprofit services (What is the dollar value of improved school ratings?), measures often involve cost-effectiveness in which outcomes are not expressed in their own units (e.g., as ratings). Cost-benefit/effectiveness analysis requires that all costs and outcomes are identified. These are usually valued from the perspective of society rather than the organizations or programs, as is the case with many efficiency measures. Program opponents frequently call for cost-effectiveness analysis, but receiving such analysis seldom allays their concerns. This is because many concerns focus on effectiveness rather than efficiency. For example, concerns about inmate vocational training often deal with recidivism (i.e., effectiveness), even though opponents express a "need" for cost-benefit analysis of inmate training programs. Thus managers do well to critically analyze calls for cost-benefit analysis.

Table 40.1 provides a comparison of various kind of measures. In conclusion, (a) most efficiency measures are determined by the availability of data; (b) measures of

TABLE 40.1
Productivity Measures

Name	Type	Example*
Effectiveness	Short-term outcomes	Increased teaching skills
	Midterm outcomes	Student test scores
	Long-term outcomes	School reputation
Efficiency	Total efficiency	All improvements/total program cost
	Partial efficiency	Specific improvements/prorated cost
	Labor efficiency	Improvements/teacher
	Marginal efficiency	Incremental improvement/ incremental cost
	Social efficiency	Improvements to society/ total cost to society
Equity	Race equity	Student performance by race
	Geographic equity	Student performance by district
	Sex equity	Student performance by sex
	Income equity	Student performance by family income
Workload	Activities	Number of students taught
	Activities/input	Students per teacher
Cost-benefit	Benefits/costs	Student performance/ total cost per teacher
Benchmarks	Workload standards	For example, 30 students per teacher
	Effectiveness standards	For example, 96% graduation rate

NOTE: *Teacher improvement program.

partial labor efficiency (units per employee) are widely used; and (c) measures of efficiency are seldom used in isolation from other performance measures.

FURTHER ISSUES IN MEASUREMENT

Guidelines for Measurement

Scientific criteria exist that assist in the development and evaluation of measures. First, measures should be valid, that is, they should measure what they are supposed to measure. A measure of the efficiency of policy response teams should take into account a broad range of their activities, not just one activity. Valid measures are sufficiently specific. They should have a meaningful range of response categories, for example, a valid measure of response time should include different degrees of being on time. Second, measurement should be reliable. Reliability means that, on repeated measurement, measurements should show little variation. Reliability is an issue when using observers to rate the cleanliness of streets or parks. To overcome this problem, raters must be trained and have accuracy of their rating verified. Reliability in surveys means that different samples of the same population should yield similar results. This is ensured by using random sampling, discussed below.

Third, measures should also be simple and easy to understand. Complex measures are often confusing to those who use them such as senior managers, elected officials, and board members. When stakeholders do not understand measures, organizations fail to increase their accountability and demonstrate their responsiveness. Measures should also be relevant to those who will use them. To deal with this problem, some managers pilot-test proposed measures among citizen groups and other potential users. Fourth, measures should reflect program activities that managers can affect. It is senseless and anxiety-inducing to hold managers accountable for things they cannot change. Fifth, measures should be practical. Data should be relatively easy to collect, and such data should conform to the above standards. The way in which measures are collected should also be foolproof. To increase the credibility of data, program evaluation frequently uses external consultants, and performance measurements are often audited by budget departments that, in some instances, are also responsible for gathering data from administrative records.

Multifaceted Indicators

Whereas some measures are highly specific (e.g., number of students taught), other measures are abstract. For example, to increase community awareness and to provide wholesome educational activities. What exactly does "community awareness" mean? What are "wholesome" activities? They are appropriate outcomes, but they also require further specificity before they can be measured. When managers are able to influence the design of their measurements, the first step is to identify different dimensions of such concepts. There is seldom one best way to measure such concepts. The first step in constructing measures is to be clear and specific about the different aspects that are being measured. Of course, not all outcomes are abstract in nature, but those that are need to be further specified. Managers need to think about the way in which different concepts are measured.

The second step is to identify how different, specific outcomes will be measured. By what means will data be collected? Typical data collection strategies are surveys of clients, staff interviews, and the use of data from administrative records. For example, awareness might be assessed through a survey of parents, whereas measurement of safety might be assessed by using data from administrative records. These different measurement approaches are discussed later in this chapter.

Using Comparison Groups

The measurement of outcomes alone does not necessarily prove that program strategies cause outcomes. Such proof is sometimes sought, especially in the context of program evaluation. For example, in programs for the homeless, the aim is often to reduce the number of homeless persons, but does a reduction in homeless persons "prove" that the reduction occurred because of assistance efforts to the homeless? Perhaps the reduction occurred because the economy improved. At stake is the need to deal with a variety of "rival" explanations about the impact or lack of impact of strategies or interventions. For reasons explained earlier, the problem of causality increases as the time frame of outcomes increases as well. Program skeptics are apt to raise questions about the efficacy of efforts, especially concerning mid- and long-term outcomes.

One approach is to identify all such rival hypotheses and to deal with them one at a time. For example, the impact of economic growth on homelessness might be estimated by comparing homeless populations in similar cities that experience different levels of economic growth, or by comparing homelessness in cities that have experienced changes in economic growth over time. The impact of efforts to mitigate homelessness needs to be assessed as well. For example, an estimate might be made based on program files of the number of homeless persons who are helped off the street and the number of those who are not recidivists after, say 6 or 12 months. An obvious challenge is to identify all relevant rival hypotheses, and to respond to them effectively.

An alternative strategy is to conduct an experiment in which subjects are randomly assigned to either a control or an experimental group. Random assignment eliminates the possibility of systematic differences between the groups; chance differences are very small in large samples. However, experiments are seldom applicable to public or nonprofit organizations.

Implementing Performance Measurement Systems

The implementation of performance measurement is usually a gradually unfolding process in organizations. Organizations must often build the capacity for gathering and analyzing data, and they must allow for changing initial performance measures as new measures are proposed and improvements are made in existing ones. Initial efforts frequently use only one or two measures as managers increase the capacity for performance measurement. Initial efforts often are limited in scope and subject to data gathering glitches; they are experimental in nature (Schwabe, 1996; Tracy, 1996).

The implementation of performance measurement often raises fears and concerns that managers must address. Performance measurement is often positioned by managers as an effort to increase accountability, to support ongoing program development, and to inform budgeting and other decision-making processes. Performance measurement is but one of several tools for this purpose. Managers find it necessary to assure employees and lower managers that decisions will not be made in isolation from other measures, and that initial efforts are understood to be experimental and not written in stone. Units should have considerable input in deciding how their performance will be measured. Managers will also need to assure employees that the performance measurement effort will not impose undue burdens.

Top leaders also need to show that they are serious about performance measurement. To this end, they often assign responsibilities to different units for developing necessary expertise. Budget offices are often used for this purpose in public organizations because they have expertise in measurement and data analysis.

The development of performance measurement can also tie into other efforts to increase stakeholder support. Key decision makers who affect the future of programs can be involved in measurement through ad hoc working groups that guide measurement and planning efforts. Key decision makers seldom object to efforts to assess and improve programs, and are apt to give their opinions about needed changes. In addition, measurement efforts can use an ad hoc "external advisory" group of program clients and community groups. This external advisory group provides feedback and a testing ground for measurement items (survey questions, etc.).

DATA COLLECTION

Productivity measurement requires the collection of data. Some principal data sources are agency records, surveys, focus groups, and the use of experts, actors, and observers. Each is discussed below.

Administrative Records

Organizations frequently produce a plethora of information in the process of managing programs. Administrative data include information on (a) staffing levels and qualifications, (b) budgets (program, indirect costs, etc.), (c) level of service provided, and (d) complaints, requests, and compliments. In addition, data from client files provide information on (e) progress, backgrounds, needs, use of services. Data from event files (e.g., repair logs) provide further information on activities. For example, to know what the most common problem is in parks, managers can examine supervisory and inspection reports about park maintenance. In these reports, managers can examine events (e.g., broken benches) as well words and phrases (e.g., things vandalized). Such events can also be examined through time or across different neighborhoods.

Administrative data are most frequently used for workload measures and workload ratios. For example, caseload data are frequently available from work logs and other administrative records (e.g., billing). These data are also readily transformed into workload ratios, such as caseloads per worker. The widespread availability of such data makes them ideal for benchmarking, and many benchmarks (or performance standards) are indeed based on workload rather than outcome data. For example, benchmarks exist for the number of calls that receptionists can handle, the number of hours needed to cut grass in public parks, and the number of swimmers that lifeguards can effectively oversee in swimming pools. However, administrative data are usually designed for the control and accountability of resources and activities, not for measuring outcomes. Outcome data are seldom collected except when the program practices Total Quality Management or benchmarking. Thus additional data collection efforts are usually needed.

Working with administrative data often involves the following challenges: (a) missing or incomplete data, (b) data that are available only in highly aggregated form, (c) data definitions that have changed over time and cannot be compared, (d) data that cannot be linked to particular events or clients, (e) data that are confidential, and (f) data that are inaccurate.

Information technology systems provide important advantages in measuring productivity. They reduce the need for analyzing data from separate case files and other paper records, and they ensure that data are captured at the point of contact. These systems also facilitate data analysis and can be programmed to produce monthly or even weekly reports of key output measures. Organizations that lack adequate information technology systems greatly increase the amount of effort involved in data collection and analysis, which may be an insurmountable obstacle.

Surveys

Surveys are increasingly used to obtain information about citizen needs and client satisfaction. Such information is often central to outcome assessment and is seldom provided through administrative records. Most surveys should be conducted on an annual basis, and some even quarterly. The following issues are involved in conducting surveys.

Sampling. Most surveys are sample surveys. This involves drawing representative samples to make generalizable statements about populations of citizens, clients, or employees. The best way to obtain a representative sample is to give each member of the population an equal chance of being selected for the sample, so that the sample is not biased toward including any specific individuals or groups. This is achieved through random sampling. A key issue is determining the appropriate sample size.

In practice, four complications may occur in sampling. First, managers may not have a list of program clients. This is frequently the case in walk-in clinics or park services. In this instance, various days and times should be randomly selected throughout the year, and a random sample of (or possibly all) users should be surveyed during these periods. The second problem is that the list that exists does not exactly match the population. This too is often the case.

Fourth, the above discussion of sampling error assumes completed responses. A larger initial sample is selected to account for nonresponses. For example, if a final sample of 400 is desired, and the expected response rate is 55%, then the initial sample should be (400/0.55=)727. Nonreponses are an important issue in surveys because the respondent group must be representative of the sample that was drawn. Response rates below 60% merit concern about possible response bias.

Types of surveys. There are three types of surveys: mail, phone, and in-person surveys. Each has somewhat different features. When many data (i.e., survey questions) are required, either in-person or mail surveys should be used. The length of most mail surveys almost always raise issues about response rates, and many cities are now using phone surveys, which are faster and usually have adequate response rates. Dillman (1978) suggests increasing the response rates of mail surveys by making them short and attractive, providing return envelopes, conducting follow-up telephone calls, and including a cover letter from senior officials.

Unbiased questions. Surveys often raise concerns about biased questioning. To avoid bias, questions should (a) be clear (i.e., unambiguous, specific), (b) avoid double-barreled phrasing, (c) be relevant and answerable by respondents, (d) be without inherent bias, and (e) avoid negative statements. Of equal importance is the selection of response scales. Closed-ended scales are preferred, because the analysis of many open-ended responses is cumbersome and prone to error. Response scales should be unbiased and complete. That is, they should include all relevant categories and have as many positive as negative response categories. A popular scale is the so-called Likert scale. For example, the question, "How satisfied are you with the services that your received?" would use the following response scale: Very Satisfied-Satisfied-Somewhat Satisfied-Don't Know-Somewhat Dissatisfied-Dissatisfied-Very Dissatisfied. Other Likert scales use Important/Unimportant; Good-Poor/Bad, Agree/Disagree; Adequate/Inadequate. Likert scales are also used that omit the "somewhat" categories (these are called five-point scales). A strategy for formulating questions is to (a) decide what information is needed, (b) decide what information target respondents can provide, (c) write preliminary survey questions, and (d) improve questions according to the above guidelines. Although existing surveys are helpful, each survey effort requires a survey that fits the unique situation.

The most common problems in doing surveys are (a) underestimating the time and resource requirements for successfully completing survey efforts and (b) failing to address significant concerns of bias, response rates and sampling, and reliability. For this reason, survey efforts frequently include outside experts hired to guide the effort (see above, "Implementing Performance Measurement Systems").

Focus Groups

The purpose of focus groups is to generate understanding of program or client needs. They do not provide information that is representative, but focus groups do provide information about the range of concerns on which information should be collected. Thus they are usually done prior to conducting surveys. Focus groups involve semi-structured, in-depth, group discussions. This technique was pioneered by companies in their marketing efforts. It is generally recommended that focus groups are homogenous, that is, that group members are selected from the same target group. This is because different target groups are likely to have different experiences, needs, and views. Different populations may also inhibit and drown each other out.

Moderators should be impartial and assist focus group members to fully explore all matters that they have agreed to discuss. Thus moderators often steer discussions back to original agendas; focus groups are not meandering conversations. Moderators are usually assisted by a note-taker who records the comments of participants.

Other Approaches

Experts are used when objective, factual data are insufficient to make judgments about program outcomes and activities, or when the assessment of such data requires the judgment of experts. Some examples in which expert judgment might be used are the maintenance of landfills, the analysis of medical records (e.g., treatment of patients), the quality of a higher education program, or the use of management techniques. Experts should only be used when it is likely that their recommendations will be acted on. A criterion for accepting expert judgment is that it is shared by other experts; hence program evaluation always uses a range (or panel) of experts. Typically, no fewer than three experts are consulted.

Trained observers are used to evaluate the condition of facilities (e.g., parks, public rest rooms, public housing, nursing homes, beach maintenance, street cleanliness) as well as events (pickpockets, authorized ticket sales, etc.). Trained observers provide unobtrusive observation.

Role-playing is a form of observer-based rating whereby observers pose as clients. Such observers are usually unknown to employees, although many do identify such "ghost" clients. The use of observers allows for spot-checks of service quality. Sometimes actors are matched with regard to race, gender, or age to observe patterns of differential treatment. An example of matched role-playing is the use of minority actors who pose as home buyers to detect discrimination in home buying or real estate services by comparing services provided to majority and minority clients. Matched role-playing is also used to detect bias in job hiring.

REFERENCES

Ammons, D. (1995). *Accountability for performance: Measuring and monitoring in local government.* Washington, DC: International City/County Management Association (ICMA).

Ammons, D. (1996). *Benchmarking for local government.* Thousand Oaks, CA: Sage.

Babbie, E. (1995). *The practice of social research.* Belmont, CA: Wadsworth.

Berman, E. (1997). [Survey of museums and social service organizations]. Unpublished raw data.

Berman, E., & West, J. (1995). Municipal commitment to Total Quality Management. *Public Administration Review, 55*(1), 57–66.

Berman, E., & West, J. (1997). [Survey of cities]. Unpublished raw data.

Brinkerhoff, R., & Dressler, D. (1990). *Productivity measurement.* Newbury Park, CA: Sage.

Campbell, D., & Stanley, J. (1963). *Experimental and quasi-experimental designs for research.* Chicago: Rand McNally.

Dillman, D. (1978). *Mail and telephone surveys: The total design method.* New York: John Wiley.

Epstein, P. (1984). *Using performance measurement in local government.* New York: Van Nostrand Reinhold.

Greiner, J. (1996). Positioning performance measurement for the twenty-first century. In A. Halchmi & G. Bouckaert (Eds.), *Organizational performance and measurement in the public sector* (pp. 11–50). Westport, CT: Quorum.

Hakes, J. (1996). Comparing outputs to outcomes. *PA Times, 19*(10), 1–2.

Halachmi, A. (1992). Evaluation research : Purpose and perspective. In M. Holzer (Ed.), *Public productivity handbook* (pp. 213–226). New York: Marcel Dekker.

International City/County Managers Association (ICMA). (1995). *Applying performance measurement* [CD-ROM]. Washington, DC: Author.

Kanter, R., & Summers, D. (1987). Doing well by doing good: Dilemmas of performance measurement in non-profit organizations. In W. Powell (Ed.), *The nonprofit sector handbook* (pp. 154–166). New Haven, CT: Yale University Press.

Keehley, P., Medlin, S., MacBride, S., & Longmore, L. (1997). *Benchmarking for best practices in the public sector.* San Francisco: Jossey-Bass.

Miller, T., & Miller, M. (1991). *Citizen surveys: How to do them, how to use them, what they mean* (Special report). Washington, DC: International City/County Management Association (ICMA).

Miller, T. (1994). Designing and Conducting Surveys. In J. Wholey, H. Matry & K. Newcomer (Eds.), *Handbook of practical program evaluation* (pp. 271–292). San Francisco, CA: Jossey-Bass.

Poister, T. (1992). Productivity monitoring: Systems, indicators and analysis. In M. Holzer (Ed.), *Public productivity handbook* (chap. 10). New York: Marcel Dekker.

Rosen, E. (1993). Improving public sector productivity. Newbury Park, CA: Sage.

Rossi, P., & Freeman, H. (1993). *Evaluation: A systematic approach* (5th ed.). Newbury Park, CA: Sage.

Schwabe, C. (1996). *Development of use of performance indicators in the city of Coral Springs, Florida* (Unpublished case study). Washington, DC: ASPA Task Force on Governmental Accomplishment & Accountability.

Sylvia, R., Meier, K., & Gunn, E. (1985). *Program planning and evaluation for the public manager.* Prospect Heights, IL: Waveland.

Tigue, P., & Strachota, D. (1994). *The use of performance measures in city and county budgets.* Chicago: Government Finance Officers Association.

Tracy, R. (1996). *Development and use of outcome information in Portland, OR* (Unpublished case study). Washington, DC: ASPA Task Force on Governmental Accomplishment & Accountability.

Welch, S. & Comer, J. (1998). *Qualitative methods for public administration.* Chicago, IL: The Dorsey Press.

Wholey, J., Hatry, H., & Newcomer, K. (Eds.). (1994). *Handbook of practical program evaluation.* San Francisco: Jossey-Bass.

NOTES

1. Historically, program evaluation preceded performance evaluation. Program evaluation was developed in the 1960s in response to increasing accountability for large federal programs. It was criticized in the late 1970s for being expensive, untimely, and divorced from decision making. During the 1980s, new approaches focused on intermediate outcomes rather than long-term goals—to increase timeliness—and involved key stakeholders in the design and use of evaluation. Performance measurement developed from these efforts.

2. Efficiency measures are sometimes called productivity measures, following the emphasis on efficiency in for-profit productivity measurement. This book takes a broader perspective on productivity.

41

City of Charlotte, North Carolina

BALANCED SCORECARD

For more than 25 years, Charlotte [N.C.] City government has measured performance because it subscribes to the belief that measurement matters. Over the years, City staff measured everything from workload, response time, and cost per unit to efficiency and effectiveness. One unintended result was an information overload—lengthy reports that few people read or utilized.

The City's Management By Objectives (MBO) process served the organization well over the years and helped staff track performance against targets. However, it did not reflect the City's emerging emphasis on strategic goals, mission-driven government, and rapid change. The old measurement system focused the city's attention backward not forward. It was an audit tool, not a planning tool. It did not relate to the City's vision, mission, or goals.

A STRATEGIC FOCUS

Charlotte wanted a performance measurement tool and report that gave a quick but comprehensive view of progress in strategic areas, and translated mission and strategy into tangible objectives and measures. In 1992 the City Council developed and articulated five Focus Areas where they wanted to direct budget resources and city staff emphasis. Focus Areas have changed little over time and include *Community Safety, City-Within-a-City, Transportation, Economic Development,* and *Restructuring Government.*

In order to communicate to the Council that the priorities in their focus areas were being addressed, the City needed a better performance measurement system that reflected the strategic focus of the City Council. The City Manager became familiar with the "Balanced Scorecard" concept through articles in the *Harvard Business Review,* and directed staff to assess its potential.

Staff found that traditional performance measurement systems often concentrate on improving the cost, quality, and cycle times of existing processes. However, the Balanced Scorecard highlights processes an organization must excel at to be successful. Robert Kaplan and David Norton, the architects of the Balanced Scorecard, describe it as the next generation of performance measurement. Kaplan says,

> "A Balanced Scorecard provides substantial focus, motivation, and accountability in government . . . the scorecard provides the rationale for their existence and communicates to external constituents and internal employees the outcomes and performance drivers by which the organization will achieve its mission and strategic objectives."

While the Balanced Scorecard was first utilized in the private sector, its concentration on four "balanced" perspectives, and not just financial results (the traditional focus), appealed to the City Manager. The Balanced Scorecard summarizes the most critical performance measures in a single management report and the Manager believed the City could adapt these concepts for use in the public sector, especially to put the focus on the citizen, or the Customer Perspective. The City customized the Balanced Scorecard, with Kaplan and Norton's concurrence, to put the Customer Perspective at the top of the Scorecard, instead of the Financial Perspective as originally designed. This Scorecard arrangement provided more flexibility for use in the public sector. In 1994, the City of Charlotte was the first municipality to implement the Balanced Scorecard.

THE BALANCED SCORECARD AS A STRATEGIC TOOL

The Balanced Scorecard is different from other performance measurement systems because it uses four balanced perspectives to answer critical service delivery questions. The Balanced Scorecard consists of the following four perspectives and helps the City to address the accompanying questions:

- Customer Perspective—"Is the City delivering the services the citizens want?"
- Financial Perspective—"Is the service delivered at a good price?"
- Internal Process Perspective—"Can the City change the way the service is delivered and improve it?"
- Learning and Growth Perspective—"Is the City maintaining technology and employee training for continuous improvement?"

City management prepared a Corporate scorecard that presently includes 19 objectives and is centered on the five focus areas—*Community Safety, City-Within-a-City, Transportation, Economic Development,* and *Restructuring Government.* The Renaissance Worldwide Consulting firm was used to develop the scorecard. The linkage of the scorecard to the five focus areas has made the Balanced Scorecard the strategic management tool the City was looking for.

CORPORATE OBJECTIVES

Each of the 19 corporate objectives has a broad definition, which provides context for what is to be achieved. For example, the definitions for four of the 19 objectives are:

- *Customer Perspective*

  Reduce Crime—Decrease crime throughout the city through the use of community-oriented policing and other strategies that target specific crime categories or offenders.
- *Financial Perspective*
  Grow the Tax Base—Increase tax revenues by increasing new business development, retaining existing businesses, and encouraging residential/commercial developments.
- *Internal Process Perspective*
  Increase Infrastructure Capacity—Increase City's capability to support growth by optimizing existing infrastructure and increasing infrastructure capacity.

- *Learning and Growth Perspective*
  <u>Close the Skills Gap</u>—Increase availability of leadership, customer service, problem-solving, technology skills, plus other skills required to support City priorities.

By using the objectives and linking those to the focus areas, all key business units are better able to identify their role in achieving the strategic objectives of the organization. The Corporate Scorecard does not and cannot represent every important service delivered. Instead, it encapsulates the strategic focus areas of the organization. However, there are a number of the 19 corporate objectives that every City business unit can embrace or impact, such as *enhance service delivery, maximizing benefit/cost, improve productivity,* and *close the skills gap.*

For example, basic city services such as fire suppression, garbage collection or animal control are not represented individually on the corporate scorecard, yet all three services can strive to "enhance service delivery." These basic services are better addressed at the business unit level scorecard, where some efficiency, effectiveness or activity-type measures may be more appropriate. The key is to identify on a high or macro level those corporate objectives that will maintain a strategic focus.

A next step for the Charlotte Corporate scorecard is to identify one critical measure for each of the 19 objectives. The Balanced Scorecard's designer, Robert Kaplan, felt this was a key step because it helps the City to advance towards its original goal to develop a quick, but comprehensive summary of progress on the City's strategic goals. It will also show how well the City is performing, while recognizing the day-to-day activities of "running the business" are measured in each business unit, and will support the critical measure identified. Budget and Evaluation staff has already begun the process of identifying one critical measure for each objective. Preliminary efforts reveal that a potential corporate measure for the "strengthen neighborhood" objective under the Customer Perspective could be the number of neighborhoods determined to be "stable" as reported in the Quality of Life index of all Charlotte neighborhoods. This Quality of Life index has been developed by the University of North Carolina at Charlotte and is being applied to all of Charlotte's neighborhoods.

CASCADING THROUGH THE ORGANIZATION

The City's goal is to use the Corporate scorecard to meet the City Council's priorities in each focus area. To do this, the Corporate scorecard has been "cascaded" throughout the organization.

Scorecards are developed at the business unit level through business plans. The business plan outlines how each business unit intends to address the strategic focus areas and Corporate scorecard objectives. It also identifies the measures that will be used to evaluate how well the business unit is addressing City Council priorities and providing service delivery. Not only are the objectives in the Corporate scorecard reflected in business unit scorecards, but also those initiatives and projects each business unit undertakes as simply a part of "running the business." Results for both the Corporate objectives and individual business unit initiatives are tracked at the business unit level.

This "cascading" of the Corporate scorecard is also reflected in each employee's performance compensation. Since 1995, the city has rewarded employees for achieving budget cost savings, if their business unit met predetermined productivity and cost savings goals that were identified in the unit's business plan as incentive targets. The link to employee evaluations has also been enhanced to where several business units now tailor individual pay-for-performance objectives to the business unit's business plan. Thus, the goals for employees are directly linked to goals of the organization. This cascading feature of the scorecard also serves as a feedback loop. If business units are not meeting their objectives, then objectives of City Council are not being met and problems can be isolated and identified.

BUDGET INTEGRATION

One of the City's most significant information tools is the budget document. Like many other municipalities, the City of Charlotte has struggled to link its performance measurement system to the budget. The budget presentation for Fiscal Year 2000 marked the first comprehensive attempt to show the City Council and citizens how the budget was tailored to meet the goals and focus areas of City Council. The integration of the focus areas and Balanced Scorecard with the budget included an overview of expenditures by focus area. In the City Manager's FY2000 budget transmittal letter, she recommended:

> "130 additional community safety officers, 20 fire fighters, and 24 positions for animal control to address the Community Safety Focus Area . . . the recommended budget also includes $32 million in neighborhood improvement bonds for the City Within a City Focus Area, the development of an Eastside Strategy Plan for the Economic Development Focus Area, more than $155 million in General Obligation Bonds for roads to address the Transportation Focus Area . . . and a reduction of 31 positions in Solid Waste Service due to a Managed Competition bid which addresses the Restructuring Government Focus Area."

In addition to highlighting the focus areas in the transmittal letter, the numerous program budgets of each business unit were also examined and placed under one of the five focus areas. Those program budgets which did not directly impact a focus area were placed in a category titled "general government" to better reflect the cost of providing municipal services that fall outside the focus areas.

The FY 2000 budget also includes performance measurement information on the cover page of each business unit's budget section. These cover pages include basic budget information such as total budget amount with a comparison to the prior year, the number of funded positions, a bulleted list of the significant budget changes, and a list of measurements that were taken from business plans, which link to the Corporate scorecard. This approach will help Councilmembers to better determine how taxpayer dollars are being spent, based upon the measures provided.

A STRATEGIC ORGANIZATION

One premise of the Balanced Scorecard is that it is more important to report on strategic processes such as promoting community-based problem solving than routine processes such as building sidewalks. The City's expectations regarding measures have changed with the development of the Corporate scorecard. In other words, it is not enough to know the level of workload or the cost of activities. It is more important to know outcomes and results.

Staff continues to strive for those measures that indicate the City's resources make a difference. For instance, the City's use of the Quality of Life index has helped to determine the impact of strategic activities in "fragile" or "threatened" neighborhoods. This index is a leap from merely measuring housing code enforcement activities to being more strategic to show what it takes to have a "stable" neighborhood.

Another measure to determine impact is the crime rate. In the past, police had measured response time which has proven to have no effect on the crime rate. The real issue with the crime rate is to prevent the next crime. The new police measures are concentrating on prevention through community-oriented policing and increasing citizen perception of safety.

The Balanced Scorecard has reinforced several important points:

1. Measurement gives clarity to vague concepts such as strategic goals.
2. Measure what matters.
3. Measurement is for communicating, not to control.
4. Building the scorecard develops consensus and teamwork throughout the organization.
5. Developing an effective performance management system takes time.

Implementing Charlotte's Corporate scorecard has helped the City become a more strategic organization by narrowing its focus and identifying better measures. This in turn has positively impacted the focus areas and those areas outside of the focus area that are part of "running the business" of providing municipal services.

BENEFITS

One of the biggest benefits of the Scorecard is just being realized, which is the ability to provide strategic information to City Council—information they can easily understand and use. By measuring what matters, the City has been able to move from the Management By Objectives system that had between 800–900 measures to the Balanced Scorecard, which in FY1998 incorporated 266 measures, including those used at the business unit level. "Measuring less" has worked better because the measures used are results-oriented or outcome-based, instead of activity measures, which do not tend to provide the full context as to what was accomplished or how money was spent.

One of the reasons the scorecard has worked so well is the tremendous support and leadership from the City Manager and City Council. The City Council is interested in performance outcomes and endorses the Balanced Scorecard because they get better information/reports that more clearly shows what a citizen gets for their tax dollar. The City Council members are also individually attuned to performance measurement and are comfortable discussing performance measurement; thus, they ask for performance information from staff. The Scorecard also represents the City Manager's commitment to performance measurement, which began with her first job with the City as an Evaluation Analyst more than 20 years ago.

The City Manager now publishes a quarterly Corporate Performance Report, which centers on the progress in each of the five focus areas and the 19 objectives of the Corporate scorecard. By linking the performance measurement system and reporting on the Council's focus areas and priorities, the City has truly developed a strategic organization that can report outcomes and progress in a simple manner. This process has produced two intended benefits:

1. City Council receives reports that include strategic results.
2. Strategy is communicated to citizens and employees.

Through its reporting structure, the Balanced Scorecard has provided the City of Charlotte with a strategic feedback loop. The loop begins with City Council setting strategic goals in the focus areas to drive budgetary decisions and concludes with reports in a strategic format that tells Council and others how well the city is progressing on its priorities and the many facets of "running of the business."

15

HONOR AND ETHICS

The complexity of behavioral motivations is one of the features of public life (see Chapter 7), but it also is the cause of one of the most complex pitfalls facing those in politics and public administration. In the private sector, corporate management is expected to be "lean and mean" in its unwavering, focused pursuit of larger profits, higher prices for shares of company stock, or growth in stockholder equity. Indeed in most corporations profits, stock prices, and the value of stockholder equity are the most important—the core—measures of how well the management team is succeeding. After all, profits and shareholders' equity are the reasons why the corporation exists.[1]

Public administrators face a more complex array of organizational purposes and thus more challenging ethical paths also. The work of the public administrator is "noble." It serves national, city, state, or tribal honor, improves the quality of life for citizens, and serves public purposes. Because of the nobility of these purposes, we expect public administrators to be above reproach—to be exemplary models of unquestionable honesty, trustworthiness, and ethical behavior. Thus, a corrupt public administrator—or a public administrator who even gives the appearance of acting unethically—becomes the focus of special contempt. Unethical actions by corporate executives are seldom tolerated.[2] But public administrators are held to higher ethical standards and are vilified when they do not live up to these standards. Unethical public administrators do not simply hurt their employers—they also betray the public trust.[3]

HONOR AND ETHICS

Noble ideals of public service have been expressed in famous speeches and slogans throughout our history. Elementary and secondary schools seek to imbue their students with a sense of respect for public values. The flag of the United States stands proudly in the front of most classrooms, and students pledge allegiance to it daily. Hence feelings of disappointment and betrayal are high when public administrators are suspected or are caught in acts of corruption, venality, self-interest or dishonor. Perhaps this helps to explain at least part of the deep cynicism and dissatisfaction with government that has pervaded the U.S. for at least the last 30 years. The Vietnam War and the Watergate experience—both cases where Presidents of the United States and their closest administrators were caught lying—ushered in an era of declining respect for government institutions and public administrators that continues today.[4]

The maintenance of national honor, public purpose, and the countless benefits that an honest and efficient public service bring to a civil society and the economy,[5] argue for the inclusion of government ethics in every course, book, and degree program in public administration.[6] Students of public administration must not only learn how to form a personal judgment about the meaning of national honor and public service ethics, but also develop an ability to navigate through the complex and often subtle ethical dilemmas that every public administrator eventually faces.[7] Students of public administration do not have a choice. They *must* develop a deep understanding and appreciation for the standards of ethical behavior and the complexity of ethical behavior in public service. The responsibility does not rest solely on public administration courses and degree programs. Ethics education begins in homes and continues in elementary and secondary schools, and in churches or temples. As we have tried to explain, however, many of the ethical choices that confront public administrators are specific to public administration and government service. "Basic ethics" is not enough for public administrators.

CONFLICTS OF LOYALTIES AND RESPONSIBILITIES

How should an administrator behave when a conflict arises between loyalty to an elected official, loyalty to her or his agency, and loyalty to the public interest?[8] How should a public administrator reconcile personal beliefs, political preferences, or professional values when they may conflict with the duties of office? Are there circumstances under which gifts may be accepted from private firms or public interest groups? Are there ways to ensure that an agency provides procedural fairness? When should a public administrator "blow the whistle" on elected officials or peers to expose malpractice or theft—even if doing so might cripple the administrator's agency for years? Are there circumstances where public administrators should—or should not—participate in public debates on public policy? Would it always be wrong—or right—to do so? In sum, can a single, coherent, shared framework of ethical principles be established for public administrators? If so, can these principles be reconciled with the widely diverse values of our pluralist society where power is divided by race, gender, age, geography, and class?

We believe strongly that general principles of ethical behavior can be articulated, that it is possible to codify such principles, and that professional associations (such as the American Society for Public Administration and the International City/County Managers Association) and governments have an obligation to publish standards of behavior that all employees are expected to exceed. Obvious crimes, such as bribery and corruption, are only one dimension. They need to be countered with effective laws and vigilant enforcement. In the noncriminal areas—in the "gray areas"—where careful judgment is needed, every possible source of guidance should be made available to help public administrators act ethically—and to avoid any appearance of not acting ethically.

Every public administrator faces conflicts of responsibilities—weekly, if not daily. At the least complicated level, there are always conflicts, for example, between the time and attention we owe to our jobs and to our families. At a more dramatic level, there are conflicts between loyalty to the president or governor, and loyalty to one's own professional standards. Unfortunately, there usually is not a simple "either-or solution" to the conflict. An upcoming decision may involve a wide variety of stakeholders. They may be residents, businesses in town, businesses that would like to locate in town, political parties, major donors, "skinheads," the ACLU, environmentalists, "right-to-lifer's," and "pro-choicers." Public administrators may have strong allegiances and share the concerns of several of these stakeholder groups that have conflicting agendas, yet public administrators must find ways to exercise their duty as ethical public servants.

Thus, every higher education program and management development training program for current and future public administrators should include a wide variety of opportunities to learn how to act ethically. We urge the widespread use of, for example, case studies, simulations, video-tape feed-back of role playing, and service-learning in education and training programs to help students learn how to anticipate conflicts between loyalties and responsibilities, and to wrestle through them to ethical—and practical—solutions.[9]

HIERARCHY OF ETHICS

Mentally organizing ethics into a "hierarchy" can be a useful approach for thinking about the conflicting roles and loyalties an administrator may face. *Personal morality* forms the base of the triangular hierarchy—a sense of right and wrong. Personal morality is inculcated through socialization processes, by parents, early teachings, social and cultural mores.[10] Directly above personal morality in the hierarchy are *professional ethics,* ethical standards that are codified by professional associations. A public administrator may belong to the American Society for Public Administration (ASPA) and the American Society for Quality Control (ASQC). Each association has its code of ethics that apply to members of the profession. *Organizational ethics* form the third level in the hierarchy. Organizational ethics define appropriate behavior in a particular city or state government, or in a department of the U.S. government. *Social ethics,* ethics that oblige members of society to behave in ways that protect all and further the interests of the group, are at the top of hierarchy. Social ethics include laws as well as informal expectations.

CODES OF ETHICS

In a code of ethics, a professional association sets out standards of conduct to guide its members. These standards often are formulated by committees of senior members of the professions, drawing on their experiences to identify the ethical dilemmas that face members of their profession. Codes of ethics do not guarantee ethical behavior. Many members of a profession will have never even seen or read them; others will read and forget about them. But codes of ethics do serve at least three very useful purposes.

- *Codes of ethics aid in the formation of a professional consensus.* Members of a professional association must pool ideas and debate what behaviors should be allowed, discouraged, and prohibited. Some behaviors are easy to identify as unethical or as ethical. It is the "gray areas" that pose problems. The mere process of discussing and debating the limits of ethical behavior is an important step beyond denial;
- *Codes of ethics provide a point of reference when a public administrator is faced with a dilemma.* They provide something to turn to for guidance when a problematic situation arises;
- *Codes of ethics provide a basis for educating members.* They provide a structure for socializing new members into the ethics of the profession and for reminding long-time members what is expected of them.

Codes need to be updated regularly. New challenges and practices arise that are not addressed by an out-of-date code. For example, the great increase in government contracting-out services to nonprofit organizations during the last decade has multiplied the opportunities for "cozy relationships" to develop—as well as for out-and-out corruption. (See Chapter 4). The Internet has made information accessible instantly and worldwide, and has created innumerable new practical questions about ethical behavior *that had not even been thought about 10 years ago.*

READINGS REPRINTED IN THIS CHAPTER

James Bowman and Russell Williams' article, **"Ethics in Government: From a Winter of Despair to a Springtime of Hope,"**[11] compares public managers' perceptions of ethics in government in 1989 and 1996. These two years were in periods of high concern about government integrity in the U.S. They also were years in which many discussions about public ethics were occurring among professionals and in the literature of public administration. Bowman and Williams sent surveys to members of the American Society of Public Administration (ASPA) and to members of the American Political Science Association (APSA) following the publication of a revised code of ethics by its Professional Ethics Committee in 1995.[12] The survey addressed three key issues: perceptions of ethics in society and government; the nature of integrity in public agencies, and the new APSA Code.

The Bowman and Williams survey found that public administrators do not believe that the current widespread concern with ethical issues is ephemeral, but rather that the concern is growing steadily. The administrators were not generally cynical. They believe that complex issues of "public virtue" are of higher interest now than in the recent past. They also believe strongly that the level of morality in business is lower than in the public sector. Virtually all administrators surveyed agreed that ethical dilemmas are a regular feature of their work and most believe that dealing with such issues could be empowering for an organization. Most disputed the idea that ethics are meaningless in organizational life (because of prevailing Machiavellian cultures), and many felt that career public administrators held higher ethical standards than politicians did. Most administrators who were surveyed responded that their agencies employed no consistent approach for addressing ethical concerns. Thus, leadership, advocacy, and publicity are needed in order to promote ethics in public organizations.

Although the views of a sample of ASPA and APSA members are not representative of public administrators as a whole, these findings provide grounds for hope. The depth and breadth of awareness of the APSA code is growing, and thus there are things that can be done. These are good signs, and as the authors suggest, they perhaps signaled the movement from the "decade of greed" (the 1980s) to the "decade of reform and reinvention" (the 1990s).

Guy Adams and Danny Balfour's book, *Unmasking Administrative Evil*,[13] is an important contribution to the expanding body of literature that reexamined and turned the spotlight on public service behavior in the 1990s. In their chapter, **"The Dynamics of Evil and Administrative Evil,"** Adams and Balfour argue that the "influence of evil" has been suppressed and "masked" in public administration. We have incorrectly viewed evil as aberrations or anomalies that result from temporary, politically induced departures from a norm of neutral or benevolent behavior. The horrible actions of the Nazi government, they argue, were carried out systematically by "politically neutral" public administrators. We must face the possibility of "systemic evil" in public administration head on, and thereby lay the groundwork for a more ethical and democratic public administration. Failure to do so will lead us toward state- sponsored dehumanization and destruction.

Adams and Balfour's strong language and their choice of examples—Hitler's holocaust and the Vietnam War—may seem removed from the everyday experience of a public administrator working on social programs or trash disposal. But, they are not. Systemic evil and willingness to tolerate it are facts of the modern world and of modern public administration. For example, we are trying to decide—today—whether we dare to permanently store nuclear weapons and spent nuclear rods near earthquake-prone faults. We are trying to decide whether we should stop shipping hazardous waste to underdeveloped nations in Africa, who are glad to have some income. We are trying to decide whether to continue burning mustard gas, nerve gas, and other World War II agents of destruction 20 miles upwind from a mid-sized city.

Many public administrators may face much more domestic and less traumatic ethical issues. Nonetheless, some public administrators face dilemmas where "administrative evil" may be committed. Adams and Balfour's perspective should be part of our awareness and the awareness of all public administrators.

As this discussion and the reprinted readings that follow show, honor and ethical behavior in public administration are long-standing and profound issues.

Their scope ranges from dealing with seemingly innocent gifts and small conflicts of interest to profound questions of national honor and the possibility of evil deeds being accomplished through the administrative machinery of which public servants are a part. These are issues that no student of public administration can avoid, or should want to avoid.

NOTES

1. All corporations have more purposes than these, but these necessarily have highest priority. Without profits and increasing shareholder equity, corporations cannot survive, grow, and attract new capital.
2. See for example: Joseph A. Petrick, and John F. Quinn. (1997). *Management Ethics: Integrity at Work*. Thousand Oaks, Calif.: Sage; and Peter Madsen, and Jay M. Shafritz. (Eds.). (1990). *Essentials of Business Ethics*. New York: Meridian.
3. See Terry L. Cooper. (1990). *The Responsible Administrator: An Approach to Ethics for the Administrative Role* (3rd ed.). San Francisco: Jossey-Bass; Harold F. Gortner. (1991). *Ethics for Public Managers*. New York: Praeger; Amy Gutmann, and Dennis Thompson. (1990). *Ethics & Politics* (2nd ed.). Chicago: Nelson-Hall; Thomas E. McCollough. (1991). *The Moral Imagination and Public Life: Raising the Ethical Question*. New York: Chatham House; and Montgomery Van Wart. (1998). *Changing Public Sector Values*. New York: Garland.
4. And more than a few other highly publicized scandals in the decades since Watergate haven't helped the situation!
5. See H. George Frederickson. (1997). *The Spirit of Public Administration*. San Francisco: Jossey-Bass; and Louis C. Gawthrop. (1998). *Public Service and Democracy: Ethical Imperatives for the 21st Century*. New York: Chatham House.
6. Bowman, James, and Donald Menzel. (Eds.). (1998). *Teaching Ethics and Values in Public Administration Programs*. Albany, NY: State University of New York Press.
7. See Terry L. Cooper, and N. Dale Wright. (Eds.). (1992). *Exemplary Public Administrators: Character and Leadership in Government*. San Francisco: Jossey-Bass; Rushworth M. Kidder. (1995). *How Good People Make Tough Choices: Resolving the Dilemmas of Ethical Living*. New York: William Morrow; and, Norma M. Riccucci. (1995). *Unsung Heroes: Federal Execucrats Making a Difference*. Washington, DC: Georgetown University Press.
8. Terry, Larry D. (1995). *Leadership of Public Bureaucracies: The Administrator as Conservator*. Thousand Oaks, Calif.: Sage.
9. Bowman, James, and Donald Menzel. (Eds.). (1998). *Teaching Ethics and Values in Public Administration Programs*. Albany, NY: State University of New York Press.
10. Kohlberg, Lawrence. (1968). "The Child As a Moral Philosopher." *Psychology Today*, *7*, 25–30.
11. Bowman, James B., and Russell L. Williams. (November/December 1997). "Ethics in Government: From a Winter of Despair to a Spring of Hope." *Public Administration Review*, *57*(6), 517–526.
12. A copy of the Code of Ethics of the American Society for Public Administration can be found in Jay M. Shafritz (Ed.), (1998), *International Encyclopedia of Public Policy and Administration*. Boulder, Colo.: Westview Press, p. 412.
13. Adams, Guy B., and Danny L. Balfour. (1998). "The Dynamics of Evil and Administrative Evil," in Adams and Balfour, *Unmasking Administrative Evil*. Thousand Oaks, Calif.: Sage.

42

James B. Bowman and Russell L. Williams

ETHICS IN GOVERNMENT: FROM A WINTER OF DESPAIR TO A SPRING OF HOPE

The issue of ethics in public service is as old as government itself. Yet "post-Watergate morality" has produced an enduring and unprecedented level of concern about the integrity of democratic governance (Garment, 1991). In the 1990s alone, the continuous stream of revelations, allegations, and investigations—involving presidents, presidential advisors, a U.S. Senator, a Speaker of the House of Representatives, a Ways and Means Committee chairman, cabinet secretaries, a Supreme Court nominee, Gulf War syndrome spokesmen, campaign contributors, and numerous state and local officials—suggests that this concern is unlikely to change any time soon. Nonetheless, this may be a Dickensian "tale of two cities": when there is despair, there also may be hope.

Indeed, ethical considerations can hardly be overlooked in a time of popular reforms that attempt to transform the public service ethos in the name of productivity (Gore, 1993). They are of fundamental importance to the quality of democracy and its administration. "Questions of morality and right conduct," Jeremy Plant (1997) points out, "are now considered as significant as the traditional concerns of Wilsonian Public Administration" like efficiency.

In the context of these events, the American Society of Public Administration (ASPA) promulgated its newly-revamped code of ethics in 1995. The association's Professional Ethics Committee subsequently requested that a membership survey, based on the senior author's 1989 survey of the same organization (Bowman, 1990), be conducted to obtain an initial assessment of the effectiveness of the code. This was especially propitious timing because the intervening years witnessed the passing of the Decade of Greed and the coming of the Decade of Reinventing Government, a period of turbulent change that has included innovations, downsizing, and, as noted, scandals at all levels of government.

A questionnaire (consisting of agree-disagree statements as well as several multiple choice and open-ended items), with a copy of the ASPA Code of Ethics, was mailed in spring 1996 to a random sample of 750 administrators who are members of the society. Usable replies were received from 59 percent of those contacted, a respectable response rate for this methodology and one comparable to earlier research.[1] A profile of the respondents, which matches the ASPA practitioner membership, reveals a group that is predominantly white, male, well educated, experienced in local government, a middle or senior level manager, relatively high income, moderate to liberal in political philosophy, and holds at least a six-year membership in ASPA.[2]

The results explore three topics in ascending order of emphasis: perceptions regarding ethics in society and government, the nature of integrity in public agencies,

and ASPA's Code. The implications of the data, and the part that a professional organization can play to enhance honorable behavior, are then examined.

ETHICS IN SOCIETY

Several questions probed respondents' perceptions of ethical concerns in the nation.
The findings indicate that these administrators do not believe that contemporary interest in morality is ephemeral. Most (83 percent) reject the claim that "The current
concern of American society with ethics in government is a passing fad" (10 percent
agree; the balance are undecided). Indeed, two-thirds (67 percent) think that this interest "seems to be steadily growing over time" (19 percent disagree; the remainder are
uncertain—proportions that are similar to those found in 1989).

Is this increased attention merely rhetorical in nature? Today a clear majority
(62 percent) disagree that "Ethics is similar to the weather: everyone talks about it,
but no one does anything about it" (28 percent concur; the rest are undecided), in
contrast with 48 percent who dissented earlier. This suggests a readiness to address
moral issues as it appears that ethics is "here to stay" and that cynicism may be on
the wane.

This willingness may stem from an impatience with—and relative unimportance
of—sensationalized scandals; nearly three-fourths of the administrators in both studies
(1996: 74 percent; 1989: 73 percent) believe that "incidents of outright criminality in
government distract attention from more subtle, genuine ethical dilemmas." Survey
participants now, in brief, see an augmented interest in public virtue, but (unlike
those in the late 1980s) hint that something will come of it. Indeed, contemporary
salience may be a result of disappointment in self-governance and the corresponding
need to renew the foundations of trust in democracy.

As part of such an effort, there is, not surprisingly, considerable unease about following the example set by corporate America so soon after the excesses of the 1980s.
Comparable percentages of administrators in both periods (now: 85 percent; then: 86
percent) reject the claim that "government morality in American is lower than business morality." However self-serving such views may be, private enterprise is not seen
as a standard in conducting the public's business—a sobering thought in an era of privatization, contracting out, downsizing, entrpreneurialism, and the 1994 financial debacle in Orange County, California. In light of these data, what can be said about
moral behavior in the conduct of daily management?

INTEGRITY IN AGENCIES

There does not appear to be any false sense that government organizations are exempt
from ethical concerns. Respondents were asked to react to this statement: "All people,
especially managers, encounter ethical dilemmas at work." As in 1989, virtually every
administrator (97 percent, 96 percent earlier) agrees that this is true, a finding consistent with that of the U.S. Merit Systems Protection Board (1993) regarding employee
observance of fraud, waste, and abuse. Ethical matters clearly "come with the territory" in the workaday life of public agencies.

Interestingly, over three-fourths of the administrators (76 percent versus 67 percent previously) believe that ethical concern can be empowering in organizations (7 percent say no; the balance are uncertain). Indeed, 60 percent of the managers (65 percent in 1989) reject the claim that "expressions of ethical concern . . . evoke cynicism, self-righteousness, paranoia, and/or laughter."[3] Likewise, approximately 60 percent in both studies (1996: 60 percent; 1989: 57 percent) dispute the assertion that ethics is "meaningless because organizational cultures encourage a Machiavellian philosophy of power, survival, and expediency (24 percent concur; 16 percent are undecided). In short, despite evidence of "squalid times," when "objective conditions are appalling . . . and discourse to deal with troubles is impossible" (Plant, 1996, 1), many of these managers are nonetheless comfortable with raising these issues at work.

Still, a large proportion (46 percent, 50 percent previously) concedes that supervisors are under pressure to compromise personal standards. The source of this stress appears to be the top levels of the organization. Many (55 percent today, 60 percent in the earlier poll) doubt that the "ethical standards of elected and appointed officials are as high as those held by career civil servants" (just 26 percent agree; the rest are uncertain). Further, nearly 90 percent dispute the contention that "senior management has a stronger set of ethical standards than I do" (as opposed to 75 percent in 1989). Apparently, the respondents agree with Paul Appleby, who warned of the harm that can be done by top officials who are "amateurs in governmental responsibility" (1952, x).

To summarize, these practitioners encounter dilemmas, believe that ethics can be empowering in organizational cultures, are able to surmount social taboos about discussing ethics, and perceive tension between top officials and careerists. What role do organizations serve in building an environment conducive to integrity? To probe this issue, organizational policies and leadership activities in agencies are examined next.

MORAL STANDARDS IN ORGANIZATIONAL CONDUCT

Organizational Approach

Since many decisions in government must supersede personal preferences, there is little doubt that individual actions can be affected by an institution's written policies and unwritten expectations. It is not unexpected, then, that nearly two-thirds (65 percent) of the executives agree that "organizations define and control the situations in which decisions are made" (25 percent disagree; 11 percent are undecided).[4] Agencies certainly are major vectors of social control.

Survey participants were asked to characterize their impressions about organizational approaches toward ethics. Nearly one-fourth of the sample in both periods believe that institutions have a reactive, negative, primitive, "low-road" approach to ethics, one that reinforces popular suspicions and focuses on wrongdoing. A "high-road," affirmative strategy that encourages ethical behavior and deters, rather than merely detects, problems describes 11 percent of organizations (versus below 7 percent in 1989) according to the 1996 respondents.

Correspondingly, just under 58 percent of the managers (vs. 64 percent earlier) believe that most agencies employ no consistent approach. If a key function of management is to create moral consciousness in organizations, imbue them with high purpose, and act as a steward of the system, then some progress may be being made—although there remains considerable room for improvement.

Thus in response to several 1996-only survey questions, a majority of managers (54 percent) indicate that their organization has never provided formal ethics training (22 percent state that training is offered at least once after hiring; 6 percent say upon hiring only); just 17 percent claim that it is given on a continuing basis. Nearly six of every ten (58 percent) report that their organization does not have "an internal ethics oversight office or a person directly responsible for dealing with ethical concerns" (40 percent say that it does with the balance uncertain). Finally, a majority (52 percent) state that their organization does not come "under the jurisdiction of an external governmental ethics commission or agency" (47 percent say that it does; the remainder are uncertain). Less than one-half of the respondents, then, report that they are provided with pertinent resources in the form of training, an internal ethics office, or an external commission. It follows that just 38 percent concur that "there is an on-going effort to reinforce an ethics code in my agency" (43 percent disagree; the balance are undecided).

Organizational Leadership

It appears that there is no agreed-upon standard or procedure to assist employees in most agencies. Consequently, many offices either ignore, shift responsibility, or simply have no strategy whatsoever for dealing with ethics. An incoherent, frequently passive, and/or reactive philosophy is not likely to support, nurture, or benefit those seeking to carefully resolve ethical dilemmas.

Accordingly, the 1996 survey participants were asked what techniques work best (and least) in fostering ethics and deterring ethical lapses in their own organizations (nearly 70 percent replied). The answers to these free-response questions were diverse, overlapping, and not readily quantifiable. It is difficult to overstate, however, the importance of management by example—i.e., the demonstration of desired conduct by department heads and elected officials. "Living the example sets expectations for all members of the organization," believes a city fire chief from a mid-Atlantic state.

The daily activities of leaders, including real instances of proper behavior, show the importance of ethics to employees and to the agency. "Ethics can only be fostered through top-level managers modeling ethical behavior and requiring the same from all others in the organization" writes the budget director of a large Wisconsin city. In short, leaders must possess integrity and practice ethics if the entire unit is to operate with a high level of morality. "Top management," says a deputy city manager from a Southwestern urban area, "must set the standard for ethical behavior for the agency." Nurturing worthy conduct is best done through advocacy, publicity, and celebration, a Kansas county administrator notes without further elaboration.

By interpolation, advocacy likely means leadership with commitment and behavior, attitude, and action. Many respondents say that what works best is to encourage discussions that test professional integrity and to identify actual problems and develop practical solutions to them. This promotes an atmosphere of trust and openness where alternative viewpoints can be examined without fear or favor. A senior higher education official from New York state believes that effective learning takes place when there are "examples of when things go wrong, and people see the episode unfold and brought to a conclusion." "Being open, honest, and truthful," holds a high official in the state comptroller's office in the northeast, "fosters ethical behavior in return." A library director from a California county adds that "clearly stated policies and written procedures also help establish baseline understandings."

Responses related to publicity, the second method to encourage rectitude, generally prescribe an advocacy role and not just a reaction when incidents occur. Routinized ethics practice and regular training to ensure awareness, support, and understanding are key. For instance, a finance director in an upper Midwest city suggests that a series of ethics-oriented policy meetings with an annual review of each policy be held throughout the year. A division deputy director in the United States Department of Education finds an internal ethics office helpful in resolving issues. Another manager, from a California city, utilizes an ethics commission hotline to discuss problems. Such activities confirm leadership support for ethical precepts, provide agency-specific examples, and offer continuing education on relevant issues.

Advocacy and publicity, finally, lead to celebration; when examples are set and issues examined, recognition should follow to cultivate honorable behavior. A New York City planner maintains that "an awards ceremony or other special recognition to those who demonstrate excellence in government, as measured by ASPA's Code of Ethics," is a productive way to nurture virtue.

These three activities ensure ongoing organizational development by demonstrating the significance of appropriate conduct in agency life. A public works director in a Midwestern city reports that his "department head believes in ethics, communicates that belief to subordinates, and always considers ethics in all actions." Another respondent from Wyoming states that her "director has the ASPA Code of Ethics on the wall and practices from the code." In short, leadership exemplars nourish a constant recognition of professionalism and employee pride in unit accomplishments.

Approaches that work least in promoting meritorious behavior include not taking the above actions; as one respondent indicates, both the best and the worst technique is the example set by leadership. Negative executive styles compiled from the responses include the sometimes overlapping approaches of neglect, hypocrisy, and exhortation.

Neglect, hypocrisy, and exhortation all reflect a passive, reactive, or defensive strategy that accomplishes little. Staff are treated like children, few resources are provided, and there are inconsistent and ambiguous policies, according to a senior administrative officer in California state government. There is frequently no mechanism to report or deal with ethical problems. Instead, respondents indicate that rule-driven procedures focus on control, not guidelines for encouraging proper conduct. A legalistic approach, according to a department assistant director in a Georgia city, where some things are allowed and others not, prevails.

> The worst technique is to leave the responsibility for organizational ethics to elected officials; often their attitude is "it did not break any laws." I had to resign a position because of pressure from elected officials that would have forced me to violate the code of ethics. (A city government housing commissioner from Michigan)

In summary, the influence of management by example, positively (when upheld by advocacy, publicity, and celebration) or negatively (when followed by neglect, hypocrisy, and exhortation), is substantial. Yet it is unrealistic to assume that role models can serve as the sole means to effect ethical behavior. While it is apparent that some progress has been made in organizational policies and leadership initiatives, it is also true that work remains to be done.

CODES OF ETHICS AND THE ASPA CASE

Many studies reveal that business and government executives regard codes of conduct as the most valuable way to promote ethics (however, see Gortner, 1991), possibly because they are seen as an important indicator of professionalism (Robin, 1989). In results comparable to 1989, just 3 percent of the respondents are satisfied that "There is no real need for codes of ethics in work organizations" (more than 90 percent disagree or strongly disagree). There is little dispute, then, that codes meet a genuine need.

Not only are they seen as important, but also there is less uncertainty today about their actual effect than was the case before. Some 44 percent discern a difference between agencies that have codes and those that do not. This compares to 38 percent in the earlier survey (approximately 20 percent in both studies do not believe that a difference exists, although the undecided proportion has declined). Once again there is a measurable, if modest, progression in perceptions of affirmative ethical practices.

Still, these data suggest that codes may not necessarily be conducive to exemplary behavior—a finding at variance with much of the literature (e.g., Bruce, 1996). How can professional associations, especially those with a broad, interdisciplinary scope, promote effective ethical standards? In 1984, ASPA adopted a 12-point code of ethics which was subsequently revamped into five overarching principles in late 1994 (Van Wart, 1996). The survey participants were asked "Are you familiar with the ASPA Code of Ethics?"

Today, nearly 8 of 10 (79 percent) members claim familiarity contrasted to 58 percent in 1989. Moreover, among those answering affirmatively, their degree of acquaintance with the code surpasses that found earlier. Thus, only 21 percent admit, "I have heard of it" (cf., 34 percent previously), while 65 percent say they "have a general familiarity" (versus 56 percent before) and 14 percent report they "are quite familiar" with the code (cf., 10 percent earlier).

These results indicate that the depth and breadth awareness of the ASPA statement has increased substantially in a short period of time. Perhaps this is partly due to the 1994 revision and its frequent reprinting in *Public Administration Review*. Coupled with survey results shown elsewhere, it is likely that the code has the potential to impact daily management. No longer is a very large segment of the membership "either unaware or has but a passing acquaintance with" the code as reported in the previous study (Bowman, 1990, 349). Such a standard, arguably, should meet at least two criteria to be productive: acceptability and enforceability. That is, not only must those governed by the code believe in (or an least acquiesce to) its principles, but the policy must also have an enforcement mechanism.

Acceptability

Most administrators (90 percent in 1996, 70 percent in 1989) affirm that the "Code provides an appropriate set of standards" to guide public administrators. There is nonetheless recognition that more tailored policies are needed for different work-places. Thus, some two-thirds in both surveys suggest that for the ASPA document to be truly effective, it "must be supplemented by an agency-specific code," a finding that suggests a possible role for the society.

The test of acceptability is, of course, whether or not the ideals embodied in the code are actually practiced. In another considerable shift, a total of 85 percent (69 percent in 1989) report that they either "often" (65 percent versus 38 percent earlier) or "occasionally" (20 percent versus 34 percent previously) use the code and/or its principles on the job.

A 1996 open-ended question provides some depth to this finding. Managers were asked to describe an ethical dilemma in their agency, and whether or not the code helped them. Those responding (40 percent of the total) were divided over its utility, as approximately one-half found it helpful and one-half did not. Among the former, most of the written comments focused on the code's value in providing a benchmark for interpreting the public interest, dealing with conflicts of interest, and coping with improper influences on decision-making by elected officials. Among the latter, administrators stated that other standards were used, the ASPA document contained incompatible provisions, the credo did not deal with specific issues, or that it was not applicable because the respondent was caught in the middle with no authority to resolve the issue.

In short, most of the entire sample either often or occasionally used the code in their work; this can go beyond inspirational and educational purposes to use in decision-making. At that point, however, its efficacy is called into question (for the reasons indicated) by one-half of those managers who answered the essay item.

More interesting results are found in the responses to the question, "With what frequency is the ASPA Code and/or its principles used by your agency in daily management?" In 1996, nearly two-thirds (65 percent) state that it is used "fairly often," with another one-fifth (20 percent) saying "occasionally," 7 percent "seldom," and 5 percent "never." In stark contrast, almost two-thirds (65 percent) indicated that it was "seldom" used in 1989 (one-fourth "occasionally," and approximately one-tenth "often"; the "never" option did not appear previously).

These data appear inconsistent with the views of the majority (54 percent), who agree that "The role of 'umbrella' professional associations such as ASPA in affecting the ethical behavior of its members—to say nothing of government as a whole—is very limited" (31 percent disagree; the rest are undecided). Perhaps these managers are being "realistic"; while the code can be helpful in thinking about problems, actual behavior may be governed by agency rules. Or possibly the apparent inconsistency is an adaptation of "thinking globally, acting locally": While only so much can be done by a voluntary association, initiatives can be taken at specific locations. It could also be a variant of the well-known finding in ethics research (e.g., Baumhart, 1961) that people generally assume that they are more ethical than others—that is, ASPA probably cannot help someone else (them), but it can reinforce the high standards in one's own agency (us).[5] Alternatively, it may be that the question was narrowly construed as dealing with enforcement, a topic to which we now turn.

Enforceability

Over 90 percent agree that in order for the code to be given weight, it must first be taken seriously by top management—apparently something that is now taking place in a number of agencies. Interestingly, in proportions similar to the earlier study, a plurality (38 percent) endorse giving ASPA power to enforce the code (31 percent are undecided; 24 percent disapprove).[6] Hesitancy on the part of members to do this may stem from questions about whether a general professional society has legitimacy to effect sanctions and whether such sanctions could be feasibly implemented.[7]

To summarize, these practitioners—unlike their 1989 colleagues—have a substantial acquaintance with the ASPA ethics document. Not only that, but they, and many of their agencies, also use the code in daily management. If one standard of an effective credo is acceptability, then the society's code is well on its way to achieving that criterion. Over two-thirds of the sample (69 percent), in fact, favor having the following statement (with a signature line) placed on the association's membership application and annual renewal forms: "I fully support and will abide by ASPA's Code of Ethics_____"
signature

CONCLUSIONS

This study shows that ethics is a matter of substantial and increasing concern in public management. Since standards of practice are inherent in the very concept of professional life and ASPA expects its members to exemplify code principles, what can be done to support them in making principled judgments?

As in 1989, most respondents want the society to take a proactive role in this area. Although no quantitative data were gathered in the earlier research, the responses to a 1989 essay question about the association's role were categorized into three partially overlapping ideas: ASPA-as-advocate, consultant, and evaluator. These functions formed the basis for the multiple-choice item in 1996 (Table 2).

Nearly 6 of every 10 members (57.2 percent) believe that ASPA should serve as an advocate to promote the public service. This includes activities such as drafting ethics legislation, offering training, and/or speaking out when officials act (un)ethically. Over one-quarter of the sample (28.7 percent) see the society in a consulting mode: developing agency-specific codes and encouraging their adoption through technical assistance, convening symposia, and/or creating curricula. A small group (6.1 percent) prefer that the association act in the capacity of an evaluator: appraising agency programs and rating them against ASPA standards, tracking unethical practices, and recognizing (un)ethical conduct. Finally, most of those responding to the open-ended choice (5.8 percent) approved either a combination of the roles or all three of them.

- I believe that ASPA should adopt a gradual process by first becoming an advocate, then a consultant, and finally an evaluator, much like the current law enforcement agency accreditation process. (A Florida law enforcement investigator).
- Start by promoting, be available to consult, and evaluate upon request. (The finance director and tax administrator of an Ohio city).
- All organizations are in need of roles 1, 2, 3, at sometime in their growth; ASPA should adapt to their needs. (A budget analyst in a Maryland county).

In short, a large majority of these administrators support ASPA ethics programs and would like them extended in an advocacy, consulting, and/or evaluative mode. The code is not seen as an alternative to creating an ethically-sensitive organizational culture. They acknowledge that problems are inevitable, and that further measures to assist decisionmakers are desirable. Frequent questionnaire comments approve the continued emphasis and steady focus on ethics as a top priority. Indeed, 60 percent support the creation of an ethics section in the society (8 percent oppose, with the remainder undecided). If the ethics section is established, 20 percent would join (making it the organization's largest section), 49 percent are undecided, and the rest would not join.

This study, to summarize, offers empirical data on ethical issues in public management and their implications for related professional associations. The respondents indicate that ethics is hardly a fad and that government has the obligation to set the example in society. They further hold that ethics in the workplace can be empowering, although not all organizations and their leaders have a consistent approach to accomplish this. The findings emphasize the key role of leadership—both by its presence and absence—in encouraging honorable public service. There is also a belief that properly-designed codes of ethics have a crucial role in fostering integrity in agencies. In fact, ASPA's code now enjoys widespread support and use among the participants in the study. Most think that a professional organization can further nurture ethics in an advocacy, consultative, or evaluative manner.

Clearly administrators think there is a genuine need for ethical guidance in the conduct of government—perhaps in response to reform movements that seek to hold public servants accountable for results instead of conformity to rules. The broad, deep consensus on the importance of ethics among these ASPA practitioner members suggests that the approaches discussed here can be meaningful when institutionalized through authentic agency leadership and professional association initiatives. As a new millennium approaches, there is reason to believe that a winter of despair is waning and a spring of hope is dawning.

NOTES

1. While respondent self-reporting, by definition, is subjective, recall this Platonic caution: perceptions are often at least as important as facts in public life (Thompson, 1992).
2. More specifically, 88 percent are white, 71 percent are male, 77 percent hold at least a master's degree, 82 percent have over 10 years of experience, 68 percent are in mid or top management

positions, 65 percent earn more than $50,000 per year, 53 percent indicate a "moderate" philosophy (23 percent say they are liberal; 21 percent conservative), and 62 percent have been ASPA members for at least six years. Their employers are state (22 percent), the federal government (20 percent), and local (55 percent); the remainder are undetermined.

This group does not differ substantially from the 1989 sample and, similar to that study, few cross-tabulations on these factors yielded interesting findings. Thus, data manipulation is rendered problematic by the homogeneous nature of the sample; the few differences that did emerge were not notable as attitudinal trends were all in the same direction.

A test for nonresponse bias in population samples comparing early and late returned questionnaires (Oppenheim, 1966) was conducted, and no significant differences emerged; thus the typical participant reflects the practitioner members at large (most ASPA members are practitioners as just 10 percent are academicians). Still, the response rate raises questions about ethical concern in the ASPA membership as well as that of the larger practitioner community. That is, by their very membership in this professional organization, members and survey participants may be more sensitive to professional values and ethical conduct than nonmembers. And yet, less than two-thirds of the sample responded.

3. Further, over 60 percent disagree in both surveys that "discussing ethics with most managers is difficult because they are concerned with appearing too idealistic or 'Sunday-schoolish.'" It appears that ethics may not be more laughable than laudable in the hurly-burly of organizational decision-making.

4. When the 1996 survey is compared to the earlier one (when over 75 percent of the respondents endorsed a similar statement), however, it appears that there is a growing emphasis on individual responsibility. The fact nonetheless remains that agencies significantly affect behaviors of their employees.

5. This is consistent with a finding by the International City/County Management Association that 90 percent of its members felt that one of the benefits of belonging to that organizations was that it promoted and enforced high ethical standards (Kellar, 1995).

6. It should be pointed out that the 1984 code made no mention of enforcement. While not a formal provision of the 1995 code, there is a statement at the end that indicates it will be enforced in accordance with ASPA bylaws (Article I, Section 4). The inclusion of the statement occurred late in the approval process, was subject to little ASPA-wide debate, and was disregarded in a definitive interpretation of the code (Van Wart, 1996).

Since this long-standing bylaw has seldom, if ever, been utilized, its appearance in the new code was in symbolic recognition of the enforcement issue—with the understanding that it was not likely to be used. Perhaps this is one explanation for why there is little change between 1989 and 1996 in the responses to this item.

7. Should the society pursue the enforcement issue, the results to the questions below—all of which confirm those found in 1989—may provide some direction. First, 80 percent of the administrators agree that "the greater congruence of a code with pre-existing values of employees, the greater its effectiveness." It appears that any enforcement role should be preceded by an effort to articulate the national code with that of the agency.

Secondly, as before, over 80 percent endorse the idea that a policy providing "a mechanism for reporting violations that includes protection for the person reporting the problem will be more effective than one which does not have such a mechanism" (4 percent disagree; 11 percent are unsure). Thus, these survey participants believe that a code must provide clear procedures to channel communication and also to safeguard employees from harassment. Finally, a large plurality (48 percent) agree that "the greater the provision of sanctions in a code for noncompliance, the greater its effectiveness" (24 percent were undecided; 25 percent disagreed), a finding reflecting the uncertain role of a professional association. These results provide support for Weller's (1988) hypotheses on the effectiveness of codes.

REFERENCES

Adams, Mark A., Jeremy W. Barber, and Hildy Herrera (1993). "Ethics in Government." *American Criminal Law Review* 30(3): 617–642.

Appleby, Paul H. (1952). *Morality and Administration in Democratic Government.* Baton Rouge, LA: State University Press.

Baumhart, Raymond C. (1961). "How Ethical are Businessmen?" *Harvard Business Review* 39 (July/August): 6–8.

Bowman, James S. (1990). "Ethics in Government: A National Survey of Public Administrators." *Public Administration Review* 50(3): 345–353.

_____. (1991). *Ethical Frontiers in Public Management: Seeking New Strategies for Resolving Ethical Dilemmas.* San Francisco, CA: Jossey-Bass.

Bruce, Willa (1996). "Codes of Ethics and Codes of Conduct." *Public Integrity Annual* 1: 13–22.

Cooper, Terry L., ed. (1994). *Handbook of Administrative Ethics.* New York: Marcel Dekker.

Cooper, Terry L., and N. Dale Wright, eds. (1992). *Exemplary Public Administrators.* San Francisco, CA: Jossey-Bass.

Frederickson, George (1993). *Ethics and Public Administration.* Armonk, NY: M. E. Sharpe.

Garment, Suzanne (1991). *Scandal: The Culture of Mistrust in American Politics.* New York: Times Books.

Gore, Al (1993). *Creating a Government that Works Better and Costs Less: Report of the National Performance Review.* New York: Times Books.

Gortner, Harold F. (1991). *Ethics for Public Managers.* New York: Greenwood Press.

Green, Richard T. (1994). "Character Ethics and Public Administration." *International Journal of Public Administration* 17(12): 2737–2764.

Kellar, Elizabeth K. (1995). "Ethics on Center Stage." *The Public Manager* 24(3): 36–38.

Lewis, Carol W. (1991). *The Ethics Challenge in Public Service.* San Francisco, CA: Jossey-Bass.

Madsen, Peter, and Jay M. Shafritz (1992). *Essentials of Government Ethics.* New York: Meridian.

Mertins, Herman, Jr., et al. (1994). *Applying Professional Standards and Ethics in the Nineties.* Washington, DC: American Society for Public Administration.

Oppenheim, Abraham N. (1996). *Questionnaire Design and Attitude Measurement.* New York: Basic Books.

Paine, Lynn Sharp (1994). "Manager for Organizational Integrity." *Harvard Business Review* 72 (March/April): 106–117.

Pasquerella, Lynn, Alfred Killilea, and Michael Vocino (1996). *Ethical Dilemmas in Public Administration.* Westport, CT: Praeger.

Plant, Jeremy F. (1996). "Public Ethics in Squalid Times: Codes of Ethics and the Deeming of Truth." Paper delivered at the National Conference on Public Service Ethics and the Public Trust. St. Louis, Missouri.

Plant, Jeremy F. (1997). "Using Codes of Ethics in Teaching Public Administration." In James S. Bowman and Donald C. Menzel, eds., *Teaching Ethics and Values in Public Administration: Program Innovations, Teaching Strategies, and Ethical Issues.* Albany, NY: SUNY Press.

Reynolds, Harry W., Jr. (1995). "Symposium: Ethics in American Public Service." *The Annals of the American Academy of Political and Social Sciences* 537 (January)

Richter, William L., Frances Burke, and Jameson Doig, eds. (1990). *Combatting Corruption/Encouraging Ethics: A Sourcebook for Public Service Ethics.* Washington, DC: American Society for Public Administration.

Robin, Donald, et al. (1989). "A Different Look at Codes of Ethics," *Business Horizons* 32 (January/February): 66–73.

Thompson, Dennis F. (1992). "Paradoxes of Government Ethics." *Public Administration Review* 52(3): 254–259.

United States Merit Systems Protection Board (1993). *Whistleblowing in the Federal Government: An Update.* Washington, DC: U.S. MSPB.

Van Wart, Montgomery (1996). "Sources for Ethical Decision Making for Individuals in the Public Sector." *Public Administration Review* 56 (6): 525–533.

Weller, Steven (1988). "The Effectiveness of Corporate Codes of Ethics." *Journal of Business Ethics* 7(5): 389–395.

43

Guy B. Adams and Danny L. Balfour

THE DYNAMICS OF EVIL AND ADMINISTRATIVE EVIL

Evil is not an accepted entry in the lexicon of the social sciences. Social scientists much prefer to *describe* behavior, avoiding ethically loaded or judgmental rubrics—to say nothing of what is normally considered religious phraseology. Evil nevertheless reverberates down through the centuries of human history, showing little sign of weakening at the dawn of the 21st century and the apex of modernity (Lang, 1991). In the modern age, we are greatly enamored of the notion of progress, of the belief that civilization is developmental, with the present age at the pinnacle of human achievement. These beliefs constrain us from acknowledging the implications of the fact that the 20th century has been the bloodiest, both in absolute and relative terms, in human history, and that we have developed the capacity for even greater mass destruction.

Well more than a hundred million human beings have been slaughtered or otherwise killed as a direct or indirect consequence of the epidemic of wars and state-sponsored violence in this century (Bauman, 1989; Eliot, 1972). Administrative mass murder and genocide have become a demonstrated capacity within the human social repertoire (Rubenstein, 1975, 1983), and simply because such events have occurred, new instances of genocide and dehumanization become more likely (Arendt, 1963). If we are to have any realistic hope for ameliorating this trajectory in the coming century, administrative evil needs to be unmasked and better understood, especially by those likely to be a necessary component in any future acts of mass destruction—public administrators, as well as all other professionals and fields active in public affairs.

Evil is defined in the *Oxford English Dictionary* as the antithesis of good in all its principal senses. A more useful behavioral definition of evil has been provided by Katz:

> Behavior that deprives innocent people of their humanity, from small scale assaults on a person's dignity to outright murder . . . [this definition] focuses on how people behave toward one another—where the behavior of one person, or an aggregate of persons is destructive to others. (1993, p. 5)

This behavioral definition suggests a continuum, with horrible, mass eruptions of evil, such as the Holocaust and other, lesser instances of mass murder, at one extreme, and the "small" white lie, which is somewhat hurtful, at the other. Certainly, at the white lie end of the continuum, use of the term *evil* may stretch our credulity, although Sissela Bok (1978) has argued persuasively that even so-called white lies can have serious personal and social consequences, especially as they accrue over time. For the most part, we discuss the end of the continuum where the recognition of evil may be easier and more obvious (at least when it is unmasked). The small-scale end of the continuum, however, remains of importance because the road to great evil often begins with seemingly small, first steps. Evil, in many cases, is enmeshed in cunning and seductive processes that can lead ordinary people in ordinary times down the proverbial slippery slope.

Where does evil come from and why does it persist? Thousands of years of human religious history have provided ample commentary on evil, and philosophers certainly have discussed it at length (Adams & Merrihew, 1990; Kateb, 1983; Katz, 1988; Kekes, 1990; Parkin, 1985; Russell, 1988; Sanford, 1981; Stein, 1997; Stivers, 1982; Twitchell, 1985). Although there was a time when locating evil in the symbolic persona of the devil provided adequate explanation of its origins, the modern scientific era both demands a more comprehensive explanation of the origins of evil and makes it nearly impossible to provide one. One author has argued that the modern age has been engaged in a process of unnaming evil, such that we now have a "crisis of incompetence" in facing evil (Delbanco, 1995, p. 3): "A gulf has opened up in our [modern] culture between the visibility of evil and the intellectual resources available for coping with it." Evil may not yet have become unnameable, although in its administrative manifestations it often goes unseen. Evil reveals itself to us depending on our approach and stance towards it, and in the modern age, the great risk is not seeing it at all, for administrative evil wears many masks.

Based on the premise that evil is inherent in the human condition, we make several key arguments:

1. The modern age, with its scientific-analytic mind-set and technical-rational approach to social and political problems, enables a new and frightening form of evil—administrative evil.

2. Because administrative evil wears a mask, no one has to accept an overt invitation to commit an evil act, because such overt invitations are very rarely issued. Rather, the invitation may come in the form of an expert or technical role, couched in the appropriate language, or it may even come packaged as a good and worthy project, representing what we call a *moral inversion*, in which something evil or destructive has been redefined as good and worthy.

3. We examine closely two of administrative evil's most favored masks. First, within modern organizations (both public and private), because so much of what occurs is *underneath* our awareness of it, we find people engaged in patterns and activities that may culminate in evil without their even being aware of it until after the fact (and often, not even then). Second, we look at social and public policies that can culminate in evil. These most often involve either an instrumental or a technical goal (which drives out ethics) or a *moral inversion* that is unseen by those pursuing such a policy.

4. Because public service ethics and professional ethics more generally are anchored in the scientific-analytic mind-set, in a technical-rational approach to administrative or social problems, and in the professions themselves, both are effectively useless in the face of administrative evil. Because administrative evil wears many masks, it is entirely possible to adhere to the tenets of public service ethics and participate in a great evil, and not be aware of it until it is too late (or perhaps not at all). Thus finding a basis for public service ethics in the face of administrative evil is problematic at best.

ADMINISTRATIVE EVIL AND PUBLIC ADMINISTRATION

The relationship between evil and public administration—is usually overlooked or dismissed as involving temporary, politically induced departures from ethical standards, which themselves are founded on the presumed inherent neutrality or benevolence of rational administration (Frederickson & Hart, 1985). Although we address public administration directly, we believe the arguments presented here hold for all professions and for practitioners of all kinds whose activities are within public life in its most general sense. We argue and present evidence that the tendency toward administrative evil, as manifested primarily in acts of dehumanization and genocide, is deeply woven into the identity of public administration (and also into other fields and professions in public life). The influence of evil has been suppressed and masked despite, or perhaps because of, its profound and far-reaching implications for the future of public administration.

Despite what may initially seem to be a negative treatment of the public service, it is not our intention to somehow diminish public administration, engage in bureaucrat bashing, or give credence to misguided arguments that governments and their agents are necessarily or inherently evil. In fact, our aim is quite the opposite: to get beyond the superficial critiques and lay the groundwork for a more ethical and democratic public administration, one that recognizes its potential for evil and thereby creates greater possibilities for avoiding the many pathways toward state-sponsored dehumanization and destruction. This approach (as with any attempt to rethink aspects of the field) is bound to bring us into conflict with some of the conventional wisdom and traditions of public administration. Our critical stance toward public administration is aimed not so much at any particular formulation of the field's identity but more at what has not been written—the failure to recognize administrative evil as part and parcel of the identity of public administration. Although it has had virtually no place in the field's literature, administrative evil is as much a part of public administration as other well-worn concepts such as efficiency, effectiveness, accountability, and productivity.

FAILING TO SEE ADMINISTRATIVE EVIL

A lack of attention to what we believe to be a vitally important concept can be explained by the understandable, yet unfortunate, tendency to lament acts of administrative evil while dismissing them as temporary and isolated aberrations or deviations from proper administrative behavior. In considering eruptions of evil throughout history, it is commonplace to think of them an emanating from a unique context. We want to believe that they occur at a particular historical moment and within a specific culture. Although this is clearly true, at least in part, it also holds a cunning deception: The effect of understanding great eruptions of evil as historical aberrations is that we safely wall them off from our own time and space, and from ordinary people in ordinary times.

It is not unusual for the Holocaust (and other, lesser state-sponsored atrocities) to be viewed in such terms, for example, perceiving that, in the midst of extraordinary circumstances, Hitler led Germany out of the fold of Western culture and into a deviant, criminal culture. As Rubenstein (1975) and Bauman (1989) have argued, however, the Holocaust, rather than being a deviation from Western civilization, was one of its inherent (although not inevitable) possibilities, carried out in large part by the most advanced, technical-rational mechanisms and procedures of modern civilization. Furthermore, it was the public service and advanced administrative procedures that made the mass slaughter possible:

> The Final Solution did not clash at any stage with the rational pursuit of efficient, optimal goal implementation. On the contrary, *it arose out of a genuinely rational concern, and it was generated by bureaucracy true to its form and purpose.* The Holocaust . . . was a legitimate resident in the house of modernity; indeed, one who would not be at home in any other house. (Bauman, 1989, p. 17)

The same can be said of other examples of administrative evil in the history of American government and public service.

In the 20th century, modern civilization has unfolded as a paradox of unparalleled progress, order, and civility on one hand, and mass murder and barbarity on the other. Rubenstein (1975, p. 91) argues, therefore, that the Holocaust "bears witness to the advance of civilization," where progress is Janus-like, with two faces, one benevolent, the other destructive. For a profession like public administration (and other professions in public life) to identify itself exclusively with the face that represents order, efficiency, productivity, creativity, and the great achievements of modern civilization is, in effect, to mask the existence of a fundamental and recurring aspect of it own history and identity—the destructive and even evil face.

Robert Bellah (1971) reached similar conclusions about contemporary American culture in reflections prompted by the massacre of hundreds of civilians, mostly women and children, by American soldiers in the Vietnamese hamlet of My Lai. He states that "both the assertion of the fundamental unity of man and the assertion that whole groups of people are defective and justly subject to extreme aggression are genuinely part of our tradition" (p. 178). From this perspective, there are not two American traditions, one good and another evil, but one tradition consisting of a paradox wherein progress in technology and human rights is accompanied by brutality, exploitation, and even mass murder. Just as Thomas Mann observed that the demonic and supremely creative were entwined in the German soul (Bellah, 1971), so freedom and exploitation are entwined in the heart of America. Likewise, public administration cannot, in the light of this realization, be described only in terms of progress in the "art, science and profession" of administration (see, for example, Lynn, 1996) without recognizing that acts of administrative evil are something other than uncontrolled, sporadic deviations from the norms of technical-rational administrative practice. Practitioners and scholars of public administration, as well as of other related fields and professions, need to recognize that the pathways to administrative evil are not built from the outside by seductive leaders but emanate from within, ready to coax and nudge administrators down a surprisingly familiar route first toward moral inversion, then to complicity in crimes against humanity.

UNDERSTANDING EVIL

We know that human beings are killers. We are (at least most of us) meat eaters who must kill for the sustenance of life. We are in the food chain and, if nothing else, we are at minimum killers of plant life. We have learned, during the course of human history, to kill as well for high social purposes, that is, for political, religious, and/or economic beliefs and systems. As uncomfortable to acknowledge as it may be, evil is as close to all of us as ourselves.

Most versions of psychology, from Freud to Jung and beyond, account for the potentially destructive tendencies of human behavior, including aggression, anger, and rage. Melanie Klein (1964), perhaps the preeminent object-relations psychologist, understands aggression, and other emotions as well, as relationships with "objects" (which are in most cases other human beings). As Greenberg and Mitchell (1983, p. 139) point out, "Drives, for Klein, are relationships." One such manifestation is hating those we love the most (as infants and children). Such a psychic contradiction is emotional dynamite and it defused through "splitting." Unlike repression, which drives unwanted or intolerable emotions underground—into the unconscious—splitting is a device that allows these contradictory feelings to coexist, albeit separately, in the human consciousness. Normally, the good aspect is held internally and the bad aspect is split off, projected outward to some external person (the "object"). This is known as "projective identification."

Organizations, social institutions, and even countries can be holding environments (or "containers") for both good and evil purposes. After all, it was a church organization that conceived and carried out the many inquisitions in centuries past. When an organization, institution, or polity "contains" the unintegrated aggression and rage (the projective identification of the split-off "bad" parts) of its members, one has the phenomenon identified in the title of a book by Vamik Volkan (1988), *The Need to Have Enemies and Allies*. The belief system, or ideology, that is manifested by the organization or polity gives the anxiety (which results from the unintegrated aggression) a name and mitigates it by making it less confusing whom to love and whom to hate. In essence, the organization or polity communicates some version (that varies according to the nature of the felt anxiety) of the following to its individual members:

> You really are being persecuted. Let me help you by naming your persecutors, and telling you who your true friends are, friends who are also being attacked by these persecutors. Together you and your true friends can fight the persecutors, and praise each other's righteousness, which will help you realize that the source of aggression and evil is out there, in the real world. And you thought it was all in your head. (Alford, 1990, p. 13)

The organization or polity has reduced the members' anxiety but reinforced the splitting off of the bad object(s) and the projective identification. Thus, the unintegrated hatred and aggression that is the source of evil is called out and is given organization and direction. This dynamic may be as benign as an amateur softball team, which makes its rival teams into "enemies." When combined with a moral inversion, in which the bad becomes good, this dynamic can lead to eruptions of evil (Alford, 1990): "To seek to destroy the bad object with all the hatred and aggression at one's command becomes good, because doing so protects the self from badness" (p. 15). From the perspective of object-relations psychology, unintegrated rage and aggression—part of the normal repertoire of human emotional responses—represent the source of evil. There may be other and perhaps better explanations, but this one provides a foundation from which we can build and elaborate more of the social and organizational dynamics of evil behavior.

Perspective and Distance

In recognizing when evil has been done, the perspective of the victim has authority. It is the body or psyche of the victim (and sometimes both) that has been marked by evil. The witness and testimony of the victim(s) carry moral authority as well and provide the foundation from which our judgments of good and evil can be made. Still, there is a distortion from the victim's perspective. From the victim's perspective, an act of cruelty or violence (or the perpetrator of the act—or both) typically is described as evil—most typically, as wholly evil. Baumeister (1997) refers to this as the "myth of pure evil" (p. 17).

The myth of pure evil is compounded by at least two related tendencies. First, the psychological concept of splitting, as discussed above, projects those aspects of the psyche seen as "all bad" outward onto some object (typically a person or persons). Second, American culture, for example, has a propensity, considerably exacerbated by popular media and particularly by television, to cast moral questions in black and white, all good or all bad terms. Villains are thus wholly evil, and we have no tolerance for a hero who is not all good. In the political arena, we ask that national leaders have a flawless and spotless past. The myth of pure evil thus represents a dangerous propensity to cast moral questions in absolute terms, which in turn makes them easier to reverse, leading to moral inversion.

The perpetrator's description of the same act differs from that of the victim, often dramatically. Baumeister refers to this as the *magnitude gap*:

> The importance of what takes place is almost always much greater for the victim than for the perpetrator. When trying to understand evil, one is always asking, "How could they do such a horrible thing." But the horror is usually being measured in the victim's terms. To the perpetrator, it is often a very small thing. As we saw earlier, perpetrators generally have less emotion about their acts than do victims. It is almost impossible to submit to rape, pillage, impoverishment or possible murder without strong emotional reactions, but it is quite possible to perform those crimes without emotion. In fact, it makes it easier in many ways. (1997, p. 18)

The magnitude gap is centrally important in seeking to understand evil. From the victim's perspective and most often in hindsight, evil is more readily identified. From the perspective of the perpetrator, however, the recognition of evil is problematic.

From the perpetrator's perspective, the act of cruelty or violence was perhaps "not so good" (not to say, evil), but considering other factors, such as prior injustices or some provocation, perpetrators rather easily produce rationales and justifications for even the most heinous acts.

Distance also is important, in terms of both space and time. It is clearly more difficult to name evil, and do so convincingly, in one's own historical time period. Consider the recent genocide in Rwanda and ethnic cleansing in the former Yugoslavia. Even from the distant perspective of a concerned nation—the United States—evidence during the time of those events was spotty. Although we would argue that the evidence was sufficient for the United States to have taken stronger action than it did, the point is that a social or political consensus is not so easily achieved when events are unfolding and the situation is murky. In hindsight, and when we are no longer called on to do anything, it is much easier to name such events as evil with very widespread agreement (but only if a Serb and Bosnian, or Hutu and Tutsi, are not part of the discourse). Geographic and cultural (or racial) distances matter as well. The Rwandan genocide was horrific, but after all, it was in Africa. Bosnia was murkier, more difficult, because it was in the West, in Europe. Naming the Holocaust as evil is made easier because it was the Germans who perpetrated it, but even so, it took the passage of nearly 25 years before there was much discussion of this signal event in the United States (Hilberg, 1985).

Both distance and perspective are powerful constituents of the mask of administrative evil. Naming any evil that American public administrators have done, even many years ago, is made more difficult because we have no distance from our own culture and profession. To recognize administrative evil in our own time is most problematic of all, because we have neither distance nor perspective without an explicit and somewhat difficult effort to create them (critical reflexivity).

Language and Dehumanization

Given that much of what we do on a daily basis is taken for granted or tacit (Polanyi, 1966), two additional elements make us especially susceptible to participation in evil, without us "knowing" what we are doing. The first of these is language. The use of euphemism or of technical language often helps provide emotional distance from what we are really doing (Orwell, 1950/1984). "Collateral damage" from bombing raids is a euphemism for killing civilian noncombatants and reducing nonmilitary property to rubble. In the Holocaust, code words were used for killing: "evacuation," "special treatment," and the now well-known "final solution." In cases of moral inversion, language can prevent us from connecting our actions with our normal, moral categories of right and wrong, of good and evil. The annihilation of a town—that is, the uprooting of an entire community, the expropriation of its property, and its evacuation to forced labor or death camps—was called "resettlement" or "labor in the East." Such language provided the minimal evidence needed to convince people that not only was such activity not evil, but it was socially appropriate or even necessary. Language often masks administrative evil.

Dehumanization is another powerful ally in the conduct of evil. If one does something cruel or violent to a fellow human being, it may well be morally disturbing, but if that person is part of a group of people who are (that is, have been redefined as) not "normal," not like the majority, or not good Americans, such action becomes easier. If those people can be defined as less than human, "all bad," rather like bugs or roaches (a classic moral inversion), extermination can all too easily be seen as the appropriate action. "They" brought it on themselves, after all. As Albert Speer, Hitler's minister of armaments, said about Jews (Speer, 1970), "If I had continued to see them as human being, I would not have remained a Nazi. I did not hate them. I was indifferent to them" (p. 315). *Dehumanization* also often masks administrative evil.

The Taken for Granted

Tacit knowing—the taken for granted nature of our daily habits of action—is essential to our ability to function in a social world (Polanyi, 1966) in which even the simplest activity is enormously and dauntingly complex if each component and step had to be articulated and thought about explicitly. The taken for granted also bears on our human capacity to participate in evil, as Baumeister notes:

> Another factor that reduces self-control and fosters the crossing of moral boundaries is a certain kind of mental state. This state is marked by a very concrete, narrow, rigid way of thinking, with the focus on the here and now, on the details of what one is doing. It is the state that characterizes someone who is fully absorbed in working with tools or playing a video game. One does not pause to reflect on broader implications or grand principles or events far removed in time (past or future). (1997, p. 268)

Most of our daily lives in social institutions and organizations is taken for granted. Not only do we stop and think about everything that we do (which would socially paralyze us), but we hardly stop and think about anything. We do not have to make a decision about which side of the road we will drive on when we start our automobile; indeed, "side of the road" does not come up on our conscious "radar screen." In most of what we do on a daily or routine basis, we are simply engaged in well-worn habits of action. There is nothing to prompt us to stop and question. So it is with administrative evil. In a culture that emphasizes technical rationality, being "at work" for most means being narrowly focused on the task at hand. This is our typical focus of awareness, which drives out, or at least minimizes, our subsidiary awareness of ethics and morality (and other contextual matters as well). Acts of administrative evil are all too easily taken for granted as well.

THE SOCIAL CONSTRUCTION OF EVIL

Individualism, one of the core values of American culture, is a barrier to our understanding of group and organizational dynamics—and administrative evil. In our culture, we are inclined to assume that each individual's actions are freely and independently chosen. When we examine an individual's behavior in isolation or even in aggregate, as we often do, that notion can be reinforced. Our culture's emphasis on individualism blinds us to groups and organizational dynamics, which typically play a powerful role in shaping human behavior.

It is an easy to make—but important—error to personalize evil in the form of the exceptional psychopath, such as Charles Manson or Jeffrey Dahmer (often without considering how they might be a product of our culture). This proclivity draws a cloak over social and organizational evil. The term "mob psychology," however, still has a resonance for most. We have a long history in the United States of public lynching, clearly a recurring example of social evil. Even more to the point, thousands of people have been subjected to administrative evil in dehumanizing experiments, internment in camps, and other destructive acts by public agencies often done in the name of science and/or the national interest (Nevitt & Comstock, 1971; Stannard, 1992).

Public administration and the social sciences have been dominated by the scientific-analytic mind-set. We have approached social and political problems with the tools of science, thinking of social and human phenomena as if they had the same tangibility and properties as physical reality. Societies and cultures, however, are human artifacts, created and enacted by human activities through time. Social and political institutions—indeed, all human organizations—are thus socially constructed (Berger & Luckmann, 1967). This means, or course, that they are not immutable; what human beings create and enact can be reenacted in some different way. This does not mean, however, that organizations and institutions are easily malleable.

To say that human social and cultural institutions and organizations are socially constructed may seem to imply that at some point groups of people rationally choose to meet together, and they consciously and intentionally set about to devise an institution. Such an activity, of course, is the very rare exception. Rather, organizations and institutions more typically emerge a little bit at a time. As children, we are socialized into a culture that already has a vast array of institutions, practices, and "rules of the road." For the most part, these come to feel natural to us, or more aptly, second nature. During a person's lifetime, most organizations or institutions will change, but usually not dramatically. Still, they *could* change dramatically. Revolutions, economic depressions, and even natural cataclysms can prompt rapid and dramatic change in a society, and of course there are new institutions. Television is a social institution that has developed within the lifetimes of many still alive. The Internet seems well on the way to developing into a social institution.

Another core value of American culture is the rule of law, based in part on the sanctity of contracts. The commercial application of such a core value may be of primary importance, but we should not overlook its social manifestation. Our political and legal systems provide the foundation for law and order in social terms. When the public order is perceived to be threatened, as it is in the contemporary atmosphere of fear of crime and random violence, the response of the citizenry is visceral, if arguably off target—solve the problem by building more prisons, instituting longer prison terms, and bringing back the death penalty while speeding up the execution process. The powerful social motivation for the preservation of social order is fueled by a fear of chaotic conditions. This fundamental need for social order helps in understanding just how strong the inclination to obey authority is for most people. Compliance accounts of human behavior thus help us understand how ordinary social life is maintained over time (stopping at traffic lights magnified into thousands of daily social interactions).

INDIVIDUAL, ORGANIZATION, AND SOCIETY

So far, we have seen how our cultural predispositions can blind us to aspects of human behavior that are crucial in understanding administrative evil. How do we develop these behavioral tendencies and bring them to organizations, and how do these dynamics link with our larger social and cultural context? These connections are the topic of Shapiro and Carr's book, *Lost in Familiar Places: Creating New Connections Between the Individual and Society* (1991). Both families and organizations, along with other social institutions, are *familiar* places for us; after all, we spend our lives in them. As the authors note, however, we increasingly experience a sense of strangeness in these places; hence, the "lost in familiar places" refrain. Old ways of understanding what a family is, for example, seem overwhelmed by changes that affect the ways in which, over time, we negotiate a sense of meaning in our lives. The old anchors do not reach bottom, and we are cast adrift. A more or less stable, shared understanding of the family or of the church or of the work organization in the past served in part as a buffer for the ideology of individualism so pervasive in American society. For most of us, our socialization into various institutions is no longer "automatic," and the socialization that we do receive is increasingly fragmented and complex.

Shapiro and Carr discuss meaning, and in particular the process by which we develop meaning, as negotiated collaborative interpretation—a fundamentally relational process. They focus on the primary human group—the family—as the context in which we first learn this process, and as providing the initial model with which we subsequently attempt to make meaningful sense out of organizational life. As they develop a phenomenology of family life, the authors suggest that curiosity is a central constant in healthy families; that is, the parents' (or caregivers') stance toward the child is captured by the question "What is your experience?" rather than by versions of the command "Your experience is. . . ." The question builds, over time, a capacity for negotiated, collaborative interpretation (the child pieces together boundaries that define "who I am), whereas the command cuts off negotiation and imposes a definition of self on the child, leading potentially to a fragmented, defensive, and often neurotic personality. In this case, the child is apt to carry unintegrated rage and aggression into adult life, along with its characteristic splitting and projective identification.

Alternatively, the split good and bad objects can be successfully reintegrated into the self, which may lead to reparation. Reparation is the motivation in mature human beings to complete worthy tasks and to make things whole again, and to do so in the recognition that there is capacity for both great good and great evil in each of us. This, then, is a recognition that moves one past splitting and projective identification, processes we learn as children as a means of coping with the otherwise unbearable knowledge that we experience hate and rage toward those we love, and the concomitant anxiety that those feelings induce. Alternatively, destructive patterns of interaction quite common in organizational life enable us to maintain the projections we grew used to as children, or even to be ready accomplices to administrative evil.

Shapiro and Carr go on to make interesting linkages to broader social institutions, such as religion. Here the key concept is the notion of a "holding environment" (or "container"), which has to do with how families (or other organizations) managed the emotional issues of their members. In the successful holding environment, empathic interpretation, valuing the experiences of others, and containment of aggression and sexuality are managed in ways that sustain the integrity of members. Organizations, social institutions, and countries also function as holding environments or containers. Religious institutions may be thought of as ritualized symbolic structures that contain chaotic experiences; that is, they act as holding environments for these difficult feelings and emotions (Shapiro & Carr, 1991). "Our proposition is that a key holding environ-ment is continually being negotiated and created through the unconscious interaction between members of a society and its religious institutions" (p. 159). As we have seen, however, organizations, institutions, and countries also serve as holding environments for evil. People who need direction—a target, really—for their unintegrated rage and ag-gression, who must split off the "bad" and project it outward, hear all too well the siren call of groups and organizations that will contain this psychic energy for them. The price tag is almost always obedience and loyalty, and sometimes moral inversion; occa-sionally, the price tag is very dear indeed—those truly evil eruptions that become the great moral debacles of human history.

REFERENCES

Adams, M. M., & Merrihew, R. (Eds.). (1990). *The problem of evil.* New York: Oxford University Press.

Alford, F. C. (1990). The organization of evil. *Political Psychology, 11,* 5–27.

Arendt, H. (1963). *Eichmann in Jerusalem: A report on the banality of evil.* New York: Viking.

Bauman, Z. (1989). *Modernity and the Holocaust.* Ithaca, NY: Cornell University Press.

Baumeister, R. F. (1997). *Evil: Inside human cruelty and violence.* New York: W. H. Freeman.

Bellah, R. N. (1971). Evil and the American ethos. In A. Nevitt & C. Comstock (Eds.), *Sanctions for evil* (pp. 177–191). San Francisco: Jossey-Bass.

Berger, P. L., & Luckmann, T. (1967). *The social construction of reality.* Garden City, NY: Doubleday.

Bok, S. (1978). *Lying: Moral choice in public and private life.* New York: Vintage.

Delbanco, A. (1995). *The death of Satan: How Americans have lost the sense of evil.* New York: Farrar Strauss and Giroux.

Eliot, G. (1972). *The twentieth century book of the dead.* New York: Scribner.

Frederickson, H. G., & Hart, D. K. (1985). The public service and the patriotism of benevo-lence. *Public Administration Review, 45,* 547–553.

Greenberg, J., & Mitchell, S. (1983). *Object relations in psychoanalytic theory.* Cambridge, MA: Harvard University Press.

Hilberg, R. (1985). *The destruction of the European Jews* (3rd ed.). New York: Holmes & Meier.

Kateb, G. (1983). *Hannah Arendt, politics, conscience, evil.* Totowa, NJ: Rowman & Allanheld.

Katz, F. E. (1993). *Ordinary people and extraordinary evil: A report on the beguildings of evil.* Albany: State University of New York Press.

Katz, J. (1988). *Seductions of crime: Moral and sensual attractions in doing evil.* New York: Basic Books.

Kekes, J. (1990). *Facing evil.* Princeton, NJ: Princeton University Press.

Klein, M. (1964). *Love, hate and reparation.* New York: Free Press.

Lang, B. (1991). The history of evil and the future of the Holocaust. In P. Hayes (Ed.), *Lessons and legacies: The meaning of the Holocaust in a changing world* (pp. 90–105). Evanston, IL: Northwestern University Press.

Lynn, L. E., Jr. (1996). *Public management as art, science, and profession.* Chatham, NJ: Chatham House.

Nevitt, S., & Comstock, C. (Eds.). (1971). *Sanctions for evil.* San Francisco: Jossey-Bass.

Orwell, G. (1984). *Shooting an elephant and other essays.* San Diego: Harcourt, Brace, Jovanovich. (Original work published 1950).

Parkin, D. (Ed.). (1985). *The anthropology of evil.* London: Blackwell.

Polanyi, M. (1966). *The tacit dimension*. Garden City, NY: Doubleday Anchor.

Rubenstein, R. L. (1975). *The cunning of history: The Holocaust and the American future*. New York: Harper and Row.

Rubenstein, R. L. (1983). *The age of triage: Fear and hope in an overcrowded world*. Boston: Beacon.

Russell, J. B. (1988). *The prince of darkness: Radical evil and the power of good in history*. Ithaca, NY: Cornell University Press.

Sanford, J. A. (1981). *Evil: The shadow side of reality*. New York: Crossroad.

Shapiro, E. R., & Carr, A. W. (1991). *Lost in familiar places: Creating new connections between the individual and society*. New Haven, CT: Yale University Press.

Speer, A. (1970). *Inside the Third Reich*. London: Weidenfeld and Nicolson.

Stannard, D. E. (1992). *American Holocaust: The conquest of the new world*. New York: Oxford University Press.

Stein, H. F. (1997). Death imagery and the experience of organizational downsizing. *Administration and Society, 29*, 222–247.

Stivers, R. (1982). *Evil in modern myth and ritual*. Athens: University of Georgia Press.

Twitchell, J. B. (1985). *Dreadful pleasures*. New York: Oxford University Press.

Volkan, V. (1988). *The need to have enemies and allies*. Northvale, NJ: Jason Aronson.

CREDITS

Reading 1, Frank Marini, "Public Administration." From *INTERNATIONAL ENCY-CLOPEDIA OF PUBLIC POLICY AND ADMINISTRATION* Editor in Chief, Jay Shafritz. Copyright © 1998 by Jay Shafritz. Reprinted by permission of Westview Press, a member of Perseus Books, L.L.C.

Reading 2, Woodrow Wilson, "The Study of Administration." *Political Science Quarterly*, 2, 1887. Reprinted by permission.

Reading 3, Camilla Stivers, "Feminist Theory of Public Administration." From *INTERNATIONAL ENCYCLOPEDIA OF PUBLIC POLICY AND ADMINISTRATION* Editor in Chief, Jay Shafritz. Copyright © 1998 by Jay Shafritz. Reprinted by permission of Westview Press, a member of Perseus Books, L.L.C.

Reading 4, David H. Rosenbloom, "The Rise of the American Administrative State." In D.H. Rosenbloom, *Public Administration: Understanding Management, Politics and Law in the Public Sector.* New York: Random House. Copyright © 1986. Reprinted by permission of McGraw-Hill Companies.

Reading 5, Andrew Gray and Bill Jenkins, "From Public Administration to Public Management: Reassessing a Revolution." *Public Administration*, (73), Spring 1995. Copyright © Blackwell Publisher Ltd. Reprinted by permission.

Reading 6, Fred W. Riggs, "Public Administration in America: Why our Uniqueness is Exceptional and Important." *Public Administration Review*, 58(1), January/February 1998. Reprinted with permission from *Public Administration Review* © by the American Society for Public Administration (ASPA), 1120 G Street NW, Suite 700, Washington DC 20005. All rights reserved.

Reading 7, Charles E. Lindblom, "The Science of Muddling Through." *Public Administration Review*, 19, Spring 1959. Reprinted with permission from *Public Administration Review* © by the American Society for Public Administration (ASPA), 1120 G Street NW, Suite 700, Washington DC 20005. All rights reserved.